Next Tech

Volume 1

Get the best from your ZX Spectrum Next

Simon N Goodwin

First published 2024

by De Re Books, Warwick, UK

Cover images are by Oliver Frey, Chris Wilkins, Stable Diffusion and the author. There are no prizes for guessing which is which, but you might have fun trying to guess both words which prompted the striking central image.

ISBN: 978-1-0685131-0-7

PoD Rev. B

DEDICATION

For Sam Goodwin, my sibling and fellow Spectrum enthusiast, who died on 8th August 2023, weeks before the Spectrum Next I'd ordered for him was delivered. I remember how Sam used his issue 1 Spectrum so keenly that he wore out the keyboard membrane, then improvised connections with strips of ZX printer paper tucked into the case, twisting them together to generate the missing key-presses. After those had worn out, he'd merge in files from a Microdrive which contained the characters he needed, deleting other lines to isolate the lost codes, and kept programming. Some of Sam's ZX BASIC programs and Z80 tips were published in *Popular Computing Weekly* issue 16, when he was 17 years old and later in issue 4 of *Your Spectrum* magazine. His name (Sam, not Coupé) was chosen for MGT's 1989 Super Spectrum. His bold font featured on the *Crash Tech Tape* and the animated end-credits for the Central ITV series *Magic Micro Mission.* It rides again in the 64-column configuration of the Spectrum Next Text Editor presented in this volume.

Rest In Peace, my brilliant brother.

Table of Contents

ACKNOWLEDGMENTS

I'm grateful to the Spectrum Next team for making this book both possible and necessary, to Sue Goodwin for providing the shed and security in which it was written, and to the online community, in particular the **BASIC on the Spectrum Next** Facebook group, for inspiration and encouragement.

Specific techie thanks are due to Phoebus Dokos and Darren Branagh for roping me in six years ago, Matt Langley for *Next Horizon*, Magnus Krook for the first version of his *NextBASIC Editor* and of course to Garry Lancaster for NextZXOS and NextBASIC.

The Tech Tips cartoon and author photo is used by kind permission of Chris Wilkins, who now safeguards the Crash magazine brand.

Other inspiration and encouragement has come from Allen Albright, Mark Gallop, Richard Hallas, Steve Knight, Matthew Logue, Matt Neale, Peter 'Ped' Helcmanovsky, Dave Reeves, Paulo Silva, Adrian Sinclair, Chris Taylor, Robin Verhagen-Guest, Matteo Vitturi, Natalie Wayland, Chris Wilkins - and my brother Sam, who did great things with his issue 1 Spectrum but sadly did not live to play with the Next that I ordered for him two years before he died.

Figure 1 - The Next Posse at Crash 2022; left to right: Tim Gilberts, David Saphier, Henrique Olifiers, Phoebus Dokos, Lyndon Sharp, Mike Cadwallader, Simon N Goodwin, Matt Davies

Chapter 1, The 21st Century ZX Spectrum

This book is about the ZX Spectrum Next, a crowd-funded 21st Century update of the 1982 ZX Spectrum computer. The Next builds upon the strengths of the Sinclair Spectrum design using modern components and design principles, so that not only the system software – NextZXOS, an update of the 16k ROM in the first Spectrum computers – but the hardware itself can be internally updated and rewired to add new capabilities.

Almost all the features of the computer are implemented in a Field Programmable Gate Array (FPGA), a mesh of logic gates and interfaces that is wired up and configured on the fly in the fraction of a second after you turn the machine on. Optional add-ons like the WiFi adapter and Raspberry Pi Zero co-processor have their own firmware, so the capability of those can be changed – though not entirely repurposed, unlike the FPGA gates – with updates to the built-in firmware. Some of the applications of the Pi Zero will be explored in this volume, though there are doubtless many more to come.

In the six years since Simon joined the early group of Next developers, the 'new' machine has more than doubled in speed, and greatly advanced in capability. This process continues and makes writing any sort of 'definitive' guide to the micro problematic – by the time you read this it's highly likely to have been reprogrammed at both the hardware and software level! For as long as enthusiasts remain excited about the possibilities – and they've been that way for 40 years, now – it will continue to be reprogrammed and enhanced. To put it another way, the Next isn't finished and never will be, and the same applies to this book.

As Phoebus Dokos found in his gallant attempts to keep the Spectrum Next manual up to date with NextBASIC and FPGA refinements, there's no room in any one book to comprehensively describe the current system, let alone project its potential. What I, Simon, have set out to do, drawing on my experience as a hobbyist and commercial software developer over decades and hundreds of technical articles, is explain some things that the new Spectrum can do which older models could not, and how they have been carefully built upon the original design rather than in place of it.

The Spectrum Next is a true Spectrum, in the spirit of the original, designed to enable rather than constrain its users, capable of almost everything earlier Sinclair and Amstrad ZX computers could do, despite their many small incompatibilities, and very much more. It is a labour of love; we hope you love it too, and this book helps you appreciate it even more.

What this book is, and is not

This book is not intended as a substitute for the manual shipped with every Spectrum Next, which is also freely downloadable for those who have yet to get the hardware. It builds on that manual, adding context, explanations and examples, aiming deliberately and explicitly at the hobbyists and tinkerers who were the intended market for all ZX micros. It presumes some familiarity with the original 1982 Spectrum, and access to the new official documentation.

This book won't teach you to write Next games, modern or otherwise – https://kevman3d.itch.io has that well covered – yet it is packed with useful insights relevant to anyone seeking to understand and use the Next, not just programmers. There are many books on game programming, both generic and specific to 8-bit micros. After decades of developing games from the first monochrome to modern 64-bit consoles I could write volumes about what's changed and what's still the same in game development. But not here. For state-of-the-art game audio insights, look no further than my book *Beep to Boom*, published by Routledge for the Audio Engineering Society.

> *We should avoid duplication of effort, because that is being done by others*
> *Arthur Mitchell*

But this book is aimed at enthusiasts not experts, and builds most on the approach I, Simon, took while writing for a dozen hobbyist magazines in the heyday of home micros, most particularly those for *Your Spectrum* magazine, the unabashedly technical precursor to the mass-market *Your Sinclair*, and my long running 'Tech Tips' columns in the best-selling ZX Spectrum magazine, *Crash Micro Games Action*, (usually just 'Crash') in which I set out every month to give tinkerers and experimenters amongst the readers a month of inspiration, beyond the twitchy world of game-playing, in just three pages. My aim is to make this 12 to 24 times better: good to last for a year or two.

You don't have to be a programmer, or even want to be one, to benefit from this book. Even if you mainly download and enjoy the efforts of others, the tips and techniques explained here will help you make better use of your Next. The book presumes that you have at least tried to read the official manual, and probably got stuck in several places. It assumes that you are interested in how Next works, why it's done that way, and how that helps or guides users of the machine.

A little practice typing in ZX Spectrum programs, recently or decades ago, will stand you in good stead. But rote re-typing is one aspect of the 1980s we can put behind us with relief. All the programs, large and small, listed in this book are freely downloadable and re-distributable, with attribution, under the Creative Commons licence.

For book-specific downloads, and links to related resources, look here:

`http://simon.mooli.org.uk/nextbook`

Please note that this is a **http** link not a 'secure' **https** one. I've nothing to hide and there's no reason to encrypt these files – indeed it makes them harder to download directly to Next or similar computers. The software is free, but please don't make copies of this book; encourage friends to buy one.

Legacy Compatibility

Much of the advice in this book is applicable to any user of the ZX Spectrum, from the 16k Sinclair original, through 48k and 128k models from Sinclair and Amstrad, whether off-the-shelf or expanded. The Next can be configured as an almost exact copy of each original Spectrum hardware implementation, more closely compatible with each of those than they were with one another, though its most spectacular capabilities show up in its native personality, running NextZXOS and NextBASIC. The philosophy behind these variants, and their differences, is an important part of this book.

Spectrum emulator users will also find useful information here, though the examples have all been tested on real Spectrum hardware and if your chosen emulator, be it CSpect, ZEsarUX, or something newer, has not kept up with the latest FPGA cores and NextZXOS distribution your mileage is bound to vary. This is a book about using the Spectrum, and particularly the latest versions, and if you've got a Spectrum Next everything here is relevant and can be done without buying or borrowing anything else.

Similarly, there is nothing here about using other supposedly more 'modern' computers to develop software to run on a Next. Given that classics like *Ant Attack* and *Lords of Midnight* were developed on the machines that ran them, relying only on cassette storage for version control, there's still less excuse now to distance yourself and complicate what you need to understand by involving muddleware and other less-dedicated machines.

There are always people willing to offer transient tips about 'PCs' but Simon sees no need to join them, having grown up and made a career before and despite the consumerist regressions of MSDOS and Windows. If you're just looking for creative fun, you need not join them, either. But it takes all sorts to make a world, and this is just one book from one of the older – and uncommonly prolific – enthusiasts among them.

> *Most of software today is glue code to get around the big packages*
> *Alan Kay*

What's here

A central aspect of this book is Garry Lancaster's NextZXOS, and particularly his advanced version of Sinclair ZX BASIC which allows users easy access to the Next system and associated hardware. There's one substantial program, split up into two banks and many small well-explained chunks, which illustrates many of the new BASIC features in context, rather than as a change-list shorn of rationale and comparative examples.

The NextBASIC Text Editor a useful program in its own right, filling one of the gaps in the early Next distro and allowing its wider capabilities to be explored and customised by reading and tweaking NextZXOS configuration files, as well as short programs and documents. It's an example that uses familiar ideas, if not cutting-edge ones.

There's far more to the Sinclair Scene than the Spectrum, before and since 1982; not only does NextZXOS ship with CP/M, and ZX80 and ZX81 emulators, the hardware can potentially be configured to implement those computers, and their peripherals, as accurately as it models the ZX Spectrum range. But progress on these new cores, and ones for later Sinclair-related machines like the QL, CST Thor, Z88 and MGT Sam Coupé has been slow. The Next team has understandably been preoccupied with the authentic and enhanced ZX Spectrum experience since work started in late 2017.

Promising but flaky cores for non-ZX micros have circulated, but those have been ported from less capable hardware made by much smaller teams, or individuals, and do not make full use of Next's potential. Team members, led by Phoebus Dokos and supported by Sinclairophiles like me, are determined to build official cores for the most relevant classic systems of the 1980s, making full use of the extended keyboard, HDMI, GPIO interface, Pi0 co-processor and external connectors, rather than just whichever bits it happens to have in common with a ZX Uno or similarly less-ambitious old-game consumption-orientated precursor.

But expert volunteer resources are limited; these official full-fat cores – for the first ZX machines, QL/Thor and MGT Sam in particular – are not yet a priority. Meanwhile there is one shining example of how Next hardware can be repurposed into a recreation of a British rival which fought hard for a place in the bedrooms and under the Christmas trees of 1980s micro enthusiasts. While it made more impact in UK schools – where Sinclair first aimed the ZX range – than at home, the Acorn BBC Micro is a great example of another way, born of the same fever that brought about the ZX Spectrum.

The 8-bit convergence

This is a Spectrum book, so I'm aware that only a minority of readers will have the BBC Micro experience or enthusiasm to make full use of the BBC Cores. Given the amount of general and specific Beeb information already in circulation, this book is not going to try to convert anyone from Sinclair to Acorn. The review is here to show how much un-tapped potential Next has, for Sinclair-related and other home computer or even console cores, and some impressive ways it's already been exploited. I plan to cover Sinclair-style cores in subsequent volumes.

I'm a Spectrum fan first, but follow Acorn with insight and experience, and advice from the real experts. The comparison between their approach and Sinclair's, to both hardware and software, is insightful even if your allegiance is firmly in the ZX camp. And the Beeb-aping capabilities of Next's hardware show how much Sinclair-related fun we have yet to look forward to, as official updates bring the same level of comprehensive support to non-Spectrum cores for Next as Hoglet and his colleagues have for the BBC Micro and its successors from Acorn.

How long is a 2MB cassette?

For readers who never progressed from ZX tape or Microdrive, still waiting hopefully for that **0:0 OK** message, there's loads of information here about file-handling and SD card support, which to my mind remove the last justifications for writing and testing Next software on anything but the Spectrum itself.

Next includes accurate hardware recreations of many rare and wonderful add-ons which only reached a minority of early Spectrum users. The SpecDrum-compatible Digital To Audio (DAC) sample converter (now extended to four channels, in stereo), the Zilog-style DMA controller, the Spectrum 128's AY 8912 sound chip (triplicated in Next, again with stereo and mixing enhancements) are all explained here, with practical examples that don't require assembly language to bring them to life, nor halting BASIC while they strut their stuff.

For those for whom square-wave beeps and attribute clash have never lost their charm, I explain how Next makes them easier to use and tame than ever before. Perhaps you'd rather not spend most of your processor power trying to get the 6¾K display to scroll smoothly, or move things on the screen without leaving a trail, re-treading challenges from the '80s?

If so, this book sets out to explain, by example and in simple steps, the new Spectrum capabilities borrowed from other systems – like the console-style tile-maps, hardware sprites, 512-colour palettes, display layers with hardware scrolling, and the Amiga-inspired Copper display co-processor. Next is similar in complexity and capability to the fourth generation of 'super home micros' like MSX2, the Acorn Archimedes, Apple GS or Amiga 1200.

This puts it ahead of the Commodore 64, Atari's 800 and ST, all 1990s game consoles and arguably the original Amiga. It's way more advanced than Spectrum rivals like the Memotech, Oric, Einstein or Acorn's Electron, not that it's every likely to sell in comparable numbers to any of those. From a hardware point of view it runs rings round the Sinclair QL or MGT SAM, though those particular 'super Spectrums' made greater strides in software than Next has yet matched, boasting Sinclair-style hardware and software integration aimed at tinkerers as much as users.

At first some of the detail may seem excessive, especially if you come to this book fresh from the fact-packed and labyrinthine Spectrum Next User Manual. Rather than restate information from that essential book, this one takes a different approach. It explains why and how aspects of the system work, drawing on history and working examples. The detail isn't waffle - it's there to help you understand the whole system and how it fits together, rather than focussing on individual features.

Next has far more features and sub-systems than can be clearly covered in a single volume, and doubtless the upgrade potential means there's more to come. But this volume is intended as the first in a series. Providing this one reaches a few hundred customers; future editions will be guided by reader feedback to delve deeper into the most exciting and enabling Nextras. Don't be shy! Just as in the original *Crash* magazine, or my later *Computer Shopper* columns, reader feedback and encouragement is the key to getting to read what you'd most enjoy.

For those tempted to dabble in machine-code, there are reviews of the main free Next-compatible assemblers, and debugging tips. The extra instructions of the Z80n, compared with Zilog's original Z80, are a moving target; but here and in future volumes I shall compare the new spells with the old subroutines, showing why they were added, and to some extent how.

This is with a view to encouraging the keenest readers to eventually edit the hardware, not just the system, or their own programs, when it won't quite do what they want, yet. But before making new stuff, it's sensible (and still fun) to take a firm grip on what we have already.

The FPGA hardware and its connections – like the extended soft-touch keyboard, ZX-style peripheral edge connector, joystick, tape and audio sockets – are designed specifically to be compatible with legacy add-ons, or logical extensions. But there are new ones too, and the ways the old ones work have changed or become more flexible as the world has turned.

Thus the fizzy dot-crawling but then still excitingly **colour** UHF TV output is replaced by a HDMI Interface, but Next also has an analogue connector, using the intermediate-tech 15-pin SVGA monitor socket, and that can equally well drive an authentic analogue CRT-based TV display via the European-standard linear RGB SCART connector. This gives a display with every detail of the original other than the grainy noise, offset colour and blurring characteristic of Sinclair's hastily-designed, barely tested and cost-reduced two-wire TV link and the 128's later and rather niche eight or 15-colour TTL digital option.

Notice how obscure numbers and acronyms have proliferated in that paragraph? They're a problem, more so now than ever before. One of the first purposes of this book is to go beyond the official 'quick start' guide in explaining what those terms refer to, how they came about, and how they relate to the screens in modern (web)shops,

ALPHABET SOUP

AV = Audio *and* Video

CRT = Cathode Ray Tube
20th-century TV display tech

HDMI = High-Definition Multimedia Interface
Modern TV AV connection

RGB = Red Green Blue
Separate colour components

SCART = Syndicat des Constructeurs d'Appareils Radiorécepteurs et Téléviseurs
1990s analogue AV hookup

TTL = Transistor-Transistor Logic
Digital on/off signalling

TV = Television

UHF = Ultra High Frequency
Broadcast TV waveband

or older – but still perhaps decades post-Sinclair – displays at the back of your loft, or awaiting recovery from a skip near you. So the first parts of this first volume will look at your options when setting up a new Next.

The initial couple of chapters set the scene for the inventions and explorations in the body of the book. To start with I shall explain how your Next manages to be compatible with the previous Spectrum models, despite their differences, and yet still capable of doing things none of them could match. Another complete chapter unravels the tangled history of display standards.

Here's an overview of the complete book. You don't need to read it all in order, and might want to skip some of the details first time through, but it's all there for a reason and makes sense as a whole, even though some of the 'history' might not seem directly relevant at first glance.

A Map of the Whole Book

Chapter 2 delves into the details of Spectrum versions and compatibility, Next personalities, Configuration menus, Kickstarter 1 and 2 hardware differences, mouse and track-ball input options. It's mostly about hardware.

Chapter 3 explains why your modern monitor or telly might not entirely be an improvement on the one you shared in 1982, and what do about it. It discusses the pros and cons of SCART, VGA and HDMI displays, analogue screen testing, screen capture, composite video converter devices, and graphics configuration commands.

Chapter 4 covers hardware connections: making a compatible tape lead, power supply issues, joystick choices and set-up, DIY optical input and output via the controller ports, adding a second SD slot, printing, configuring floppy discs and other plug-in interfaces.

Chapter 5 turns towards software, and NextBASIC in particular. It covers BASIC benchmark speed-ups and remaining bottlenecks, program source tokenisation, variable-name look-ups, avoiding memory leaks, stream and esxDOS file operations, backups and file comparisons. It also discusses programming the Copper co-processor from BASIC for sound and graphical effects, WiFi downloading and custom system menus.

Chapters 6, 7 and 8 demonstrate recently added features of NextBASIC. They present a carefully-designed Text Editor program while exploring the history of BASIC programming. The program demonstrates mouse selection and menus, keyboard polling, character sizes, integer optimisations and the practicalities of splitting large programs and data into banks. In its own right, the text editor is a neat utility for tweaking configuration files and short texts.

Chapter 9 details the history and development of Next systems, including ways to identify particular hardware and software versions and detect the availability of the Z80n processor. This will help you decide whether or not to upgrade your Spectrum Next and which older versions you might want to keep on spare SDs for backward-compatibility testing.

Chapter 10 dives into Z80n machine code with the first of two open-source drivers, capable of regularly running up to 64 'slot' routines in parallel with NextBASIC. This driver is written with the Odin native assembler.

Chapter 11 demonstrates some driver 'slot routines' in action. The Z80n programs vary in length from three to almost 200 instructions. All are explained, step by step, without presuming machine-code expertise.

Chapter 12 builds substantially on the 'slot' driver and automatic sprite update system introduced in NextBASIC 2.06, with support for smoother movement and more complicated paths, including fast fixed-point arithmetic routines which take advantage of Z80n processor extensions.

Chapter 13 is all about Next's memory, explaining the difference between BASIC Banks and MMU Pages, with programs to read any RAM page and replace system fonts. After that it shows by example how to help out the Z80n by using the DMA co-processor for animation and audio streaming.

Chapter 14 tunes into Next's three built-in AY-3-8912 programmable sound generators, providing procedures to emulate BEEP better and play multi-channel audio without stopping the main NextBASIC program.

Chapters 15 and 16 introduce a second driver, this time written with the NextBASIC inline assembler and extending NextZXOS to allow BASIC programs to set up and PRINT Layer 3 hardware TileMap graphics, for larger, faster displays, animated fonts, and image rotation. These chapters include examples of machine-code optimisation to trade speed for space.

Next's FPGA chip is reprogrammable in hardware as well as in software. **Chapter 17** introduces Virtual Hardware Design and VHDL, contrasting synthesising an FPGA core with conventional programming, using examples from Next's own circuits and logic design. It shows programmers and old-school electronics hackers the principles of FPGA design, by comparison with familiar hardware and software, including contributions by SpecNext core maintainer and VHDL expert Allen Albright.

Chapter 18 demonstrates how much Next still has to offer beyond the SpecNext default configuration. It shows ways to run BBC BASIC inside NextZXOS, giving a massive increase in floating-point performance, while comparing Sinclair and Acorn languages and operating systems.

NextZXOS can be temporarily replaced with two alternative cores that implement Acorn computer hardware, including very capable audio and graphics add-ons, and the 'tube' co-processor interface which runs extremely fast and capacious programs on the Pi0 in parallel with Next's FPGA, with hardware display acceleration via the second HDMI port.

Unmodified BASIC program performance can be thousands of times faster than the original BBC Micro and hundreds of times faster than any native Next BASIC. Programs to explore disc images and convert source between Sinclair, Acorn and Z80 BBC BASICs are included.

Reading order

The book has been designed, with occasional cross-references and reminders, so that most of the chapters can be read independently. The key exceptions are Chapters 7 and 8, which expect you to be familiar with the introduction to the NextBASIC Text Editor in Chapter 6, and Chapters 11 and 12 which build upon Chapter 10's Slot Driver. Chapters 15 and 16 are the most advanced and challenging, and should be read together, in order, once you're familiar with the Next-specific concepts previously introduced.

Example program downloads

All the substantial programs listed in this book are available for download from the book's support page at http://simon.mooli.org.uk/nextbook, or via GetIt, direct to your Next or net device, under the following titles:

GraphTech, an archive collating the little character set and font utilities, screen scrollers, fractal routines from the NextBASIC Facebook group, and **VGAgrid.bas** from Chapter 3, for setting up and comparing displays.

Bumper.bas, EsxDOShooks.bas and **NextDiff.bas** from chapter 5.

TextEditor examples from Chapters 6, 7 and 8, including fonts.

SlotDriver, the Slot driver and demo methods from Chapters 10 and 11.

SpriteHax from Chapter 12, with graphics.

DMAdemos from chapter 13, including example 8-bit audio samples.

VBEEP procedures from Chapter 14, including frame rate correction.

TileDriver source and demo programs from Chapters 15 and 16.

Beeb2Next from Chapter 18, with SSD image and BASIC converters, written in NextBASIC, and example BBC BASIC programs.

GetIt will soon be part of the SpecNext distro, and, if you don't have it yet, it can be downloaded for free from https://em00k.itch.io/getit

The cutting-room floor

I've been compiling notes for this book for more than six years. There's still rather a lot left over. WiFi, networking in general, deeper details of the palette system, interrupts, esxDOS, bus expansion and the recently-introduced CTC timers will have to wait till a future volume. The same applies to analogue inputs, CP/M, NextBASIC 2.10, MIDI, I2C, Core 4 and other Sinclair cores. I look forward to hearing your priorities and suggestions, but you've waited long enough – the next 17 chapters give you something to be going on with!

Chapter 2, Next Personalities

Next is not an emulator. It is several computers in one box. Each 'core' is one electronic configuration of the gate array, but the SpecNext core can be synchronised in several different ways, depending on the state of internal registers. Once loaded, the Next core can still switch between further wiring and timing arrangements. This is essential for 'Spectrum compatibility', because original Sinclair and Amstrad hardware products work in subtly different ways; software for any particular original system may not run as expected unless the Next core is fine-tuned to match.

These hardware configurations are known as 'personalities'. Current Next cores include four distinct personalities which implement different memory and display timings, independently of options that, for instance, tailor the video output for particular screens. Many programs are not fussy and run acceptably on any personality. This is how Amstrad were able to claim that the Spectrum +3, for example, was still a ZX Spectrum. But some programs are tightly bound to the specific hardware version they were developed and tested on. They look, sound or play differently on other versions.

Gremlin's 128k game *Auf Wiedersehen Monty* is one example. It won the Crash Readers' Best Game award in 1987, and includes 32k of sampled sound. This plays as expected on a Sinclair Spectrum 128, the black 'Toast-rack' model, or the first light grey Amstrad 128 +2 revision. But on later Amstrads, running the same program, the sampled speech is garbled. This is because Spectrum memory runs at different speeds, depending on whether it is shared between the Z80 Central Processing Unit (CPU) and the Ferranti ULA (Uncommitted Logic Array) custom-chip, or only accessible to the Z80. In a 16k Spectrum, all the RAM is shared. The extra 32k of memory in a 48k system is faster because it is implemented in a separate set of eight chips, and the Z80 has exclusive access to those.

Figure 2 – Cover art from the 48k Monty tape

The Spectrum 128 also uses two sets of memory chips, but this time each set can hold 64k bytes. One set is slower because sometimes the processor is made to wait, for a microsecond or so, while the ULA video circuit fetches information from that RAM. The other set of chips is 'uncontended' which means that it runs at a steady speed.

128 incompatibilities

Spectrum 128s manage their memory in 'banks' of 16k, four from each set of chips. Banks are numbered from 0 to 7, and Sinclair arranged that the even-numbered banks, 0, 2, 4 and 6 use the fast, uncontended chips, while odd-numbered banks 1, 3, 5 and 7 gave priority access to the display. When there's no video data to be fetched, while the screen border is being drawn, the Z80 doesn't have to wait. But as pixels and attributes are rendered to the middle of the screen, the CPU is delayed between 0 and 6 clock cycles, up to 1714 *billionths* of a second, while the display data is read.

These tiny delays add up, though the effect they have on a running program depends upon the exact mixture of machine-code instructions under test. Some need more access to RAM than others. The wait might stretch to seven cycles on later Amstrads.

ROM is not slowed down, which is why the 48k Spectrum isn't as much faster than the 16k Spectrum as you might expect, at least when running BASIC where the data is in RAM but all the code is fetched from fast ROM. In the most pathological case – a CPIR instruction running from contended RAM at the exact point when CPU and ULA access requests overlap most tightly – the ULA may seize two-thirds of the available time. In realistic programs, measured over many instructions and points in display output, the slowdown is between 20 and 25 per cent. The more time the Z80 spends 'thinking', processing already-fetched data rather than talking to the external memory, the less the effect. These irregular interactions explain why Gremlin's game sounds fine on an original 'Toast-rack' Spectrum 128 (nicknamed for its black gunmetal heatsink) yet unintelligible on a +3.

Graphics updates are similarly affected. Some games have enough slack time in their update loop that they look and play the same whether they run from contended or uncontended memory. Some run slow, or unevenly, if the code or data intended for fast memory ends up competing with the ULA.

Amstrad allocated these banks differently when they cost-engineered their original light-grey Spectrum 128, closely modelled on the Investronica design Sinclair adopted, into their final +2A,+2B and +3 variants. Those Spectrums run their first four banks at full Z80 speed, but allow ULA contention for banks 4..7 (the two dots denote a range: 4, 5, 6 or 7 in this case). For economy, ULA screen data must be in bank 5 or 7. This suits both 128k arrangements.

When Shaun Hollingworth and Pete Harrap wrote *Auf Wiedersehen Monty* they had Sinclair's specification, so they deliberately put the extra speech for the 128k version into banks 4 and 6, knowing that those were uncontended. Amstrad victims found they need a patch, devised decades later by *XoRRoX*, to divert the data into banks 1 and 3.

Rather than patch every other 128k program that runs awry, Spectrum Next users simply need to pick the personality that matches the expectations of the original programmer. ZXDB's 'machinetypes' field can help determine that. If a program does not run as you remember it, try another personality before saying Next is incompatible. There are quite a few corrupt snapshots in circulation, so it might also be worth looking for a different file download or digging out your original cassette.

Other differences between Spectrum versions affect the timing of display lines and the exact clock frequency. On early machines, contention slugs input port as well as memory accesses. The *Contended Memory* page at sinclair.wiki.zxnet.co.uk delves deep into the weeds of 128 system variations. I've simplified this discussion to highlight the most significant differences.

Next's modelling is very detailed, but not a perfect match for every computer Sinclair's sub-contractors ever shipped. Different batches of Ferranti ULAs contained workarounds and fixes that imposed even more subtle variations, though they're minor compared with the four cases Next specifically models. For subtleties of the original Spectrum, consult Chris Smith's masterwork, *The ZX Spectrum ULA*, ISBN 978-9565071-0-5

Personal choices and ROM revisions

Next starts up in a personality matched to Amstrad's final products. You can change this when a program loads, or via the configuration menu that Next puts up (while running an earlier core intended only for bootstrapping the system) if you hold down the space bar immediately after powering up:

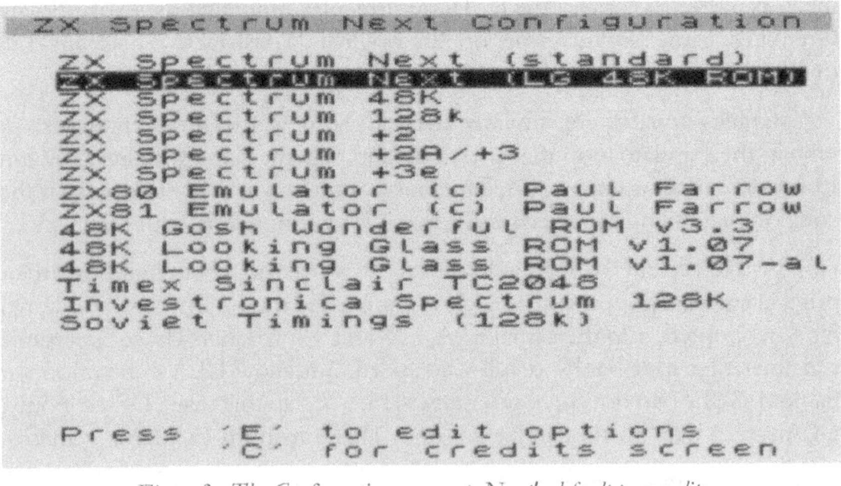

Figure 3 - The Configuration menu sets Next's default personality

The options in Figure 3 vary between NextZXOS releases. They are read from the **menu.def** file in the Machines/Next subdirectory of your startup SD card. They don't correspond directly to personalities, but are labelled to help users match specific models; for instance the 1985 Sinclair ZX Spectrum 128 and 1986 Amstrad ZX Spectrum +2 settings differ only in ROM.

Despite the different plastic cases, the same circuit designs are used in either of those. The only change in the personality configuration menu after 2.06 up to 2.09 is that *Soviet Timings (128K)* has been revised to *Pentagon 128K*. The Eastern European *Pentagon* micro was an unlicensed Spectrum clone with uncontended memory and eccentric display timing, which some hackers in Eastern Europe exploited to make demos which only look good if the video output is bent to suit.

The LoadZX Museum tells of the Timex Sinclair TC2048, a variant of the 48k Spectrum made in Portugal for sale in Poland in 1984, adding a Kempston-standard joystick socket, calculator-style keys, and a US-made custom chip giving Timex HiColor and HiRes output via composite video, as well as the Spectrum's default display. Respectively, those configurations match NextBASIC's LAYER 1,2 and 1,3 and LAYER 0.

Figure 4 - A Timex TC2048 (loadZX.com)

The five Configurations with '48' in their name all use original Sinclair timings. They differ only in their 16k ROM software. GW stands for Geoff Wearmouth, who patched Sinclair's ROM to fix bugs and add features, including letter-by-letter or abbreviated rather than keyword entry, BASIC renumbering and block-erase commands prefixed by REM.

LG stands for Looking Glass. It is an alternative without bulk editing commands but better suited for PS/2 external keyboards. Type STOP – as a keyword or in full – to toggle between input modes. Next's docs/roms directory gives more detail. The Next (standard) option uses an exact copy of Sinclair's original ROM, bugs and all, when switched into 48k BASIC, but the default is the LG ROM as that's very compatible – it makes ZX BASIC work the way the 1982 manual says it should – but less orientated around what *Computing Today*'s editor Henry Budgett dubbed the 'dead flesh' keyboard.

+2A/+3 and +3e options match the later Amstrads which introduced Plus3DOS; the +3e is Garry Lancaster's replacement 64k ROM set for those, with bug fixes and new features including IDEDOS hard-disc support. Pentagon/Soviet timings suit amateur-made Russian clones, which have no RAM contention and longer display frames. The rest, including the emulators, use original Spectrum 128 'Toast-rack' timing.

You are free to remove menu.def options that you'll never use, or shuffle the order to please yourself. If you have access to other ROMs, such as the 16k hardware diagnostics **testrom.bin**, or the 32k **ace.rom** from the formerly freely-distributable *Jupiter Ace* emulator for 128k Spectrums, you can add them to the menu. This is how I added those, after putting the 'ROM' files in my Machines/Next folder, using the program listed in Chapter 6, The NextBASIC Text Editor:

```
menu=Jupiter Ace,1,8,ace.rom
menu=Diagnostics,0,8,testrom.bin
```

The **1** selects a Toast-rack 128 personality, the **0** is for 48k hardware. The second digit can over-ride the display output configuration, but **8** is a sensible default which uses whatever you've previously selected from the Test Screen. Instructions are in the first Next manual, downloadable from SpecNext.com, and on the Quick Start card shipped with Nexts from the second Kickstarter batch, dubbed KS2. I shall explain why those options exist and what they do.

Over and above the four Personalities, which tweak the logical behaviour of Next's FPGA, the screen settings alter the speed of all Next's logic to suit the beam – or lack of beam – on TVs and monitors that would not otherwise match the TV standards Sinclair Spectrum's expected. Chapter 3, Screen Selections, explains all the grisly details.

So far we've only configured features of the original Spectrum, but Next has lots of add-ons built in, and you might want to tweak those to customise your set-up further, especially to plug in and use 1980s peripherals which might clash with Next's optional extras. Most of these options, like the Personalities, can be adjusted later with BASIC commands or via the Browser file-selection menu, but you can preset the defaults by pressing E from the first configuration menu and moving the cursor around in the usual way.

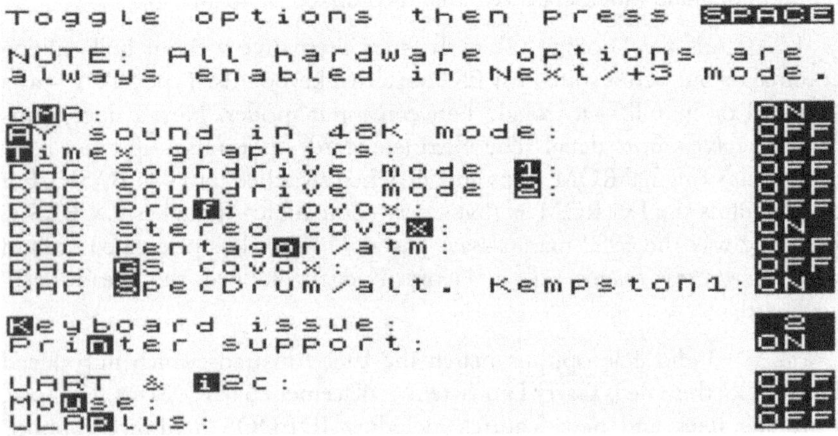

Figure 5 - Advanced hardware options revealed in Next's Browser .tap and snapshot load menu

Config Options explained

The initial Options menu has changed several times over the years. Figure 6 shows how it looked in 2018. Some items have been moved or renamed since, but it's still helpful to see them in their original places. We can still run any earlier Core and its matching NextZXOS on any Kickstarter 1 (KS1) board, by booting from the original SD card and pressing C to replace the current core with the older one. It's just as easy to swap back. Kickstarter 2 machines use a larger FPGA so they only suit cores made after the Spartan 6 chip became obsolete. There's lots more about this in Chapter 18, Alternative Cores.

The menus are a user-friendly way to alter values in the **config.ini** file read from Machines/Next when Next starts up. If you prefer typing to tapping you can edit this directly; reboot for the changes to take effect, and take care because if you get the syntax wrong Next could fail to start up till you revert the file to the previous version. Always keep a back-up copy!

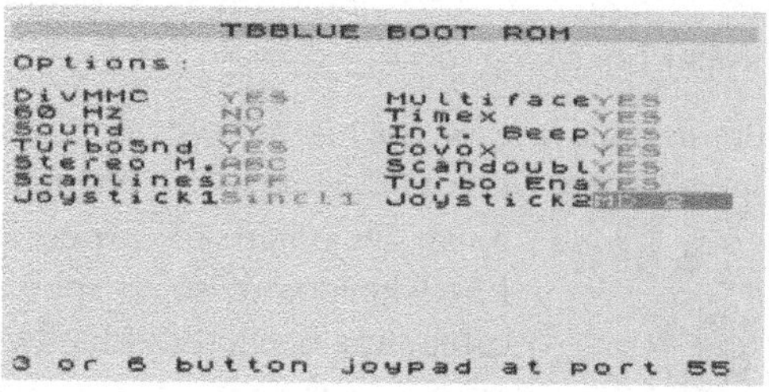

Figure 6 - The Options Menu from Next release 2.00

DivMMC is a Spectrum storage interface designed by Mario Prato, used by Miguel Guerreiro's esxDOS to read and write files on SD cards when NextZXOS is not available, usually in hardware personalities pre-dating +3e. Its hardware ports clash with Sinclair Interface 1 and MGT +D add-ons, as well external DivMMC and DivIDE hardware, so it's useful to have a way to turn it off, beside the REG commands noted later. Along similar lines, Romantic Robot's Multiface came in versions for each Spectrum variant, adding a 'magic button' with options to grab memory contents while a program runs. Multiface hardware built into Next works if that option is set to Yes, otherwise it's hidden for compatibility. Next's green button triggers it, using custom NextZXOS code while running NextBASIC or looking for original Multiface ROM images for older sorts of Spectrum. For licencing reasons these ROMs are not shipped as part of the Next SD distro. The same applies to the closed-source esxDOS.

Scanlines is a cosmetic option that spaces out pixel rows, vaguely like the striations visible close-up on an old non-interlaced TV tube. The **60 Hz** option is best left off, unless your screen is so alien to European standards that there's no other way to get it working, as it's not very compatible.

Scandoubl adjusts the display output from interlaced format, like analogue broadcast TV, to the 'progressive' format required by HD and PC monitors, by simply sending each line twice, at double speed, 31 kHz. Newer systems incorporate this into the R and V screen selections, as most VGA-spec monitors need it but RGB (SCART) screens only expect 15.6 kHz scanning. **Timex** enables port 255 and the HiRes and HiColor LAYER 1 display options. It's optional because a few games like *Arcanoid* read that port, expecting undocumented pre-Timex behaviour, for beam synchronisation – that technique doesn't work on later Amstrads, anyway.

Turbo Ena sets bit 7 of REG 6, enabling the F8 hotkey to change the CPU speed. I worked this out by scanning through editor.c in the app/src directory. Controller options are explored in the Joysticks section, leaving only a mixed bag of audio-related switches.

Covox is stereo sample-replay hardware. **Turbo Snd** puts three Spectrum 128 chip-music synths in place of the original Spectrum 128's one. **Sound**

selects between subtly-different Programmable Sound Generator chips (see Chapter 14, Better BEEPs) while **Stereo Md.** distributes the three soundchip channels between left and right stereo channels in two different ways to match incompatible non-standard stereo output modifications. **Int. Beep** determines whether all the audio or just original BEEP clicks are routed to the optional internal 'loudspeaker' – Figure 88 shows how I hacked one of those onto my Issue 2A development board.

By the time NextBASIC 2.06 shipped the menu had grown to match Figure 7, alongside. Originally Next defaulted to expect a PS/2 keyboard, so a 'splitter cable' was needed to plug in a mouse at the same time. The PS/2 socket contains wiring for two serial interfaces, respectively intended for a mouse and a keyboard. Once the beautiful new case was ready the hardware default was switched from keyboard to mouse, so people without an adapter could easily plug in a PS/2 mouse (or any trackball or touch-pad that uses the same IBM-standard interface) and type on the Rick Dickinson keyboard.

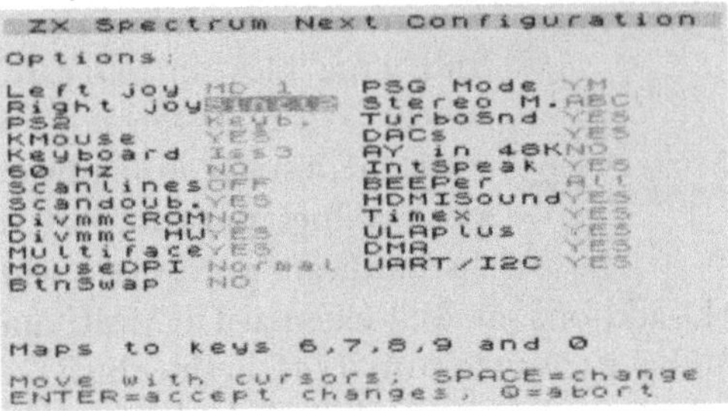

Figure 7 - The Expanded Options menu of Next 2.06

This can get confusing when swapping between cores, so the new **PS2** option lets you switch the default from **Mouse** back to **Keyb**.

If you have a splitter cable you can achieve the same effect, or more confusion, by swapping the mouse and keyboard leads over. If it works, leave it alone. If not, swap the leads or the menu option – but not both, or you'll be back where you started!

Figure 8 - A rather rare Sinclair-branded PS/2 mouse, dished out to the faithful by Henrique at one of Chris Wilkins' Crash shows in Kenilworth

Since you need to cold-start Next to access the menu that's rather inconvenient, so the dot command **.ps2mode** will flip the configuration bit in REG 6 without resetting your micro; parameters **-k** and **-m** give priority to the keyboard or mouse.

PS/2 devices are not meant to be 'hot-swapped' and liable to stop communicating if you swap them around while Next is powered up. Turn off your Next while you are plugging them in, and turn it off again before you unplug them.

There are three more mouse-related options. **KMouse** turns on three ports associated with Datel and Kempston mouse interfaces, for dozens of Spectrum programs compatible with those **BtnSwap** exchanges the interpretation of the buttons to suit some left-handed people. **MouseDPI** adjusts the mouse sensitivity, so that a rodent designed for a giant megapixel screen doesn't shift our relatively low-resolution cursor too fast for accurate positioning. Chapter 8, Banked Editor Procedures, shows how to read those ports in NextBASIC or Z80 code. As with any built-in hardware, it's best to leave this switched on unless you plan to connect peripherals that use those port addresses for another purpose.

Figure 10 - This unbranded PS/2 trackball is fully compatible with Next

Arguably the killer app for Next mouse-pushers is *Krystle Designs*, a freely-downloadable editor for sprites, fonts, palettes, tiles and screens, with excellent documentation, written entirely in NextBASIC. Snarf it from leeorg.itch.io/krystle-designs

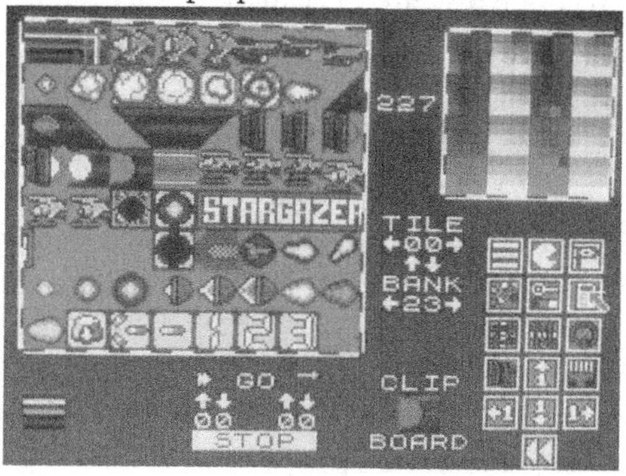

Figure 9 - Lee Duke's Krystle Designs in action

Those more into bleeps than pixels should check out *NextDAW* in the demos folder on your Next SD card, a 9-channel Digital Audio Workstation for creating chiptunes with a PS/2 mouse, written in Japan by Gari Biasillo.

By the time you read this there may be even more embedded hardware and switches to turn it on and off. CTC timers were recently added, but have yet to surface in that menu. A radical re-think of the options led to Figure 11, the latest Options menu as I write this. The Next team realised that, rather than give an ever-increasing set of global menu options, to be tweaked with REG commands or by restarting the system and toggling menus, it made more sense to separate hardware-setup controls from those which affected how the system worked with particular software, especially games and demos.

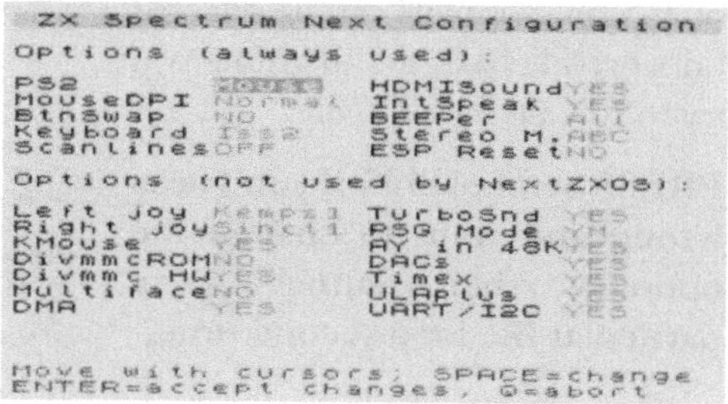

Figure 11 – Options in NextZXOS 2.07 to 2.09

The best default for one title might clash with another, so the second set of options, now captioned 'not used by NextZXOS' in Figure 11, provides ***defaults just for the legacy personalities,*** unless over-ridden by file-specific settings that can be tweaked via Figure 5 when a program is first launched from the browser, customising the hardware personality for that particular title. This means a game that expects TurboSound or a Sega joypad can automatically select those settings, while another that auto-detects the programmable sound generator and has different audio on 48k and 128k systems can be configured to work either way by the new **AY in 48k** setting. Likewise games that may use an extended palette can run without it (in traditional colours) by tweaking the **ULAplus** toggle.

Sound has been renamed **PSG Mode**, **Covox** is now **DACs**, **Int. Beep** is **IntSpeak** and the old **DivMMC** option has been split into **ROM** and **HW** versions so either the software or hardware can be hidden or replaced independently. **DMA** hides or reveals the Zilog Z8410 Direct Memory Access hardware explained in Chapter 13, Memory.

UART/I2C controls the WiFi and Real Time Clock hardware serial interfaces, to be explained in a later volume. Meanwhile, leave them switched on if you want NextZXOS to work normally, and turn them off if your custom hardware clashes with the relevant ports listed in **The ZX Spectrum Next Hardware Ports List**, which is in the manual right after the big cryptic list of **The Next Registers**, which are discussed throughout this book.

Browser auto-configuration

The Spectrum Next's file browser makes several adaptations to boost compatibility. Snapshot files with names ending **.sna** or **.z80** have contention turned on automatically after loading. Multi-part tape **.tap** files run with contention on and Timex features off, in 48k mode only. Other options can be selected on a per-file basis the first time you try to run a legacy ZX file.

PRESS Symbol Shift if you guess wrong and want to change the options when launching a particular file for a second time.

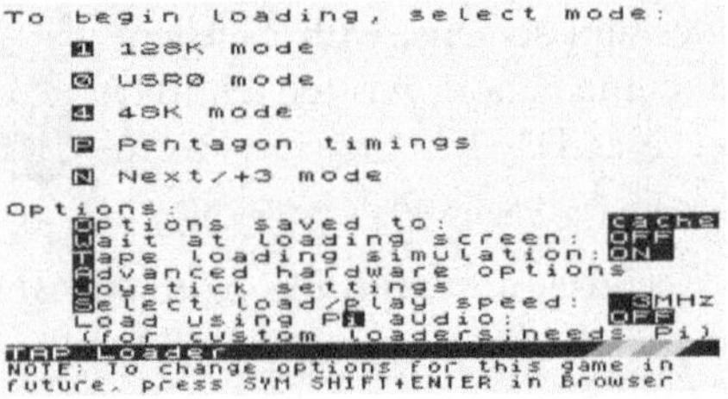

Figure 12 - Browser Snapshot file options

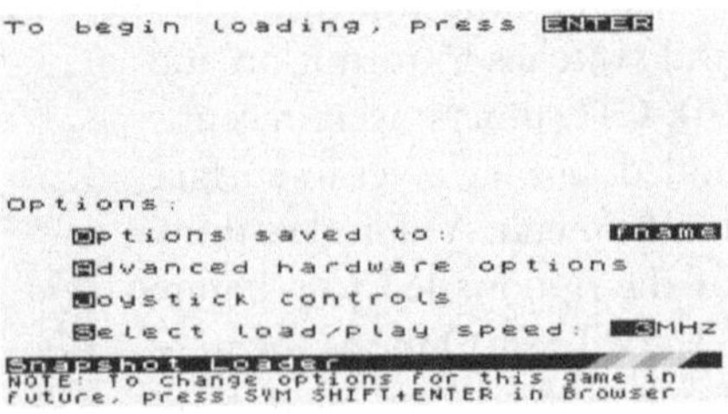

Figure 13 - Browser .tap cassette file options

I'm certain we've not seen the final version of these menus, which is why I've spelled out how they've developed. You might still need to know about the old menu if you've swapped to an older release, perhaps in order to load alternative cores for Spartan 6 Nexts that are not compatible with changes to the core menu and bootstrap system which arrived with NextBASIC 2.06h and Core 3.01.05. There are a few that require the old system, mainly quick ports by FPGA pioneer Victor Trucco.

All the cores for the original Spartan 6 FPGA need updating for the new larger Artix 7 chip in Kickstarter 2 Nexts. While we're still waiting for multicore support on those systems it's understandable that the old projects haven't been updated. There may be third-party cores that only work on Kickstarter 2 or later hardware, but SpecNext Ltd has committed to continue to support all versions, from the Issue 2A developer boards through the official clones like N-Go and Xberry Pi, which also use the Spartan 6, to the KS2's Issue 4 and whatever future Kickstarters and clone efforts may bring.

Future core files will hold bitstreams for both old and new FPGAs, but I've decided not to delay this volume waiting for them. Chapter 18, Alternative Cores, sets out the situation for early adopters, and what Kickstarter 2 backers can look forward to when the dust settles and volunteers find time.

Next board hardware versions

I have an issue 2A Next board from 2018 and an issue 4 (internally known as issue 2H) from the second Kickstarter, delivered in 2023. There are more than a dozen groups of hardware changes between these, involving over a hundred components. None of these affect the logical performance of the boards – they're fully compatible, digitally – but there are many changes in the analogue performance, nanosecond timing and signal thresholds between the batches. Without quite drilling down to the details of individual components, here's my hobbyist-level summary of the story so far.

Logical comparisons

The Ferranti ULAs Sinclair and Acorn chose in 1981 contained the equivalent of 1000 logic gates. MGT's 1988 SAM ASIC (Application Specific Integrated Circuit, a step from ULA to FPGA) had ten times that capacity. Next's FPGAs are so much more flexible that comparisons are necessarily vague; they could model between 120,000 and a million gates, depending on the particular arrangement the designer needs.

Most of the following information comes from Allen Albright via Mike Cadwallader's YouTube videos tagged @SpectrumNextStuff, and Mike's blog on the SpecNext.com website. There's stacks of useful information there, but after seven years much of it is out of date. The product numbering gets confusing; the missing Issue 3 boards were labelled 2E; work on those stopped when Xilinx put their Spartan 6 FPGA chip fabrication plant offline for two years, suggesting that developers switched to their Artix 7, made on a higher-resolution process, still in Taiwan, with 'only' one year of lead-time.

Mike explained the Artix part chosen has 'slightly larger' capacity in terms of logic but uses a four-times bulkier bitstream for configuration, so the on-board startup memory was increased from 16 megabytes to 32. Either way this dwarfs Next's RAM, but it's only used to hold cores read into the FPGA at startup, leaving a capacity for 30 alternative cores on Spartan 6 systems and 14 – still plenty – with KS2. The rest of the system, including ROM programs, loads from SD once the FPGA is initialised.

Cased KS1 boards are labelled issue 2B and very similar to the earlier dev boards. The new case and keyboard required an extra couple of connections to the internal GPIO connector, a grid of user-configurable interface signals popularised by the Raspberry Pi project, and a capacitor was added to smooth the 9 volt DC power input. The main aim for Kickstarter 2 was to fix known weaknesses of the first batch and production-engineer its electromagnetic performance, to the point where the complete unit met commercial standards for handling interference in and out of the system.

Kickstarter 2 board revisions

The KS2 connectors were variously filtered, buffered and decoupled, giving a less 'noisy' analogue VGA output, more powerful edge connector bus and HDMI signals, and a fix for the 'back-power' issue that meant disconnecting HDMI to be sure of resetting a KS1 system properly. N-Go clones include the HDMI fix but not the other KS2 enhancements.

KS1 backers got used to a quiet background burble of bleeps and clicks caused by interference between the ESP01 WiFi add-on and the stereo audio output. This can be temporarily muted by disabling WiFi with the REG 2,128 command; REG 2,0 brings it back.

KS2 uses a more modern but still-compatible ESP12F, soldered-down, decoupled and moved away from the audio circuits. New machines no longer chirp like they're haunted, and communication is more reliable at speed as the ESP12F has extra 'flow control' signals, but it's no longer possible for avid hackers to reprogram the unit. They can use the CN9 connector to disable the on-board WiFi and put their own customised ESP01 in its place, but it's not a recommended hack.

Besides better buffering, greater power capacity and 5V compatibility, the KS2 edge connector gives more control for bus request and interrupt signals from external devices, but it still lacks three of the power rails present on the 48k Spectrum it was copied from. The old -5V supply was only intended for obsolete 16 kilobit DRAMs and the pulsed 12V 'AC' line was even less useful, but serial ports in the Interface 1 and similar peripherals need +12V which Next does not directly provide.

Adding a DC to DC converter for these expansions was ruled too costly, but KS2 boards have extra ringed pads showing where a third-party supplies can be tacked on. I'd start with a £1 MT3608 DC upconverter board, running like the rest of the Next from an external *regulated* 9V supply so it is always stepping the input voltage up. If you try this, let me know how you get on!

Infernal Squeaker

Next's internal speaker connector was originally only meant for BEEP and authentically quiet, running from the FPGA's 3.3V supply on KS1. Other audio can be routed there but is distorted and barely audible from a tiny-Sinclair-style speaker, which must have an impedance above 30Ω. The second setup includes a 5V supply and provision for a more sophisticated amplifier, but you still need to add your own parts to bring out the potential. Sinclair boosted volume in 1982 by adapting the Issue 2 Spectrum to use the 9 volt rather than 5 volt supplies, but it was always rather quiet. The later Sinclair QL speaker was so much more powerful that SuperBASIC designer Jan Jones recommended 'a woolly hat' in the absence of a volume control!

The Spectrum's remarkably tolerant cassette input was a tribute to the hybrid analogue and digital skills of Ferranti. Although Next uses a similar conditioning circuit it's less sensitive, especially on the Artix 7, so one of the diodes has been replaced with a lower-drop Shottky type to close the gap. There's more about cassette compatibility in Chapter 4, Simple Hardware Projects.

One extra feature of the new FPGA is a set of very fast 12-bit analogue to digital converters; they're not currently used by Next, and absent from the Spartan 6, but Issue 4 boards include three points, labelled J11, J22 and J24, where hardware experts can inject analogue input signals. The sampling hardware can be triggered and read by reference to the new REG 248..250 set.

It's not over yet

That was a potted history of Next versions. There's much more that has been and could still be said, some of it in Chapter 9, Next variations and History. There's even the possibility of getting the hardware or system software extended to suit your own designs. But there's a wealth of good stuff already up for grabs. This book is one expert hobbyist's attempt to catalogue and explain that.

As with my magazine articles in the 1980s, this is the best I can work out by experimentation and scouring published information. We're all volunteers and I have no special access to any secret source for Next. Apart from NextZXOS, which only Garry gets to see as text, the project is entirely open-source. Be wary when looking through old Wikis and Forum posts; Next is a moving target and much of the information accumulated there was correct in 2019 but could have changed since.

> ***The journey is the reward***
> *Steve Jobs*

The most profound way to learn about Next is to experiment with it. This will remain true, just as it was in 1982 for the original Sinclair ZX Spectrum. Enjoy!

Chapter 3, Screen Selections

You've got a Next, and after experimentally connecting several screens and restarting it several times while tapping D, V or R – for HDMI/DVI, VGA or SCART cables – you've probably got a readable picture. With luck you've also got sound, either via the headphone-style stereo or HDMI TV sockets on the back. If not, please carefully re-read the instructions that came with your computer, replies on the Spectrum Next Facebook groups, or the latest SpecNext.com website pages. This book gives context and much more detail.

TVs, monitors, LCDs and CRTs

It may seem that as fast as any new tech becomes commonplace it's swept away by a new, incompatible semi-replacement so we all have to go shopping again, learning a new set of acronyms and hidden misfeatures. As a Spectrum Next enthusiast you've probably seen this happen several times over the last four decades. Such obsolescence is a particular problem for retro-computers as they need to remain true to the original display standard, while usable with modern replacement screens for those who cast out their old analogue displays sometime last century.

> ***If it works, it's obsolete***
> *Marshal McLuhan*

The 1982 Spectrum was designed to connect to most UK televisions via the socket intended for broadcast TV reception. This determined the shape of the screen, the amount of detail it could display, and the rate at which pixels were transmitted. That standard lasted for 30 years, until desktop computers demanded higher resolution, achieved by shrinking the fuzzy dots on a vacuum tube display, speeding up the scanning beam to fit more in, and separating the component signals to reduce the smearing of colours.

Such VGA (Video Graphics Array) systems were increasingly constrained by analogue connections, so when liquid crystals and similar electronic matrix displays delivered comparable performance makers pivoted to bigger arrays of square pixels, first via DVI (the office Digital Video Interface) then at home with HDMI. This progressively-doubled resolution from the million-pixel *HD Ready* format to the modern *8k* standard for 33,177,600 million pixels. An original Spectrum, or a Next in most configurations, puts up just 49,152 pixels. If those were mapped one-to-one onto a modern screen it'd occupy a postage-stamp sized rectangle. Spectrum pixels have to be duplicated and stretched to remain readable.

Complicating this further, modern screens are a different shape, wider for a given height, and expect data at several rates. 1980s games were designed around the display rate, which varied then around the world and even more now. Next works hard to adapt authentic ZX images for new displays, but the results inevitably depend on the particular screen you're trying to connect, what is was made for and where you bought it. If you're just tinkering for your own amusement, this hardly matters. But if you plan on sharing your efforts, or running programs made by other people, it makes a big difference.

For maximum authenticity without sacrificing clarity you'll use a 20th Century monitor with stereo sound and an analogue RGB input, such as a Philips CM-8833 or Commodore 1040S. If, like me, you've dropped yours and it won't work anymore, you can get close with a late 20th-century European telly with a full implementation of the SCART standard. These can be linked to Next's VGA analogue display socket with a simple cable. The original Next manual, and the 'Quick Start Guide' included with later production, summarise the way display outputs and standards are selected. This longer text explains why those options exist, the implications of choosing each one, and how to get the best out of your Next, depending on your priorities and the audio and video hardware at your disposal.

Considerations include screen shape or 'aspect ratio', pixel resolution, and frame rate. Analogue displays try to adapt to whatever you feed into them, but digital ones are fussier and show nothing at all, or a taunting message, if the data doesn't match their built-in expectations. The muddle started last century, so let's try to catch up before the rules change again.

Frame rate

A century ago, mains electricity supplies used DC current, like the nominal 9V supply into most Spectrum models. The exact voltage – and hence size of your TV picture – depended on the supply and length of the wire from the generator. My grandparents' black-and-white TV picture used to shrink as the farm's batteries ran flat, till one of them gave up squinting and trudged out into the stables to kick the DC diesel generator on again.

Transformers were needed to boost the voltage for efficient distribution. Those require AC (alternating current) so after a tussle between power companies, involving dog-electrocution demos to highlight the danger of rival systems, mains power was made to alternate up and down so it could be transformed magnetically between voltages. In Europe and down under we settled on 50 cycles per second, later known as 50 Hertz, while North America and Japan opted for a lower delivery voltage and smaller transformers, pulsing at 60 Hertz. Neither was a good match for the 24 Frames Per Second (FPS) rate of cinema, as we'll see later.

Films and analogue TV pictures are redrawn or 'refreshed' many times a second, exploiting the persistence of vision so that the image appears continuous. To simplify the design and minimise annoying flicker when TV was introduced, the rate of display refresh was matched to the AC mains.

50 Hertz was so finely guaranteed in the 1960s that Ferranti made office computers with front clocks run from the AC mains, and (mostly shellac or vinyl) disc turntables frequently used mains cycles as a timing reference. That's why fairground singles played flat while the Waltzer was spinning up…

Similarly, the displays of early Tandy micros imported into Britain wobbled distractingly as their unadapted 60 Hertz American screens struggled with UK 50 Hertz mains. Conversely, Acorn Atom displays used US chips that struggled to sync with 50 Hertz tellies. It was a mess. It still is.

Modern HDMI TVs are all required to support some TV-standard signal. But these may run at 50 or 60 Hertz; European sets may only support 50 Hertz, although it's common for ones made for sale elsewhere, and digital computer monitors worldwide, to only work properly at around 60 Hertz.

This matters to us because the only regular timing signal in a Spectrum is the 'frame interrupt', and almost all ZX software was created on the assumption that this would occur 50 times per second. If it comes more often, as it must to accommodate 60 Hertz display frame updates, games in particular get upset. They may run 20 per cent fast, if their code can reliably finish in 16.7 rather than 20 milliseconds, or at 60% of the proper speed if it needs the extra time, and it over-runs so it's only updated at alternate frames. Such titles will alternate between these rates, depending on what's going on, which can make them hard to play.

Modern action games like *Old Tower* by RetroSouls achieve high-resolution colour effects which would seem incredible last century, but rely on such precise timings that they're almost unplayable unless the display matches their expectation. There's also a handful of 'Nirvana Engine' games that work this way. There are faster and easier ways to program such effects on Memotech, MSX, Next and SAM computers that allow larger attribute files, but they remain acute tests for retro display compatibility.

Next's display rates

Ideally we'll all have 50 Hertz displays compatible with all classic ZX software and almost all the new stuff – there are a few perverse titles that are set up for 60 Hertz PC monitors, but they are outliers. The further from 50 Hertz your display runs, the less compatible it will be. But Next was designed to be used, rather than to force the re-opening of 70s TV factories like the ones that later churned out Tatung Einsteins and Commodore computers, and many computer monitors won't synchronise to the 50 Hertz European TV standard.

Almost all modern screens can work at 60 Hertz, but that's a poor match for Spectrum software. In fact many monitors, especially those with an analogue VGA interface, start to behave themselves somewhere between 50 and 60 Hertz. In a grand hack that impressively shows the flexibility of its design, the entire Next system can be sped up to match arbitrary PC screens while minimising the impact on game-play, music and sound-effects.

Three bits in the custom-chip register REG 11 correspond to the current display output. They're normally set from the start menu, but can be read later with the REG function if you've forgotten which setting is in effect.

You can't currently change them without resetting. VGA0 is the most compatible while VGA1 to 6 progressively speed up the entire computer – not just the screen but also sounds, file transfers and program execution – to bring it in range of whatever LCD panel you found in a skip and hope to repurpose. The eighth setting, which could be VGA7, is reserved for the digital HDMI output. Next originally ran that at 48.2 Hertz but it's been experimentally cranked up to 50 Hertz by reprogramming the hardware.

I recommend that you step through all the test-cards displayed after you turn on Next with the V key held down, till you find the first one your display can handle. The lower the setting the more compatible it will be with golden-age Spectrum games. The higher it is, the faster Next will be forced to run to keep up with your alien screen technology!

REG 17	Display output	MHz	Rate
0	SCART/VGA0	28.0	50.0
1	VGA 1	28.6	51.0
2	VGA 2	29.5	52.6
3	VGA 3	30.0	53.6
4	VGA 4	31.0	55.4
5	VGA 5	32.0	57.1
6	VGA 6	33.0	59.0
7	HDMI	27/28	48.2/50

Table 1 - Display output frame rates in Hertz

Allen Albright has explained: "What happens with increasing VGA setting is that the system clock is increased at each step but all the timing relationships are kept the same. This means the display will still work as expected but the computer will actually be running faster so games will run faster and audio will be higher pitch. 50Hz VGA0 is where the standard Spectrum speed will be found and ideally is what you want to use for this kind of thing. The other VGA modes are for monitors unable to sync to a 50 Hertz frame, which is outside the VGA spec."

Almost every VGA monitor will sync happily to VGA 6, 59 Hertz, and many PC monitors accept VGA 2, leaving games pretty playable and only musicians with perfect pitch discomfited. Simultaneous output of 50 Hertz graphics through both VGA and HDMI is possible, though not all cores support it and it's incompatible with the VGA2 to VGA6 compromise settings. I've used it to show the difference between analogue and digital displays at Crash shows. On KS2 hardware, VGA0 and VGA1 settings also drive HDMI output. The original KS1 HDMI output was accompanied by slow VGA, but the beta 3.02.01 HDMI core for those systems does not output anything to the VGA port at the same time.

HDMI may be convenient for us but in the California tech cartels cinema is still more lucrative than interactive media so original Next cores serve that at 48.2 Hertz for interpretation as doubled-up 24 Hertz cinema. Don't expect even borders or exact aspect ratios; Sinclair and analogue broadcasters just aimed towards the middle. From Core version 3.02.01 VGA7/HDMI output has been tweaked for 50 Hertz output, though work continues to improve compatibility with weird screens out in the wild. There is a handy list of over 300 modern monitors that support 15.6 kHz analogue RGB signals online at 15khz.miraheze.org.

This leaves only the 60 Hertz switch, shown in alternate menus, for further experiment. Sinclair's 60 Hertz products (Timex TS-series and Samsung QLs) had VHF RF outputs and lots of timing eccentricities to complicate things like porting Aquaplane from Quicksilva's hacked up original PAL border effect onto the 60 Hertz Timex 2068. On the American QLs even the fonts had to scrunch up so the Psion business software suite fitted onto a 192-line NTSC telly! There is a separate 60 Hertz mode, toggled by bit 2 of REG 5, but this is disabled when SCART output is active; it relies on eccentric hacks, altering the timing of each screen line and suppressing some completely, so it's only recommended as a last resort. It's certain to upset many machine-code games more than VGA 6 or – if compatible – one of its lower-numbered brethren.

Next VGA Tester

The following little program reveals how Next's VGA output is mapped onto the preset pixels of a digital LCD or plasma screen. It plots a simple grid of lines at the maximum pixel resolution. On a HDMI display all the lines are equally and precisely placed. On a CRT, they're fuzzier but unless the resolution has been compromised, by intermediate filtering or conversion to composite or UHF formats, the lines should still be regularly-spaced vertically and horizontally, each line within the text characters clearly visible.

```
 80 INK 2: PAPER 0: LAYER 1,2
100 FOR i=0 TO 255 STEP 2
110   PLOT i,0: DRAW 0,175
120 NEXT i
130 FOR %y=0 TO 88 STEP 2
140   PLOT 0,%y: DRAW 511,0
150 NEXT %y
170 PRINT AT 12,33;
   "1234567890ABCDEFGHIJKLMNOPQRST"
180 PRINT AT 13,33;
   "!@#$%&'()_<>=+-^*/?`:UVWXYZ|\{"
190 PRINT AT 14,33;
   "}1234567890ABCDEFGHIJKLMNOPQRS"
200 PRINT AT 15,33;
   "][!@#$%&'()_<>=+-^*/?`:UVWXYZ;"
```

Like all the programs in this book, this VGAgrid example is available for download via *GetIt* or from my homepage, but if you're still setting up it won't take long to type in; it's the first seven lines which draw the vital grid.

Figure 14 is an oversampled photo of part of the display from that program on a typical small LCD monitor, a DGM L3619DD. With DVI as well as VGA video input, this is a reasonable match for Next's output as it syncs down to 50 Hertz, the VGA0 setting, giving authentic timing for classic games. Its 4:3 aspect ratio avoids black sidebars or stretched pixels; a stereo analogue sound socket feeds its front-facing speakers. The VGA plug leaves the Next's expansion connector clear for plug-in goodies from your original Spectrum collection, but at a price – the monitor interprets the analogue VGA signal as an unusual 660x560 resolution and in order to map that to the screen's XGA 1280x800 LCD pitch, *some pixels end up wider than others.*

This is particularly noticeable across the screen, with uneven vertical bands appearing when the two grids – from the computer, and the screen – interfere. You can move these bands around by adjusting the analogue TV input settings – phase, clock and image position – but you can't make them go away unless your LCD happens to be an exact match or integer multiple of the resolution it infers from the analogue signal. Almost all VGA displays show this issue, which is particularly obvious when using Timex HiRes or 16-colour TileMaps. Those layers are otherwise ideal for editing documents and programs, so these VGA artefacts are most annoying for tinkerers and native software developers.

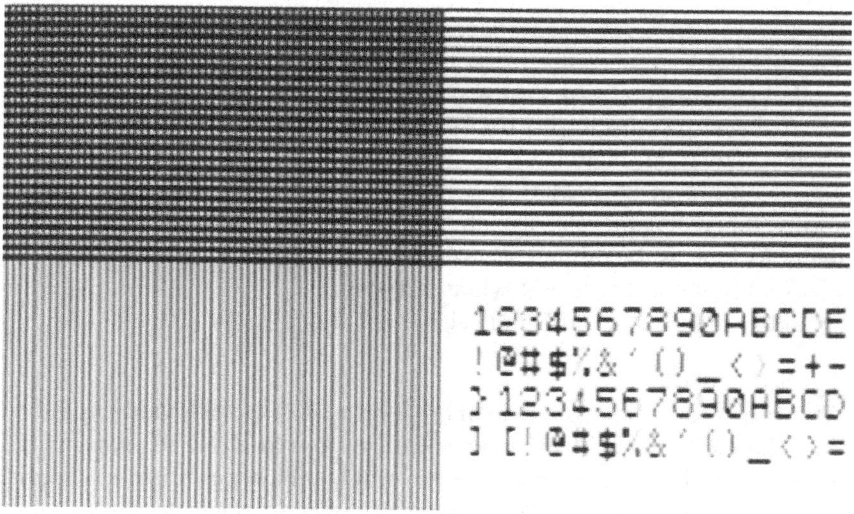

Figure 14 – Digital display artefacts exposed by the VGAgrid test

The bands are still present but less obvious when playing old games, as their lower resolution means pixels tend to be rounded to multiples of two or three, or three or four, rather than just one or two. The higher the native resolution your display has the less conspicuous the bands become, but they remain present and are more obvious on some images than others, depending on their contrast and edges, introducing a shuttering flicker during horizontal scrolling which would not appear on HDMI and gets smoothed out by CRTs.

HDMI (or the video-only equivalent DVI) maps each of Next's pixels to an exact and regular grid – 720 by 576 pixels for Spectrum 50 Hertz PAL pixels and borders – so the same program displays this on an HDMI screen:

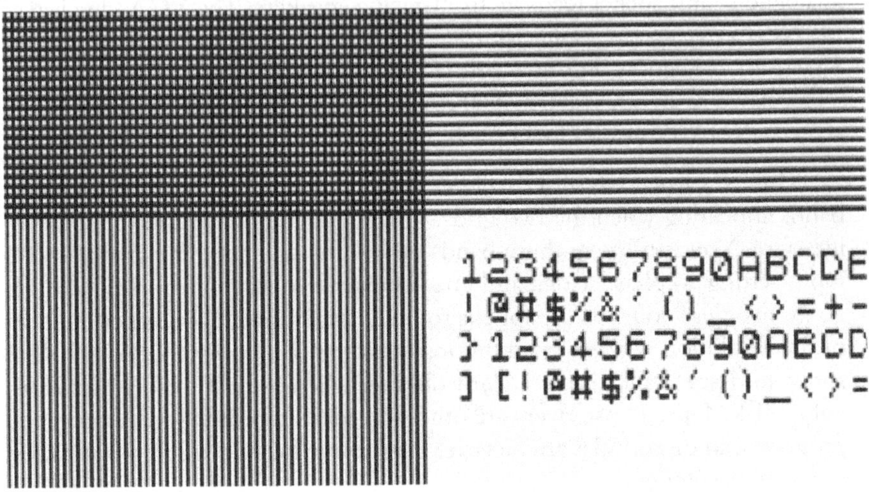

Figure 15 – HDMI displays map Spectrum pixels exactly

Rather than photograph the screen with my iPhone 7+, as I've done for the analogue pictures in this book, I used the HDMI Video Capture USB dongle shown in Figure 16 to display Next's output in a QuickTime window and grabbed Figure 15 digitally from there. As long as the printers have done a good job, all the black and white lines should be identical in width and height.

Figure 16 - £10 HDMI capture dongle

TV 'standards'

A particular and unique problem of broadcasts and especially video tapes first made on the National Television Standards Committee (NTSC) system used in Japan and USA was interplay between the luminance (brightness) signal previously standardised for black and white reception, and the chrominance or color (sic) components added later. The fake US-TV bulletins by 'Barabra Wintergreen' in Armando Iannucci and Christopher Morris's news spoof *The Day Today* sent this up for nerd-triggering and comic effect. NTSC was said, quite plausibly, to stand for 'Never Twice Same Colour'.

This led to the development of the mostly European alternative PAL (Phase Alternate Line) system which cancelled out the worst of these errors by reversing the phase-bending applied to alternate lines of the picture, giving less interference and better backward compatibility, but more flicker. The optionally more-interlaced but otherwise PAL-like 'Sequential Colour and Memory' scheme gave Thomson and Oric micros an extra toehold in France.

SECAM was jokingly known as 'System Essentially Contrary to the American Method.'

The interplay of standards is still an issue for retro-computing enthusiasts, though Next skirts it by only directly supporting output of separate red, green and blue colour components, via HDMI/DVI and SCART/VGA interfaces. The former include audio, while the later are video-only.

By the time PAL TV had been worked out, NTSC was entrenched in the early-adopter territories and they had to live with its wonky colours. It also suffered severe temporal jitter in 24 FPS film transfers, which interleaved three and two original images, with some frames mixing them in slices, giving them a six Hertz strobing effect, and extra flicker on a third of the frames!

Raw PAL TV, as opposed to film transfers, flickered more than material made for US TV – unless the phosphors were adjusted for longer persistence, which happened less as globally production lines became dual-standard – but by using almost the same line time in longer fields PAL gained extra vertical resolution which was well-used on Acorn and Amiga software made in and for Europe, but incompatible with US and Japanese tellies. This affects Next 'overscan' LAYER 2 and 3 displays that fill up to 256 lines. NextBASIC does not support those directly, and they don't entirely fit on NTSC screens.

British broadcasters 'fixed' the timing of cinema transfers more smoothly by creating each interlaced frame from two 50 Hertz fields, each derived from a single 24 FPS film still image, but that made the films run faster and most of a semitone sharper in pitch, as you would notice if you tried to strum a guitar or tinkle a piano along with the soundtrack of a PAL movie broadcast. This is still a giveaway on some archive footage played on modern systems.

> *People who design computers don't know a lot about displays*
> *Mary Lou Jepsen*

This non-standardisation of both recordings and corrective bodges has special repercussions for ZX Spectrum Next, causing games to play fast or slow, and vary in pitch, even more as the author's display differs from that of the player. Chapter 14, Better BEEPs, provides fixes and explanations for audio issues. Attempts to fix the video often make things worse.

Gamma and grey-scales

And then there was (and still is) inconsistent grey-scale gamma, the reason most turn-of-the century UK games look washed out on US tellies and US films and games were often too dark to show much of the details, however you set the brightness and contrast – shifting or tilting a straight line can't fix a mismatch between two curves, except at one or two points along them.

The non-linear curve between dark and bright, like that of the eye, was analogue-compressed for broadcast then expanded differently on NTSC versus PAL screens. Alas modern digital monitors come closer to the US TV transfer function than the PAL curve our Spectrum games were made on and intended for. This is yet another reason classic European games look wrong on new screens.

While I'm here I might also note that during the 1970s CRT manufacturers changed the green phosphor (which had a long persistence, being derived from wartime radar tubes, unlike the red and blue components added later). That's why 1970s colour arcade games – especially titles set in space which exploit a black background to claim part of the surround, so the playfield appears wider – leave a characteristic ghostly green trail behind moving sprites which you don't see on later TV tubes, let alone digital matrix displays.

The spatial offset of colours within CRT pixels varies with the set design and in particular the layout of red green and blue stripes or triangles on the front surface of the tube. This is most noticeable when comparing Sony Trinitron displays with earlier rivals built around a triangular matrix projected from offset tubes, through an image-dimming shadow mask. Ambient light is also a factor. Naive Retro scanline or phosphor 'shaders' don't get much of this right, which is why they're often inauthentic to the point of regression. To fix this properly, the screen hardware and display signals need to be designed together, to match the intended effect.

Texas Instruments and Sinclair's approach of having big borders adds further trade-offs. Spectrum pixels are not aligned with the colour boundaries assumed in the TV 'standard'. By contrast, US-made micros from Atari and Commodore were synchronised to multiples of the standard limit of 160-colour-changes per line, giving the 80/160/320/640-pixel lines of early US colour consoles and micros. But our wide borders were important to cope with varying overscan, allowing time for the ZX81 and TS1000 to process video and code in a single chip, and to give power-of-two pixel line counts convenient for binary-logic hardware and programming.

Perhaps the final nail in the coffin of the ZX Spectrum's TV ad-hockery is the offset timing of pixel and colour data fetches. Despite running the DRAM faster than recommended, the Spectrum staggers the application of attribute data to corresponding pixels, shading colours into the following colour cell. We needed £40,000 of corrective hardware to bring breakthrough full-screen ZX game graphics into spec for UK broadcast for the *Magic Micro Mission* series I helped make at Central ITV in 1983.

Another complication if you crave photorealism is that even when RGB works it excludes some of the colours at either end of the spectrum from its gamut. Scottish inventor John Logie Baird's 1930s colour TV recordings, preserved on gramophone records, used only red and greenish components to save bandwidth, ending up with a yellowish tinge rather than the CRT blue we got used to 40 years later. Undaunted, Baird also had a fair crack at 3D TV in the thirties. But it was EMI founding engineer Alan Blumlein who set the standard for electronic TV which dominated the 20th century, forming the basis for both PAL and NTSC video signals, which later imposed colour on Blumlein's system by wiggling the pixel timings. I've oversimplified a bit, but in summary: colour TV is a hack, especially when Brits are doing it empirically on a tight budget.

Composite video output from Next

You might think that Next's TV output can only be used with SCART CRTs that support component input – separate red, green and blue signals – but in fact even old tellies and video recorders that expect a single-wire composite video input can be simply adapted to put up a decent picture, though not as clear as component SCART or VGA, still less HDMI.

I borrowed a little HDMI2AV box from a friend who said it'd cost him £3.49 from eBay and found to my surprise that it would accept Next's HDMI signal and output stereo audio, via two phono plugs, usually colour-coded red and white for right and left channels, alongside composite video for the yellow phono socket on many 1990s TVs. Spectrum 128s support composite video, as well as RGB component output, via a 7-pole DIN socket on the back. The traditional way to get this – and a much improved picture – from an original 48k Spectrum was to run a wire from the input to the TV modulator – the silver box under the hump at the back of a classic Spectrum – to a phono plug, since the LM1889 encoder on the board creates a PAL composite video signal en route to UHF TV aerial output.

Figure 17 - The Mini HDMI2AV adapter

As the name suggests, composite video is a mashup of monochrome and colour-difference signals which bypasses the analogue aerial connection and its broadcast-channel filters but remains backwards-compatible with ancient black and white tellies by shifting pixels around subtly to provide hints for the colour decoder in later sets. The picture is not as sharp as you'd get from distinct component signals, with colours still smeared to the right, scintillating due to timing interference, but clearer than de-modulated UHF.

Figure 17 shows the Mini HDMI2AV adapter. It's a little black box, about 20mm deep and 60mm square, with a HDMI socket on one side and three photo sockets for the video and audio out on the other. A third side contains a switch to select NTSC (US/Japan) or PAL (Europe, Australasia) video output, and a micro USB socket for power from a 5V adapter.

I found my TVs could cope with either setting of the TV-standard switch and Next's HDMI output provided enough power to run the box, so it was, for once, truly plug-and-play. I tested it on two Japanese TVs made for the

UK market – an authentic 4:3 aspect Panasonic CRT model TX21 MD4, using the front-panel inputs, and a Toshiba 36L2333D wide-screen HD LCD, with both KS1 and KS2 Nexts running recent cores, in every case, within the limitations of the composite signal, it Just Worked.

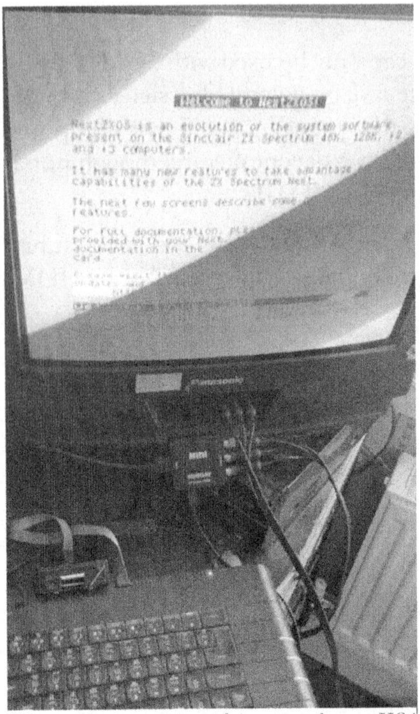

Figure 18 - composite video output from a KS1 Next to a Panasonic TX-21 TV

Figure 18 shows the Panasonic output from my TV test set-up – the diagonal stripes are artefacts of the camera imaging matrix interfering with the slower CRT scan, so the grey triangles can be ignored as a human eye won't notice them. You can still see that the text is quite readable, and the wiring is as simple as it could get.

If your telly supports full-spec SCART RGB you're better off with a Next SCART cable, but if it only has phono inputs or the SCART is one of the less capable sorts, like those on most video recorders, this nifty gadget gives you a decent display with authentic phosphor blur, matching the images Cameron Pound captured for Crash magazine in its heyday.

The adapter is made in China and unbranded so I can't tell you exactly where to buy one, or if a similar-looking model will work as well – the 'UP Scaler 1024P' marking is doubly misleading as the analogue output falls far short of HMDI so it's really a down-scaler to 576i or 480i resolution. But it does adapt most TVs that suit an old Spectrum to work with Next. If your set requires a UHF input you'll also need a modulator, such as the silver Astec box from an old TV game, a redundant Rediffusion cable TV box, or a video recorder with a phono input for composite video and a TV aerial output.

Differences between Spectrums

Even if your display is authentic, Spectrums are not identical. The timing of display and memory access varies slightly between models, and that has repercussions for software – especially graphics demos – that assumes they all match the original hacker's set up. Next can run at the erratic speed of original 16k and 48k models, the slightly different rate of early 128k machines, as well as further changes introduced by Amstrad's cost-engineering for the final +3 and +2A/B units. It even supports the skewed timing of Pentagon Spectrum clones beloved by Russian demo coders.

The snag is that you need to know, or find out by experiment, exactly what the original programmer expected, or you might see something rather different, and more flickery, than they intended. Complaints about Nirvana engine games – equivalent to Timex HiColor or SAM MODE 2, but done by hammering the CPU rather than redirecting attribute fetches for each scan – generally come from beginners running mismatched Amstrad +3 timings.

Configuration commands

We can also fine-tune Next's timings with a dot command. Starting from NextBASIC, Quicksilva's *Aquaplane* runs properly on a suitable display after explicitly selecting 48k timing, turning on contention (which slows access to certain banks, and Next normally turns off) and disabling Timex modes, so the game can read attributes from the ULA bus to find the beam position:

```
.config t=48 c=on tmx=off
.run aqua*
```

That **.config** command changes those settings till the next full reset; **.run** finds and launches aquaplane.tap, or the first ZX program file it finds starting with 'aqua'. Type **.config -h** for other options, or inconsistently **.run** with no parameters to see how that categorises 'ZX files' by the end of their names.

Hidden metadata

The Next file browser stores configuration 'metadata' by appending text to the associated filename, which is normally hidden by the file browser, or in a subdirectory on the SD card, determining the personality and settings that file will subsequently be loaded with. This behaviour can be controlled with the %FORMAT keyword, added to NextBASIC 2.08.

%FORMAT works like an integer variable but controls parts of the system, rather like %CODE. It's value is 0 when the system starts, but if you set bit 1 with %FORMAT |= 2 the TAP/TZX/SNA/Z80 loaders will to store metadata in the filename instead, so that when you copy the file, without renaming, those aspects of its configuration will be copied with it. If you restore the original name, the custom configuration will be lost.

Bit 2 of the %FORMAT pseudo-variable in NextZXOS 2.09 disables writes to the cache at c:/nextzxos/metadata. You can set it, when required, with %FORMAT |= 4. If you update your SD you may want to copy the old metadata file to the new one, along with programs in your C:/home directory. It's easier to update the system if you put all your own files there, rather than scatter them around in Tools, Docs and other folders created by SpecNext, which are liable to be moved or updated in new releases of the system.

Chapter 4, Simple Hardware Projects

My Tech Tips columns for Crash magazine featured a mixture of commercial software and hardware reviews, plus news, advice and tips for developers and serious users. The Spectrum Next scene is tiny by comparison – with fewer than one per cent of the potential 'market', no one will make a living out of Next, so there are no commercial products for me to test and critique. That said, there are still hundreds of active developers and perhaps a thousand more who'd like to learn, refine and create extensions to what they might reasonably think of as the *Last True Home Computer*. I'm here for them all.

Next's FPGA core straddles the divide between hardware and software, but even if you stay outside the box there are simple things which can be cobbled together by users who wish to customise their systems. This chapter introduces and explains a handful of those, concentrating on the connectors which are readily accessible on the outside of the Spectrum Next. For those willing to open the box there's fun to be had with keyboard, GPIO, I2C and co-processor mods, which I'm keen to write up another day.

Expansion potential

Early-adopters may have soldered in a clock chip, expanded RAM or added Pi0 and WiFi boards. Those add-ons were clearly documented in the KS1 manual, and standard features of most later production, so I won't re-tread that ground, having surveyed it in the 2019 and 2021 Crash annuals.

Unlike subset clones and emulators aimed at nostalgic gamers, Next is a hardware-expandable home computer, with an almost Amstrad/Sinclair-compatible 54-way edge connector on the back. Most 1980s peripherals plug in and work just as they used to, as long as you configure Next to match the hardware they were designed for. After weeks of testing, I wrote up my KS1 compatibility findings in the Crash annuals. KS2 boosted the signals and brought a few marginal devices into the fold. But five years down the line we're still waiting for the first Next-specific expansion cards, and I shall be sure to review them (hi, Charlie!) when they surface.

Easy pickings

Meanwhile we have low-hanging fruit to harvest. The vast majority of ZX software was supplied on cassette tape and Next includes a two-way cassette interface. But there's no bundled tape cable, and original Sinclair leads let us SAVE but not LOAD. Audio replay and recording devices have changed a lot in 45 years, so our first project is to make up a modern two-way adapter that supports LOAD and SAVE on analogue tape and new digital devices.

Next's front-panel joystick sockets provide an obvious and welcome new way to get data **into** the system. After some FPGA tweaks I requested which Allen Albright kindly delivered in 2021, those ports can be used for digital **output** as well as inputs. The scope for this feature is enormous, not least because you don't need to open your precious computer to take advantage of it – my DIY proof of concept sets that ball rolling.

The SD slot tucked away on the side of every Next and compatible system is a game-changer, but a limitation for developers who want to keep up with the latest system updates without shuffling their work-in progress laboriously around via drive M or – perish the thought – some other computer! So I'll open the box briefly to explore options for adding a second SD drive. Finally I'll revisit how to hook up floppy drives from the ZX era, for those who still have those and software they'd like to update for NextBASIC or continue to run in the Classic Spectrum personalities. The potential is enormous, so let's get cracking!

Cassette connection

The cassette interface was a central feature of most early micros. Even the original 16k IBM PC had cassette ports when it trailed our ZX Spectrum into the UK market, priced at £2,890 – the equivalent of £12,700 in 2024 pounds, back when a 16k Spectrum set us back £125 (£553 now). This puts whinges about SpecNext non-profit pricing into context. For those willing to forgo Rick Dickinson's last great casework, yet missed the first Kickstarter's £99 bare-board deal, the N-Go and Xberry Pi clones are amazing bargains.

Next expects a cassette lead compatible with Amstrad's final offering, the Spectrum +3, and that's where our ZX history lesson must begin.

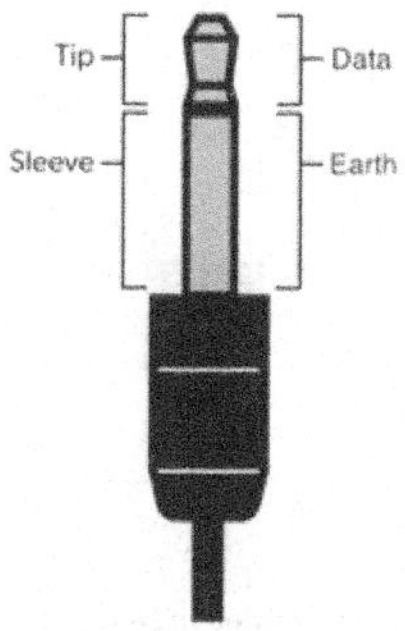

Tip-sleeve (TS) plug

There are two common types of 3.5 mm jack plug, known as TS and TRS. Sinclair ZX computers came with a cassette cable joining two light grey plugs, for output from the Spectrum to the MIC input of a tape recorder, and a separate circuit for two black plugs. That linked the cassette recorder EAR output to the correspondingly-labelled Spectrum socket, which is what LOAD commands read from.

In the 40 years since, there have been big changes in analogue audio conventions, most noticeably in that portable cassette machines were usually mono and capable of both playback and recording, whereas Sony's Walkman introduced stereo output but usually ditched recording capability.

Mobile phones and CD players followed the stereo-output convention, making them compatible with Walkman headphones and their many clones. Amstrad attempted to do away with the external cassette dependency, 'gluing on' a cassette mechanism to Spectrum +2, +2A and +2B models. This approach was copied from Amstrad's earlier CPC range, also seen in the UK years before as a feature of the EACA Video Genie, the TRS-80 compatible Z80 home micro I used to write all my 1980s Tech Tips columns. From Alan Sugar's point of view it was a way to avoid the tangle of cables around his son's ZX Spectrum, and helped to reduce the many customer returns caused by beginners trying to apply worn or mis-connected external music cassette recorders to the more sensitive task of computer storage.

Amstrad soon did away with the EAR and MIC sockets on the back of every Sinclair Spectrum, and earlier ZX computers, but despite the built-in floppy drive on the Plus 3 most software was still sold on cassette, and punters still needed a way to load those tapes.

Reasoning that one socket was cheaper than two, and leaving third parties with the slim pickings of making and selling +3-compatible cassette leads, Amstrad put a single TRS socket in place of the two TS sockets on Sinclair machines. The earth (sleeve) connection was common to both input and output, and the output from the computer to the tape MIC input was wired up to the tip connector of the new socket, leaving the ring connection for input from the tape EAR output.

Short of back-panel space after allocating a similar socket for the new stereo audio output, Spectrum Nexts follow Amstrad's lead (sic) and pack both EAR and MIC signals in the same hole. This has an unfortunate consequence for anyone who has disinterred their old Sinclair set-up and tried to use either of their black and grey TS cables to LOAD classic cassettes or homebrew files into their new Next. The old cables are fine for SAVE, but short out the EAR input to the Next, so they're useless for loading.

T, R and S stand for Tip, Ring and Sleeve (or Shaft). The diameter is 3.5mm, inaccurately known as ⅛ inch in the USA. You may also come across TRRS plugs, with four poles, or even five-way TRRRS plugs, the same size as Sinclair's mono ones but with more rings for extra connections. The TRRS type allows a mono microphone input as well as stereo audio out, and is mostly used for mobile phone headsets. Next sockets are both three-way TRS type, so no advantage is gained by using more poles – you just make getting a good connection for the required signals harder.

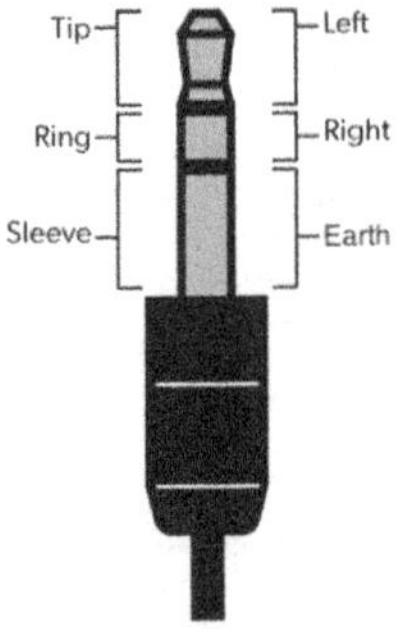

Tip-ring-sleeve (TRS) plug

You can use an Amstrad-era +3 cable with Next and it'll work as well as ever – indeed, just as well as your cassette recorder still does, or doesn't – but there's another potential pitfall. These days, analogue audio output sockets are almost always stereo, expecting a TRS plug, whereas cables made to link a +3 to a Sinclair era cassette recorder normally have mono TS plugs at the non-computer end. These plugs route the left side of the stereo to the computer's EAR input but, lacking the ring innovation, short out the right stereo channel. Apart from an increase in power consumption, audio players are generally resilient to such abuse, but we'd be better off using a TRS plug in the stereo socket, whether we take the signal to the computer input from the tip, the ring, or both at once.

If your cassettes are unevenly spooled or DIY recordings on only one tape channel, joining them together may improve your chances of getting a clear signal from one or other side into your Next.

That's why I generally recommend linking tip and ring together in parallel to the ring of the computer-side plug. But if the tape is worn or frayed, interference between signals spread on either channel could make things worse. And if you're struggling to recover data from an old tape or stereo player you might cope better by connecting just the two rings, as it's the outer 'left' cassette tape track that's most prone to mechanical damage.

Conversely, if things are severely mis-aligned, there can sometimes be interference between the two 'right' channels recorded in opposite directions down the middle of a tape! There's no right answer, except that a stereo TRS plug at the player end gives you a better chance of extracting the required signal.

Bulk cassette-duplicating plants, like the massive CBS factory at Aylesbury which I visited with other Quicksilva programmers in 1984, sped up manufacturing by recording tape for eight or sixteen cassettes at once on a fat one or two inch reel, then slitting that down into eighth-of-an-inch slivers for each cassette case. In

Power Struggles

Old timers may remember that Sinclair got a better bulk price on ZX80 and ZX81 boards by fitting three 3.5mm sockets, using one of those for the DC power input as well as tape connections. These had the snag that sparks would literally fly if the power plug was inserted while the mains adapter was turned on, as a momentarily short-circuit occurred before the plug-tip reached the back of the socket. This fault was fixed for the Spectrum. Amstrad screwed this up again by using a five pin audio plug for the 12 and 5 volt power to +3 and +2A/B computers. Ben Versteeg worked out that this arrangement had a nasty tendency to blow up the few expansion devices still compatible with Amstrad's rehashed edge connector. It became a matter of luck rather than science which connection came up first, and if that wasn't the earth pin, devices using multiple supplies were quite likely to be damaged - see www.bytedelight.com/?page_id=6233

There's another potential problem with Next, because it was designed in Brazil where 9V power supplies are wired up the opposite way around from the way Sinclair (and Casio, among others) did it. Spectrums, up to and including Amstrad's first grey +2s, expect at least +9V on the outer (shaft) part of the power plug, whereas Brazilians, and some other manufacturers, standardised with the positive lead in the middle. Sinclair and SpecNext DC supplies are NOT compatible.

Take care if you are using a 1980s keyboard or in-line device, such as an audio booster, that passes through power from the supply to the Spectrum board. A Next in a 48k case upgrade, like some Saga or Fuller keyboards, requires power the opposite way round for the expansion and computer. If you plug a Next supply into one of those you'll probably break the daisy-chained peripheral. To fix this, use the original Spectrum supply and swap over the DC pass-through wires from the peripheral to your Next.

the early days the outer slices, most prone to flutter, were discarded, but once demand peaked these often ended up in the shops with their more reliable neighbours. To avoid a five-minute wait to record each batch of 48k tapes, the recorders span at sixteen times the original speed, 30 inches per second, as fast as a Sinclair microdrive loop. Although extra-powerful magnets were used, that still left a weaker signal recorded on the tape than obtainable at home when making one-off mono tapes at the standard speed.

Level up or drop out

There is one more fly in the ointment, which stems from variations in recording and replay levels. Ferranti and Sinclair designed the Spectrum input to suit signals from portable cassette recorders running from a four-cell six-volt power supply with the output set close to maximum volume. Sony's Walkman range dropped down to two AA cells, giving a maximum swing of 3 volts.

Modern phones and audio players usually run from a single Lithium cell, providing fewer than four volts. So unless the original cassette recording was at a healthy level on good tape – neither likely for bulk-manufactured product – you may find that the signal from a modern player is barely enough to get the loading border-stripes up on Next, and some sort of signal booster, such as a 6 or 9 volt headphone amplifier, is needed for reliable loading.

When all is said and done, Sinclair learned a lot from their three previous attempts at reliable cassette loading. The Spectrum interface is relatively good by the standards of other home micros, which were typically slower, less reliable and harder to diagnose, lacking the border stripe feedback, header tones to stabilise automatic level controls, input signal conditioning and Ferranti ULA analogue/digital compatibility. The Next input was tweaked for extra sensitivity during the Kickstart 2 revision, which also helps; earlier Nexts, and their clones, tend to be less sensitive.

Signal level is amenable to analogue fixes – you may find the output of a mains-powered HiFi separate cassette deck more compatible than that from a cassette Walkman, for example. If you try that, use the headphone output via a suitable adapter from 6.3 to 3.5mm calibre, as the back panel output to phono or DIN sockets is generally weaker. Solid border stripes are, as ever, a good sign. Weak ones imply the need to turn things up or interpose an amplifier, while wobbly ones indicate uneven spooling which may be fixed by playing the tape back and forth, at normal speed, to the end and back again so it's evenly wrapped around the drive hubs. Frequent use of fast forward and rewind can make that worse. Even if your car still has a cassette player, don't be tempted to respool your data tapes as you're driving around!

Now we know the difference between TS and TRS plugs it's time to design the ideal cassette lead for Spectrum Nexts and modern audio players. They're not currently available even from retro specialists, so this makes a good project to get this chapter underway. Soldering enthusiasts will already have finished making their own cable, and perhaps burned their fingers a bit, but this project is aimed at less expert people so I'm going to start with cheap ready-made widely-available cables rather than expect anyone to solder the insides of a jack plug, which is fiddly even if you remember to put the sleeve on the wire first; if not, you'll need to leave it nude or do it again, and after 50 years that's still a mistake I sometimes make. Prebuilt cables are usually cheaper than the plugs at either end, so we're going to cut those down to suit rather than build up from fiddlier bits requiring twice as much wiring-up. To avoid *any* requirement for melting things, I shall suggest two ways of linking the wires mechanically.

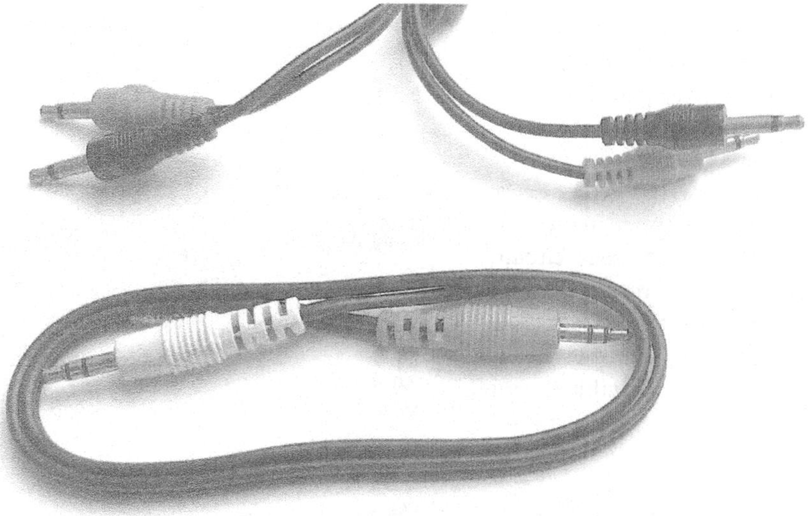

Figure 19 – Ingredients for a Spectrum Next (and Amstrad +3) -compatible cassette cable

To make a Next-compatible cassette cable you'll either need one of the cables shown above and a quarter of an original Spectrum or ZX81 tape lead (top), or half of each. The half-and-half cables are readily available, and still suit 1980s mono portable tape recorders. The other sort is compatible with most stereo replay devices, such as a mobile phone or Walkman, as long as they deliver a loud enough signal to trigger Next's cassette input circuit.

To wire this up without solder you could use the modern Wago clip connectors my game-dev pal Adam Sawkins suggests (left) or the retro option of a translucent nylon screw-retaining 'chocolate block' barrier strips (right) like those often seen dangling in alarm systems and behind car stereos, if soldering is scary but Meccano didn't put you off screwdrivers. There are pros and cons to each approach; the Wagos require long

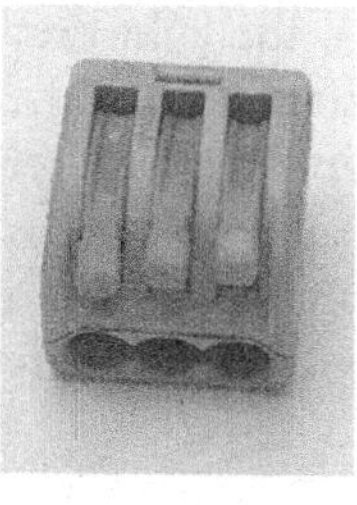

leads as the connecting parts are recessed right at the back. Terminal strips allow you two bites at each connection as the holes on opposite sides are connected together, but it's easy – especially with a stranded copper cable – to end up poking the bit you want to screw down past the side of the bolt rather than under it, so that it falls out. However you choose to make the connection, don't be afraid to tug it when you think it's complete; if it's done properly it will hold fast, and if not you'll need to try again, sooner rather than later.

If you have access to a multimeter with a low resistance range, or any sort of continuity tester, check that the shafts of all the plugs you have hooked together are connected, and that there is no connection from there to the tip or ring of the connector that will plug into your Next. It's easy to introduce a short-circuit between them by failing to twist together every one of the copper strands for each part of the circuit, accidentally roping in a strand or two from the adjacent conductor. That won't break anything, but won't work.

Figure 20 - Connections close-up: Left-side cables go to your tape recorder, the wire on the right connects to Next

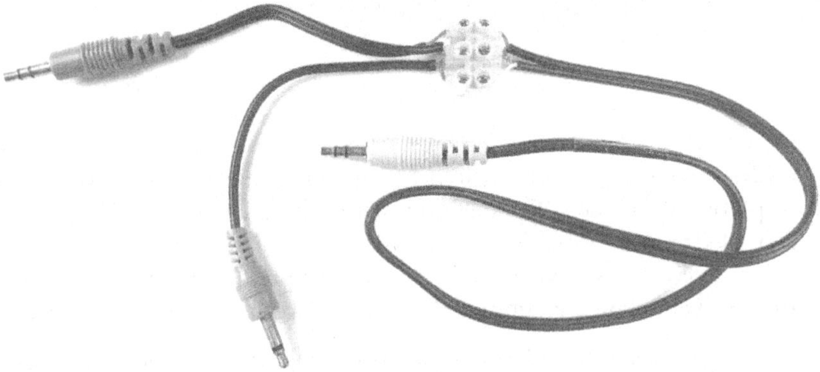

Figure 21 - The finished modern SAVE/LOAD cable for Next and Spectrum +3

The next step is to check is that the tip of the MIC lead – the light grey plug on Sinclair mono cables – is connected to the tip of the connector at the Spectrum Next end. Slightly fiddlier, make sure that the **tip** of the other stereo plug, which will go into your phone or similar stereo audio player, is connected to the **ring** of the new Spectrum plug. If you've opted to use both sides of a stereo output, check finally that both rings of the TRS plugs are connected.

This cable will also work with a Spectrum +3, and is more compatible with stereo audio signals than the type recommended in the Plus Three manual. Glue it up or box in the connector, for mechanical reliability.

Digital input and output

The cassette port handles **analogue** audio-level signals. The easy way to get **digital** bits in or out without creating circuit boards or opening the box is to make up a custom cable for the two joystick ports on the front edge of Next.

So far it's all been about plugs and wire. Our next project adds a one-bit video output, matching BEEP in the visual domain! Persistence of vision means this can't be seen to blink more than about a dozen times a second unless you use a stroboscope, but BASIC or Z80 REG instructions can flip it *hundreds of thousands* of times a second. Other computers can read the pulses using a suitable lead to a digital input, like any of the six input pins of each joystick port. Such arbitrary pulse-trains can control MIDI synthesisers, colour LEDs, DMX stage lighting, infra-red remote controls, tape drives or wired Sinclair networks, sometimes via a resistor or transistor to match the expected signal.

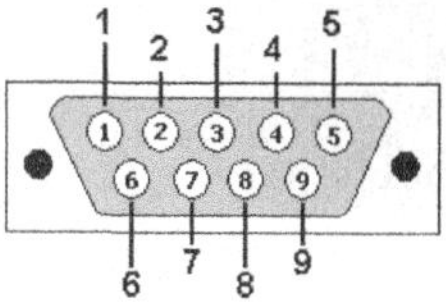

Figure 22 – Front edge joystick pin numbers

Figure 22 shows how the joystick port connections are numbered, looking into Next from the front. Conveniently this is also how the plug looks from the back, when we come to solder it. Pins 1 to 4 are for the cardinal directions, Up, Down, Left and Right, Pin 6 reads the main fire button and pin 9 is for an optional second button, not usually supported by ZX Spectrum interfaces. This leaves pins 5 and 8 for power, +5 volts and earth respectively, and pin 7 which is labelled 'select signal' in GitLab and originally intended to enable the extra buttons on Sega Megadrive controllers – but we have greater plans!

When first I investigated pin 7 on a prototype board and early next core I found that it carried a periodically-pulsed signal intended for an optional Sega controller hardware state-machine. While this prevented me from controlling it directly, it proved that it was wired as an output, and after some online discussion FPGA maestro Allen Albright was persuaded to bring pin 7 fully under software control, so that it could be set high or low or carry output from the FPGA's UART (serial port) when the Sega controller option was disabled via REG 11. Ain't FPGA wonderful!

Baby Blinkenator

We're going to control a Light Emitting Diode (LED) from our Next. Any small Red, Green or Yellow ones are suitable; White and Blue LEDs generally require a higher voltage. Infra-red remote control lights can be used – to check they're working, use a mobile phone camera as they generally respond to infra-red we can't see, showing it as white on the camera preview.

Figure 23 - Proof of concept - the Pin 7 LED plugged in to my Next

Light is generated once a voltage across the LED's two legs passes a chemically-determined threshold: just under 2 volts for the recommended LEDs. Being diodes, LEDs only pass current in one direction. If you wire them up the wrong way around, nothing happens.

The longer lead of most LEDs is the 'anode', a reference to the top plate in a thermionic 'radio valve', expecting a positive voltage. The other end is the 'cathode'. The 0.2" (5 mm diameter) yellow LED in the middle of Figure 24 has its anode on the left, like the smaller red LED alongside. My first prototype used a green one.

If you were to collect the anode of any decent-sized LED directly to the five volt supply on pin 8 and the cathode to pin 7, a KS2 Next could make it glow brightly, delivering just over 20 mA of current and 35 mW of optical power, by grounding pin 7.

But this approach of sucking on Next's one readily available digital output also generates a similar amount of waste heat inside Next, and while that won't cook it immediately I'm going to tone it down with another classic electronic component, a resistor. If all this seems like small beer, bear in mind we've got an introduction to FPGA at the end of this volume. Let's get something simple working, first!

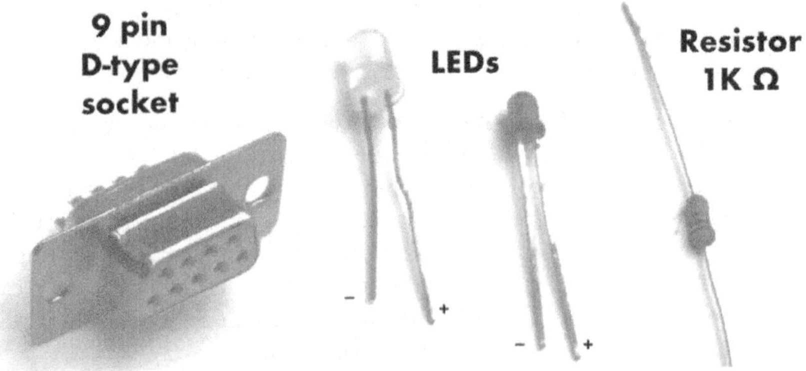

Figure 24 – Choice ingredients for today's ZX Spectrum Next Blinkenlight demonstration

Resistance isn't futile

Resistors are usually marked with four bands of colour roughly denoting the resistance value in 'ohms', usually suffixed with an Omega symbol, Ω, the last letter of the Greek alphabet. As long as the resistance is suitable, any size, tolerance or power rating will do, for this purpose. A little one fits neatly in a bit of shrink-wrap tube, as I've done in the prototype, Figure 25.

For any given voltage, the resistance (measured in ohms) limits the continuous current through an electrical circuit. Unlike semiconductors, including our LED, a resistor works identically either way round so it doesn't matter which end you connect to either leg of the LED. The current from Next will be limited, taming the intensity. I plucked a 1k Ω resistor from the carpet – colour-code stripes brown, black and red – but the exact value isn't critical. Anything between 330 and 1500 Ohms will limit the drain on Next to a few milliamps with still-visible blinks.

Figure 25 - The resistor is shrink-wrapped into the LED's left leg

Making it blink

The following program takes control of pin 7, after checking whether or not either joystick port is configured to read the extra buttons of a Sega Megadrive controller. If so, that option is temporarily turned off by tweaking REG 11. Line 160 saves the old value in %R before forcing direct control by setting the most significant bit of the register, and clearing bit 0 which holds the value to control the digital output, 0 or 1.

```
100 REM Demonstrate Joystick port PIN 7 bit-banging output
110 REM Simon N Goodwin November 2022, updated August 2024
120 %j=% REG 5:%f=0
130 IF %j & @1000 THEN IF %(j & @11000000=@01000000) OR
    (j & @11000000=@10000000) THEN %f=1:
    PRINT "Megadrive clash on  LEFT port 1"
140 IF %j & @0010 THEN IF %(j &@00110000=@00100000) OR
    (j & @00110000=@00010000) THEN %f=2:
    PRINT "Megadrive clash on RIGHT port 2"
150 IF %f THEN PRINT "MD disabled REG 5 was %@"; STR$ (%j,2)''
160 %r=% REG 11 & @01111111:%b=%r & @01111110 | @10000000
```

Now we have control over the output control bit we can make the light flash, or send information bit-by-bit to another computer, by setting and clearing the least significant bit of REG 11. This demonstration continues until the space key (character 32) is pressed. If you hold down any other key you'll see the blinking speed up because the PAUSE statements that determine the timing are interrupted. For this reason, you need to hold rather than just tap space to get out. Then it only remains to restore the other bits of REG 11 to their original values, and display reassuring messages:

```
170 PRINT "Current pin 7 state ";%r'"Blinking; SPACE to stop"
180 REPEAT : REG %11,%b: PAUSE %5: REG 11,%b|1: PAUSE %10:
    REPEAT UNTIL CODE INKEY$ =32
190 REG 11,%r
200 PRINT '"Output setup restored."
210 IF %f THEN PRINT  "Megadrive control restored."
220 STOP
```

Figure 26 – the display of the joystick output demo

Unfinished business

Blinking a little light quickly demonstrates that arbitrary binary data can be output from Next without opening the case or making a complicated interface for the expansion port. We could always read up to a dozen binary **inputs** via the other pins on the joystick ports, but the FPGA change was crucial to allow **output** in the opposite direction. This should be enough to enable MIDI input for notes, rhythms and synthesiser patch data, as well as Sinclair networking using a QLAN QL-based file server or the closely-related *Interface 1 ZX-NET* protocol.

I haven't finished implementing those yet, though I have written a driver to use the QLAN hardware as a MIDI output interface. Sandy White did something similar to drive a synthesiser via the Sinclair *Interface 1* network port, as part of his *Quicksilva* game *Zombie Zombie*, the follow-up to *Ant Attack*.

There are similar programs for the Spectrum 128 which use its one-bit MIDI output port to play music. Although Next lacks that hardware, and the ROM routines to drive it, those programs can potentially be patched quite simply to write to the Next controller ports rather than the absent Sinclair or Amstrad hardware. For new programs, Next's DRIVER model gives us a flexible way to send network, music or appliance control data from BASIC or any system-friendly program.

The output from pin 7 is weaker than that from 1980s five-volt TTL chips, so it's quite likely that a booster might be needed before it can communicate with older hardware. This could be as simple as a single transistor. I started work on this soon after that hardware output was enabled then got distracted by software projects and accidentally dropped my only MIDI synthesiser and haven't had time since to fix it, or experiment with other peripherals. This is certainly a topic I am keen to return to, as long as this book is successful enough to justify a follow-up volume.

Next registers currently only support one front-panel OUT bit – the same signal is sent to pin 7 on both joysticks – but they allow two sets of inputs, each including four directions and two select or 'fire' buttons. We can potentially use those as inputs for any other switch-like signal. My next even simpler project adds up to a dozen light-sensing inputs to Next. There are still seven front-edge inputs free while using a standard single-button joystick.

We're going to test just one input, set up to act like 'button 2' but controlled with light rather than a modified Kempston or Atari joystick.

Let there be Light-Dependent Resistors

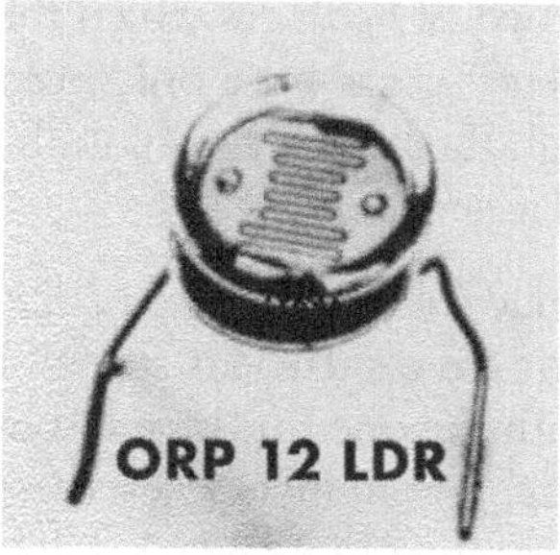

Figure 27 – A light-dependent resistor, also used in my 1979 ETI ***Optical Autowah*** *invention*

When I was a schoolboy in the 1970s one of my favourite components was the ORP 12 **Light Dependent Resistor** (LDR). The resistance of the wiggly line of Cadmium Sulphide on the top falls by a factor of a thousand or more when exposed to light.

We can wire one of these directly to any of Next's dozen joystick input pins. Those are designed for switches, so no limiting resistor is needed, beyond the LDR itself. One leg of the component needs to be connected to Next's pin 8, the earth or 'ground' wire. The connection of the other determines exactly what signal Next receives. To mimic the second button, connect the other leg to pin 9, leaving remaining inputs free for a normal joystick. Or choose pin 6, beside the output pin, so that the light-detector seems to press the default fire button: key 0 on Sinclair or Cursor interfaces. You don't even need a program to test this – just wire the LDR between joystick socket pins 6 and 8, and observe the zeros automagically typed in whenever you let light shine on the detector.

You could use such signals in a BASIC program to adjust the palette of your Next at night, synthesise a dawn chorus, distinguish burglars from housebreakers, or for other light-dependent purposes. The response is no faster than the eye's, so flickering is averaged out; an LDR could read semaphore, but not fast-spinning fan-blades.

This hack will work just as well on any Spectrum with a joystick interface. Look for changes in the value of IN 31 after wiring it up, either way round, between pins 6 and 8 of a Kempston-compatible interface. The LDR will 'press the fire button' when in direct light, and let go when in shadow.

Adapting KS1 hardware for external SD cards

If you're interested in creating content for and on your Next you're likely to find the single SD slot a limitation. This has to hold the version of NextZXOS you're testing and all the programs you'd like to test. Ideally your own files would be stored separately from the operating system, so you can easily swap to an older or newer version when checking compatibility. Even if your priority is running stuff from other people, you'll periodically want to update your Next to the latest release, to take advantage of new features and bug-fixes, and it's best to keep the old version till you're quite sure that everything you like suits the new one. After that, you'll probably have a load of files that need copying from the old SD to the latest, and that's much easier if you can have two cards plugged in at once.

Every Next, from the early Issue 2A bare boards of 2018 to the Kickstarter 2 versions shipped in 2023, supports two SD sockets which the operating system sees as drives C and D. But so far Nexts have only been shipped with a full-size SD slot for drive C. Though there's provision on the board for a second SD card it's not been supplied as standard.

I discussed this with SpecNext director Henrique Olifiers at Crash 2023. He explained that the plastic case mould does not have sufficient space or rigidity for a second SD slot to be added underneath the one for drive C, but took my point that it would be handy for future machines to include a second card, even if it was relatively inaccessible. A built-in drive D could work like an internal hard drive in some other computer, holding the user's own files, leaving the accessible slot for the system and NextZXOS updates.

In fact there are solder pads for an internal second drive inside the Next. Anyone skilled in surface-mount soldering can tack a micro SD socket to the underside of the main board, or equivalent pads on the daughter-board that holds the main SD socket and coloured side-buttons, shown in Figure 31.

Readers who have followed my articles in electronics and computing magazines since 1979 will be well aware that soldering is not my strong point. I am capable of globbing together prototypes that work, but rely on production engineers to make them robust and nice to look at. Indeed my first successful invention, an analogue wah-wah effect for guitars and other electronic instruments, was only fully-formed and useful when I abandoned my wobbly efforts to make a foot pedal to control it and resorted to controlling it with light (Optical Auto Wah, in *Electronics Today International* Tech Tips, December 1979).

Age hasn't improved either my eyesight or dexterity, but I've been lucky to work with production engineers who have the professional skills to turn my inventions into reliable products. I was also impressed by the work of staff at ICL and Samsung who reworked Sinclair's part-baked UK designs into the robust and standards-compliant North American version of the QL.

The *One Per Desk* appliance went further, after a long development by Sinclair standards, albeit a bit quicker than SpecNext's – it ended up being used for more than a decade by UK fire and ambulance service call handlers, despite the apparent handicap of depending on Sinclair Microdrives for external storage. ICL's OPD was rebadged by British Telecom as the *Merlin*, then dubbed the *BT Tonto* (presumably by *Lone Ranger* fans unaware that the nickname means fool, in Spanish) and marketed by Australian Telecom as the *Computerphone*. It took the skills of a traction-engine enthusiast to sort out the rubber rollers in the drives, to the point where production workers at the

Thorn-EMI plant at Feltham took to borrowing parts from the parallel ICL production line to get Sinclair-branded QL microdrives running smoothly.

Adapters off-the-shelf

Somewhere between me and Samsung lies Richard Spencer, Next enthusiast and boss of Active Consult Limited, a one-man UK supplier that has supported Spectrum Next users through thick and thin. I wrote about his first solution to the Next-drive dilemma when I revived my Tech Tips column for the 2019 Crash annual, and have been testing and making suggestions ever since. Richard is in the tradition of small-scale makers from the 1980s Sinclair Scene, hand-making all sorts of niche add-on for Spectrum Next enthusiasts, selling them sporadically at unprofitable prices as a service to the community.

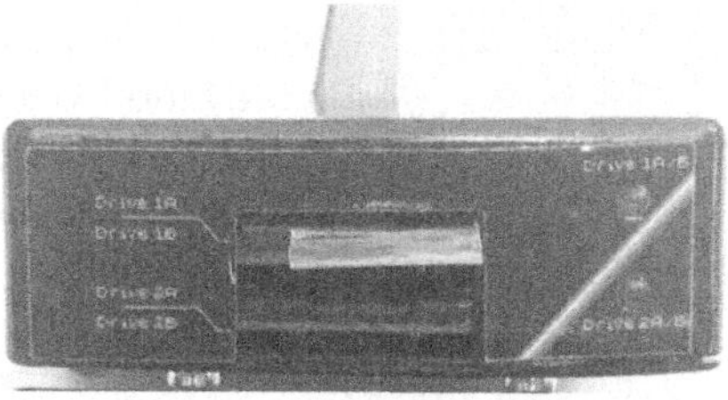

Figure 28 - Active consult's external drive box for Next and N-Go

Richard's first solution to the Next drive drought was a plastic box containing four SD sockets – two standard-sized, with two micro-SD alternatives tucked underneath – plus two red LEDs which blink brightly and reassuringly as either drive is accessed. The sticky-labelled black box, about 70 by 50 by 20 mm in size, is shown in Figure 28. The loop of Sellotape on the card in the top socket shows that I've had trouble prising it from the unexpectedly tight slot on a Kickstarter 2 Next. That is the official bodge for those who, like me, find that it does not 'loosen up with usage' as we were told when customers first identified the issue. Richard's box tended to float around my desk a bit on the end of its 40 cm ribbon cable, till I opened it up and weighted it down with some plasticine. There's a long tradition of controller manufacturers doing similar things to improve the heft of joysticks, and light-guns like Cheetah's obsolete *Magnum* pistol.

I found this little box invaluable in my early work with the Issue 2A Next board, but gather that one developer considers it unreliable, blaming the long un-screened cable. I suspect that variability between SD cards accounts for the difference between their experience and mine. Later versions used a shorter cable, and were cost-reduced from the already-reasonable £18 black-box version to a bare-bones 'plug and play Dual SD Reader' held together with shrink-wrap and hot glue (Figure 29). It's a bargain at £6 if you have a KS1 Next or N-Go and can live without the flashing lights and micro-SD option.

Figure 29 - cheap but effective – the two-slot external SD card adapter from Active Consult

However many sockets you connect, Next supports only two SD inputs, for drives C and D. The micro-SD sockets in the black box are alternatives to using an adapter in one of the big sockets – the flimsy adapters are entirely passive, containing metal strips to bridge from the big plug to the smaller socket, and a couple of springs to implement the write-protect slider. If you have a card in Next's built-in slot you can't simultaneously access another drive C, of any size, in an external adapter. If you try this, don't expect either of them to work. But you can plug the card you want to boot from into any one of them, and a second card into any drive D socket, be that internal or on a flying lead. Just don't put more than one card in the same logical drive.

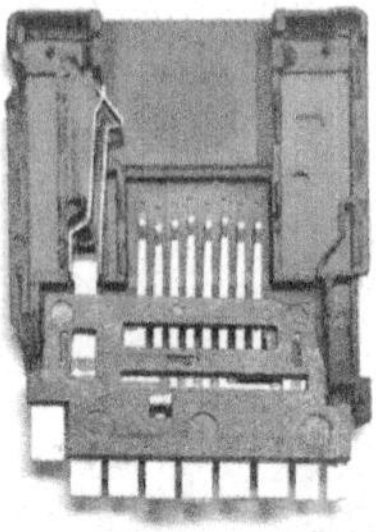

Figure 30 - nothing but springs inside a μSD card adapter

The chunky rectangular connector used to connect SD drives on the first hardware was replaced by a relatively flimsy one for Kickstarter 2; adapters are in the works and I've been promised an early chance to preview them, but in the meantime the accompanying pictures presume a Kickstarter 1 Next or similar clone such as ManuFerHi's N-Go.

The ten-pole J13 connector is on the main Next board between the SD socket for drive C and the five-way keyboard membrane socket. It carries all the signals needed for both SD cards and the coloured side-buttons, but if you plug something else into it and want to use a Next in its Rick Dickinson-designed case, rather than as a naked circuit board, you'll need some way to wire the buttons up. Figure 31 shows how I did it, soldering four coloured wires between the main board and the side-switches. The top connection provides the earth return for all three buttons, as the top pins of all the switches are already wired together through the printed circuit board. This is a relatively simple feat of soldering as there are no sensitive components in the places where the wires need to be added, but if you're unsure of your skills, get someone more practiced to do it for you, or at least practice on a less precious circuit-board first.

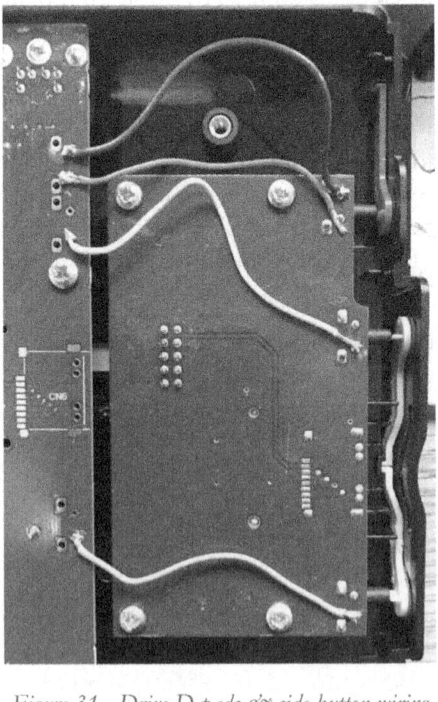

Figure 31 - Drive D pads & side-button wiring

You can see CN6, the pads for an internal SD drive, on the left of Figure 31. The grid of silver pins on the adjoining extension-board is where the wire from J13 would go if we'd not diverted it to external SD slots, and you can see a couple of those track further across and down to another, unlabelled, duplicate set of pads. This is an alternative place where an internal μSD holder could be fitted, with the possibility of external access if you don't mind wrecking your Next's box. Both sets of pads have an address-selecting wire swapped compared with the drive C slot on the other side, so a card fitted to either of those appears to NextZXOS as drive D.

Edge-connector expansion

Before the Spectrum Next case was finished the early boards were designed to fit inside a Sinclair 48k Spectrum case, using the dead-flesh keyboard and additional holes for the extra connectors like HDMI, one SD slot and front joysticks. The extension board central in Figure 31 was needed to bridge the gap in the wider case so that the coloured buttons and drive C slot remained accessible. The profusion of new connectors is a potential problem for Next owners who wish to use HDMI at the same time as classic ZX interfaces which extend to the side of the Sinclair-compatible edge connector, as many of those block the new HDMI port. You could revert to VGA or SCART video output if your TV or monitor can handle that; otherwise you will need some way to extend the edge connector so that the HDMI plug and ZX peripheral box can co-exist. Spanish N-Go makers ManuFerHi have anticipated this and offer a *Expansor del conector edge del N-Go* which works just as well with machines from the first SpecNext production run.

Figure 32 - N-Go's expansion port extender

Should €9.08 plus the additional European postal charge seems steep, ZX paupers from the 1980s might find an equivalent extension by plugging in the similar-looking *Fixer,* designed by MGT to unscramble the ROM control signals Amstrad changed when they released the +3. As long as the device you're trying to connect does not contain any ROM or RAM, the other unchanged signals from the *Fixer* board will be passed through past the HDMI obstacle to your add-on; I used mine to connect an HDMI display and a RAM Music Machine sampler, both at the same time, to my cased Next. But *Fixer* won't help with Interface 1 or Spectrum disc controllers, which also include ROMs.

> *Connector trouble is responsible for most of the peripheral problems that I hear about*
>
> *John Wase, Format #2*

Multi-port adapters like Byte Delight's *kMouse* or MGT's metal-boxed *TwoFace* can also extend the edge connector, and potentially allow several old interfaces to be plugged in at the same time; but everything you plug in to a Spectrum increases the risk of signal interference or an accidental open or short-circuit, so don't add adapters you can live without. Next already has Multiface, Datel Mouse, DivMMC, Kempston and other joystick capabilities, so you should always use the built-in interfaces rather than old ones, which will force Next to slow down to 3.5 MHz to match the (lack of) speed of the original gadget while the expansion port is activated.

Getting into print

There are dozens of classic ZX peripherals, and in my experience most of them work with a Next if you enable the external bus with REG commands and find a way to load and run the 'driver' software that came with them. Alphacom and Sinclair ZX printers are directly supported, even in NextBASIC when 128k system variables clobber memory reserved for the original Sinclair printer buffer, because NextZXOS supports them directly – just power down, plug in the printer, and LPRINT, LLIST and COPY away.

Third-party parallel printer interfaces will work in theory, but probably require a new driver, especially if the original one, loaded from tape or ROM, only worked on a 16k or 48k system. Nextpert Chris Taylor has written a text-only driver for WiFi printers which works in NextZXOS. It suits the majority of modern WiFi printers but lacks pixel-level support for COPY.

If you're keen to bring up your Centronics gear, and know the Z80 ports used by your original parallel printer interface, Chris's code at github.com/taylorza/zxn-wifiprn is a good start for making a new driver for an old interface and printer. Two drivers are listed later in this book; neither is printer-specific but the TileDriver handles text output and control codes similar to the Epson and HP PCL sets commonly used by parallel printers.

Owners of MGT Disciple and Plus D floppy disc interfaces are in luck as those are known to work on Next, as long as a suitable 48k or Sinclair 128k hardware personality is selected – Amstrad deliberately broke compatibility with add-on disc systems when they introduced their +3 variant, and this limitation also applies to NextZXOS as it is derived from +3e ROMs which rely on Amstrad's 64k ROM paging system.

Figure 33 - MGT's original +D advert, from when they shared Cambridge premises with Sinclair's Z88 team

Here's how to use any model of Spectrum Next with an MGT Plus D or later Datel or Byte Delight branded Plus D disc interfaces. This setup enables you to load and run programs from your original Spectrum discs in any compatible Next personality. You could also transfer them to SD, as long as you've installed esxDOS as described in the manual, though not both at once. If they rely on features of the MGT expansion ROM, such as hook codes, GDOS or the Microdrive command syntax, they'll need modifications to run alongside NextZXOS, much as they would for an Amstrad +3.

I tested this combo for the 2019 Crash annual, and got my newer Plus D to work with KS1 hardware and the firmware of the time, but struggled with an older interface, probably a very early one. Both work fine on KS2 Nexts!

This section is derived from posts I wrote for the MGT disc Facebook group (facebook.com/groups/862380571579326). It explains how to use any Plus D, or the earlier and bigger *MGT Disciple* add-on, with any Next or clone. I concentrate on the disc interface aspect, but the same approach can be used for other ports and expansion devices. The main difference is the ports that need to be opened up, which vary between devices. In general it's a matter of setting the startup menu suitably and pressing the right keys a few seconds later. I'll cover the more common Plus D interfaces first and *Disciple* differences later on. Both support double-sided double-density floppy discs of any diameter from 3" to 5.25", giving a formatted capacity of 800k with 780k available for files, the rest reserved for up to 80 directory entries.

MGT Plus D and its clones

Figure 34 - testing Plus D interfaces on my KS2 Next

I'm glad to report that both my +Ds work perfectly and identically on KS2 hardware in all 48k and pre+3 128k personalities, with either G+DOS 1A or the recommended upgrade BetaDOS 1.3. I suspect the bus driver improvements explain the fix for the prototype interface. I've not tried the printer yet, as my Epson MX80 has been in the shed for 23 years and needs careful awakening.

I've saved and loaded 48k and 128k snapshots, *Alchnews*, *Flexibase*, *Fractal Collection*, *Scene 75* and other floppy discs. All worked fine. I checked standard Sinclair 48k and 128k (Toast-rack) personalities, GW and LG 48k ROMs,

Timex TC2048, Investronica (Spanish, 1985) and the Pentagon 128 personality. The sole Amstrad personality that works as expected and authentically is the grey 128+2; after that Amstrad cost-reduced the hardware to the point where only their own disc system was usable.

There is work underway to fix this from NextBASIC, as the ZX and Alphacom printers have been made compatible already, but it's not finished yet. As Figure 35 shows, Timex, TurboSound, 48k AYs, kMouse, UART /I2C, DMA and ULAplus options can all be left on. HDMI, VGA and SCART all worked fine. I mostly tested in VGA 2, which runs the bus slightly faster than Sinclair's; some peripherals might object to the modified timing in higher VGA modes; start with VGA 0 if your display is compatible with 50 Hertz.

Figure 35 - Options for MGT +D compatibility

The only things that **must** be disabled before you can access Plus D floppies – shown in the startup menu here – are the built-in DACs and the two DivMMC options, because those use some of the same hardware port addresses the Plus D needs. Press space at startup and again to get to that menu. After they're set you can leave the menu alone.

Once in 48k or 128 BASIC, with the Plus D plugged into the back like any other Sinclair Spectrum, you must press the yellow button and digit 5 (or F5 on a PS/2 keyboard, or left in a cursor joystick, etc!) **or** issue the following single-line command to enable the expansion bus:

```
OUT 9275,128: OUT 9531,128: NEW
```

The keypress is more convenient when trying stuff out, but the OUTs are handy inside programs where you want to access the drives periodically but then revert to esxDOS at 28 MHz when processing. F6 toggles the bus off. To do this from BASIC or Z80 code use OUT 9275,128: OUT 9531,0.

After that, put a floppy with a G+DOS or BetaDOS system file in D1 and type RUN to boot it as usual. The DOS will persist in Plus D RAM through a reset, and you can soft-reset to 48k as ever with RAND USR 0 and carry on discing. If you use the red reset button that'll turn off the edge connector again till you re-enter those two OUTs, but there's no need to reload the disc system as the DOS is held inside the Plus D.

If it doesn't work first time, check the numbers in the OUTs. The token letters for OUT and NEW are O and A. Press EXTEND MODE then hold Symbol Shift with letter O in 48k, or use one of the ROM personalities that allows keywords to be typed in full. I tested this with firmware 1.44 and Core

3.2.0 but expect it to work like this on any 2.08 or later release including the one shipped with KS2.

For this and similar flat-box interfaces, make sure the feet on your Next are folded away, or the Plus D interface will end up hanging from the edge connector, which isn't electrically or mechanically a good idea. This doesn't apply to the Disciple which lifts and tilts the computer, as Sinclair's Interface 1 and SixWord's Swift Disc also did.

MGT Disciple and Next

The steps for Disciple users are almost the same as for Plus D except that the Disciple uses 'Kempston' port 31 for one of its own joysticks, as well as several control outputs. So as well as disabling Next's DACs you have to configure both joysticks to **any setting other than** the default Kempston 1 or MD 1 options via the same startup menu, or MGT's larger interface will be unable to select its floppy drives. Sinclair joystick options work fine as they use keyboard ports.

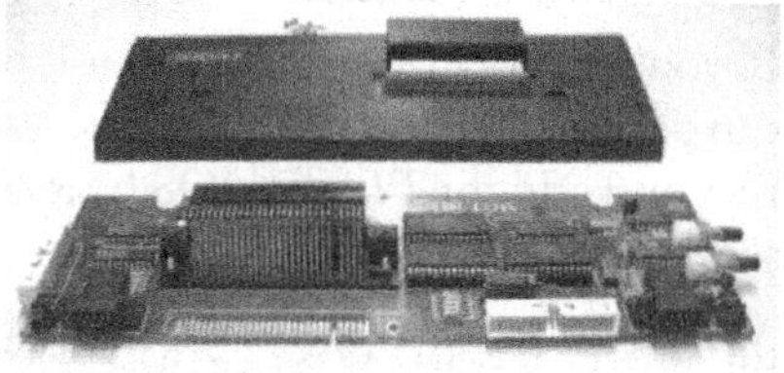

Figure 36 - An MGT Disciple, inside and out

The bonus is that if you've installed esxDOS (not part of the distro, but documented there) you can safely turn on the DivMMC Next menu options and use that alongside the Disciple! Disciple was compatible with Sinclair's Interface 1 but Plus D and DIV interfaces (including the default internal Next one) are NOT because – to avoid other port clashes, once Interface 1 production was discontinued – those cheekily clobber the ports Sinclair had previously reserved, and therefore also clash with one another.

Edge connector edge-cases

One chink in Next's compatibility is that there are no 12 volt or negative supplies available on the edge connector, so RS-232 serial ports on Interface 1 and some other plug-ins will not work. This could potentially be fixed, internally or externally, by adding modern high-efficiency DC to DC converters between row 4 on the bottom row of the edge connector and rows 20 and 22 of the top side, for -5V and +12V respectively. The one most worth adding is the +12V supply. The -5V rail supplies very little current and is rarely needed except by early 4116 DRAM chips, used in the original 16k display-memory section and famously wobbly ZX81 RAM packs.

Don't let the numbering of bus connections in the Amstrad manuals put you off – they didn't count the slot occupied by the locating key, four pads in from the edge. This is why Next manuals number expansion bus signals from 1 to 28 each side, with a gap for the slot at 5, whereas Amstrad counts skip that and only reach 27.

I've only had my old Disciple working in the 48k personalities, so far, but Tim Gilberts has it working in 128 too – this may depend on the Disciple firmware revision. 48k is the best bet as esxDOS is almost completely incompatible with the Spectrum 128 ROM changes. Some readers may have seen Tim Gilberts' setup at Spectrum shows, with Interface 1, running both refelted microdrive tapes and vDrive SD images, underneath his twin-floppy Disciple adapter, underneath his Next!

You can plug in all these at once, and shuffle files between them. You do need to use the Disciple's INHIBIT button selectively when you want the Sinclair shadow ROM rather than Bruce Gordon's one, but that'd apply equally to any Spectrum. But there's no inhibit button on a Plus D, and no through-port either. The upside is that Byte Delight are still making and selling those, and it can be exchanged for DivMMC with REG commands.

The Software Solution

If you're got access to MGT disc images but no compatible interface, you can use my *Next MGT Reader* utility to extract standard ZX program and data files and add the PLUS3DOS headers expected by NextZXOS and esxDOS.

This utility can read the 800k floppy disc image files, most often with names suffixed .DSK or .MGT. These files contain raw sectors from GDOS, G+DOS, UniDOS or SAMDOS discs – plus either BetaDOS or MasterDOS, as long as those are formatted for the standard directory capacity of up to 80 files. It reads, sorts and displays the directories and lets you select files to read or convert. As it's all in BASIC it's easy to adapt for batch conversion. It doesn't yet reshuffle the Z80 register data from snapshots, but could easily be extended to do so.

```
+SYSTEM     6656                       ZIP LOADER 875
STAR BASE4  3827                       ZIP 2.4C   22414
ZIP2.4SNAP  49152                      AUTOLOAD   931
STARBASE4C  5051                       SB4CLOADER 119
2068ZIPLIB  1530                       ZIP1.6 SRC 18404
ZIP1LIBSRC  15303                      CAT1       160
CAT LOADER  77                         CAT2       160
CAT3        160                        READHEADER 3189
AUTOHEADER  1780                       HEADREADER 1630
MMM 2       7191                       MMM 1.1    7831
2068ZIP1.5  15720
Filename? "zip1.6 src"
View ZIP1.6 SRC Extract or Both, V/E/B?"█"
```

Figure 37 - NextBASIC MGT Reader output

Download this from simon.mooli.org.uk/nextech/#NextMGTreader, or directly to any Next with WiFi set-up, via GetIt from em00k.itch.io/getit – use ID c82eb9 for the specific file. You can get source and object files for all the projects listed in this book from the same places.

Joysticks

In the 1970s Atari popularized simple joysticks with four directions and one fire button for game control. These became a standard for most Spectrum gamers, even though there was no built-in interface. From the ZX80 to the rubber-key Spectrum, Sinclair computers have wired 40 keys as eight groups of five buttons, so it was simple to wire an Atari stick in parallel with any of those groups. I demonstrated this with *Interface Zero*, a rudimentary but effective wires-only adapter featured in issue 5 of *Your Spectrum* magazine.

Leading ZX developers Quicksilva had picked the top row of digits for their joystick interfaces, either mapping digits 1 to 5 to one stick – with fire effectively pressing the '1' key, and keys 2 to 5 picking up the four directions. A second stick uses 0 for Fire and 6 through 9 to move. In NextBASIC, %31& IN 63486 reads keys 1..5; substitute IN 61438 to poll keys 0 and 6..9.

Sinclair followed Quicksilva's lead when they finally got around to releasing an official Spectrum joystick adapter, the Interface 2, which mapped Atari joysticks, and Commodore copies, to those same digit keys. In another nod to Atari boss Nolan Bushnell, Interface 2 also allowed games to be instantly loaded and played from small, expensive ROM cartridges.

Figure 38 - Atari's original one-button joystick. You'll break before it does - unlike the later QuickShot 2

But by then there were two unofficial and different joystick interfaces competing for the support of Spectrum game developers. One of those, from Bedfordshire hardware manufacturer Kempston, used two cheap chips to expose five inputs independent of the keyboard. An IN 31 instruction, from BASIC or machine code, returned a byte with the lower five bits set by pressing Fire (bit 4) or Up, Down Left and Right directions, (bits 3 to 0 respectively). Led by Ultimate, many software houses supported the 'Kempston standard' (for Atari one-button joysticks) which left the keyboard free for other inputs.

Since the ZX80, Sinclair's BASIC editor had used another set of four digits to position the cursor: 5, 6, 7, 8, each labelled with arrows on the keyboard. CAPS had to be pressed to distinguish BASIC cursor-movements from numeric entries, but ZX games soon also adopted those for unshifted directional control. The snag, from a programmer's point of view, is that 5 is in a different port group from the others, so two IN commands were needed to read the set. The advantage, compared with Quicksilva or Sinclair's own approach, is that key labels match joystick directions; either way, fire was still mapped to key 0. Pioneered by AGF and Protek, these were known as 'cursor' joysticks. Like the keyboard, but unlike Kempston interfaces, 0 rather than 1 denotes a pressed button or direction.

Next hardware supports all these arrangements. Each of its two joystick ports can be configured to send the same signals Kempston, AGF, Sinclair or Quicksilva accepted. Games often support one or all of those schemes, as well as keyboard input, via menus or automatic detection code. One snag, which was not considered a biggie in the 1980s, was that only one button was available for Fire. Atari, like Apple, reckoned one button was enough for their style of software, arguing that games that occasionally needed more could read keys for extra actions like pick up and drop.

The browser screen to load snapshot and tape image files includes a sub-screen which can map controller inputs to keys from the original 40-key Spectrum matrix (though not the extra keys added later). The mappings can be saved as part of the file-name, which is handy when copying it to a different SD card, or in a system 'cache' database file on your current card, selected by pressing O from the snap or tap menu.

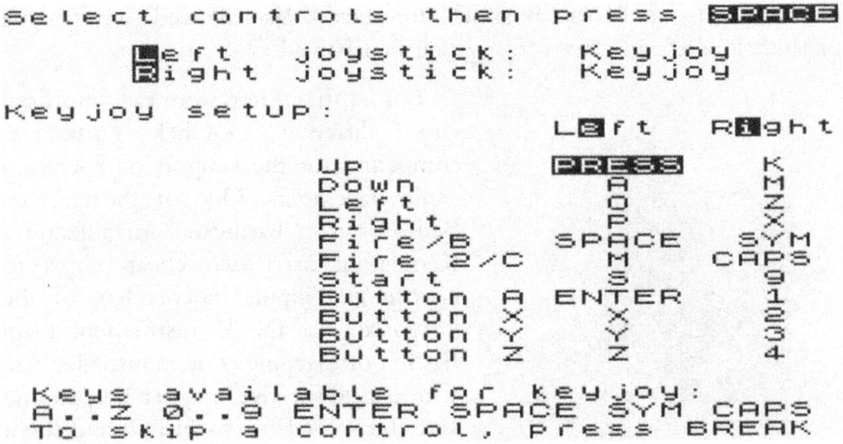

Figure 39 - the Keyjoy menu recently added to Next's browser – press J from the TAP or SNAP menu

You need a Sega Megadrive-compatible controller to assign the A/X/Y/Z and Start buttons to keys, or additional fire buttons. Old games rarely expect more than one fire button, but this way you can map new buttons to old keys for games that need extra inputs or only normally work with keyboard control.

Autofire or bonus buttons

Later game consoles had increasingly complicated input schemes and lacked keyboards, so modern gamers have come to expect more buttons. Next keeps up by reusing signals on the nine-way D-type joystick port, most simply to provide a second button connected to pin 9, which Atari reserved for an analogue 'game paddle'. Bit 5 of port 31 gets set when Next is configured for Kempston input and pin 9 is shorted to earth on pin 8. It's just a sixth switch, with no clever logic.

A second dual-fire Kempston-style input is available on port 55, though only a few new games check it. But that's not enough for modern gamers, so Next follows a scheme Sega invented to support an extra four buttons on 16-bit Megadrive controllers, which have extra hardware to support more buttons than the 9-way socket can directly read.

This explains the MD1 and MD2 configuration options, which still work like one or two button joysticks unless Sega-compatible hardware is plugged in. From a software point of view, two more buttons, labelled A and Start by Sega, can be read with IN from the remaining bits of the Kempston input ports. Four more, labelled X, Y, Z and MODE, are latched in Next's REG 178, using four bits for each joystick socket.

With nine pins on each port, even after reserving one for the 'common earth' return you might expect eight buttons. But pin 7 is reserved as an output, and Sega and Next put a low-current 5 volt supply for external logic on pin 5, the last one remaining. This introduces a slight incompatibility, as Atari reserved pin 5 for a second analogue paddle input and put power on pin 7, as did Kempston.

1980s joystick manufacturers looking to distinguish their bundle of switches from rivals used pin 7 to power optional 'auto-fire' hardware, which is unlikely to work on Next unless you make a little adapter linking Next's pin 5 with pin 7 on a second plug, passing through connections 1, 2, 3, 4 for directions, and 6 and 8 for fire and earth. Otherwise, leave the auto-fire switched off, or wait for someone to implement it in the FPGA.

The curse of Amstrad

Once Atari, Sinclair, Sega, Memotech, MSX and other micro companies had settled on the nine-pin joystick connector, at least for the four directions and fire, Amstrad took over Spectrum production and deliberately made the joystick ports they 'glued on' to their Spectrum 128 remix incompatible with all the sticks in existence, even their own CPC range. They did this not by changing the circuit or the connector – which was not patent-protected – but by scrambling the wiring!

Howard Jacobson of joystick importers Cheetah Marketing told me at the time that Alan Sugar had demanded a price of one dollar per unit for the flimsy SJS-1 joysticks he got manufactured for the Spectrum +2 bundle, and had to commit to order a million units to get that price. The scrambling meant that only SJS-1 sticks would work on the Amstrad Spectrum. Standard ones don't cause any damage, they just don't work. Cheetah and their rivals swiftly arranged for their products to come with two plugs, a grey one for the Amstrad +2s and a black one for everything else!

Figure 40 – Curse of Amstrad – the grey joystick plug wiring is scrambled

Unless you still use one of the eccentric Amstrad Spectrums, you'd be wise to chop off the grey plug. The black plug works with Next and everything else, but the grey one can potentially damage a Kickstarter 1 system by shorting out the Sega SELECT output.

Cordless connections

People with more faith than me in batteries have grown accustomed to playing games via cordless controllers. These incorporate a battery-powered radio transmitter in the hand-held device, and a matched receiver at the other end, plugged into a socket normally expecting a wired controller. As long as you get the specific Sega variant that fits Next's 9-pin D-type sockets, and don't forget to charge the remote part regularly, these work well on Next, though there's inevitably a slight lag introduced by the radio system.

The £19 wireless adapter for Sega Megadrives made by 8BitDo is a good match for Next, and links with some cordless Sony and Nintendo joypads you may well already have kicking around. I've tested mine with a WiiMote and a PlayStation 3 controller, both left over from my former career developing mainstream games on PowerPC-based consoles.

The £22 Retro-bit wireless Arcade Pad, meant for similar Sega systems, includes a console-style pad as well as the wireless bits. But don't make the mistake of buying the USB versions, wireless or otherwise. There are what look like micro-USB ports on the back of so-called accelerated Nexts, but one of them is worse than useless, as the Quick Start Guide warns, and the other is only connected to the optional Pi0, not directly to our Z80n. It's left-over from when SpecNext Ltd worried they'd not be able to afford a HDMI licence and designed-in the Pi0 to get one by proxy. Chapter 18, Alternative Cores, explains more productive uses for this optional extra.

Startup defaults

If your Next has both WiFi and the real-time clock options you should consider adding a command to update the clock periodically. The startup program autoexec.bas in your SD's NextZXOS subdirectory runs whenever you reboot. Add this line, suggested online by Maciej M-klas:

```
IF (REG 2&@11)=2 THEN .nxtp time.nxtel.org 12300 -z=GMT
```

Adjust the parameter after -z to suit your time-zone if you're not in the UK. A list of time-zone codes is in Robin Verhagen-Guest's .nxtp project's wiki at: github.com/Threetwosevensixseven/nxtp/wiki/Timezone-Codes

The REG 2 test means that Next will synchronize the clock only after a hard reset (power on) but not after a soft reset (red button tap). Bear in mind that from a cold start the WiFi might take longer to start up than NextZXOS. This partly depends on your router.

You can set other convenient defaults in the same file – I use SPECTRUM CHR$ 64 to over-ride the gaudy syntax colouring in the 128 BASIC editor by switching it into Timex HiRes, and RUN AT 3 to default my programs to use the 28 MHz CPU setting.

Chapter 5, NextBASIC Performance and Tips

In my reviews of Next for the 2019 and 2021 Crash annuals I included – with my tongue firmly in my cheek – updates of the standard BASIC benchmark timings published by *Computing Today* magazine in their 1982 review of the 16k ZX Spectrum.

> ***Bill Gates and I both believe you can write any good program in BASIC, period, end of discussion***
> *Chuck Peddle, PET designer*

As the 16k RAM was slowed by video access, yet nine out of ten purchasers bought the faster 48k model, these oft-repeated figures helped form the rather misleading perception that ZX BASIC was relatively slow. Hacks in 128 BASIC didn't help, but there's been a lot of progress since, most obviously because Next can be clocked up from 3.5 to 28 MHz – or beyond, by adjusting the VGA scan rate to support PC monitors which can't handle UK PAL TV timing – but also because of sterling work by Garry Lancaster to undo some of the 128k regressions, fix bugs and optimise key routines.

This chapter drills down on performance details, but in general NextBASIC is fast enough for most things, including twitch games, though you may need to experiment to find the quickest techniques now, if you've grown up with the simpler ZX BASIC. New string operations with IN and square brackets can replace whole loops in the old language.

Next's integer variables, hardware sprites, scrolling and DMA are discussed later, in the context of real and useful programs. There's also necessary explanation of the way a processor only designed for a maximum of 64k now juggles two megabytes of RAM, covering the differences between BASIC banks and MMU pages, and ways to manage the RAM which don't hamstring the debugging of large programs.

Benchmark history

At the start of the 1980s almost every micro review included a table of timings for seven or eight little programs which were designed by Tom Rugg and Phil Feldman of the US magazine *Kilobaud* to run on any BASIC micro. An eighth test, to check maths function speed without concern for precision, was added by John Coll of *Personal Computer World*.

Benchmark timings are often misleading, sometimes deliberately so, because they test the speed of tiny programs which are not representative of any useful workload. I explained their flaws, especially in the context of comparisons between different micro architectures and interpreters and compilers, in my demolition-job *Nailing Jelly to a Tree* which was published in the debut issue of Computer Shopper magazine in March 1988. Old and new PCW benchmark listings appear there, and were re-printed in many eighties mags.

By the time I reviewed the Amstrad Spectrum 128+2 alongside the BBC Master Compact and C64C for them, *Personal Computer World* had ditched the benchmarks along with most coverage of home micros, BASIC and creative programming. I moved on to *Crash*, *Computer Shopper* and *Sinclair QL World*. But Next is a child of the 1982 Spectrum, running almost all of the original ROM code written for Sinclair by John Grant and Stephen Vickers of Nine Tiles, so the benchmark comparison is still apt.

NextBASIC performance update

I included Benchmark timings for an early NextBASIC in the 2019 *Crash* annual, and updates for 2.06 and the 28 MHz hardware boost in the 2021 issue. Both compared Next with the 16k Spectrum timings from *Crash* issue 19. The following table updates those figures for NextBASIC 2.09. They also apply to 2.08 as those releases mainly differ in features and bug-fixes, rather than performance enhancements.

Columns correspond to the eight benchmark tests, ranging from BM1, an empty 1000-step FOR loop, BM2 a similar loop using IF THEN GOTO, to 100 calculations of exponentials, logarithms, and ridiculous trigonometry (the Sine of 99 Radians is hardly a commonly-needed value) in BM8. The rest add extra code inside the IF loop for variable and constant arithmetic (BM3 and BM4), then a GO SUB, nested FOR loop, and array update, in tests 5 to 7. The INT tests are modified to use NextBASIC's integer expression evaluator.

Numeric precision Test:	BM1	BM2	BM3	BM4	BM5	BM6	BM7	BM8
Z80n NextBASIC 2.09, FP	0.55	0.69	1.97	1.91	2.2	5.8	8.02	3.08
Z80n NextBASIC 2.09, INT	0.30	0.45	0.72	0.71	1.01	3	3.83	N/A

Figure 41 graphs how much faster NextBASIC runs the benchmarks, compared with a 16k Spectrum. The Next was running at 28 MHz in SCART 50 Hertz display and could be 18% faster, albeit less compatible, in the 59 Hertz VGA6 mode.

The 3.5 MHz 1982 Spectrum timings could also be slightly faster if measured on a 48k system, as the ZX BASIC and Z80 stack are running from contended RAM in the 16k system, but the difference is relatively small as BASIC interpreter code runs at full speed from the 16k ROM. Bars are proportional to speed, not time, so bigger means faster. We've come a long way! There's no integer bar for BM8 as that test requires decimal arithmetic.

In the meantime I also tested the update from 2.06 to 2.07 and reported back to the NextBASIC Facebook group that "integer FOR loops haven't sped up at all, and benchmark 8 (the transcendental nonsense) is almost unaffected. But simple IF loops, in tiny programs where the line-search overhead is insignificant, were about ten per cent faster in normal BASIC and a third faster (i.e. doing four work units in the previous time for three) in integer format."

Figure 42 shows that NextBASIC runs all the tests substantially faster than it did in 2021, apart from the integer FOR loop, which regressed a little because of necessary bug-fixes in its LOCAL and EXIT statement-handling.

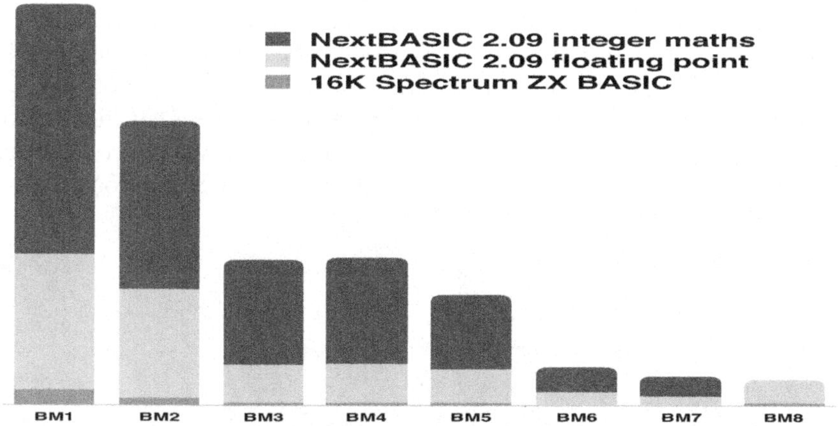

Figure 41 - Progress in Spectrum BASIC Benchmark performance from 1982 to 2023

Despite the progress on integer arithmetic and loops in general, the maths-heavy Benchmark 8 is no faster than it was in 1982. Apart from the RND function, not included in John Coll's test, it's still running code from the ZX81 ROM, although later systems like MGT's SAM and BBC BASIC Z80 have proven that our CPU can do floating-point arithmetic substantially faster if those routines, optimised for size rather than speed, are updated.

It's fair to compare Spectrum BASIC with BBC BASIC Z80 as that's been ported to run natively on Next. Chapter 18, Alternative Cores, shows that's there's still lots of potential to speed up Next's floating-point maths package, and also perhaps the implementation of FOR loops. Figure 108 in particular highlights the potential for much faster mathematical functions.

But what does all this mean in our own programs? There's no definitive answer because real programs, unlike benchmarks, do useful work in varying ways, with far more lines, procedures, strings and other confounding factors.

I timed a short demo, heavy in integer arithmetic, which spins sprites on elliptical paths at various speeds. On 2.06H I got at most 27 animated sprites flying around independently, with their speeds and positions curvily updated from BASIC every frame, and keyboard and mouse input included in the REPEAT loop. Using the same approach on 2.07A, I got 32 sprites flying at once without dropping a frame.

Bottlenecks and BASICs

NextBASIC keeps getting faster and more capable. It is still being actively developed. Compatibility is still the priority, rightly, and a big constraint. One remaining bottleneck is the way variable names are looked up while a program runs. The new longer array names in 2.08 make programs easier to read, but can also slow them down.

This is because every reference to a name, other than the single-character integer ones prefixed in programs with %, involves a sequential search through the VARS area of memory. The longer the names used since the last NEW, LOAD or CLEAR command, the more slowly each later one will be found. This will be tricky to fix compatibly, though I have a few ideas, since many useful programs rely on the internal structure of VARs which has been documented in every Next manual as well as the original Sinclair one.

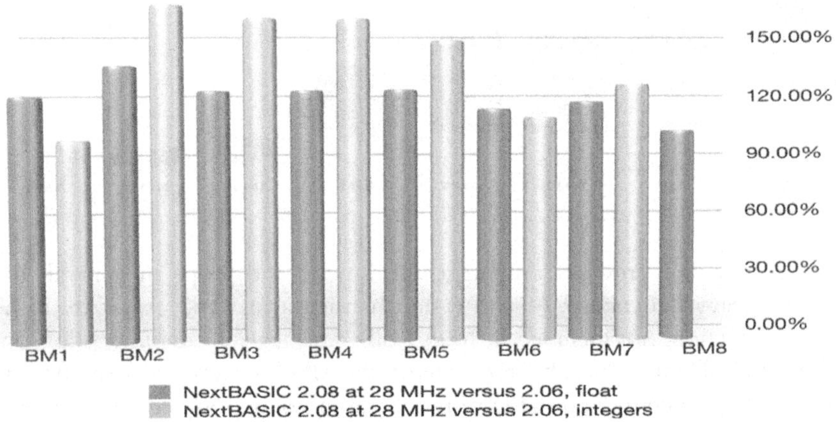

Figure 42 – Benchmark performance changes between NextBASIC 2.06 and 2.08

Variable lookup times depend on the order of encounter after CLEAR. Integer variables avoid this by limiting the name length and preallocating storage at fixed addresses, like *Acorn Atom* and *Camputers Lynx* BASICs, and most Tiny BASICs, but this makes non-trivial programs famously hard to read even though it's great for misleading benchmarks. BBC BASIC is egregious in this respect, potentially five times slower with meaningful names, while Sinclair's QL SuperBASIC runs at the same speed even with hundreds of 250-character names, because it contains a 'name table' and the tokenised program directly indexes into that, like 8-bit Atari BASIC.

Eschewing Microsoft's two-character limit, ZX BASIC allows arbitrarily long descriptive names for scalars, even names that include nonsignificant spaces, as Algol 68 could. NextBASIC 2.08 extends this to arrays and strings. But existing programs rely on the long-documented VARS data format, so user-name tokenisation is problematic; this disproportionately slugs long programs written for readability. So, for now, it helps a lot to first cite variables after CLEAR or LOAD in order of likelihood of later use.

One advantage of the tokenised format of ZX BASIC, unlike the text format used by SuperBASIC, is that the dictionary of names and values in VARs is saved with the program, so we can optimise the order of variables, moving the most used to the front, via judiciously-timed SAVEs and assignments. This makes the files bigger, which is why my line 9999 SAVE commands tend to be prefixed with a CLEAR command.

Contrary to early Sinclair adverts, which compared ZX80 BASIC with text-only Tiny BASICs from the 1970s, the tokenisation does not save much memory and it makes reading and printing our BASIC programs on other computers harder, as they expect ASCII text rather than Sinclair-special codes. We can convert programs files with **.bas2txt** and back again with **.txt2bas**, for easier bulk editing and searching, and the updated file browser makes this even easier through new menu options.

Optimisation should always be guided by measurements – static analysis is pointless, especially for an interpreter where sequential context is vital. My biggest single contribution to whole-program optimisation is Next's Profile driver, available since the 2.07 distro at apps/dev/Profiler, with comprehensive instructions now in the docs/guides folder on your SD card. This driver runs alongside your program, building up a table showing how much time is spent on each line.

BASIC PRINT remains rather slow as is uses the generic stream system which works one byte at a time, adding a lot of per-call overhead. It was designed for a 1k computer with a dynamically allocated display map and very limited ROM space and has been complicated further by additional display modes. Next's TILE commands (not to be confused with hardware tiles, explored in Chapter 15, Tiles and Layers) may help here. Graphics commands like PLOT and DRAW are fastest in LAYER 0, but still slow by Acorn standards.

In general ZX BASIC is fast at referencing constants, especially decimal ones, compared with other BASICs, because it precomputes and stores their binary representation. This preparation does not apply to integer expressions, saving bytes; the conversion code for small numbers is fast enough for this not to affect performance.

Memory leaks

A brilliant program or algorithm is useless if you can't make it fit, and a nightmare to test if it soaks up ever more memory, the longer you run it. Questions about memory leaks are a recurrent theme of Facebook's *BASIC on the Spectrum Next* group; here's the distilled wisdom. Worked examples of how to partition and test a large program appear in Chapter 6, The NextBASIC Text Editor.

The statement M=65536-USR 7962 sets M to the amount of free memory left for BASIC variables, GO SUBs etc. This works on all Spectrums and all Next personalities. If it's going down as your game runs, you have a leak.

Use this expression to work out where and how fast your program is leaking, e.g. PRINTing it periodically, and check later that the issue is fixed.

GO SUBs without matching RETURNs will only cause a slow leak, but it will be cumulative. GO SUB in Next BASIC stacks four times as much data – 12 bytes, rather than 3 in Sinclair versions. This change can break ZX BASIC programs on Next if they ran close to the memory limit. Try this:

```
10 GO SUB 20: STOP
20 PRINT 65536-USR 7962: GO TO 10
```

Replace the GO TO with RETURN to fix the leak.

Jumping out of a procedure except via END PROC has a similar effect.

CLEAR will recover the memory but lose all variable values and return lines. Either way, the return address has to be stored until you RETURN or END PROC. If you never return, that memory cannot be recovered otherwise than by NEW or CLEAR. Using GO TO out of loops causes the same issue as jumping out of subroutines or procedures – stuff will be pushed onto the stack but never removed. That's why Garry recently adopted the EXIT keyword from Sinclair SuperBASIC to augment WHILE with a generic memory-safe way of quitting REPEAT loops or integer FOR loops.

> ***It is practically impossible to teach good programming to students that have had a prior exposure to BASIC: as potential programmers they are mentally mutilated beyond hope of regeneration.***
>
> *Edsger Dijkstra, 1975*

NextBASIC utility programs

This section of the book contains programs that serve two purposes. They make NextBASIC easier and more pleasant to use, and they demonstrate language features and techniques which may be useful in your own programs.

Along the way, they also reveal some of the potential pitfalls or gotchas of programming on a small computer system. Small doesn't necessarily mean simple, and the open-to-all nature of Sinclair products means that not all advice in circulation is necessarily helpful, or even tested!

All these programs have been tested, which means that rather than think up an idea, invent a solution and check it does what was intended, I've actively tried to break them, and then fix them, and try to break them again, before bothering you with them. Many ideas – perhaps half – get abandoned along the way, but that's fine. Ideas are cheap. Solutions are not. Remembering Marshall McLuhan's quote, I hope these examples encourage you to make obsolete things that please you. And don't forget the Chinese proverb, tastefully appropriated by Steve Jobs, cited at the end of Chapter 2.

It's fun to make things, and easy to get started, contrary to professional wisdom (which may be a tautology). Isaac Newton told Robert Hooke, "*if I have seen further, it is by standing on the shoulder of giants*". Thankfully, you no longer need to know Latin, to do that.

We can't all be John Grant or Steve Vickers, or Garry Lancaster. Those jobs are already taken. But none of them were born expert Z80 programmers or language designers. Like me, and you, whether in the 1980s or now, they learned by experiment, first staring confusedly at other people's work, then tentatively fiddling with it, growing in understanding till they came up with something that was – perhaps for them alone – an improvement. And they found that it was fun.

So they kept at it. All it takes to learn with and from a computer is the inclination, uninterrupted time, memory and imagination. The original Spectrum was a hit because people could get pleasing results from it quickly, and it rapidly rewarded further effort. It was small, elegant, and more than the sum of its parts. You don't need to understand everything to see why – time permitting – it's worth continuing to delve.

The Spectrum Next is still small, and more complicated, but you can still engage with it almost as immediately as ever. A lot of the frustrations, like slow loading and limited space, have been addressed, and there are mountains of new features; but they're all optional and you don't need to grasp them to make a start. A Spectrum Next is like an 80s micro but with many of the expensive add-ons built in, ready when you are, and unprecedented support for more, by building on the existing software or hardware, plugging in gadgets you treasured and learned about long ago, tweaking or making new ones.

You may never write 'from scratch' a 'complete program'. This is rarer than you may think, even for professionals. Most of us just kept fiddling till there wasn't much of the original left, and we felt justified in saying that what remains was ours – our creation, our art. It doesn't need to be clever, or useful, as long as you find the creative process interesting. Keep at it. *Share and enjoy*, to quote the motto famous creative procrastinator and micro dabbler Douglas Adams attributed to the Sirius Cybernetics Corporation Complaints Division.

Time is the greatest constraint. In the early '80s computer clubs, before the commodification of software, it was rare to see people with jobs and families at meetings. Most of the keenest attendees were considered too young to be taken seriously, or retired people. Either way, they had time to learn, and curiosity about what they might achieve. Many went on to build a career; most didn't, and that's fine. They all had fun, found things out, and shared the experience.

If you're preoccupied with raising a family, propping up Capitalism or simply staying alive, this part of the book may not suit you. Yet. But one day, with luck, it or some well-written user-guide will open up a world of creativity that can be shared, and enjoyed, without running out, hitting a wall or using up anything up you don't have already. So hang onto this book, regardless!

Backing up

If you're creating something step by step, it's vital not to lose tweaks along the way. It's also important to keep track of the changes, in case one of them is a mis-step and you need to 'roll back' to an earlier version.

NextBASIC has access to vast amounts of SD storage, but limited support for rolling back. When you save a program, if you re-use the filename, the old one will be renamed from **filename.bas** to **filename.bak** and the update will take the name **filename.bas**. You can turn this off with %FORMAT |=1 but it's handy if you soon realise you've accidentally made the file worse.

Just call up the browser, rename the mis-step to, say, filename.bad, and wind time back with by renaming filename.bak to filename.bas. It's not unknown for a mistake to be salvageable, or at least instructive, after further thought, so don't be in too much of a hurry to purge the 'bad' versions. It's not as if you're likely to run out of SD card space, though the directory listing might eventually get a bit unwieldy. At this point, you can wipe out all the false-turns in your current subdirectory with:

```
erase "*.bad"
```

Since computer memories may fail at any time, it's sensible to make backups to another card. From the very first prototypes, Spectrum Next allows two SD cards to be connected at once, but there's only one SD socket on the standard machines. I hope that will be fixed for Kickstarter 3.

If you're mainly interested in emulation you've doubtless got other computers and can use them to back up your Next creations. But if you prefer to concentrate on Next itself, like me, a twin card adapter (and a few spare SD cards) is the best investment you can make. There's a socket for such an adapter on every KS1 or N-Go board, labelled J13.

I've moved mine to my boxed KS1 Next, with a bit of fiddling to run the ribbon cable through one of the gaps around existing sockets. Pick a gap to suit your desk layout and what else you want to plug in. The easiest choice, and biggest gap, is around the ZX edge connector, but if you're keen to use that and don't have an edge extender (needed to avoid many ZX peripherals blocking the HD socket) you could run it through the hole for the second HDMI output, unless you've blocked that with a Pi0.

On my 2018 dev board I now use the equally effective but less prettily cased Dual Micro SD Reader from the same maker, Richard Spencer. It's just a board on the end of a ribbon cable but still 'plug and play' and at £6 for two latching SD sockets, mapped to drive C: and D:, it's a bargain.

You do need to undo the six screws on the underside of a cased Next, or open up your N=Go, to access J13, but the machine has been designed to be 'user serviceable' and if you can fit a mains plug you can do it. I've seen a picture of a prototype version of a similar expander for the KS2 Next, but haven't had a change to test it yet.

Now, on with the software.

Automatic versioning

The .bak file is better than nothing, but no help if you save again before realising the previous version was faulty. When working on large files I've got into the habit of saving numbered versions, such as Editor13.bas, Editor14.bas and so on, by editing a SAVE command with the current filename, traditionally placed at line 9999 in ZX BASIC projects.

But what if I forget to bump up the version number before saving? Renaming a **.bak** file might still save me, but only once. So here's a small procedure (around 500 bytes long) which can be merged at the end of any program and will make sure that every time you SAVE with GO TO 9990 the number in the filename is bumped up automatically, leaving you with a full history of all the changes. I've used line 9990 rather than 9999 just because I wanted to show the PROC call and subsequent SAVE on separate lines, for clarity, and found it useful to have a message confirming the name of the new file. You may prefer to merge lines 9990 and 9995, with the command LINE MERGE 9990,9995, and then edit the line number to 9999. It's your program now – tweak it as you wish!

```
9690 REM Save Bumper, SNG October 2023
9700
9710 DEFPROC Bumper(n$)
9720 LOCAL latest,t=0
9730 LOCAL f$,t$,n=1+ LEN n$
9740 DIM t$(999)
9750 CLOSE # 4: OPEN # 4,"v>t$"
9760 CAT #4,n$+"*.bas"
9770 GO TO #4,0
9780 REPEAT
9790   INPUT #4; LINE f$
9800   WHILE LEN f$
9810   WHILE f$<>"No files found"
9820   IF f$( TO n-1)=n$
9830     t= IN (f$,".")
9840     WHILE t
9850     IF f$(n)>"0" AND f$(n)<="9"
9860       t= VAL (f$(n TO t ))
9870       IF t>latest THEN latest=t
9880     ENDIF
9890   ENDIF
9900 REPEAT UNTIL 0
9910 CLOSE # 4
9920 ENDPROC =n$+ STR$ (latest+1)+".bas"
9930
9990 PROC Bumper("Bumper") TO f$
9995 SAVE f$: PRINT f$;" saved"
```

I've put the routine into a procedure, PROC Bumper, which can be called from any line by passing the stem of the required filename as a string parameter, e.g. PROC Bumper("Editor"). If the SAVE command was inside the procedure the resultant file would be larger, because it would include the names and values of temporary variables used to work out the new name, including a fairly large string array, with the saved program.

Putting it outside, and making the variables local, means the only extra thing that must be saved is f$, the string returned by PROC Bumper( ). You may want to be able to continue your program from any point previously reached, immediately after loading. If so, its own variables will be saved along with the program lines, including this procedure. But if your intention is to start it with RUN, which clears variables, you might as well add a CLEAR statement at the start of line 9990, before the PROC call. This will reduce the size of the saved programs.

Bumper( ) uses five local variables besides the parameter, **n$**. Variable **n** is just a convenience to save repeatedly working out one more than the length of **n$**. In **latest** we store the highest version number of the previously-saved files, and **t** is a temporary working variable. Line 9720 explicitly sets them both to zero, though the =0 isn't really needed as that's the default value of all variables newly declared as LOCAL. The other two variables are strings, which default to 'null' or empty. The directory catalogue will end up in **t$**, and **f$** is used to read and analyse individual lines from that.

Unlike, say, Unix systems, NextZXOS does not allow the programmer to open the directory as a file and read the names from it, line by line. But NextBASIC does allow output from commands to be redirected into a file, by specifying a stream for the output. By default this is stream #2, connected to the upper screen, but ZX BASIC was advanced for its time in being 'device independent', so that any command that allows a stream specification, like PRINT or INKEY$, can write or read a file instead if given a stream number of a previously-opened file.

Thus CAT #3 will output to the printer, mapped to stream 3, and PRINT #0; diverts output to the lower part of a LAYER 0 screen. Consistently but less usefully, LPRINT #2; works exactly like PRINT because the only difference between LPRINT and PRINT, like LLIST and LIST, is that the former generally write to stream 3 while the later default to stream 2.

This ZX BASIC feature was preparation for serial adapter and ZX Microdrive support, but Sinclair's rush to market meant that the Spectrum shipped before the other devices, other than a simple serial port, were working reliably. Interface 1, and compatible disc systems from Opus, MGT and others, completed this feature, and although Amstrad dropped support for serial files in the Plus 3, Garry Lancaster restored it, and more, in his +3e update, which became the foundation for NextZXOS via IDEDOS.

Like MGT in their SAM Coupé, Garry extended OPEN to allow output to memory, as well as to a file, and even to a string. In NextBASIC the maximum size of this string must be preset, hence the DIM on line 9720, for the string T$ which has previously been declared LOCAL, so that its use inside the procedure doesn't affect the value of T$ outside, and the memory allocated is automatically cleaned up when the procedure ends. We want F$ to exactly fit each line read from the directory file, so it's neither necessary nor desirable to preset the length.

The procedure, and all the variables inside it, necessarily limits the total size of the rest of the program, so the dimensioning of T$ needs to be long enough for all the directory entries (including file sizes) output by CAT, but no longer. I chose 999 to support about 40 versions, or at least four even if the names are extremely long. If that's not enough, the program will stop with an End of File error in line 9760. To fix this either delete some of the old versions, move them elsewhere, or increase the value in the DIM statement, and try again.

The wildcard specification **n$+"*.bas"** limits the number of lines by including only those starting with the stem of the project name and ending with **.bas**, but if you're busy you might have lots of those in the current directory, and each line of the catalogue will need about 25 characters, including the size in K printed after each name – more if you insist on UsingExceptionallyLongFilenames; the file-system limit is 255 characters, except on drives A, B and M which ape the ancient CP/M system and only cater for eight characters of name followed by a dot and up to three more characters of extension, e.g. **AUTOEXEC.BAS**.

Line 9750 connects stream #4 to the variable t$, so that CAT #4 puts the entire output of the CAT command in the string array. The CLOSE makes sure the stream's not already in use, as otherwise OPEN fails with an error message. GOTO #4,0 winds back to the start of the stream, so that INPUT #4;LINE can read the catalogue, line by line, from the start. The WHILE statements inside the REPEAT loop make it stop if a blank line is encountered, marking the end of a list of files, or none match the wildcard and CAT outputs "No files found".

In ZX BASIC the WHILE *condition* statements would be written IF *condition* THEN GO TO 9910, and the REPEAT UNTIL 0 (which passes control back to the prior REPEAT, for another line) would be written GO TO 9790. The REPEAT/WHILE/UNTIL approach is faster, especially on long programs, as there's no need for BASIC to search for numbered lines, but requires more discipline as if you use GO to leave the loop a dozen bytes of memory will remain allocated, keeping track of the start, until an ENDPROC or REPEAT UNTIL is reached, or LOAD, NEW, RUN or CLEAR release all the memory allocated since the last of those commands.

Once we have a catalogue line in F$, lines 9820 to 9890 use other Nextras to see if it starts with the stem of the filenames we care about, followed by at least one digit greater than zero and no more than nine, and then a dot. If there's no dot the WHILE t statement leaves the loop, otherwise line 9860 reads the number on each suitable line from after the stem, up to the dot which it interprets as a decimal point. If this number **t** is greater than the value of **latest** it updates latest to the new highest version number found.

We can't just assume that the last filename will have the highest number, because files are listed by CAT in their order in the directory. This is not necessarily ascending order, as when files are deleted the gaps they leave are re-used for the next new file written.

It only remains to close the stream and return the full name of the next file to be saved, with the incantation **=n$+ STR$ (latest+1)+".bas"** after the ENDPROC. This gets copied into the global f$, or any other string variable, as the local strings have been forgotten when the procedure ends, by the TO keyword after the PROC call on line 9990, ready for the SAVE and reassuring PRINT on the last line.

Tokens and text

A .bas, or .bak, file contains a program in the form it will run from memory, with keywords like PRINT and REPEAT packed into a single byte and numbers like -1 or 2.718281828 encoded, in a hidden Z80-ready binary form, within the file. It also includes all the current variable values.

To save memory on the ZX81, without sacrificing readability, some tokens even contain spaces, such as OPEN # or GO TO. In NextBASIC a few keywords allow abbreviations, like RAND for RANDOMIZE or CONT for CONTINUE, to ease typing.

If you want to print or edit a program outside NextBASIC you need the text rather than the binary. This is why, if you view the .BAS file on another non-Spectrum computer, it's mostly gibberish, with only the variable names, constants and string values readable as plain text.

It's handy to file variable values with the program but sometimes more convenient to edit the text alone, for comparisons, printouts, or complicated editing of groups of lines. NextZXOS provides dot commands to convert a .BAS token file into text, or back again. Dot commands are machine code programs, loaded on demand from the **C:/dot** directory or a path on the current drive, which extend BASIC in useful ways when their names are typed as if they were BASIC commands, preceded by a full stop. Don't confuse this with a decimal point, or the dot before an extension in CP/M-style filenames.

The dot commands include a more capable version of CAT, cryptically called **.ls** in Unix style, and many others which form extensions to the system, like **.more** to view text files (which is puzzled, as you'd expect, by **.bas** ones), **.date** and **.time** to access the optional clock hardware, **.mem** and **.nextver** to check memory usage or the system version, **.find** to search for filenames, **.browse** to select files, **.guide** to read *NextGuide* documents, and many more.

Most of the dot commands may be followed by parameters, such as file paths, to control their behaviour; the better-written ones provide help if you enter them without any parameters. For instance, these commands convert **Test.bas** into **Text.txt** and back again. Remember that the final version of **Test.bas** will not contain any variable values!

```
.bas2txt Test.bas
.txt2bas Test.txt
```

Program comparisons

If you have saved numbered versions of a file you may want to compare them to work out what's changed, especially if a new bug has appeared. I got bored of moving my Next SD cards to a bigger computer and using *Beyond Compare* to work out what had changed, so I wrote a simpler program to compare two text files on Next.

NextDiff is intended for analysis of NextBASIC programs, so it uses line numbers at the start of each line to recover synchronisation after a change. It could be extended to match any later pattern, but I don't recommend that as a first project. Here it is:

```
100 REM NextDiff 20230728 by Simon N Goodwin, NextBASIC 2.08+
110 a$="EditorProcs15.txt"
120 b$="EditorProcs17.txt"
125 LAYER 0: PAPER 7: CLS : INK 0
150 CLOSE # 5: OPEN # 5,b$: INPUT #5; LINE b$: PRINT "B: ";b$
130 CLOSE # 4: OPEN # 4,a$: INPUT #4; LINE a$: PRINT "A: ";a$
140 aMax= DIM #4:aNum,bNum=0:aGo,bGo=1
160 bMax= DIM #5
170 REPEAT
180   IF aGo
190     IF POINT #4<aMax THEN INPUT #4; LINE a$ :
           aNum= VAL a$( TO 4): ELSE a$=""
200   ENDIF
210   IF bGo
220     IF POINT #5<bMax THEN INPUT #5; LINE b$ :
           bNum= VAL b$( TO 4): ELSE b$=""
230   ENDIF
240   bGo=aNum>=bNum
250   aGo=bNum>=aNum
260   IF a$<>b$
265     INK 2-(a$[-(" ","")]=b$[-(" ","")])
270     IF aGo THEN PRINT INVERSE 1;" A "; INVERSE 0;a$
280     IF bGo THEN PRINT INVERSE 1;" B "; INVERSE 0;b$ :
           IF aGo THEN PRINT
290     PAUSE 0
300   ENDIF
330 REPEAT UNTIL(NOT aGo OR LEN a$=0) AND(NOT bGo OR LEN b$=0)
340 CLOSE # 5
350 CLOSE # 4
360 INK 0: STOP
```

I won't go into as much detail as I did for **Bumper.bas**, as the file-input part of this program is very similar, and if you want detail, history and insights into how and why BASIC works, there's plenty to come later, especially in the chapters about the NextBASIC Text Editor. The names of the files to be compared are set in the first two lines. Those variables are later re-used to hold and compare lines from each file. Changed lines from each are distinguished in the output by the prefix A: and B: respectively. As bas2txt puts the filename, preceded by a hash, in a dummy line at the start of its output, these always differ and are output for reference at the start.

The DIM # statements read the number of bytes in each file to aMax and bMax, so we can tell when we're finished. POINT # reads the current pointer positions. The line numbers in each file are stored in aNum and bNum, and the flags aGo and bGo are set while differences are apparent. The output includes only the changed lines, with A: or B: prefixes depending on where they come from. Line 265 is the only clever bit, setting the ink colour to 1 (blue) or 2 (red) depending on whether the difference between two lines with the same number is just spacing, after reformatting, or more significant.

Other aspects of NextZXOS, such as sprite and mouse handling, will be addressed in the larger examples, but there are a few hardware features that need direct OUT, POKE or REG commands whether accessed from BASIC or machine code. Chapter 14, Better BEEPs, coddles the Programmable Sound Generators in user-friendly PROCs, and also demonstrates program timing adjustments, LAYER PALETTE and pixel graphics. There's more about pixels and palettes in Chapter 15, Tiles and Layers, and Chapter 13, Memory, explains how to access the DMA controller for graphics, sound or memory-management.

File operations with esxDOS

Most of the functions of NextZXOS have NextBASIC keywords to make them easy to use, but there are a couple of file operations that can currently only be performed efficiently with machine-code. Both are particularly relevant when processing large files. Currently there's no way for BASIC programs to reduce the length of an existing file without copying the first part to another file and deleting the longer version.

Operations on binary files are also slow because unless the file has line-end markers at regular intervals, making it compatible with INPUT, it's necessary to load the entire file with LOAD CODE, or chunks with **.extract**, or resort to reading a byte at a time with INKEY$ #.

My alternative approach is about a hundred times faster than INKEY$ and works however the file is structured. The routine is used in the example of streaming audio samples from SD in Chapter 13, Memory experiments, but presented here as a BASIC extension, and an example of how to interface BASIC streams with PLUS3DOS and esxDOS system routines.

Converting stream numbers to file handles

The first challenge is that DOS knows nothing of the stream numbers entered after a # character in BASIC commands like OPEN, PRINT and CLOSE. The system uses its own internal 'file handles'. Amstrad might have mapped these numbers directly onto the general-purpose BASIC streams #4 to #15 but chose to keep them distinct, probably because they were hurriedly adapting CP/M code from their CPC and PCW computers.

So here's a PROC that takes the number of an open BASIC stream and returns the corresponding file handle expected by PLUS3DOS and the esxDOS software layer above it:

```
890 ;Return PLUS3DOS handle of a stream or 0 if invalid/closed
900 DEFPROC S2H(stream)
905 LOCAL p,h
910 IF stream<4 OR stream>15 THEN PRINT "4..15": ENDPROC =0
920 p= DPEEK ((stream+3)*2+23568)
930 IF p=0 THEN PRINT "#";stream;" CLOSED": ENDPROC =0
940 h= PEEK (p+12+ DPEEK 23631)
950 IF h<2 OR h>15 THEN PRINT h;" Eh?": STOP
960 ENDPROC =h
```

Truncating a file

To truncate an existing file we need to open it in the usual way, then pass the corresponding file handle and the desired length in bytes into esxDOS with an extended USR call. This reserves memory and stores the code; it can run from any otherwise-unused 15 bytes of RAM:

```
100 REM esxDOS hooks demo
110 CLEAR 49099
120 %b=49100
130 POKE %b,197,121,207,160,225,56,4,
    125,207,162,216,6,0,207,147
```

```
TRUNC:
 PUSH BC
 LD A,C
 RST 8
 DB F_GETPOS
 POP HL
 JR NC,ERR
 LD A,L
 RST 8
 DB F_FTRUNCATE
 RET C
ERR:
 LD B,0
 RST 8
 DB M_GETERR
```

Figure 43 - File truncation routine, assembly source

The corresponding assembly language is shown in Figure 43. You don't need to understand the code to use it, but it shows Z80 veterans the general way esxDOS file operations are invoked. It uses three API hook codes, each preceded by a RST 8 instruction. F_GETPOS reads the current pointer position for the file handle in the accumulator. We copy the handle number from the USR parameter passed in the BC register, keeping a copy of its value on the stack for the next call. If F_GETPOS is successful it returns with the carry flag set and the 32-bit file pointer position in registers B, C, D and E. We pop the file handle into HL, copy it from L to the accumulator, then use the F_FTRUNCATE hook to adjust the file length. It expects the 32-bit position in the same four registers. If anything goes wrong the Carry flag is cleared by the hook routines and we quit via the M_GETERR hook, with register B clear to tell it to generate an appropriate BASIC error report. Concise descriptions of all the Next system's hook codes are in the *NextZXOS_and_esxDOS_APIs* file in your C:/docs subdirectory.

The following NextBASIC uses the code POKEd in at %B to truncate "BigFile" to **newLength** bytes. Notice that the filename is prefixed with "U>" to indicate that we want to 'Update' the file, by changing its length.

```
140 OPEN # 4,"U>BigFile": GO TO #4,newLength
150 PROC S2H(4) TO %h
160 IF %h THEN %h = USR (%b,%h)
170 CLOSE # 4
```

```
PUSH DE
POP IX
LD A,(DE)
RST 8
DB F_READ
RET
```

Figure 44 - Fast INPUT$ Z80 code

Fast binary file input

The second example also uses PROC S2H(), but this time it passes a string to the USR code. This parameter serves three purposes: firstly, it tells the code how many bytes are expected, implied by the string length. Secondly, it gives the code a place to store the resultant input bytes. Thirdly, we use the first character of the string to provide the DOS file handle. That gets clobbered by the result, so be sure to set it again before calling for the next chunk of the file. Reading always starts from the current file pointer position, and the number of bytes actually read is returned by the USR call.

```
1020 CLEAR 49099:%b=49100:count=256:start=512
1030 POKE %b,213,221,225,26,207,157,201
1050 OPEN # 4,"BigFile": GO TO #4,start
1060 DIM b$(count): PROC S2H(4) TO h: b$(1)= CHR$ h
1070 PRINT "Got "; USR (%b,b$);" up to "; POINT #4
1080 CLOSE #4
```

This example reads 256 bytes from offset 512 in the file into **b$**. Adjust **start** and **count** for other bytes. See page 323 for a more detailed example. Figure 44 is assembly source for the seven-byte routine POKEd by line 1030. USR puts the start address of the string parameter in DE and the length into BC. We read the first byte of that into the accumulator to set the file handle, after copying the address for the result into register IX, then F_READ (hook 157) does the all the hard work for us, returning the actual number of bytes in BC just where USR expects its numeric result.

Copper magic

Here's one more neat trick, before we get back to BASIC in the next chapter. The Copper is a simple beam-synchronous co-processor, copied from a feature of the Amiga's custom chip-set. It's less powerful than the Amiga implementation, as Next lacks the companion Blitter co-processor which can be programmed by Amiga's Copper to reprogram the Copper to reprogram the Blitter to generate completely new screen modes, as I demonstrated in my *Banging The Metal* columns for *Amiga Format* magazine. Even so, our Copper is well capable of adjusting Next's audio and display registers as specific lines and columns are output to the screen. There's a tantalising example of its use at the end of the *Time and Motion* chapter of the official Next manual. Here's more.

The Copper recognises just two instructions, both packed into 16 bits. If the most significant bit is set, this is a WAIT instruction. The next six bits specify a column of the playfield or border, with 0 on the left and 55 at the end of the previous line. Columns 56 to 63 are never reached, and only columns 0 to 31 correspond to on-screen attribute positions.

The other nine bits, including the least significant bit of the first byte and all of the second, specify a screen line, numbered from 0 to 311 to include all the border lines and frame-fly-back time. Lines 312 to 511 are never reached, so the copper program can be deliberately stalled by telling it to wait for a non-existent position – by convention, column 63 and line 511 are used, synthesising a HALT instruction that has all 16 bits set.

The Copper ticks at eight pixel intervals until a specified line or character-column is reached. It can also move eight-bit values to any of the first 128 Next registers. If the most significant bit of the Copper instruction is clear, this is a MOVE. The remaining bits of the first byte select a Next register, 0..127; the second byte is a new value for that register. If your main loop or interrupt handler modifies that value, by replacing it in the 'copper list', different effects can be achieved in successive frames. 2K of RAM embedded in the FPGA allows up to 1024 Copper instructions to be scheduled, either running freely as display frames are output, or winding back to the first instruction when a new frame starts. For sub-pixel horizontal positioning, an all-zero instruction delays by one clock cycle, and a MOVE of any value to register 127 gives a two-cycle shift to the right.

Copper stereo sound

It's important to be able to do things even when a non-displayed line is output, which is why the Copper counts lines up to 311 rather than 191 for a normal screen or 255 for displays that overscan into the border. I gather that Lyndon Sharp's early Next game *Pogie* interleaves three Copper WAIT instructions on each of the 312 lines with MOVE instructions that copy music samples to the DAC hardware. As long as the sample data is updated as part of the regular frame interrupt, continuous music plays at a rate of up to 50*312*2 samples per second.

I believe *Pogie* outputs samples at 15600 Hertz, every line of a PAL display. This uses at least 624 instructions - one WAIT and one MOVE per line, leaving 400 for other register updates in each frame. If you put two MOVEs after each WAIT you can output stereo, or mix two mono channels through both speakers. The same principle can be used to play two stereo streams at half that rate, giving roughly dial-a-disc sound quality, using all four DACs with room for 88 WAIT or MOVE instructions left over. There's an explanation of another way to play samples, at potentially higher sample rates, on page 295 in the chapter about DMA. Try both at once!

Copper slice scrolling

There's not yet a programmer-friendly interface to the Copper display co-processor, so here's an example of how to use it to slice a screen up and send parts of it scrolling around, *Frogger*-style:

```
100 LAYER 0: BORDER 0: PRINT FLASH 1,"ENTER to stop",
110 LIST 170: REG 97,0: REG 98,0: REG 97,0: REG 98,0
120 REG 96,128: REG 96,0:  REG 96,38: REG 96,0
130 REG 96,128: REG 96,32: REG 96,38: REG 96,0
140 REG 96,136: REG 96,64: REG 96,38: REG 96,0
160 REG 96,255: REG 96,255: REG 98,%@11000000: %t=0
170 REPEAT :%t=%t-1&255: REG 98,192: REG 97,7: REG 96,%t
180   REG 98,192: REG 97,11: REG 96,%255-t
190   SPRITE MOVE INT : REPEAT UNTIL 13= CODE INKEY$
200 REG 98,192: REG 97,7: REG 96,0
210 REG 98,192: REG 97,11: REG 96,0: SPRITE MOVE INT
220 REG 97,0: REG 98,0: PRINT AT 0,0,,: STOP
```

Line 110 momentarily stops the Copper, before we send a new program to it by repeated writes to REG 96. The manual warns that you may need to do this twice, if your update falls at exactly the point the Copper is about to re-start. Line 120 to 140 set up three pairs of WAIT and MOVE instructions, active on screen lines 0, 32 and 64. Three subsequent MOVEs set REG 38, the ULA horizontal scroll offset. To start with, they all just reset the scrolling.

This creates a framework for scrolling parts of the screen. Line 160 sets it running. Then the loop at the end updates the seventh and eleventh bytes of the Copper program to scroll slices of the screen according to the value in %T. Text lines 5 to 8 roll one way, lines 9 to 12 the other. To avoid input interference, SPRITE MOVE INT does the frame synchronisation, rather than PAUSE 1. Use HALT or frame interrupts in Z80 code. Press Enter to stop the demo. The lines after REPEAT UNTIL restore a normal display.

The Copper can provide split-screen views for multiplayer racing, re-using colours and sprites each side of the split, or separate panes into the ideal pixel format for fast updates without loss of colour, like *Elite* on the BBC Micro. We can put a bitmap at the top, over a Layer 3 TileMap for captions (see Chapter 15, Tiles and Layers), or even alongside, in the style of *Atic Atac*. A graphics package could use a LoRes or Rajastan (16-colour LoRes) pane for zooming into the pixels. Registers 21..27, 34..38, 44..57, 96..99, 104..108, 110, 111 and 117..121 are amenable to such manipulations.

Next's layers could also be used for overlays not practical on earlier single-layer micros, but the Copper allows more efficient use of memory for partial displays – for instance a 256x128 pixel LAYER 2 window can be mapped into 32k of Z80 RAM while at the same time the program has access to Tiles or ULA graphics elsewhere.

Chapter 6, The NextBASIC Text Editor

Small examples are just fine for explaining basic principles, but sometimes it takes a substantial project to show how bigger things fit together. In 1983, when Roger Munford launched *Your Spectrum* magazine, he had already published my sprawling ZX disassembler **Spectramon** over eight pages in *ZX Computing* magazine, and was looking for something more challenging as an example of 'structured programming' for the new mag. With half a degree in computer science under my belt and a friendly landlord, Jon Smith, to help with the expression evaluator, I proposed a Z80 compiler for ZX BASIC, written entirely in ZX BASIC.

This gave me an opportunity to contrast the inner workings of BASIC and machine code, showing how to translate programmatically from one to the other, and lots of scope for complex data-structures and algorithms like expression evaluation, binary searching, error recovery, recursive descent parsing and the use of an intermediate language to manage complexity.

The entire compiler was written on the Spectrum itself, using only cassette storage during development, and a single software dependency, the very early Z80 assembler Ultraviolet from ACS, which allowed me to put build tools and Z80 mnemonics for the code library in the same BASIC source format – with the assembler instructions in REM statements – as the compiler itself.

This became **Zip**, the first of ten compilers I published during the 1980s, and a series of four articles in *Your Spectrum*. Later versions of this compiler were made for the Timex 2068, a Spectrum-based machine sold mainly in the USA, and the MGT SAM Coupé, an early attempt – rather like Next – to extend the ZX legacy after Sinclair dropped the ball.

So where's the NextBASIC compiler? While a compiler for NextBASIC would be a splendid example, it's a much tougher target than Zip addressed, even for a subset of the language (which Zip can already compile, of course, as NextBASIC is a superset of ZX BASIC). ZX BASIC was originally written to fit an 8k ROM, including the character set and underlying operating system, and well-documented with an excellent disassembly of the entire implementation available in book form from Ian Logan.

But NextBASIC already spans more than 80k of binary protected even against PEEKs. No source code is available, and there are no documented entry points to share ROM code, beyond the 16k ROM, which knows nothing of banks, procedures, sprites, tiles or layers beyond 0, and some esxDOS hooks. Most problematically, for a would-be compiler, the language changes whenever someone comes up with a good idea to extend it.

After several failed attempts to keep up, and a lot of time disassembling ephemeral code and obscure data-structures, I have backed away from the idea of publishing a BASIC compiler tutorial for Next, partly because it is such a large, moving target – and the better a compiler is, the less most users will care about its intricacies – but also because there are many new aspects of Next programming – such as the handling of memory banks, custom fonts and character sizes, mouse control – which deserve a substantial and useful example but don't have much relevance to a program translator.

Roger Munford's brief for 'structured programming in BASIC' was quite a challenge in the original ZX BASIC, inevitably requiring a raft of line numbers, PEEKs, POKEs and GO SUBs which were a puzzle for anyone to understand, even if the publishers hadn't misprinted the second accompanying article in scrambled order, and missed out a vital GO SUB.

NextBASIC has grown up in the meantime, at first in rather superficial ways reminiscent of BBC BASIC, and later picking up serious language features like those in Sinclair's later SuperBASIC, for the QL micro, and BetaBASIC for the Spectrum which became SAM BASIC on MGT's Super-Spectrum SAM Coupé. I'm itching to write more about those and will certainly do so once we have SAM and QL cores for Next, comparable with the existing Spectrum ones – but right now what I feel is most needed and deliverable is a non-trivial example program that does something useful and understandable while taking full advantage of the new 'structured' features of NextBASIC.

There are many example BASIC programs that run on Next, but most were written by people familiar with the original unstructured ZX BASIC, at the time or since. As I was drafting this text, still awaiting the delivery of the second Kickstarter, recent NextBASIC updates had made a few classic ZX hacks obsolete or incompatible, while introducing very cool new ones which have yet to get much exposure.

So when I came across a public-domain text editor, written from scratch in NextBASIC 2.06 by Magnus Krook, I was impressed by how clearly written it was, using procedures and banks, as well as traditional ZX BASIC string handling. I was equally excited by the potential to speed it up and make it more useful by building on the framework he'd started, taking advantage of NextBASIC 2.08 features as well as my own experience translating and optimising interpreted code.

I wrote a BASIC to BASIC translator – in fact, a suite of six programs – in my first job as an apprentice programmer at Racal in 1980. It translated PDP-11 minicomputer BASIC-PLUS, DEC's model for Microsoft's MBASIC, into MCZ micro BASIC running on hardware designed by Zilog themselves in 1976. Since then I've used a dozen other BASIC dialects, the most impressive of those being Sinclair's later SuperBASIC and the ROM BASIC of the Sam Coupé. With each update, NextBASIC comes closer to the capabilities of those 80s classics, without – and this is the key point – sacrificing compatibility with the original ZX BASIC, known to millions.

One of the frustrating things early in the life of Next, which persisted for several years after the first Kickstarter, was the dependency of the system on plain-text configuration files, despite the peculiar absence of any native tool to edit them. Next pioneers were forced to write little programs to read and rewrite files in need of changes, or (more often) move the SD card to a more mature computer, just to be able to add or remove a line in some key file.

It was possible to work around this by installing software like **WordStar** for CP/M, or **Tasword 3**, one of the few Spectrum editors designed for random-length lines, but these workarounds were complicated and inflexible, as neither allowed full access to the Next SD file system.

Earlier editors like the best-selling **Tasword 2** were not suitable because they presumed fixed-length lines and a hard-wired display format. This was for reasons we'll soon understand, which were also followed by collaborative editor projects like **SamScratch**, built using similar data-structures.

A couple of crude editors were ported from the big computers, in the form of cross-compiled dot commands, but showed an uncomfortable combination of the modal inscrutability of Unix and a poor fit for the unique features of Next. And if you don't like the way those work, you've no chance of changing it without also changing your computer, because none of them were compiled on Next itself.

And that's why both the following chapters are devoted to so prosaic a task as editing small text files, using a program written entirely in NextBASIC. This takes advantage of the latest features in NextBASIC 2.08, using separate memory banks for graphics, data and BASIC procedures. It is interoperable with alien systems like Unix, Qdos, AmigaOS, both macOSes, CP/M, MSDOS and Microsoft Windows, automatically adapting to and for variations and incompatibilities in the way they organise text documents.

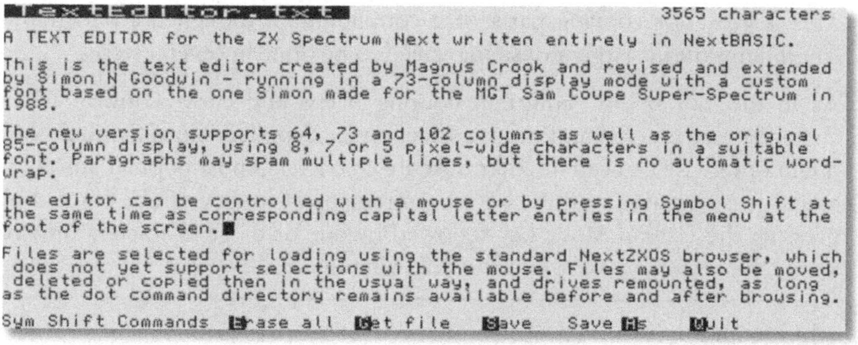

Figure 45 – The NextBASIC text editor showing 73 columns per line

Features

The Editor comes with a short text file listing its features, which I shall summarise here. Text can be entered, edited and shuffled around either as individual characters or paragraphs which may span several lines of the screen. Four display formats, trading visibility for legibility, offer from 64 to 102 characters per line. Figure 45 shows the 73-column layout. Later images illustrate the other resolutions.

The Editor can be controlled with a mouse or by pressing Symbol Shift at the same time as corresponding capital letter entries in the menu at the foot of the screen. Files are selected for loading using the standard NextZXOS browser, which does not yet support mouse input. When it does, since the Editor directly calls the system, mouse control will be added automatically. Besides user-familiarity, this is a good reason for not rolling your own file selector, let alone relying on checking an unprompted INPUT.

While in the browser, called from the Editor, text files may also be moved, deleted or copied, in the usual way. Drives can be remounted, as long as the dot command directory remains available before and after browsing. This is handy if sometimes you still feel tempted to put your SD cards in some other computer. The Editor sniffs each new file and uses the same line-end sequence when saving as it found when the file was loaded, to suit less flexible computers of your choice (or someone else's).

The custom fonts and mouse pointer load when the editor starts up. Three 16k banks are used, as well as the usual BASIC programming area. All memory allocated is released afterwards.

Cutting, pasting, block moves and deletion

Block operations work a paragraph at a time. Short lines can easily be merged into one paragraph, and separated later, with the Delete and Enter keys. Symbol Shift D, or a corresponding Delete menu, deletes the current paragraph, non-destructively. Symbol Shift I will then insert it, once or many times at any paragraph boundary, providing a simple cut-and-paste capability. This is great for copying parts of a configuration, though the paragraph-length limit means large moves may need to be done in several steps.

As in the 128 BASIC editor, reassuring beeps and clicks confirm when characters are entered and mouse selections are applied. Since Symbol Shift might otherwise be used to enter obscure characters, most popular among C language programmers, these have been remapped so they can be entered by pressing the Extend Mode key followed by one of those characters printed above the keytop, as shown in the following table:

Obscure character	[	]	©	~	|	\	{	}
EXTend + keypress	Y	U	P	A	S	D	F	G

Table 2 – Characters entered into the Editor by pressing EXT followed by a letter key

A short beep sounds when EXT is pressed, and a lower tone if it is pressed again without entering any special character. This approach allows the file commands to work normally with Symbol Shift.

There is one standard ASCII symbol which cannot be entered on Next, in any program, not just this Editor. This is the grave accent, `, CODE 96, which Sinclair, Acorn and Teletext replaced with the £ currency sign. This symbol makes most sense on typewriters or daisywheel printers, where it can be used in conjunction with backspace and over-typing to drop a French accent over a vowel. That's not the way screen editors work.

CODE 96 lives on mostly in shell scripts where (like almost every symbol up for grabs) it has a specialist meaning: in fact, it has at least two special and incompatible meanings. In Unix command shells it is known as a backtick, indicating that the following symbol should be treated as a command rather than parameter data. In Microsoft's PowerShell it does what Unix uses the backslash for, prefixing a sequence that cannot otherwise be typed literally. So please do not try to use this Editor, or Next, to edit alien shell-scripts. Be glad, instead, that Sir Clive didn't expect proud Britons to use dollars as a currency sign.

Regardless of turbo clock-speed or how cleverly you use other language features, characters dribble out onto the Next screen rather slowly. The Editor takes pains to avoid redrawing more than the current paragraph, but when scrolling back and forth through a document that's sometimes necessary, and scrolling line-by-line makes that even more tedious. So the TRUE VIDEO and INVERSE VIDEO keys allow fast navigation in steps of eight paragraphs back and forth through the text.

Find and Replace

There is another way to move purposefully through the document, or to make bulk changes quickly and reliably in many places. NextBASIC 2.08 has allowed a fast search and replace capability to be included. To get started, press **Symbol Shift F** then enter the text you'd like to Find. A corresponding menu option also appears if the screen is wide enough to display it.

Searching always starts from the first paragraph of the document but you can quickly step on to any later match. Comparisons are case-independent and the character © (on the P key) is a 'wild card' that matches any character, rather as a question mark can be used in a filename – so f©n will match Fin, fun or FAN, for example.

A low-pitched beep sounds if the text is not found in any paragraph. Otherwise you are invited to **Replace** it, find the **Next** match, or **Quit**. Press **R**, **N** or **Q**. If you have not yet specified a replacement you will be prompted for it, otherwise it will be put in place of the search text, and the next match sought.

All spaces are significant within the search pattern and replacement. Search and replace works fine within paragraphs, but not across paragraph boundaries, so it won't find 'ZX BASIC' if ZX happens to be right at the end of one paragraph, even if 'BASIC' starts the following one.

Limitations

I inherited several key design decisions from Magnus, most notably the determination to implement the editor entirely in NextBASIC – allowing full access to almost every aspect of the system, and the potential for customisation to suit the things we do most often.

There are a couple of limitations built in, implied by the use of BASIC string arrays to hold the text. The maximum number of paragraphs – logical lines separated by newline characters – and the maximum length of each paragraph is preset when the main array is dimensioned. BASIC variables, other than the 52 single-letter integer ones prefixed with %, must all fit within the area of almost 41k primarily dedicated to the program and its runtime state. This requirement imposes a limit of 100 paragraphs of up to 256 characters each, though it's easy to redistribute this space, e.g. for up to 300 paragraphs each no longer than 80 characters, by tweaking lines 210 and 220.

The maximum total size of the file is also limited to 16k bytes. This rule allows the entire file to be quickly loaded in one step into a bank, and then scanned to find the type of newline characters – necessarily, as BASIC's INPUT LINE statement can only cope with one of the three common possibilities used on other computers, and hence in some Next files.

After explaining the current approach I'll explore ways to remove both limitations, at some cost to the clarity and elegance of the program. In practice Next configuration files and most program examples are less than 16k long – as were most of my *Crash* Tech Tips columns – so the editor is still pretty useful, and easy to follow, despite these limits.

The Editor uses the Timex HiRes screen mode, LAYER 1,2, which has a resolution of 512 by 192 pixels, normally in 24 lines each eight pixels high. A standard Spectrum font would only allow 64 columns per display line, but Next allows the number of pixels per character to be reduced from eight to seven or six, or further still if readability is not important: the *Tasword 2* font allows ransom notes of up to 128 columns per line to be cobbled together.

This approach was also used on the Sinclair QL (which offers seven-pixel character spacing in Quill on a TV, and six- or eight-pixel widths in standard BASIC) and on the MGT SAM in its four-colour HiRes MODE 3, which goes up to 85 columns without loss of readability. Since I designed the font for that ROM, I've converted it back to the Spectrum and extended Magnus's code to automatically use it when a standard ZX font would not fit. Figure 46 shows the SAM font being used on an 85-column screen.

The NextBASIC editor supports four display formats, with 64, 73, 85 or 102 columns per line. The code to work out when to split paragraphs across multiple lines adjusts accordingly, depending upon the value of the variable L, set when it is first run.

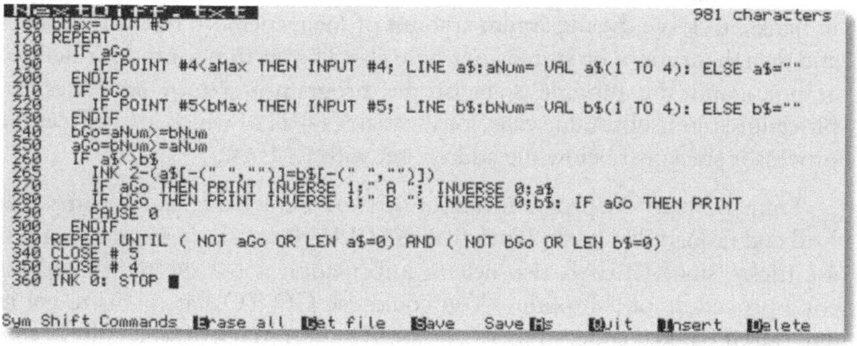

Figure 46 – The NextBASIC text editor configured to show 85 columns per line

Any standard Spectrum font can be used in the 64-column mode – by default the program loads the Bold font from the 1988 *Crash* Tech Tape, but any other 768-byte font file can be substituted if preferred, or you can skip the font loading entirely in which case the original Sinclair character shapes will be used. The following image illustrates the Bold font in a 64-column display:

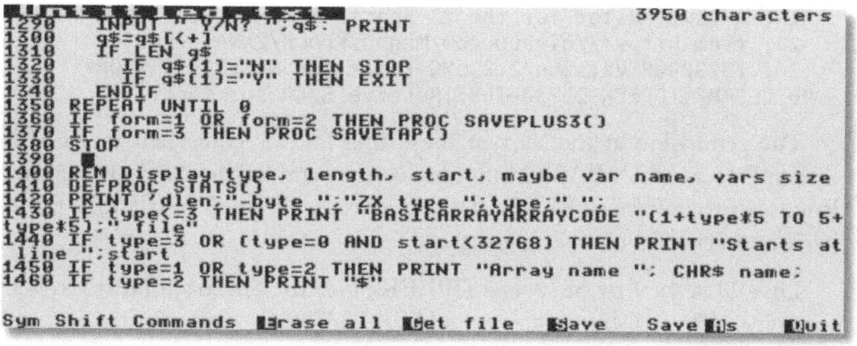

Figure 47 – The NextBASIC text editor showing 64 columns per line in a ***bold*** *font*

For narrower characters, the font file must be the same size but bits on the right of each binary pattern must be left zero as those columns won't fit. For instance, if you want 73 characters per line, each no more than seven pixels wide, each byte of the font data must be an even number, so the least significant bit is zero.

The NextZXOS system file browser is not currently font-adaptive, so the editor switches back and forth before calling **.browse** to select a new input file. The code to do this provides another useful example, and insight.

The main program

This section explains the part of the editor which remains in Z80 main memory, rather than copied to a bank like the contents of EditorProcs.bas.

In general, you want as much of your program as is practical to be stored in banks, to leave the maximum amount of main memory free for variables and data that cannot be stored anywhere else, like custom fonts, user-defined graphics and the runtime state of the program – return addresses for procedures and subroutine calls, local variables – all of which are held on the processor stack just below the address set with CLEAR.

Some parts of the program cannot be stored in a bank, like the lines that load and unload that bank. Lines that use CLEAR to adjust memory bounds are tricky, since CLEAR also deletes information about the return address for a procedure or subroutine. You could use GO TO statements to get in and out of banked code, so there's no need to keep track of where they came from, but it's neater and easy to shuffle stuff between banks if the code is wrapped in procedures, functions or subroutines with unique line numbers.

The main Editor program starts by reserving memory for a custom font in the Sinclair format. The font defines patterns for 96 characters, those with ASCII codes from 32 to 127, using eight bytes for each, for the eight rows of pixels in each character. We therefore need 96*8 bytes for the set.

Here's how Editor.bas starts:

```
 1 ; A text editor for the ZX Spectrum Next, derived
 2 ; from https://github.com/MagnusKrook/ZXNext-Editor
 3 ; 20230908 Version 1.8 SNG remix for NextBASIC 2.08+
90 CLEAR % DPEEK 23730-768:;Reserve 3/4k for font.
```

The semicolon at the start of these first lines is equivalent to REM in earlier dialects of ZX BASIC, but more concise and familiar to Z80 assembly-language programmers. REM still works just as well, since NextBASIC prides itself on backward-compatibility.

Line 90 is the first of several DPEEKs into the Spectrum Next's system variables. The 16-bit value at address 23730 is documented by the penultimate line of the System Variables chapter in Spectrum programming manuals, where it's called RAMTOP. It holds the address of the last byte of memory available for BASIC. Bytes at higher addresses, above RAMTOP, are typically used to store machine code or graphics data. Here, line 90 moves RAMTOP down by 768 bytes, the size of the font.

It's good style to create variables with the names of system variable addresses used in your program, since RAMTOP is more descriptive and less prone to typing-errors than the corresponding magic number. On line 90 that'd be of little help since the assignment RAMTOP=23730 would be wiped by the CLEAR statement that uses it, but later we'll set up just such a mnemonic variable, and another for CHARS, the system variable indicating the address of the character set. There's a reference table, naming and describing all the main variables used in the Editor, at the end of this chapter.

Apart from the DPEEK, which is Next's shorthand equivalent of two PEEKs, two additions and a multiplication in original ZX BASIC: **DPEEK p = (256 * PEEK (p+1) + PEEK p)**, the only other Next-specific feature in line 90 is the per cent sign after CLEAR, which gives NextBASIC permission to take short cuts in evaluating the subsequent arithmetic, using its 'fast integer evaluator'.

The main saving here is eleven bytes of precious main RAM since there's no need for BASIC to precompute and store the binary form of the simple integer values 23730 and 768 invisibly in the program, as it normally would to avoid the overhead of converting them from decimal to binary at runtime. That optimisation dates back to the ZX81 and saves a lot of time for values like -123456789e-11. However the Z80n, with its hardware MUL instruction, has little need of such tricks for integers that will fit entirely into a 16-bit register pair, and memory is scarce.

Integer precedence

After a per cent sign, numeric values are treated as positive whole numbers in the range 0..65535, overflows are ignored and negative values expressed as if they'd been added to 65536: so **%2-4** yields **65534**! This way of counting is easy for the Z80n, and consequently quick, and only needs two bytes per value rather than five for a signed decimal. It demands more concentration from the programmer, especially as the integer evaluator doesn't comply with conventional operator precedence rules. Consequently **%2+2*2** is **eight**, working strictly from left to right, as 2+2 is four and 4*2 is eight. However mathematicians rule that multiplications and divisions should be done before adding and subtracting so that, without the per cent prefix, **2+2*2** yields **six**! The invisible forms mean that, despite appearances, that line takes 17 more bytes of RAM than the integer version – three lots of six bytes for the invisible binary forms of 2, minus one for the per cent sign.

This confusing simplification was introduced when Garry had 'only about 300 bytes' left for Next ROM features, and decided to forgo conventional niceties to make best use of the space. Since then he's freed up extra space for system code by using DivMMC RAM pages for parts of the BASIC interpreter (allowing further hairy optimisations, like the use of self-modifying code) but the need for backward-compatibility has left us with some tricky implications especially when working code is embellished with % signs and then falls over mysteriously.

For example, an earlier version of the editor used a sequence of IF AND THEN statements to sift out certain value ranges. This worked fine till the variable **col** was replaced with the integer **%C**, which can be found and processed much more quickly:

```
IF col>=19 AND col<=27 THEN POKE LASTK,%200:; Erase
```

After 'optimising' this to

```
IF %C>=19 AND C<=27 THEN POKE LASTK,%200:; Erase
```

the POKE was executed for any value of %C 19 or more, including values greater than 27 which were previously skipped. This is because BASIC treats AND and OR as part of the arithmetic expression between IF and THEN, and after a per cent sign processes these 'operators' strictly from left to right, rather than working out the parts either side of the AND before checking to see if they are both non-zero.

Assuming %C=50, NextBASIC interprets the second version as IF 50>19 which is TRUE, yielding the result 1, then 1 AND C, which is also TRUE as C is non-zero, and finally 1<=27 so the POKE happens regardless of the last value checked. The code is faster, but the result is wrong! The cure for this is to add brackets so the second comparison takes place before the AND is worked out. This works as expected:

```
IF %C>=19 AND (C<=27) THEN POKE LASTK,%200:; Erase
```

Finally, for now, note that the % sign is not repeated before the second instance of the variable name C. This is the most confusing part for people brought up on Microsoft BASIC which uses a % *suffix* to denote integer variables, much as $ denotes a string in both dialects. Next uses the % symbol as a *prefix* for the entire following expression (up to THEN, a comma, a final closing bracket or similar non-arithmetic punctuation), so this statement cannot even be entered:

```
IF %C>=19 AND %C<=27 THEN POKE LASTK,%200:; Erase
```

it is rejected at the second % sign – and the following, while valid since NextBASIC 2.08 allowed integer subexpressions to be included anywhere, prefixed by '(%' and ending with ')', wastes a byte needlessly:

```
IF %C>=19 AND (%C<=27) THEN POKE LASTK,%200:; Erase
```

The last per cent sign in every version of the line, at %200, saves another five bytes by telling NextBASIC to convert the value 200 from text to binary on the fly. In older versions of ZX BASIC you'll sometimes see VAL("200") where 200 might otherwise appear. This still saves one byte, because VAL is tokenised to a single byte (CHR$ 176, as listed in Appendix A of the manual) for a total of eight bytes, whereas the literal 200 without quotes is stored as the text '200' followed by an invisible marker byte (CHR$ 14) and five bytes of the corresponding binary value – nine bytes in all.

More common, and even slower, ways to save memory were to use expressions like SGN PI in place of 1, NOT PI for 0, INT PI for 3 and so on. PI is a keyword so that it only occupies one byte in the program, whereas 3.14 would take ten bytes and be less accurate. The approximation 22/7 would use twenty bytes and also involve a division, which is one of the tardier floating-point operations, though exponentiation with ^ is by far the slowest. Next's approach of allowing % prefixes for easy values, instead of the binary form, is more economical, and quicker too.

Having written 4000 words just getting to the first executable line of the program, and skipping REMs which – while wasting precious bytes – serve only to make the program readable and easy to maintain, let's pick up the pace a bit, as we complete the initialisation of the editor, or we might never get as far as the loop that reads and displays characters.

Finding lines

In classic ZX BASIC lines 100 to 527 of the program, before the main loop starts, would ideally be shunted away to the end of the listing, accessed with a GO SUB and RETURN as they only run once at the start. This will speed up searches for earlier line numbers in the program, because every time GO SUB or NEXT or RESTORE refer to a line-number while a Sinclair BASIC program runs, the interpreter performs a slow sequential search from the very start of the program till it finds the relevant line number, or the one after.

The more lines precede the one referenced, the longer this searching takes. In modern NextBASIC we can often leave the initialisation at the start, since there are no GO TO statements in the main loop that follows. NextBASIC is more efficient, and therefore less fussy about the order of lines in a program, because its new keywords keep track of the memory address, rather than just the lines numbers, for REPEAT and integer FOR statements, making those loops relatively quick.

In versions of NextBASIC up to 2.07 this optimisation also caused problems because editing of the program while testing could invalidate the stashed address, so that CONTINUE did not work. This was a particularly painful regression for ZX devotees who'd grown used to the way they could carry on debugging after changing a program, when an Acorn or Microsoft programmer would have to re-run their program from the start, making debugging progressively harder for non-trivial programs.

As of NextBASIC 2.08 Garry made the new loops more compatible, while speeding up even the old sort, made with FORs and GO TOs, and procedure and GO SUB calls, by adding a hidden table of line addresses to simplify the searching. One consequence of this is that there's less room for BASIC statements in each bank since the last part of each 16k bank file is reserved for the hidden table, and you only find out you've run out of space from the new **No room for line** error message when you try to copy the program lines to a BANK.

On balance though, especially for large programs, this is a positive change because it removes one of the greatest bottlenecks in ZX BASIC, which its inventors at Nine Tiles were keen to fix in 1982; alas Sinclair was not willing to either wait or pay for improvements to the original interpreter designed for a 1k ZX81, despite all the Spectrum's extra ROM and RAM.

Finding files

```
100;---------------------------------------------------
110;-                    Initialise                   -
120;---------------------------------------------------
130 ; Path to the supplementary files "EditorProcs.bnk",
140 ; "Sam6FONT"/"BOLDFONT" and "Pointer.spr". Edit if needed.
150 F$=""
```

Line 150 shows how Magnus made provision for the Editor to run from any location on any Next drive, even though it depends on data files for graphics and banked code. By default, when F$ is null, those files are loaded from the current directory – often the same one containing Editor.bas, assuming you just loaded it without prefixing the name with another path, such as "D:/Utils/Editor/Editor.bas".

Wherever the original program is loaded from, it can't start unless the data files are in the current directory. To fix this, edit line 150 to say where you've put the data files, e.g. **F$="D:/Utils/Editor/"**. After initialisation **F$** is re-used to store the current file-name, or "Untitled.txt".

Text resolution

```
160 %w=%73:; Set %W for 64, 73, 85 or 102 columns.
170 IF %w<>64 THEN IF %w<>73 THEN IF %w<>85 THEN IF %w<>102
   THEN PRINT "Line width %W does not suit 5 to 8 pixel
   character-widths.": PAUSE %0: CLEAR %768+ DPEEK 23730: STOP
```

The original Editor only supported an 85-column display using the standard character set, but one purpose of this example is to show how to write programs that adapt automatically to other character widths. The variable %W – an integer which can be quickly accessed, sacrificing readability for space and speed – should be set to the number of characters which will fill one line of the Timex HiRes display, using the four most readable character sizes available, with widths of 5, 6, 7 or 8 pixels corresponding to a display of 102, 85, 73 or 64 columns respectively. Figure 48 uses the 102-column narrowest-character option.

Alter line 160 to suit your preference and visual acuity. Line 170 makes sure you've picked one of the four tested possibilities. It could equivalently have been written IF %(w=64) OR (w=73) etc. Later we'll see cases where IF THEN IF structures are usefully faster than IF AND THEN or IF OR THEN, but it makes little difference here as the line is only run once.

The program stops if %W is not set to a supported value, but not before printing a message – designed to look neat in both 32 and 64 column displays, since we've not yet set the LAYER – and releasing the memory previously reserved for the character set. The PAUSE %0 waits for a key-press, as otherwise the error message would be promptly erased by the CLEAR statement.

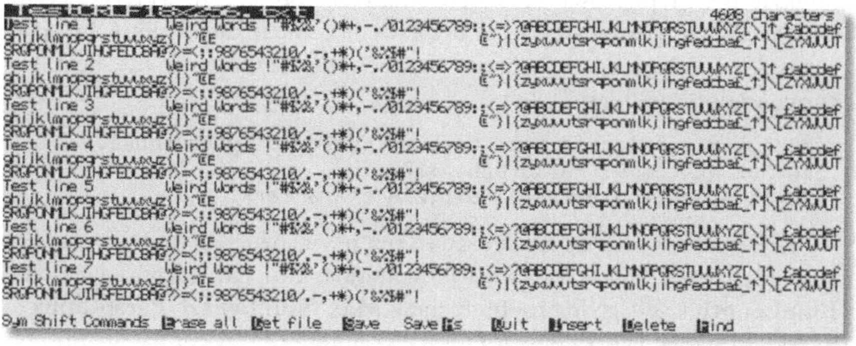

Figure 48 – Five-pixel wide characters boost resolution to 102 characters per line

```
180 ; Save the current CPU Speed then run CPU at 28 MHz.
190 %C=% REG 7&3: RUN AT %3
```

The Editor is designed to be used while developing software, so it takes pains not to mess up the configuration of the Next's memory, CPU or display. It needs all the speed it can get, hence the RUN AT %3 statement later on line 190, but notice how Magnus saves the previous CPU speed setting before turning it up to maximum. When the program ends the value of %C is used to return the machine to whatever speed you had previously set. This is particularly useful if you're experimenting with classic ZX peripherals or software that can't cope with a 28 MHz speed setting. If you've already RUN AT 3, or selected 28 MHz via the menu, it makes no difference.

Variable bottleneck

Currently – unlike say Beta BASIC 4, or SAM BASIC for MGT's 1989 Super-Spectrum – NextBASIC stores all variable values in the original 48k RAM reserved for programs in 1982. This means that existing programs load and run without conversion, 16-bit system variables can be PEEKed and POKEd as usual, and utilities for editing the BASIC area continue to work. This is not true for SAM BASIC, because that uses 24-bit pointers to allow much larger programs and arrays, at the price of some incompatibility and a LOT of extra systems-programming effort.

Despite the extra 80k RAM in the Spectrum 128, or the much larger RAM of Next, almost all NextBASIC variables, including strings and arrays, have to fit the same area of almost 41k originally reserved for ZX BASIC programs and data, below the address set with CLEAR. The exceptions are the 52 new integer variables tucked away in nearly 4k of private and undocumented Next system RAM, but there's no way to expand that secret stash.

The larger the main program, the less space is left alongside it for variable values. That's why most of the Editor code, and the mouse pointer image, are stored in separate banks, accessed indirectly. The remaining space is dominated by a large two-dimensional string array, with each row big enough to hold paragraphs that fill several lines of the screen. The longer the paragraphs are permitted to be, the fewer of them can fit into the space available, so there is a trade-off between the settings of the next two configuration variables:

```
200 ; Limit files to this maximum number of paragraphs.
210 Max Number Of Paragraphs=%100
220 Max LineLength=%256:; 64..256 characters.
```

These default settings are chosen to suit most small text files. If you know your files never have more than 80 columns, you can safely reduce **Max LineLength** to 80, giving room to crank **Max Number Of Paragraphs** up to 300. You could also adjust for a smaller number of longer paragraphs, but there's a practical limit imposed by the programming assumption that at least two paragraphs will fit onto the screen at once, so arbitrarily long paragraphs would require a substantial re-write of the display procedures.

Notice how spaces are (almost) freely used in the variable names. This rare readability benefit stems from the way BASIC is tokenized, and has been in ZX BASIC since the start. The spaces are no more significant than use of capital or lower-case letters, so **MAXNUMBEROFPARAGRAPHS** is equivalent to **Max Number Of Paragraphs**, but a lot less readable. This broke down somewhat when the Spectrum 128 editor was bolted on to the original BASIC, as that required keywords to be typed letter-by-letter, preventing the use of variable names like AT, TO, LN, LEN and LINE. Those were previously unambiguous as the corresponding tokens were entered in one step, rather than letter-by-letter. That's why there's no space in **LineLength**. If there was, NextBASIC would be confused by an apparent reference to the LINE keyword.

Long variable names cost bytes but make programs more readable. They were one of the reasons I found Magnus's original program so easy to follow and extend, but they come at a cost in performance as well as memory. Unlike say Atari or Sinclair QL SuperBASIC, which tokenise user-defined names into index numbers just as ZX keywords are packed, the full text of each long variable name is stored in the program, and again (shorn of spaces) in the VARS area which is slowly and repetitively searched from the start, every time the value associated with a name needs to be found.

Since this is a complicated example, and meaningful variable and procedure names make it much easier to follow, I've resisted the temptation to trim most of Magnus's names, or his explanatory code comments, but in several places I've used short integer variable names, such as %W, %C and %F to record aspects of the configuration, or %I within key routines to speed up loops.

It's a tough call, but if in doubt leave such optimisations till your program is well-tested with meaningful names in place. By using **MultiSearch** from http://simon.mooli.org.uk/nextech/#NoGo directly on a stored program, or this Editor on the text version, it's easy enough to replace long names with short ones, but trickier to go the other way. The shorter the pattern you seek, the more likely it is to crop up with a different meaning in other places.

Bank management

```
 230 ; Find free memory banks.
 240 BANK NEW ProcArea:; Bank for other procedures of the
program.
 250 LOAD F$+"EditorProcs18.bnk" BANK ProcArea
 260 BANK NEW WorkArea:; Temporary storage for load and save.
 270 BANK NEW SpriteArea:; Memory bank for sprites.
```

The Editor uses three 16k banks to relieve the pressure on main memory. Each is allocated with BANK NEW, which sets the subsequent variable to the number of a bank not previously allocated to NextBASIC. So line 240 reserves 16k of memory and sets **ProcArea** to the corresponding bank number. The next line loads version 18 of the EditorProcs into that bank. Notice how F$ is prepended to the filename, so it doesn't have to be in the current directory if F$ contains some other valid path.

Version numbers and backups

The number I've embedded in the bank filename has proven to be a lifesaver over the 16 major revisions of this program; when new bugs cropped up I was able to isolate the causes by converting the relevant bank files to text with the **.bas2txt** dot command and comparing them side-by-side with professional programs like *p4merge* and *Beyond Compare*, till I wrote NextDiff.bas to bring the Next work entirely in-house.

Disc space is rarely an issue on Next, so the only thing to be wary about if you follow this back-up history rule is the need to update lines like this, and the ones around line 9990 of each BASIC file, before testing the new version. Expect new errors and weird regressions if you forget that and load the old EditorProcs bank with a new editor!

Two 1970s operating systems, which I used in my first job at Racal, integrate version numbering into their file-system, including a number (from 1 to 32767) as an attribute of every file, separate from the filename, bumping it up at each SAVE and allowing old versions to be retrieved by specifying the number after a semicolon, e.g. BASIC.BAS;3 – this was a feature of DEC's RSX-11/M and VMS, both designed by Dave Cutler who went on to rescue Microsoft with Windows NT.

Sadly, version numbers were lost along the way, leaving them – and us, aping CP/M – with just the crude device of **.bak** files that discard the filetype encoded in the original extension. You can turn this off, if you dislike the clutter and have a better backup system, by setting bit 0 of the file-system control variable %FORMAT:

```
%FORMAT|=1
```

The vertical bar sets the bit without changing the values of other bits, such as bit 1 (value 2) which invites the loader for legacy file-formats like SNA and TAP to store details of the system set-up they expect by adding characters to the file-name, which can be copied around, rather than making an entry in your local metadata cache, as you're less likely to share that (**c:/nextzxos/metadata**, controlled with the .metadata dot command). It's not hard to create a better backup system – you could for instance get line 9999 to bump the version number in a filename at every SAVE, checking the directory for the last-used value with a wildcard search.

The short example **Bumper.bas**, presented earlier in this book, automates this numbering, though it's much longer and initially slower than maintaining the latest number by hand-editing line 9999.

Lines 260 and 270 reserve two more banks. **WorkArea** is used as a temporary store for the file to be edited, limiting it to a maximum size of 16384 bytes. This includes line-ending characters, but doesn't count the optional Plus3DOS file header, which it strips during loading.

Banks stay allocated until they're released with BANK CLEAR, unless the Next is reset, another program is loaded, or NEW is typed, when all banks allocated by NextBASIC are released. More than 100 banks are initially free on a 2 MB Next, but it's still possible to use them all up while testing a program if you don't release them between test-runs. It's easy to lose the variables holding the numbers of allocated banks, with no easy way to retrieve them, if you accidentally use CLEAR or RUN during testing.

The quick way to prevent this 'creep', short of starting again after NEW or LOAD, is to type GO TO 830 which runs the program epilogue. That resets RAMTOP and the default character-set as well as releasing all 48k of **ProcArea**, **WorkArea** and **SpriteArea** allocations.

Initialisation

We've nearly reached the main loop of the Editor now. The final dozen lines of the set-up code prepare variables that will be used later, and call three procedures in the BASIC bank to initialise the display, mouse and text arrays.

```
280 Dirty=%0:; There are no edits yet.
290 DIM C$(Max LineLength):;Paragraph cut/paste buffer.
300 Cut Size=%0:; Nothing to paste yet.
310 BANK ProcArea PROC Init Display()
315 PROC NewFile():; Create a new, empty file.
320 BANK ProcArea PROC Init Mouse()
330 Remove Header=%1:; Set to 1 to SAVE without +3 headers.
360 LASTK=%23560:; Newly-pressed key-code system variable.
370 MODE=%23617:; Cursor mode (0=Normal, 1=Extended mode)
```

Line 280 makes provision for the prompt to save your text edits before erasing, quitting or loading another file. As soon as the loaded file is changed, the 'Dirty flag' is set. Before Load or Erase clobber the current text this flag is checked and the user is prompted to either save or lose those changes.

Lines 290 and 300 prepare for paragraph cut and paste actions later. C$ is a fixed-sized string variable, big enough to hold any single paragraph of the file being edited, and **Cut Size** is initialised to zero because nothing has yet been cut. Three PROC calls set up the display, text arrays and mouse input.

PROC Init Display( ) is defined in the ProcArea bank, previously loaded by line 250. It gives mnemonic names to two more system variables, CHARS and RAMTOP, used to prepare and remove the custom character-set. It loads the corresponding font then sets the character width according to %W.

Similarly-banked PROC Init Mouse( ) loads the mouse driver and pointer image to the mostly-empty Sprite Area bank. PROC NewFile( ) prepares and displays an empty editing area. It appears later in the main program.

The flag **Remove Header** is set to 1 by default, so that when a file is written out the 128-byte PLUS3DOS header at the start is stripped off. This is irrelevant to Next itself, which can load files of text lines or CODE blocks with or without headers, but important if you want to edit the file as text on some other computer which will be confused by the 128 bytes of binary book-keeping information Amstrad introduced as the start of Spectrum Plus Three disc files. The next chapter includes an example of BASIC to detect and skip over headers, in PROC Calculate File Size( ).

Two more assignments give names to system variables PEEKed and POKEd as the program runs, both bytes associated with the keyboard. The byte at address **LASTK** contains the ASCII code of the most recently pressed key, or zero, updated 50 or 60 times a second as each display frame is drawn, and **MODE** is a flag toggled whenever the EXT key is pressed. Like ZX BASIC, the Editor uses this to allow extra key-combinations to be typed and distinctly interpreted.

At last we're ready to do some editing! The main part of the program follows, with just two set-up steps before the REPEAT loop.

```
500;-------------------------------------------------------
501;-                      Main loop                      -
502;-------------------------------------------------------
510 ; Reset key input before polling.
520 POKE LASTK,%0
525 %CODE|=%2:ON ERROR GO TO %530:; Catch BREAK or errors.
```

Line 520 clears the LASTK system variable, where NextZXOS puts the most recently-typed key code. Without that POKE, the editor might reinterpret the ENTER (CR) keypress that started it and insert a new line before you even start typing into a fresh document.

Line 525 should be commented-out while testing, by inserting REM or semicolon at the start of the line, as it's designed to stop the Editor from stopping if BREAK is pressed or an error is detected. **%CODE** is a special integer variable added for NextBASIC 2.08, which works like a system variable but doesn't require POKE to change it. Setting the second bit of %CODE prevents the BREAK or SHIFT SPACE keystrokes from stopping the program.

The operator |= is used, rather than a simple = assignment, as the bitwise OR operator | doesn't change other bits in the word. So **%CODE|=%2** sets the second bit, whether or not it was set before, and leaves the other bits in %CODE alone, as they could be reserved to control entirely different options.

The ON ERROR statement means that if a subsequent error occurs and is not trapped by a later ON ERROR statement, execution restarts at the start of the main loop, at line 530. No attempt is made to try to diagnose the fault or recover in any context-specific way, but this approach catches rare errors like running out of memory while scanning for a line-end marker in a binary file, or loading errors caused by finger trouble or hardware failures.

The main loop

The main loop of the Editor is between lines 530 and 820, starting with **REPEAT** and ending with **REPEAT UNTIL Last Key Pressed=199**. 199 is the code for Symbol Shift Q, the 'Quit' menu option. Each time round the loop a single keyboard entry or mouse click is processed. The mouse handler simulates keyboard input by changing the value of **Last Key Pressed**. To avoid slowing down every lap, the comment on line 527 explaining the first line inside the loop has been moved outside the REPEAT block, so it doesn't need to be skipped over by the interpreter each time.

```
527 ; Wait 1 frame for a key to be pressed.
530 REPEAT
550 PAUSE %1:Last Key Pressed= PEEK LASTK: POKE LASTK,%0
```

Line 550 reads keys indirectly, by waiting one frame – PAUSE 1 – to ensure that the keyboard has been freshly polled by the system frame interrupt, then reading the latest character code, if any, from the LASTK system byte. While we could have used CODE INKEY$ to find the currently-pressed character this approach copes properly with auto-repeat (when a key is held down for more than a short time, configured with the system variables REPDEL and REPPER) whereas INKEY$ ignores those, soon leading to lost or repeated characters, or both.

What's a Frame Interrupt?

You might wonder how LASTK gets updated, especially if the term 'system frame interrupt' goes whoosh over your head. It did for me too, long ago, so here's a proper explanation. The internal timing of ZX computers has always been intimately related to the output of display information to the screen. Each full screen, usually comprising 192 rows of pixels, is known as a 'frame' and output to the TV 50 times per second.

Next is able to vary this rate somewhat to suit modern displays, which may not exactly match the PAL standard Sinclair aimed at, but for most compatible results 50 Hertz is the best choice. Programs, especially demos and games, that make full use of the original Spectrum's capabilities will not run at the right speed unless synchronised with 50 frame per second video output. Hertz is the international standard term for what used to be called 'cycles per second'. It's named after the German physicist Heinrich Hertz who proved the existence of electromagnetic waves.

There are two ways an interpreter can read the keyboard – either directly by accessing the hardware, taking account of shift states, EXT and graphics entry modes to convert switch signals into a symbol or keyword code, or indirectly by reading a value which the system promptly updates with the required number when a key is pressed. Either way, it's vital that this value is up-to-date as, besides catering for INPUT and INKEY$, the user must be able to stop a running program promptly by pressing BREAK at any time.

Traditional BASIC interpreters let the user keep control by polling the keyboard hardware after each statement is interpreted. This works, but the less time the interpreter spends on each statement, the greater the proportion of time is taken up not actually running the program but checking if it should have stopped. Back in the pre-ZX days this was well-known and magazines featured risky POKEs which would speed up Microsoft BASIC by disabling these checks. This often wasted more time than it was expected to save – a few per cent of total runtime at best, depending on the complexity of the statements being interpreted – when the user was accidentally locked out, unable to run the keyboard re-enabling POKE, and forced to RESET and reload the program to regain control.

Sinclair came up with a better solution, but this problem still crops up, for instance a few years ago when the *EhBASIC* interpreter for 6502 CPUs was ported to BBC Micro systems. StarDot forum member Gordon Drogon found out that almost ten seconds – 14 per cent of the total runtime of a fractal-making program – could be saved by disabling a regular call to check for the break key combination, with the cryptic Beeb command POKE $47F,1. The overhead was caused because the interpreter was calling the slow OSBYTE routine, like our INKEY$ #, to try to read a key code after every statement. This was fixed by using a faster, less obvious system call, but shows that interruptions should never be treated as an afterthought.

Since ZX computers derive their timing from the display output it's easy enough to include a keyboard check as part of the code which runs once for each output display frame. The Z80 has a hardware mechanism to allow fast switching from the main 'foreground' program to a separate Z80 routine called an 'interrupt handler' which takes care of regular housekeeping then returns control to the foreground. NextZXOS DRIVERs also use this interrupt, and custom hardware like serial ports and CTC (Counter Timer) devices can generate interrupts at other times, but display synchronisation and keyboard input are the default applications.

As part of the recursive exploration that brought you this book, I've done some experiments to measure the overhead of the frame interrupt on Next and original Spectrums. The good news is that it's negligible on modern hardware – between 0.33 and 0.37 per cent of a frame when running the CPU at 28 MHz.

The variation depends on whether a key is actually pressed when the interrupt occurs, and to some extent which key, too. You can see this by running a short BASIC loop that puts stripes in the frame border, and pressing keys as it runs e.g. the following (not part of the Editor program):

```
5 BORDER 0: BORDER 1: BORDER 2: BORDER 3: PAUSE 1: GOTO 5
```

Type RUN AT 0 before trying this, as otherwise the pattern might be drawn invisibly by the faster processor, in the top or bottom border. The PAUSE 1 statement causes the BASIC interpreter to run a HALT instruction, which stalls the Z80 till an interrupt occurs. The BORDER lines put horizontal stripes in the display border either side of the screen.

Run that loop, and press SHIFT. Notice that the stripes move slightly down the screen. This is because of the extra time taken each frame because there's a key down. When you press SPACE more work is needed to work out the ASCII key code, and the pattern moves further down. Press BREAK to stop the loop, and give thanks for our interrupt-driven keyboard updates.

It takes a PAL TV 64 microseconds to trace each line of the display, so you can work out the time a routine is taking – as long as it's less than 20 ms – by wrapping it in BORDER statements, with a PAUSE 1 for synchronisation, though the extra statements will distort the measurements.

There's no ZX BASIC POKE to turn off keyboard polling, and the obvious approach of making a USR call to the two-byte routine 243 201 (Z80 DI and RET instruction codes) doesn't work because the system turns interrupts back on (with the EI code, 251) every statement. The main times they're disabled for longer is during BEEPs, tape and SD card access, where timing is too critical to allow interrupts to run; extra hardware checks are included so we can still interrupt them with SHIFT SPACE or BREAK, or sometimes just SPACE when time's particularly tight. This explains why keypresses get lost and the TIME function falls behind if you're doing a lot of loading and saving, or – perish the thought – a cacophony of BEEPs.

The interrupt routine can also be called synchronously from Z80 code by the RST 56 instruction, code 255, so that's how I measured its overhead when the DI/EI USR calls were ignored. I POKEd a block of 20 RST 56 instructions, followed by a RET, into memory and wrapped the USR call in BORDER and PAUSE statements. To make it easier to count the number of screen-lines output while that block was executed, I printed a grid of alternate black and white pixel lines in the main screen.

Even into the 21st century this 'raster counting' was a standard way to measure the speed of critical game loops. It's less used now as few displays have a 'beam' for the code to chase, and modern processors have sub-nanosecond 64-bit timing hardware built in. But it's a very intuitive approach.

Since Next works the traditional way, even on a modern screen, to suit old programs and new ones using the Amiga-style Copper display co-processor, I've been able to reuse my PS2 and GameCube experience, from ATD and Codemasters, when optimizing Next display routines, just as I did decades before on Spectrums and Amigas.

It took the industry a long time to get this right; one of the snags of my first micro, the 1977 Apple 2, was that it had no frame interrupt and therefore no software technique for beam synchronization. As a result, most fast Apple 2 games show 'tearing' when display memory updates clash with TV output. But this was not as bad as on other early machines, like the original IBM PC display adapters, where pixels were lost if the CPU tried to access display memory at the same point as the video output. This meant that short black lines sparkled annoyingly across the TRS-80 monitor during games, and *Space Invaders* on an Acorn Atom appeared to take place in a snowstorm, as white dots took the place of aliens whenever the CPU took precedence.

Other 8-bit systems, such as Memotech, MSX and Tatung Einsteins, all based on Texas Instruments Video Display Processors, have the opposite fault, blocking access to display memory except while the screen border was being drawn. This limits screen updates of *Speculator*, Tony Brewer's hardware Spectrum emulator for those systems, to less than half the original speed.

Even our beloved Spectrum was not immune to display-related slow-downs, though these can be – and usually are – disabled on Next unless precise timing compatibility is required. The Spectrum ULA has to share access to the bottom 16k of our 48k RAM, or half of the RAM on a 128, between CPU and display. As we saw in Chapter 2, it does this by making the CPU wait for access to that RAM while pixels are being output, so that a memory access that would otherwise need three or four cycles actually takes eight, unless the beam is in the screen border.

Even with the generous ZX borders, this drags the effective speed of RAM on a 16k Spectrum down to 2.66 MHz on average. The ROM and the top 32k of main memory are not 'contended' in this way, racing along at the full 3.5 MHz, but this is still a factor 1980s Spectrum programmers needed to account for, especially in full-screen updates such as those performed every frame by the classic Ultimate games. It also meant that most Spectrums run faster than you'd expect from the first (endlessly re-published) BASIC benchmark timings, which were measured on a 16k machine, with code in fast ROM but data including the CPU stack in slowed-down RAM.

The uneven timing also meant that custom cassette loaders could not run reliably from the RAM of a 16k Spectrum. Similarly, the 'speech synthesis' feature in Quicksilva's early hit *Meteor Attack* became unintelligible, even allowing for the one-bit input and output, because the data captured on a 48k machine was played from contended 16k RAM when the game was released for all models.

This was before developers found out that – to Sinclair's surprise – sales of the 48k machine had surpassed those of the cheaper 16k Spectrum nine times over, even in 1982 when there was £50 price difference.

The overhead of NextZXOS interrupt-driven key polling increases to between 500 and 600 microseconds of each 20,000 microsecond frame at 50 Hertz, when Next runs at the original speed of 3.5 MHz. This is between 2.6 and 3.0% of total available CPU time. It's slightly more in 48k BASIC (3.0 to 3.4%) though both soon become insignificant once we crank up the CPU clock.

128 BASIC took an additional hit every frame when Investronica introduced the add-on keypad, never released in the UK, as part of their 128k upgrade of Sinclair's hardware, vital for them to get around arbitrary Spanish import restrictions on 'toy' computers with less memory.

The extra code needed to query the keypad, via a slow serial connection to a feeble PIC microcontroller, was so slow that Sinclair patched the ROM so it was only polled every other frame.

That wasn't much help for games hoping to use all the spare time in every frame, and that routine – along with the keypad hardware interface – is one part of the Spanish Spectrum 128 design Next chooses to leave out. For gruesome details of the keypad interface, consult Paul Farrow's ZX Resource Centre at http://fruitcake.plus.com. Now, having worked out where LASTK comes from, let's get back to the Editor.

As soon as we've read the new key code – bearing in mind that there's just been an interrupt to scan for it – we clear LASTK back to 0, the value used when no key is pressed.

This has become the standard way to read key-presses on the fly from ZX BASIC, though technically it's a bit of a hack – if you're not sure of polling the keyboard regularly it's more reliable to clear bit 5 of the system variable FLAGS (POKE 23611,PEEK 23611 & @11011111) when waiting for a key and only reading LASTK when that bit is set by the interrupt (checked with IF PEEK 23611 & @100000), but in practice I see no need to change the way Magnus did it.

Figure 49 – Detail of the issue 1 Spectrum circuit board, hand-routed by Stewart Honeyball, showing the last-minute 'dead cockroach' modification needed for reliable keyboard input.

Before closing the book on interrupt-driven keyboard input it's worth noting that the first ZX Spectrums off the production line had to incorporate a bizarre bodge, known as 'the dead cockroach', to fix a hardware bug in the first Ferranti ULA which would otherwise have made keyboard input unreliable. Figure 49 shows my issue 1 Spectrum board, with the modifications added by hand on the assembly line at Timex to fix the problem. Notice there are a couple of pins near the top right corner of the ULA turned up and connected by flying wires to a small circuit board mounted on four stiff wires by the Z80A processor, hooking up a cheap chip containing four NAND gates in a way that prevented display scanning corrupting keyboard input.

Later, to save money, the little board was eliminated leaving just the 74LS00 chip on its back with its legs in the air – hence the 'dead cockroach' description. The reason for this is explained in Chapter 18 of Chris Smith's brilliant Spectrum book, rather more technical than this one, "The ZX Spectrum ULA – How To Design A Microcomputer", where he notes:

'This fault passed undetected initially because the ZX Spectrum Operating System reads the keyboard via an interrupt service routine, executed while the television electron beam is returning to the top of the screen, and therefore during a period when contention does not occur. As soon as software began to be written in machine code that read the

keyboard port directly, it was discovered that the read was unreliable… Sinclair was faced with the prospect of discarding the first batch of ULA chips, at a huge financial loss."

The dead cockroach allowed Sinclair to release the Spectrum on 23rd April 1982, without waiting months for a fix from Ferranti. In fact the same bodge was still used in later Spectrum production, but built-in to the revised issue 2 ULAs first produced in August 1982. By then it was not practical to redesign it away, because a proper fix would have affected existing software timings.

Character tests

One thing I have changed substantially, since the first version of this editor was published, is the software bagatelle that acts upon specific key-presses. It's tempting to use a sequence of IF statements for each possibility, but this gets slower and slower as cases are added and more and more of them need to be skipped in order to find the one – if any – which has matching code.

Since there are only 256 possible values of PEEK LASTK we could sift them all to different lines, starting at N at intervals of G, with GO TO N+G*PEEK LASTK, using up to 256 lines to catch each possibility and a RETURN or GO TO instruction to go back for the next.

In fact some blocks of codes, such as those for ASCII characters, could be handled by a single statement, exploiting the way ZX BASIC falls through to the next higher line number if an exact match is not found, though the arrows and Symbol Shift patterns would still need a custom block of code each.

This might be a viable approach on 2.08, with its faster line-lookups, but on earlier versions of NextBASIC it would have made things worse by introducing a slew of extra lines for the interpreter to skip over while seeking later ones. It'd also make the code more long-winded and harder to read, as the order of possibilities would depend on the mnemonic correspondence of arbitrary key-codes, rather than any deeper logic.

I've opted for a 'divide and conquer' approach instead, sifting character codes into groups to minimise the number of tests in each group, especially for the most often-expected key-presses. This is partly because it gives me a chance to demonstrate the multi-line IF ... ENDIF blocks introduced with NextBASIC 2.08, and also to make the code more interesting to read.

The computed GO TO approach is still worth considering in some cases, e.g. in a joystick controlled beat'em'up game where a single read of 31 & IN 31 yields 32 possible codes for all combinations of joystick direction and fire button state (plus a few impossible ones involving opposite directions being active simultaneously). For the editor there are four main categories of input:

- no input, signified by a code of zero
- control keys like arrows, delete and enter, with codes less than 32

- displayable ASCII characters, codes 32 to 127
- Symbol shift and EXT combinations with codes greater than 127

So as soon as it has a key-code in **Last Key Pressed** the Editor switches four ways:

```
552 IF NOT Last Key Pressed
554   IF Character Count<>Old Count THEN BANK ProcArea
   PROC Display Character Count():; Refresh if count changed
   and no key is pressed.
558   DRIVER %126,%1 TO %b,%x,%y: IF %b&@111 THEN
   BANK ProcArea PROC Handle Mouse Click(%x,%y)
560 ELSE IF Last Key Pressed<=127
570   BEEP 0.002,%0: IF Last Key Pressed>31 THEN
   BANK ProcArea PROC Insert Char(): REPEAT UNTIL %0
```

The no-input case is handled by lines 552 to 558. Whereas the original editor used to check the mouse buttons every time round the loop, and redisplay the current character-count every time a character was added or deleted, line 558 only check the mouse buttons when no key is pressed. The mouse pointer still moves freely, as it's handled by the driver, which reads the mouse position registers and updates the corresponding sprite position every frame, as part of the same system interrupt that polls the keyboard.

It seems reasonable to assume that mouse-buttons and keys are unlikely to be pressed simultaneously, or within the same 20ms interval between interrupts, and this approach makes text entry faster. The driver command puts the mouse button status in %B. Five of the bits are used for the mouse-wheel, so the formula %B&@111 is used to isolate only the least-significant three, associated with mouse buttons. The value is non-zero, causing the Mouse Handling procedure to be called, if any of the mouse buttons is currently pressed.

My other trick – very effective during fast typing and cursor movement – uses a variable called **Old Count** to keep track of the **Character Count** most recently displayed. The slow PROC Display Character Count() is only called, from line 554, when the user stops typing **and** the count has changed. This means it lags behind the input during bursts of fast typing, but catches up as soon as the typist catches a breath.

Line 560 introduces a multi-line block that handles ASCII characters, whether printable or not. These have codes no greater than 127, and all the displayable ones, from space onwards, have codes of 32 or greater. After a very brief key-beep – for consistency with the ZX BASIC editor, and the reassurance of old-timers still using a dead-flesh keyboard – line 570 parcels off displayable codes to the banked Insert Char() procedure, which uses the value of Last Key Pressed internally, followed by the rather cryptic REPEAT UNTIL %0 which jumps as fast as possible back to the most recent REPEAT statement, on line 530, to pick up the next character.

Since REPEAT UNTIL normally marks the end of a REPEAT loop, and NextBASIC has no equivalent of the QL's END REPEAT or SAM's LOOP terminator, anyone who has been bitten trying to jump out of integer FOR loops might be worried about conditionally jumping back to the start of a loop by terminating it early, potentially multiple times. Might this not waste memory, or make it unpredictable where the program continues after the loop has finished? It might, but in this case it doesn't.

In fact, conditional REPEAT UNTIL statements are the officially-sanctioned way to do what NEXT would do inside a SuperBASIC REPEAT loop, i.e. jump back to the start. Block structure is preserved as long as you eventually terminate the loop by falling through an unconditional REPEAT UNTIL statement where the UNTIL condition is true, a WHILE test fails, or via the new EXIT statement (derived from BLISS) which leaves the loop likewise. **WHILE t** is the equivalent of **IF NOT t THEN EXIT**.

Cursory attention

The next thing we want to do as quickly as possible is move the cursor, so the following block of code, handling character codes 1 to 31, checks for arrow keys first of all.

```
600   ; Move the cursor.
610   IF Last Key Pressed=9 THEN IF Cursor Col<(%w-1) THEN IF
   PosIn Current Paragraph<>L(Current Paragraph)+1 THEN PRINT
   AT Cursor Row,Cursor Col;OVER %1;CHR$ 143;CHR$ 143;:Cursor
   Col+=%1:PosIn Current Paragraph+=%1: REPEAT UNTIL %0
620   IF Last Key Pressed=8 THEN IF Cursor Col>0 THEN Cursor
   Col-=%1: PRINT AT Cursor Row,Cursor Col; OVER %1; CHR$ 143;
   CHR$ 143;:PosIn Current Paragraph-=%1: REPEAT UNTIL %0
640   IF Last Key Pressed>=8 AND Last Key Pressed<=11 THEN
   BANK ProcArea PROC DisplayCursor():
   BANK ProcArea PROC MoveCursor()
```

Magnus's original Editor had a single banked PROC to handle arrow codes 8 to 11 – respectively corresponding to the ASCII backspace (ZX left arrow, code 8), horizontal tab (right, 9), line feed (down, 10) and vertical tab (up arrow, 11). To make horizontal cursor movement much faster, on average, my version sifts out the two most common cases, stepping the cursor back and forth along the same line, and handles them immediately.

Only if the cursor is not at the first or last column are lines 610 and 620 allowed to move the cursor and adjust two key variables – **Cursor Col**, giving the horizontal position of the cursor, between 0 and %W-1, and **PosIn Current Line**, between 1 and **Max LineLength**, which tracks the place where characters will be inserted or deleted within the current paragraph. Some of the spaces which would ideally appear in these variable names have had to be omitted because the 128 BASIC editor would treat IN and LINE as keywords, causing syntax errors which did not affect earlier ZX BASICs.

The code for each direction is very similar, except that moving right increases the corresponding variable values and moving left decreases them. In both cases the new 'accumulation assignment' syntax is used, adopted by NextBASIC 2.08 from the C programming language.

Cursor Col+=%1 is equivalent to **Cursor Col=Cursor Col+1** in traditional ZX BASIC, but faster because Next only has to look up the variable **Cursor Col** once as it will be used as both source and destination. The numeric value is also more concisely stored, as %1 takes five fewer bytes than the tokenised decimal value 1, encoded within the BASIC program as the bytes 49,14,0,0,1,0,0.

Overprinting

The same approach repositions the cursor either way, but when moving left **Cursor Col** is adjusted beforehand, as opposed to later when moving right. OVER 1 ensures that the character pattern swaps ink and paper for each pixel which is set in the pattern. This means that printing CHR$ 32, the space, in OVER 1 has no visible effect, while printing any character over itself leaves a blank, converting all the ink pixels to paper colour.

The magic number 143 is the code of the all-ink block graphics character. Overprinting this on top of a normal character swaps every pixel between ink and paper colours, giving the familiar reversed appearance of a character with the cursor on top, and avoiding the complication of the cursor being a character in its own right, as it was in the original ZX line editor.

Regardless of direction, both lines overprint the cursor pattern twice, in successive columns. This has the effect of making the existing cursor highlight disappear, as overprinting any character twice with the same symbol restores the original, **and** moving it left or right depending on whether we've already reduced Cursor Col (to move left) or will do so later (to move right). Either way, to keep the speed up we use REPEAT UNTIL %0 to loop straight back for the next key-press.

The other cursor-movement possibilities could potentially cause the screen to scroll or the cursor to move between lines. Those are handed in the all-purpose and hence relatively slow PROC MoveCursor( ), which we'll explore later when we look at the code in the ProcArea bank. Before the cursor is moved we call Display Cursor( ) which also has the counterintuitive effect of hiding the cursor in its current position, as explained later.

This leaves us with just the codes between 1 and 31. Not all of those can be entered from the Spectrum keyboard and some, like the codes 18 and 19 reserved for FLASH and BRIGHT in attribute modes, are irrelevant to a Text Editor running in Timex HiRes LAYER 1,2. The next lines deal with those, in order of simplicity and likelihood so that the slowest and most complicated cases are only checked if none of the simpler ones have matched before.

Edit functions

```
650   ; Edit functions.
660   IF Last Key Pressed=12 THEN BANK ProcArea PROC Handle
    Delete Key(): REPEAT UNTIL %0
665   IF Last Key Pressed=13 THEN BANK ProcArea PROC
    Insert Paragraph(%1)
```

Line 660 is easy to understand once you know that 12 is the keycode for DELETE. Like all the other codes, it is tabulated in Appendix A of the Spectrum BASIC manuals. When the delete key is pressed it might remove a single character from the screen, or an entire paragraph if the cursor is at the start of one. Anything else on the current line gets appended to the one before, as long as it fits.

Since the simple case of deleting the last character in a line is very common, often done several times in quick succession, and may involve little updating of the display, we wind straight back to the REPEAT after handling CHR$ 12. As we'll see later, deleting can get complicated, and may require the whole screen to be re-drawn. To leave more room for text, this procedure is stashed away in the ProcArea bank.

Inserting a paragraph is a relatively costly operation that involves shunting paragraphs around to make space, as well as a full redraw of the display. The PROC that does all this is also used by the paragraph Paste operation (Symbol Shift I, for Insert) so Insert Paragraph( ) takes a parameter which is 0 when pasting and 1, as here, when it involves dividing the current line between two paragraphs.

Faster scrolling

One of the slowest aspects of the original implementation was scrolling from the start to the end of a multi-page file, or back the other way. Each paragraph shift required the entire screen to be redrawn, and that means a lot of short waits in a 100-paragraph file. So one of the first things I did when looking to make the prototype more user-friendly was add a way to move quickly through the text, in steps of eight paragraphs backwards and forwards.

Since these are common operations, often repeated almost immediately while looking through a file, I assigned the TRUE VIDEO and INV VIDEO keys to movements back and forth. These keys return codes 4 and 5 respectively.

As I worked on this, the built-in NextBASIC program editor was updated to move backwards and forwards by single words within a line, using the same keys. Since horizontal cursor movement is not such a bottleneck here, I decided fast scrolling was our priority.

If you feel otherwise, it's easy enough to change the following couple of code blocks to scan the current paragraph with IN – as demonstrated in PROC Find( ), later – and adjust **PosIn Current Paragraph** and the cursor position to match the previous or next space there. There's a ready-made PROC to do that, used by the editor in nine circumstances, such as the default fast-scrolling routines: PROC Calculate Cursor Position InText( ).

```
669 IF Last Key Pressed=4 THEN BANK ProcArea PROC Scroll(-8):
   ; True video key, back 8 paragraphs.
670 IF Last Key Pressed=5 AND Current Paragraph<>Last
   Paragraph THEN BANK ProcArea PROC Scroll(%8): BANK ProcArea
PROC Display Cursor()
```

Scrolling backwards is handled by line 669. If you find eight paragraphs is too big a step – perhaps because you usually write long lines, or use wide characters – feel free to change the value -8. The great thing about writing software tools in BASIC is that it's very easy to customise them to please yourself. Scroll(-4) will move backwards through the file more slowly, ensuring that every paragraph is shown along the way. Line 670 scrolls the cursor eight paragraphs, or however many you prefer, forwards when the INV VIDEO key is tapped.

After PROC Scroll( ) redraws the display, the new location of the cursor and value of **PosIn Current Paragraph** will depend upon what's just been drawn. PROC Calculate Cursor Position InText( ) sorts this out, ready for redrawing of the cursor in the new place. Like 'PosIn', the potential for misinterpretation of an IN keyword by the 128 BASIC tokeniser means we're not allowed a space within the 'InText' part of the procedure name.

Keyboard EXT modes

One of the most notorious features of ZX BASIC implementations was the number of functions performed by each key. From the 1k ZX80 to the 48k Spectrum, just 40 physical keys were progressively laden with extra symbols and control capabilities, engaged by pressing Shift, Symbol or Function key combinations, and eventually by using two shifts at once – the EXT combination – to get even more capabilities by switching the cursor to another mode.

When the Spectrum keyboard was redesigned with extra-key-tops, in 1985, the same underlying electronics was used, so we got even more shift keys, like Graphics (formerly Caps Shift 9) and EXT (formerly Caps Shift and Symbol Shift pressed together) which didn't help at all if the following character required Symbol Shift anyway.

This also meant that Spectrum Plus and Toast-rack 128 keys were even harder to press, as two rather than one internal switch needed to be activated, but eliminated the need to change the circuit-board, or the 16k BASIC ROM. Since Sinclair had alienated his Spectrum programmers and electronics designer by then, but kept industrial designer Rick Dickinson sweet, there was not much choice!

This obsession with cost-reduction by making keyboards more complicated for customers pre-dates the ZX range. Back in 1977 Clive Sinclair was working with Chris Curry, who went on to found Acorn, and trading as 'Science of Cambridge', having been squeezed out of his old company Sinclair Radionics in a refinancing deal. One of their schemes to raise money for the pre-ZX80 MK14 bare-board micro was to repackage old calculator parts in an ergonomic disaster called the 'Science of Cambridge Wrist Calculator', briefly powered by six watch batteries; 15,000 kits were sold under the ominous slogan 'now 10 keys can do the work of 32'.

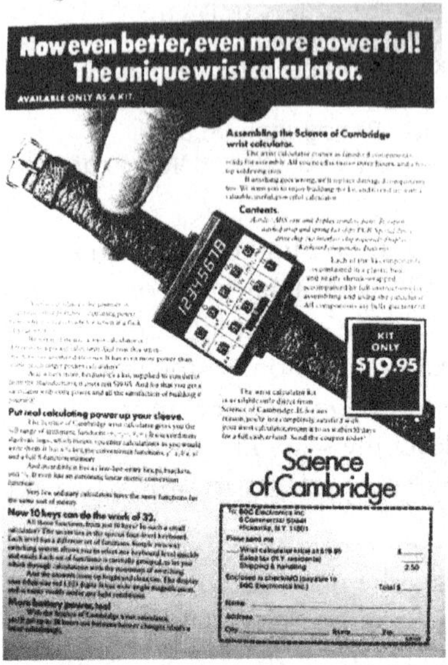

Figure 50 - this US advertisement for his 'unique wrist calculator' looks like a typical Sinclair advert. Though Clive was briefly blocked from trading under his own name after Sinclair Radionics failed, Science of Cambridge and Sinclair Research used the same advertising agency, Primary Contact.

Later Amstrads rethought this with a more complicated membrane, plus electronics to remap the new keys to mimic combinations of the old 40 keys, so software could not tell them apart. After many experiments while sticking with the 13-wire keyboard matrix, to make the boards drop-in replacements for original Sinclair Spectrum and Plus cases, SpecNext gave up on multi-layer membranes, fixing related problems by repurposing two wires intended for the Raspberry Pi0 GPIO expansion interface. This is one reason the Kickstarter 1 Next was so late, but also why its keyboard feel is so much lighter and more reliable than the earlier attempts, without breaking backward-compatibility.

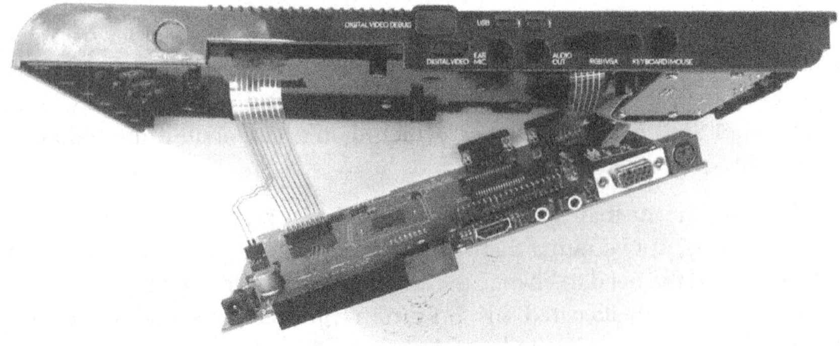

Figure 51 – A partially-dismantled Kickstarter 1 Next, showing the extra two wires that improved keyboard input, trailing down to the main board from the side of the keyboard.

The EXT key allows access to additional character codes that would not otherwise be available from the keyboard. The Editor handles this the same way BASIC does, by setting or clearing the value of the system variable MODE each time the key is pressed. There's no display of the temporary mode change, as there was in 48k BASIC when the cursor was a character in its own right, rather than an overlay, but a beep sounds to warn you that the next key-press may be unusually interpreted.

```
680 IF Last Key Pressed=14 THEN POKE MODE,1- PEEK MODE:
   BEEP 0.1,8* PEEK MODE :; Toggle EXT mode.
```

Notice how the value of the byte at **MODE** is toggled between 0 and 1 with the same statement regardless of the previous value. 1-PEEK MODE yields 1 if PEEK MODE is 0, and 0 if it's 1. This is more concise than the obvious:

```
IF PEEK MODE THEN POKE MODE,0: ELSE POKE MODE,1
```

but would go wrong if the initial value of MODE was anything other than 0 or 1. In fact it is set to 2 in graphics mode, but we're safe as there's no way to go into graphics mode – or edit graphics characters – in the Editor itself. Just in case someone is ingenious enough to leave the file browser or an INPUT statement with graphics mode selected, the value is POKEd back to 0 after letting the operating system handle input directly.

If the user presses EXT but then wants to type normally, without using a special key-press, they need an easy way to cancel the unwanted mode change. As in BASIC, pressing EXT again does this. Notice how the pitch of the PEEK is different – eight semitones higher – the second time EXT is pressed. The helps users understand the changing input context, without distracting them from the screen.

```
684 ENDIF
685 IF Last Key Pressed>127
690 ; Ambiguous codes
695 BEEP 0.004,%3
```

The ENDIF ends the block which deal with input codes less than 128. We don't use ELSE here as it's possible that Last Key Pressed has changed from 0 to some high value associated with a Symbol Shift combination, because there's been a menu selection made with the mouse while the keyboard was idle. The BEEP when those codes are entered is a little longer and higher in pitch than for standard ASCII characters.

Key features

In fact, there are eight more ASCII key-codes that may need to be inserted after translating them from EXT or Symbol shifted keypresses that generate higher non-ASCII keyboard codes. The helper PROC Stuff() is used to insert these replacements, after setting **Last Character Code** suitably.

These ten codes are in fairly random order, so the simple, obvious and verbose approach would be to add an IF statement for each, e.g.

```
IF Last Key Pressed=188 then PROC Stuff("{")
IF Last Key Pressed=189 then PROC Stuff("}")
```

Since space is precious, I've reduced the ten statements to four by sifting the input into four groups of adjacent codes. The only one that gets a line to itself is the translation of EXT P, for the copyright sign, into CHR$ 127, on line 700. Since this is not a standard ASCII character – officially code 127 is for the teletype DEL signal – I've used CHR$ 127 in this printed listing, but in the first BASIC implementation "©" did the trick in seven fewer bytes.

Explicit integers are not yet allowed immediately after CHR$ – CHR$ %127 is a syntax error – but CHR$(%127) will profitably trade visible characters for invisible ones.

```
700 IF Last Key Pressed=173 THEN PROC Stuff(CHR$ 127)
710 IF Last Key Pressed>=197 AND Last Key Pressed<=198 THEN
   PROC Stuff("]["(Last Key Pressed-196))
715 IF Last Key Pressed>=227 AND Last Key Pressed<=229 THEN
   PROC Stuff("~\|"(Last Key Pressed-226))
720 IF Last Key Pressed>=188 AND Last Key Pressed<=194 THEN
   PROC Stuff("{}...[]"(Last Key Pressed-187))
```

Line 710 is a bit more complicated since it handles both 197 and 198, which were traditionally entered with a combination of EXT and Symbol Shift on the Y or U keys. This was no inconvenience as ZX BASIC made no special use of those brackets, but NextBASIC uses them to extend the indexing range of some integer arrays, allowing %A[1663] as a synonym for %Z(25), for example.

NextBASIC 2.08 goes further, allowing square brackets after a string expression to trigger handy translations such as the removal of leading or trailing spaces, case conversions or substitutions. We could have used this for all the remapping in lines 700 to 720, by building up two strings containing the codes we want to trap and replace: CHR$ 173, CHR$ 197 and so on – and replacements "©[]~\|{}[]" in any order.

But as the translation feature arrived during development, and the CHR$ patterns are greedy for memory, I've saved demonstrating the new string trickery for PROC Find( ) and used IFs to equivalent effect. Line 715 is the first where handling adjacent codes together brings a useful saving, as the adjacent codes 227, 228 and 229 all correspond to shifted ASCII characters we need to remap, so one line sifts out and remaps all three to '~', '\' and '|' respectively.

Line 720 takes this approach furthest. Codes from 188 to 194 include those for curly braces '{' and '}' and two alternative ones, avoiding the need for EXT, mapped to square brackets. All four – and three intermediate codes with no single-symbol equivalent, 190 to 192 – are translated by the final call to PROC Stuff( ). Since there are no ASCII characters associated with the three in the middle, I've put dots in their place. Including them means we can handle the important four with line 720, rather than one line for each sort of bracket.

Anyone curious about ASCII should research the career of Bob Bemer, the man who introduced curly brackets to the computer character set, persuaded IBM (eventually) to put letters in contiguous groups, and (for better or worse) invented the backslash \, which barely existed before 1960. Backslashes became useful when Unix deployed them as an 'escape' character to prefix ones that would otherwise be difficult to parse – it was deliberately-chosen as otherwise useless. In 1961 when it was considered for inclusion in ASCII, it only made the cut because the non-IBM representatives who stubbornly opposed it couldn't agree on a better candidate.

Backslashes were forced to the attention of non-programmers because Microsoft co-founder Paul Allen copied DEC's TOPS command-line syntax when adapting a 'quick and dirty' unlicensed clone of CP/M for IBM's first Personal Computer DOS. TOPS and Allen dedicated the forward slash / as a prefix for command options, to differentiate them from file-names, where Unix and our dot commands use a dash. This choice meant that when MSDOS belatedly gained support for sub-directories the conventional separator was not available, and IBM refused to allow existing commands to be changed – even though only two MSDOS 1.0 commands had any options!

Bob's rationale for adding backslash was nothing to do with file paths or directories, but drawn from mathematics via the influential European programming language Algol, which expresses the logical operations of exclusion and inclusion visually, with pairs of slashes in opposite directions: /\ for AND and \/ for OR. NextBASIC, like C, uses **&** and **|** (another ASCII innovation) for bit-wise versions of these mathematical operations.

Programming languages like C and Java might have been more readable without Bob, but this editor would probably have been much less compatible. He was most proud to have invented 'escape sequences' which were vital to the implementation of the first terminals, and therefore feature in CP/M, Atari TOS and MSDOS, though those were never used by Sinclair.

NextBASIC defines character 27 as a rarely-useful symbol to fill an entire window with the following character code. Some of the other multi-byte codes in ZX BASIC use the same principle with different control-codes, such as 16 and 17 to set ink and paper, 23 to tab across up to 65536 columns, or 22 to position the cursor.

The equivalent would be ESC Y x y on many terminals, in CP/M-86 or GemDOS and most pertinently in Amstrad's Locomotive BASIC for the Spectrum +3. The escape sequence encodes x columns and y rows, counting from 32 to avoid needing invisible characters, so printing CHR$(27)+"Y$!"

in those systems will put the cursor on the fourth column of the second line. For more of Bob's anecdotes, start here:

`http://web.archive.org/web/20090903184346/http://www.bobbemer.com/BRACES.HTM`

The literal transliteration in lines 700 to 720 of the Editor makes some of the late additions to ASCII a little harder to type, but frees up eight Symbol Shift combinations for the menu shortcuts, as follows:

Menu item	Key press	CODE
Save As	Symbol Shift A	226
Delete paragraph	Symbol Shift D	205
Erase everything	Symbol Shift E	200
Find and replace	Symbol Shift F	204
Get new file	Symbol shift G	203
Insert paragraph	Symbol Shift I	172
Quit	Symbol Shift Q	199
Save over existing file	Symbol Shift S	195

Table 3 – Mouse menu options and corresponding keys

You may wonder how I worked out those codes, as they're not listed by keypress combination in the manual. As often in BASIC, it's quicker to write a program to find out what the computer knows than it is to look it up in a book, let alone posting a plea to a ZX-related social media forum. I used this:

```
REPEAT: POKE LASTK,0:PAUSE 0:PRINT AT 0,0;PEEK LASTK,:REPEAT UNTIL 0
```

That displays the corresponding code at the top left corner of the screen after each keypress. There remains just one still-unused Symbol Shift combination: Symbol Shift W, code 201. That pulls up the **<>** token which must be entered as two characters since 128 BASIC did away with keyword entry. Use it wisely to add whatever missing feature you crave most.

File commands

```
730 ; File commands
735 IF Last Key Pressed>=200 THEN ON Last Key Pressed-200:
  PROC NewFile()::: PROC OpenFile(): BANK ProcArea PROC Find()
740 IF Last Key Pressed=226 THEN PROC SaveFile(%1)
750 IF Last Key Pressed=195 THEN PROC SaveFile(%0)
```

Five of the commands invoke corresponding procedures. Lines 740 and 750 call the same PROC but with a different parameter: %0 to save over the previously loaded or saved file, and %1 for **SaveAs**, which prompts for a new filename first. The other three are handled by line 735, exploiting the way that **Erase**, **Get** and **Find** shortcuts all return codes in the range 200 to 204 and using the new single-statement switch construct.

After checking we have a code of 200 or more, ON Last Key Pressed-200 tries to pick one of the following statements on the same line, counting the first of those, PROC NewFile( ), as statement zero and the fifth and last as PROC Find( ). That one's tucked away in the ProcArea bank, so I'll reveal its workings in the next chapter.

The two empty statements between the three colons account for codes 201 and 202, which are ignored. Codes greater than 204 are rejected silently by ON as there's no corresponding statement for them on that line. If that were not the case we'd need to check IF Last Key Pressed>=200 **AND IF Last Key Pressed<205** but in practice there's no need because of the way ON is implemented. We have the option of providing an ELSE clause to catch values for which there's no matching statement, but that's not necessary here.

The cut and paste (paragraph **Insert** and **Delete**) operations are each implemented in a single line, reusing five **ProcArea** routines:

```
780 IF Last Key Pressed=205 THEN C$=P$(Current Paragraph):Cut
   Size=L(Current Paragraph):Character Count-=Cut Size:Cursor
   Col=%0: BANK ProcArea PROC Delete Paragraph(Cut Size)
```

This is where **C$** and **Cut Size**, initialised at the start, step up. We needed to preset them to empty values in case someone decided to paste before cutting anything. In that case a blank paragraph is inserted. They get customised when a paragraph is deleted with Symbol Shift D. The number of characters cut is used to adjust the character count, then passed to PROC Delete Paragraph( ) where it's used to determine whether the Cursor Row and Column need to be updated.

Since deleting character-by-character gets quite slow for a substantial block, you can use Symbol Shift D to speed this up, even within an existing paragraph, by pressing Enter either end of the characters you wish to lose, then deleting the paragraph thus formed, and deleting once more to rejoin the parts either side.

Symbol Shift I, to insert or paste a paragraph, and Symbol Shift Q are handled last. Code 172 handles pasting by calling PROC Insert Paragraph( ) with a zero parameter, to indicate no splitting of the current paragraph is required. It then copies the paste buffer from **C$** to the **Current Paragraph** and its length from **Cut Size** to the corresponding line-length array entry, and increases the **Character Count** to match, before refreshing the display:

```
790 IF Last Key Pressed=172 THEN BANK ProcArea PROC Insert
   Paragraph(%0):P$(Current Paragraph)=C$:L(Current Paragraph
   )=Cut Size:Character Count+=Cut Size: BANK ProcArea
   PROC Refresh Display(): BANK ProcArea PROC Calculate Cursor
   Position InText(): BANK ProcArea PROC Display Cursor()
```

```
810 ENDIF
820 REPEAT UNTIL Last Key Pressed=199
```

Line 810 marks the end of the program block that handles non-ASCII input codes, which began at line 685. If bytes were free – as is the case in BASIC banks that don't fill the entire 16k – intermediate lines could have been indented by a couple of spaces to make the scope of the block more obvious. But that only really improves legibility when the intervening lines are short, and has a tiny associated speed penalty, as the interpreter skips over the spaces, one by one, every time. Code 199, the **Quit** combination, breaks out of the main loop.

Cleaning up

The remaining code which is not part of a PROC is the epilogue of the main loop, which undoes the work of lines 90 to 320, cancelling the error-trapper, releasing memory and restoring the original font.

```
830 ON ERROR
840 BANK ProcArea PROC Quit(): BANK ProcArea CLEAR
860 DPOKE CHARS,%F: PRINT CHR$ 30;CHR$ 8; CHR$ 2; CHR$ 3;
870 CLEAR ( DPEEK RAMTOP)+768
880 STOP
```

Most of the clean-up code has been tucked into the ProcArea BANK, but the line that releases that bank has to be part of the main program – think about it! Line 860 restores the character-set address previously stashed away in %F by the Init Display( ) procedure, then prints a few control-characters to remind the system to use it.

Printing CHR$ 2 restores the previous font for standard eight-pixel-wide characters, the default width restored with CHR$ 30 and CHR$ 8, then CHR$ 3 does the same for the narrower versions. The CLEAR undoes the effect of line 90, returning all the memory allocated for the custom character set to NextBASIC, and wiping the screen as a side effect. A dozen bytes could be saved here by using the (%) idiom, or 15 with the cryptic CHR$ PI at the end. Like most functions expecting a whole number parameter, CHR$ rounds values to the nearest integer. This means that CHR$(4*PI) yields the CR code, as 4*PI is nearer 13 than 12. But beware: since NextBASIC 2.08 CHR$ 3*4 yields a string of four code 3 characters, rather than character 12, or a syntax error as in other Sinclair BASICs.

One more little procedure simplifies the input-translation lines 700 to 720 by stashing the replacement character code in **Last Key Pressed** before passing it on to Insert Character( ). If you recode those lines to use the NextBASIC 2.08 character-replacement modifier, as mooted earlier for lines 700 to 720, you can also remove this PROC:

```
900 DEFPROC Stuff(T$)
910 Last Key Pressed= CODE T$
920 BANK ProcArea PROC Insert Char()
930 ENDPROC
```

Chapter 7, Main program Editor procedures

Most of the Editor procedures are stored in a separate bank, to free space for text in the main program area. They're the subject of Chapter 8, so this one covers only the procedures in the remainder of the main program file. All of the program line numbers are unique, so that procedures can be MERGEd back and forth between the .BAS and .BNK files. The remaining procedures in Editor.bas deal with file loading and saving, and the setting up of data arrays. It's convenient when testing to have these in the main area – though if the ProcArea bank was not already full I'd probably have tried to shoe-horn some of the simpler loading code there, too.

This brings up one of the main purposes of this example, the demonstration of how to split up a large program into banks while still being able to develop and extend the whole thing efficiently. It is much harder to edit code in a bank than program lines in the main area. Even tracing the code is fiddly, because you need to specify the bank number after the line or procedure name, e.g. LIST PROC Scroll( ) BANK ProcArea, where LIST PROC Scroll( ) would be enough otherwise, and leave the BASIC editor conveniently on the first line of that procedure afterwards.

Editing code in a bank is a much more tortuous process, especially at first before you memorise the steps needed to swap back and forth between banks, when there's a risk of losing changes, or leaving them in the wrong place, if any step is accidentally skipped. We're not allowed to add lines piecemeal into a bank – when we use BANK LINE to copy a range of lines there, only one range can be specified and it overwrites any lines previously copied to that bank. It's all-or-nothing when it comes to reading code the other way, from a bank to the editor. BANK MERGE copies the entire bank contents into main memory, space permitting.

I find it convenient, quicker and less error-prone to keep a copy of program lines to go into a bank in two forms, as a standard .BAS file which can be loaded, merged and edited as normal, and a corresponding 16k .BNK file for direct loading. This means the slow interactive BANK LINE step only needs to be performed once, probably after making several changes, while keeping track of the amount of free space left in the bank and taking necessary steps to trim lines or extract procedures to another file immediately, if it won't all fit.

The editor is supplied as two standard BASIC files, Editor.bas and EditorProcs.bas, and a duplicate version of the procedures bound up into a 16k bank file, EditorProcs.bnk. The files are not quite identical and the difference reveals the technique I use to make sure they're kept in step, yet easy to edit. The technique to do this is explained at the end of the next chapter, after the detailed explanation of the EditorProcs. Figure 53 is a guide to the organisation of the editor, and the distribution of procedures between the two program files. Line numbers are shown below the box which names each procedure; the shading differs and numbers are prefixed with L to indicate which PROCs are in the in the banked file.

For clarity, links to the one-line Display Cursor() procedure at line L2460 are not shown in the diagram. It's called from these procedures: Delete Char(), Delete Paragraph(), Find(), Handle Mouse Click(), Insert Paragraph(), Move Cursor() and Scroll(). The even tinier PROC Limit() at L 3910 is likewise omitted, as it's only called from Scroll().

The two large blocks at the top of the figure are not procedures. They represent the first part of Editor.bas. These blocks invoke procedures, as shown by arrows to boxes for each procedure they call. We can see that the INITIALISATION block directly calls PROC Init Mouse() and PROC Init Display(), which are self-contained within the bank, and PROC New File() which is also part of the main file. That calls PROC Set Up View() among the banked EditorProcs, which in turn calls Calculate Cursor Position In Text(), Refresh Display(), Display Character Count() and Display Menu() procedures elsewhere in the NextBASIC bank, at the lines shown.

.RET – tracing GO SUB, FN and PROC calls

When a program stops it may be hard to know the flow that led it to report, and the scope of variables which may have been temporarily replaced by LOCAL versions. Fear not, help is at hand!

The .RET command was written by Garry Lancaster for NextBASIC 2.08, in response to a NextBASIC tool I put together for earlier NextZXOS versions and circulated privately. Both show the sequence of calls outstanding when a program generates a report or reaches STOP statement.

They scan back through the stack of procedure calls, parameters and local variables, listing them in reverse order of calling, with the most recent call at the top. Figure 52 shows output from .RET after stopping editor initialisation within PROC Display Menu(). Reading from the top upwards, we can see that PROC NewFile() was invoked by line 315, which called PROC Set Up View() in the BASIC bank from line 4964 of the main program.

From line 5060 in bank 107 this called PROC Refresh Display(), which set up two local variables %I and Row, before calling PROC Display Menu() which declared one local variable, T$, currently containing a block-graphic symbol. This process is non-destructive so you can CONTINUE, perhaps after editing variables or the program, to continue testing.

```
LOCAL: T$="▌"
107:2160:1 PROC Display Menu()
LOCAL: %I=2
LOCAL: Row=2
107:5060:1 PROC Refresh Display()
4964:1 BANK ProcArea PROC Set Up View()
315:1 PROC NewFile()
```

Figure 52 – Output from the .RET command just before completing PROC NewFile()

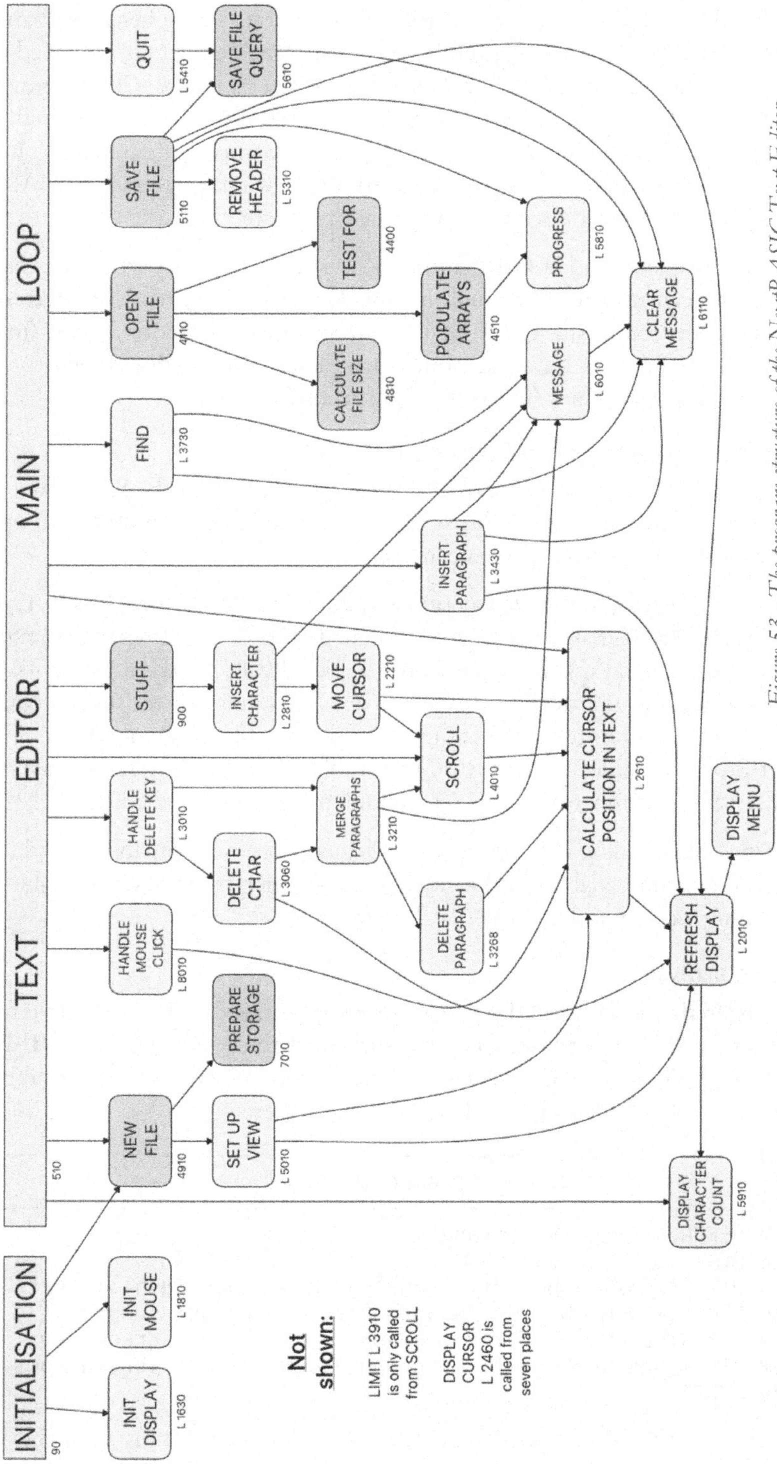

Figure 53 - The program structure of the NextBASIC Text Editor

I've decided not to list my prototype PROC HC() here because changes for NextBASIC 2.08 invalidated the reverse-engineered details I worked out to trace earlier versions. That hack was named after a HOW_COME routine I wrote in Sinclair SuperBASIC for *Popular Computing Weekly* in September 1985, and later included in the QL *Turbo Toolkit* demos. If you need to trace older programs before you can convert them for the latest NextBASIC, please contact me for a copy of the prototype source.

The dot command is faster and its Z80 source code is part of the distro so anyone can now look through it to work out how NextBASIC currently structures the return stack. Best of all, Garry maintains the code, so any future internal changes will be sorted out via updates in the **/dot** directory and documented in the **/src/asm/dot_commands** folder.

Files, arrays and the WorkArea

Eight procedures in the last part of Editor.bas implement the Save, Save As, Erase and Load commands. Most of these procedures are required to open a new document; Erase and Save are relatively simple.

Besides several of the display procedures we've seen before, PROC Open File( ) calls PROC SaveFileQuery( ), Calculate File Size( ), Prepare Storage( ) and Populate Arrays( ), as well as a little helper PROC TestFor( ) to work out how the lines in the newly-opened file are separated. All those procedures appear at the end of the main Editor.bas program file. The only others there are PROC NewFile( ) and PROC Save File( ), which handle the last two Symbol Shift commands we've yet to implement: Erase and Save.

Since file opening is the most complicated remaining capability, and uses much the same variables and arrays as the simpler commands, I'll take the code out of order and nail the easy bits first.

Editing arrays

Last in the file comes DEFPROC Prepare Storage( ), which sets up empty arrays to store the text during editing, and clears the WorkArea bank. BANK ERASE could also be used to set only one part of a bank to any chosen byte value, but by default it clears all 16384 bytes to zero.

```
7000;------------------------------------------------------------
7001;-                    Prepare storage                        -
7002;------------------------------------------------------------
7010 DEFPROC Prepare Storage()
7020 BANK WorkArea ERASE
7030 DIM P$(Max Number Of Paragraphs,Max LineLength):; Text
7040 DIM L(Max Number Of Paragraphs):; Paragraph lengths
7050 DIM R(Max Number Of Paragraphs):; Starting screen row
7060 DIM N(Max Number Of Paragraphs):; Number of screen rows
7070 ENDPROC
```

The four DIM statements dedicate most of the memory available for variables to the text being edited. Biggest by far is the two-dimensional array

P$, with one string element per paragraph, each initialised to hold **Max LineLength** characters, all spaces at first.

String padding

ZX BASIC string array elements are fixed in size and filled with spaces when they're dimensioned. This means that when you assign to a string array element the text you supply is put at the start, and any spare characters allocated in the array are left empty, usually holding spaces.

Sometimes this is handy, for instance if you want to print integers neatly in six-character wide columns: DIM Z$(6): Z$=STR$(%Z) will give you a nicely-padded value of the required width in Z$, with between one and five spaces at the end to align output ready for the next column. But often it's fiddly, requiring the actual length – as opposed to the maximum, set in the DIM statement – to be stored somewhere else so that the spaces at the end of a long string don't get spat out when they're not relevant.

This approach is potentially wasteful. However it only applies to string arrays, where it may in practice save RAM if the strings are always short. Consider for example a table of Z80 assembler mnemonics, where the length and address 'descriptors' for an array of variable-length strings would waste more bytes than the padding spaces after "LD " and "OR ".

Otherwise, if your entire text can fit in a single ZX BASIC string, which may be up to 40k long without needing any DIM declaration, an undimensioned string might be just what you need, as long as you leave enough space to edit it: A$="*"+A$ temporarily needs enough RAM for two copies of A$, making adding characters at the start slow and expensive as A$ grows. A$=A$+"*" is no better but NextBASIC 2.08 comes to the rescue with A$+="*" and even ZX BASIC can be persuaded to append efficiently with A$(LEN A$+1)="*", exploiting its relatively rare ability to slice destination as well as source strings.

When we explore the EditorProcs we'll see other ways to optimise Sinclair BASIC string handling. As many Spectrum and some Next users had only previously encountered the non-standard DEC BASIC approach to string handling (which was copied by Microsoft and, reluctantly, on the insistence of the BBC, by Acorn), getting to grips with string arrays is an important part of learning Sinclair BASIC.

Other ways with strings

Our approach is unlike most other BASICs, which typically limit the length of any string to 255 bytes, stashed wherever they fit at the time. Those must unpredictably pause for 'garbage collection' to recover fragments of space, as a result. The ZX approach is a trade-off, also used in Atari's 8-bit BASIC (which is similarly and unusually tolerant of long strings). BBC BASIC takes a hybrid approach which tries to guess the actual amount of space a string will need, periodically doubling its guesses; depending upon the program this might be the best of both worlds, but it is sometimes even more wasteful than the Sinclair/Atari approach and certainly a lot harder to predict.

It's worth noting that Sinclair, informed by experience of Microsoft, Acorn and ZX BASIC trade-offs, came up with an even cleverer approach on their final micro, the Sinclair QL. This handles dimensioned arrays like ZX BASIC except that it reserves an extra two bytes per string element to store the actual length, automatically hiding later bytes unless those are explicitly sliced out. The effect is like having arrays P$( ) and L( ) packed together, with the actual lengths automatically handled.

Sinclair SuperBASIC – first proposed by Jan Jones for the unreleased Z80-based LC3 Spectrum follow-up – limits each undimensioned string to 32,766 characters. These are allocated from sections of a memory heap containing entries a multiple of eight bytes long. That's just enough space to store the 32-bit address and length of any other entry, on machines of up to 4 GB RAM – the architectural limit of the QL's 68000-series processors. We'll have to wait for an official QL core from SpecNext before we can experiment with Sinclair SuperBASIC on our Nexts – and (rather less likely) some external RAM expansion before we can approach the theoretical limit.

Keeping track of ZX string lengths

To avoid printing 256 spaces when an empty line is all that's needed, the Editor keeps track of the actual number of characters assigned, from 0 to the limit **Max LineLength**, in a separate numeric array L( ). So if paragraph %P is full, L(%P) will hold **Max LineLength**. Shorter paragraphs use lower values in the L array. If it represents a blank line, L(%P) is zero. This is the usual approach people take adapting string routines from Microsoft to ZX BASIC.

I considered tweaking this scheme to use Next's faster integer array %L(), which has its own pre-allocated memory outside the main variables area, but this was difficult in earlier versions of NextBASIC where integer variables could not directly be used in the context of string expressions, when slicing or copying parts of strings around. More fundamentally, it would also limit **Max Number Of Paragraphs** to 63, at most.

NextBASIC 2.07 gave us a way to steal elements from later letters of the alphabet, so that %L[64] referred to %M(64) but this only gets us up to %L[127] (also known as %M(63)) before we run into the next array we might want to treat similarly, N( ) and %N( ). Changing the array name N to something even less memorable than the single letter allowed (standing for Number of lines) seemed too awful a hack, even for me. So L( ) remains.

There are two other numeric arrays of the same size which retain the names chosen by Magnus, N() and R(). We'll see those used when we delve into the EditorProcs. The R( ) array contains the screen row, from 1 to 20, where display of that paragraph *starts*. The companion N( ) array handles paragraphs that span more than one screen line, tracking the *number of rows* of the screen display the paragraph occupies.

So if the current paragraph is 200 characters long and the screen width is 64 characters, R(Current Paragraph) will be 4, as 192 characters will fill three lines and the last eight characters will occupy the start of a fourth. Assuming the whole paragraph fits on the screen, it will start on row N(Current Paragraph) and extend to row

```
N(Current Paragraph) + R(Current Paragraph) – 1
```

In conjunction with the screen width in %W, these arrays enable the cursor update code to identify the paragraph it's pointing into as it moves around the screen. It might be practical to use smaller arrays – in a long document, most of the paragraphs will not be on the screen so their N( ) and R( ) values are not used – but it'd be more complicated. Since these two arrays use only 10 bytes per paragraph, compared with 261 for the other two arrays, I've opted to take the hit to keep things relatively simple, and fast.

Opening and loading any file

The Open File procedure has three helpers, PROC Calculate File Size( ), PROC Populate Arrays( ) and the tiny PROC TestFor( ), which is the only procedure it calls more than once. The others have been separated out to make the code easier to follow and to allow local error-trapping, since file handling is one of the least predictable parts of any program, especially on systems like Next with removable storage.

Notice that OPEN is not a keyword, so it can be used with spaces around it in a procedure or variable name. The keyword is OPEN #, and oddly enough – for reasons soon to be explained – that's not used to load the file, but only to check for a PLUS3DOS header in case that needs to be removed. But before we load anything, we must check the 'Dirty' flag and give the user a chance to save recent changes before they're over-written.

```
4000;-----------------------------------------------------------
4101;-                           Open file                     -
4102;-----------------------------------------------------------
4110 DEFPROC Open File()
4120 LOCAL e,X$,file Size
4124 ; If there are unsaved edits, save the current file.
4125 IF Dirty THEN PROC SaveFileQuery()
```

Since it's very straightforward, I'm going to skip forward to explain SaveFile Query( ) before finishing off the discussion of Open File( ).

```
5600;-----------------------------------------------------------
5601;                         Save file query                  -
5602;-----------------------------------------------------------
5610 DEFPROC SaveFile Query()
5620 LOCAL k
5630 PRINT AT %22,%0;" Save changes (y/n)?",
5635 REPEAT
```

```
5640    POKE LASTK,%0: PAUSE %0:k=32| PEEK LASTK
5650    IF k= CODE "y" THEN PRINT "y";: PROC SaveFile(%0): EXIT
5660    IF k= CODE "n" THEN Dirty=%0: EXIT
5670 REPEAT UNTIL %0
5680 BANK ProcArea PROC ClearMessage()
5690 ENDPROC
```

PROC SaveFile Query( ) is called if you try load another file or quit the editor after making changes that have not yet been saved. The LOCAL k statement ensures that if the variable k is used elsewhere changes made inside this procedure don't affect the outer or 'global' variable with that name. The local copy initially has the value 0.

The procedure prompts for a single-key Yes/No response and loops indefinitely till either Y or N is pressed. The PAUSE %0 waits for a keypress and the POKE to LASTK makes sure it's not misled by a stale menu keypress still lurking in the one-byte input buffer.

Caps Lock and Shift are irrelevant thanks to a neat bit of Boolean algebra on line 5640, which allows the subsequent lines to check for just lower-case letters regardless of what was actually input. The way this works is explained in detail in the discussion of PROC Find( ) in the next chapter.

The lines after the call to SaveFile Query( ) handle file selection, showing how to call the browser so that the user can pick a file from a list rather than have to type the name manually. Unfortunately the browser did not support mouse selections at the time this program was written, so you'll need to use the keyboard unless it's been updated since.

```
4127 @Browse: ON ERROR GO TO @Bad Browse
4128 DPOKE CHARS,%F: PRINT CHR$ 3;:;NextBASIC font for browser.
4130 .BROWSE -t TXT -t MD -t CFG -r -d -k -m -p
    "Please select a file (.txt, .md or .cfg)" X$
4140 @Bad Browse: ON ERROR : DPOKE CHARS, DPEEK RAMTOP-255:
   PRINT CHR$ 3; CHR$ 2; CHR$ 31; CHR$ Font Width;:
   ; Restore editor font.
4142 POKE MODE,%0: POKE LASTK,%0
4145 IF X$="" THEN BANK ProcArea PROC Refresh Display():
    BANK ProcArea PROC Display Cursor(): ENDPROC
```

Before calling the dot command **.browse** a couple of preparatory steps are needed to ensure the standard font it expects is in use, and to catch any errors it might return. Character 3 is the code to 'regenerate small fonts' and needed because the browser uses its own custom character width which might not suit the font the Editor is using. Later we restore our font and it's chosen width with CHR$ 31, the 'redefine character set' code, which is described in more detail in the discussion of PROC Init Font( ) in the next chapter. Character 2 updates the definition of standard eight-pixel wide characters.

The eight command-line parameters passed to **.browse**, each prefixed with a dash, configure the browser to only allow specific file extensions. This removes the risk of loading a block of code or tokenized .BAS file, neither of which are compatible with a plain text editor. Besides the obvious **.txt** extension, the command supports **.cfg** files, which are used to configure NextZXOS and one of the key reasons a native editor is handy, and the **.md** (Mark Down) files used on Git, the version-control system where Spectrum Next source files are maintained.

If you want other file extensions to be allowed, and are confident they contain text rather than binary data, you can and should add them to the command line and prompt. Besides the three **-t** file-type parameters there are five which give the browser extra powers: **-r -d -k -m -p** respectively allow files to be renamed, deleted, moved or shuffled between memory cards while in the browser. Since you can get back without loading anything, by pressing Break, this means that the editor (or any similar program you write) gains these Sidekick-style file-handling capabilities without having to add them explicitly to the program menus.

The big snag of using the file browser, as opposed to a simple INPUT LINE statement, is that like all dot commands it must load code from a drive – usually the C:/dot directory, unless you specify otherwise – in order to work. This is not much of an issue if you have the two drives every Next supports, or keep small texts on drive M: or a Plus3DOS disc image in drives A: or B: but it otherwise means you need a valid NextZXOS system in drive C before trying to open a file.

This is a restriction, especially as other files the Editor needs are only loaded at startup and via the custom path in F$, but on balance it's worth it. If you disagree, use INPUT AT %22, %0;"Load file: "; LINE X$ at 4130. You can then skip the font shuffling PRINTs, but definitely not the error-trapping.

Indeed, a fail-safe sequence like CLOSE # %15: OPEN # %15,X$: CLOSE # %15 should follow the INPUT, so the file name is immediately checked for validity while the local error-trap is still in place, or make the equivalent call to PROC Calculate File Size( ) earlier, after copying the name to F$ first. Do not bother if X$ is null. I deliberately use that temporary string for the input selection so that the previous default in F$ doesn't get clobbered if nothing new is entered or selected.

Error trapping

Error-trapping is one of the few places where we still need to use GO TO statements, now NextBASIC supports multiline conditional blocks, which previously had to be slowly emulated using GO TO. Dot commands can only return a simple success or failure indication, so there's no scope for helpful messages indicating what went wrong. However, the risk of errors is much less when an existing file is selected from a menu than if the file name, path and extension had to be typed in full, every time.

I've given the error-handling target lines 4127 and 4140 symbolic labels, prefixed with @ signs, rather than relying on cryptic line numbers. These are symbolic names which can be used by GO SUB, GO TO, RESTORE, EXIT, SAVE LINE or BANK LIST, in place of the corresponding line numbers, or even within a line. They make programs easier to read.

Labels are a bit slower than line-number references in NextBASIC, so you might think twice before using them in inner loops, but in this case they're only looked up in the course of file selection and the overhead of that swamps the few microseconds needed to look up a meaningful name.

The label **@browse** is at the top of the file-selecting code, so we can branch back there for a fresh selection if needed,. The label **@bad browse** is used just after the attempt to read a file name, where it resets the error trap and restores the character width expected by the Editor.

Notice that line 4145 checks for X$ being empty, and returns immediately after tidying the display if so, leaving the currently-loaded document intact. Otherwise line 4150 sets F$ to X$ and calls PROC Calculate File Size() which opens the file specified in F$, setting the global variable **file Size** with its length after adjusting for a 128-byte PLUS3DOS header if it finds one.

```
4150 F$=X$: PROC Calculate File Size()
4160 IF file Size>16384 THEN BANK ProcArea PROC Message("File
   larger than 16k ("+ STR$ file Size+")"): GO TO @Browse
4175 ; Set up the variables to store the file data.
4177 PROC Prepare Storage(): BANK ProcArea PROC
   Refresh Display()
4180 BANK WorkArea ERASE : LOAD F$ BANK WorkArea
4182 IF file Size<16383 THEN BANK WorkArea POKE file
   Size,%13,%10
```

The editor has a 16k limit on the length of files it will edit (not counting any header) so we check that next. See how line 4160 helpfully includes the actual file size in the error message if it finds the chosen file is too large to fit, and then goes back to allow a different file (or nothing) to be selected. As we've seen before, PROC Prepare Storage( ) simply sets up empty arrays to hold the file text and line details.

It would then be possible to load a standard ZX BASIC text file line by line with INPUT, though rather slow for a file with many lines. Instead we load it all in one go, as long as it will fit, into the WorkArea bank, having previously cleared that with BANK ERASE.

The LOAD BANK command is a lot faster but the key reason Marcus opted to use a temporary bank and LOAD command is because that works whatever characters are at the end of each line, whereas INPUT insists on a single CHR$ 13 at the end of each line. That's fine for genuine Spectrum, TRS-80 or Classic Mac data, but if the file came from CP/M, Windows, Qdos, AmigaOS or Unix it probably wouldn't work.

The end of the line

The global variable B$ is a practical concession to the inconsistent ways other computers handle files. When the ASCII character set was invented, shortly before the advent of home computers, the default output of a program was not to a screen but to a mechanical terminal with a moving print-head or 'carriage' that printed characters in ink on paper rolls. Two separate motors were used to advance the paper and prepare for the next line. One rolled the paper up – a so-called Line Feed operation, abbreviated LF and encoded as CHR$ 10 – while the other returned the print-head to the left margin, an operation called Carriage Return or CR, CHR$ 13.

Almost always these characters were sent as a pair known as CRLF, but in some obscure cases, mostly to do with underlining and overprinting to obtain new character patterns, old computers might send more CRs than LFs, or more LFs than CRs when 'printing' blank lines, where only the paper needed to move, and the Carriage could be left alone.

By 1980 printing terminals were obsolete, but old operating systems like CP/M – and Microsoft's MSDOS, an unlicensed clone of CP/M – persisted in sending both CR and LF codes, and storing them together at the end of each line of a file. This was clearly wasteful for screen-editing and most other purposes, when all you need to know is that the current line has ended, which could be signalled by any single character-code.

About then a 'Holy War' broke out. Companies like Tandy standardised on CR alone, in their more sophisticated Z80 operating system TRSDOS. The Unix world settled on LF for the same effect. For a while Sinclair ignored both, creating a non-ASCII character set for the ZX80 and ZX81, using just 64 codes, mostly to save ROM space. Like Apple, Tandy, Dragon and Acorn, at first they didn't see the point of lower-case letters but eventually the penny dropped that word-processing might be a useful application and the ASCII character set took hold, adding 30 more character-shapes including lower-case letters and obscure punctuation characters.

Before ASCII, character sets were often computer-specific, variously packing three characters into two bytes (DEC RAD50 – for good measure, the 50 is in octal, base eight, where $50_8*50_8*50_8=175000_8$, which is 64000 decimal, neatly fitting within the 0 to 65535 capacity of a pair of bytes), or one character into six bits; this was convenient for machines with 18 or 24-bit words, or ROM-starved micros like the ZX80 and ZX81, which used the seventh bit to swap black and white pixels and the eighth for tokens.

IBM scrambled digits and letters around in a seven- or eight-bit soup called EBCDIC (Extended Binary Coded Decimal interchange code) based around the quirks of punched cards and Selectric typewriters, yet still used in some IBM and Fujitsu mainframes. The fact that letters were not even grouped conveniently into alphabetical blocks was even more annoying than the small regression for ZX hexadecimal enthusiasts when Sinclair adopted ASCII and 'A' was no longer the character after '9'.

When the Spectrum came along, designed by TRS-80 enthusiast Richard Altwasser, it picked up ASCII and naturally followed the Tandy convention of ending lines with just CR, as did many other small micros. Sinclair's slightly later QL, with firmware by Unix enthusiast Tony Tebby, opted for LF, as did the team developing AmigaOS, soon after. They in turn were followed by Linux and macOS, in a late switch from the ZX-style CRs used on Classic Macs. Amstrad remuddied the water by using both CR and LF in Spectrum CP/M, so the same applies to CP/M on Next.

NextZXOS uses CR characters to mark the end of lines and to move the cursor in PRINT. Sinclair's Interface 1 hedged its bets by providing two 'channels' for printer output, one known as channel "T', for Text, which translated CRs into CR LF pairs and stripped out other control and graphics codes, and channel 'b' for 'Binary', which sent 8-bit codes unmolested down the same wires.

To be generally convenient, our Editor has to cope with all three types of line-ending found in the wild: LF, CR or CR LF. Since NextZXOS is partially developed on Mac, Linux and Windows systems, the Next file browser is similarly permissive. But our Editor has to write files as well as reading and displaying them, so it can't just translate lone LFs or suppress them after CR. You may want to re-edit a file on the alien system that created it, in which case you'd reasonably expect the editor to preserve whichever convention was originally used for that file.

This is why the global variable B$ is needed. This string contains the one or two characters expected to terminate lines of the current file. It may be changed later if the loading process reveals that a newly-loaded file uses different line-end markers.

I recently found out that Acorn Atoms, and BBC Micros too, saved a couple of bytes of ROM by using the sequence LF CR – which has the same effect as CR LF on a printing terminal – but I've yet to be bitten by that combination. The following two calls to PROC TestFor() cater for either or both line-endings, setting the line-break string in B$ to CR or LF depending on the file contents, or CR and LF, in that order, if both are found:

```
4185 ; Check which control characters are used for line breaks.
4186 ; Possibilities are 10 (LF), 13 (CR) or 13,10 (CR LF).
4187 ; Note special cases where file is empty or there is only
4188 ; one line and no line break. B$ is the line break string.
4200 PROC TestFor(%10) TO B$
4210 PROC TestFor(%13) TO X$
4220 B$=X$+B$
4230 IF NOT file Size THEN B$= CHR$ 13:file Size=%1: BANK
   WorkArea POKE %0,B$
```

PROC TestFor( ) returns an empty string if the specified code cannot be found in the work area. Line 4230 converts an empty file into one of a single carriage return, so the Editor always has something to chew on. The penultimate steps, before setting up the view of the newly-loaded file is to call Populate Arrays to read the lines from the Work Area into the BASIC arrays where it can be easily edited. If anything goes wrong we loop back to line 4127, labelled **@Browse**, for a new file to be selected; at this point the old text has been lost.

```
4240 PROC Populate Arrays() TO e
4250 IF NOT e THEN GO TO @Browse
4294 IF Last Paragraph>Max Number Of Paragraphs THEN BANK
    ProcArea PROC Message("Too many paragraphs"): GO TO @Browse
4297 BANK ProcArea PROC Set Up View()
4300 ENDPROC
```

Magnus devised an ingeniously fast way to determine which control characters are used in the text file. The obvious way would be to PEEK all **file Size** bytes from BANK WorkArea and check their codes one by one. Even at 28 MHz, this is painfully slow. Hence the next PROC, TestFor, which takes a single parameter, the ASCII code of the character we're hoping to find.

```
4400 DEFPROC TestFor(c)
4405 LOCAL T$: ON ERROR ENDPROC =""
4410 T$= BANK WorkArea PEEK$ (%0,~c)
4420 ENDPROC = CHR$ c
```

Line 4405 saves the current value of T$ so that variable name can be re-used locally inside the procedure, then sets up a local error-trap which means that TestFor( ) returns an empty string if anything goes wrong. The PEEK$ incantation reads bytes in BANK WorkArea from the start, offset %0 till it finds a character with the ASCII code specified in the C parameter. The squiggle "~" (called a tilde, ASCII code 126 and the last standard ASCII character Sinclair defined) tells NextBASIC that the second parameter of PEEK$ is not a length but an indication of how the end of the string is marked in memory.

If the file contains text with the specified line-ending, T$ ends up holding the first line. But if it's a binary file, or uses some other end-marker, that character might not exist in the bank at all. The 'new commands and features' list in which this function was introduced didn't say anything at all about that possibility, and even if the required character is found by chance in a random file it could be anywhere in the bank.

If it's right at the end, NextBASIC is quite likely to run out of RAM creating the temporary string. But a loop PEEKing and checking each character code in the bank up to **Max LineLength** (+2 for the LF in a full-sized CR/LF terminated line) would be slow, and the IN function to search a string was not available when the Editor was designed.

Magnus's approach is safe, as long as there's enough free RAM for a single valid paragraph, because of the ON ERROR trap. If anything goes wrong (e.g. a memory or parameter error) the PROC restores T$ and returns an empty string, just as it would if the required character was not found. The local error-trap is automatically forgotten after ENDPROC, and any previous error trap is reinstated.

Copying Banked text to string arrays

All this sets us up for the helper routine Populate Arrays( ) which copies paragraphs from the WorkArea to the array of paragraphs P$( ) and sets the length of each paragraph in the corresponding element of numeric array L(). We still don't know if the file contains any paragraphs longer than **Max LineLength** but we have the codes for the end of the first one and will use those, in B$, to identify and strip later paragraphs from the file.

```
4500;-------------------------------------------------------
4501;-              Open file: populate arrays             -
4502;-------------------------------------------------------
4503 ; Extract paragraphs from the file stored in the WorkArea
4504 ; and store them in the P$ array. Since a string array is
4505 ; fixed in size, we also need to store the length of each
4506 ; paragraph in the L array.
4507 ; This procedure exits with a value 1 on success.
4510 DEFPROC Populate Arrays()
4520 LOCAL R$,pos,row length,%i,%t
4540 Last Paragraph,Character Count=%0
4553 ; We identify paragraphs by searching for the paragraph
4554 ; break string (B$). If the file ends without a break,
4555 ; there will be an error so we need to catch this and
4556 ; extract the last paragraph separately.
```

Line 4520 clears the local R$ to an empty string and sets the other local variables to zero. This is particularly important for **pos** which will be used to keep track of the position in the file being read. The value zero indicates the start of the file.

Progress report

It's good practice to give an indication of progress while file operations that might take more than a second or so are underway. The Editor supports a simple progress bar which fills up, with reassuring sound-effects, during loading and saving.

Once again there's a risk that a very long PEEK$ might exhaust available memory, so an error handler is set up to get us back to the caller, returning a value of 0, if that happens.

```
4560 ON ERROR GO TO @No Break
4565 %t=(Max Number Of Paragraphs+9)/10
```

The progress bar has up to 10 sections so we work out how many paragraphs to allocate to each of them on line 4565. The number of paragraphs per section in **%t** is rounded up so that it must be at least one; if

Max Number of Paragraphs is less than one there's no work to do, so adding nine to that before dividing by ten gives us a safe value to divide by later when we're indicating progress through the file. Dividing by zero would cause an error if **Max Number Of Paragraphs** was set to a value less than ten, which might be the case during testing.

We're now ready to start filling the arrays, using **%i** in a loop to index each entry in turn. The local variable **pos**, set to zero at the start of the PROC, keeps track of the current offset in the WorkArea being scanned. When this reaches the **file Size** we must have finished; line 4580 checks for this.

```
4570 FOR %i=%1 TO Max Number Of Paragraphs
4580 IF pos>=file Size THEN ENDPROC =%1
```

Lines 4589 to 4610 process each line of the file in turn, reading its text (without the line-end markers) into the temporary local string R$. Before reading the next prospective line, starting from **pos** up to the first line-ending code in B$, we make sure that string is empty. Remember that memory for variables is scarce, and the old value of R$ is still in memory till we have a replacement for it ready to be copied in. This extra step makes sure that however BANK PEEK$ is implemented there's no risk of both old and new values of R$ having to be held in RAM at the same time, as the loop proceeds.

```
4589 ; Extract a paragraph ending with a break string.
4590 R$="":R$= BANK WorkArea PEEK$ (pos,~ CODE (B$(1))): GO TO
   @Check
4598 ; When no break string is found, extract what remains
4599 ; of the file.
4600 @No Break: ON ERROR : IF pos<fileSize-1 THEN R$="": IF
   file Size-pos<=Max LineLength THEN R$= BANK WorkArea PEEK$
   (pos,file Size-pos)
4601 ; Check the paragraph is within the allowed size.
4610 @Check: IF LEN R$<=Max LineLength THEN row length= LEN R$:
    ELSE GO TO @Too long
```

R$ now contains the text for a normal paragraph and all that remains is to make sure it'll fit in the array P$, which is done at line 4610 labelled **@Check**. But what if some line after the first exceeds **Max LineLength**? Much as in TestFor( ), we use ON ERROR to catch the possibility of a whopper that also exceeds available memory. Line 4600 catches this, clears the error-trap and makes sure there's at least one valid character left, and no more than **Max LineLength**. The assumption is then that the file was saved with no line-end characters after the final line, so we scoop the remainder up and carry on.

```
4619 ; Store the paragraph and metadata.
4620 P$(%i)=R$
4630 L(%i)=row length
4640 Character Count+=row length
4650 pos+=row length+ LEN B$
4660 Last Paragraph=%i
4670 IF % NOT (i MOD t) THEN BANK ProcArea PROC Progress(%i/t)
4680 NEXT %i
```

The rest of the loop updates P$( ) and L( ) with the new paragraph text and length and bumps up two variables which keep track of the total amount read so far. **Character Count** is displayed in the top right corner of the screen while editing, and includes all visible characters including spaces, but not the line-end markers which are not explicitly stored. However when we update **pos**, the offset of the next line within the WorkArea, we also add the length of the line-end string B$, remembering that it could be either one or two characters long.

Since the file end is usually reached before the loop limit of **Max Paragraph Count**, we update **Last Paragraph** to refer to the total loaded so far after adding each line. The final step of the loop checks if we've read enough to justify updating the progress bar.

The cryptic expression **% NOT (i MOD t)** is true only if **%i** divides exactly into **%t** with no remainder. If so, we derive and display the new progress factor, from 1 to 10, by dividing the current paragraph number **%i** into **%t** and passing the result to PROC Progress( ).

Notice how we don't do this every paragraph, as the call and particularly the display update would slow things down without visible benefit. The integer modulo test is much faster and ensures the progress display is not updated unless we have something new to show.

There are three ways this PROC can end. Either it runs out of room to store paragraphs, finds one too long to store, or manages to stash them all away. The last three lines, including two ENDPROCs returning different values, and a couple of explanatory messages, sift out those cases.

```
4685 IF pos<>file size THEN BANK ProcArea PROC Message(
    "File truncated to "+ STR$ Last Paragraph+" paragraphs"):
    F$="Untitled.txt"
4690 ENDPROC =%1
4700 @Too long: BANK ProcArea PROC Message("Paragraph "+
    STR$ (%i)+" too long ("+ STR$ LEN R$+")"): ENDPROC =%0
```

Line 4685 warns if not all the file has been consumed. In this case the lines that could be loaded are complete and can be edited, but should not be saved over the original because that's likely to discard the extra paragraphs that were not loaded. To reduce that risk the stored file name in F$ is replaced with "Untitled.txt", which is interpreted by SAVE as an indication that a new file name is required, so it should work like SAVE AS.

As long as all the paragraphs fitted, even if there were some left over, the PROC returns 1 to the caller, signifying that there's valid text to edit. The **Character Count** and **Last Paragraph** global variables indicate how much of it has been loaded.

But if any paragraph exceeded the **Max LineLength** limit, 0 is returned after a suitable message. Notice how this message shows the actual length of the 'too long' line – that comes in handy if it only slightly exceeds the limit, as you could try loading that file again after editing the program to increase that. That might take a few goes, as it doesn't check if later lines are even longer, and might not work at all if any are too long for at least two to fit on the screen at once. But it's more helpful than a bald 'line too long' message.

The true file length

The next procedure is likely to be useful in other programs, especially if you tweak it to accept F$ as a parameter (in the brackets) and return **file Size** as a result, rather than use global variables. If so, you should also include **file Size** with the local variables on line 4815, and stick = **file Size** at the end of line 4890, so it can be transferred to a global variable such as **bytes** with a call like this: PROC Calculate File Size("Unknown.txt") TO bytes

In principle it's easy to find the number of bytes in a file – just open it and use DIM # to read the length. In practice there are two things that might go wrong – the OPEN could fail, or the actual length might not correspond to the number of data bytes, because of padding at the end or a header at the start, skipped over by LOAD, but still visible to OPEN.

Since the value F$ comes from the file browser, it's almost certain to exist, unless the user has unplugged their memory card in the intervening milliseconds! But unlike most BASICs, the Spectrum OPEN # statement fails if the chosen stream is already open. This can easily happen while testing, either because a later line gives an error or the program is interrupted before reaching the CLOSE # statement.

Rival BASICs close the old file before opening the new one, without an error. CLOSE # doesn't return an error, whatever the state of the stream. So this is why it's customary for Next and ZX BASIC programmers to include a dummy CLOSE # command before each OPEN #. It eases testing, while taking only four or five bytes and negligible time compared with OPEN #.

```
4800;-------------------------------------------------------
4801;-             Open file: Calculate file size          -
4802;-------------------------------------------------------
4810 DEFPROC Calculate File Size()
4815 LOCAL %i,X$
4820 CLOSE # %15: OPEN # %15,F$
4830 DIM #%15 TO file Size
```

If the file had been created from NextBASIC with OPEN and PRINT, that'd do the job. But in order to quickly adapt the Spectrum system to the CP/M based DOS they'd already written for CPC and PCW computers, Amstrad introduced a 128-byte header at the start of every file created by SAVE. This prefix contains the extra information which BASIC LOAD needs, such as the array DATA name or program VARS offset, which directories in operating systems like CP/M or Windows can't accommodate.

Only a handful of bytes are needed, but because of the way CP/M works in 128-byte sectors to suit its original 8-inch floppy disc format, Amstrad padded those out with a hundred or so dummy bytes and a tell-tale marker "PLUS3DOS" at their start. The following block of Editor BASIC checks if that is present and discounts the true file-size accordingly.

Under rare circumstances a genuinely headerless file might start with exactly those characters, all in capitals, and so be wrongly lopped. If this bites you, and you can afford the bytes, borrow the **checker** code from my **ReHead.bas** utility (at http://simon.mooli.org.uk/tt2020/, from my column in the 2021 Crash annual) and only lop off the front of the file if the checksum of the first 127 bytes matches the 128th character code in the file.

```
4840 IF file Size>127
4850   GO TO #%15,%0
4860   FOR %i=%1 TO %8
4870     X$=X$+ CHR$ NEXT #15
4875   NEXT %i
4880   IF X$="PLUS3DOS" THEN file Size-=128
4882 ENDIF
4885 CLOSE # %15: PRINT ;:; Reselect stream "s".
4890 ENDPROC
```

If there are at least 128 bytes in the file, so a header might be present, line 4850 winds the file pointer back to the start and the FOR loop collates the first eight bytes from it in X$, which is initially empty as it's local. As long as you don't start your plain-text files with exactly those eight characters, this fixes the incompatibility. If not, clear the configuration variable **Remove Header** to zero on line 330, so that every file saved by the Editor always has a header at the start, leaving no risk of your Next getting confused. The price of this is that editors on other systems will see 128 bytes of Amstrad junk at the start of the file. You can't please all the people all the time.

New File – starting from scratch

The NewFile( ) procedure is called when the editor starts up and also when the current document is erased.

```
4900;-----------------------------------------------------------
4901;-                          New file                        -
4902;-----------------------------------------------------------
4910 DEFPROC NewFile()
4920 IF Dirty THEN PROC SaveFile Query()
4930 F$="Untitled.txt"
4935 B$= CHR$ 13
4940 PROC Prepare Storage()
4961 Current Paragraph,Last Paragraph=%1
4962 Character Count=%0
4964 BANK ProcArea PROC Set Up View()
4970 ENDPROC
```

If any changes have been made to the file in memory since it was loaded, the variably Dirty will be non-zero. This prompts the Editor to invite you to save first. Otherwise all the assumptions about the current document are discarded: the filename defaults back to 'Untitled.txt', the line-end character to the Spectrum default of CR (ASCII code 13), and the arrays are cleared.

Line 4961 saves a couple of bytes by using the NextBASIC 2.08 extension to assign two variables to the same value in a single statement. This means that when the view is set up we are at paragraph 1, and that's the last paragraph, an empty one since the character-count is zeroed. Paragraphs are numbered from one, not zero, because 1 is the first subscript in ZX BASIC arrays, unlike NextBASIC's integer ones which are inconsistently, but 214 nanoseconds more quickly, indexed from 0 to 63.

Saving a text file

The two commands to save a file differ in that **Save** uses the current filename in F$, while **Save As** prompts the user for a suitable new filename. If no filename has been supplied, or you were perverse enough to deliberately call your document 'Untitled.txt', (perhaps it's a list of Parliamentarians excluding peers – in which case Commoners.txt could solve the problem) Save is treated as Save As. If you enter nothing, nothing gets saved.

```
5100;--------------------------------------------------------------
5101;-                          Save                              -
5102;--------------------------------------------------------------
5110 DEFPROC SaveFile(saveAs Flag)
5120 LOCAL pos,X$,t,i
5130 IF saveAs Flag OR F$="Untitled.txt" THEN BANK ProcArea
    PROC ClearMessage(): INPUT AT %22,%0;"Save as: "; LINE X$:
    BANK ProcArea PROC ClearMessage(): IF X$="" THEN ENDPROC
```

The local temporary variable X$ is used so the old filename is not lost till a new one is supplied. We then make sure that B$, the line break sequence, is valid, clear the **pos** and work out a temporary factor **t** for updating the progress bar in ten steps, proportional to the actual number of paragraphs.

```
5135 IF LEN X$ THEN F$=X$
5140 ; Store the file contents in memory.
5150 ; Ensure that we have a line break code.
5160 IF NOT LEN B$ THEN B$= CHR$ 13
5170 pos=%0:t= INT ((Last Paragraph+9)/10)+1
5175 PRINT AT %23,%0," ",
```

Line 5175 clears the menu line in a way that works regardless of the display and character width, using one space and two commas. The commas print enough spaces to get to the middle of the current line or the start of the next, depending on where the next character would otherwise appear. The space makes sure that this is always half a line after the current position. Without it, the second comma would be ignored as the print position is already at the start of the second column.

This behaviour is different from that in SAM BASIC, where extra columns are introduced so they're always 16 characters apart, in any screen mode. Next always has just two columns, even in Timex HiRes LAYER 1,2 and regardless of character-width, so a comma might move the cursor by 16 or 64 characters depending on the current layer and font.

While we could write the file a paragraph at a time with PRINT, which currently calls the file system once for every character output, that'd be much slower than doing it as a block with SAVE. Marcus opted to speed this up by again using the ProcArea as a staging-post, poking each paragraph there, adjusting pos, the offset in the bank, by only the number of characters actually used in the string array element in line 5200. The next line tacks on the line-end characters from B$, and 5220 updates the progress bar, much as we've already seen in the OpenFile( ) procedure.

```
5180 FOR i=%1 TO Last Paragraph
5190   BANK WorkArea POKE pos,P$(i, TO L(i))
5200   pos+= L(i)
5210   BANK Work Area POKE pos,B$:pos+= LEN B$
5220   IF NOT (i MOD t) THEN BANK ProcArea PROC Progress(1+
    INT (i/t))
5230 NEXT i
5235 IF NOT pos THEN pos= LEN B$: BANK WorkArea POKE %0,B$
```

Line 5235 makes sure that the file always contains at least one line-end. After this we have **pos** bytes in the WorkArea and can save them immediately if we're not expected to remove the DOS header. Otherwise we call a procedure in the ProcArea to strip it and save the remainder, as explained in the next chapter. Notice that **Remove Header** can be the name of a variable *and* a procedure, without confusing NextBASIC.

```
5240 IF Remove Header THEN BANK ProcArea PROC Remove
    Header(pos): ELSE SAVE F$ BANK WorkArea,%0,pos
5245 BANK ProcArea PROC ClearMessage()
5250 BANK ProcArea PROC Message("Saved.")
5260 Dirty=%0
5270 BANK ProcArea PROC Refresh Display()
5280 BANK ProcArea PROC Display Cursor()
5290 ENDPROC
```

Once the file is saved it only remains to tidy up the display and clear the **Dirty** flag, indicating that there are no changes still un-SAVEd. The last line of the file isn't strictly needed, but has become a convention among ZX BASIC enthusiasts. GO TO 9999 – the highest permitted line number – saves the current version of the program being worked on. In this case the line includes a file version number, updated when major changes are made, and starts with CLEAR so we don't also save the variables, including 20k of arrays, unnecessarily.

```
9999 CLEAR : SAVE "Editor17.bas"
```

Glossary of the main Editor variables

The following table of variable names used in the Editor was created by the **ListVars.bas** utility from my website: http://simon.mooli.org.uk/nextech

All these variables are global apart from **file Size**, used only while loading. To save memory, F$ is repurposed after the editor components have loaded.

The glossary is divided into five sections.

1. The **Initial Configuration** values can be tweaked to customise the Editor's display, file usage, and capacity.

2. The **Display Representation** group tracks what's shown on the screen.

3. The **Editor Internal State** variables record character and paragraph counts, line-ends, the file name, cut and paste buffer and of course the text being entered and edited.

4. The **Memory Banks** variables are set when the program asks NextZXOS for three 16k banks.

5. The last group, **System Variable mnemonics,** names structures described in Chapters 24 and Chapter 25 of the Next User Manual.

Variable name	Default	Purpose
Max Number Of Paragraphs	100	Document new-line character limit
Max Line Length	256	Limits the length of each paragraph
%W	64	Display line width in characters
Remove Header	1	Set to 0 to output PLUS3DOS headers
F$	empty	Path to Editor component files
Display representation		
Cursor Row	1	Cursor line number, 1 to 20
Cursor Col	0	Cursor column, 0 to %W-1
First Visible Paragraph	1	Top paragraph shown on screen
Last Visible Paragraph	1	Bottom paragraph shown on screen
Font Width	6	Pixel width of editor characters
R( )	1..20	First screen row of visible paragraphs
N( )	1..4	Count of rows in redrawn paragraphs
%F	15360	Previous character-set address

Editor Internal State		
Last Key Pressed	0	Latest key code, 0 if no key pressed
P$(,)	blank space	2D character array of paragraph text
L( )	array of 0s	Length of paragraphs in characters
F$	Untitled.txt	Name of the file being edited
B$	CHR$ 10	Line terminating sequence e.g. CR LF
C$	empty	Paragraph cut/paste buffer
Cut Size	0	How many characters cut for pasting
Dirty	0	Set to 1 if the file has been changed
PosIn Current Paragraph	1	Character index within the paragraph
Current Paragraph	1	The paragraph the cursor is shown in
Last Paragraph	1	The final paragraph index used in P$
Character Count	0	File byte count without line-ends
Old Count	0	Character Count last displayed
file Size	0	Number of valid bytes in the text file
%C	0	Previous CPU setting for RUN AT, 0..3
Memory Banks		
ProcArea	107	Number of the bank of procedures
WorkArea	106	Bank used while loading and saving
SpriteArea	105	Bank for the mouse pointer sprite
System variable mnemonic	Address	Meaning of contents
LASTK	23560	ASCII code of latest keypress, or 0
CHARS	23606	CHR$ 0 font base (256 before space)
MODE	23617	1 in EXTEND input mode, 2 for GRAPHICS characters, otherwise 0
RAMTOP	23730	Address of last byte of BASIC RAM

Table 4 – Glossary of editor variables

Chapter 8, Banked Editor Procedures

This chapter explores the inner workings of the Editor, explaining all 24 NextBASIC procedures in the **EditorProcs.bnk** file. With one exception, all the PROC calls within this file are to other procedures inside it. The exception is in PROC Quit( ), which may call PROC SaveFile Query( ) in the main program, if the Dirty flag is set when the user shuts down the Editor.

Over the next few pages we'll see how to set up, shut down and use the Next mouse input driver for menu and cursor-placement, select, show and remove fonts customised for varying display resolutions. We'll strip PLUS3DOS headers so files written with SAVE can be read easily on other systems, format numbers neatly, insert or delete string array elements and show other general-purpose Next programming techniques.

Besides all that, the main purpose of these procedures is to maintain two representations of the text being edited, one in the pair of arrays P$( ) and L() and the other on-screen. These change as the Editor runs, most often when the main loop updates **Last Key Pressed** and calls procedures in this bank to move the cursor, insert and delete characters and paragraphs, scroll the screen or update the menu, messages or progress bar.

The Glossary of editor variable in Table 4 divides the variables associated with editing into two groups. The **Display Representation** group keeps track of the cursor and the characters displayed on the screen. The **Editor Internal State** variables look after the entire document, including the character and paragraph counts, cut and paste buffer and of course the text being entered and edited.

Initialisation helpers

```
   1 ; A text editor for the ZX Spectrum Next, based on
   2 ; https://github.com/MagnusKrook/ZXNext-Editor
   3 ; Version 1.8 for NextBASIC 2.08+ in 64/73/85/102 columns
1600 ;-----------------------------------------------------
1610 ;-     Load font to RAMTOP and set character size       -
1620 ;-----------------------------------------------------
1630 DEFPROC Init Display()
1640 LAYER CLEAR : LAYER %1,%2
1650 Font Width= INT ((%192-w)/17+.5):; Map from line width
   in %W, 64->8, 73->7, 85->6, 102->5.
1670 CHARS=%23606:%F= DPEEK CHARS:RAMTOP=%23730
```

PROC Init Display( ) is called early in the Editor's initialisation. Before selecting a LAYER 1,2 Timex HiRes display, line 1640 restores the internal state of the display system to the default with LAYER CLEAR. This is important because otherwise the order, offsets and margins of the display might still use values from whatever program ran before.

Line 1650 uses ad-hoc arithmetic to infer **Font Width**, the width in pixels of each character, from the number of characters per line previously stashed in %W. The magic numbers 192, 17 and 0.5 were chosen by experiment to give the required answers in all four cases. The next line names two system variable addresses, **RAMTOP** and **CHARS**, which will be used to prepare and remove the custom character-set. The address of the font previously used is stashed away in **%F**, and gets restored when the user quits the Editor.

The following block, from line 1680 to 1730, tries to load the custom font into memory previously reserved with CLEAR. It uses the NextBASIC 2.08 multi-line IF extension to skip the font setup completely, unless there's at least enough RAM for the font to be loaded. 768 bytes are required, for 96 eight-byte character patterns corresponding to ASCII codes 32 to 127.

It's always possible that the font file will fail to load, perhaps because it's not in the expected place, or the SD card has been removed without remounting it, so lines 1690 and 1720 wrap up the font initialisation in an ON ERROR block. If anything goes wrong between those lines, the Editor continues to run, using the system default font.

```
1680 IF DPEEK RAMTOP<(65536-768)
1690    ON ERROR GO TO @NoFont:; Custom fonts are optional.
1700    LOAD F$+(%w>64)?("BOLDFONT","Sam6FONT") CODE 1+
    DPEEK RAMTOP
1710    DPOKE CHARS, DPEEK RAMTOP-255
1720    @NoFont: ON ERROR
1730 ENDIF
```

Line 1700 attempts to load a suitable font file to the address immediately above RAMTOP. The **1+** is vital because DPEEK RAMTOP returns the last byte which BASIC will try to use, rather than the first free address which was passed to CLEAR. The most suitable filename is selected by the rather weird expression (%W>64)?("BOLDFONT","Sam6FONT") which uses an extension to NextBASIC 2.08 that resembles the 'conditional expression' syntax of the C programming language from 1978.

Language lawyers refer to the **?** sandwiched between the brackets as the 'ternary operator', perhaps because they like languages so much that a bit of Latin is irresistible! Just as NOT is a 'unary' operator, taking only one parameter, most of the others in BASIC like /, *, >= and **OR** are termed 'binary' (because they must sit between the two values they operate upon, not because they necessarily work on single bits). In both languages + and – can be either unary or binary, as in **+3 + -1 - 2**.

While the C idiom is limited to three values – the first one selecting between two alternatives, separated with a colon which would really confuse BASIC – the Next remix can select any one from an arbitrary number of subsequent expressions, depending on the value before the question mark. If this is zero the first expression is evaluated, and in this case we get the string "BOLDFONT".

If %W>64 is true, indicating that the characters would be too narrow for that font, the selection value is one (Sinclair's Boolean convention meaning true) so we get "Sam6FONT" which uses a 5x7 pixel matrix, so it's still readable when there are more than 64 characters on a line. You could extend this line to support more fonts by elaborating the first expression, e.g. (%W>64+(W=102)) would return 2 just for the 5-pixel width, selecting a third string (e.g. **,"ThinFont"**) which could be added within the second pair of brackets, and so on.

I designed the Sam6 font in 1988 for MGT, the makers of the Sam Coupé computer, so that Bruce Gordon's Timex-like 512x192 pixel four-colour MODE 3 display would be capable of supporting the 80-column 24-line display then standard for CP/M business systems. It ended up, ingeniously compressed, in the SAM firmware.

I included additional accented characters, chosen to match European variants in the then-commonplace Epson printer set, but those were squeezed out of the ROM and shipped as a CODE file on the tape or floppy disc bundled with Bo Jangeborg's *Sam Flash* graphics package. They're not included here because the Next team chose not to implement this experiment in European localisation, leaving those codes for block graphics which were an optional compatibility feature on the Coupé.

The last line of the procedure tells NextBASIC about the character set, using the previously calculated Font Width and a couple of Next-specific control codes. CHR$ 31 causes the default NextZXOS font to be replaced with the one defined by the CHARS system variable. This is not needed in ZX BASIC but vital now because NextBASIC supports different font patterns for widths from three to eight pixels per character, storing them in hidden memory within BANK 8. The next character-code picks one of those sizes for subsequent output. PRINT CHR$ 30 is also followed by a width-code, and changes the pixel interval between successive characters output to the screen to match.

```
1740 ; Select Timex HiRes mode and 64, 73, 85 or 102 columns.
1750 PRINT CHR$ 30; CHR$ Font Width; CHR$ 31;
    CHR$ Font Width;: INK %0: CLS
1760 ENDPROC
```

PROC Init Mouse( ) loads the mouse driver and pointer image, both created by Gilsoft *Quill* maestro Tim Gilberts for the NextZXOS distro. This wastes 16,128 bytes at the end of that bank as the mouse pointer only takes up 256, but the SPRITE BANK command expects an entire 16k bank. You can use the rest for other sprites, or any other data you choose to BANK POKE and PEEK from there. Once again, the loading is error-trapped – in this case, if the driver is not found or can't be installed the Editor still runs but unless the driver was previously loaded you must use keys rather than the mouse to control it.

SPRITE PRINT turns the pointer on and off and SPRITE BORDER allows it free roam across the screen. The DRIVER 126, 2 command determines which pointer to use, defaulting to sprite 0, pattern 0. By adding parameters you could use a different BASIC sprite number, or add a 'busy' pointer as pattern 1, like an hourglass or the 'busy bee' image in Digital Research's GEM. The final DRIVER line disables mouse acceleration, the option to make fast movements pan the pointer further.

```
1770;-----------------------------------------------------
1780;-                Initialise mouse pointer           -
1790;-----------------------------------------------------
1800 REM Mouse input uses the standard driver and a new
   pointer.
1810 DEFPROC Init Mouse()
1820 SPRITE PRINT %0
1830 ON ERROR GO TO @Eeek:; Skip if driver is already
   installed.
1840 .Install /nextzxos/mouse.drv
1850 @Eeek: ON ERROR ENDPROC :;Skip pointer setup if it fails.
1860 LOAD F$+"Pointer.spr" BANK SpriteArea
1870 SPRITE BANK SpriteArea: SPRITE PRINT %1: SPRITE BORDER %1
1880 DRIVER %126,%2:; Use sprite 0 from first sprite bank.
1890 DRIVER %126,%6,%255:; No horizontal acceleration.
1900 ENDPROC
```

The Editor only needs three of the six mouse driver commands. DRIVER %126,4 requests a character- rather than a sprite-based cursor, and is not used by the Editor. DRIVER %126,3 and DRIVER %126,5 can temporarily disable either type of cursor. While not needed here, those options are documented in the MOUSEreadme.txt file in the **docs/extra-hw/mouse** folder of every NextZXOS distribution.

Refreshing views

PROC Refresh Display( ) clears the screen and redraws the entire editor display, including the heading and menu, wrapped around the document text. The top left corner of the screen shows the current document file name, in double-width reverse video; CHR$ 28 turns on or off double-width output, depending on whether it's followed by CHR$ 1 or CHR$ 0, like CHR$ 20 and CHR$ 21 for INVERSE and OVER. The character count appears at the end of that line.

```
2000;-----------------------------------------------------
2001;-                    Refresh display                -
2002;-----------------------------------------------------
2010 DEFPROC Refresh Display()
2020 LOCAL row=%1,%i=First Visible Paragraph
2030 ; Print the file name double-width in the top left corner.
2040 CLS
2050 PRINT AT %0,%0; INVERSE %1;" "; CHR$ 28; CHR$ 1;F$;
   CHR$ 28; CHR$ 0;" ";
2060 PROC Display Character Count()
2070 ; This loop prints paragraphs to fill rows 1..20. The
2071 ; strings are stored in the P$-array, which has a
```

```
2073 ; preset Max LineLength in bytes; the L-array contains the
2075 ; actual length of each paragraph. After each paragraph
2076 ; has been printed the row at which it starts is stored in
2077 ; the R-array and the number of screen lines it takes up
2078 ; is stored in the N-array. This information is used later
2079 ; to calculate where in a paragraph the cursor is located.
```

The repeat loop between lines 2090 and 2150 scans through the visible paragraphs to find twenty consecutive lines to display in the middle part of the screen. It uses the text in P$( ) and the corresponding paragraph lengths in L( ) to populate two other arrays, R( ) and N( ), with the first screen row where the paragraph starts and the number of lines it needs, respectively.

Even an empty paragraph takes up one line, while longer ones need an extra line for every %W (line width) characters they contain, as calculated on line 2120. Local variable **%i** counts paragraphs from the first one visible till the screen is full, and **row** counts screen lines.

```
2090 REPEAT : WHILE (%i)<=Last Paragraph
2100   PRINT AT row,%0;P$(%i)( TO L(%i));
2110   R(%i)=row
2120   IF NOT L(%i) THEN N(%i)=%1: ELSE N(%i)=
     INT (1+(L(%i)-1)/(%w))
2130   row+=N(%i)
2140   %i+=%1
2150 REPEAT UNTIL row>20
2155 Last Visible Paragraph=%i-1
2160 PROC Display Menu()
2170 ENDPROC
```

Once past row 20 we stop, taking note of the **Last Visible Paragraph** for later updates, finishing off by displaying the menu at the bottom.

Cursor control

The MoveCursor( ) procedure is usually called from line 640 of the main program, with **Last Key Pressed** set to a cursor direction code, 8, 9, 10 or 11 for left, right, down and up respectively.

There are two other places MoveCursor( ) can be called from within EditorProcs, at the end of the InsertChar( ) and DeleteChar( ) procedures, coming up soon. As well as editing the text those calls fake the pressing of a horizontal arrow key so that the cursor moves in sympathy with the editing operation. An attempt to move left or right from the start or end of a line is translated within this procedure into a vertical cursor movement, so the horizontal direction codes are handled first.

```
2200;-----------------------------------------------------
2201;-                      Move cursor                  -
2202;-----------------------------------------------------
2210 DEFPROC MoveCursor()
2220 ; Move the cursor to the right, or to the beginning of the
2225 ; next row when the end of a row has been reached.
2230 IF Last Key Pressed=9
```

```
2235   IF PosIn Current Paragraph>L(Current Paragraph) THEN
PROC Display Cursor(): ENDPROC
2237   PosIn Current Paragraph+=%1
2250   IF Cursor Col=(%w-1) THEN Last Key Pressed=%10:Cursor
    Col=%0: ELSE Cursor Col+=%1
```

Horizontal cursor movement

Lines 2230 to 2250 cope with movement of the cursor along the line to the right. Usually this is quickly and simply handled by line 2237, which advances the cursor and the edit position along the current line. But first, line 2335 makes sure that's safe by checking that we're not already past the end of the line, in which case we just redraw the cursor and return.

Another complication comes if we're currently at the end of a row, when **Cursor Col** would equal **%W-1**, allowing for columns being counted from 0 by PRINT AT. We can't move right if we're already at the end, so line 2250 converts that movement into a downward shift to the first column of the next screen row.

Cursor movement to the left works similarly, but the logic is a little simpler; it's easier to trap an attempt to move back from the top of the document than one heading past the end:

```
2260 ELSE IF Last Key Pressed=8
2265   IF NOT Cursor Col THEN IF NOT (Current Paragraph=1 AND
    Cursor Row=R(Current Paragraph)) THEN Cursor Col=%w:Last
    Key Pressed=%11
2270   IF Cursor Col THEN Cursor Col-=%1
2272 ENDIF
```

The ELSE IF at line 2260 means that this code for movement to the left is ignored, without even checking **Last Key Pressed**, if the right-arrow code was detected. Otherwise this test sifts out CHR$ 8, the ASCII backspace and Sinclair cursor-left code, and adjusts Cursor Col suitably.

Line 2265 starts by checking if the cursor is in column 0; only then, in the unusual case when **NOT Cursor Col** returns true, does it attempt a couple more checks, making sure that we're neither in the first paragraph nor at the beginning of the first paragraph. The twin IFs and negative logic are efficient, but cryptic at first glance. A slower but perhaps clearer way to express the same condition would be:

```
IF Cursor Col=0 AND (Current Paragraph<>1 OR
        Cursor Row<>R(Current Paragraph)) THEN …
```

The key to understanding this is that R(Current Paragraph) is the row on which the current paragraph starts; if the paragraph extends beyond one line the cursor will be on a later row and it's safe to move it up, momentarily positioning the cursor at the end of the line with **Cursor Col=%w** and translating the move left into a cursor-up movement by **Last Key Pressed=%11**, which will be acted upon later in the procedure.

The advantage of using the IF NOT... THEN IF NOT... approach is that there's no need to consider either Current Paragraph or Cursor Row unless the cursor is in the first column, which is rarely the case. If we'd used AND and OR all three comparisons would have to be worked out every time.

Line 2270 handles the common and simple case of moving the cursor left. The IF test checks there's at least one column to move it into, otherwise the cursor stays at column zero.

Vertical Cursor movement

Now we must consider the case of vertical motion, either because the up or down arrow key was pressed or the equivalent motion was caused by moving the cursor across the boundary between rows.

```
2275 ; Move the cursor down and scroll the text if needed, but
2276 ; first check that we don't move down past the last row.
2277 ; An exception is when the last row is completely filled.
2278 ; In that case the cursor must be allowed to move down
2279 ; one row to column 0.
2281 IF Last Key Pressed=10
2283   IF Current Paragraph=Last Paragraph THEN IF Cursor
    Row>=R(Last Paragraph)+N(Last Paragraph)-1 THEN IF L(Last
    Paragraph)-(%w)<PosIn Current Paragraph THEN PROC Display
    Cursor(): ENDPROC
2290   Cursor Row+=%1: IF Cursor Row>20 THEN Cursor Row=%20:
PROC Scroll(%1)
2295 ENDIF
```

The Line Feed code 10 signifies a downward movement. Line 2283 simply redraws the cursor and returns if the move would take us past the end of the last paragraph. Once again, notice that IF THEN IF means that the entire line is quickly skipped unless we happen to be at the very last paragraph of the document. %W is in brackets so the integer variable can be used in the context of the floating-point arrays. If the cursor has nowhere to go, we redraw it and return. Line 2290 tries to increase the cursor row by one; if that takes it past the last row available for editing, row 20, we keep the cursor there and scroll the document down to show the next paragraph.

Code 11, ASCII's vertical tab and Sinclair's cursor-up code, works similarly but in the opposite direction. Line 2305 makes sure we don't try to move up if we're already in the first paragraph and the cursor's on the first row of the editing area. Otherwise we try to move the cursor up; if it reaches row 0, reserved for the filename and character count, we put it back on row 1 and scroll the document up around it.

```
2302 ELSE IF Last Key Pressed=11
2305  IF Current Paragraph=1 THEN IF Cursor Row=1 THEN PROC
    Display Cursor(): ENDPROC
2310   Cursor Row-=%1: IF NOT Cursor Row THEN Cursor Row=%1:
    PROC Scroll(-1)
2320 ENDIF
```

All that remains is for MoveCursor( ) to is correctly record the current paragraph number , adjust **PosIn Current Paragraph** and maybe tweak the cursor column before displaying it in its new position:

```
2330 ; Adjust the cursor position if it is placed at a point
2340 ; where there is no text, by moving it to the left until
2350 ; the last character on the row is found.
2400 PROC Calculate Cursor Position InText()
2410 PROC Display Cursor()
2440 ENDPROC
```

You may be relieved or disappointed to hear that the next procedure is only one line long. The name Display Cursor( ) is potentially misleading, as it uses OVER 1 printing, which has the effect of cancelling out the first PRINT in a position if you then PRINT the same character the same way over the top of it. This means line 2475 can draw a cursor (reversing the ink and paper) over any character, *or* erase one already there. The procedure could equally well have been called Draw Cursor( ) or Undraw Cursor( ) as it does both jobs.

Amazingly a US Corporation managed to patent this mathematically-obvious technique in 1978, back when the US Patent Office had a deliberate policy of not hiring any computer scientists to check applications. Playing it safe, Apple and IBM paid millions of dollars for a licence to display cursors that way, even though programs had been using it at least five years before the patent was filed. It lapsed in 2007; I think we're safe.

Cursor placement

```
2450;-----------------------------------------------------
2451;-                      Display cursor               -
2452;-----------------------------------------------------
2460 DEFPROC Display Cursor()
2475 PRINT AT Cursor Row,Cursor Col; OVER %1; CHR$ 143;
2480 ENDPROC
```

The short PROC Display Cursor( ) could have been copied out in all 19 places where it's called, though that would make the Editor a bit longer and less readable. Early on I tried both, and have opted for now to leave the PROC calls in, since they're concise and relatively clear. The main place they slowed things down was in movements left and right inside a line, when the cursor needs to be undrawn in one place and then immediately redrawn alongside. My later optimisation of lines 610 and 620 in the main loop sped this up greatly by overprinting the cursor twice from a single statement, without calling PROC Display Cursor( ) even once.

The next procedure is one of the most time-consuming yet vital in the entire Editor. It scans through all the paragraphs on the display, using the current **Cursor Row** value to work out which paragraph contains the cursor and updating **Current Paragraph** and **PosIn Current Paragraph** to suit:

```
2600;-------------------------------------------------------
2601;-           Calculate cursor position in text          -
2602;-------------------------------------------------------
2610 DEFPROC Calculate Cursor Position InText()
2620 LOCAL %p=First Visible Paragraph-1
2630 ; Calculate which paragraph the cursor is positioned in
2640 ; by looping through the visible paragraphs, and match
2650 ; the cursor row and column with the paragraph metadata.
2670 REPEAT
2680   %p+=%1
2690 REPEAT UNTIL (%p)=Last Paragraph OR (Cursor Row>=R(%p)
   AND Cursor Row<R(%p)+N(%p))
2700 Current Paragraph=%p
2720 PosIn Current Paragraph=(Cursor Row-R(%p))*(%w)+
   Cursor Col+1
2730 ; If the cursor is beyond the end of a paragraph, move it
back.
2740 IF PosIn Current Paragraph>L(%p)+1 THEN PosIn Current
   Paragraph=L(%p)+1:Cursor Col=L(%p) MOD (%w)
2760 ENDPROC
```

The cursor position is determined by scanning the R() and L() arrays that hold the first row and number of screen lines for each paragraph, starting from the First Visible Paragraph. In line 2720 the expression **(Cursor Row-R(%p))*(%w)** works out the number of characters, if any, in rows of the current paragraph before the cursor, and adding **Cursor Col+1** gets us the position of the cursor in the string, indexed from one.

You may wish the top left character coordinate was numbered (1,1) rather than (0,0) but it's too late to change that now. In fact Sinclair did, very briefly, try having AT coordinates in X, Y order in QL SuperBASIC, PRINT like ZX PLOT and DRAW commands, but they swapped it back to match AT in ZX BASIC after two very buggy QL ROM releases.

This meant that the first bundled QL software from Psion included something like IF VER$="FB" OR VER$="PM" THEN AT X,Y: ELSE AT Y,X. It'd be nice to have a function like VER$ in NextBASIC, to check the exact version running a program, but even nicer not to need it! Page 194 has a workaround.

There are two complications of working out the cursor position this way: at the end of the file the display may not be full, as it could have been fast-scrolled so only the upper part of the screen contains text when the last paragraph is reached. Also, it's vital not to scan past the Last Paragraph of the document, or leave the cursor floating in the blank space past the end. If so, line 2740 repositions the cursor at the end of the paragraph.

Character insertion

PROC Insert Char() is typically the most-used procedure, as it's called every time a character is added to the document, and there are never more deletions than insertions!

```
2800;-----------------------------------------------------
2801;-                    Insert character                -
2802;-----------------------------------------------------
2810 DEFPROC Insert Char()
2830 IF L(Current Paragraph)>=Max LineLength THEN PROC
   Message("Paragraph full"): ENDPROC
2840 ; Insert the character.
2850 P$(Current Paragraph,PosIn Current Paragraph TO )= CHR$
   (Last Key Pressed)+P$(Current Paragraph,PosIn Current
   Paragraph TO L(Current Paragraph))
2860 L(Current Paragraph)+=%1:Character Count+=%1
```

After checking that there's room, returning with a **Paragraph full** message otherwise, line 2850 inserts the new character into P$(Current Paragraph) and moves everything after the current position one character along to make room. Notice how the assignment to a slice of the array leaves earlier parts of the line in P$( ) unchanged; few other BASICs allow this optimisation. Line 2860 bumps up the document character-count and current paragraph length, then we update the display, which is much the slowest aspect of text entry.

If the current line has overflowed, a full display refresh is needed to make room for a fresh line. This is detected by checking if the remainder of the line length divided by the screen width shows we are one character over. Otherwise we take the ELSE branch on line 2880 and re-draw the entire paragraph in place, soaking up some of the empty space there must be at the bottom of the text area.

```
2870 ; Check if the paragraph expands to a new line. If so,
refresh the display.
2880 IF L(Current Paragraph) MOD (%w)=1 THEN PROC Refresh
   Display(): ELSE PRINT AT R(Current Paragraph),%0;P$(Current
   Paragraph, TO L(Current Paragraph))
2900 ; Move the cursor to the right.
2910 Last Key Pressed=%9: PROC MoveCursor()
2920 Dirty=%1
2930 ENDPROC
```

Remember how horizontal cursor movements may be translated into vertical ones when crossing the start of a line? Line 2910 assumes that moving the cursor rightwards (code 9, ASCII tab and Sinclair's right arrow) will accommodate the insertion. Elegantly, as we've just seen, PROC MoveCursor( ) checks this and, if necessary, adds the required vertical move, possibly involving scrolling. Complicated logic is required to keep text and display in step, managing the risks of running past the end or start of the paragraph, document or screen, so it pays not to have to work it out more than once!

Line 2920 makes sure the **Dirty** flag is set, since the text has been changed by the insertion. This ensures the user will get prompted to Save first, if they Quit or try to Load another document in the meantime.

Deleting characters

```
3000;-----------------------------------------------------
3001;-                  Handle Delete key                -
3002;-----------------------------------------------------
3010 DEFPROC Handle Delete Key()
3020 IF NOT Cursor Col AND Current Paragraph>1 AND PosIn
    Current Paragraph=1 THEN PROC MergeParagraphs(): ELSE IF
    PosIn Current Paragraph>1 THEN PROC Delete Char()
3030 ENDPROC
```

When the user presses DELETE two things might happen, depending on where the cursor is in the paragraph. If it's right at the start, we must merge this paragraph with the previous one, if any. Otherwise PROC Delete Char() removes a character from P$( ) and the screen. That procedure comes next.

```
3050;-----------------------------------------------------
3051;-                  Delete character                 -
3052;-----------------------------------------------------
3060 DEFPROC Delete Char()
3090 ; Delete the character to the left of the cursor.
3100 P$(Current Paragraph,PosIn Current Paragraph-1 TO
    )=P$(Current Paragraph,PosIn Current Paragraph TO L(Current
    Paragraph)):L(Current Paragraph)-=%1
3110 ; If the paragraph now is a row shorter, refresh the
    display, otherwise just print the new paragraph content.
3120 IF L(Current Paragraph) MOD (%w)=(%w-1) THEN PROC Refresh
    Display(): ELSE PRINT AT R(Current Paragraph),%0;P$(Current
    Paragraph, TO L(Current Paragraph));" ";
3150 Last Key Pressed=%8: PROC MoveCursor()
3160 Character Count-=%1
3170 Dirty=%1
3180 ENDPROC
```

Line 3100 updates P$(Current Paragraph) by moving the characters beyond the cursor back one place, effectively deleting the character there, and reducing the number of characters, L(Current Paragraph), by one. Apart from the direction of movement, the rest of the procedure resembles PROC Insert Char( ). Most of the time all we need to do is reprint the edited paragraph in place, adding one blank space to shorten it – otherwise we'd end up showing two copies of its final character.

But if the deletion has made the paragraph one screen row shorter, a complete display refresh is needed, triggered by the test on line 3120. Either way we finish by moving the cursor left, reducing the character count by one, and setting the **Dirty** flag because there is now an un-saved change.

Juggling paragraphs

The next three procedures work on paragraphs rather than individual characters. There are routines to delete and insert paragraphs, used by cut and paste as well as character operations. Another merges a pair of adjacent paragraphs. This runs when the delete key is pressed while the cursor is at the start of a paragraph which you want to join on to the preceding one:

```
3200;-----------------------------------------------------------
3201;-                    Merge paragraphs                      -
3202;-----------------------------------------------------------
3203 ; This procedure is called when <DELETE> is pressed at
3204 ; column 0. It merges the current and previous paragraphs.
3210 DEFPROC MergeParagraphs()
3220 IF L(Current Paragraph)+L(Current Paragraph-1)>Max
    LineLength THEN PROC Message("Maximum paragraph length
    would be exceeded by "+ STR$ (L(Current Paragraph)
    +L(Current Paragraph-1)-Max LineLength)): ENDPROC
```

The first thing to check is that the result will fit into a single paragraph after merging. Line 3220 adds up the length of the current and previous paragraphs and returns without doing anything except displaying a message if the combined paragraph would be too long. Otherwise we check if the current paragraph is empty, as would be the case when deleting a blank line. In that case the paragraph length in L( ) is zero, which IF interprets as FALSE, and the ELSE path of the following multi-line conditional block is taken, calling the Delete Paragraph procedure with a zero flag indicating that there's no need to update the cursor position. **Character Count** never changes when paragraphs are merged, as line-end characters are not counted.

If there are characters to merge, they all end up in the previous paragraph (Current Paragraph - 1) as Delete Paragraph will remove the current one. Line 3240 works out the first empty space in the previous paragraph and puts the entire contents of the current one there. Notice that the first part of the current paragraph is not touched by line 3245.

This approach only works in BASICs that support preset string lengths and appending by slicing. The obvious alternative approach, with variable-length array elements, would be to use P$(Current Paragraph-1)=P$(Current Paragraph-1)+P$(Current Paragraph) but on average that copies four times as many bytes as line 3240 does. If neither string was dimensioned we could use NextBASIC 2.08's string concatenation operator +=, but P$(Current Paragraph-1)+=P$(Current Paragraph) has no effect, since the dimensioned array element is already padded out to full length with spaces at the end. However the last statement on line 3245 does use that operator, in a numeric context, to add up the two paragraph lengths:

```
3230 Cursor Col=L(Current Paragraph-1) MOD (%w)
3240 Cursor Row-=1+ INT ((PosIn Current Paragraph-1)/(%w)):
    IF Cursor Row<1 THEN Cursor Row=%1: PROC Scroll(-1)
3245 IF L(Current Paragraph) THEN p$(Current Paragraph-
    1,L(Current Paragraph-1)+1 TO )=p$(Current Paragraph, TO
    L(Current Paragraph)):L(Current Paragraph-1)+=L(Current
    Paragraph)
3250 PROC Delete Paragraph()
3260 ENDPROC
```

PROC Delete Paragraph( ) comes next. The loop to delete the current paragraph, between lines 3270 and 3320, simply copies each paragraph record up into the immediately previous array entry. There's no need to touch the characters left in P$(Last Paragraph) because they've been copied up to the previous paragraph, and Last Paragraph will soon be adjusted to hide them.

```
3264;--------------------------------------------------------
3265;-                   Delete paragraph                    -
3266;--------------------------------------------------------
3267 ; Move up all the paragraphs after the current paragraph.
3268 DEFPROC Delete Paragraph()
3270 FOR %i=Current Paragraph+1 TO Last Paragraph
3280   L(%i-1)=L(%i)
3290   P$(%i-1)=P$(%i, TO L(%i))
3320 NEXT %i
3330 IF Last Paragraph>1 THEN Last Paragraph-=%1: ELSE L(Last
    Paragraph)=%0
```

Line 3330 reduces the paragraph count by one as long as it remains at least one: the smallest document is a single empty paragraph. If so, the ELSE part clears the length of the old Last Paragraph. All that remains is to tidy up the display, with three procedure calls, and to set the **Dirty** flag:

```
3340 PROC Refresh Display()
3350 PROC Calculate Cursor Position InText()
3370 PROC Display Cursor()
3380 Dirty=%1
3390 ENDPROC
```

The next procedure deals with the opposite action, inserting rather than deleting a paragraph. Apart from the cursor positioning and direction of paragraph movement, it starts and ends very similarly to Delete Paragraph().

```
3400;--------------------------------------------------------
3401;-                   Insert paragraph                    -
3402;--------------------------------------------------------
3410 ; This procedure is called when the user hits <ENTER>, to
3420 ; split the paragraph at the cursor into two paragraphs,
3425 ; or when split is zero to make room to paste a paragraph.
3430 DEFPROC Insert Paragraph(split)
3440 ; Check that the maximum number of paragraphs is not
3450 ; exceeded.
3460 IF Last Paragraph>=Max Number Of Paragraphs THEN PROC
    Message("Too many paragraphs"): ENDPROC
3470 ; Move the cursor to the first column and down one row.
3490 IF NOT (Cursor Col=0 AND PosIn Current Paragraph<>1) THEN
    Cursor Row+=1: IF Cursor Row>20 THEN Cursor Row=%20: PROC
    Scroll(%1)
3495 Cursor Col=%0
3500 ; Move all paragraphs below the cursor down.
3520 FOR %i=Last Paragraph TO Current Paragraph STEP -1
3530   P$(%i+1)=P$(%i, TO L(%i))
3540   L(%i+1)=L(%i)
3550 NEXT %i
3551 Last Paragraph+=%1
3552 Dirty=%1
```

Moving versus copying or clearing

Notice that the STEP in line 3520 is negative, and we start copying down from the last paragraph, moving upwards to earlier array elements till we get to the one after the current paragraph. This is because we don't want to change the current paragraph and if we copied the other way we'd end up with copies of it all the way to the end of the document, rather than the required upwards move. Let's quickly see how fast the Z80 could do it.

```
CLEAR8K:
 LD B,0
 LD D,B
 LD E,B
 LD
(STK+1),SP
 DI
 LD
SP,END+1
LOOP:
 PUSH DE
 PUSH DE
 PUSH DE
 PUSH DE
 PUSH DE
 PUSH DE
 PUSH DE
 PUSH DE
 PUSH DE
 PUSH DE
 PUSH DE
 PUSH DE
 PUSH DE
 PUSH DE
 PUSH DE
 PUSH DE
 DJNZ LOOP
STK:
 LD SP,0
 EI
 RET
```

Z80 programmers will be familiar with this requirement, where LDDR (LoaD, Decrement and Repeat) must be used to move bytes within a block upwards from the end, and LDIR (LoaD, Increment and Repeat) for moves in the other direction. You can use either as long as the blocks don't overlap, but if they do the direction is crucial. However, the incrementing LDIR is sometimes deliberately used to clear memory, as if the destination for copying is one byte after the source you'll end up with BC copies of the first byte following it. For example, you could put the value you want to store in A, the number of bytes in BC and the first address in HL then CALL CLEARMEM, which uses DE internally.

```
CLEARMEM:
 LD (HL),A
 DEC BC
 LD  D,H
 LD  E,L
 INC DE
 LDIR
 RET
```

```
CLEARMEM2:
 LD E,A
LOOP:
 LD (HL),E
 INC HL
 DEC BC
 LD  A,B
 OR  C
 JR  NZ,LOOP
 RET
```

That eight-byte program reads more than it needs to, but it's still faster than CLEARMEM2, an equivalent-sized loop avoiding the complex LDIR instruction. This loop takes 38 cycles per byte whereas LDIR needs only 21, despite the extra work it does. The saving comes from the reduced overhead of instruction decoding while the specialised instruction loops internally.

Zilog's LDIR is a two-byte single-instruction equivalent of the 8080-compatible SIMLDIR, which takes 32 cycles in all but the last step; it needs eight more bytes of code, when not implemented in hardware, and one extra register, presumed to be A in the example alongside.

```
SIMLDIR:
 LD A,(HL)
 LD (DE),A
 INC HL
 INC DE
 DEC BC
 LD A,B
 OR C
 JP NZ,SIMLDIR
```

In Zilog's repeating instructions this copying goes via the memory data register inside the Z80, also used for (HL) and bit instructions, which cannot be accessed directly. LDDR works identically except that it uses three 16-bit DEC instructions.

Unlike their faster equivalents for single 8-bit registers, 16-bit INC and DEC do not set the zero flag so each version of the loop has to check this by combining the B and C registers in the accumulator; only if they're both zero will the Z flag be set by the OR C instruction.

There are faster ways for the Z80 to clear memory, involving the stack pointer, but CLEARMEM is concise and works fine even if interrupts (which will affect stack contents) are enabled. Otherwise, consider CLEAR8K, which clears the 8k *before* END, about twice as fast. The performance boost comes because each PUSH reads only one byte of code and writes two bytes of data. It's copied out many times to minimise the loop overhead, and DJNZ operates the maximum 256 times so the 'zero' count in B can also be used to blank DE! To wipe 6k of LAYER 0 pixel data, use 12 rather than 16 PUSH instructions, starting END at 22529; since PUSH descends through memory, the initial stack pointer must point just *past the end* of the block to be cleared.

The much easier way to set a block of memory to any value from BASIC is to use **BANK %B ERASE offset, count, value** – where **offset** and **value** default to 0 and **count** to 16384 unless explicit values are supplied – just don't confuse that with BANK CLEAR! DMA is the fastest method, but also much fiddlier. Chapter 13, Memory, explains how, and why.

Splitting, the difference

Back in BASIC, the 'split' parameter is zero when inserting text with Symbol Shift I, indicating that the work is nearly done, as the update of the L$() and P() arrays will be handled by code in the main loop. It works out the new cursor position and then bumps up the current paragraph number if we're at the start of the document.

There's another little trick here, which removes the need for a second IF test and putting the END PROC on another line for just the NOT split case. The expression **(Current Paragraph=1)** returns **1** (true) if we started at the first paragraph before, and **0** (false) if we were any later in the document. Adding this expression onto **Current Paragraph** has the desired result without complicating the flow:

```
3555 IF NOT split THEN Current Paragraph+=(Current
    Paragraph=1): ENDPROC :;Caller updates L() & P$().
```

The remainder of the paragraph insertion procedure splits one paragraph into two at the cursor position. It copies the remaining part of the current paragraph into the next one and adjusts the lengths of both paragraphs to reflect the position of the split, in lines 3580 and 3600. There's no need to touch the characters left in the current paragraph after the split-point, **PosIn Current Paragraph**, as adjusting the length effectively makes them invisible. All that remains is to tidy up the screen,

```
3560 ; Prepare the new paragraph.
3570 P$(Current Paragraph+1)=P$(Current Paragraph)(PosIn
    Current Paragraph TO L(Current Paragraph))
3580 L(Current Paragraph+1)=L(Current Paragraph)-PosIn Current
    Paragraph+1
3600 L(Current Paragraph)-=L(Current Paragraph+1)
3620 PROC Refresh Display()
3640 PROC Calculate Cursor Position InText()
3650 PROC Display Cursor()
3660 ENDPROC
```

Search and replace

Search and replace was the final feature added to the Editor. At first I wrote a machine-code routine to search strings and arrays, as there was no quick way to do that in NextBASIC 2.07, but Garry came to the rescue in the next release which extends the IN function to accept two string parameters and return the first character index where the second string occurs in the first, or zero if there's no match.

This function was called POS in the original Dartmouth BASIC and is similar to the INSTR function in DEC BASIC-PLUS and its imitators, though on Next there's no parameter to set the start of the search to somewhere after the start of the string being searched. It's simple to emulate that in NextBASIC by slicing the front off the first (pattern) string and adding back the corresponding offset to the result, if a match is found.

After setting up some local variables the procedure asks the user to enter the string they'd like to find. If nothing is entered FIND returns at once.

```
3700;-------------------------------------------------------
3710;-                          Find                        -
3720;-------------------------------------------------------
3730 DEFPROC Find()
3735 LOCAL X$,T$,R$,i,%t,k
3740 INPUT AT %22,%0;"Find: "; LINE X$
3750 IF NOT LEN X$ THEN PROC ClearMessage(): ENDPROC
3755 T$=X$[-]
3760 FOR i=1 TO Last Paragraph
3770   %t= IN (P$(I, TO L(i))[-],T$)
```

Otherwise another 2.08 feature is used to convert any capital letters in the entry to lower-case, so that the search is case-independent, like ZX BASIC variable-name matching, meaning that "the" will also match "The" or "THE". The lower-case version of the entry is stored in another variable, T$, so that if the user decides to search again for the same pattern we can display it as entered, from X$, rather than after folding it into lower-case, which is a change the user doesn't need to know about.

Line 3760 sets up a loop from the first to the current last paragraph, thus skipping any unused elements at the end of the array. Notice how the incantation to fold down capital letters **[-]** is applied to the paragraph being searched but not the search pattern. We could have avoided the need for T$

by writing **X$[-]**) at the end of line 3770, but that would have been slower because it would have meant re-converting X$ to lower-case before searching each paragraph. As we only look inside paragraphs one by one, if the pattern is split between two paragraphs FIND won't spot it.

Note also that we don't look in all of P$(i), but only up to the actual length used, in L(i). This saves time when paragraphs are not all the maximum length, as it usually the case.

The next ten lines, before the NEXT i which moves to the following paragraph, run only if the search was successful, with **%t** representing the character index in P$(i) where the pattern was found. The comment after the ENDIF makes it easier to work out which of the previous IF tests it ends:

```
3775   IF %t
3780     First Visible Paragraph=i: PROC Refresh
    Display():Cursor Row= %t/w+1:Cursor Col=%t MOD w-1: PROC
    Display Cursor(): PROC ClearMessage(): PRINT AT %22,%0;
    "Next ";INVERSE %1;X$;INVERSE %0;" Replace or Quit (n/r/q)"
3785     @query: PAUSE %0:k=32| PEEK LASTK
3790     IF k= CODE "q" THEN EXIT
3795     IF k= CODE "r"
3796       IF R$="" THEN PROC ClearMessage(): INPUT AT
    %22,%0;"Replacement? "; LINE R$
3797       IF L(i)+ LEN R$- LEN X$>Max LineLength THEN PROC
    ClearMessage(): PROC Message("Line too long."): ELSE L(i)+=
    LEN R$- LEN X$:P$(i, %t TO )=R$+P$(i,(%t)+ LEN X$ TO ):
    PROC Refresh Display(): PROC Display Cursor()
3798     ENDIF :;"r"
3800     IF k<> CODE "n" AND k<> CODE "r" THEN GO TO @query
3810   ENDIF :;%t
3820 NEXT i
```

Line 3780 displays the matching paragraph and positions the cursor on the first line of the match. It does this by splitting the value of **%t**, the index of the search pattern in the paragraph, into two parts: the line number in the paragraph, and the column number within that line, both counting from 0. The calculations use integer arithmetic so Cursor Row is rounded down to a whole number after dividing %T, the position in the paragraph, by %W, the line width in characters; the **+1** is needed because screen rows are counted from 0 and the first line, row 0, is used for the status display.

Off by one, or backwards?

Cursor Col numbers columns from 0, the left margin, but **%t** returned by the string IN function counts the first character as number 1, hence the **-1**. I stress this because some of the most common errors in programming are caused by using an off-by-one value.

ZX BASIC tried to be user-friendly by counting characters and array elements from 1, rather than 0 which would be easier to implement. However, the text and graphics coordinate systems count from zero, and differ about whether 0 is at the top (for characters, sprites and tiles) or bottom of the screen, for pixels you PLOT and POINT to.

Making things even more confusing, the bottom of the LAYER 0 screen is just above the two lines reserved for editing and error messages, as Sinclair had it, but lines in all other layers are counted from 16 pixels lower down, the first visible pixel line, including the editing area. This inconsistency also affects rectangles specified with LAYER DIM and LAYER ERASE.

There is a better way. Spectrum BetaBASIC, and SAM BASIC, got the best of both worlds, and support for variable-height lines, by allowing negative coordinates and defining an extra variable YOS (for Y offset) which was added to vertical positions.

When YOS is zero SAM works like the original Spectrum. Setting YOS to -18 allows plotting to the bottom of a screen with two 9-pixel high editor lines at the bottom; SAM can allow extra space between lines, which is why the font looks rather cramped vertically on Next. YOS=88, XOS=128 puts the origin in the middle of the main screen, conveniently for plotting sines and cosines or other graphics like the Mandelbrot set which extend either side of both axes.

Even more powerfully, and equivalently to the SCALE command in Sinclair QL SuperBASIC, XRG and YRG are scale factors SAM BASIC applies to pixel coordinates; setting both to 0.5 halves the size of a vector-drawn image and using 3.0 triples it in both dimensions. Scaling factors can be different vertically and horizontally, and negative scales are both valid and useful, flipping coordinates to run from top to bottom, or right to left! We can still get this effect in NextBASIC, but have to explicitly add and multiply each coordinate and line offset to get the same effect.

Replacement label

Back at PROC Find( ), the user is shown the match and invited to type R, N or Q – standing for Replace, Next (look on, without replacing) or Quit – stop looking. Line 3785 start with a label @query which is returned to if the next keypress doesn't match any of those letters. PAUSE %0 waits till a key is pressed, and as we saw in the main loop of the editor PEEK LASTK picks up the character code of that key-press.

The prefix **32|** shows another approach to case-independent input, by making sure that bit 5 (as 2^5 is 32) of the character-code is always set. If you study Appendix A of the Spectrum manual, which lists the character set, you'll notice that lower-case letters have the same ASCII codes as their capitalised counterparts, except that the lower-case codes are 32 greater.

The bitwise OR operator sets the specified bits, whether or not they're already set. This means that capital-letter codes, in the A to Z range 65 to 90, are mapped to the lower-case range 97 to 122, and small letters, which already have bit 5 set in their code, are unaffected. The ASCII set was deliberately designed, by expert bit-wranglers, to make this easy.

Even IBM's earlier EBCIDIC worked that way, but by making all letter codes *greater than 128*, with lower-case *first*, bit 6 *set* (+64) denoting capitals, and *gaps of seven or eight undisplayable characters* breaking the two alphabets into six sections! So if you think Sinclair's version of ASCII is eccentric, with **£** and © plugged in, give thanks that they didn't copy IBM mainframes.

Line 3790 catches an entry of **q** or **Q** and uses the new EXIT keyword to break cleanly out of the FOR loop, continuing at line 3830 after NEXT i. The multi-line IF block from 3795 to 3798 replaces text if **R** is pressed. Line 3800 loops patiently until one of the three valid keys is typed.

Line 3796 only asks for a replacement string, in R$, if one has not already been entered. You can replace the pattern with nothing – deleting it, in effect – by pressing Enter without any replacement text, but if you've already entered a replacement for a previous match it will be immediately used again if you press **R**. If you press **N** to skip to the next match the replacement text is not used, but still remembered for next time, or the time after.

Line 3797 shows all the steps needed to safely and efficiently replace part of a string with another, when the two parts may differ in length. The first thing to check is that the replacement will fit; we're safe if the current length of the line, in L(i), plus the length of the replacement, LEN R$, minus what we're replacing, LEN X$, is no more than **Max LineLength**. Otherwise we spit out a 'Line too long' message and scan on to the next match.

Replacing the text involves adjusting the current length of the line, and inserting the replacement text in place of the search pattern. To save time and memory, the first part of the paragraph, before the match, is left untouched. The slice P$(i, %t TO) refers only to the part from the start of the match onwards. The replacement R$ is inserted there, followed by anything else in the paragraph that came after the pattern.

The expression P$(i, (%t) + LEN X$ TO) isolates that remainder, starting from the match-point after skipping as many characters as were in the search pattern **X$**. The only weird aspect is the brackets around %t, which are needed because, despite all the consistency improvements in NextBASIC 2.08, LEN X$ is still not a valid integer expression.

Although the length of a string is always in the integer range, the integer expression evaluator can't handle strings, so the integer part is worked out inside the brackets and converted to floating-point form before the standard expression evaluator gets to grips with LEN X$.

Once the replacement has been made, we refresh the display and redraw the cursor, so the modification is visible while the next search continues. After all paragraphs have been searched, or the user presses the **Q** key to stop sooner, a long deep BEEP tone sounds if nothing has been found, and the procedure ends by clearing the message line.

```
3830 IF % NOT t THEN BEEP %2,-52
3840 PROC ClearMessage()
3850 ENDPROC
```

Reference parameters

The next procedure is exceptionally short but generally useful, and illustrates another NextBASIC 2.08 advance. In previous incarnations of NextBASIC, and the original BBC BASIC, parameter passing was one-way. The parameters in brackets after the DEFPROC were treated as local variables, with values from the calling PROC line copied in and discarded later, when the old value of that variable (if any) was restored.

While it's possible to return several values at the end of a PROC, there's was no way for a procedure to modify its parameter and have the corresponding external variable updated with the new value on return. In other languages and more versatile versions of BASIC this is known as 'call by reference', as distinct from the usual 'call by value'. REF is often more convenient than the earlier approach of specifying the inner and outer variable names twice, on the way in and out of the procedure.

Where REF is used in DEFPROC, the corresponding parameter in each PROC calling it must be a variable, not an expression. This makes sense, because if you passed the value 0, say, there would be nowhere for the changed parameter to be stored. Changing the value of 0, even if that was possible (hello, Forth language programmers) would be counterproductive!

Our simple example is a one-line procedure that makes sure the first parameter, which must be a variable, does not exceed the second parameter, which may be a number, another variable, or a numeric expression. The first parameter may be changed, as it has REF before its name in the DEFPROC, whereas the second is local, as in earlier NextBASICs.

```
3900; -----------------------------------------------------
3901; -                       Limit                       -
3902; -----------------------------------------------------
3910 DEFPROC Limit( REF v,c)
3920 IF v>c THEN v=c
3930 ENDPROC
```

PROC Limit(A,B) clamps the value of A to no more than B. Although the procedure has a conditional effect internally, it can be called from within a multi-statement line without disrupting the flow to later statements, as an in-line IF test would. The value of A may be changed, but B is never touched. We'll see how handy this can be in the next procedure.

Scrolling the screen

The Scroll( ) procedure takes a signed numeric parameter, the number of paragraphs to move up or down through the document. Before the call to refresh the display the revised **First Visible Paragraph** number is clamped to prevent scrolling off the start or end. We keep a copy of its original value, in the local variable **old top**, so we can easily detect if the first visible paragraph has changed, and safely limit **Cursor Row** if necessary.

```
4000;-------------------------------------------------------------
4001;-                        Scroll                              -
4002;-------------------------------------------------------------
4010 DEFPROC Scroll(direction):;+ down or - up direction lines.
4012 LOCAL old top=First Visible Paragraph
4015 First Visible Paragraph+=direction
4020 IF First Visible Paragraph<1 THEN First Visible
    Paragraph,Cursor Row=%1:Cursor Col=%0
4025 IF direction<-1 THEN PROC Refresh Display(): PROC
    Calculate Cursor Position InText(): PROC Display Cursor():
ENDPROC
4030 PROC Limit(First Visible Paragraph,Last Paragraph)
4035 PROC Refresh Display()
4036 PROC Calculate Cursor Position InText()
4037 IF old top=First Visible Paragraph THEN PROC Display
    Cursor(): ELSE PROC Limit(Cursor Row,r(Last Visible
    Paragraph)+n(First Visible Paragraph)-1)
4040 ENDPROC
```

Utility procedures

PROC Set Up View( ) gets called when the Editor starts, after a new file is loaded, or from the **Erase all** menu item. Like Scroll, it uses the NextBASIC 2.08 comma extension to assign one value to several variables in a single statement. Notice that columns are counted from 0 (to suit PRINT AT) but rows from 1 as the first row of the screen is the status line. Paragraph numbers are also counted from 1, but that's because ZX BASIC arrays do not allow a zero subscript.

Unable to pick an ideal default, Microsoft's GW BASIC provided an OPTION BASE statement to set the start of all array indices to either 1 or 0, depending upon the parameter, but stops the program with an error if this is changed after any arrays have been dimensioned.

```
5000;-------------------------------------------------------------
5001;-      Set up the view of a New file/Opened file             -
5002;-------------------------------------------------------------
5010 DEFPROC Set Up View()
5020 Dirty Flag,Cursor Col=%0
5030 First Visible Paragraph,Cursor Row=%1
5040 PROC Refresh Display()
5050 PROC Calculate Cursor Position InText()
5060 PROC Display Cursor()
5070 Old Count=Character Count
5090 ENDPROC
```

Beheading Plus3DOS

PROC Remove Header( ) is called from PROC SaveFile( ) if the **Remove Header** flag was set when the Editor started up. Recall that's it's OK to use the same name for a variable and a PROC. It takes one parameter indicating the number of bytes – including the header – in the WorkArea, and uses the EXTRACT dot command to strip the first 128 bytes of the file created by SAVE, doing away with a file header which is liable to confuse computers that don't run Plus3DOS. We still use SAVE because it's far quicker than it would be to OPEN a file for output and PRINT it piecemeal, even using BANK PEEK$ and appending B$ manually to each paragraph.

The two-step process starts by saving the text in the WorkArea to a temporary file with the same name as the document being edited but '.tmp' tacked onto the end. The local string **T$** holds that filename and is used later to delete it. In the meantime the final output file is generated by passing the name of the temporary file to **.extract** from along with the offset **+128**, so it skips that many bytes from the start of the temporary file; then comes **F$** the name of the file to be extracted. The **-f** option at the end of **U$** confirms that it's safe to overwrite the previous version of the output file.

To see the full set of options for this versatile dot command, which can also shed bytes from the end of a file or split it into multiple sections, type **.extract** with no parameters. Most dot commands have this sort of help, which is just as well as they're barely documented otherwise. In fact two dot commands are used: **.$** is a sort of wrapper for other dot commands which allows variable parameters to be passed, combined into a single string, rather than requiring them to all be explicitly supplied on the same line after the name of the command.

One consequence of the Editor's reliance on dot commands is that the C:/dot/ directory has to be available whenever it is running. This rule applies to many NextBASIC programs, since, along with drivers, dot commands are a standard way to add commands beyond those built-into BASIC. They're MUCH slower than built-in commands as their code is loaded from SD every time they're used – even if the same dot command is called several times in succession, as in my MGT_Reader which performs a succession of **.extract** commands to read 510-byte sectors from a floppy disc image.

It is possible to run a dot command from a path other than the default C:/dot/ but the path must be on the current drive and literal, rather than read from a variable. Thus **./dash/echo** will look for the **.echo** dot command in a folder called dash, but there's currently no way to use F$ to customise the path, as we can for BASIC commands like CAT and LOAD.

```
5300;-----------------------------------------------
5301;-           Remove +3 header from saved file           -
5302;-----------------------------------------------
5310 DEFPROC Remove Header(toPos)
5320 LOCAL T$=F$+".tmp"
```

```
5330 LOCAL U$=T$+" +128 -o "+F$+" -f"
5350 SAVE T$ BANK WorkArea,%0,toPos
5360 .$ Extract U$
5370 ERASE T$
5380 ENDPROC
```

Resource Management

One of the principles of good programming is to release resources and restore the system to a known state when your program quits. It's rude to force the user to reset the machine, especially if they're developers who might have a non-trivial setup to restore after that. It would be worse still to lose the work the user was doing before, so PROC Quit( ) starts by testing the Dirty flag and inviting the user to file any unsaved changes. Then it undoes the work of PROC Init Mouse( ) and most of the initialisation done when the Editor starts.

Two steps can only be done in the main program: releasing the ProcArea bank itself (which cannot be done from inside the bank) and releasing memory allocated above RAMTOP for the font, which requires a CLEAR command that stops ENDPROC working. Those tasks are performed after the call to PROC Quit( ) from line 840.

```
5400;--------------------------------------------------------
5401;-                          Quit                          -
5402;--------------------------------------------------------
5410 DEFPROC Quit()
5430 IF Dirty THEN BANK %255 PROC SaveFile Query()
5450 SPRITE PRINT %0:; Hide the mouse pointer.
5470 BANK SpriteArea CLEAR
5480 BANK WorkArea CLEAR
5500 ON ERROR GO TO @Uninstalled
5510 .Uninstall /nextzxos/mouse.drv
5520 @Uninstalled: ON ERROR
5530 REG %7,%C:; Restore CPU speed.
5540 ENDPROC
```

May I see the menu?

This procedure displays the menu across the bottom line of the screen:

```
5700;--------------------------------------------------------
5701;-                      Display menu                      -
5702;--------------------------------------------------------
5710 DEFPROC Display Menu()
5720 LOCAL T$= CHR$ 133+ CHR$ 20+ CHR$ 1:; Block and INVERSE 1
5730 PRINT AT %23,%0;"Sym Shift Commands ";T$;"E"; INVERSE
    %0;"rase all ";T$;"G"; INVERSE %0;"et file  ";T$;"S";
    INVERSE %0;"ave   Save";T$;"A"; INVERSE %0;"s   ";T$;"Q";
    INVERSE %0;"uit";
5740 IF %w>84 THEN PRINT AT %23,%66;T$;"I"; INVERSE %0;
    "nsert  ";T$;"D"; INVERSE %0;"elete";
5750 IF %w>90 THEN PRINT AT %23,%84;T$;"F"; INVERSE %0;"ind";
5760 ENDPROC
```

The local temporary string T$ is printed at the start of each menu item, so that the first letter stands out. It contains the code for a vertical block, paper colour on the left and ink to the right, then two control codes that work like the print item INVERSE 1, making the next letter match the block graphic.

When you're working entirely on Next it's convenient to press the Graphics key followed by 5 to get the block character, but printed listings won't show that correctly unless you're using the ZX Spectrum font, which is alas not yet one of the Postscript or TrueType printer standards! Having inflicted long ZX Printer listings on the world often enough (most egregiously in my contributions to mid-80s *ZX Computing* and *Personal Software* magazines) I've opted to use CHR$ to keep this one (almost) in standard ASCII code.

The original five menu items fitted neatly on a 64-column screen line, but when I added paragraph cut and paste via INSERT and DELETE buttons they needed extra space only available in an 85-column or wider display. Those menu items don't appear on a 64-column screen, but the Symbol Shift I and D work as well as ever even though they're not mouse-clickable or displayed as a prompt. FIND came even later, so you only see that button at bottom right if you've configured the Editor for more than 90 columns.

Call that progress?

When files are being loaded or saved, the menu buttons are disabled and a progress bar is shown instead. The following procedure displays that on the last line of the screen. The length of the bar signifies how much of the file has been saved or the proportion of the total available number of paragraphs loaded so far. The parameter **p** slices a string of vertical bars so that as **p** is increased more bars appear. The value of **p** normally ranges from 1 to 10 but in case of rounding errors, and as a gesture to *Spinal Tap* fans, the procedure can cope with the range 0 to 11.

```
5800;--------------------------------------------
5801;-                    Progress bar          -
5802;--------------------------------------------
5810 DEFPROC Progress(p)
5820 PRINT AT %22,%w-22;"|||||||||||"( TO p): BEEP 0.01,%3
5860 ENDPROC
```

The beep provides synaesthetic feedback – for added tension or chromatic variety you could replace the preset pitch **%3** with the value of **p** to hear a rising scale rather than a sequence of identical blips. The coordinates **%22, %w-22** position the bar near the right side of the penultimate line of the screen regardless of the character-width.

The following procedure updates the character count displayed in the top right corner on the screen. PROC Display Character Count( ) is only called when there's no typing underway, so it can afford to spend a little time keeping the display neat.

```
5900;------------------------------------------------------------
5901;-                   Display character count                 -
5902;------------------------------------------------------------
5910 DEFPROC Display Character Count()
5920 LOCAL X$= STR$ Character Count
5930 PRINT AT %0,(%w-12)- LEN X$;X$;" character";"s" AND
    Character Count<>1
5940 Old Count=Character Count
5950 ENDPROC
```

Rather than let PRINT convert the count from numeric to text form we use the STR$ function to put the text into X$, and then adjust the print position according to both the screen width in characters, in %W, and the number of digits in the count. This means that the number stays left-aligned even when the number of digits changes. The same approach can be used to neatly line up columns of numbers, or varying-length texts.

Some other BASICs have a PRINT USING statement to handle such formatting based, like **printf** in the C standard library, on the 1957 Fortran concept of 'format edit descriptors', and with similar limitations – it's great as long as the actual value will fit and you get all the values and patterns in the same order in two parts of the program. The ZX BASIC approach brings all this under your control, in conjunction with much more flexible character handling than in either compiled language, and usually ends up simpler when decimals and exponential representations are not required.

The embellishment at the end of line 5930 serves only to make sure we display '1 character' or a plural number of characters – perhaps 0 character**s**, or 16000 character**s** – for any other count. ZX BASIC allows AND to be applied to a string and a number, not just a pair of numbers. The result is the string if the number after AND is non-zero (true) and an empty string otherwise. The effect is that the 's' at the end of 'characters' is suppressed if **Character Count** is one, without needing an extra IF … THEN … PRINT sequence.

Line 5940 helps us avoid re-writing this display if the value has not changed, by copying the **Character Count** just displayed into **Old Count**. This is efficient because the procedure is only called from the main loop if no key is currently pressed *and* **Character Count** has changed from the **Old Count** previously shown.

The next two procedures are complementary; indeed PROC Message( ) calls Clear Message( ) after a suitable delay and alerting BEEP. Spaces are printed either side of the message so it stands out when displayed in reversed ink and paper colours, usually white on black.

There's no check that T$ will fit the line, so keep it to 62 characters at most so it doesn't overflow onto the last line of the display, where the menu is shown. If you find it disappears too soon for your taste, adjust the value after PAUSE in line 6030. If you feel it hangs around too long, you can reduce the value to a minimum of 1 – 0 would wait indefinitely – or cancel it by just carrying on typing.

```
6000;-------------------------------------------------------------
6001;-                       Display message                     -
6002;-------------------------------------------------------------
6010 DEFPROC Message(T$)
6020 PRINT AT %22,%0; INVERSE %1;" ";T$;" ";
6030 BEEP %1,%3: PAUSE %99: PROC ClearMessage()
6040 ENDPROC
6100;-------------------------------------------------------------
6101;-                        Clear message                      -
6102;-------------------------------------------------------------
6110 DEFPROC ClearMessage()
6120 PRINT AT %22,%0," ",
6130 POKE MODE,%0: POKE LASTK,%0
6140 ENDPROC
```

The combination of spaces and commas used to clear the message line was explained in the discussion of PROC SaveFile( ) in the last chapter. The POKEs to System Variables at the end make sure that any menu selection key is flushed from the buffer at **LASTK**, and graphics or Extended input mode is no longer selected in **MODE** after this procedure has been called.

This is vital as those commands don't sift out the EXT and GRAPHICS key modes and could return with normal text input disabled in favour of special key-codes. If so, it might subsequently be difficult to enter the ASCII characters the editor expects.

I could have put these POKEs after each INPUT LINE or **.browse** statement but as they all clear the message line before accepting any more input it simplifies the code, and makes further INPUTs easier to add safely, if it's in done once in PROC ClearMessage( ). Even though it may not always be needed, the time overhead of interpreting a single POKE is dwarfed by that taken to write a whole line of spaces to the screen. The first version of the editor cleared **MODE** every time round the main input loop, which was safe but slow.

Mouse integration

There's just one procedure left to explain, and it's a feast. Lines 8010 to 8110 do all the work needed to position the cursor anywhere in the text with a mouse-click, regardless of the character-size, and to translate clicks on the bottom line into menu command-codes that'd otherwise be entered with Symbol Shift key-combinations. I shall discuss the cursor-positioning first, and save the two magic lines that work the menus for pudding.

```
8000;-------------------------------------------------------------
8001;-                     Handle mouse click                    -
8002;-------------------------------------------------------------
8010 DEFPROC Handle Mouse Click(%x,%y)
8020 ; Translate X Y pixel coordinates to text column and row.
8030 LOCAL %k,%c=%x-64/ INT {Font Width},%r=%y>>3-4
```

```
8050 ; If the mouse points in the text area, move the cursor.
8060 IF %c<w THEN IF (%r)<R(Last Visible Paragraph)+N(Last
    Visible Paragraph) THEN PROC Display Cursor():Cursor
    col=%c:Cursor Row=%r: PROC Calculate Cursor Position
    InText(): BEEP .3,%0: PROC Display Cursor()
8070 IF %r<>23 OR (c<19) OR (c>88) THEN ENDPROC
```

PROC Handle Mouse Click( ) is called from line 558 in the main input loop whenever any mouse button but no key is held down. The DRIVER command on that line picks up the current mouse pointer coordinates and passes them to this procedure if it also detects that one of the mouse buttons is pressed.

Border points

Line 8030 immediately converts the pixel coordinates %X and %Y returned by the driver into character row and column positions %R and %C, adjusted according to the font width and fixed border area. Pointer coordinates may range from 0 to 639 horizontally and 0 to 255 vertically. This allows the pointer to move outside the 512 by 192 HiRes display area, by the equivalent of 64 pixels on either side and 32 above and below. %X-64 takes care of the 64-pixel left-hand border, while integer division by the **Font Width** converts the horizontal position from pixel to character units.

The INT{ } formula is required so that a standard variable name can be used in an integer expression. For example, **Z = %X + INT {X}** would set **Z** to the total of the floating-point and integer variables, both called **X**.

The vertical border is 32 pixels and Spectrum characters are always 8-pixels high, so **%r=%y>>3-4** divides the position by 8 (three bit places, or halvings) then subtracts 4 from the result to get rid of the border. I could equally well have written **%r=%y-32/8**, which is the same number of bytes, but division is slower than shifting.

Line 8060 uses these character coordinates to position the cursor, after first checking they're plausible. Since we're using the integer expression evaluator, which is optimised for whole-numbers in the range 0 to 65535, we only need to make sure that **%r** and **%c** are low enough to fit on the screen. If the calculation of **%c** on line 8030 would normally yield a negative number, in the screen border, the Z80 just wraps them round into large positive values, shown in NextBASIC by adding 65536 to the 'negative' value, so -1 becomes +65535, -64 (the lowest value expected) becomes +65472; either way the misplaced click gets ignored.

The rest of line 8060 makes sure that the value in %R corresponds to a row that's actually visible on the screen. It'd be bad news if we were able to position the cursor beyond the last paragraph of the file. This works out the active last screen line by adding the display line number of the last visible paragraph to the number of screen-lines it uses. If that test passes it first wipes the existing cursor by redrawing it in place, copies %C and %R to the global variables **Cursor Column** and **Cursor Row**, uses PROC Calculate Cursor Position InText( ) to update **Current Paragraph** and **PosIn Current Paragraph**, and redraws the cursor before returning with a satisfied BEEP.

Whether the cursor has been moved or not, line 8070 returns unless the pointer is on the last row of the screen, in the menu, and neither before nor after the menu option texts, which start in the 18th column and extend no further than the 89th, regardless of the character width. Then the real fun begins.

Mouse commands

At first sight the last two lines of this procedure are deeply mysterious. Somehow the column number in %C is converted into a key-code in %K, in such a way that the corresponding mouse menu option is entered as if it'd been typed in conjunction with Symbol Shift:

```
8080 ; Handle clicks in the command area.
8090 %k= CODE "FFFFFFFFFF  IIIIIIII  AAAA  £££££££   EEEE
   *******  KKKKKK  JJJJJ"(%c-18)
8100 IF %k>32 THEN Last Key Pressed=%k+130
8110 ENDPROC
```

To understand this spell it helps to look at the original version, which used a sequence of lines like these, where **mCur** stood for Mouse Cursor:

```
8090 IF mCurRow=23 AND mCurCol >= 32 AND
     mCurCol <= 37 THEN POKE LASTK,190: ; Open
8100 IF mCurRow=23 AND mCurCol >= 39 AND
     mCurCol <= 44 THEN POKE LASTK,229: ; Save
```

After accounting for the four floating-point values hidden in each line, these weigh in at 70 bytes apiece. Each line checked both **mCurRow** and **mCurCol** to identify the group of characters on the bottom line associated with a menu option. For instance, the OPEN menu entry, allowing one character of slop either side, occupied half a dozen character-positions from column 32 to 37. A click there would poke the token for PEEK, 190, into LASTK as if it'd been typed. PEEK is on the "O" key, as 48k BASIC enthusiasts probably know by muscle-memory (I checked).

After adding three more commands to the original five I was running out of space to move PROC Find( ) from the main program, where I tested it, into the bank. The main issue was not speed, though the entire procedure ran whenever a mouse button was pressed, but space. I also wanted a quick way to visually check the mapping between the menu text and the positions where each 'button' was detected, since any tweak to the menu line otherwise required error-prone changes to all the numbers demarcating buttons shown after the change.

The first and simplest change was to replace the repeated checks for **mCurRow=23** with a single line, 8070, which returns immediately if the cursor is not on that line or off the menu on either side. I'd previously replaced **mCurRow** with **%R** to take advantage of the integer shift operation when dividing the pixel coordinate by eight. At this point all we really need is some way to translate clicks in any column of the menu line into corresponding button codes, or none for the space between the menu items.

The no-limits Computing Science approach would be to use three arrays, each with one entry for each menu item, holding the start and end columns of each button and the associated key-code. Looping over those arrays I could eliminate the duplicated program statements, but I'd still need three arrays, plus code and data to set them up. None of the values are larger than a byte so I might prefer to pack all the data into 21 bytes of RAM somewhere and use PEEK to read them all. That's still a lot of BASIC.

Instead I decided to use a literal string constant, the same length as the active part of the menu with the buttons in, to store characters corresponding to the buttons, with gaps in-between. Allowing some slack either side, six adjacent characters would denote the code for OPEN, six later for SAVE, and so on. The widths and spacing would line up with the buttons in the menu.

The lowest code I needed was 172 for Insert, Symbol Shift I. The highest was 226, for Save As, as tabulated in the Glossary of editor variable. The NextBASIC editor makes it fiddly to enter character codes greater than 143, the last block graphic, but subtracting 130 from both gave me an easy-to-enter range from 42 to 96, asterisk to the pound sign.

ASCII officially defines character 96 as a weirdly-detached grave accent, known to Unix fans (for which every character has several cryptic purposes, and often multiple names) as 'back tick'. Microsoft's Outlook mail client mischievously replaces a closing single-inverted comma with this code, or a yet more obscure Unicode, as part of its campaign to make it impossible to paste plain ASCII into an email and get back what you typed. This is especially programmer-hostile if you regularly share program snippets or roll your own HTML.

Sinclair's local variation on this cultural imperialism was to redefine ASCII code 96, which must have seemed one of the least useful, as a British currency sign, "£". When I imported this program for editing, the £££££££ sequence displayed on my Next screen, mysteriously but correctly, changed into ``````` – if I'd anticipated this I might have used a code offset other than 130, but by then I'd been seduced by the row of asterisks, and manually substituted the Sinclair glyphs above.

The rest should be near-obvious. The first menu item is **Erase all**, mapped to key E which returns the token for **>=** when symbol-shifted, character 200 in Appendix A of every good Spectrum manual. 200-130 is 70, and CHR$ 70 is "F" so the first clump of letters in the lookup string on line 8090 is a bevy of Fs, the same width as the 'Erase all' button.

Get file comes next in the menu, mapped to key G, which returns the token for THEN, 203, when symbol-shifted. 203-130 is 73, so the next clump uses the letter three places further down the alphabet, "I" – and so on. You probably need to refer to Appendix A, or write a little program to find the codes by experiment, but once you've done so, all that remains is to double-check that the lookup string matches the menu items, column for column.

Looking back at line 5710, PROC Display Menu( ), it's hard to work out where any of the button texts will be displayed. Since Sinclair block graphics are rarely found in programming fonts, and hard to re-type even if you can print them, I have deliberately re-expressed the half-block character as CHR$ 133 rather than a literal symbol. This translation, and the flipping in and out of inverse ink and paper used to highlight menu letters, makes it ever harder to count columns and work out where each button starts and ends on the screen. Luckily, there's no need. The numbers no longer matter – we only need our lookup string to line up with the menu entries, and PROC Display Menu( ) is all we need to display those.

My check process is to make a copy of line 8090 and edit it to print the lookup string on the line above the menu, with the PRINT modifier **AT 22,18**. Line 22 is the one above the menu and 18 is the first column checked for mouse menu-clicks. If anything doesn't line up, edit the lookup string to fix that, and copy it back to 8090. Complicated though it may still seem, that's much easier than counting columns, and less error-prone. It also saved about 400 bytes, so I was able to move PROC Find( ) into the banked code.

Unless you're writing another mouse-menu system you're unlikely to find this technique directly useful. But any time you need to translate irregularly-distributed small numbers into key-codes, or different small numbers, this is a quick, concise and flexible way to do it.

Advanced Bank Management

The last couple of lines of EditorProcs.bas are not included in the corresponding EditorProcs.bnk because they appear only as helpers to push the BASIC procedures from the editing area into a bank, and to back-up the full version (including those lines) to an SD card when it next needs editing.

```
9997 BANK NEW B: BANK B LINE 1630,9990: SAVE
    "EditorProcs18.bnk" BANK B: BANK B CLEAR :
    GO TO 9998:;Command to update bank
9998 SAVE "EditorProcs18.bas"
```

The last line is the traditional ZX BASIC 'autosave' command, often seen on line 9999, the highest line number permitted. Zxperts are accustomed to typing GO TO 9999 to save the current program, whatever its name. In this case it's one slot earlier, at line 9998, to prevent confusion if the normally-banked EditorProcs are merged with the main program. If you use more than one BASIC bank I recommend you use a distinct line number, at the end of that particular section of the program, for each part. But you should not GO

TO those lines when the files are merged together, or you'll end up clobbering each of the separate files with the combined one, and needing to use ERASE to remove the extra lines from each.

More excitingly, line 9997 converts the currently-loaded EditorProcs.bas into a .BNK file containing all its procedures, but shorn of the introductory REMs, which serve no purpose, and the two lines above which are only needed to create the bank file and would only waste space if included within it. There's little need for % characters before the line numbers in line 9997 as, though they'd save 15 bytes, that line isn't loaded while the Editor runs.

Line 9997 starts by temporarily claiming a 16k bank, assigning **B** with the bank number. It assumes that at least one bank will be free, which is usually the case unless you've been skipping the clean-up step at the end of the main loop many times during testing. If your changes introduce an error you should get into the habit of typing GO TO 830 before you RUN the program again, as that restores the standard character set and releases the banks previously claimed, as well as the 768 bytes the custom font borrowed from just above RAMTOP.

The second statement on line 9997 copies the procedures into the temporary bank **B**. Notice how the range of line numbers 1670 to 9990 includes all the procedures we'll later want to call, but none of the identifying REMs at the start or these two lines at the end. SAVE BANK writes the rest out to a new file, and BANK CLEAR releases the temporary bank **B** once we've finished with it.

Line 9997 ends with a GO TO because – as you'll find if you try it – the bank-copying command is not allowed as part of the program, but only as part of a command line with no line number. The 9997 is only present to keep the updating commands at a convenient place in the .BAS file. To use it you must first select the line (e.g. with LIST 9997) then use the BASIC line editor to remove the line number from the start, and enter the rest, starting BANK NEW B, as a direct command.

Reports of line numbers and remaining space will scroll up the screen as the bank is populated. This process can fail if any copied line is more than 255 bytes long. There's no such limit in ZX BASIC, but the new restriction on bank contents greatly simplifies Garry's paging code, and many BASICs, like the MBASIC and BBC dialects, impose a 255-character limitation on every line, not just hidden ones.

Uploading can also fail if the specified range of lines will not fit into 16k, after allowing a few bytes for offset pointers (stored in the last 8 bytes) and – since NextBASIC 2.08 – for a table of line-start offsets, using two bytes per banked line to record how far into the bank each program line has been inserted.

Fast line look-ups

This ROM 2.08 enhancement means line-number references, such as those after GO TO, GO SUB and RESTORE, are resolved while a program runs up to five times faster than they were by Sinclair's code and earlier NextBASIC releases. Those walked through every line of the program, from the start till the chosen line number, every time the location of a line was required. On a 1k ZX81, this was reasonable, but on a 48k Spectrum, let alone a 2 MB Next, it slugged performance of large programs more and more as they grew, and encouraged ugly hacks like copying the most time-critical lines of a program to the start of the listing, with one slow GO SUB at the start to invoke less time-critical setup code moved up to higher line-numbers.

The implementation of the speed-up is buried in the secret ROM code, but analysis of the file contents reveals that it must use the line-start table, probably via a 'binary chop' algorithm, to skip the sequential search through the entire program or bank, finding the address of the target line more quickly. Since the table includes the offsets, but no line numbers, it must still take advantage of the numbers tokenised – in big-endian byte-swapped order – at the start of each program line.

For instance, the line number of the 'middle' line in a bank can be determined by reading the middle entry in the table of offsets and PEEKing its number from an address two bytes further on in the bank, within the tokenised program line, stored in the format documented in the NextBASIC data structures part of Chapter 24 of the BASIC manual.

The term 'binary chop' refers to the way we could quickly probe such a table for a specific line, without having to check each entry in turn, in a way that gets pleasingly proportionally faster the more lines there are. I used this technique in Pass 3 of my Zip Compiler, first listed in *Your Spectrum* magazine issue 4, to scan a table of ZX BASIC line numbers and Z80 code addresses, converting slow GO TO and GO SUB statements into fast Z80 JP and CALL instructions.

It works like this. From the middle line number we can work out if the required line is in the first or last half of the bank. If we're very lucky, or there are only three lines, we may hit the jackpot right away. Otherwise we 'chop' the table in half, as we know from the first test that the required line number – or the closest match after it – must be in either the first or last section. So we repeat the process, picking the middle line in *that* section and checking if it comes sooner or later than the one we want.

Progressive halvings – the 'binary' part of the algorithm – quickly home in on the exact match. For instance, if there are 1001 lines in the bank, no more than eight probes are needed to divide them into 500, then 249, 124, 63, 31, 15, 7 and 3 possibilities, at which point a simple check for greater, less or equal is enough to pinpoint the start address of the required line number.

A sequential search would have to scan 500 lines, on average, for the same result. Even with the extra hassle of finding the middle, and indirectly looking up the line numbers (to avoid needing two copies as Zip requires, since there are no line numbers in compiled code) this is a great speed benefit for all but the shortest BASIC program.

Testing banked programs

The last thing that needs explaining in this discussion of splitting up BASIC programs into banks is how you test them after dividing them up for the convenience of NextBASIC. You can't edit the lines in the bank in the usual way. You can't even post modified lines into the bank from the editing area, because the BANK LINE command doesn't do a MERGE – it replaces the entire bank with the line or lines you specify.

You can however examine the lines in the bank with BANK LIST, e.g. BANK ProcArea LIST to view the entire bank contents from the start, BANK ProcArea LIST 3000 to start about half-way through, or BANK ProcArea LIST PROC Scroll( ) (don't forget the redundant brackets) to start listing from the specified procedure.

The long-winded approach to updating any NextBASIC program spread across multiple files is to test the combined combination and make notes of changes needed in banks. Sometimes you can test these by making temporary tweaks to the main program. For instance if a banked procedure is missing the line **LOCAL T** you can work around the issue, and verify the fix, by saving the value of **T** in another variable before the PROC call and restoring it afterwards.

The only general approach is to temporarily replace the main program – and the variables and state you're trying to test – by loading the .BAS file corresponding to the uneditable .BNK, checking your notes and making the required changes, saving the updated bank routines as both .BAS and .BNK, then reloading the original main program and re-running it, reloading the dependent banks along the way. Even this only works if you always remember to save the latest main program with GO TO 9999 before loading the bank, perhaps after removing temporary bodges before you forget about those… These are the seven steps, which include loops, and woe betide you if you forget any of them:

1. Test the combined program, fixing issues in the main part and making notes about bugs buried in the banks.
2. Save the modified main part, probably after CLEAR as including lots of variables wastes space and slows down the file-handling.
3. Load the .BAS file corresponding to the banked code you need to tweak, e.g. EditorProcs17.bas
4. Apply the notes to correct (you hope) issues in the bank.

5. Save both the .BAS and the .BNK with GO TO 9997 or similar.

Consider changing the version numbers in the file names if you use those (e.g. EditorProcs17 becomes EditorProcs18). You only have to do this for the .BAS, but if you decide to keep backups of old versions of the .BNKs as well, for regression testing, don't forget to alter the main program to load the remix rather than the unfixed previous version!

6. Repeat steps 3 to 5 for lines that need changing in any other banks.

7. Reload the main part of the program and resume from step 1.

This is a tedious and error-prone process. It replaces the convenient edit-and-continue cycle of developing a single-file program with a sequence of steps that must be followed carefully, at a great risk of confusion or wasted effort. Unless you have perfect focus and a great memory, backups are vital. It's also wise to keep notes of the changes required and plan how you'll test them as you go along.

It's almost (but not quite) as painful as working in a traditional separate-compilation programming language without edit and continue, like an old-school Computer Scientist who knows no better. It's a high price to pay for having more than 40k of code in your program, but if you're willing to go through all the hoops it does allow very large BASIC programs to be developed, potentially more than a megabyte long in total, spread over 100 banks or more.

The only reason we put up with this, and Garry went to all the trouble of ingeniously implementing it, is because it preserves backward-compatibility with ZX BASIC programs from the original Spectrum. Almost anything a 48k Spectrum can LOAD and RUN will also work, unmodified, in NextBASIC. The 40k limit remains because both BASICs use 16-bit pointers to keep track of the program and variables, and these are saved as part of every BASIC program. While 16 bits could address up to 64k, the first 24k are reserved for the ROM, LAYER 0 screen and system variables.

Cambridge comparisons

Acorn's BBC BASIC has similar limitations, made worse by the fact that the original machine had a maximum of 32k of RAM, needing up to 20k of that for the screen and 3.5k for system variables. Their hardware-heavy, software-light solution, faithfully duplicated in the BBC Micro cores for Next hardware, was to add an entire CPU, as well as 64k more RAM.

Thus the BASIC program could use a full 64k, without direct access to any of the original ROM or RAM, and stick all the programs and variables in the new 64k area, leaving the original CPU and memory for display and other system input-output functions. This precluded the use of PEEKs and POKEs to access that from BASIC, breaking many early programs, while still limiting the total of both variables and program to 64k (in fact a bit less, because of the need for an inter-processor communications area). Later Beebs, in the Master series, could cope without the second 6502 by using a slower 128k RAM bank-switching approach, similar to that used in Spectrum CP/M.

Compatibility was maximised either way, as these approaches preserved the 16-bit limits assumed in the design of the BBC BASIC data-structures, frozen by LOAD and SAVE. The only change required, and performed automatically by LOAD, was to run through the program updating the pointers from each line to the next to account for the variation in start-address (set by PAGE, Acorn's equivalent of Sinclair's PROG system variable). This step was needed anyway because the BBC disc systems were liable to gobble anything up to 3k of the 8k left for programs on a HiRes cassette-based Beeb for their own buffers and system variables, changing the base address to accommodate the file system. Sinclair's Interface 1 does a similar thing with PROG, but less so and only when microdrives or serial ports are used; it also has more RAM to start with!

The other way to handle banks

MGT's SAM BASIC works very differently. It sacrifices strict binary compatibility in order to allow a single program and its variables to span hundreds of kilobytes, or to have up to thirty screens in memory. SAM manages this by changing the system variables to use an extra byte for every pointer, shuffling the program and data through an invisible 32k RAM window that could safely PEEK and POKE any address in a +/- 16k range without need for bank-switching. Arrays of hundreds of K became usable, but most ZX BASIC programs that relied on POKEs into BASIC – such as my own Next-friendly **MultiSearch** – became incompatible.

This change didn't even slow down SAM BASIC, since it allowed further optimisations of the stored data formats and BASIC tokens, automatically handled by a small conversion program, BASCONV, needed to load ZX BASIC. But it took almost a year to get right, during which time any program more than 16k long was liable to fail in mysterious ways. Understandably but sadly the SAM BASIC author, my friend Dr. Andy Wright, is no longer interested in programming Z80s! Ironically the 32-bit Sinclair QL suffered from similar issues in its first year, because of accidental use of slightly-faster 16-bit instructions and offsets in the SuperBASIC ROM.

Bigger BASIC without (as much) pain

Back in NextBASIC, there are ways to live more comfortably with this Z80 addressing legacy than the seven-step dance, but the best choice depends on how your program is organised. If there's any possibility that your project might one day burst the 40k limit set in 1982, it pays to think about how you might split it up while you're designing it, rather than as an afterthought later, when you may already be boxed into a corner.

Since BASIC variables must all be in the main 40k, apart from the few K reserved for Next's integer values, we should consider ways to reduce the pressure to keep variable values there.

Using integers helps if your code can work with 16-bit values, preferably whole numbers between 0 and 65535, but even %A[ ] is limited to subscripts from 0 to 1663, plus 26 integer scalars, and that only by stealing space from the other 25 variables %B( ) to %Z( ). A more capacious approach, almost as fast, is to reserve bank space for integer values.

Rather than use %A[0 to 1663], you can store up to 8192 16-bit values in a single bank with DPOKE and %DPEEK, so %A[X]=%A[Y] becomes BANK %A DPOKE %X<<1,%BANK A DPEEK(Y<<1) after you reserve the bank with BANK NEW %A. If your values can be limited to the range 0 to 255 there's room for 16384 of them in each bank and you can skip the <<1 steps, otherwise equivalent to *2. Those are just a slightly faster way to double the index in order to address 16-bit words rather than 8-bit bytes.

This approach is especially attractive if the array values are data, such as graphics coordinates or paths for a sprite, which are loaded and read by the program as it runs but already set-up from the start. You can do the same sort of things for strings, either by padding each element out to the maximum length with spaces, the way ZX BASIC string arrays work, or more economically by storing just the characters you need, packed together at one end of the bank, and a table of offsets and lengths at the other end of the bank. Working from both ends towards the middle means all the remaining space is always available for either text or the table. The only variable you need to keep outside the bank is the number of strings already packed away.

In fact, we can get by without explicitly storing any lengths, since we can infer the length of any entry by comparing the offset where it starts (from the table) with the offset of the entry after, as long as you make sure the table always contains one more offset than the number of strings it's tracking. This is easily done by ensuring that the last entry in the table always holds the offset pointing *after the last stored string*. Conveniently, this is the place where the *next* string will be stored.

To add another string, use the last table entry to find the unused space and make sure there's room for the text and two bytes (at the other end of the free area, extending the table towards the text) for the new 'last entry'. Deleting strings from anywhere but the end is painful, requiring moving the text and table entries after the change, but that's almost the same for array editing, as we've seen in PROC Delete Paragraph( ). The only difference is that, as we use the same offsets to find both starts and lengths, it's also necessary to subtract the number of characters removed from the shifted entries for strings stored after the deletion.

Moving large arrays into banks does get fiddly if you need more than 16k of data as you'll then need to divide it between banks. BetaBASIC 4 can store arrays in RAM Disc, but NextBASIC can't. One way to make this *slightly* less cumbersome is to use an integer array to store the bank numbers. Here's how to implement an array of 250,000 bytes. First we allocate sixteen 16k banks:

```
FOR %B=%0 TO INT(250000/16384): BANK NEW %B(B): NEXT %B
```

Now we read byte N (which cannot be an integer as it may exceed 65535) with BANK %B(INT{N >> 14}) PEEK INT {N & 16383} and update it with BANK %B(INT {N >> 14}) POKE INT{N & 16383}, byte. This is much slower than the single-bank approach because of the need to split the value N into two halves.

The >> 14 is the speedy equivalent of division by 16384 (which could be written as 2^14 if you *really* wanted to slow things down) which discards the bottom 14 bits of the value of N, yielding a 16k bank number, while & 16383 extracts only those bits (as 16383 is 2^14-1, or BIN 11111111111111) to get a byte index into the bank.

For 16-bit values, either make sure the index is always even by counting in steps of 2, or double it every time e.g. BANK %B(INT{N >> 13}) PEEK (INT{N} & 8191 << 1). The INT{} business is needed because N may be more than the integer limit of 65535. If you decide to go off and buy a SAM, port SAM BASIC to Next or implement a SAM Coupé core, rather than do this, I quite understand. Until IBM rescued Intel by designing the 32-bit 80386 for them, this was the sort of shenanigans that made IBM PC programmers prematurely greyer.

Don't READ this

If your program relies on numeric or textual data you may be tempted to follow standard BASIC practice and include the values in DATA statements held in the program and copied into arrays when the program starts. This is convenient for short programs, especially as it keeps all the code and numbers together in one file, but also very wasteful on any Spectrum, where each numeric value ends up stored three times over in that precious 40k – as text, separated by commas, in the DATA statement; as an invisible 6-byte binary value embedded in the program; and as a 5-byte value in the array where it'll actually be used.

One of the great strengths of Sinclair BASICs, dating back to the ZX80 and aping languages like APL, is that when you type SAVE you're not storing just the program lines, as in other BASICs, but also the names and values of all the variables that have been set since the last RUN or CLEAR. It follows that if you're short of space the first thing you should do is move any DATA lines out of the program entirely. Put them in a separate program which contains only variable assignment statements or the DATA and loops to copy it into pre-dimensioned arrays. Run that program once to set up the variables, then type ERASE to get rid of the program lines, leaving only the variables, and SAVE the resultant 'empty program'.

Instead of assigning the variables from DATA in your main program, simply MERGE that empty program with it, and you'll end up with all the variables ready for its use and no duplicate copies of the values in memory. SAVE that as a single combined file; it will be smaller and start faster. But beware – if you start it with RUN, rather than GO TO or the SAVE LINE auto-start option, you'll clobber all the preset variables, and need to merge them back in.

For the same reason, any CLEAR command to adjust RAMTOP must be in an earlier program. Cassette software often put this in the short loader program that also draw or loaded the title screen.

These are the main techniques used to condense NextBASIC variable values. Shrinking the program lines has been an obsession among Sinclair hackers since the 1k ZX80, and most of the techniques recommended for ZX81 and ZX Spectrum programs apply to Next, with the same caveats: SGN PI may be five bytes more concise than the single digit 1. That's because of the way SGN and PI are tokenised to single bytes, whereas 1 is encoded as the digit text, CHR$ 49, followed by six hidden bytes: a CHR$ 14 marker and a five-byte generic numeric representation, with the binary word 1 tucked away in the middle, surrounded by all the space reserved, just in case, for the binary form of values like -123456789e-12.

These hidden bytes speed up ZX BASIC compared with most others, including Microsoft and BBC variants, which laboriously convert numbers from decimal to binary *every time* they interpret them! But it costs extra, invisible, bytes to hold both forms of the number, and for simple values like 0 and 1 the conversion overhead saved is unmeasurable, unlike the memory cost, which soon adds up in a large program. Working out PI-PI or PI/PI for 0 and 1 saves bytes, but not time.

Sinclair's QL SuperBASIC takes another approach, storing only the binary form (in six bytes) *without* the numeric text originally entered, and letting LIST do the conversion, favouring both runtime speed and memory-saving over quick and exact listings. This has a snag: it means values are only ever LISTed one way. You may enter 10e-1 or 0.01e2 but it'll always be listed as 1.

By default Next sticks with the ZX BASIC approach, for compatibility, but if you're assigning small integers the cost outweighs the benefit, especially as the Z80n has a hardware multiplier which is quicker than bitwise arithmetic or a table look-up when converting between bases. Consequently Next works like the lesser BASICs inside integer expressions, storing only raw digits and converting them to binary on demand. Thus you save five bytes by clearing a numeric variable, of any type, to **%0** rather than **0**, and time if not space by using **%3** rather than the old subterfuge of **INT PI**. You can see this done several times at the start of Editor.bas, and elaborated in line 4961 of PROC NewFile( ) which assigns the value **%1** to two Paragraph-counting variables in a single NextBASIC 2.08 statement.

The classic way to make programs shorter is to remove all comments and insignificant spaces, and only use short cryptic variable names. Since that makes the program hard to read and even harder to maintain, it's a last resort. If I'd done that for the longer examples in this book I'd never have been able to explain them to you, in the unlikely event that they'd ever worked. So I shall leave detailed advice on code-pruning to the mass of articles about it already online and in old ZX books, pausing only to remind you of the incantation:

```
PRINT 65536-USR 7962
```

which tells you how many bytes from that 40k remain free. You could put a % after the above PRINT, momentarily saving 15 bytes, but as it's only a temporary command it makes more sense to type the minimum required. If you're not sure if a change is really saving space, use this command before and after editing, and learn. The Spectrum is a great teacher: patient, consistent, and pedantic.

Merge for testing

Although I've spattered %s liberally around Magnus's once-beautiful code to shoehorn more functions into the editor, and removed a few REMs that duplicated the text of the following program line, I've stuck with the main-program plus one-BASIC bank approach, as adding extra BASIC banks won't make the examples any more helpful.

Fans of line renumbering may have tutted about the ragged line numbers used in this project. Part of the procedure to 'finish' a program before publication used to be to renumber it, usually to start from line 10 or 100 and proceed in even steps of 10. This suited people whose BASIC included an AUTO line numbering command, which eased program entry by providing line numbers for each new line at a selected interval. NextBASIC 2.09 added LINE NEW for this; it has long had a LINE command to renumber listings.

This existentially-unfinished program uses uneven line intervals which reflect edits since it was started; it has deliberately not been renumbered since, mostly because PROCs have been moved back and forth between Editor.bas and the EditorProcs bank in a trade-off between leaving RAM for the text (by minimising Editor.bas) and making updates easier (noting that EditorProcs are harder to tweak).

The current split leaves EditorProcs almost full and Editor.bas rather smaller. Once you have reserved a 16k bank you might as well use as much of it as you can, while still leaving space for the banked line lookup table. The smaller Editor.bas is, the more room it leaves for arrays and temporary string storage.

Unbankable assets

But there are a few things that can't be put in a PROC, like the line that loads the EditorProcs BANK, or CLEAR commands which would stop ENDPROC or RETURN working. Customising options are also best left in the main program, like %W to set the character size and F$ to indicate where supplementary files are stored. Among those options are **Max Number Of Paragraphs** and **Max LineLength**. Normally those are chosen in a trade-off between support for big paragraphs and having lots of them, while bearing in mind the 16k limit on total file size.

But if we trim either of those down, momentarily, it becomes possible to temporarily merge the EditorProcs into the main program, making editing and debugging a lot easier. There are a few other tweaks that need to be made for this to work, and the interleaved code blocks mean it's necessary to re-apply fixes to the separate files later, but on balance it's a productivity booster especially if you have a list of bugs or features to explore and none of them absolutely require more than a screen or two of text in the Editor while you test them.

Of course, many lines in the main program use BANK ProcArea to divert execution to the EditorProcs bank, but you don't need to change any of those to test the merged code. Remember how we reserved space for EditorProcs.bnk at the start of the program?

```
240 BANK NEW ProcArea
```

This assigns the number of a reserved bank into ProcArea, so after that's loaded we can use BANK ProcArea PROC commands to call code there. There also needs to be a way for banked code to call procedures in the main program, and as we saw in PROC Quit( ) this can be done from any other BASIC bank by referring to BANK 255:

```
5430 IF Dirty THEN BANK %255 PROC SaveFile Query()
```

You can save time and typing by putting procedures that call one another in the same bank whenever possible, but BANK 255 works well at other times. If ever your program needs to know which bank it's running from, it can determine that with **PEEK 23415**, reading the system variable NXTBNK. To stop the merged program looking for a non-existent bank, change line 240 to:

```
240 ProcArea=255
```

Now all procedure calls will look in the main area, *whether or not* they are prefixed by BANK ProcArea. You'll need to temporarily comment out line 250 by adding a semicolon or REM at the start, as there's no longer any need to load the EditorProcs bank, as well as the last statement on line 840, which normally clears that bank after use.

Making Space

To allow more room for program lines, at the temporary expense of text capacity, edit line 210 to dramatically reduce **Max Number Of Paragraphs**. Eight is still enough to test scrolling, if your test data uses multi-line paragraphs. Finally, just as you would while testing just the main program, comment out line 525 so that the fallback error-trap doesn't prevent you from breaking into the program or analysing errors in it.

As long as you stick to short documents, and keep notes on tested changes to be copied back to the separate BASIC files, these temporary tweaks allow you to test the entire editor without having to hop back and forth between bank-specific files. Even if you lose track of the changes, the NextDiff program listed in Chapter 5 will enable you to scan through text versions of each BASIC file and identify just what's been altered, skipping the identical sections. That's why I wrote it.

There will come a time when your own programs are too large for the main area, even with reduced array dimensions, or when you need more data than will fit at the same time as all the procedures. In this case you can still temporarily move a subset of the banked procedures – just the ones you expect to need to change. I did this for PROC Scroll( ) when extending it for multi-line moves, merging the changes back into EditorProcs later, and for some of the Paragraph-handling procedures while getting cut and paste to work. I also temporarily merged **Display Menu** and **Handle Mouse Click** while I was catering for extra menu options and character widths.

The process is like that when merging all the PROCs into the main program, except that fewer edits are needed there, as most of the banked code stays where it was. To extract just the procedures you'll be working on, load EditorProcs.bas and delete all except the lines you need to move. For just PROC Scroll( ), which uses line numbers 4010 to 4040, type:

```
LOAD "EditorProcs.bas"
ERASE 1,4009
ERASE 4041,9999
SAVE "Scroll.bas"
LOAD "Editor.bas"
MERGE "Scroll.bas"
```

There are two other temporary changes you'll need to make in Editor.bas. Lines 670 and 675 are the ones that call Scroll to move back and forth in eight-paragraph steps, and those normally call **BANK ProcArea PROC Scroll**. The old version of Scroll is still in the bank, but while testing we want to temporarily use the new merged one.

Remove the **Bank ProcArea** prefix from those two lines for the time being. Restore those lines and the error-trap at line 525, when you're finished. Don't forget to copy your changes to PROC Scroll( ) back to the bank file, and remove it from the main program. It should now be quite clear why renumbering either part of the program would be counterproductive.

Library banks

All this juggling is only needed because of the close coupling between components of the editor. If your program is more easily separated into modules, especially if those are stable and have a well-defined interface, you should rarely need to shuffle banked code around. In practice, especially while developing such modules, the above hard-won advice may make the difference between finishing a large program and abandoning it.

NextBASIC banks come into their own when you use them for handy procedures which you never intend to edit. If you wrote these yourself it's still almost irresistible to fiddle with them, with all the hoop-jumping previously discussed, but much less of a temptation if they've been written and carefully tested and documented by someone else, especially if they do the sorts of thing that should not need to be re-invented for every program – managing data-entry and storage, implementing user-interface elements, and other things most large programs have in common.

This is where Matt Langley's magnum opus, the Horizon library, comes to our rescue. Next Horizon is a large collection of ready-made procedures in themed BANKs, including a set of audio-related PROCs for AY and DMA sound – donated by me after drafting Chapter 14, Better BEEPs, for this book – plus Window, Palette, Menu and Icon banks, and others specialised for Debugging and Memory management.

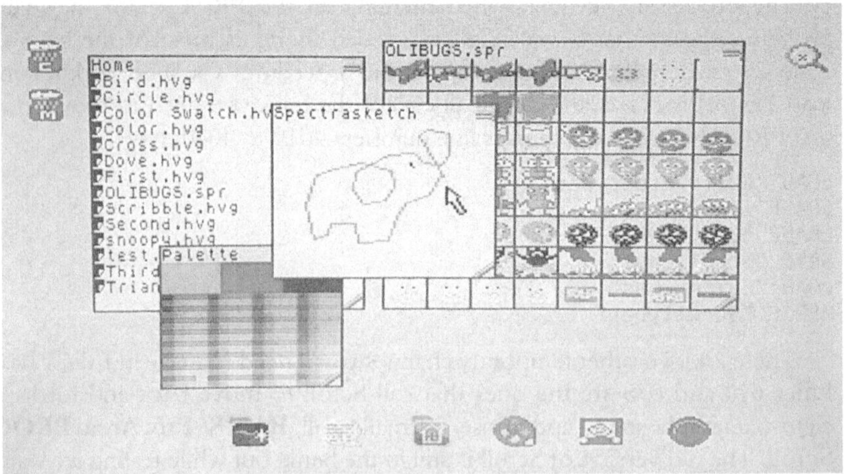

Figure 54 - Next Horizon GUI components. It still won't draw an elephant for you.

You request the ones you need and Horizon itself makes sure that any dependencies are satisfied by loading other banks with necessary shared routines. Updates of Horizon add new capabilities and route around internal changes, so your client program doesn't have to. The result works rather like shared libraries in compiled languages, but with the advantage that you get all the source and can still BANK LIST the things you're using.

If you build up a coherent set of NextBASIC procedures to do something not easily possible with NextBASIC commands, I encourage you to talk with Matt about the possibility of making them into a Horizon module. There will probably need to be some changes to tie them into the rest of the system but it's well worth the effort. Together we can develop feature-filled programs without having to re-invent wheels, concentrating on writing just the new code needed for the specific utility or game you're after. It'll also be easier to document since its common elements will work just like other Horizon-based applications.

Improving the editor

I said earlier that the Editor is unfinished. If you compare this version with the original at https://github.com/MagnusKrook/ZXNext-Editor you'll see many tweaks, but some unchanged aspects. Editing is still done in NextBASIC arrays, there's a 16k limit on total file-size, only ASCII text is supported, paragraph counts and lengths are preset (though adjustable). Since the program is entirely in BASIC, and well-commented, you're free to change any aspect to make it suit your own needs better.

You might alter F$ to keep the helper files somewhere more convenient on your SD card, or alter the paragraph count and length limits to allow more but shorter lines, or vice versa. If you make a lot of use of obscure characters you might prefer to ditch the Symbol Shift shortcuts and rely on mouse-control for the menu actions. You might like to change the step-size when scrolling, or reassign the INV and TRUE VIDEO keys to some other purpose. You could swap in your own font, add a help screen, or programmable keys that enter a whole pre-set string at a time.

The most obvious bottleneck remains screen update and scrolling but we can see this is generally a NextBASIC rather than a NextZXOS limitation, because it also affects machine-code programs like **.browse**. Scrolling down the document could be faster if it provoked the screen to scroll, by printing at the bottom, rather than redrawing from the top, and adding only the changed lines, leaving the old text to scroll off the top.

You'll need to restore the filename and character count on the top line, or move these somewhere else. Backward scrolling, up the file, tends to be less common and would require a routine to move existing lines the opposite way. That can be done with POKE and PEEK$, BANK COPY commands or a short machine-code routine, as documented half a dozen ways on page 160. However you do it, you'll need to cope with the way alternate characters of each Timex HiRes screen line are stored in separate memory areas, described in Chapter 15, Tiles and Layers. But as you're moving whole lines vertically that's just a matter of updating both areas of display memory the same way. Programs like the Odin assembler use hardware TileMaps rather than high-resolution bitmaps but they're limited to system-supported tile sizes, so 5 by 8 pixel packed text isn't any easier.

There are faster ways of writing characters, especially when they're eight pixels wide, but the ROM has to cater for all combinations of LAYER, OVER, INVERSE and colours, even though this Editor is just designed around Timex HiRes. You might want to write an optimised routine to copy characters from the font to the HiRes screen, though that'd probably require Z80n code or clever use of DMA to beat the ROM performance. Or you could extend the Editor to print in colour on other layers and with larger characters, working with NextBASIC rather than around it. At the moment, the action is the same whichever mouse-button you press.

Mightier mice

You could handle each button differently by swapping 1s for 0s in the expression **%B&@111** used to read mouse buttons at line 558. The optional mouse wheel is not currently used, but **%B>>4** yields a four-bit value from it. To use that, you need to read it twice and compare values before and after. If they differ, the wheel has moved in the meantime; the values 'wrap around' from 0 to 15 or vice versa depending on which direction the wheel's moving.

The following example reads the hardware directly. If **old** is the first value read and **now** the second, and you read often enough for the step to be no more than 15 units in either direction, you can convert it into a positive or negative count like this:

```
300 DEFPROC WHEEL( REF delta)
310 LOCAL now=% IN 64223>>4
320 PRIVATE old=now
330 IF old<=now THEN delta=now-old: ELSE delta=now-old+16
340 IF delta>7 THEN delta-=16
350 old=now
360 ENDPROC
```

This example is not part of the current editor, but could be added (at appropriate line numbers) if you have a mouse-wheel and find a good use for it. Notice how this uses another NextBASIC 2.08 goodie, the PRIVATE variable **old**. PRIVATE variables are rather like LOCAL ones except that they retain their latest values between calls. Line 320 only changes the value of **old** the first time the procedure is called. After that, it will contain the previous value up till line 350, when it's updated for next time.

PRIVATE variables are useful when implementing a Computer Science concept called a 'closure', a packet of persistent data and code. They're not often essential, but sometimes handy if you want to keep track of a list of items, like memory blocks or allocated banks, by storing the number of the first one (or 0, if none) in a PRIVATE variable and pointers to any number of others within the memory area before each one.

You don't need the mouse driver to read the hardware, though it's convenient to do so as it updates a sprite for you every frame, counts up the pulses to give an absolute rather than relative position, and provides extra features like mouse acceleration, where the cursor moves further when the mouse is moved more quickly. **IN 64223** reads the buttons and wheel directly, and horizontal and vertical movements can be sensed with **IN 64479** and **IN 65503** respectively – just as they could be on any Spectrum with an original Datel or Kempston mouse interface add-on.

Editing bigger files

The biggest Editor revision would be to remove the 16k limit. I'm not going to attempt that in this book – there are too many other, shorter examples that should be shared sooner – but I'll outline some of the issues and possible approaches.

The 16k limit comes not just from the array dimensions but the way the entire file is loaded in one step to a single bank. Larger files would require more banks to be allocated. To split the file between them, use the dot command **.extract** to pull sections of the file into separate banks, rather as PROC Remove Header( ) snips out the later part.

Deletion and insertion can be made acceptably fast – though some copying between banks will still be needed – by starting with the entire file loaded to the end of the allocated banks, leaving free space at the start, where the cursor starts out. This approach is used by the no-limits Unix Editor Emacs.

As the cursor moves down the file, copy each character or line from the end to the start of the set of reserved banks, so there is always free space at the cursor position. Characters can be added or deleted from there without needing to move anything else. You will still need a table of line start offsets, or line lengths; 16-bit entries would limit the file to 64k, but at the price of one extra PEEK per line you could extend that 24-bits, far more than the total RAM available on Next.

You don't need lengths as well as offsets, because you can find any line-length by comparing the start offsets of adjacent lines, as long as you also know where the end of the last one is. This is reminiscent of the earlier 'Bigger BASIC' ideas for storing random-length strings at one end of a bank and an index at the other end. It's similar to the way 'multi-session' CD-Rs were recorded, allowing updates on a write-once disc by writing from the outsides inward and reading the opposite way, so the old index is over-ridden by the new one written beside it. In this case it's wise to keep the text – including line-end characters – in one set of banks, and the index elsewhere.

A single 16k bank could track 5460 paragraphs each up to 16 MB long, or you can re-use the main-program space previously allocated to P$( ) for an expanded L( ) line array with similar limits, wasting a couple of bytes per element (as each float value needs 5 bytes) but avoiding the need to combine eight and 16-bit values to find any particular line. The N( ) and R( ) arrays should be trimmed so that they only keep track of lines actually visible on screen, starting from the top paragraph displayed.

Just as when handling screen lines and string array elements, all the complications arise at boundaries – when moving the editing point between banks (especially for pasting) and when writing out the combined file. Consider using PRINT #n BANK b PEEK$(offset, size) to read and write, but limit the size of each temporary string so you don't run out of main memory, even though fewer large PRINTs will be quicker than lots of small ones, for a given total size.

These are just a few suggestions. There's loads of scope for Editor editing, and even more for re-using these techniques in your own programs.

Please let us all know how you get on, either via the SpecNext forum at https://specnext.com/forum/viewforum.php?f=14 or the NextBASIC Facebook group: https://facebook.com/groups/ZXNextBasic which I check almost every day. It's a great resource for people learning about NextBASIC.

Chapter 9, Next variations and History

This chapter collects information about differences between the original ZX Spectrum and six years of Spectrum Next development. It includes machine-code that runs on any Spectrum but is guaranteed to work differently, and predictably, on a Next as opposed to a Sinclair or Amstrad model. This can be used when writing assembly-language programs that could take advantage of Next's advances, while remaining compatible, if slower and less flashy, with the millions of earlier Spectrum systems.

I considered writing a paragraph about each of the extra instructions in the Z80n repertoire in this book, but such summaries have been written before and all have the weakness that they lack context showing how the new instruction is useful. So instead I've used Z80n instructions freely in the examples in this book, and any that haven't been covered yet in context may be cited in future volumes – or ignored, if I still can't find a use for them.

Z80n specialisation test

This ZX BASIC will run on any Spectrum, and detects NEXT's Z80n if available:

```
8000 RESTORE 8100
8010 LET a=23708
8020 FOR i=a TO a+9
8030  READ d
8040  POKE i,d
8050 NEXT i
8060 LET d= USR a
8100 DATA 62,1,237,36,0,0,79,6,0,201
```

```
LD A,1
MIRROR A
NOP
NOP
LD C,A
LD B,0
RET
```

Figure 55, Z80n sifting subroutine

This returns 1 on any Zilog CPU, and has been tested on an original grey Spectrum +2 in 128k and 48k BASIC. But it returns 128 on a Z80n, thus identifying any ZX Spectrum Next, checked in +3e and 48k personalities.

The example puts the 10 bytes of code *very* temporarily in the middle two ZX BASIC calculator memories, but is relocatable to any address. The NextBASIC equivalent is simply:

```
POKE 23708,62,1,237,36,0,0,79,6,0,201: d=USR 23708
```

but that's less useful as it requires NextZXOS which in turn expects a Z80n!

The code works because it uses the 'mirror A' opcode $ED $24 on Next, and this is ignored by the original Z80. Rare MSX2 micros use Zilog's Z380 CPU which implements those bytes as a rather useless TST H instruction, so they're correctly identified as not-Z80n. The zero bytes after that are padding, interpreted as NOP instructions by Spectrums old and new, but put there just in case some other Z80-derivative uses the $ED $24 sequence to prefix a three or four-byte instruction. The last four bytes copy the accumulator to the C register, clear B and return, yielding a conventional USR function result.

Identifying the SpecNext Core version

Specific versions of the SpecNext FPGA core are identified by values in REG 1 and REG 14. This program prints out the three version numbers, in order of priority. The major version has been 3 since early in development, and even the minor version changes infrequently – recently only when support for the Artix FPGA was added.

```
100 LET %t= REG 1
110 PRINT "Major version ";%t>>4;
120 PRINT ", minor version ";%t & 15;
130 PRINT " sub-minor version "; REG 14
```

Sifting out a particular NextZXOS release

There's a dot command to check the version of Next's system software, as opposed to the FPGA hardware. By default **.nextver** neither prints nor returns anything at all, but if you suffix it with -v (short for verbose) it will spit out a number like 2.09, and if you put a name after the command the value will be copied as a decimal into that variable, e.g. **.nextver version**

Unfortunately this command doesn't uniquely identify release candidates or updates of a numbered NextBASIC release, which incorporate bug-fixes you might need to know about or work around. For the time being, the best way to check for these, if for some reason you can't simply write version-independent code, is to wrap a test in an ON ERROR block at the start of your program, check to see if the bug manifests itself, and if necessary merge in alternate code to suit the particular system you find yourself running.

Dot commands are slow and limited because they must find and load the implementation file from SD whenever they're invoked. But **.nextver** doesn't contain the version number – it just calls the M_DOSVERSION esxDOS function, which returns version-specific information in Z80 registers. The following snippets find and display the NextBASIC version number and system 'language code', via esxDOS hooks.

```
100 REM esxDOS hooks demo
120 %b=23708
130 POKE %b,207,136,66,75,201
140 REM RST 8;M_DOSVERSION;LD B,D;LD C,E;RET
150 %u=% USR b
160 PRINT "NextZXOS version   ";
170 PRINT CHR$ (%u>>12+48);CHR$ (%u>>8&15+48);".";
180 PRINT CHR$ (%u>>4&15+48); CHR$ (%u&15+48)
```

The machine-code poked by line 130 invokes Z80 restart 8; this is one of eight preset ROM entry points defined by Zilog e.g. Reset (RST 0), Interrupt handling (RST 56) and other routines so commonly-used that it's worth allocating them a single-byte instruction to jump into reserved slots at the start of the ROM, rather than a more general three-byte CALL instruction. BASIC reserves RST 16 for character output to the current stream, RST 40 to enter the floating-point calculator, RST 48 to reserve memory, and the other three for scanning the current program. The numbers indicate the ROM addresses, at eight-byte intervals, called by these Z80 instructions.

RST 8 was initially reserved by Sinclair for error reporting, then extended by Interface 1, esxDOS and various other mass-storage systems to issue system commands, known as 'hook codes'. These allow machine-code programs to access files and other resources without having to call arbitrary ROM routines, which are liable to vary in address between system releases.

Specific commands are indicated by the byte immediately after the RST op-code. 207 is the op-code of RST 8 and 136 denotes M_DOSVERSION. The last three bytes return to BASIC after copying the DE register pair into BC, where USR expects to find a result. Lines 170 and 180 unpack the digits of the version number from four-bit 'Binary Coded Decimal' format, adding 48 to each digit 0..9 to convert it into printable ASCII code, and slotting a dot in the middle to match the output of **.nextver**.

Language localisation

The next snippet returns the system language as a two-character code; currently 'en' and 'es' are supported, for English and Spanish (from España) and other languages may be added in future. Multilingual programs can check this and output messages in the appropriate language, assuming they've been pre-translated. The machine-code is almost identical, except that the result is two ASCII characters, copied to BC from the HL register pair. The BASIC just separates them out from **%U** for display with an 8-bit shift and a mask:

```
200 POKE %b,207,136,68,77,201
210 REM RST 8;M_DOSVERSION;LD B,H;LD C,L;RET
220 %u=% USR b
230 PRINT "System language "; CHR$ (%u>>8); CHR$ (%u&255)
```

These five-byte routines can run from any address. Once again I've stashed them very temporarily into memory used by the system when evaluating arithmetic expressions, which saves reserving space with CLEAR and putting the code up there. If you intend to call these routines several times in a program it's wiser to reserve space for them, as the space at 23708 is liable to be clobbered as soon as NextBASIC needs to evaluate any non-trivial arithmetic expression. But the answers won't change until the system is rebooted, so you might as well keep them in a variable after first fetching them, if your program needs to check the version or language in more than one place.

NextZXOS history

The software component of Next – the equivalent of the 16k ROM developed for Sinclair by Nine Tiles in Cambridge – is called NextZXOS and has been seven years in the making, picking up that name just as the first bare-board systems were reaching developers and Kickstarter backers. Over the previous year it had progressed from version 1.84, which was an elaboration of the 64k +3e ROM upgrade for Amstrad's disc system, to 2.00 which surfaced in September 2018.

Programs in this book have been enhanced to take advantage of NextBASIC improvements introduced for 2.08 and the second Kickstarter. At the time of writing 2.07 is still the latest packaged release for Spartan 6 (Kickstarter 1 and clone) systems; an early 2.08 shipped with Kickstarter 2. Newer systems are still being tested pending a fresh update package for both old and new hardware; the latest files are always available for download from:

https://gitlab.com/thesmog358/tbblue

NextZXOS 2.xx Milestones

2.00 **September 2018:** system release for Kickstarter 1 Issue 2A boards.

2.01 Conversion between tokens and text, for editing BASIC either way. Browser and snapshot file-handling improvements.

2.02 **September 2019:** CP/M plus integration.

2.03 ZX Printer (and compatible) support. 28 MHz clock option. Many improvements to the integer expression handler. String POKE and PEEK$. Better 48/128k compatibility.

2.04 **January 2020:** integration of the FPGA Core 3.01 series.

2.05 Major internal re-organisation to support code in DivMMC RAM and make room for new features.

2.06 Automatic SPRITE animation – requiring Core 3.01.03 or later. Fixes for bugs in the original Sinclair ROM. Support for system-friendly Plus3 .DSK image files.

2.07 **February 2022:** major update, featuring work mostly done in 2021.

Many Menu, Editor and File Browser enhancements. NextBASIC expression-evaluator optimisations. New Tools sub-menu. Extended User-defined graphics.

2.08 **June 2023:** Big improvements to NextBASIC, supporting long string and array names, default, array and DATA parameters, a line-address look-up cache, ENDIF, EXIT, PRIVATE, REF and TIME keywords, base conversions, consistency of expression evaluators.

2.09 **April 2024:** Block renumber and automatic line numbering. Better tape image file support. BANK 8 Sprite data hook. Many bug-fixes.

The full version history is in the docs/nextzxos-changelog.txt file, some 2,600 lines at the time of writing. I've condensed that to list key milestones which brought us from 2018's version 2.00 up to 2.09 in 2024. Each major release has a new number after the decimal point, with intermediate tweaks and bug-fix updates denoted by suffix letters. For instance, 2.06N corrected bugs in VERIFY and the Calculator described in Appendix D of the manual.

Mapping Next's 'ROM'

ROM stands for read-only memory, and technically there's no 'ROM' in Next, apart from the serial EPROM used to load the chosen core, but not the system code it depends upon, into the FPGA at start-up. The 64k space allocated by Amstrad is part of 256k of reserved system RAM which gets loaded from SD after the boot menu, and then write-protected in hardware so that it is effectively read-only, as the RO of ROM implies.

Over the years the OS, which includes NextBASIC, the file browser, and the menu system, has spread into several other 'ROM' files loaded at the same time, accompanied by megabytes of examples, optional system extensions, documentation and applications on the SD. This summary concentrates on the NextZXOS system, which loads the following components from the Machines/Next subdirectory:

`enAltZX.rom enNextLG.rom enNextMf.rom enNextZX.rom enNxtmmc.rom`

As of NextBASIC 2.09 RC11, discounting duplicates, these add up to 104k of system software, of which about 16k is free for future expansion. RC stands for Release Candidate. In the run-up to a full release these test versions are regularly updated and replaced as bugs are logged and fixed.

The two 64k files **enNextLG** and **enNextZX** are almost identical – the only difference is that one depends upon the original Sinclair ROM and the other uses the bug-fixed LG 'Looking Glass' version in 48k configurations. Both have about 8k of unused space. We'll have to wait till Garry opens the kimono before the details of these are revealed – it's still work-in-progress, and code is often duplicated or shuffled between files. It seems that the file browser comes first, then other system components, followed by Plus3DOS, the Spectrum 128 editor, and the 'original' 16k ROM at the end. New NextBASIC keywords are in the 32k **enAltZX** file, which also duplicates some of the NextZXOS menu system.

The memory browser, snapshot support and other 'green button' code is in **enNextMf.rom** which has only about 50 bytes of its 8k free. This is paged over the main ROM. It is Next's replacement for the Multiface software originally developed by Romantic Robot. **EnNxtmmc.rom** is an overspill from the main system, loaded into one of the 8k RAM pages originally reserved for the built-in DivMMC storage interface. I believe that parts of the OS that benefit from self-modifying code, such as DPOKE, are in here.

There are several other ROM files which change relatively infrequently, all associated with pre-Next personalities. These include the 1982 original **48.ROM**, the almost-identical Timex TC2048 version, and several of Geoff Wearmouth's patched variations. 32k ROM configurations are supported by the Toast-rack's **128.rom**, or its incompatible Spanish precursor which differs mainly in the first 16k of editor code, with Spanish error messages in the ZX BASIC half, or Amstrad's warmed-over +2 version **128-2.rom**. The last two big files are 64k images of Amstrad's **Plus3.rom** and Garry's hard-disc version **128-3e**, each associated with Plus Three legacy support.

ZX80 and ZX81 ROMs are just a small part of the files with those names; both are 32k long, though the ZX81 ROM and font occupy only 8k of one and the ZX80 Integer BASIC and OS takes just 4k of the other. The rest is support for Paul Farrow's software emulations of those earlier ZX micros, which run in Next's Spectrum 128 hardware personality, using interrupt-driven code to expand the byte-per character display files into a 6k Spectrum bitmap.

Backward Compatibility

Backward-compatibility is rightly seen as vital – if it won't run ZX BASIC programs and peripherals, it'd be misleading to call Next a ZX Spectrum – but sometimes users have come to rely on hacks that hamper improvements to the system, forcing Garry Lancaster to make a tough call. This applies particularly to the integer BASIC extensions, which are inconsistent with ZX BASIC in terms of operator precedence, loops and error reporting. But those are independent extras which never appear in ZX BASIC from the 80s, clearly marked and sifted out by the per cent prefix, so they preserve compatibility even though their semantics is inconsistent.

A trickier case applies to DEF FN, which was rather eccentrically implemented in the Sinclair ROM by patching invisible values into the program when a user-defined function was called. Guided by a hint in the 1982 manual, programmers wishing to pass multiple parameters to machine-code have exploited the DEFADD system variable in at least 20 published extensions to ZX BASIC.

NextBASIC's USR function now supports multiple parameters, and many of the old extensions have counterparts built in to NextBASIC. DEF FN used to be very slow, but has been recoded to work like PROC. This upsets old programs that use it to pass parameters via the DEFADD system variable, so NextBASIC 2.09 has added an option to allow old-style definitions to still be entered or tokenised by .txt2bas. Use **%CODE|=%4** to set bit 2 of the pseudo-variable %CODE if you need to enter such lines; old and new FNs co-exist happily once they're in the program.

I have worked with hundreds of programmers and find that Garry is exceptionally responsive to bug reports and very likely to fix anything that can be demonstrated as a regression with a short example program that has different effects on old and new systems. If he can reproduce the problem, he probably can and usually will fix it. But don't underestimate the difficulty of maintaining backwards compatibility or the amount of time it takes to investigate bug reports, especially vague ones.

Most of us are well aware that Next is a labour of love, subsidised by volunteers on the team and beyond, but it's worth reminding everyone that they're all very busy; if you contact them with a problem be sure to document it in a way that allows it to be reliably reproduced, and be willing to wait.

Before you report an apparent bug, make sure it still occurs on a newly-reset Next powered up from cold. Take a note of the exact version of NextBASIC displayed in the first menu screen, and try to check if the bug occurs on older versions, or has been fixed in the latest one on GitLab. If you've made any changes to the ROMs, all bets are off. Bug checks and reproductions should only be attempted on original system files, rather than custom tweaks. Create an 'issue' on GitLab so it can be tracked by everyone.

SpecNext Core versions

While Garry works on the system software in the UK, with support from the team and expert users, Allen Albright in Canada has been responsible for Next's FPGA hardware updates since Victor Trucco returned to his first love, enhancing MSX micros. Core changes are periodically logged in the **cores/zxnext/changelog.md** file at:

https://gitlab.com/SpectrumNext/ZX_Spectrum_Next_FPGA/

The following table summarises changes to the SpecNext Core. As in the OS history, I've skipped listing small tweaks and fixes to concentrate on showing more major changes. This information helps us identify which core version we need to take advantage of a particular feature, or which old one was 'current' when an old program with compatibility problems was written.

The pause in 2022 does not reflect a slump in activity so much as the need to reimplement the Spectrum Next design to suit the Artix 7 FPGA when the original Spartan 6 chips became unavailable in quantity for Kickstarter 2.

The comments below are terse and necessarily technical. You may need to experiment or read the FPGA source to fully understand some of them. Terms like ULA, PSG and HDMI are decoded elsewhere in this volume. UART refers to the two internal Universal Asynchronous Receive/Transmit interfaces, more often known as serial ports; DMA and CTC are Z80 add-on chips designed by Zilog and partially implemented inside Next. *Multiface*, *DivMMC*, *Opus Discovery* and *Wafadrive* are external hardware expansions for the original Spectrum; the first two of these are built-in to Next's FPGA; Core changes improve compatibility when the other two are plugged-in.

As the old FPGA fills up, it takes longer and longer for the Xilinx silicon compiler to re-synthesise new features into it. It's important to realise that neither Allen nor Garry are paid to work on Next – indeed, they've both got demanding full-time jobs. That limits their time for hobby projects but helps to qualify them for the painstaking work of maintaining and extending Next.

SpecNext Core update history, 2020 to 2023

3.01.01 *March 2020:* Audio tweaks, REG 142 added for easier Spectrum 128 bank switching, Sinclair joystick 1 and 2 addresses corrected.

3.01.02 DMA changes. Bit 4 of REG 138 propagates ULA fetches to the bus.

3.02.03 REG 128 now allows internal DivMMC banks 14 and 15 to replace external 16k ROMs, for floppies and similar smart peripherals.

3.01.04 *April 2020:* Multiface 48/128 fixes, joystick pin 7 output, Pentagon 512 paging, direct access to the new keys via REG 104, 176 and 177.

3.01.05 Amstrad +3 port contention removed. Mouse scaling and button swap. New REG 100 sets video line read offset to align overscan etc.

3.01.06 *May 2020:* Multicore changes allowing up to 1MB to survive reboots, easier 16-bit RAM access for other cores, Pentagon 1024 paging.

3.01.07 *June 2020:* Multiface and DivMMC can now coexist. All four versions of the Multiface are now supported. Opus Discovery and Wafadrive compatibility (REG 129 bits 5&6). F5/F6 keys toggle expansion bus.

3.01.08 *August 2020:* CTC counter/timer hardware. Provision for eight units, but only four are currently implemented, to preserve FPGA space.

3.01.09 *November 2020:* better UART flow control, Interrupt vectors for all peripherals, less intrusive snapshot NMI, current PSG chip detector.

3.01.10 *April 2021:* UART buffering rewritten, DivMMC breakpoints on restarts, PS/2 keyboards can now generate composite key-presses, hardware-programmable joystick/pad key mapping, Amstrad disc port access traps, Kickstarter 2 edge connector bus buffer control.

3.02.00 *June 2023:* Artix 7 and Spartan 6 code merge. Better tape input and ESP flow control on KS2. Sega pad MODE input added. Interrupt and PS/2 keyboard fixes.

3.02.01 *September 2023:* Kickstarter 2 HDMI timing corrected, for correct 50 or 60 Hz VGA *and* HDMI at once. Kickstarter 1 hardware requires separate cores for *either* improved HDMI *or* VGA/RGB output.

Work continues on updates for both FPGAs, with a commitment not to 'fork' the system by adding features on new hardware that are inaccessible to early-adopters. As we see with improved HDMI, sometimes this means that Kickstarter 1 users must choose one particular core, while those with the later and larger Artix 7 gate arrays might find both options combined in their core.

Next is a community effort, and there are far more volunteers with Z80 and BASIC software skills than able to chip into Next's VHDL development. That's why I've written Chapter 17, Hardware Programming, to encourage Next enthusiasts to explore the FPGA source and potential improvements.

Chapter 10, NextZXOS DRIVERS

Drivers are a central feature of NextZXOS, which is why I've written two as examples for this book and another, the NextBASIC Profile driver, which has already become part of the system distro. This also enables us to compare three of the tools available to write assembly language directly on Next.

Drivers can do two things which are logically district but often useful together. They can run a short machine-code routine regularly every display frame, typically between 50 and 60 times a second. Since this is triggered by the maskable interrupt it doesn't happen during BEEP, cassette or SD access because those fail if interrupted. Drivers can also implement character input and output for a new input/output device, such as a parallel printer, serial port, network adapter or sound chip. And they provide commands for both.

The Spectrum system is 'device independent' which means that the same PRINT, INPUT, INKEY$ and similar keywords can be used to access any device, or a file, once the hardware is selected with an OPEN command, which binds a letter associated with the device **channel** to a **stream** which can be indicated as a parameter for the input or output statement, usually in the range #4 to #15 as lower numbers are reserved by the system. Streams may support input or output, e.g. for serial or network transfers to or from the Next, but some only work one way, e.g. keyboard input or printer output.

Sinclair shipped the unfinished 1982 Spectrum ROM while Nine Tiles were still working on support for Interface 1 and microdrives, so only three devices are defined by default and these are connected to low-numbered streams: "k" handles input, originally using stream #0 and #1 for the lower and upper screen areas. Stream #2 is connected to channel "s" and stream #3 to the ZX printer.

The only difference between PRINT and LIST versus LPRINT and LLIST is that the former default to use stream #2 while the latter use stream #3. But you can change this with OPEN, e.g. after OPEN #3,"s": LPRINT will output to the screen, which may be handy if you don't have a printer, and after OPEN #2,"p" normal PRINT and LIST statements will be sent to the printer channel. When you CLOSE # any of these system streams they automatically revert to their usual binding.

Character streams

Add-on printers replaced the output routine for #3 so that LPRINT and LLIST were re-directed to their own interface. Filenames are treated as a special case of channel names, with the first character determining the form of file access ("o" for output to a new file, "u" to read **OR** write (Update) an existing one and "i" to read input from an existing one. Input is the default so you don't need to specify it if opening an existing file with a name more than one character long. To avoid problems with filenames starting with stream letters, a > sign is needed after the file stream letter to separate it from the file name and path. Hence LPRINT output can be diverted to the file 'test.txt' in directory 'output' with OPEN #3,"o>output/test.txt". Files are collected in a small buffer and written to the file whenever it fills up. To make sure the last few characters are flushed out to the file, you need to CLOSE the file, e.g. with CLOSE #3. This will reconnect stream #3 to the default ZX or Alphacom printer driver in Sinclair or NextBASIC, or leave higher stream numbers available for re-use for other files or devices.

Generally the examples in this book pick specific stream numbers like #4 and #5 for file input and output, but the choice of stream number from #4 to #15 is arbitrary. They all works the same way, so the key thing is not to try to use the same number for different things all at the same time. Unless you're very forgetful that's rarely a problem in your own programs, but when adding code to someone else's it helps to have a way to find a stream number which you can be sure is not currently in use, like this:

```
530 REM Return lowest open stream number 4..15
540 REM or 999 if all streams are already open
550 DEFPROC FREESTREAM()
560 LOCAL %c,%p
570 FOR %c=%4 TO %15
580   %p=% DPEEK ((c+3)*2+23568)
590   IF %p=0 THEN EXIT
600 NEXT %c
605 IF NOT p THEN %c=999: ; No free streams
610 ENDPROC =%c
```

Address 23568 holds the system variable STRMS, +3 skips over internal streams used only by the ROM, and the DPEEK and *2 allow two bytes per entry. Call this with something like:

```
PROC FREESTREAM() to %s : IF %s<=15 THEN OPEN #%s,"myfile"
```

Don't forget to CLOSE #%s when you're done with the file, so the stream can be re-used but also to make sure the final output is saved.

For more about Next streams, including channels **M** and **V** for limited output to memory or a string variable, **W** for a custom window using part of the screen, or driver output, refer to Chapter 21 of Next's original manual. Chapter numbers are one lower in the KS2 edition of the manual, so 20 there.

In this first example driver we're going to concentrate on the interrupt-handling part of the driver system. Interrupts are already used in NextZXOS, to regularly scan the keyboard for BREAK or other keys, and to provide an ingenious sort of multi-tasking that allows sprites to animate and move automatically at regular intervals, once prepared with NextBASIC SPRITE commands.

This driver allows up to 64 additional 'methods' comprising Z80n code and data to run every frame, while BASIC carries on at the same time. I'll show how to visualise this 'time sharing' and do cool things with it.

Thanks for Interrupting

On the original Spectrum hardware Z80 programmers could add a single interrupt handler by switching the CPU to interrupt mode 2 and setting up a table of 257 identical bytes selected unpredictably (depending on the add-ons connected and how they're wired). This value is used as the address of a Z80 code routine, in one of almost 200 fixed places in RAM, starting from $4040 (in the layer 0 screen) and extending to $FFFF at the end of RAM. I explained this in an article about *Realtime Games* in Tech Tips long ago, and won't labour the details because none of this works in NextZXOS.

Instead NextZXOS catches the display interrupt itself, scans the keyboard and updates TIME, then calls each driver which is loaded and registered to respond to interrupts. There's room for up to four drivers in memory at once, but by the time you've added one for a printer or serial keyboard, one for profiling NextBASIC, and one or two more for music and sound effects, you soon run out of slots.

This is a shame if all you really need is a way to run a short interrupt routine regularly. There are lots of reasons you might want to do this in an app or game, e.g. to check when DMA has finished and queue another buffer from banked RAM, or to animate the screen in more intricate ways than the Copper or SPRITE CONTINUE will let you.

NextBASIC fan Mark Gallop is writing a sprite animation application that allows arbitrary movement paths to be entered, edited and followed, rather than the straight-lines allowed by SPRITE CONTINUE, which are fine for *Pong* and maybe a simple platformer, but not much use for a flock of aliens in an arcade game like *Galaxian*. More on this in Chapter 12.

I was dithering about writing a custom driver as an example for this book, perhaps to sequence long streams of pre-banked audio samples, implement a BBC-style ENVELOPE system for AY chip effects, spool bytes out to a parallel printer or check network input while BASIC continued to run, or to help Mark convert his system to update any number of animated objects automatically every frame. Those are all great applications for an interrupt-based driver, but we've only got room for four. So I decided that this example would be a sort of meta-driver, allowing several short Z80 routines to be added or removed, external to the driver itself.

Time management

This scheme means a single driver can service lots of machine-coded methods, in easily-configurable order. The limitation is that all the interrupt code must run to completion in a short fraction of a second, before the next interrupt turns up, 50 to 60 times per second depending on the display speed.

The total amount of code that can run in all 64 slots, plus the system overheads, must not take more than 20 ms even with a 50 Hertz display, and perhaps only 16ms on a PC-type monitor. After allowing some foreground time, for the main program to run between interrupts, and slack for variation from one frame to the next, there's still time each frame to run tens of thousands of Z80 instructions, but not hundreds of thousands.

Later I'll show how to measure and visualise the amount of time taken by the system and each slot. Before saying more, it's important to note that NextZXOS is not generally re-entrant, so system calls can't be made from within an interrupt handler. Not only might they take too long, as in the case of SD card access, they might literally interrupt another call to the system, re-using memory or system variables that both calls might depend upon. Either or both could go wrong, and corruption of the SD card might result.

Memory management

You can remap memory inside your interrupt routine, e.g. by changing the values of REG 82, 83, 84 or 85 to put different banks into the address space from 16384 (after the ROM) to 49151, where RAM disc files and NextBASIC BANKs are swapped in and out, but it's VITAL that your code reads and restores the original values before it returns, or the running program might find the expected memory contents have disappeared. This will usually require a reset to recover, so make sure you've saved your work before testing any sort of machine code.

Any of the Next's RAM can be swapped in or out of that 32k window in the middle of Z80 address space. The first 16k is off-limits because the system uses that for ROM, driver code and the Z80 stack, and the top 16k is not safe to use for your own interrupt-handling code because an interrupt can come at any time, and BASIC might have put something else there at just that moment, so the driver will run arbitrary code – usually crashing – when it fails to find your routine at any address above 49151.

32k is still room for a lot of code alongside your resident or banked BASIC and the system variables, especially as the LAYER 0 screen area from 16384 to 23295 is free if you're only using LAYER 2, and the 768 byte attribute area from 22528 to 23295 is not used by LoRes, Timex HiColor or HiRes screens, LAYERs 1,0, 1,3 and 1,2 respectively.

Otherwise CLEAR 46*1024-1 will reserve a couple of K from 47104 upwards, and keep the top 16k for BASIC or data banks and any part of the Next's RAM your code may temporarily drop there with REG 86 or REG 87, as long as you save and restore the old MMU settings so NextZXOS doesn't get confused. In this way you're not limited to the 32k in the middle of Z80 RAM but can extend your interrupt handling stubs with code to swap any two other 8k pages, or several in sequence, in and out, to access far more RAM than the Z80 can see at once. The examples in Chapter 11 put a handful of routines in reserved RAM, just under the 48k watershed.

Secondly, those routines don't have to be built in to the driver, but can be put anywhere safe in Z80 memory. This means they can be tested independently by stepping through the code in main memory, which would be problematic for the driver code itself as it runs from DivMMC RAM mapped under the ZX ROM, requiring quick reflexes when you only have 20 ms, at most, before the code normally would be re-triggered!

A better example

Another reason I wanted to write a new driver is to show how one can be built from a single file using Odin, until recently the most capable Z80 assembler designed specifically for Next. The examples supplied with NextZXOS assume a multi-megabyte program, *Pasmo*, which only runs on other larger computers, yet they still expect the driver to be merged together from separate source files that create data and code blocks.

In 2020 I wrote an example driver with *Zeus*, the classic 48k Spectrum assembler in the Next distro, which used a single source file – for the NextBASIC Profile driver, now part of every Next distro SD. Because of the way Zeus relies on BASIC to load and save files this still required a stand-alone BASIC program, grandly called the 'driver compiler', to combine the main driver code after assembly with the driver setup data – originally from a separate file, now baked into the BASIC. This makes a file suitable for the DRIVER command to load, removing the PLUS3DOS header which DRIVER won't accept but SAVE CODE tacks on regardless.

Helped by Ped Helcmanovsky filling gaps in the Odin documentation, I made a single example file that outputs a complete ready-to-load driver. So the fourth reason for this example is that it shows everyone they don't need another computer, or even a second program, to create a new driver. Feel free to slice and dice this, or the Zeus profiler source, to make whatever new driver tickles your fancy. And if you'd like to dabble in interrupt-driven Z80, you can use this one as it is, and extend it far beyond the dozen examples shown in the next two chapters.

The Interrupt Slot driver

I've called this metadriver the 'interrupt slot driver', because it manages a set of 'slots', each containing a code address called indirectly from another program. As well as the code address, each slot holds a 16-bit data value which is passed into your code whenever the driver fires up that slot. You can use that for a single input data value, such as a colour or line number, or to pass the address of a table of any number of values which the code in the slot can read and *write*.

Separating the code and data means that several slots can use the same code with different data, or share data between different code routines, set up to run in whatever order suits you by appropriate choice of slot numbers, or with BASIC or any other program running in the foreground. And if you don't want to use any of the slot data values, you don't have to.

DRIVER commands

You load the driver, like any other, with **.install**. And you remove it, releasing the slot, with **.uninstall**. Once a driver is loaded it will start monitoring channels, if they're OPENed using its stream letter, running interrupt code if configured to do so, and be ready to accept configuration parameters via the DRIVER command, which can pass values to any loaded driver selected with the corresponding identifier (ID). Usually the first value is the driver ID, then a number from 0 to 127 to indicate the required action, and one or two more integer values to customise it.

The Interrupt Slot driver has been assigned ID 8 by Garry Lancaster. That number is easy to type and recognise in DRIVER commands, without resort to the CODE function. This choice also leaves alphabetic IDs for drivers that use OPEN, unlike this one.

It's important for each driver to have a unique ID, which is why Garry maintains a central list. This is the `docs/nextzxos/DriverIDs.txt` file on your latest distro SD, updated as new drivers are added. Contact Garry before using one of the remaining IDs, or circulating an incompatible driver that re-uses one of the already-allocated IDs.

This driver's Application Program Interface (API) includes four custom commands, to select any slot and set the code and data addresses, to read either one of those addresses back to BASIC, and a quick way to deactivate all the slots, which is needed anyway as part of the driver's start-up sequence:

DRIVER 8, 101, S TO C reads the *code* address for slot **S** into **C**

DRIVER 8, 102, S TO D reads the *data* address for slot **S** into **D**

DRIVER 8, 128 turns off all the slots in one step.

The main command, used to set up any slot, reserves 64 command codes so it can set both data and code addresses for any slot in a single step:

DRIVER 8, S, C, D

S may be 1 to 64. Slots are processed each frame in ascending order. **C** is the address of the service code and **D** is a data address for that slot, passed in register DE. You can use this as a data byte, word, or address of more data (allowing output as well as input, and data sharing with BASIC or other slots).

Make sure there's valid code at address **C**, ending with a RET instruction and leaving nothing on the stack, before doing this. Don't push more than a hundred words onto the default stack, because DivMMC RAM space is limited. Alter SP to point to your own RAM, and restore the old value before the RET, if you must PUSH and POP more. There's a more detailed introduction to stack handling later, in the code commentaries.

To disable a slot, pass a value of **C** less than 256, e.g. DRIVER 8,1,0. In general **C** and **D** should be in the range 16384 to 49151 as NextZXOS swaps the ROM/RAM outside that range without warning, which is bad news for code that expects it to be unchanged 50 times a second, but you are free to live dangerously and use any value from 256 to 65535 if you are quite sure what'll be there and promise not to moan to me if it isn't.

Later I'll show an extension to the original design which allows slot routines to run from the top 16k, as long as they've been loaded into BANK 0, which is the default used by BASIC. This feature is built into the published version of the driver, but to keep this example easier to follow I'll miss it out of the first example. There will be scope for more complicated drivers later in this book, and hopefully in subsequent volumes, too.

Here is a little BASIC loop to test the commands, using dummy code addresses less than 256 so no Z80 code is needed:

```
390 FOR i=1 TO 15
400   DRIVER 8, i,i*5, i*50
410   DRIVER 8, 101, i TO a
420   DRIVER 8, 102, i TO b
430   PRINT "Slot ";i;" code ";a;" data ";b
440 NEXT i
```

The generic driver error message is output if you try to use a command code lower than 101 and greater than the number of slots, or in the range 103 to 127. Values above 128 are reserved by Garry for stream operations, and 1 to 64 are allocated to specific slots, so IDs 65 to 100 and 103 to 127 are free for future expansion. Code 0 is reserved in case one day we run out and need an 'escape mechanism'. Similarly, if Zilog hadn't left most of the opcodes prefixed with $ED free we'd have struggled to add the Z80n extra instructions.

The Character Set section of the Spectrum manual shows how $CB, $DD, $ED and $FD opcodes unused by Intel enabled Zilog architects Faggin and Shima to more than double the Z80 instruction set, compared with their earlier 8080 design. This might have played a part in protecting them from being sued into oblivion by furious Intel bosses, but Zilog's early finance deal with oil giant Exxon probably did more to dampen the ardour of Intel's litigation 'profit centre'. Either way, they got away with it; good news for us!

The driver source

This is the second-biggest Z80 example in this book, but still barely 100 bytes of code and data. It was assembled and tested with Odin of 2021, the latest version when it was written. You don't need to re-type it – like all the code in this book, it is freely downloadable from simon.mooli.org.uk/nextbook You don't even need Odin, as ready-assembled code and examples are also available from the same web-pages.

There are plenty of other resources to teach Z80 assembly language so my comments will be confined to the general quirks of driver-writing and the specific needs of this one, along with Odin features when they're not common to all Z80 assemblers. As I'm aware that some readers will be familiar with BASIC but easily baffled by some of the quirks of Z80n history, I'm going to take some time to explore those, along the way.

To make it easier to see the structure, the driver source is presented in two chunks. The first is a minimal but complete, tested and working driver. After that I shall list some optional code which provides extra flexibility for the methods that run within driver slots. Here's how it starts:

```
; TTN1 Vertical blank vector driver
; Simon N Goodwin 1st November 2023
;
limit   EQU  512                   ; Size of dot arena
slots   EQU  64                    ; Number of slots
stride  EQU  4                     ; Bytes per slot
headlen EQU  8                     ; Driver header size
base    EQU  49160                 ; Code assembly address
; Lifecycle API codes defined by NextZXOS
getinit EQU  128                   ; Initialisation API
getshut EQU  129                   ; Shutdown API, unused
; Special API codes to read from slots
getcode EQU  101                   ; Return code address
getdata EQU  102                   ; Return data address
recount EQU  (length-relocs)/2
; This is the header used to load the driver
        ORG  base-headlen
        DEFB "NDRV"                ; Magic start marker
        DEFB 8+128                 ; Includes interrupt flag
        DEFB recount               ; Number of relocations
        DEFB 128                   ; Call Init, no DivMMC
        DEFB 0                     ; No additional banks
```

The first few lines give symbolic names to 'magic numbers' that appear later. The 'equ' assembler directive stands for equate, and can be read as if it was something like `limit=512` in BASIC, except that the value corresponding to the name should be the same throughout the program. Unlike a variable, changing the associated value with a later EQU line is an error in Z80 assembly language, as it contradicts the mnemonic purpose of the directive.

In this case **limit** is the standard amount of memory allocated for each driver, though additional RAM pages can be requested when the driver starts up. The symbol is used to make sure that the code and data inside this driver fits neatly within that space. The symbol **slots** determines how much memory therein is allocated to the storage of slot details, in chunks of **stride** bytes per slot. The term 'stride' represents the interval in bytes when 'stepping' from one slot to the following one.

Each .drv file is prefixed by an eight-byte header which identifies it to NextZXOS and enables it to be properly linked into the system. The DEFB assembly language directive, sometimes abbreviated to DB, is used to prepare data bytes.

The symbol **headlen** gives a name to the length of this header. The first half of it must contain the characters 'NDRV', so the system can be confident it's really a driver file. The extension '.drv' is just a file-system convention and a hint for directory-browsing humans; the **.install** command couldn't care less what the file is *called*, as long as it has a valid header.

The next four bytes are specific to the way each driver works. The first of these bytes contains the driver ID, 8 in this case; since bytes are precious and ASCII only needs seven bits the eighth is purloined to indicate whether or not this particular driver expects to be called every interrupt. The value 8+128 indicates that this is driver ID 8 and includes an interrupt handler.

Relocating Z80 code

The next byte can be zero if the driver program is relocatable, with no call or absolute jump references, or addresses of data within its 512 byte region. Otherwise, and almost always, it holds the number of 'relocations', or 16-bit address references that will need adjusting depending on exactly where NextZXOS decides to put the code.

There is currently 2K of system memory reserved for four add-on drivers, which can all be active at once. If you need more, you need to **.uninstall** one of the four, or petition Garry to reserve space for more. The exact address where any driver is loaded and run from depends on the system version and how many drivers have previously been loaded. That's problematic for Z80 code and data that includes 16-bit address references within the driver itself, because those specific addresses depend on where the code ends up.

The pragmatic solution is for us to assemble each driver as if it was going to be loaded to address 0, usually the start of ROM, and give the system enough hints to be able to add the actual load address onto all such 16-bit internal references after the driver is loaded and before it is first run. The sixth byte of the driver header contains the 'number of relocations', a count of how many such corrections are needed.

Additional data, in words from offset 520 at the end of the .drv file, identifies all the specific offsets earlier where relocation offsets must be added. We'll see the exact format of that data at the end of this example. The key thing to remember is that if you include a JP or CALL in your driver code you must label it and add it to the table of offsets to make sure that it gets relocated. Otherwise the code will jump off to the wrong place, probably crashing the Next.

This caught me out when I changed a JR instruction into a JP, because additional code meant the target address was no longer within the -128 to +127 byte relative range of JR, but forgot to include the address of the JP instruction in the count and table of references requiring adjustment. Until I realised my mistake, perfectly 'good' code crashed, because it wasn't jumping to the right place *after it had been loaded into the system.*

This explains why the next line of the file has two parameters rather than the usual one. ORG, short for Origin, indicates the start address where the following block of Z80 code is expected to run from once it's been assembled. Sometimes we want this to be a place which will be available later but is currently busy, e.g. the low memory addresses where drivers run in place of the usual ROM, or attribute memory used by LAYER 0 but free when LoRes, LAYER 2 or Timex 'hi' displays are active. In this case ORG takes two parameters: the first is the address which the code will be temporarily stored by the assembler, and the second is where it will eventually be loaded and run from.

Before memory paging enabled dot commands and other ingenious expansions, game developers often wanted to write code that would later run from the addresses used by their assembler, temporarily loaded into the same 48k RAM. The two-part ORG variant directed the code to be stored at the first address so it could be SAVEd from there after assembly, but told the assembler to fix up internal CALLs and other memory references as if the code was actually stored at the second address. A subsequent LOAD CODE to the second address meant that the final project could re-use RAM which the assembler had occupied when the project was assembled.

The following code shows how ORG is set up for a driver; **base** can be any address protected by CLEAR or otherwise known to be free while the assembler runs. Since ORG originally had only one parameter, the extension syntax is assembler-specific. In Zeus, used to build the Profile driver on your SD, the equivalent syntax would be `ORG 0 DISP base`.

Driver entry points

Two addresses at the start of the driver are special, because they're the 'entry points' the system calls when interacting with it. The first three bytes – just enough room for a jump instruction – are invoked when a DRIVER command is typed. Parameters from the command-line are loaded into specific registers before the system jumps to the start, labelled API. A subroutine called COMMS checks those register values and implements whatever command corresponds to those values, such as `getcode`, `getdata`, `getinit` or `getshut` in the API documentation.

Drivers that also respond to interrupts can't just put the implementation of the API at their start, because there is a second entry point just three bytes into the 512-byte driver space. This entry point is used not when a DRIVER command is entered, but as part of the system update which occurs 50 or so times per second, whenever a new display frame is about to be generated. On a standard Spectrum this just increments the system variable **FRAMES** and polls the keyboard, updating **LASTK** and associated system variables, depending upon which keys are held down and for long. Timing in-between frames is also a factor for keyboard auto-repeat and 'debouncing'. These delays were introduced so that cheap switches don't accidentally trigger multiple entries when they've only deliberately been pressed once; then auto-repeat was added to make it easier to move the cursor within long lines.

Next extends the Sinclair frame interrupt scheme, to animate sprites and call driver-specific interrupt routines, as well as to run the standard or updated keyboard one. The loop labelled **SCAN** is in this second entry-point within DRIVER 8. As the name suggests, it scans the slots every frame to work out which need updating.

The immediately-previous instruction NOP pads the two-byte **JR COMMS** code to make sure that **SCAN** appears at the fourth byte of the driver, at offset 3; assembly-language programmers get used to counting from 0, whereas BASIC DIMs, string offsets and indeed our own driver slots count from 1, the way humans tend to be taught.

```
; This is the actual 512 byte driver code and data
        ORG  base,0

api     JR   comms
        NOP                         ; Pad to offset of 3

scan    LD   HL,slot1               ; Test code vector high bytes
        LD   B,slots                ;   for this many slots
        LD   DE,stride              ;     at this interval
        XOR  A                      ; Zero means slot is inactive
```

The SCAN routine above starts by pointing the 16-bit register pair HL to the beginning of the slot-specific information, labelled SLOT1. It loads the number of slots into 8-bit register B, and the size of each slot – the 'stride' between them – into register-pair DE. The choice of these registers is not arbitrary but necessitated by the way the Z80 designers extended the Intel 8080 instruction set by adding quirky little special-purpose instructions, often bound to a particular one or two of the seven original data registers, A, B, C, D, E, H and L.

Every register or unmixable pair has unique properties as well as shared ones. A and HL are accumulators. Often instructions force you to use only those. HL doubles as the main register for indirect memory addressing, while B specialises in counting backwards!

Register C addresses ports and pairs only with B; DE can be swapped with HL, multiplies into itself on our Z80n, and tracks DEstinations... then there are Zilog instructions and registers which usually take longer and more code bytes than that core set but save spilling values, in 16-bit pairs, to that luxurious but bandwidth-hungry 64k 16-bit stack. So they're worth using – seven more registers on Next than on an 8080, or five on earlier Spectrums plus IX (but not always IY): 16+8 bit index registers which are rather clunky and limited, but still useful for things like draughts-boards and arrays of small structures, especially packed bits like the flag bytes in the Spectrum system variables. And then there's the geek candy, specialised compound instructions like CPDR and LDI that usually do slightly more or less than you want, and alter up to seven registers at a time - all hard-wired, of course.

Programming algorithms efficiently on the Z80 is often a matter of deciding which registers to use for what, then regretting and refining that recursively over several pages till it nearly all fits.

BASIC programmers with 26 integer variables that all work the same should be very grateful. But Z80 programming is eccentrically fun and satisfying, like *Tetris* with a purpose.

CPU register history

The most-used register pair, H and L, was a special case even on the 8080, working as a 16-bit accumulator and also as a 'memory pointer' referred to as M rather than (HL) in Intel's assembly language. Almost every operation that can refer to any of the seven 8-bit registers may also refer to a byte in memory, at the address held in register-pair HL.

This arrangement was inherited from the earlier and much slower 8008 processor, which was not designed by Intel but by the peripheral company Datapoint. They sold dumb screen-and-keyboard combos called 'VDU terminals', intended to enable teletype-style access to remote computers, using a scrolling screen rather than a paper-roll for output. Datapoint's original product was built from dozens of small TTL chips.

To save money they asked semiconductor companies to pitch a single-chip replacement for their boardful of logic. Texas Instruments, who stood to lose a lot of TTL sales if they could not be the ones replacing those, tried to make an 8-bit microprocessor to fit the spec, but their TMX-1795 apparently never worked.

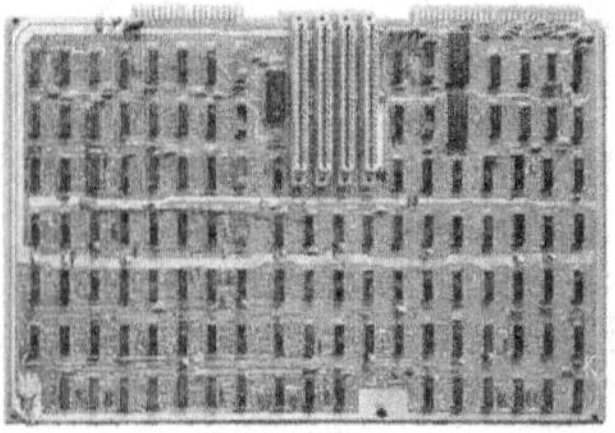

Figure 56 - the main CPU board from a Datapoint 2200 terminal – Intel packed this into a single 8008 chip, precursor to the Z80. Photo credit: `oldcomputers.net`

Intel's speciality was RAM production. They were reluctant to consider making processors for fear of upsetting their primary customers of the time, the big computer manufacturers. But they had a small department looking into the potential of making custom chips for embedded systems.

That group put in a bid for the Datapoint contract and eventually succeeded, thanks in great part to recent hire Federico Faggin. He had designed his first CPU, with 6k of 12-bit core memory, while a teenager working for Olivetti in Italy, and went on to found Zilog. But in the meantime Datapoint lost interest and Intel kept the rights to their chip.

Thus Intel, a chemical engineering company tooled up to make memory chips, ended up shipping three of the most significant early microprocessors, without ever giving any serious thought to the instruction set with which they were programmed!

The first, the 4004, was specified by Japanese calculator manufacturers Busicom to process decimal digits, so four bits were enough and the instruction set came directly from the calculator design. Entering and displaying characters needed more bits – the Datapoint terminal ASCII code included 94 symbols – so the later 8008 was designed around 8-bit character codes. The Intel 8080 was an improved version, using the same main registers and memory model to make conversion of 8008 programs relatively simple. There's a detailed analysis of the changes at https://bread80.com/2022/07/09/comparing-datapoint-2200-8008-8080-and-z80-instruction-sets

Instruction-set strategy

The upshot is that a quarter of the 256 possible single-byte 8008 or 8080 instruction opcodes are reserved just to move values between the seven single-letter registers or the memory byte M, pointed at by the 16-bit register pair HL. Seven of these are futile time-wasters like LD A,A and LD B,B. The eighth, the even more useless LD (HL),(HL), would in theory just copy a byte over itself, but the designers sensibly hijacked that opcode for the HALT instruction, which stops the processor until an interrupt occurs; that one is used in our BASIC PAUSE command.

Many other instructions were generalised for these eight possibilities. Eight Zilog LoaD instructions (similar to LET in BASIC, written backwards as MOVe in 8080 assembly language, but using the same codes) will load any 8-bit value from the following instruction byte to any one of the seven registers, *or* to memory addressed by HL. Thus Zilog's (HL) mnemonic, or M in Intel assemblers, can be written in place of a register letter, though it's slower due to the extra overhead of memory access. Likewise, the 16 8-bit INC and DEC instructions can add or subtract one, increment or decrementing any of the seven registers *or* any byte of memory – providing its address has been preloaded to registers H and L.

Intel stuck with this eight-fold access to registers or memory bytes, and approach of pairing registers for 16-bit addressing, for more than a decade, in the 8085, 8086 and 8088 processors. Meanwhile Zilog was founded by the team of Federico Faggin and Mastoshi Shima (from Busicom) that had created the 4004, 8008 and 8080. Their Z80 was boxed into the same corner by the need for Intel software-compatibility. When Zilog came to add extra features to the Z80, to attract new customers, improve performance and fend off claims from Intel that they were just copying an older design (albeit Datapoint's, rather than Intel's) they knew that the requirement for most of the old instructions to work with seven different registers, or (HL), had used up most of the possible 8-bit instruction codes.

The 8008 carried over 174 of the Datapoint instructions, and added 22 new ones: 8-bit INC and DEC, the RSTs and nine-bit rotation through carry. The 8080 shuffled the Datapoint operation codes (opcodes) and shoehorned in another 48, mostly new instructions to manipulate registers as 16-bit pairs.

Figure 57, Intel crammed the 8008 CPU into an 18-pin RAM package

In order to add more instructions using the twelve opcode bytes left over, Zilog had three choices. They could retain the generality by using eight codes for register-or-memory versions of each new instruction. That way they'd only have been able to add one and a half sets.

They could have added a dozen instructions by making new ones specific only to certain registers. Or they could use some of the left-over codes as a 'prefix' to tell the CPU to interpret the following byte as a completely new instruction. This opened up hundreds of new combinations, at the expense of making programs longer, since all the new instructions would start with 16-bits of opcode, instead of just eight.

Zilog predictably opted for a mix of the second and third approaches. Six relative jump instructions, and two for exchanging 8080 and new Z80 register banks, left just four byte-prefixes. Zilog used the lot.

From Z80 to Z80n

This history lesson is directly relevant to Next, because the same challenge applied to Next's original FPGA designer Victor Trucco when the team wanted to add new instructions for the Z80n. Almost all Zilog's extra instructions were forced to use prefix bytes, as you can see from the Z80 assembly language columns alongside the character codes in the Character Set chapter in the Spectrum manual. Prefixes 221 and 253 ($DD and $FD in hexadecimal) were used to ease the pressure on HL by diverting Intel instructions that interpreted (HL) as a memory address M to instead access memory pointed to by one of two new 16-bit registers, IX and IY.

Since it is often necessary to access several adjacent memory bytes, Zilog extended the new instructions with a third byte, a signed offset which would be added to the index in IX or IY before accessing the combined memory address. This looks great in the spec sheet – every instruction previously bound to the single address M can now access 512 bytes around the addresses held in IX or IY – but came at quite a heavy cost in overhead and complexity.

LD (HL),A, which stores the byte in register A at the address in HL, has a single-byte opcode and runs in 7 clock cycles – four to fetch the instruction and three to write to memory. But the similar-looking LD (IX),A or LD (IY),A instructions are more than twice as slow and need three times as many bytes of code.

Some assemblers require the offset +0 to be specified, as a reminder of the wasted byte. Worse still, the mechanism to divert CPU references from

HL to IX or IY hides registers H and L, so the codes for LD (IX),H or LD (IY),L don't work as expected; they actually, unofficially and not very usefully, store one or other half of the associated index register rather than the main H or L. Eight codes are needed for just five useful cases, A, B, C, D, E, when reading or writing 8-bit register values to indexed addresses.

This is partly why optimised Z80 programs tend to stick to the old 8080 instruction set most of the time, using the Zilog extras only when the extra code bytes are not enough to wipe out the advantage. Often it works out quicker to shuffle values between the original 8080 registers than to accept the overhead required by new Zilog registers and instructions. So Zilog allow any 8-bit register to be shifted left or right, whereas Intel confined such instructions to the Accumulator. But the 8080 instructions upon A are half the length of equivalent, sometimes functionally identical, Zilog extras, so if you're shifting any value by more than two places it's more economical to copy it into A and back out again, than to use several of the new slower instructions directly on the required register.

Zilog, and later SpecNext, often used the second approach of adding instructions that were quite-literally hard-wired to work with specific registers. A case in point is Next's MUL instruction, which yields a 16-bit result in two registers from two 8-bit values, also in registers.

Rather than provide all the variations like MUL DE,H,L (for DE=H*L) MUL BC,D,E, MUL HL,B,C – which would amount to 126 combinations just for input in A, B, C, D, E, H or L and the result in HL, DE or BC, we get just one: MUL D, E which reads values in D and E (it doesn't matter which, as multiplication is commutative) and returns its 16-bit result to the same places.

> *Bloody instructions which, being taught, return to plague the inventor*
> *William Shakespeare*

Perhaps the team agonised over which registers to dedicate, but with BC optimised or essential for loop counts and port access, and HL and A specialised as 16-bit and 8-bit accumulators, there wasn't really much choice to those who already know the Z80 inside-out. Even if you end up using four of the 56 register-copying instructions to marshal the inputs and outputs from other registers, the total time of 32 Ts (clock-ticks) is about the tenth that of the equivalent generic loop, and needs fewer bytes of code.

Barrel-shifting Nextras

Similar decisions affected the 16-bit BS-prefixed 'barrel shift' mnemonics, all of which move bits in DE according to a count in the bottom four or five bits of register B. There's a single byte instruction to swap HL and DE, added after the Datapoint spec, which gives a quicker way to get values into or out of DE. This is Zilog's EX DE,HL (equivalent to EX HL,DE, or simply if cryptically XCHG on the 8080).

SpecNext are more generous, providing Nextras to add 16-bit constants to register pairs, or an 8-bit register to a pair. There are three of each, updating BC, DE or HL, but the 8-bit value to add can only be the accumulator, register A. Along with MUL these instructions and all the other Nextras use the 237 ($ED) prefix byte, which Zilog had allocated to 59 instructions (and 13 undocumented duplicates) leaving 188 free for Nextras. 160 of those opcodes remain available, but seem unlikely to be allocated for fear of breaking compatibility, or bursting the KS1 FPGA.

The most extreme example of operands gobbling up instruction space comes with Zilog's fourth prefix byte 203 ($CD), which adds 256 potential new codes but uses three-quarters of those for just three classes of instruction: BIT, SET and RES, which each have 64 register/bit variants. The other 64 codes prefixed by 203 are taken up with eight sorts of shift or rotate instructions, of which sixteen should be duplicates and half those don't work as planned, so the intended 'SLL' codes $ED30 to $ED37 are simply missed out of Zilog's (and Sinclair's) documentation because they accidentally add 1 to the shifted value and if that'd been fixed to match that mnemonic they'd just have been dupes of the eight SLAs defined elsewhere.

Next could have included a BSLL version of BSLA but sensibly opted not to, since when shifting left logical and arithmetic shifts have identical effect. Only when shifting right is it necessary for the top (sign) bit to be preserved in arithmetic as opposed to logical shifts, so we have and need both BSRA and BSRL, for signed and unsigned values respectively, but BSLA ($ED28) has no BSLL counterpart because BSLA already does the same thing.

For similarly reductionist reasons the new 16-bit rotate instruction BRLC (Barrel (i.e. multi-bit) Rotate Left can also rotate right N bits by supplying 16-N in register B. So there's no BRRC. I've no idea what the C stands for, and given that the instruction, like most Nextras, doesn't affect the carry flag (the reason for the ADC and SBC mnemonics) it may be a mistake. But consistency is not something Z80n programmers should rely upon!

In fact part of the charm – or horror, depending on how busy you are – of the Z80 is the quirkiness of the instruction set, which Next has only increased. The need to make sure the right registers are available for each special instruction leads to repeated local re-writing of optimised Z80 code by experts with time on their hands, and a pidgin-Z80 style using only the simplest and most generic instructions among those new to the processor or with bigger fish to fry. I compare this process with the country skill of dry-stone-walling, building a solid and regular wall out of random pieces of stone, where each placement has consequences for subsequent choices. Programming a modern 32-bit RISC chip is far simpler, because you have lots of large registers that can be used interchangeably, but a lot more verbose in terms of code length and other resources.

Since you're still reading, we assume you're up for the Z80n challenges – the purpose of this digression, among others, is to explain the underlying design decisions that give our little CPU its many annoyances, quirks or delights, depending upon when you notice them. I find that understanding the history of the 8080 makes the Z80 more logical in some cases and at least explicable in others. This is despite the fact that I have never actually owned or programmed an 8080 chip – nor an 8085, 8086 or 8088, for that matter.

Back to the driver

A few pages ago we were explaining the SCAN routine of DRIVER 8. Before we access slots, using our new-found insights into (HL) and register allocation, there's one more quirky line to understand. Our final preparation is to clear the accumulator, register A, by the peculiar but economical method of exclusive-oring its contents with themselves.

The binary AND operation combines two bytes, setting only bits which were previously set in both operands. OR sets any bits which had been set in either or both. So eXclusive OR, XOR in Z80 code, sets only bits which differ between the two operands. When applied to two identical values, XOR logically clears all the bits in the result.

This is one of the tricks experienced Z80 programmers use automatically. The more obvious instruction LD A,0 would work as well in this situation, but needs an extra byte of code, for the value 0, and takes three additional clock-ticks to fetch that from memory.

The next five lines loop over all the slots, testing the first byte of each to see if the slot contains a valid code address. It's normal for Z80 code to store 16-bit values with the units first and the most significant (multiples of 256) part in the second byte. Thus, HL is usually stored as L followed by H. This approach is called 'little-endian' and makes multi-byte arithmetic easier since the carry from the lowest-order bytes is available for each following byte when memory is scanned in ascending order.

Every standard has its exceptions, and since the earliest ZX BASIC it's made sense to store some values the other way round. Not only does this make them easier to read in a multibyte hexadecimal dump, storing the most significant byte first makes it easier to sift out large values quickly This approach, favoured by Motorola and IBM, is named 'big-endian', in a wink to the holy war among boiled-egg eaters in Jonathan Swift's satire *Gulliver's Travels*. ZX BASIC uses it for line numbers, to make checks for the end of the program quicker, and I use it here to scan the slots slightly more efficiently. Since the slots are read and written a byte at a time, the internal byte order makes no difference providing we do it consistently when storing and retrieving.

> *You don't understand something until you understand it more than one way*
>
> *Marvin Minsky*

The OR (HL) instruction labelled TRY sets the processor Z flag if the byte pointed to by HL is zero. Otherwise, the next line jumps on to the USE routine. The ADD HL,DE at the label NEXT which advances HL to test the next slot, since pages ago we set DE to the size of a slot, currently 4 bytes.

The loop is completed by the DJNZ instruction, a register-specific Zilog special that takes one away from the value in register B and jumps back to TRY until B becomes zero. DJNZ is a concise way of making a loop that goes round between 1 and 256 times. Start with 0 for the maximum count.

The alternative would be DEC B : JR NZ,TRY but that uses one extra byte, and three more clock-ticks, so Zilog felt it worthwhile to make a special fast version hard-wired to register B, and Z80 programmers ever since have tried to avoid using B for anything else in small loops.

Once B ends up zero, the interrupt handler ends with a RET instruction. This returns control to NextZXOS, so the next driver can take its turn. Since RET reads the return address from the memory addressed by SP, the stack pointer, it's essential to make sure that SP has the same value when you RET as it did when the subroutine was called. We're safe here, having not used any PUSH or POP instructions or otherwise adjusted SP. In bigger programs, beware – an 'unbalanced stack' is a frequent cause of program crashes.

```
try     OR   (HL)                 ; Check if slot is active
        JR   NZ,use
next    ADD  HL,DE                ; Advance to next slot
used    DJNZ try
        RET
```

Stack magic

The Z80 stack is intended for two purposes: to hold the return address to the point after an RST, CALL instruction or hardware interrupt, or to save and restore temporary values to free up registers during a complicated routine. In either case it is used in a first-in, last-out order (or last-in, first out, if you prefer). This is necessary so that when one subroutine CALLs another the return addresses are used in the necessary order.

RET reads the two bytes at the 'top' of the stack into the program counter. Confusingly, the Z80 stack grows from higher to lower addresses, so after a RET the value of SP is increased by two bytes. CALL stores the program counter for the immediately following instruction at the 'top' of the stack, moving SP down by two bytes. PUSH and POP instructions work similarly except that the 16-bit values they store or retrieve come from other registers such as BC, DE, HL, IX, IY or the odd couple AF, which pairs the accumulator with the processor state flags (zero, negative, borrow or overflow, etc) to make a two-byte set.

Not all CPUs have a stack; if not, a sequence of register store and load operations can achieve the same effect, but much more slowly. For instance we could use HL as a stack pointer and store DE there with this sequence:

```
DEC HL
LD (HL),E
DEC HL
LD (HL),D
```

However, those four instructions take 26 cycles to execute, versus just 11 for the single-byte PUSH DE using the stack. The Z80 is generous in that all of RAM can be used for the stack – the 6502 allows only 256 bytes, or just 16 on the 8008 – but there's no check on its range or to stop it clobbering data or code at lower addresses. Because PUSH stores two bytes at once and adjusts the stack pointer ready to push more, repeated PUSHes are a quick way to clear blocks of memory. Many games wipe the screen that way, but remember that the stack is also used by hardware interrupts which may be requested at any time. . See page 160 - use the DI instruction to delay this, and EI as soon as you are ready for normal system stack operation to resume.

How slot methods are invoked

The USE routine runs only when a slot is active. Since most of the 64 slots will be inactive most of the time, yet any of the 64 could be active, the TRY loop is optimised on the assumption that most slots will be inactive, since this minimises the system overhead of having the driver loaded but no slots set up. Consequently USE starts by saving BC, containing the loop count, on the stack with PUSH BC – there's no PUSH B, two bytes are always PUSHed or POPped – then re-reads the first, most significant, byte from the slot into B and the lower byte into C. We have the address of the slot code, in little-endian order, in BC. Similar steps read the next two bytes, the data address, into DE. As we progress from byte to byte we've been incrementing HL, so we save the address of the next byte – the start of the following slot – on the stack with PUSH HL. This way the slot method can do whatever it likes with that precious register-pair and we can easily restore the next slot address with POP HL when it returns.

```
; HL -> an active vector slot; find code and data
use     PUSH BC                 ; Save slot loop count
        LD   B,(HL)             ; Code vector to BC
        INC  HL
        LD   C,(HL)
        INC  HL
        LD   D,(HL)             ; Data vector to DE
        INC  HL
        LD   E,(HL)
        INC  HL
        PUSH HL                 ; Save address of next slot
```

As noted earlier, there is no JP (BC) instruction, and to call the slot code what we really need is something like CALL (BC). The next few lines implement this in four steps. The line labelled REL1 calls a three-byte routine labelled jpBC. The REL label addresses are stashed in a table at the end of the driver, so they can be adjusted from ORG 0 to match whatever address offset was used when **.install** put the driver code into system-reserved RAM.

The CALL puts the return address of the following label, PROCEED, on the stack. The code at jpBC copies the B and C registers into H and L and uses JP (HL) to jump to the start of the slot method. We've already stacked HL, the next slot address, so nothing gets lost.

Every method must end with a RET that uses the return address to get back to PROCEED. This recovers the stacked values of HL and BC, reloads STRIDE into DE and 0 into the accumulator, then jumps back into the slot-scanning loop at USED.

```
rel1    CALL jpBC
proceed POP  HL
        POP  BC
        LD   DE,stride              ; Reload slot size for stepping
        XOR  A                      ; Reload empty slot marker
        JR   used

jpBC    LD   H,B
        LD   L,C
        JP   (HL)
```

The next routine makes sure that all slots are marked as inactive as soon as the driver starts. The NextZXOS **.install** command calls every newly-loaded driver with the GETINIT API code (128) in the accumulator, to give the driver a chance to perform one-off initialisation. Likewise **.uninstall** passes GETSHUT (code 129) to the driver before removing it from memory. This gives the driver a chance to reset or release any external resources it might have been using. This driver simply ignores GETSHUT, but the GETINIT call can also be used during a session to turn off all the slots at once, with the command DRIVER 8,128.

The INIT routine should look familiar. It's a simpler version of the SCAN code we've seen before, moving HL through all the slot addresses, counting down in B, clearing the first byte of each slot to mark it inactive. Since we know the stride between slots is less than 256, we can be sure the value in D is zero, so the line labelled EMPTY re-uses that value when clearing. One extra step is used before the RET; driver commands signal success or failure by setting the carry flag C (not to be confused with register C) if something has gone wrong. We use AND A to make absolutely sure it is clear before we return. In fact for any reasonable values of SLOT1 and STRIDE the earlier ADD HL,DE is sure to leave carry clear, but the extra byte does no harm and makes for more robust example. None of the other instructions – not even DJNZ – have any effect on the processor flags.

```
; Clear first byte of all slots at initialisation
init    LD   B,slots
        LD   DE,stride
rel2    LD   HL,slot1

empty   LD   (HL),D                 ; We know that stride < 256
        ADD  HL,DE
        DJNZ empty
```

```
        AND  A                       ; Clear carry = success
        RET
```

How DRIVER commands work

Back at the start of the driver code we jumped to label COMMS from the entry-point reserved for commands. Now it's time to see how the DRIVER 8 commands are interpreted. The command API (the value after 8, in the DRIVER instruction) is passed to us in register B. First we must deal with out all the system commands, which have codes greater than 127, by testing the top bit of B and jumping to SYSTEM if it's set. If not, we must have an API code in the range 0 to 127. Values between 1 and SLOTS put subsequent parameters in corresponding slot addresses, so we sift those out with a jump to SETSLOT, if comparing the SLOTS limit with B leaves the carry flag clear.

Otherwise B must be greater than SLOTs, implying this must either be a GETCODE or GETDATA call, or an error. The next entry in the DRIVER command must be a slot number. This arrives in DE and is checked for validity by the next three conditional tests, which also reject erroneous references to slot 0. If the slot value is in-range we use EX DE,HL to swap it into HL, which is the quickest place we can double a 16-bit value, and use ADD HL,HL twice to find the offset of the chosen slot, effectively multiplying HL by STRIDE. To work out whether to return the code or data address we compare B with GETCODE and GETDATA and return via ERROR if any other API was selected. ERROR alerts BASIC that something has gone wrong by setting the carry flag. Adding 128 to itself in the 8-bit accumulator is a sure way of doing that, as the total is 0 carry 1.

```
; Commands 0..slots-1 initialise the chosen slot
; GETCODE and GETDATA commands read corresponding fields
comms   BIT  7,B
        JR   NZ,system

        LD   A,slots
        CP   B                       ; Is B a slot number, or 0?
        JR   NC,setslot

; Validate parameter in DE, the slot number to read

        LD   A,D
        OR   A
        JR   NZ,error                ; Reject DE > 255

        OR   E
        JR   Z,error                 ; Disregard slot 0

        LD   A,slots
        CP   E
        JR   C,error                 ; Reject E > slots

        EX   DE,HL                   ; Move parameter into HL
        ADD  HL,HL
```

```
        ADD  HL,HL                ; Scale parameter by stride
        LD   A,getcode
        CP   B                    ; Check for code-reading ID
        JR   NZ,notcode
```

The implementations of GETCODE and GETDATA are identical except that GETDATA must read the second rather than the first word from the slot. The NOTCODE path uses a pair of INC HL instructions to skip the code address, leaving HL pointing at the data word. Both commands exit via REL3, which adds the relocated start address of the slot table to HL and reads the relevant word from memory into BC for return to BASIC.

```
rel3    LD   DE,slot1             ; Find slot from offset in HL
        ADD  HL,DE
        LD   B,(HL)               ; Return BC
        INC  HL
        LD   C,(HL)
done    AND  A                    ; Flag success
        RET

notcode LD   A,getdata
        CP   B                    ; Check for data-reading ID
        JR   NZ,error

        INC  HL                   ; Point at data field in slot
        INC  HL
        JR   rel3
```

The SYSTEM routine handles the GETINIT and GETSHUT system calls, rejecting any others via ERROR. If B contains GETINIT we run the INIT loop, and we simply ignore GETSHUT, since there's nothing this driver needs to clean up but we don't want **.uninstall** to return an error. The other system codes are used by PRINT and similar interactions with drivers, and irrelevant to this simple example; some of those will be demonstrated in Chapter 15, Tiles and Layers, which includes a more intricate driver that supports character output.

```
system  LD   A,getinit
        CP   B
        JR   Z,init               ; Mark all slots free for use

        LD   A,getshut
        CP   B
        JR   Z,done               ; No specific shutdown action

error   LD   A,128
        ADD  A                    ; Carry flag signals failure
        RET
```

With the two system APIs and the two slot GET routines out of the way let's see how SETSLOT processes DRIVER 8 APIs up to 64. The DRIVER command puts the third and fourth parameters into HL and DE. After checking for the non-existent slot 0, we temporarily stack the data address so we can use HL to convert the slot number into an offset from SLOT1. REL4 forms the slot address in HL then restores the data parameter value to BC.

Notice how it's quite legal to POP different registers than you PUSHed. Some programs use this as an easy way to copy a register pair, but a couple of 8-bit LD instructions is no longer and much faster as it avoids moving SP back and forth or writing and reading 4 bytes of memory, so a PUSH/POP pair is best avoided unless you need one of the registers (B, in this case) in between, or the code is not part of a time-critical loop.

```
; DE is the code address for slot B, HL is the data address
setslot LD   A,B
        OR   A
        JR   Z,error                ; There is no slot 0
        DEC  B
        PUSH HL
        LD   H,0                    ; Form 16-bit offset
        LD   L,B
        ADD  HL,HL                  ; Double twice to fit stride
        ADD  HL,HL                  ; Slot offset is in HL

rel4    LD   BC,slot1
        ADD  HL,BC                  ; HL -> slot B
```

The last few lines of the driver code copy the four parameter bytes into the slot and return with carry clear, indicating success:

```
        POP  BC                     ; Get data address in BC
        LD   (HL),D                 ; Store high byte first
        INC  HL
        LD   (HL),E                 ; Store low byte next
        INC  HL
        LD   (HL),B                 ; Data address high byte
        INC  HL                     ; Advance to store low byte
        LD   (HL),C
        AND  A                      ; No carry, flag success
        RET
end                                 ; Must be <= limit-slots*size!
```

All that remains is data; the rather complicated ORG statement after the code END label advances the assembler output to point half-way into the 512-byte driver size LIMIT, so the last half contains not code but room for SLOTS (64) records of STRIDE (4) bytes each. It doesn't matter what bytes are initially in this space, as INIT will prepare it for later slot-specific words, so the data at SLOT1 contains a description to help identify the .DRV file to anyone in the habit of scanning code for interesting text. Fans of *Design Design* games will be used to doing this, and waiting a little longer for tapes to load as a result (0 bytes in the gaps would've loaded faster).

```
; Allocate slots up to the limit; pad space with temporary text
        ORG base+limit-(slots*stride),limit-(slots*stride)
slot1   DEFB "Interrupt Slot Handler ©2023 Simon N Goodwin",13
```

This bonus text makes no practical difference to the size of the driver file because the **.install** command always seeks 520 bytes on from the start, to pick up and process relocation offsets. A third ORG statement ensures this starts in the right place, after the 8 byte NDRV header and 512 bytes loaded into system space for one of the four permitted driver extensions.

```
; Relocation data follows slots, at the end of the driver
        ORG base+limit,limit
relocs  DEFW scan+2
        DEFW rel1+2
        DEFW rel2+2
        DEFW rel3+2
        DEFW rel4+2
length
        SAVE "slot.drv",base-headlen,length+headlen
```

Notice how the start and end of the relocation offsets are labelled, RELOC and LENGTH respectively. These values get cited right at the start of the listing, to work out RECOUNT, the count of relocation entries in the driver header. This is cross-checked against the file-length by **.install**, so you get an error message if they don't match, but if you simply forget to label and table any instruction that needs relocation, you won't know till the driver misbehaves of crashes. Take care out there!

Modifications

The first version of the slot driver only saved the main Z80 registers (AF, BC, DE, HL) and could not cope with code or data loaded into BANK 0 which BASIC usually maps to the top 16k of the Z80 address space. The following tweaks fix both those issues, at the cost of making the example more complicated, and slightly slower in the simplest applications. The following code replaces everything previously listed between the labels API and REL1. A few lines soon after the label USE are unchanged, but have been restated here to make the patch easier to follow.

```
api     JP   comms                 ; Interpret DRIVER commands

; This is the frame interrupt handler which calls the slots
intr    EX   AF,AF'                ; Save alternate AF
        PUSH AF
        PUSH IX                    ; Save index registers
        PUSH IY
        EXX                        ; Save alternate register set
        PUSH HL
        PUSH DE
        PUSH BC                    ; 12 bytes stacked
```

Beside the index registers IX and IY, Zilog added an extra set of seven registers and flags, and two instructions to switch between the original and (identical) extra group. The EXX instruction swaps over BC, DE, and HL with their 'alternate register' counterparts BC', DE' and HL'. Notice that all six are hidden or exposed in one step. There's no direct way to copy between them or use both normal and alternate registers in a single instruction. The flags and accumulator get swapped separately, by the EX AF,AF' instruction. Using both before and after we call the slot code, and stacking IX and IY similarly, driver slots have 16 registers and two sets of flags at their disposal.

We only need to save the extra registers once, before processing all the slots, as their values are not touched while transitioning between slots. Doing this in the driver, rather than each method, saves time when several slots use them, though it slightly increases the overhead of each interrupt when none of the slots are active, or none need the index or alternate register set.

```
scan    LD   HL,slot1          ; Test code vector high bytes
        LD   B,slots           ;   for this many slots
        LD   DE,stride         ;     at this interval
        XOR  A                 ; Zero means slot is inactive

try     OR   (HL)              ; Check if slot is active
        JR   NZ,use

        ADD  HL,DE             ; Advance to next slot
used    DJNZ try

        POP  BC                ; Restore alternate regs
        POP  DE
        POP  HL
        EXX                    ; Revert to default set
        POP  IY                ; Restore index registers
        POP  IX
        POP  AF                ; Restore alternate AF
        EX   AF,AF'
        RET
; HL -> an active slot; find corresponding code and data
use     PUSH BC                ; Save slot loop count
        LD   B,(HL)            ; Code vector to BC
        INC  HL
        LD   C,(HL)
        INC  HL
        LD   D,(HL)            ; Data vector to DE
        INC  HL
        LD   E,(HL)
        INC  HL
        PUSH HL                ; Save address of next slot
```

Safe memory paging

The following block of code could be removed as when driver code runs the stack pointer will be in the area normally reserved for ROM. I've left it in to show how to check this, as that may be vital for USR code invoked without a precautionary CLEAR to reserve the top 16k or more:

```
; Check if SP is below 48k before attempting any paging
        LD   HL,0
        ADD  HL,SP             ; The official way to read SP
        LD   A,%11000000       ; Bits set in address 49152+
        AND  H                 ; Ignore the lower-order bits
        CP   %11000000
        JR   Z,rel1            ; Never page out the stack!
```

The next block is essential if slot code or data is in the BANK 0 area normally mapped by ZX BASIC to addresses from 49152 upwards. Rather than adjust the MMU regardless, which might slow down the handling of each slot needlessly, we check the top two bits of both the code and data addresses and proceed as before unless one or both of those addresses is in the top quarter of Z80 space. If either the code or data address is above 48k we must make sure that the normal BASIC bank 0 is mapped there while the interrupt handler runs, then restore whatever was mapped there afterwards, as NextZXOS may change it.

```
        LD   H,%11000000          ; Mask top address bits
        LD   A,D                  ; Consider data address
        AND  H                    ; Ignore other bits
        CP   H                    ; Are both still set?
        JR   Z,setBank

        LD   A,B                  ; Consider code address
        AND  H
        CP   H
        JR   NZ,rel1              ; Nothing needs saving
```

The following block is only executed when the top 16k of memory needs to be temporarily set up as it would be when BASIC is being interpreted. We start by giving symbolic names to the custom Next hardware we're going to need to twiddle. Notice that although we can **set** any Next register, such as MMU6 and MMU7 which control access to the top 16k, using a custom NextReg instruction, but if we want to **read** one of those registers we have to do it using the SELECT Z80 port, as documented in the manual.

```
; NextReg interface constants
select  EQU  9275                 ; NextReg select port
MMU6    EQU  86                   ; Penultimate MMU register
MMU7    EQU  87                   ; MMU register for top 8k

; Save and restore the top 16k bank mapping from REG 86 and 87
setBank PUSH BC                   ; Prepare for port input
        LD   BC,select            ; Address REG select port
        LD   A,MMU6               ; MMU6 maps 48k to 56k
        OUT  (C),A
        INC  B                    ; Advance to REG data port
        IN   L,(C)                ; L = REG 86
        OUT  (C),0                ; Put start of BANK 0 at 48k
        LD   A,MMU7               ; Index MMU7, 56k to 64k
        DEC  B                    ; Back to REG select port
        OUT  (C),A                ; Select MMU7
        INC  B
        IN   H,(C)                ; H = REG 87
        LD   A,1                  ; Top 8k of BANK 0 page number
        OUT  (C),A                ; Map the rest of BANK 0 at 56k
        POP  BC                   ; Restore code address
        PUSH HL                   ; Save MMU6 & MMU7 contents

rel0    CALL jpBC
```

```
        POP  HL                 ; Recover stored MMU contents
        LD   A,L
        NEXTREG MMU6,A          ; Restore 48k to 56k mapping
        LD   A,H
        NEXTREG MMU7,A          ; Restore 56k to 64k mapping
        JR   proceed

rel1    CALL jpBC               ; CONTINUE AS BEFORE
```

Notice too that the additions and performance optimisations mean that the COMMS routine is no longer within 127 bytes of the entry point at API, so the JR instruction and NOP have been replaced with a three-byte JP. That's faster but means we need to add API+2 to the list of relocation addresses at the end of the driver file.

Two other 16-bit references to absolute addresses are introduced by the changes, at SCAN and REL0, so version 2 of the code must end as follows:

```
relocs  DEFW  api+2
        DEFW  scan+2
        DEFW  rel0+2
        DEFW  rel1+2
        DEFW  rel2+2
        DEFW  rel3+2
        DEFW  rel4+2
```

The formula labelled RECOUNT adapts automatically to these additions.

The version number of the driver in the line labelled SLOT1 was also updated, to 1.9 at the time of writing. Using a text literal rather than a comment means this ends up in the assembled code as well as the source, which makes it a lot easier to keep track of which data file generated a specific lump of code.

One sure way to waste time and let bugs slip by is to have several versions of the same source file and not be sure which is the latest. While file dates may resolve the doubt, they're easily lost or changed; it's wiser to make the version number explicit in both the source and binary code, ideally from the same single source line.

Try to avoid storing the version number in more than one place, as that risks inconsistency. Resist the temptation to leave it unchanged for a 'small tweak' – otherwise, you're liable to run out of patience long before you run out of version numbers!

Chapter 11, MULTITASKING

This chapter presents tiny examples – just 93 bytes of Z80n magic – which give a multi-tasking feel to NextZXOS by running five little routines via the Interrupt Slot driver. They illustrate how to measure and adjust the time taken by each slot, and one way (not necessarily the best way, but authentically) to create static multicolour borders like those used in Quicksilva's *Aquaplane*. They also demo background output to custom hardware, intercepting and changing system-variable updates, continuous layer scrolling and modulated sound effects that run at the same time as NextBASIC – even while you're editing the program, and even if it's rolling around while you try to do so!

These example methods are complete, but deliberately minimal. They vary in length from 4 to 22 bytes. More extensive examples appear elsewhere in the book, for useful applications like sampled audio streaming from banked RAM, or to make sprites follow curves and arbitrary paths on and off the screen. These examples, assembled with Odin like the interrupt driver source, are starting-points for your own experiments.

Organisation of the demos

Each demo uses a smidgeon of BASIC to set it up and illustrate how it works. The background processing is implemented with just enough machine code to keep it running independently. Since slots are updated alongside NextBASIC, the examples can poll for input and display the inner state of the demos as they run. Each example ends by cleaning up after itself, a necessary discipline in a paged-memory system that was never designed for multi-tasking or resource-sharing.

The demos are individually discussed here, but supplied for download in combined source files, one for the BASIC demo framework and one for the machine code and data. Each file is archived twice, as ASCII text for ease of reading or conversion, then again as tokenised BASIC or Odin-format assembly-language. The ready-assembled machine code is in a fifth file, called simply **slotest** – a contraction of Slot and Test.

So the full set is **slotest.asm, slotest.txt, slotest.odn, slotest.bas** and **slotest**. The code is assembled to address 49000, with room for expansion and data up to 49150, but everything – even the data – is fully relocatable, so you can load and run it from any RAM address, providing you adjust code and data references from outside to match the place you've moved things to.

Along the way, I shall demonstrate how Z80 code running in a slot – or potentially anywhere else – can be written in a relocatable style, whether invoked from a driver slot or via a USR call. This is rarely necessary nor even desirable for the main part of a program, as it adds complexity and processing overhead, especially for programs with many subroutines. But in the context of re-usable slot routines it's a perfect fit, and worth knowing about now we've seen how NextZXOS handles the relocation of code and data when drivers are linked into the system. The examples are linked by one BASIC program that runs all of them in sequence. This chapter reveals them one by one, with explanations of their workings.

All of the routines run from addresses from 49000 upwards, so BASIC should be prevented from encroaching into that space. The following lines reserve memory, load the assembled code, then install the driver that will link the code with BASIC:

```
100 CLEAR 48999: LAYER 0
110 LOAD "slotest" CODE 49000
120 .install slot.drv
```

Background whooshes

The first slot demo generates continuously-varying sound. While I show that this can be done using the AY-3-8912 chip alone, in Chapter 14, Better BEEPs, the envelope control demonstrated there can only pulse the volume of sounds playing as your BASIC or other program runs. The slot driver allows *any* AY soundchip register to be periodically updated. This example sweeps the random-noise generator pitch across its full range, as other programs run as normal:

```
270 PRINT AT 3,0;"Pitch"
280 OUT 65533,8: OUT 49149,15
290 OUT 65533,7:%s= IN 49149
300 %s&=@11000111: OUT 49149,%s
310 DRIVER 8,1,49004,49151
320 REPEAT
330   PRINT AT 3,7; PEEK 49151,
340 REPEAT UNTIL CODE INKEY$
350 DRIVER 8,1,0
360 %s|= BIN 111000:; No noise
370 OUT 65533,7: OUT 49149,%s
380 STOP
```

The general approach for efficient use of the slot driver is to do as much one-off initialisation and clean-up as possible in BASIC, leaving only the parts that *must* run every frame in machine-code. Referring on to the Better Beeps chapter you can confirm that line 280 sets AY register 8, the volume control for channel A, to 15, the maximum loudness. The next two OUTs select the mixer control, register 7, and enable the three noise output bits, in a simplified version of PROC AYNOISE().

Line 310 links the slot driver to our demo code. It points the first driver slot at 49004 for code and 49151 for a single data byte, the current noise pitch. This command sets the sound playing, starting at whatever pitch happens to match with PEEK 49151, soon settling into a repeating pattern.

The REPEAT loop does three things. It waits for a key to be pressed, and in the meantime reads the byte at 49151 and displays it alongside the caption 'Pitch:' printed outside the loop. The comma at the end of line 330 blanks up to the next half-line boundary, so that the display is correct even when the pitch wraps back to a single-digit value. The caption is only printed once, as it'd be a waste of time to rewrite it every time round the loop. PRINT AT is used to align the caption and value together.

So far, we've not heard anything that could not be done with standard BASIC. Instead of PEEKing 49151 to show the latest value from the driver slot, the loop could be changing the noise pitch directly with an OUT to soundchip register 6, like the loop between lines 1130 and 1170 in the demo in Chapter 14, Better BEEPs.

To prove we're not cheating, press BREAK so the REPEAT loop stops prematurely. The driver slot is still running, so the sound keeps changing, even though we're no longer displaying the latest value. In fact the noise will continue to play and vary while you LIST or edit your program. Type CONT to re-enter the loop and see where the pitch value has got to.

When another key is pressed, line 810 disables the driver slot. This stops the noise changing, but the AY-3-8912 continues to play the last-selected sound until the OUTs on line 370 re-select the mixer and turn off the noise controls. Notice that the previous register value retained in %S is used to make sure that the other five bits are unchanged when the mixer is updated to turn off the three control bits specific to noise routing.

Hence the bitwise OR on line 360 affects only bits 3, 4, and 5 of the mixer; setting those disables noise output on channels A, B and C respectively. Mixing in the previous value of the other bits means that tone outputs are unaffected. This is important when one register controls several parts of the sound chip, as applies most particularly to the soundchip mixer, register 7.

Here's the machine code, which by default assembles to address 49004. You could use a different ORG address or simply load the relocatable code anywhere else that's not liable to get clobbered, as long as you change the code address in line 310 to match the new address of the following routine:

```
wobbler LD   BC,65533            ; AY-3-8912 select port
        LD   A,6                 ; Noise period register
        OUT  (C),A
```

The twelve-line Wobbler routine closely resembles the sequence of OUT commands used in BASIC. The first three lines are effectively OUT 65533,6, though Z80 machine language requires the port address (65533 or ayR) and soundchip register number (6, noise period) to be loaded into registers BC and A respectively before the OUT instruction.

Driver slots are invoked with register pair DE pointing at their data, so the next three lines read the byte at 49151 (unless you set another address in the DRIVER 8,1 call), add one to it, and store it back in the same place:

```
        LD   A,(DE)              ; Get first data byte
        INC  A
        LD   (DE),A
```

The final lines of the wobbler point BC at the **ayD** port, where we shall store the updated noise period that determines the change in sound. The AY-3-8912 only has a five-bit noise pitch control so three 'shift right logical' instructions are used to divide the count by eight, clearing the top three bits of the accumulator, before writing to the noise period register and returning from the slot handler.

```
LD   BC,49149
SRL  A                       ; Map 0..255 to 0..31
SRL  A
SRL  A
OUT  (C),A
RET
```

The division by eight means that although the counter varies every frame the pitch only changes every eight frames. We could safely have skipped seven out of eight updates, but that'd make the example longer and a little harder to follow. When a routine is so short, it's not worth complicating it for such a tiny win. As it happens, a later demo will use the full 0 to 255 range of the data-byte, even though 0 to 31 is enough for the sound effect.

Borderline timing

The next slot demo is even shorter and simpler. It just sets the display border colour by directly writing to port 254, the only Z80 hardware port implemented on an original Spectrum. Like the BASIC command OUT 254,0 this is much quicker than the command BORDER 0 as it goes directly to the hardware and doesn't change the lower-screen line colour to match, as the BORDER command would.

Run this example in LAYER 0 to be sure of seeing its border changes. Not all Next LAYERs respond to the BORDER command; the same applies to changes made with OUT 254. The border of a 512x192 pixel two-colour HiRes display is separately controlled by port **255**, added by Timex, to match up the full-screen PAPER with contrasting INK colours; those are always linked, in LAYER 1,2. The slot code is just three lines and four bytes:

```
; 49000 Clobber border colour with data value 0..7
border  LD   A,E
        OUT  (254),A
        RET
```

Remember that slots are invoked with the data parameter in DE. This routine ignores the high byte in DE and copies whatever turns up in the E register to port 254. Values 0 to 7 determine the border colour, controlled by the three least-significant bits of the port. Other bits affect the cassette and BEEP outputs, as noted in the IN and OUT chapter of the Spectrum manual, but there's no sound interferences as long as each OUT leaves those bits unchanged; border colours from 0 to 7 leave those unrelated bits clear.

Setting the border colour is nothing new, but the slot driver lets us do it *several times each frame*. If we add a short delay between colour changes we can create a multi-colour border, like that in the 1983 Spectrum game *Aquaplane* which used carefully-timed OUT 254 instructions to extend its cyan sky and dark blue sea beyond the main screen and out into the border.

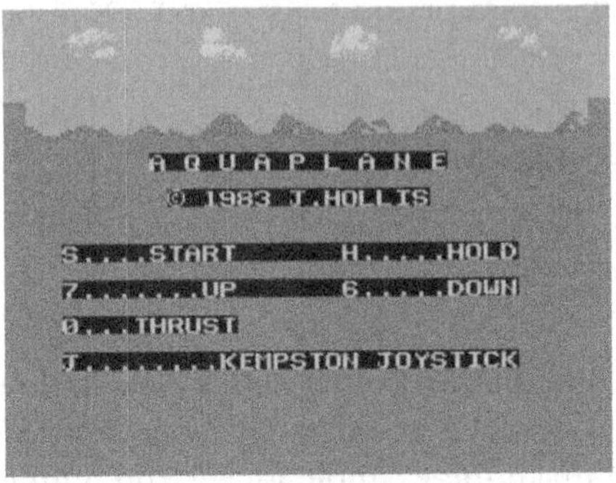

Figure 58 - Quicksilva's Aquaplane, as mis-represented by shovelware site archive.org. Notice abrupt changes in sea level caused by lazy screen-grabbing, on a broken emulator.

More elaborate trickery along the same lines allowed David Webb's later game *Starion*, published by Melbourne House, to render a giant count-down that extended into the screen border. Effects like this rely on tight synchronization between the code and TV display, which is why *Aquaplane* needed tweaks to run on the NTSC display of the Timex 2068 Spectrum variant made for 60 Hertz US tellies, and shows up short cuts in ZX emulators that don't allow accurate beam-tracing effects – compare the mangled Figure 58 with the proper capture in Figure 59.

Quicksilva founder John Hollis soaked up the necessary delay, as each Aquaplane border was aligned, to scroll the clouds. In this example we're just going to use a 16-bit counting loop to implement a variable-duration delay:

```
delay   DEC  DE
delay0  LD   A,D
        OR   E
        JR   NZ,delay
        RET
```

This normally runs from address 49054, unless you relocate it; no changes are needed even so, since a JR relative branch instruction determines where to continue from until the count is complete. The counting is done in the DE register pair since that's where the slot data parameter turns up. The first line DEC DE takes one away from the current value but doesn't set the processor flags to indicate whether the count has reached zero or underflowed.

The 8-bit single-register DEC instructions from Intel's 8080 remix *do* set the flags, but the 16-bit Zilog add-ons – like most of Victor's Z80n extras – are not connected to the CPU flags. If the Z flag got updated when DE counted down to zero we could do away with the next two lines. In practice they're both needed, and often seen in program loops.

The last two lines of the slot code return only when DE reaches zero, otherwise continuing the count-down with another DEC DE at the line labelled DELAY.

The flags are closely associated with the Z80 accumulator register so the quick way to check if other registers are zero is to OR them together in A; the Z flag will only be set if all the registers thus combined hold zero, otherwise that will leave a non-zero result.

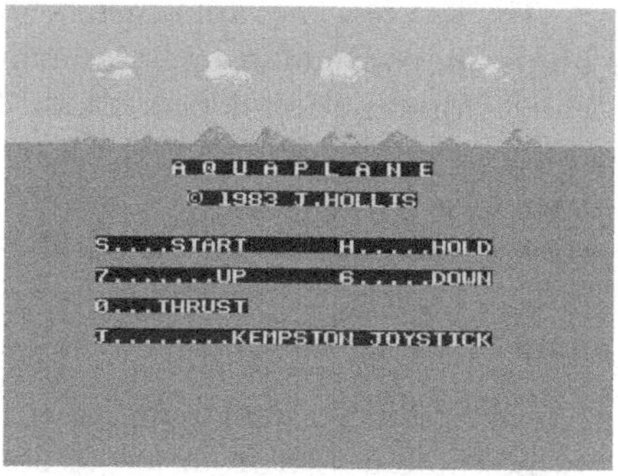

Figure 59 – Aquaplane again, this time correctly showing the intended border effect

The recent addition of counter-timer (CTC) hardware to Next's FPGA provides more elegant ways to wait a certain number of machine cycles, but we're just going to burn CPU cycles in this demo. Thus we can graphically illustrate what happens when a driver slot out-runs the available frame time. Our delay is under keyboard-control, so it can be matched up with any screen line regardless of frame rate or display type, though the delay to reach a given line depends upon the exact rate at which that particular display is scanned.

Off-by-one, off by 65536

One slight snag of this loop is that if we always start at the top a count of 0 will generate the *maximum* possible delay, rather than the *least*. This is because we decrement DE before testing the result for 0, so an initial zero will 'borrow' from an imaginary bit 16 and become 65535 (%1111111111111111 binary) before DE is first tested. There's a simple fix for this inconsistency: the driver slot is programmed to start from the *second* line, labelled DELAY0, rather than the top of the loop. Now the delay routine returns immediately, without looping, if it starts with zero in DE. Hence the driver jumps in at address 49055, after the DEC DE, even though the slot code starts at 49054.

Here's the BASIC part of this demo. It uses three driver slots to set the border colour in two places with an adjustable delay, visible as a screen offset, between them. PROC WAIT() just displays the supplied message and waits for a key-press, so you can see the changes as each slot is prepared:

```
410 BORDER 7
420 PROC WAIT("Press key for blue border")
430 DRIVER 8,2,49000,1
440 PROC WAIT("Press key for  red border")
450 DRIVER 8,2,49000,2
```

Here's the WAIT PROC, so I'm not guilty of keeping anyone waiting unnecessarily. Note how it checks for no key before awaiting a new keypress:

```
1100 DEFPROC WAIT(prompt$)
1110 PRINT prompt$
1120 REPEAT : REPEAT UNTIL NOT CODE INKEY$
1130 REPEAT : REPEAT UNTIL CODE INKEY$
1140 ENDPROC
```

The first few lines implement a boring static display. Line 410 sets a white border the conventional way, assuming that you've not reprogrammed palette entry 7 for some non-default colour. This also puts white paper in the bottom two lines of a traditional LAYER 0 screen, where INPUTs would normally take place. After a key-press, line 430 configures driver slot 2 to use machine code at address 49000 to output the data value 1, corresponding to blue, to port 254, every frame. The input area is unaffected, but the screen border turns blue even though BASIC still records that it's white.

Unless there's something rather time-consuming already running in slot 1, the entire border from top to bottom becomes blue. That's because the NextZXOS driver system is invoked during the 'vertical blanking' part of the display frame, so we don't usually see the point where the first new colour is set. In the absence of anything else – like a SAVE command – writing to port 254, we see a solid blue border all round. After the next key-press, line 450 does the same except with a different data value, 2, turning the border red. SAVE and BEEP turn off slots while they're running, by disabling interrupts.

Notice that it's not essential to turn off slot 2, with DRIVER 8,2,0, before giving it new code or data values. When using several slots together it's sometimes neater to do so, or to choose the order in which you set, tweak or run slots carefully, to avoid momentary glitches becoming apparent.

Now we're ready to use more slots and implement our multicolour border. Unlike the obvious `3 PAUSE 1: BORDER 1: BORDER 2: GO TO 3` BASIC one-liner, which surely inspired John Hollis, the driver approach leaves NextBASIC running for the rest of the frame after the colour-change, and the stripe doesn't drift about when a key is held down…

Try pressing SHIFT, or ENTER, while running that line 3 to see how PAUSE 1 is affected by the system keyboard polling that takes place every frame, unless interrupts are disabled. Pressing SHIFT alone moves the border pattern down slightly, while other keys require more system decoding effort, increasing the display offset. The effect is most obvious after RUN AT 0; just holding a key down measurably – indeed visibly, here – reduced the speed of ZX BASIC on the original 3.5 MHz Spectrum.

Next keyboard polling also takes time, though proportionately far less at 28 MHz after RUN AT 3, despite the more elaborate keyboard. But it doesn't obviously affect driver display synchronisation, because the four custom drivers all run *before* the default system driver polls the keyboard.

After the next keypress line 470 gives somewhat cryptic names to four variables. The delay value is held in **split** in units of DE-countdown loops. The duration of these loops depends on the screen configuration and CPU clock speed. Assuming RUN AT 3, a value of 4000 gives a delay long enough for the transition to appear high on the main part of the display, soon after the normal top border. The four instructions in the loop take 6+4+4+12 =

26 cycles for each repeat, so a 4000-unit delay soaks up 100,400 CPU clock ticks, and there are 560,000 of those in a 50 Hertz frame at 28 MHz.

```
460 PROC WAIT("Press key for both borders")
470 split=4000:hop=100:limit=30000:old=split
```

Since changing the delay duration by less than a microsecond at each keypress would make for a tedious demo, **hop** presets the amount **split** will change by when up or down arrow keys are pressed to adjust the delay. The default factor of 100 makes sure that even a few presses will visibly move the border pattern – the interval between output of successive analogue TV lines is about 64 microseconds. Feel free to tweak either value to please yourself.

The other two variables, **limit** and **old**, set a maximum for **delay** and keep track of the previous setting of **split**. Having a maximum confines the delay to an interesting range and avoids integer overflow problems. We use **old** in the repeat loop that checks for input, so that the driver slot 3 delay isn't updated unless one of those arrow keys has been pressed and **split** is not already at either end of its range. If we were to interpret line 560 every time, regardless of whether or not **split** had changed, the display might sometimes flicker even if no key was pressed.

Line 450 set up driver slot 2, holding the border red. The following two lines put a delay in driver slot 3, then re-use the border method to switch the colour back to blue (1). The result is that the border changes part-way down the screen, from red to blue, at a height determined by the value of **split**.

```
480 DRIVER 8,3,49055,split
490 DRIVER 8,4,49000,1
500 PROC WAIT("Press up/down to move split")
```

The subsequent REPEAT loop uses INKEY$ to detect up or down arrows and adjust **split** either way, in steps of **hop**, while one of those keys is held down. Find out what happens when **split** is so large that the delay adds up to more than one whole frame; press and hold the down-arrow key.

Running out of time

The red area at the top grows, as the blue transition comes later and later. Keep pressing, driving the split into the lower border, and beyond. Eventually the solid blue area becomes replaced by a flickering purple zone, as the delay time becomes so long that alternate frames are shown in red, while the loop grinds on in slot 3, and the blue part is only visible half of the rest of the time. Even longer delays would make it redder and flickerier, as slot 4 was getting to run fewer and fewer times every second.

Now press up arrow again till the delay is trimmed to fit within one frame, and the solid border display is visible once more. Phew. Nothing has broken, but interrupts were missed so the TIME function and system FRAMES count will fall behind, as they always did during BEEP or LOAD or any other command that had to disable interrupts to work, literally, uninterruptedly.

```
520 REPEAT
530   IF INKEY$ = CHR$ 10 THEN IF split<limit THEN split+=hop
540   IF INKEY$ = CHR$ 11 THEN IF split>hop THEN split-=hop
550   IF old<>split
560     DRIVER 8,3,49055,split:old=split
570     PRINT AT 0,6;split,
580   ENDIF
590 REPEAT UNTIL INKEY$ =" "
```

The border method is particularly useful for measuring how much of each frame slot methods need to do useful work. We can visualise how long routines in slots 2 to 11 are taking by putting the border method in both slot 1 and slot 12, but with different colours. The depth of the band in the first colour in the border is proportional to time spent processing intervening slots. The more it jumps around, the more we could gain by optimising the slowest path though our code.

Of course, this is no different in principle than spattering the main loop of a fast BASIC game with BORDER statements before the PAUSE 1 or SPRITE MOVE INT that maintains a constant frame rate, but the Z80 method is over a hundred times faster, hence much less likely to add to the delay you're trying to minimise!

On average, Z80 instructions each take about eight clock cycles, known to Zilog as Ts (Time-states). A more optimistic way of reckoning would be to count 4 Ts per code-byte. These formulae underestimate the time taken by complicated instructions that churn internally or access multiple bytes of non-code RAM, like LDIR, PUSH and POP, but conversely the simplest instructions like OR A or LD D,C go twice that speed. At 28 MHz with 50 Hertz display output the 8T rule of thumb allows for 28e6/(50*8) = 70,000 instructions per frame. Which is quite a lot, until you get stuck in a loop…

There are a couple more things we can learn from this demo. The first is that the keyboard response seems to slow down at around the point where the frame delay only just fits in the available time. I reckon this is because the system keyboard driver, and in particular the auto-repeat logic, ends up running erratically as it runs short of time before the next poll should begin.

The second insight is apparent if you happen to set the delay to a duration which causes the red to blue transition to occur in a visible part of the border. Sometimes this point will be rock-steady. Other delays will show it flickering over a short distance, a few pixel-widths, in various parts of the border, but always the same size.

It seems this happens when the OUT command is occurring at almost but not quite exactly at the point when the display hardware is ready to fetch another few pixels from RAM. The CPU is delayed a tiny amount, but the border is such a sensitive real-time meter that the hold-up becomes visible.

The exact fraction of a microsecond when this contention occurs depends upon just when the interrupt was triggered and whatever else the CPU/video combination was doing at the precise time when the frame interrupt was generated. Maybe Allen Albright will read this and tweak the FPGA to eliminate the tiny jitter, or provide another explanation. In any case, it's not a problem as long as we're prepared and aware of it.

Bigger and more variable timing jumps may be problematic, though – they indicate that earlier parts of the update, or perhaps lower-numbered slot methods, are running erratically. If this is allowed to get out of hand, games become inconsistent and hard to play, because the smooth and steady working of the eye-brain-hand-keyboard-screen update loop is disrupted, and the façade of interactivity crumbles…

When you tire of this excitement, press SPACE to leave the REPEAT loop. Three driver commands turn off slots 2, 3 and 4, and NextZXOS sets the border back to white – the colour we set with BORDER 7 earlier – when it next decides to tidy up the whole screen.

```
600 DRIVER 8,2,0
610 DRIVER 8,3,0
620 DRIVER 8,4,0
```

Stop the world, I want to get off – ULA scrolling

Let's introduce a demo that scrolls the ULA screen. Since it's under driver slot control, the scrolling will carry on even while you're editing your program, or trying to type commands to turn the slot off!

Remember that we can't call BASIC commands to reposition the screen from a driver, because we've no way of knowing when an interrupt occurs what NextZXOS might be in the middle of doing. It could be half-way through a different or related graphics statement, or fiddling with system variables it'd need in a consistent state before embarking on a new command. We could ensure synchronisation by just setting a value in memory in our driver slot, and having our own NextBASIC program check that address periodically and jump off to do the required command when it spotted the 'signal' change; that's slower, but safe.

Alternatively we could live a little more dangerously and write directly to a NextReg from within the slot code. This is still risky if NextZXOS happens to be trying to update the same hardware when the driver interrupts. Imagine that it's turning a soundchip channel on or off by flipping bits in the mixer register. If our change comes in just after it has read the old state and before it sets a new one, it's not clear which update will take precedence. NextZXOS could get very confused.

This is another instance of the 'two writers bad' situation and can generally be avoided, in a simple system like Next, by steering clear of any commands that could alter the same registers your driver wants to tickle. But there are some commands, like LAYER CLEAR, which touch lots of Next registers and memory areas while they're working. It's wise not to turn on driver slots till this sort of one-off initialisation is complete, and to toggle them off again promptly before loading new levels of a game, quitting or doing anything else out of the ordinary.

That said, there's nothing to stop you issuing REG commands or equivalent OUTs anywhere in a program, and often that's a good way to work out how more complicated NextBASIC commands are implemented, or get part of their function without having to put up with bits you might not want, like the repainting of screen lines by the BORDER command.

The ULA horizontal scroll register is a case in point; BASIC won't touch that unless you tell it to, and as it's a single byte you can be sure that a change will reach the hardware in one 'atomic' step, whereas *Zaxxon*-style diagonal scrolling would involve adjusting both X and Y registers separately and a risk of momentary – but visible – inconsistency between one change and the other. The beam-synchronous nature of driver operation, and the way changes timed to occur during vertical blanking are invisible, means that drivers certainly can give impressive yet stable effects by adjusting multiple registers, but such techniques require careful testing.

Our penultimate little driver demo combines the sweeping noise effect with screen-scrolling, so the display pans about in perfect sync with the whooshing of the sound generator. I'll start by presenting the new Z80 code that moves the display, then tie that in with the noise effect via NextBASIC.

```
; 49036 Slide ULA layers annoyingly with wobbler
scrolly LD   BC,9275               ; REG select port
        LD   A,38                  ; ULA pan register
        OUT  (C),A                 ; Select register

        LD   A,(DE)                ; Data byte
        BIT  7,A
        JR   Z,move
        NEG                        ; Flip direction

move    INC  B                     ; Data port 9531
        OUT  (C),A                 ; Pan screen
        RET
```

The 18-byte scrolly slot-routine, typically loaded to address 49036, uses REG 38 to pan the ULA screen; LAYER 2 has its own independent positioning registers. The first OUT instruction selects the X scroll register and the last one puts a new value into it.

The value is read from our data parameter pointed at by register DE. To give a two-way scrolling effect I check if this value is greater than 127 with BIT 7,A (setting bit 7 adds 128 to the byte value) and negate values in the unsigned range 128 to 255. This has the effect of creating a sequence that counts up from 0 to 127 then turns around at 128 and counts back down to 1, at which point the byte overflows from 255 to 0 and the smooth cycle repeats.

Now we can show two slots sharing data, and creating a synaesthetic audio-visual experience, albeit a simple one. Here's the BASIC to tie these together. The audio wobbler runs in slot 1, prepared, just as before, by line 740. The scrolling is done from slot 3; slot 2 is skipped or could be used for some intermediate purpose. Before starting up the wobbler, line 710 links slot 3 to the scrolly routine above and gives 49151 as the address of its data. You may remember that this is where the wobbler kept its update count. Any other address could be used – perhaps even a system variable, like one of the byte counters in FRAMES – but for the sound and vision to be synchronised both slots must share the same data address.

```
710 DRIVER 8,3,49036,49151
720 POKE 49151,0
730 REM Set data byte cycling
740 DRIVER 8,1,49004,49151
```

This time we make sure the count starts at 0, so the screen doesn't jump immediately from its default pan position. Ideally the next three lines, which we've seen before setting up the noise demo, would claim the noise channel before activating the slots but as long as we start with channels muted it doesn't matter if the noise output is enabled a few lines later.

```
750 OUT 65533,8: OUT 49149,15
760 OUT 65533,7:%s= IN 49149
770 %s&=@11000111: OUT 49149,%s
```

At this point, assuming you have a ULA layer on display, the whooshing noise will restart but this time the entire playfield will be sliding back and forth in time with the changing sound. The following loop displays the data value as it's updated and waits for a keypress, but it's rather exciting to press BREAK and carry on trying to use your Next.

```
790 REPEAT
800   PRINT AT 7,6; PEEK 49151,
810 REPEAT UNTIL CODE INKEY$
```

The sound and video effect will continue as you edit or browse. Everything still works perfectly – NextZXOS doesn't mind where your screen is offset, it just updates the usual places in memory and leaves us to keep track of the cursor by eye. Type CONT or GO TO 820 to recover.

The clean-up sequence is important. First we turn off slot 1, to stop the value at 49151 cycling round, and slot 3, to stabilise the screen. Then we manually reset REG 38, the horizontal pan position, to the default offset of zero. Finally we turn off the noise output, either by setting the volume to zero or, in this example, by disabling noise channels in the mixer.

```
820 DRIVER 8,1,0
830 DRIVER 8,3,0
840 REG 38,0:;Reset pan
850 %s|= BIN 111000:; No noise
860 OUT 65533,7: OUT 49149,%s
```

Blinking in the background

The example files include another slot routine which fiddles with the system variable LASTK. It can be used along with the NextBASIC Editor to remap the keypress that normally displays the 48k BASIC <> token to give a copyright sign instead, but it's not generally useful because the system keyboard driver would clobber the change later the same frame, at least as far as INPUT and INKEY$ are concerned. So I'll leave that method (**rekey**, at 49026) for you to ponder if so inclined, and return to the flashing-light example I used to demonstrate control over pin 7 of the joystick ports in Chapter 4, Simple Hardware Projects.

Back then I used a BASIC loop to blink the LED. This time we'll do it from a driver slot, so the lighthouse doesn't go out (or get stuck on) whenever you break into the program. In fact you can leave this running as you write or edit a completely different project, just as long as you don't **.uninstall** the driver or overwrite the 23 bytes of code and data that keep the light flashing.

This example is different from the others in that it doesn't use the data address in DE. Instead it accesses private data alongside the code, making it a sealed unit – a 'closure' in Computing Science jargon. It could work just as well if the data was pointed-at by DE, but encapsulation lets me demonstrate another neat trick that could be very handy in other applications.

The Z80 code within a driver must be relocatable, because there are four different places NextZXOS might run it from. Any CALLs, 16-bit jumps or data references within that area need to be 'fixed up' after loading to point to the places it's ended up, rather than the default base address of 0.

But also bear in mind that when a slot is active the code is located and started up by jumping to an address copied from BC to HL by the driver. This means that the code knows where it's running from, even though that final load address was unknown when the code was assembled.

The blink routine needs three variables. One is used to count down till the frame when the light is next to be toggled off or on. Another contains the interval, in frames, between blinks. This **rate** is set from BASIC and copied into **count** as the countdown to the next blink begins.

The third byte preserves the state of the other bits in REG 11, as only one of those is needed to control the output to pin 7 on the joystick controller ports, and the others shouldn't be changed because that could cause unwelcome side-effects such as hooking up one of the serial ports to the pin we're trying to toggle. Since four of the bits in REG 11 are currently reserved, writing junk there could potentially do *anything* on future SpecNext cores.

Here's the table of variables, which is normally held at RAM address 49080, immediately after the RET instruction which ends the blink routine.

There are no explicit references to any of these addresses in the code, because it works them out relative to wherever the routine has been loaded.

```
count   DB   0                      ; Frames till next blink
rate    DB   0                      ; Frames between blinks
oldOut  DB   0                      ; Last output to port
```

The first two lines of **blink** point HL at the variables. We know that HL initially contains the code start address, labelled blink, because it's been invoked with a JP (HL) instruction from the driver. The first variable is labelled **count** so we can find the offset to it from the start of the code by letting the assembler compute **count-blink**.

This is a better approach than loading BC with a literal value such as 20, because no error-prone manual counting is needed, and the assembler will adjust the value for us automatically if either **blink** or **count** need to move in relation to one another, perhaps because extra code got added to the **blink** method later.

```
blink   LD   BC,count-blink         ; Offset to data
        ADD  HL,BC                  ; Point at data
        DEC  (HL)                   ; Count down
        RET  NZ
```

Most of the time, the blink routine will return after just four instructions. As soon as it has the address of **count** in HL it uses DEC to decrement it. Unless the result is zero, the method returns immediately. Otherwise we need to blink the light and reset the counter. This involves accessing the other two variables, **rate** and **oldOut**. That's easy, as we know they're right after **count** and HL already points at that. Here's the code that copies **rate** into **count**:

```
        INC  HL
        LD   A,(HL)                 ; Read rate
        DEC  HL
        LD   (HL),A                 ; Reset count to rate
```

Before we blink the light we need to know what to store in the other seven bits of REG 11, and the value already being output to pin 7, so we can toggle it from 1 to 0 or vice versa. A couple of INC instructions winds us past **count** and **rate** to **oldOut**, which we read into the accumulator.

A naïve approach would be to test bit 0, which is hooked up to the joystick port output, and alter it to 1 if it was 0, and 0 if it was 1, with something like BIT 0,A: JR NZ,ON: LD A,0: JR DONE: ON: LD A,1: DONE – but that's ten bytes of code including two slow relative branches.

After a week's practice a Z80 beginner might trim this to: AND 1: JR NZ,ON: INC A: JR DONE: ON: XOR A: DONE – which saves a couple of bytes. But all we really need to achieve is to replace a 1 in bit 0 with a 0, or a 0 with a 1, while making sure none of the other seven bits is inadvertently changed. That can be done in a single two-byte instruction: XOR 1, as shown overleaf:

```
INC  HL
INC  HL
LD   A,(HL)                ; Read old port state
XOR  1                     ; Toggle output bit
```

It only remains to update REG 11 and store the new value of **oldOut** in preparation for the next blink. Handily HL is already pointing where we need to save the tweaked accumulator value, and the update can be neatly achieved with one of the custom Z80n NextReg instructions, equivalent to the two OUTs used earlier to access the FPGA's SELECT and DATA ports:

```
NEXTREG 11,A
LD   (HL),A                ; Update port state
RET
```

This version of NextReg writes the value in the accumulator, register A, to the FPGA DATA port. The register number for the SELECT port is stored as the third byte of the instruction. There's also a four-byte variant, which stores both the SELECT and DATA bytes as constants in the code.

Here's the BASIC to get the blinker going. This is trimmed from the earlier example in Chapter 4, as it needs to go through the same rigmarole to turn off polling of the extra buttons on a Megadrive pad:

```
930 %j=% REG 5:%f= %0
940 IF %j&8 THEN IF %(j&192=64) OR (j&192=128) THEN %f=%1
950 IF %j&2 THEN IF %(j&48=32) OR (j&48=16) THEN %f=%2
960 IF %f THEN PRINT "Megadrive buttons temporarily disabled"
970 %r=% REG 11 & 127: %b=%r & 126 | 128
980 POKE 49080,100,25,%b: DRIVER 8,1,49060
```

This leaves the LED blinking away till you unload the driver or disable the slot with DRIVER 8,1,0. By default it will blink on and off again once every second. To halve the blink rate, POKE 49080,50. POKE any value up to 255 (for a cycle time of 10.2 seconds on a 50 Hertz Next); you may need a stroboscope to work out the rate for low values, as a rate of 1 will give 25 blinks per second.

As noted in the discussion of the **delay** method, 0 is taken as the maximum when the count-down is done before the check for zero, so POKE 49080,0 will give the slowest rate of all, rather than the fastest. Feel free to move the code and data, but if you store them somewhere else don't forget to change **both** addresses in line 980!

When you've finished playing with the LED, especially if you're nimble-fingered enough to be a Megadrive joypad enthusiast, you should turn off I/O mode and restore the other bits of the joystick port mode selection register by typing: REG 11,%R

Relocatable USR code

There are more intricate examples of slot methods in the next two chapters. Before closing this introduction I should note that the approach to relocatable code and data used in the driver **blink** method may also be applied to USR routines on any Spectrum. USR code called from the original ZX ROM will awaken with the start address in BC, so it can address local variables or relocatable subroutines by adding the relevant offset, e.g: START: LD HL,VAR-START: ADD HL,BC will leave HL pointing at VAR.

The multi-parameter version of USR recently introduced to NextBASIC is not quite backward-compatible, because it stores the value of the first integer parameter in BC, rather than the start address. I raised this as issue 95 on GitLab while regression-testing NextBASIC 2.08.

Garry Lancaster pointed out that we can still run old relocatable code by passing the start address *twice* to the revised USR function: **USR(start, start)** will invoke the code at **start** from the first parameter *and* pre-load BC with that address via the second parameter. So I closed the issue.

Chapter 12, Advanced Sprite Animation

NextZXOS 2.06 introduced SPRITE CONTINUE, allowing sprites to move automatically. This was a giant leap for NextBASIC, making much more complicated games possible without resort to machine code. It led a group of us to investigate how it worked, and ways to make it better.

This chapter describes eight demos that animate sprites in increasingly ingenious ways, starting with the features in NextBASIC 2.06 then adding PEEKs, POKEs and USR routines to do more advanced things. It uses an extensible framework I grandly call the Sprite Director, developed using Object Orientated Programming techniques (yes, OOP, in BASIC and Z80), to build up a library of methods for extending NextBASIC SPRITE facilities.

Nine of us have been investigating this since 2020 and it was one of the last things holding back completing this book early in 2024. This chapter explains, by example, the SpriteHax NextBASIC and Z80n assembler demos, with particular emphasis on the use of fixed-point arithmetic to allow smoother and more flexible sprite animation, and fast curve generation. All this is because Garry Lancaster kindly let us disclose the sprite data table:

I agree it makes sense to allow access to this data so that extensions can be produced, and saves me the job of adding sprite path functionality into NextBASIC, at least for the time being. I don't have any plans to change the data structures (there are no free bits anyway, so any further extensions would need to be added as additional separate structures). The data may well need to move in future versions, but I have now added a vector to locate it in RAM8; I've also added my own documentation for the data structures; you seem to have deciphered this exactly :)

Bit	Purpose
0	See text
1	Stop at limit
2	Auto-flip Y
3	Auto-flip X
4	Bounce/Cycle
5	Stop at end
6	Y changing
7	X changing

Figure 60 - Byte 5 flags

The second part of this exploration explains a shorter but more sophisticated demo that swirls 64 sprites at 50 Hertz, accessing the system sprite table directly, leaving most of the CPU time free for other processing. This builds on SLOT.DRV, the interrupt slot handler, and comes in two parts: SPRITEHAX0, a tutorial, then a fuller demo, SPRITEHAX1.

How Sprite Continue works

NextBASIC uses two data tables to animate sprites. Garry generously allowed us to publish details and provided a mechanism to find them, in case they need to move from their current position early in BANK 8. Our aim, demonstrated in this chapter, is to allow SPRITE CONTINUE to do all the existing magic while allowing short slot routines to implement smoother movement along arbitrarily complex paths. The first table is 2K long, comprising the 16 bytes shown in Figure 61 for each of 128 sprites. It is a stunning feat of efficient data-packing, and well rewards a few hours of investigation and experiments.

These bytes have purposes well-defined by the hardware and SPRITE command syntax. The first five bytes closely correspond to REG 53..57 except that five hardware bits are re-used by NextBASIC for other purposes. In all, sixteen bits of those five bytes are 'flags' tracking things like visibility, orientation and relative parameters. So the four flags in the low bits of byte 2 match REG 55's XM, YM, R and X8 mirror, rotation and X offset bits.

Byte	Purpose	Flags
0	Sprite X	
1	Sprite Y	
2	Palette Offset	4
3	Pattern number	2
4	Magnification	4
5	Behaviour flags	8
6	Path X Start	
7	Path X End	
8	Pattern Start	2
9	Pattern End	2
10	X step	
11	Path Y start	
12	Path Y end	
13	Y step	
14	Movement rate	
15	Initial delay	

Figure 61 – Usage of Sprite table bytes

Byte 3 packs the six-bit pattern number alongside the anchor or relative and visibility flags from REG 56, as described at www.specnext.com/sprites and byte 4 starts like REG 57, with four bits to control sprite magnification, but uses the top two for palette and pattern anchoring, and bit 0 for travel flipping.

Since sprites can move in the border, X co-ordinates may be more than 256 – their ninth bits are tucked into the least significant bits of bytes 2, 8 and 9. Byte 2 has the palette offset in the top four bits – sensibly, as it's a range from 0 to 240 in steps of 16 – and signals rotation, Y and X mirroring in bits from 1 to 3. The top bit of byte 8 is set to animate stationary sprites, and the top bit of byte 9 is only set while counting downwards through animation patterns.

Figure 61 reveals the main purpose of each byte, with a column noting the number of 'flag bits' in each entry. Byte 5 does the most work. It's bit 4 is clear if animation is to 'bounce' backwards through the sprite numbers at the limit, or set for it to cycle back to the start. Bits 0 and 1 are treated as a pair, determining the behaviour when X/Y limits are reached. 0 means reflect this direction; 1 means stop this direction and start the other; 2 just stops this direction of motion, while 3 will stop and make the sprite invisible.

The second table immediately follows the 2k block. It is just 32 bytes long, allocating two bits for each sprite to indicate if it is moving or that the corresponding data is 'Dirty' from a SPRITE command update, and thus needs reprocessing to render the next frame. Each pair of bytes handles eight sprites, from 0..7 in the first pair to 120..127 in the 16th. Bits set in the first byte show that sprite needs updating; the second byte shows that it's moving.

Introductory SPRITEHAX0

The SpriteHax0.bas demo shows seven ways of manipulating sprites, starting with the official SPRITE commands and building up to make direct access to the sprite data table in BANK 8. The GEMSPRITES file contains 32 rudimentary sprites adapted from public domain images, with eight frames each showing gems in four different colours.

The embedded machine code needs to be assembled before any of the USR calls will work, so start by making sure you have ASM in your dot directory and type GO TO 1000. This invokes the assembler, stores code from address 48000 upwards, and saves the program and generated code to SD as long as no errors occur. If you forget this, or the alternative of typing LOAD "FixedPoint" CODE 48000 to put pre-assembled code in the required place, later demos in this set will crash your Next, though no long-term harm will result. Let's examine the BASIC first:

```
 90 REM SpriteHax0 © Simon N Goodwin 2022..2024
100 REM Primer to move eight sprites on screen in various ways
110 REM The first 8k of BANK 8 may be poked at 48k..56k
120 REM Put any other page at 56k, test routines at 48000
130 RUN AT 3: CLEAR 47999: SPRITE CLEAR : LAYER CLEAR
140 LAYER 1,2: BANK NEW %a: LOAD "gemsprites" BANK %a
150 SPRITE PRINT 1: SPRITE BORDER 1: SPRITE BANK %a
160 SPRITE 1,150,192,1,1,0,0,0: SPRITE 6,50,192,1,1,0,0,0:
   SPRITE 2,30,150,1,1,0,0,0: SPRITE 5,75,150,1,1,0,0,0
170 SPRITE 3,150,120,1,1,0,0,0: SPRITE 7,150,30,1,1,0,0,0:
  SPRITE 4,150,90,1,1,0,0,0: SPRITE 0,24,30,1,1,0,0,0
180 SPRITE CONTINUE 0,0 TO 304 STEP 2 RUN ,48 TO 192 STEP 5
   RUN ,24 TO 31,0,1,0: SPRITE CONTINUE 1,0 TO 304 STEP 1 RUN,
   48 TO 192 STEP 1 RUN ,0 TO 7,0,1,0
190 SPRITE CONTINUE 2,32 TO 272 STEP 2 RUN ,48 TO 192 STEP 3
   RUN ,8 TO 15,0,1,0: SPRITE CONTINUE 3,0 TO 304 STEP 1 RUN
   ,0 TO 240 STEP 2 RUN ,0 TO 7,0,1,0
200 SPRITE CONTINUE 4,32 TO 272 STEP 2 RUN ,32 TO 224 STEP 4
   RUN ,24 TO 31,0,2,0: SPRITE CONTINUE 5,0 TO 304 STEP 2 RUN
   ,64 TO 192 STEP 5 RUN ,8 TO 15,0,2,0
210 SPRITE CONTINUE 6,32 TO 272 STEP 2 RUN ,48 TO 192 STEP 6
   RUN ,16 TO 23,0,3,0 : SPRITE CONTINUE 7,0 TO 304 STEP 3 RUN
   ,48 TO 192 STEP 3 RUN ,16 TO 23,0,3,0
220 PRINT "(0) Normal SPRITE MOVE INT... tap key to continue"
230 REPEAT : SPRITE MOVE INT : REPEAT UNTIL CODE INKEY$
```

The first part laboriously sets eight sprites moving on straight-line paths with the commands introduced in NextBASIC 2.06. CLEAR 47999 reserves main memory from address 48000 upwards for test code and data. I picked an address below 49152 to avoid issues caused by paging of the top 16k. The 8k from 49152 to 56k will be used to map the first half of BASIC BANK 8 into main memory so the Z80 can see it and NextBASIC can PEEK and POKE at it. The 'protection' of BANKs 7 and 8 only applies to commands like BANK 8 POKE; if MMU registers are used to put either bank into main memory they can be PEEKed and POKEd using original 48k BASIC commands, or non-BANK updates of those.

The next thing the demo does is search for the sprite data table. We used to use this to check that the sprite data hasn't moved in NextZXOS updates, but don't need to do that in future since Garry has given us a safe way to find it, in NextZXOS 2.09 RC11 and later. In fact it hasn't moved since 2.06 and even if it does one day DPEEK(page16+8190)+page16 will reliably locate it somewhere within that 8k in any future NextZXOS. So this is for 2.08 and earlier, and a general example of table-scanning through protected banks.

```
250 REM SpriteFinderGeneral 0.1, locates sprite 0
260 CLEAR 47999: PRINT "(1) Seeking sprite data"''
270 REG 86,16: REM Map start of bank 8 to 48k
280 SPRITE CONTINUE 0, STEP 1,2 TO 3 STEP 4 STOP ,,,5,6
290 FOR %i=49152 TO 49152+8192-6
300   IF % DPEEK i=513 THEN IF % DPEEK (i+2)=1027 THEN IF
   % DPEEK (i+4)=1541 THEN %s=%i-10: PRINT
   "Sprite 0 spec in bank 8 at ";%s-49152;"  ";
310 NEXT %i
320 SPRITE 0,45,123 : REM Confirmatory check
330 IF % PEEK s=45 AND (PEEK (s+1)=123) THEN PRINT "Confirmed"
```

After a precautionary CLEAR call to protect higher RAM addresses, REG 86,16 puts the 16th 8k page at address 49152 in Z80 space. Since banks are twice the size of pages, and both count from 0, page 16 corresponds to the first 8k of BANK 8. The second half of BANK 8 is at page 17, but we don't need to look there to manipulate sprites.

The previously-secret Sprite data table has been fully documented in the updated release 2.09 NextBASIC_New_Commands_and_Features files in the docs/NextZXOS SD directory, and briefly at the start of this Chapter. Sprite 0 data starts at offset 1247 in BANK 8 (till further notice) with 16 bytes for Sprite 0, then 16 more for sprite 1 at offset 1263 into the page (49152+1263 when accessed via MMU6) and so on up to sprite 63.

Line 280 puts a pattern of six consecutive bytes into the normally hidden SPRITE 0 data. The sequence 1, 2, 3, 4, 5, 6 is chosen to be easy to find and not very likely to crop up by accident. The FOR loop searches for them all through the 8k. The values DPEEKed correspond to $0102 (513), $0304 (1027) and $0506 (1541, 5 + 6 * 256) and the SPRITE CONTINUE parameters were picked to hit the last six bytes which happen to hold singular values without odd flags to complicate things. We're looking for these entries:

```
10   X step
11   SPRITE CONTINUE Y start
12   SPRITE CONTINUE Y end
13   Y step
14   Movement rate
15   Initial movement delay
```

Once the data is found at %I, line 300 sets %S to the presumed start of the sprite 0 data 10 bytes before, then use a simple SPRITE command to verify that the first two bytes change as expected.

The next demonstration is a minimally-simple confirmation that we can now change the coordinate of a sprite with a POKE rather than a SPRITE command. It works but doesn't get us any advantage, yet.

```
350 REM Demos of direct access to sprite engine from BASIC
360 SPRITE STOP : SPRITE CONTINUE 0, STEP 0
370 REPEAT : REPEAT UNTIL NOT CODE INKEY$
380 PRINT AT 10,0;"(2) POKEd pixel movement... press a key
   to continue"
390 SPRITE 0,10
410 REM Pixel movement
420 FOR %d=0 TO 255
430   POKE %s,%d
440   SPRITE MOVE : PRINT AT 22,0;%d;" ";: GO SUB @show0
450   IF CODE INKEY$ THEN EXIT
460 NEXT %d
```

The SPRITE CONTINUE command after SPRITE STOP clears the first sprite's movement rate back to zero. This is necessary, as Paulo Silva realised, because the SpriteFinderGeneral previously POKEd it to 5.

Since we'll move between the demos by pressing a key, and don't want to skip them all after the first key-press, lines like 370 occur periodically to make sure there is no key pressed at the START of each demo. Line 450 here breaks out of the loop, using the 2.08 EXIT extension. If you are still on 2.07, replace EXIT with **%d=256** but bear in mind these demos were mostly written on 2.08 and tested on 2.09 so you might need to update or add other tweaks to run on an older system.

The label used at the end of line 440 is a relocatable reference to a subroutine on line 800, which PRINTs out the 16 bytes of sprite 0 data at the start of the area in BANK 8, after checking that MMU6 still maps that to 48k. The NextBASIC editor changes MMU registers without restoring them so GO SUB works fine in a program but not from a command that doesn't also set REG 86,16 before the GO SUB. If you're looking for a simple starter project, you might rewrite line 820 to show the sprite 0 data fields more clearly; this example is just enough to alert us to which bytes are hit, not necessarily which bit-fields change.

```
800 @show0
810 IF REG 86<>16 THEN PRINT "Editor clobbered REG 86?": STOP
820 FOR %i=%s TO %s+15: PRINT % PEEK i;" ";: NEXT %i
830 PRINT '': RETURN
```

Smoother and further

The sprite system has several limitations which these advances systematically eliminate. Two of those are that positions and speeds are in whole pixels so slow and smooth movements cannot be progressively applied - the step between one pixel movement per frame to two is abrupt, so a sprite takes at most five seconds to move all the way across, and the next faster step is double that, crossing the screen in 2.5 seconds. We can make that smoother.

Also, there's only enough space in the system table for on-screen coordinates (e.g. one byte for Y, with all values from 0 to 255 corresponding to visible locations) so you can't put a sprite far above or below, or partway along a side-scrolling playfield, before or after the current screen position, without complicated and slow conditional tests to check whether it's become visible as a platform-style game scrolls across a larger than screen-size graphic background in memory. Big game worlds are more fun, so we'll fix that, too.

Fixed-point resolution

My solution to both these issues is to use two bytes for each coordinate, but rather than consider the 16 bits as a signed value from -32768 to +32767, or an unsigned integer 0 to 65535, the way NextBASIC's integer evaluator prefers to work, our 16-bit value has four bits for the fractional part, giving a range from 0 to 15/16, eleven bits for the whole number (0 to 2000ish) and one bit for the sign. Now we can express offsets before or after the overscan screen coordinates from 0 to 319. For instance –640 would be a position two full screens to the left of the current display window, in a virtual coordinate space up to eight screens wide in either direction and 21 screens tall.

The next loop introduces this idea minimally. %D counts from 0 to 255 * 16. The POKE >>4 divides the count in %D by 16, so the sprite coordinate only changes once every 16 times round the loop. We don't gain any smoothness yet, but now the sprite moves at 1/16th the slowest speed it could otherwise go, if its position was still being updated every frame. The SPRITE command has a parameter to skip alternate updates, or more often, for the same effect, but that can't handle fractional steps. A fixed-point step of 3 (meaning 3/16ths) at line 510 would move 9 pixels every 48 frames, a step of 4 would up that to 12 pixels in the same time, and likewise for finer intervals, without the costly conditional tests that would otherwise be needed.

The choice of 16 subdivisions is a compromise between smoothness and preserving enough other bits for a wider range beyond the screen, while still staying within the 16-bit limits of Z80 native arithmetic. Later, when we draw curves, we'll use a different fixed-point format, counting 64ths, for rounder circles; these 'fixed point' formats are known as 12:4 and 10:6 respectively. The numbers add up to the 16-bit word size. The value before the colon counts bits reserved for the whole number and sign, followed by the number of fractional bits, after the colon, giving 2^4 (16) or 2^6 (64) fractions before the next whole number, respectively.

```
480 REM Demo of fractional movement
490 REPEAT : REPEAT UNTIL NOT CODE INKEY$
500 PRINT AT 10,0;"(3) POKEd fractional
   moves... press a key to continue"
510 FOR %d=0*16 TO 255*16
520   POKE %s,%d>>4
530   SPRITE MOVE : PRINT AT 22,0;%d;" ";
540   IF CODE INKEY$ THEN EXIT
550 NEXT %d
```

Since the other seven sprites are moving every time, it's easy to tell which one we're moving with POKE, as it's a lot slower than the others.

Curves without cosines

The next demo loop uses Marvin Minsky's 1972 algorithm from the HakMem collection to generate consecutive sine and cosine approximations using only simple arithmetic. Page 229 of my Beep to Boom book discusses the algorithm; here I've replaced multiplication by a fraction with a right shift, for greater speed on the Z80n. The smaller the fraction (or further the shift) the more points in the circle are calculated and the smoother the curve. I use shifts of five and six places (for the X, Y and U, V coordinate pairs) to get two different Sine/Cosine pairs every time round the loop. The magnitude of the initial values of X and Y (or U and V) determines the radius of the circle by SQR(X^2+Y^2) and SQR(U^2+V^2), and their relative values give the initial angle. So if one value is zero the other is the radius starting vertically or horizontally, and if the lengths match you get a 45-degree diagonal.

It's probably easier to understand this by watching the code, maybe with fewer sprites and a PAUSE between steps while you get the hang of it:

```
580 REM Circular path with only trivial arithmetic
590 FOR %d=0 TO %7: SPRITE %d,%d*20: SPRITE CONTINUE %d,
    STOP , STOP ,0 TO 31,64,0,%d*8 : NEXT %d
600 PRINT AT 10,0;"(4) POKEd fractional curves till keypress",
610 REG 86,16:x=2500:y=0:v=1000:u=1000
630 REPEAT
640   y=y+(x>>6)
650   v=v+(u>>5)
660   x=x-(y>>6)
670   u=u-(v>>5)
680   POKE %s,x>>5+150,y>>4+96
690   POKE %s+16,v>>5+150,u>>4+96
700   POKE %s+32,70-y>>4,100-x>>5
710   POKE %s+48,70-u>>4,100-v>>5
720   POKE %s+64,80-x>>4,100-y>>5
730   POKE %s+80,100-v>>4,100-y>>5
740   POKE %s+96,127-u>>5,100-y>>5
750   POKE %s+112,100-v>>5,x>>4+70
760   SPRITE MOVE INT
770 REPEAT UNTIL CODE INKEY$
```

Ideally this demo would use % integer arithmetic, with SGN{} to accommodate both positive and negative offsets around the centre of the circular path, but a NextBASIC bug (#114 on GitLab) in signed-shift handling means I've chosen to use normal variables here, till the fix is widely available.

Lines 640 to 670 work out two coordinate pairs. The eight POKEs update the sprite 0..7 positions with shuffled values from those, to derive eight distinct circular paths. The constants in the POKE lines set suitable centres for each path. I shall re-express all this in fast Z80 assembly language, later.

Before we get into the assembly language there's one more demo. It is a hybrid of the eight-sprite POKEing NextBASIC twirler we've just seen, and a Z80n equivalent soon to be revealed. The same four variables X, Y, U and V are calculated, but this time only U and V are used to update four sprites via a machine code USR call. The calculations of X and Y on lines 912 and 914 are not used in the graphics, but printed on-screen alongside U and V by line 915, so we can check that they roughly correspond. The values are nearly but not identical; this is because the >>6 operations on X and Y are more precise than the 16-bit numbers DPOKEd and DPEEKed for U and V. But they're close enough for graphics, in either case.

The variable T came in handy when I wanted to step through the values generated after lots of calls. After –T fast steps the test at the end of line 935 inserts a PAUSE 0 between subsequent steps. With T set to –1000 you get a few fast twirls before the pauses start; to keep the loop going between those, replace CODE INKEY$ with 0 in line 960.

Two new integer variables, %C and %P, give the address of the code and the parameter data passed on line 910. The code is the short block labelled TRIG at the start of the assembly language section coming soon. First I'll discuss the first eight bytes of parameter data, because they're the start of a per-sprite data-structure, re-usable for many advanced updates.

The fixed-point sprite object

This demo uses four sixteen-bit parameters. In order these are known as X, Y, U and V. X and Y are 12:4 fixed-point coordinates, typically positions in the fixed-point sprite space from -2048 to +2047.9375 (15/16 = 0.9375). Depending upon the code, U and V might be another coordinate pair, or integers or (in this case) 10:6 fixed-point 'phase accumulators' that count in 1/64ths, otherwise like the normal BASIC variables X and Y.

```
865 PRINT AT 10,0;"(5) ASM reflected curves until keypress",
867 REPEAT : REPEAT UNTIL NOT CODE INKEY$
870 %c=48000:%p=49000:%s=49152+1247: REG 86,16
880 REM Set start position, radius and angle
885 x=15:y=1406:u=x:v=y:t=-1000:; Pause after this many steps
890 DPOKE %p,120*16,88*16,u,v
900 REPEAT
910   RANDOMIZE USR (%c,%p)
912   y=y+(x>>6)
914   x=x-(y>>6)
920   u= % DPEEK (p+4): IF u>32767 THEN u=u-65536
930   v= % DPEEK (p+6): IF v>32767 THEN v=v-65536
935   PRINT AT 2,0; x;" ";y,u;" ";v;"  ";:t+=1:
      IF t>0 THEN PAUSE 0
940   SPRITE 0,166+u/16,96+v/16
942   SPRITE 1,150+u/16,116-v/16
944   SPRITE 2,166-u/16,116+v/16
946   SPRITE 6,150-u/16,96-v/16
950   SPRITE MOVE
960 REPEAT UNTIL CODE INKEY$
```

The USR routine just updates U and V in place. It doesn't touch X or Y, yet. Line 890 stores the initial values and lines 920 and 930 read back the updated ones, with IF tests to convert unsigned results from DPEEK into signed values in the range -32768 to 32767 according to the rules of two's complement arithmetic, the way the Z80 works. Note that RANDOMISE clobbers the random number seed; see page 423 for a neat way around this.

SPRITE commands control the motion, rather than POKEs, dividing integer values from the Z80 by 16 before combining them with the centre coordinate. We can't use the faster >> 4 here because we need the sign to be preserved, but division will do that. Notice how negating the signed results reverses the direction of sprite rotation. This happens because it has the same effect as flipping both the X and Y axes.

Assembly-language sprite methods

There are a couple more demos later in SpriteHax0, but let's consider the machine-code part next. To take advantage of the new multi-parameter USR function, and the 'slots' for machine code routines in my interrupt slot driver used by the SpriteHax1 demo, the demo code uses a standard 'object orientated' interface.

Each routine or 'method' takes two address parameters. The first is the USR code entry point, and the second is a data-pointer. The C++ programming language tries to hide this parameter, but sometimes has to expose it as a pointer called 'this'. In my current scheme the 'this' pointer to parameter data (the 'instance' of the 'object') is copied to the IX register by the first two lines of each method.

The technique predates C++ (I first encountered it at Racal when we had a load of prototype code written in Forth by tyros in California, and I was one of the programmers expected to translate that into pre-OOP C code). You may have encountered something very similar in classic 'callback' APIs.

Stripped of the language-lawyer hurdles this approach combines and separates code and data in a way that is very handy for efficient re-use of either. So we can set up a load of parameter blocks, one for each actual or potential sprite, path generator or related 'object', and a load of 'method' routines which do different but useful things with whatever parameter block they're linked to by a USR or DRIVER-slot call.

We'll see that one call can invoke several methods in succession, passing values via the parameter object, and each object can point to another object or table of parameters. This allows the object data as well as the code methods to be shared, to build up complicated behaviours without code duplication.

We've just seen a method to generate circular coordinates. Another one adjusts coordinates by preset and adjustable amounts whenever it's called, in this case wrapping between the bottom and top of the screen. Another example method combines coordinates with a 2D offset, crops them into screen-space and then converts the fixed-point result into bits scattered across the BANK 8 sprite table.

There are *lots* of other such methods that could be useful. This research, inspired by Mark Gallop's Sprite Path Generator, forms a framework to share and re-use existing and new methods to efficiently implement all the complex sprite behaviours that we currently have to hand-roll in NextBASIC when the automated capability falls short of what we need – for arbitrary animation paths, clipping to a screen window from a multiple-screen backdrop, scroll-relative offsets, 3D projection, automatic mouse pointer tracking, etc.

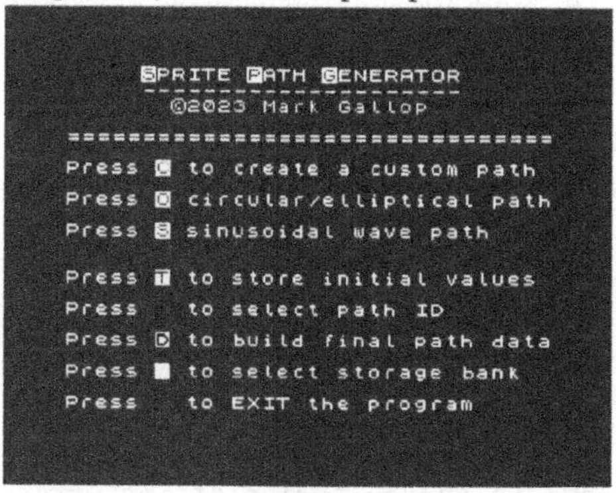

Figure 62 – Mark's Prototype Sprite Path Generator

Thus behaviours can be built up with any combination of NextBASIC and Z80n code that fits the profile and eases development and debugging. The slot driver can readily be used to invoke methods on chosen objects automatically, in configurable order at regular intervals, alongside BASIC. It works just like the 2.06 sprite system, in a way that is both compatible and extensible. So sprite movement may use new methods, while animation and rotation continue to use SPRITE CONTINUE, or vice versa. Now as well as fixed-offset 'relative sprites' we could link sprite objects with scaling, offsetting, swapping, wrapping, bouncing, grouping and cropping methods.

The object structure is designed to be extended. The first twelve bytes are enough to build upon, and intended to prefix every Sprite Director object. The comments and equates on lines 1032 to 1044 document the current set. We've seen that the first eight bytes of the object are two pairs of fixed-point coordinates. These are the minimum needed to combine relative and absolute pairs, support input and output, or embed other state like step sizes, scales, angles or oscillator phases. The fifth word is the 'escape mechanism' to link objects or add arbitrary extra data for specific methods. Typically it will point to another such object, to pick up more coordinates or other parameters, as I'll soon show. The more we use this 'standard' structure, the more effectively we'll be able to share methods.

At least two additional single-byte parameters complete the structure. After X, Y, U, V and O the offset to another object, we often need a way to bind an object to a particular sprite. The 11th byte, S, 0..63, is reserved for that input. Since we now allow off-screen sprites, and automatic updates independent of the NextBASIC ones, we also need a way to know if an object has been cropped off the screen.

The top bit of the twelfth byte, F, is set when a sprite is visible and 0 otherwise. Other bits may be defined for similar independent state outputs in future. Initially the flag is reset, before the sprite is updated. If it is off-screen, nothing changes and the code flies on. If the sprite is visible (however the method defines that - there could be methods for each window, or shared parameters) the flag gets set. This can be a cue for NextBASIC updates, or a hint to other methods about work they should now do or can safely skip. T is temporary; at some point I might trim the structure from 13 to 12 bytes by storing the value held there, a cache for the number of the page we swap out to access the system sprite table, in an alternate register or on the stack.

```
1000 CLEAR 47999
1005 .asm
1010 ; org 48000
1015 ;trig
1020 ; push bc
1030 ; pop ix             ; Use IX to access parameters
1032 ;; defw x,y,u,v,o ; O points to shared sprite offset words
1033 ;x equ 0            ; Fixed point X coordinate
1034 ;y equ 2            ; Fixed point Y coordinate
1035 ;u equ 4            ; Fixed point workspace 1
1036 ;v equ 6            ; Fixed point workspace 2
1037 ;o equ 8            ; Address of fixed-point offset data
1038 ;; X & Y are 12:4 coords, U & V trace out curves in 10:6
1040 ;; defb s,f,t       ; S is the sprite number 0..63
1041 ;; F is 128 when the sprite is visible, T is the old page
1042 ;s equ 10
1043 ;f equ 11           ; 0 initially, updated automatically
1044 ;t equ 12           ; 13 bytes of parameters (so far)
```

With these offsets established we can look at our first simple method, the oscillator seen first in BASIC, called from the 'reflected curves' demo:

```
1050 ;; Update Sine, Signed V = V + U >> 6
1060 ; ld e,(ix+u)      ; Load U to DE
1070 ; ld d,(ix+u+1)
1080 ; ld c,e           ; Save a copy of U for later
1085 ; ld b,d
1090 ; call asr6        ; DE = U/64, by signed shifts
1100 ; ld l,(ix+v)      ; Load V to HL
1110 ; ld h,(ix+v+1)
1120 ; add hl,de
1130 ; ld (ix+v),l      ; Store new V
1140 ; ld (ix+v+1),h
1145 ;
1150 ;; Update Cosine, Signed U = U - V >> 6
1160 ; ex de,hl
1170 ; call asr6        ; DE = V/64
1180 ; ld l,c           ; (ix+4) Load U to HL
1190 ; ld h,b           ; (ix+5)
1200 ; or a             ; Clear carry
1210 ; sbc hl,de
1230 ; ld (ix+u),l      ; Update U
1240 ; ld (ix+u+1),h
1250 ; ret              ; Old U in BC, new U in HL
```

The ASR6 subroutine shifts a 16-bit value six places to the right, preserving the sign, like a bug-fixed version of the SGN{ >> 6} operator. As we'll also need an ASR4 for 2:4 fixed-point maths, I've put them end to end with a well-known hack at line 1880 to remove the need for a slow JR $+1 between them to skip the first set-up line only needed at the start of the shift sequence. The value 254 is a CP opcode, causing the next instruction to be interpreted as a value rather than code. Then we ignore the results of the comparison, in effect skipping one byte ahead without wasting a two-byte JR instruction. This hack was used in MGT ROMs to fit SAM BASIC into 32k.

Although it's DE that we need to shift, the old 8080 instruction to shift register A is twice as fast as the Z80-specific RR E so it saves time and bytes to keep half the value in A rather than E while we shuffle it. 16-bit left-shifts can be done in one step with ADD HL,HL, but we need 16-bit right shifts with sign extension here, and without resort to table look-up that requires three bytes of code per bit. I wanted to test this code from BASIC which passes the first data parameter in BC rather than DE so there's another PUSH POP pair before the start of ASR6 so a call to address 48100 can be used for testing. Uncomment lines 2003 and 2005 to return the result to USR via BC:

```
1760 ; org 48100
1770 ; push bc
1775 ; pop de     ; Harness for USR testing
1780 ;
1790 ;; Shift DE arithmetically 4 or 6 places
1800 ;ASR6
1810 ; ld a,e     ; Use accumulator for speed
1820 ; sra d
1830 ; rra        ; RR E is longer and slower
1860 ; sra d
1870 ; rra        ; DA = DE/4
1880 ; db 254     ; cp n opcode, skips next code byte
1890 ;ASR4
1900 ; ld a,e     ; Divide DE by 16
1920 ; sra d
1930 ; rra
1940 ; sra d
1950 ; rra
1960 ; sra d
1970 ; rra
1980 ; sra d
1990 ; rra
2000 ; ld e,a     ; Result in DE
2003 ;; push de
2005 ;; pop bc    ; Copy to BC for USR testing
2010 ; ret
```

The most trivial yet useful four-byte 'slot' object follows. This will be used in SpriteHax1 to show progress through the object update slots. It takes a parameter in E, 0..7, immediately setting the border colour. A BORDER statement could be used but also redraws the LAYER 0 lower screen colours, taking much longer than a single OUT instruction.

```
2017 ; org 48130
2019 ;border
2021 ; ld a,e          ; Data parameter 0..7
2022 ; out (254),a     ; Force border colour
2023 ; ret
```

Another trivial routine follows. Call ADDUP at 48134 to chain two methods together. In this case we call ADDON, a method to increment a fixed-point position by a preset X, Y measure at each call, then fall into the UPDATE method which transfers coordinates from the object into the system sprite table. In this case we skip the first two lines of UPDATE, entering at gotIX, because the work of transferring the USR parameter to register IX has already been done by ADDON. The pair of instructions at 48194, on lines 2193 and 2194, are very like ADDUP, except this time they call the TRIG curve generator before falling into UPDATE.

```
2025 ;; X+=U, Y+=V; then offset, clip and update sprite
2027 ;addup
2030 ; call addon
2032 ; jp gotix
2034 ;
2040 ;; Update X and Y by adding U and V
2043 ;addon
2045 ; push bc
2050 ; pop ix
2060 ; ld e,(ix+y)      ; Y = Y + V; first fetch Y
2065 ; ld d,(ix+y+1)
2070 ; ld l,(ix+v)      ; Fetch V
2072 ; ld h,(ix+v+1)
2074 ; add hl,de        ; Apply delta to Y
2075 ; ld a,15          ; Wrap Y to +0..255 range
2076 ; and h
2077 ; ld (ix+y),l      ; fine: 0..15.9375
2078 ; ld (ix+y+1),a    ; coarse: 0..240 step 16
2080 ; ld e,(ix+x)
2085 ; ld d,(ix+x+1)    ; X = X + U
2086 ; ld l,(ix+u)
2087 ; ld h,(ix+u+1)
2088 ; add hl,de        ; Apply delta to x, no checks
2089 ; ld (ix+x),l
2090 ; ld (ix+x+1),h    ; Update X, no clip or wrap
2095 ; ret
2190 ; org 48194 ; Enter here to move then update
2193 ; call trig
2194 ; jp gotix  ; Both routines in sequence
```

After setting IX from BC, ADDON is a simple method that adds the parameters in U and V to X and Y respectively. This method can move an object in any direction by a fractional step. The X motion is unchecked, so it can run off the left or right side of the screen, eventually re-emerging on the other side of the 4096-pixel arena of this demo. The Y delta is wrapped into the range 0..255 by lines 2075 and 2076 which discard the top (256..3840) four bits of the coordinate so objects wrap between the top and bottom of the screen, or vice versa, again for demo purposes. Depending your game, either or both might be set to wrap, run on or clamp; customise accordingly.

Let's see the EXPOSE and UNPAGE subroutines that provide temporary access to the system sprite table, along with UPDATE, sometimes entered at gotIX. The former pair serves all methods that read or update the table. Three equates point at the SELECT I/O port, the MMU6 register which controls access to addresses 49152-57343, and TABLE, the current offset within that page of the system data for SPRITE 0. The recommended way to find this offset is now to DPEEK it from 8190 bytes into BANK 8. Future programs should do that, so that they'll work on NextBASIC updates.

```
2200 ;; Apply offset and range check to sprite position
2204 ;SELECT equ 9275          ; NextReg selection port
2206 ;MMU6   equ 86            ; MMU register for 48..56k
2208 ;TABLE  equ 49152+1247    ; Sprite 0 address in MMU6
```

The UPDATE routine needs to know which sprite coordinates mark the edge of the visible screen. These demos use overscan XRANGE and YRANGEs of 320 and 256 rather than the Sinclair screen dimensions of 256 and 192 pixels. Like ADDON and TRIG, UPDATE starts by copying the USR parameter from register BC to IX so that object data bits and bytes can be easily picked out from the parameter area.

```
2210 ;XRANGE equ 320           ; Number of sprite columns
2212 ;YRANGE equ 256           ; Number of overscan lines
2218 ;
2220 ;update             ; Enter at 48200 to run this
2230 ; push bc
2240 ; pop ix             ; Index parameter table
```

GotIX labels the most intricate of these routines and the one most likely to be worth specialising and elaborating. Beyond the customary Z80 register-shuffling complications, required because so many operations can only be done efficiently in A or HL, the logic is as follows:

a) Find the offset pointer to the screen-start coordinates (default 0,0)
b) Add the first offset from there to the object's fixed-point X position
c) Check to see if the total is beyond XRANGE; if so, exit fast via HIDE
d) Convert the fixed-point X to an integer 0..XRANGE-1 with ASR4
e) Add the second offset from o+2 to the object's fixed-point Y position
f) Check to see if the total is beyond YRANGE; if so, exit via HIDE
g) The sprite is on-screen; update system table X, Y and visibility data

```
2245 ;gotix
2250 ; ld l,(ix+o)      ; Point HL at 12:4 X,Y offset
2260 ; ld h,(ix+o+1)
2270 ; ld b,h           ; Save base of offset table
2280 ; ld c,l
2290 ; ld e,(ix+x)
2300 ; ld d,(ix+x+1)    ; DE = sprite X
```

```
2310 ; ld a,(hl)
2320 ; inc hl           ; For LD HL,(HL)
2330 ; ld h,(hl)
2340 ; ld l,a           ; HL = delta X
2350 ; add hl,de        ; HL = fixed-point absolute X
2380 ; ex de,hl         ; Prepare for visibility check
2390 ; or a
2400 ; ld hl,XRANGE*16-1 ; Rightmost fractional pixel
2405 ; sbc hl,de
2410 ; jr c,hide        ; Off screen
2420 ; call asr4        ; Form integer X coordinate
2430 ;; push de
2440 ;; pop bc          ; Old test code to check X
2450 ;; ret
2460 ; inc bc           ; Point BC at Y offset
2470 ; inc bc
2480 ; ld h,b           ; Shuffle BC to HL and DE to BC
2490 ; ld l,c           ; HL -> Y offset
2492 ; ld a,(hl)
2494 ; inc hl
2496 ; ld h,(hl)
2498 ; ld l,a           ; HL = fixed point Y offset
2500 ; ld b,d
2510 ; ld c,e           ; Save screen X in BC
2520 ; ld e,(ix+y)
2530 ; ld d,(ix+y+1)
2540 ; add hl,de        ; HL = fixed point absolute Y
2550 ; ex de,hl
2560 ; or a
2570 ; ld hl,YRANGE*16-1 ; Lowest fractional pixel
2580 ; sbc hl,de
2590 ; jr c,hide        ; Off screen
2600 ; call ASR4        ; Fixed point to integer
2610 ; ex af,af'        ; Hide screen Y in A'
```

At this point we have the new screen coordinates in BC for X and A for Y. Commented-out test code stashed these values temporarily in U and V so they could be checked with PEEKs from BASIC. The next step is to remap the system sprite table where we can access it (so make sure method code is not in the same 8k area!) by calling EXPOSE to set IY to point at the start of the system table entry for this sprite.

```
2620 ;; ld (ix+v),a     ; Save screen Y for inspection
2630 ;; ld (ix+u),c     ; Same for X (temporarily)
2640 ;; ld (ix+u+1),b   ;   which may be up to 319
2650 ;
2660 ;; Temporarily page in the system sprite table
2670 ; push bc          ; Save sprite X during paging
2680 ; call expose
2690 ;; HL and IY now point at sprite table entry S
2700 ; pop bc
```

The following block of lines updates the system table entry. The revised Y value drops directly into the second byte but the X position may exceed 255, so its most significant bit has to be slotted into the least significant bit of the word after the Y byte. That'd be a little easier if Y came before X in the table, as both parts of X might be rewritten, with the 7 unrelated bits, in one fell swoop, but ROMability and alphabetical logic prevailed; the key requirement is to set the right bits and preserve the others.

The convenience of indexed bitwise operations is clear from the two SET 7 lines which set single bits in the object and the table to mark this sprite as visible. The ZX BASIC ROM uses IY to access system variable flags for just this reason, but there's no need to preserve IY here because versions of NextZXOS that support sprites also leave IY free for general use.

Notice that the flags get set whenever the sprite is visible. It's quicker and simpler to do this every time than it would be to check the current flag and only set it if it's not already. As long as a newly-created sprite object starts with F clear, we can rely on it being current after the first call to UPDATE.

```
2870 ; ex af,af'        ; Recover Y coordinate
2880 ; ld (iy+1),a      ; Update sprite Y in table
2890 ; ld (hl),c        ; (iy+0) Set low bits of sprite X
2900 ; ld a,@11111110 ; Mask for all but bit 0
2910 ; and a,(iy+2)
2920 ; add b            ; B is 0 or 1 as BC = 0..XRANGE-1
2930 ; ld (iy+2),a      ; Complete X preserving other bits
2940 ; set 7,(ix+f)     ; Update local (in)visibility flag
2950 ; set 7,(iy+3)     ; Confirm that sprite is visible
```

Three short subroutines remain. UNPAGE simply restores the previous page at 48k by reading the its number, stored by EXPOSE in T, and setting MMU6 back to the earlier value.

```
2970 ;unpage
2980 ; ld a,(ix+t)      ; Retrieve previous MMU page
2990 ; nextreg MMU6,A ; Restore MMU configuration
3650 ; ret
```

The **hide** routine is optimised to avoid paging unless a sprite that was previously visible has just disappeared. This, and the convenience of revealing the visibility in the object, is why I duplicate the flag in the object as well as the system sprite table.

```
3670 ;; Turn sprite visibility off if it's out of bounds
3680 ;hide
3690 ; bit 7,(ix+f)     ; Did we think it was visible?
3700 ; ret z            ; Not set, nothing to change
3710 ; call expose      ; Map in the system sprite table
3720 ; res 7,(ix+f)     ; Clear visibility cache flag
3730 ; res 7,(iy+3)     ; Clear system visibility flag
3740 ; jr unpage        ; Exit with sprite off and MMU tidy
```

At last it is time to EXPOSE the eponymous routine that pages the system table into memory. There's no perfect place to map it, but CLEAR protects high CPU addresses, NextZXOS paging generally takes place in the first (ROM) or last (49152..65535) 16k BANK, and RAM-hungry mixed-code and BASIC programs are likely to prioritise the top 8k for USR code and data, so – for now - I've chosen to put it at 48k during the microsecond or two it's being read and written. This brings two requirements - the Sprite Director cannot be used if objects or methods directly associated with the system sprite table update are there, as they'll vanish most inconveniently while we're trying to read them. The system stack (SP) also needs to be above or below that area, for the same reason, but methods called from a DRIVER slots are safe as they use a small temporary stack in the ROM area.

On entry IX must point to the sprite object so the sprite number can be read from IX+S and the current MMU6 page stored in T. Z80 gurus are invited to improve this code and eliminate the need for the odd thirteenth byte T by storing the temporary on the stack or (more easily) in alternate registers via EXX. That's partly why the slot driver preserves all the Z80 registers, not just the most commonly-used 8080 subset.

The routine clobbers registers IY, BC, HL and A. The only non-obvious lines are 4180 and 4190, which limit the sprite parameter at IX+S to the range 0..63 before scaling it by 16 to find the relevant system sprite data. I consider this essential to prevent writing outside the system table into undocumented parts of BANK 8 if the value of S is overwritten or incorrect. Bogus sprite numbers 64..255 are interpreted modulo 64. The calling program should leave the upper two bits of S, and the seven lower bits of F, alone until we agree a new common purpose for those bits. On exit both HL and IY point to the system sprite table entry and the value of IX is unchanged.

```
4070 ;expose
4090 ; ld bc,SELECT
4100 ; ld a,MMU6
4110 ; out (c),a
4120 ; inc b
4130 ; in a,(c)          ; Read current MMU6 page
4140 ; ld (ix+t),a
4150 ; ld a,16           ; First page of BANK 8
4160 ; out (c),a         ; Map sprite data at TABLE
4180 ; ld a,63           ; Reduce sprite number MOD 64
4190 ; and a,(ix+s)
4200 ; ld l,a            ; Table occupies 2K
4210 ; ld h,0
4220 ; add hl,hl         ; *2
4230 ; add hl,hl         ; *4
4240 ; add hl,hl         ; *8
4250 ; add hl,hl         ; *16 bytes per sprite
4260 ; add hl,TABLE      ; NEXTRA applies offset to Y field
4270 ; push hl
4280 ; pop iy
4290 ; ret
```

SpriteHax0 has two more eight-sprite demo routines. The next calls TRIG and UPDATE for a single sprite, using a single Sprite Director object at 49000, %P. The DPOKE sets the centre X and Y coordinates, the start angle to 45 degrees (as U=V) and initialises the radius to the square root of $2*(1475/16)^2$ - around 128 - to make full use of the overscan screen height.

The formula is Pythagoras's; adjacent and opposite side lengths are both 90.625. The only tricky bit is the way O is made to point back into the object, to its own U and V values updated by the TRIG routine, so that the subsequent USR call to UPDATE uses X and Y for the centre of the path and U and V to swirl around it. A larger program could DPOKE X and Y just when the screen scrolls or the centre of the sprite path needs to change.

The call to TRIG from line 8280 updates the UV component angles. Add a PRINT before line 8290 to see their values as they change, converted from fixed-point to pixel coordinates by FN fp(). Line 8290 calls UPDATE to refresh the system sprite table and SPRITE MOVE transfers the changes to the hardware in the usual way.

```
8190 REM Combined demo of asm path generation and update
8200 REPEAT : REPEAT UNTIL NOT CODE INKEY$
8210 PRINT AT 10,0;"(7) ASM TRIG and UPDATE until keypress",
8220 %p=49000
8230 u=1450:v=1450
8250 DPOKE %p,150*16,128*16,u,v,(%p+4):; Use UV as offsets
8260 POKE %p+10,0,0: REM sprite 0, visible
8270 REPEAT
8280   RANDOMIZE USR (48000,%p): REM Update U,V
8290   RANDOMIZE USR (48200,%p): REM Move sprite
8400   SPRITE MOVE INT
8410 REPEAT UNTIL CODE INKEY$
8420 REPEAT : REPEAT UNTIL NOT CODE INKEY$
```

Eight sprite objects at addresses from 49000 upwards bring the other seven sprites back to life, starting each oscillator at a random angle in the first quadrant and a radius between 35 and 50 (line 8520) with centre positions arrayed diagonally. Rather than call TRIG and UPDATE sequentially, the double-call routine from line 2190 avoids the overhead of extra USR calls.

```
8490 REM Twirl eight sprites at different angles and radii
8500 PRINT AT 10,0;"(8) 8 sprite twirls ... until keypress",
8510 %n=0: FOR %p=49000 TO 49000+8*13 STEP 13
8520   u= RND (800):v=800-u
8530   DPOKE %p,%p&15<<8+320,%p & 15<<7+620,u,v,(%p+4)
8540   POKE %p+10,%n,0
8550   %n+=1
8560 NEXT %p
8570 REPEAT
8580   FOR %p=49000 TO 49000+8*13 STEP 13
8590     RANDOMIZE USR (48194,%p)
8600   NEXT %p
8610   SPRITE MOVE :; INT
8630 REPEAT UNTIL CODE INKEY$
```

Advanced SPRITEHAX1

This section explains the demo SpriteHax1.bas. First comes the initialisation:

```
100 REM Direct driver Sprite animation, SNG 24 March 2024
110 .install slot.drv
120 RUN AT 3: CLEAR 46999: SPRITE CLEAR : LAYER CLEAR
```

```
130 REM Slot code addresses
140 trig=48000:update=48200:both=48194: ;Calls trig then update
150 borda=48130:addup=48134:addon=48140: ; Parameters are at %R
160 LOAD "FixedPoint" CODE 48000: ;asm source in SpriteHax0.bas
170 POKE trig,213: REM Push DE not BC to find driver parameters
180 POKE update,213: POKE addon,213
```

The slot driver (ID 8) is installed and memory gets reserved from 47000 up. Not much of this is used; a few code routines assembled from source in SpriteHax0.bas are loaded from "FixedPoint" CODE to address 48000, and to run from addresses outside the MM6 (48..56k) area. Objects occupy the gap at 49000. Lines 140 and 150 give names to the code entry points.

Later we'll build a table of parameter objects elsewhere in protected RAM, with its start address in %R so it can move around. All the code in this demo is invoked every frame from driver slots, so that it runs in parallel with BASIC, like the SPRITE CONTINUE statements it builds upon.

Interface 1.5, USR notes

One difference between the USR API introduced in NextBASIC 2.08 and the driver object interface documented below is that driver slot code is entered with the address of parameter data in register DE, whereas the new USR call syntax puts the first parameter in BC, which was the entry address in earlier single-parameter USR calls. There are several ways round this; the simplest but least elegant is the POKEs in line 170 and 180, which replace the PUSH BC lines at the start of relevant methods with PUSH DE, to suit the driver.

Ideally USR would support three parameters without recourse to fiddling with the maths stack, putting a third parameter in half of the space reserved for a string descriptor, so the driver-friendly code could call USR(%c,%c,%p) preserving the established convention of passing the entry address in BC, handily for relocatable code. DRIVER 8 could be changed to pass the data pointer in BC instead of DE instead, but that would break existing code and undermine the USR relocation convenience we've been able to rely on for 42 years. I find it reassuring to be able to test DRIVER slot routines with USR before letting them run 50 times a second under interrupts, so I'm willing to pay the price of POKEs or secondary entry points for that convenience.

```
190 BANK NEW %a: LOAD "gemsprites" BANK %a
200 SPRITE PRINT 1: SPRITE BORDER 1: SPRITE BANK %a
210 FOR %d=0 TO %15: SPRITE %d,%d << 2,100,%d&7 >> 1 <<
   3&31,1,0,0,0: SPRITE CONTINUE %d, STOP , STOP ,%d&7 >> 1
   << 3 TO %d&7 >> 1 << 3+7,64,0,%d*4 : NEXT %d
220 LAYER 1,3: PAPER 0: CLS : PAPER 3: SPRITE RUN
```

That loads a sprite set to bank %A and primes sprites 0..15. These will still have pattern animation handled by SPRITE CONTINUE (due to the 64 on line 210) but defer positional updates to the Sprite Director framework.

The manipulations of the loop counter %D just line up the sprites with distinct graphics.

The demo runs in Timex HiColor LAYER 1,3 so that it can use unique colours on each pixel line without claiming LAYER 2 or clobbering the LAYER 0 attribute memory at 22528 to 23295, which is a handy place for small objects when neither LAYER 0 nor LAYER 1,1 is needed. HiRes LAYER 1,2 isn't suitable because BORDER stripes will be used to illustrate demo frame timing. HiColor text is printed even more slowly than LAYER 0. PRINT is a very expensive command compared with updates using sprites, so consider POKEing tiles or using sprites for score updates.

Two fast Minsky oscillators generate fixed-point sine and cosine values. The object data for these is stored at %P onwards, 47000 and 47013; other objects follow at 13-byte intervals. The demo generates reflected copies of the data from these oscillators in a buffer at %R.

```
230 DRIVER 8,1,borda,3: ; Magenta border for oscillator slots
250 REM Start two oscillators on driver slots 2 and 3
260 %p=47000: ; Put 64 object structures at %p, %p+13 etc
265 u=800:v=u: ; Radius SQR(u+v)=40, initial angle 45 degrees
270 %r=59000: ; Space for reversed coordinates
280 DPOKE %p,120 << 4,88 << 4,u,v,%p+4: ;Oscillator parameters
290 POKE %p+10,0,0: ; Sprite 0, invisible, uses driver slot 2
300 DRIVER 8,2,both,%p
310 u=0:v=800: REM Radius 28.3 (SQR v), angle 90 degrees
320 DPOKE %p+13,240 << 4,88 << 4,u,v,%p+17: ;Second oscillator
330 POKE %p+23,1,0: ; Sprite 1, invisible, using slot 3
340 DRIVER 8,3,both,%p+13
```

The first three interrupt slots are associated with this code. Slot 1 just sets the screen border to magenta - on most displays this will occur invisibly in flyback but if the magenta leaks over to the top of the screen that's a sign this code is taking longer than expected. Slots 2 and 3 call the unimaginatively-named 'both' method to run the oscillator then reposition sprites 0 and 1 to spin round centres at 120, 88 and 240, 88, the fixed-point coordinates DPOKEd to the start of each object.

The O 'offset' is pointed into the object as in SpriteHax0 demo 8 so the changing UV values are used as sprite coordinate offsets. The next 14 sprites re-use those pairs of UV coordinates to move elsewhere but sympathetically:

```
350 REM Link those oscillators to 14 other offset sprites
360 FOR %d=2 TO 7
370   DPOKE %13*d+p,%d*480+160,%d << 2+96*16,0,0,%p+4+(d&1*13)
380   POKE %13*d+p+10,%d,0
390   DRIVER 8,%d+2,update,%13*d+p
400 NEXT %d
410 FOR %d=8 TO 15
420   DPOKE %13*d+p,%d*240,%d << 4-40*16,0,0,%d*2&14+r
430   POKE %13*d+p+10,%d,0
440   DRIVER 8,%d+2,update,%13*d+p
450 NEXT %d
```

Each of sprites 2..15 has its own parameter object which reads its offset from the first pair of the table of objects at %R. The controlling DRIVER slots 4 to 17 only need to call UPDATE as they derive their fresh positions from U and V changes in slots 2 and 3. This shows how related, offset and reflected paths can be economically created and shared within the Sprite Director framework. Incidentally, I realise that the constant multiplications by 16 (or 13) could be optimised away, but deliberately left them so it's easier for readers to identify sprite or object data by the 'stride' between elements.

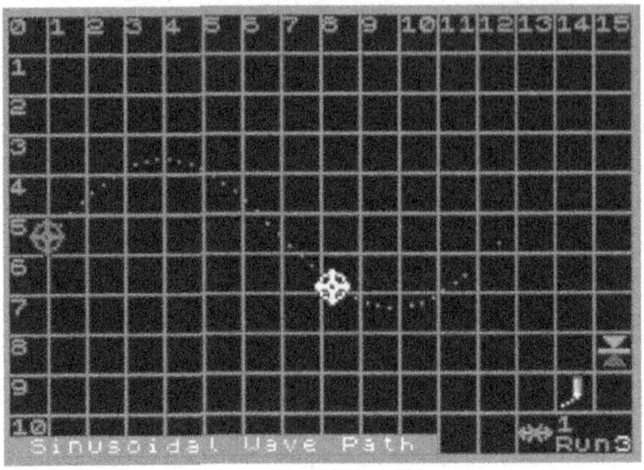

Figure 63, Authoring a sinusoidal sprite path

Since I want to demo all 64 sprites in motion, and we only have 64 driver slots, some of which will be needed for border colouring, and I want to show SPRITE UPDATE working in parallel alongside the Sprite Director methods, the next loop sets eight sprites dropping down the right side of the screen entirely under NextBASIC control, at the eight slowest standard movement rates of 1 to 8 pixels per frame. They're obvious as the 8 TO 23 animation parameter makes them use the lemon and lime (yellow and green) sprite patterns alternately as they drop. They also reveal the limits on speed and smoothness of system sprites which the fixed-point Sprite Director approach ameliorates!

```
470 REM Set eight BASIC sprites dropping at speeds 1 to 8
480 FOR %d=16 TO 23
490   SPRITE %d,%d+4*11,0,1,1,0,0,0
500   SPRITE CONTINUE %d, STOP ,0 TO 255 STEP %d-15 RUN ,
      8 TO 23,0,0,%d
510 NEXT %d
```

That leaves 40 hardware sprites, all animated in much the same way, but with fine speed variations that show how much smoother fixed-point fractional updates look, compared with single-pixel integer ones.

```
520 DRIVER 8,18,borda,5: ; Cyan border for the 40 smooth slots
550 DPOKE %13*64+p,0,0: ;Alternative offset for the 40 sprites
560 FOR %d=24 TO 63
570  SPRITE %d,0,0,1,1,0,0,0
580  SPRITE CONTINUE %d, STOP , STOP ,%d&24 TO %d&24+7,64,0,%d
590  DPOKE %13*d+p,%d-24*128,0,0,%d-22,%13*64+p: ;Or try %p+4
600  POKE %13*d+p+10,%d,0
610  DRIVER 8,%d-1,addup,%13*d+p
620 NEXT %d
730 DRIVER 8,63,borda,3: ; Magenta, slots done; other drivers?
```

DRIVER 8 slots 23 to 62 animate these sprites. The ADDUP method combines increments in each object's U and V fields to the corresponding X and Y with the ADDON routine (explaining why that demo wraps Y in the visible range 0 to 255), then falls into the UPDATE method to tell NextBASIC where to put them. As listed above, these sprites just move down the screen, at different and increasing speeds from left to right, because line 590 sets their O (offset) field to point to 64*13+P, just after the 64 object parameters, and we store 0, 0 there in line 550, so the offset-adding has no visible effect. But we can have fun by tweaking this slightly.

Additional swirly effects

A single fixed-point DPOKE to %13*64+P moves all the 40 sprites using that offset left or right, potentially off-screen or back again. DPOKE the next word to shift them all up or down. As line 590 suggests, replacing '13*6' in that line with 4 will causes all 40 sprites to get their offset from the U and V fields of object 1, the first oscillator, sending the whole lot swirling on and off the screen in addition to the wrapping vertical motion first seen!

The two other DRIVER calls set the border colour to cyan (5) at the start of this processing and magenta (3) at the end. This reveals what proportion of the total frame time is spent in the 80 ADDON and UPDATE methods that move these 40 sprites, and the speed-up when they go off-screen.

Slot 18 turns the border cyan immediately after the first 16 sprites have been processed. Top slot 63 is reserved for the final border change to magenta, showing the interrupt driver has finished and NextZXOS is back in control. If you tweak the main loop to ignore input you'll see the magenta area grow while a key is held down, when the system frame interrupt handler must do extra key-decoding work.

Just before the main loop at line 760 we add a little eye-candy in the form of a title and captions for the border stripes. The PLOT loop puts coloured marks on alternate pixel lines of the HiColor LAYER 1,3 screen, highlighting the effect of timing changes on border stripe positions.

```
640 FOR %d=0 TO 191 STEP 2: PLOT PAPER 0; INK %d&3+4;1,%d:
   PLOT PAPER 0; INK %7-(d&3);254,%d: NEXT %d
650 PRINT AT 6,1; CHR$ 28; CHR$ 1; CHR$ 29; CHR$ 1; BRIGHT 1;
   FLASH 1;"SPRITE DIRECTOR";
660 PRINT AT 9,1; CHR$ 28; CHR$ 0; CHR$ 29; CHR$ 0; PAPER 5;
INK 7;"59 SLOT DRIVER updates in cyan";
670 PRINT AT 11,1; PAPER 3;"Other DRIVER time in magenta";
680 PRINT AT 13,1; INK 5; BRIGHT 1; PAPER 1;"BASIC SPRITE
   MOVE use blue";
690 PRINT AT 15,1; PAPER 2;"PRINT statements show as red";
700 PRINT AT 17,1; PAPER 6;"BASIC update DPOKEs in yellow";
710 PRINT AT 19,1; PAPER 4;"BASIC keyboard poll in green";
720 PRINT AT 21,1; PAPER 0;"Free frame time in black";
760 REPEAT : BORDER %0: PAUSE %1: BORDER %1: SPRITE MOVE
770    ;BORDER %2: PRINT AT 2,4;% DPEEK (p+4);" ";% DPEEK (p+6),
780    ;PRINT AT %4,%4;% DPEEK (p+17);" ";% DPEEK (p+19),
```

```
790    ;PRINT AT %3,%4;% DPEEK (13*24+p+2);
800    BORDER %6
810    DPOKE %r,% 65535- DPEEK (p+4),% 65535- DPEEK (p+6),%65535
   - DPEEK (p+17),%65535- DPEEK (p+19),% 65535- DPEEK (p+6),%
   65535- DPEEK (p+4),%65535- DPEEK (p+19),%65535- DPEEK
   (p+4),%65535- DPEEK (p+17)
820    BORDER %4
830 REPEAT UNTIL %31 & IN 254 <> 31
```

This loop deliberately uses PAUSE 1 and SPRITE MOVE rather than the faster combined SPRITE MOVE INT, so the border stripes reveal how much time is spent in NextBASIC as well as while processing DRIVER slots. The border is black (0) during the spare time in each frame soaked up by PAUSE 1. The driver then runs on the frame interrupt, and only after that BORDER 1 turns the border blue (1) while SPRITE MOVE does its stuff.

Lines 770 to 790 of SpriteHax1.bas print U, V and Y values from various objects. The lines are commented-out because three PRINTs and BORDER 2 to set a red border take more time than everything else, soaking up almost all the slack time in the frame update! Remove one or two of the semicolons to see how costly PRINT is. Compare LAYER 0 (a bit better) or LAYER 2 (worse!). The BORDER statements are quite slow as they do a lot more than just OUT 254. Each one soaks up several scan lines! The BASIC parts set a black border during PAUSE, yellow for the laborious line 810 DPOKEs, green for the key polling loop and red if you uncomment the PRINTs.

Line 830 uses a variant of the CODE INKEY$ check for a keypress which also responds to SHIFT as it reads all eight rows of the keyboard matrix at once. Unfortunately the bit-masking soaks up most of the advantage of avoiding the overhead of evaluating CODE INKEY$ using the default string and floating-point ROM routines.

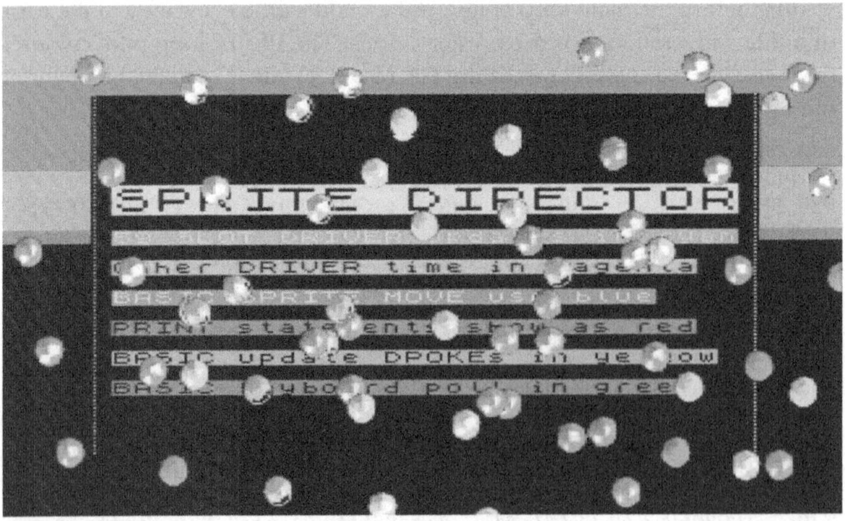

Figure 64 - The Sprite Director in action, 64 sprites whirling and still most of the CPU time free

This leaves only one ugly line to explain. The border is yellow (INK 6) while line 810 does nine consecutive DPOKEs to the communications area at %R, using nine separate DPEEKs and eighteen integer arithmetic operations to scramble and reverse the U and V offsets from the two oscillators. Sprites 8 to 15 use adjacent pairs of these values to swirl in opposite directions from the first eight. It's messy but it works, showing the cost of integer arithmetic and potential for a handful more lines of Z80 code to provide an equivalent or better linkage using one of the remaining five driver slots. The offset at %64+13+P comes into its own in the clean-up routine, which uses it to roll the 40 dropping sprites smoothly off the right hand side of the screen:

```
850 FOR %d=0 TO 363 STEP 3
860  DPOKE %13*64+p,%d << 4,%d << 3: SPRITE MOVE INT
870 NEXT %d
880 .uninstall slot.drv
890 BANK %a CLEAR
895 BORDER 0
```

The last three lines uninstall the driver, which is vital before you risk overwriting the objects it's accessing thousands of times a second (you could alternatively turn them all off, with the driver still in memory, with the standard INIT command DRIVER 8,128) and release the memory where the sprites were loaded - avoiding the need to reset later when you eventually run out of banks during repeated testing. BORDER 0 cancels whatever colour the driver OUTs might have imposed, synchronising BASIC and the hardware.

Fixed-point conversions

Two DEF FN lines at the end of the file slowly but usefully convert values between 12:4 fixed-point and 40-bit floating point formats. Replace the 4 with 6 for 10:6 fixed-point format, or similarly for other representations. The INT should not be necessary but is needed till Garry fixes GitLab issue #115, because currently 0 << 1 <> 0! FN fp() could be faster but it works as-is and should only be needed for diagnostics and setup outside your main loop.

```
920 REM Convert fixed-point 0..65535 to floating-point +/-2048
930 DEF FN fp(t)=((t < 32768)*t-((t > 32767)*(65536-t))) >> 4
950 REM Convert floating-point +/-2048 to fixed-point 0..65535
960 DEF FN f124(t)=(65536 AND t < 0)+ INT (t << 4)
```

After getting this far you may feel there's one missing fixed-point routine, and you'd be right. Both Matteo Vitturi and I have written fixed-point multiplication routines for co-ordinate scaling but neither of us has had time to roll the code into a demo yet. If you come up with methods complementary to the ones in this chapter, please share them for possible inclusion in a future update of the SpriteHax download package.

Chapter 13, Memory

The original ZX Spectrum had just 16k of RAM, with about 9k available to BASIC. Another 16k, not all used, was reserved for ROM, leaving room for 32k of add-on memory before the Z80s 64k address space was full up. The Zilog hardware also allowed up to 64k of 8-bit I/O (Input/Output) ports to be addressed, but design economies mean that few of those port numbers are unique. There are still enough of those, thankfully, to allow extra RAM beyond the 64k limit to be selected by writing to a port before reading or writing data. The port provides a few extra address bits, greatly increasing the address space at the expense of making each access a two to four-step process, depending on whether you care to restore the previous set-up afterwards.

From a 21st century perspective, the 64k corset looks like a mistake. But in the 1970s when the Z80 was designed, 64k was a vast amount of memory few microcomputer users could afford. The picture alongside shows a memory card made for a Z80-based RML 380Z computer, common in UK schools before Acorn and BBC piled in. The 50p coin shows it's almost as large as a Spectrum circuit board from a couple of years later. Yet the card was a similar price to Sinclair's micro, slower, with a capacity of just 2K bytes.

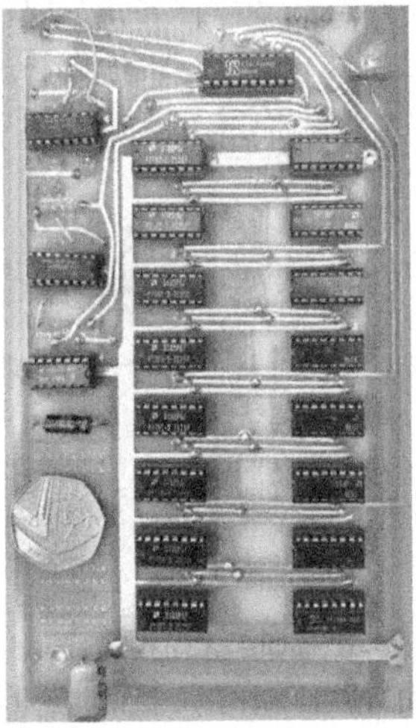

Figure 65 - 2K of RAM for a pre-Spectrum Z80 system

Every pin on a chip carries a production cost whether it's needed or not. The smallest packages are manufactured in largest volumes, making them cheaper through economies of scale. Intel crippled the performance of the 8008 CPU by shoe-horning it into a cheap 18-pin package, and limited it to 16k bytes, far more than most customers could afford in the days when a kilobyte of affordable memory came in eight chips of similar dimensions.

Sinclair paid extra for the 1984 QL's 68008 because it required a 48 pin package, thereby addressing more RAM than the 40 pin Z80 but still limited to an 8-bit data interface by the remaining pins. The 64-pin package of the 68000 CPU in later STs and Amigas was a substantial part of its cost – in fact the much cheaper 68008 chosen by Sinclair, made in Motorola's Scottish plant at East Kilbride, was a slightly *more* complex chip.

Next's 2 MB RAM

Memory on the Spectrum Next is managed in 8k pages, so that at any time the Z80 CPU can access eight separate pages from the megabyte or two on Next's circuit board. To select any one byte within two megabytes of RAM we need a 21-bit address, since 2^21 (2*2*2*2*2*2*2 * 2*2*2*2*2*2*2 *

2*2*2*2*2*2*2) is 2097152, the total byte count of a full-spec Next's 2MB memory. The early KS1 boards came with half this soldered down, in the form of two chips, and sockets for another pair of chips to make up the total, filling the second megabyte of address space from 1048576 to 2097151.

256k of this memory is reserved for ROM, DivMMC and Multiface pages. The rest is available to NextBASIC and for screen layers.

MMU registers

The memory-management implementation is simple – the top three bits of the address on the Z80 processor bus is used to select one of eight 8-bit registers. Each of those holds an 8-bit value. The 21-bit memory address in your 2 MB RAM is formed by combining up eight bits from those registers with the lower 13 bits of the Z80 address. The result is that each 8k of Z80 address space can be mapped to a different 8k from within the 2 MB potentially accessible. In fact you could even put the same 8k of main memory eight times in Z80 space, by setting all eight registers to the same value. This isn't much more useful than Z80 instructions like LD H,H or LD E,E – it's just a consequence of the generality of the design.

The 8k areas are called 'pages', by analogy with printed books. Since Zilog call two consecutive bytes a 'word' (and coined some two-letter words, in the form of assembly-language mnemonics like LD, JR and EX to justify that) you might argue that each page can hold 4096 words, BT WE WL NT AL SE YR PT. In these pages I've resorted to longer words whenever necessary!

The eight registers are known as MMU0 to MMU7, and someone brilliant assigned them to slots 80 to 87 of the NextReg set, so that humans and BASIC programmers comfortable with decimal can work out the slot for a particular 8k page by adding 80 to the slot number, hexadecimal enthusiasts can add $50, addressing NextReg $50 to $57, and Intel diehards can stick with Octal and confuse the rest of us by referring to registers 0120 to 0127. The acronym MMU stands for Memory Management Unit. The following procedure displays the page number associated with each 8k slot:

```
590 DEFPROC SHOWPAGES()
600 PRINT "Memory Management configuration"
610 FOR s=0 TO 7
620   t= REG (80+s)
630   PRINT "Slot ";s;" @";( STR$ (s*8192)+"     ")(1 TO 5);
635   PRINT " holds 8k page ";
640   IF t=255 THEN PRINT "ROM": ELSE PRINT t
650 NEXT s
680 ENDPROC
```

In fact it's possible to access 80k, as long as you're willing to accept that reads and writes from the bottom 16k of the Z80 address space are mapped to different pages. I shall demonstrate how to do this, from NextBASIC, in this chapter.

Banks versus Pages

It's important to realise that PAGE and BANK refer to two different but overlapping concepts. Zilog's 64k may equally well be considered as eight pages of 8k, or four BANKs of 16k, where the 16k banks start at address 0 (normally ROM), 16384 (LAYER 0 pixels), 32768 (the upper limit for a 16k Spectrum) or 49152, the address where extra memory on a 128k Spectrum is swapped in and out. 128 BASIC mostly used the extra 80k for RAM disc storage, but NextBASIC also allows programmers to store parts of their program or 16k blocks of data, accessed via the BANK keyword.

While a BANK statement is being interpreted NextBASIC converts the bank number, in the range 0..111 on a 2 MB machine, into a pair of consecutive page numbers, by doubling the BANK number and adding one to turn to the second 8k page. It restores the old values of MMU6 and MMU7 afterwards, so your program still gets the correct results if it PEEKs addresses above 48k even though the default, BANK 0, isn't always there.

NextBASIC uses 16k BANKs rather than 8k pages because it was designed before the MMU system. The original Sinclair code for access to the RAM disc and ROM added for the Spectrum 128 presumed 16k chunks and only allowed free mapping of RAM into the space above 48k.

Some people are picky about which scheme they use – when I asked Odin author Matt Davies to consider showing 16k bank numbers in his assembler he replied "*16k banks are entirely a BASIC invention. The hardware uses 8k banks and so Odin will remain using those.*" But Garry Lancaster is equally if not even more committed to 16k banks, and has the non-BASIC precedent of Investronica and Amstrad Spectrum hardware usage since 1985 to bolster his case. The rest of us just have to accept this is another holy war, be aware of it, try not to get confused, and make adjustments when necessary.

The reason I raised this as an Odin issue was because there was no hint in the assembler documentation of how to find code after assembly, other than looking up the hexadecimal object code page numbers listed in reverse order in Odin's INFO command, which varied between runs of the dot command, then "*converting hex 8k offsets to decimal 16k ones and adding 8192 for luck (or not)*" as I wrote in my plea for help on GitLab. Matt later relented, revealing a workaround that had remained undocumented in four years: "*You can save generated code from within Odin using the SAVE command. It takes the format SAVE "name", <offset>, <length> and you can add a + before the filename to append. E.g.: SAVE +"filename", ...*" – phew!

Flat addressing, pros and cons

In an ideal world we'd be able to PEEK or POKE any byte just by specifying its address, so PEEK(262143) would read the last byte of the first 256k. Sinclair's later SuperBASIC works that way, because the QL's Motorola 680xx architecture allows linear or 'flat' addressing of any byte from 0 to the top of RAM, potentially byte 4294967295 on a fully-expanded system. The QL's PEEK and POKE commands extend all the way, matching the 32-bit range of numeric values, which applies equally well to ZX BASIC.

The BASIC interpreter of the MGT SAM Coupe allows flat addressing, even though its Z80B has the same 64k addressing limitation as the original Spectrum's Z80A and Next's Z80n. Whereas NextBASIC only allows up to about 40k of array and variable values, using the same upper part of the 64k address space as a 48k Spectrum, the only limit on the length of SAM BASIC programs and arrays is the memory inside the computer.

NextBASIC does not work that way, because an understandable priority in its design was to retain compatibility with ZX BASIC programs from 1982 and ever since. Their System Variables and file header records use 16-bit counts and address values, limiting them to a 64k range, of which the first 16k is allocated to ROM and the next 7k or so dedicated to the display, ZX printer buffer and the system variables themselves.

Program lines and variables occupy the following 40k, with provision for User Defined Graphics (UDGs) and the processor stack, a temporary store that expands downwards from RAMTOP through memory as register values are backed up for re-use and subroutines are called. The CLEAR command empties this stack and positions RAMTOP so graphics, code or other data can be tucked away higher up. The top address is 65535, the 64k limit imposed by Zilog.

SAM BASIC comes with a one-way converter that reads ZX BASIC and replaces the 16-bit pointers with 24-bit ones, allowing larger programs. The snag is that those ZX utilities that directly access the interpreter data-structures, stored program and system variables, won't work if they rely on the 16-bit pointers to variable values and program lines.

Many of the system variables most often tweaked by Sinclair programmers, like the font addresses CHARS and UDG, LASTK and the upper-case flag, are in the same places and work the same way on SAM, but this compatibility cannot be maintained for pointers to the program memory, because there's just not enough space there to address SAM's extra RAM, and old programs wouldn't know how to find or interpret that if it was added.

Fiendish code in SAM's 32k ROM shuffles memory around as a program runs so that all the memory appears accessible to BASIC even though the CPU can only see 64k of it at a time, in two 32k RAM areas with two optional 16k ROM overlays. Beyond observing that SAM BASIC is available as well-documented open source Z80 code, and could just as well run on SpecNext with tweaks to the memory-paging routines, I'm not going to discuss it more in this volume since NextBASIC takes a very different approach, prioritising compatibility.

AnyPage – a routine to read, update or copy any RAM page

NextBASIC BANK PEEK and POKE statements block access to interesting – albeit volatile – data-structures in BANKs 7 and 8. SAVE and LOAD commands use the default paging, rather than whatever you may have set up with the MMU registers, even above RAMTOP. This is tricky if you're curious about how the system works so I've written a little NextBASIC program, with 55 bytes of machine-code support, to allow access to any page of RAM independently of NextBASIC. This routine is used later in a version of the NextBASIC Text Editor for Layer 3, which renders text with the custom driver introduced in Chapter 15, Tiles and Layers. It's needed there to prevent tile data in BANK 7 being clobbered by the file browser. There's a simpler application, for directly updating the fonts hidden in BANK 8, after the code explanation.

> *Warning, these commands could damage your sanity*
> *Bob Brenchley, Format #1*

You need to reserve a few bytes at the top of RAM with CLEAR, and POKE the source and target memory details into the machine code up there, before invoking it with a USR call. The addresses where those details are stored are shown in Figure 66, the output from PROC REPORT() listed below. This PROC, and its BYTE() and WORD() output helpers, depends upon three global integer variables set when the corresponding machine-code is assembled. The address of the start of the code is in %S, and the length of the code is in %L. These values are used when saving the assembled routine.

Midway through the code, starting just after the label POKES, there's space at %P for five bytes and three 16-bit words to be stored. These determine how much memory is copied to and from particular addresses. The bytes hold MMU register and page numbers, and an indication of the direction of transfer. The words indicate the source and target addresses, in Z80 memory space, and the number of bytes to copy.

```
1990 DEFPROC REPORT()
2000 PRINT %L;" bytes of paging code at ";%S
2010 PRINT '"POKE configuration after ";%p''
2020 PROC BYTE(2, "Source MMU register")
2030 PROC BYTE(3, "Source Page number ")
2040 PROC BYTE(6, "Target MMU register")
2050 PROC BYTE(7, "Target Page number ")
2060 PROC WORD(9, "Number of bytes    ")
2070 PROC WORD(12,"Source address    ")
2080 PROC WORD(15,"Target address    ")
2090 PROC BYTE(17,"235 swaps direction")
2100 source=% DPEEK (p+12):target=% DPEEK (p+15): PRINT
2110 %c=% DPEEK (p+9): PROC CHECK("source",% PEEK (p+2))
2120 PROC CHECK("target",% PEEK (p+6))
2130 PRINT '"Current configuration copies ",% DPEEK (p+9);
2140 PRINT " bytes in page ";% PEEK (p+3);" from"
2150 IF % PEEK (p+17) THEN source,target=target,source
```

```
2160 PRINT source;" to ";target;
2180 PRINT " in page ";% PEEK (p+7)''
2200 ENDPROC
```

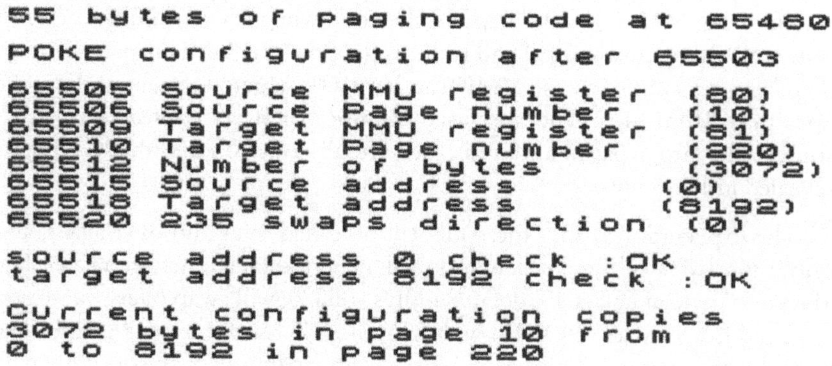

Figure 66, Configuration output from PROC REPORT(), part of AnyPage.bas

Two helper procedures use %P to label bytes and words in the report:

```
3000 DEFPROC BYTE(%b,t$)
3010 PRINT %p+b;" ";t$;" (";% PEEK (p+b);")"
3020 ENDPROC

3040 DEFPROC WORD(%b,t$)
3050 PRINT %p+b;" ";t$;" (";% DPEEK (p+b);")"
3060 ENDPROC
```

The following CHECK() procedure ensures that the chosen MMU page is compatible with the corresponding source or target address. It takes two parameters: the name of the area, 'source' or 'target', and the MMU register address, 80..87. The name, rather than the address, is passed so that messages can refer to it descriptively; the VAL function gets the corresponding address for checking. If it's in the correct page, OK is printed; otherwise an error message indicates what needs fixing.

```
3080 DEFPROC CHECK(a$,%r):; Uses global %c byte count
3085 PRINT a$;" address "; VAL a$;" check :";
3090 IF %r>87 THEN PRINT '%r;" is <80, not an MMU REG": ENDPROC
3100 IF %r<80 THEN PRINT '%r;" is >87, not an MMU REG": ENDPROC
3110 LOCAL %t=%r&7*8192,%a= VAL a$
3115 IF %a+c>(56<<10) THEN PRINT '"Clobbers code in top 8k":
   ENDPROC
3120 IF %a<t THEN PRINT '"Address too low, min ";%t: ENDPROC
3130 IF %a>(t+8191) THEN PRINT '"Address too high, max";
   %t+8191: ENDPROC
3140 IF %(a+c)>(t+8192) THEN PRINT '"Count ";%c;" off page":
   ENDPROC
3160 PRINT "OK"
3200 ENDPROC
```

AnyPage copies up to 8k from any Next RAM page to any other. The copy cannot cross an 8k page boundary, but still works if both source and target pages match. The addresses it temporarily remaps should be below 56k, as using MMU7 would map out the code while it was running, but as it runs with interrupts disabled and restores the previous MMU register settings there's no reason not to use MMU0 and MMU1, which normally address the Spectrum ROM area. The area used, number of bytes copied, 1 to 8192, source and target pages and addresses are all configured with POKEs, as revealed in Figure 66.

The expectation is that the code will be called over and over again, and only a few bytes of the configuration will need to change between calls. The 'direction' byte at offset 17, default address 65520, will swap over source and target addresses when POKEd with 235, the EX DE,HL opcode, and leave them alone if zeroed. The Layer 3 Text Editor patch uses this to copy data back and forth without needing to read and rewrite all four address bytes.

```
 100 CLEAR 65399
1000 .asm
1010 ;; Copy up to one page anywhere. Put this code above 56k
1020 ;
1022 ;SOURCE equ 80  ; MMU0
1023 ;TARGET equ 81  ; MMU1
1024 ;
1026 ; org 65480
1028 ;START
1030 ; ld a,TARGET
1040 ; ld bc,9275     ; REG select port
1050 ; out (c),a
1060 ; inc b
1070 ; in a,(c)
1075 ; db $dd         ; Use IX not HL
1080 ; ld h,a         ; IXH is old MMU TARGET
1090 ; ld a,SOURCE
1100 ; dec b
1110 ; out (c),a
1120 ; inc b
1130 ; in a,(c)
1135 ; db $dd
1140 ; ld l,a         ; IXL is old MMU SOURCE
1150 ;
1160 ; di            ; Protect stack
1165 ;POKES
1170 ; nextreg SOURCE,14
1180 ; nextreg TARGET,0
1190 ; ld bc,96*32    ; ASCII set of 4-bit tiles
1200 ; ld hl,0        ; MMU0 start
1210 ; ld de,8192     ; MMU1 start
1220 ; nop           ; POKE 235 EX DE,HL to swap direction
1230 ; ldir
1240 ; db $dd
```

```
1250 ; ld a,l
1260 ; nextreg SOURCE,a
1270 ; db $dd
1280 ; ld a,h
1290 ; nextreg TARGET,a
1300 ; ei
1310 ; ret
1320 ;END
1330 ; LET %P=POKES
1340 ; LET %L=END-START
1350 ; LET %S=START
```

Figure 67 – In 1981 Computing Today listed 88 Z80 instructions never documented by Zilog

AnyPage expects you to know what you're doing. If you POKE the wrong values, it may crash your Next. If you POKE the wrong *places* that's even more likely! The source is wrapped up with demo and check routines in **AnyPage.bas**. The demo copies 3k from a newly-allocated bank to the first half of the LAYER 0 screen. Figure 66 shows sample output. PROC CHECK() in the same file scans this in case of attempts to use addresses beyond the range of the MMU pages, or page out the code while it's running.

The source was assembled using **.asm** 0.7a which does not support direct access to eight-bit halves of IX and IY, so **db $dd** has been inserted to divert standard instructions from HL to IX; as all Z80 chips support these unofficial instructions, many assemblers recognise IXL, IXY, IYX and IYL where H or L would otherwise be used by an 8080 and issue code to update half of an index register. If not, the example shows how to uses these instructions, which are slow – half the speed of register transfers to L or H – but handy when you don't want to use the stack, as in this case, and EXX would require more intermediate steps. I learned of these instructions from an article by D. S. Peckett for Computing Today. The **$fd** prefix targets IY. Chris has since added IXL, IXH, IYL and IYH support to his assembler.

Hacking System fonts

NextZXOS's new layers support custom character sizes, from 3 to 7 pixels wide. Unlike the standard font that is eight pixels wide, the narrow character patterns are not held in main memory, but hidden where they cannot be directly addressed. Well, now they can be, with AnyPage, and some caution.

Chris Taylor did some unofficial digging in BANK 8, warning his Facebook followers, *"I know I am going to get shot for this, but I always find problems like this intriguing and I am just too curious not to look..."* and discovered the three-pixel wide font, also used for a width of four with a blank column alongside, stored at offset 3328. Immediately after it, half-way through the first page of BANK 8 at offset 4096, the second custom font appears – this is the one used for character widths of five or six pixels. In that case, the least-significant three bits of each byte are empty.

NextZXOS uses the barrel-shifting instructions to slide those bytes to the required character boundaries for most LAYER 1 screens, and expands the bits into bytes for LAYER 2 and LoRes text output. Now we know where they are, we can directly load our own fonts into BANK 8, for immediate use, without affecting the wider default font. Of course, as Chris made haste to explain, *'this was on 2.08 – this could be in a totally different location between OS versions'* – so I've checked 2.09 RC 11 and the same hack works there. Cool, but risky, of course.

Figure 68 - Narrow fonts revealed, via BANK 8 PEEKs and LAYER 1,1 PRINT commands

The official way to do this, which should always be used in programs intended for public distribution, is to load the replacement font into 768 bytes of RAM 256 bytes past the value in CHARS, with the character patterns shifted left into the most significant three or five bits of each byte, leaving the lower bits zero. Then tell the system to copy them into its cache for character-width N with the obscure command PRINT CHR$ 31;CHR$ N;

After this, you'll need to restore the default font, or your preferred full-width character set, at CHARS, which will work as documented by Sinclair for LAYER 0, then PRINT CHR$ 2; to tell NextZXOS about the change.

Here's the little program I used to generate Figure 68. It uses two procedures, Show() and Tell(), to put the small fonts on the attribute screen. I've used LAYER 1,1 rather than LAYER 0 because the new layers support font selection control codes, while LAYER 0 requires the extra step of setting up a 'user window' to bypass the Sinclair-standard default behaviour.

The CLEAR allows us to map any BANK into the top 16k; in this case we only need the first 8k page of BANK 8, but the second 8k would be revealed if REG 87,17 was added to line 120. The constant K makes the addresses a bit more readable. K*18 is the middle third of pixel data for the attribute screen, and (48+4)*K points at the second half of the page controlled by REG 86.

```
100 REM FontWanger 0.0
110 LAYER 1,1: CLEAR 49151
120 K=1024: REG 86,16: REM Map BANK 8 start to 48k
130 PROC Show((48+4)*K)
140 PROC Show(K*48+3328,K*18)
150 PRINT AT 3,0; CHR$ 30; CHR$ 6;: PROC Tell()
160 PRINT AT 11,0; CHR$ 30; CHR$ 4;: PROC Tell()
170 PRINT : STOP
```

Legacy Pixel Addressing

PROC Show() copies bytes from the parameter address, diverted to BANK 8, to the screen. Notice how, in both LAYER 0 and LAYER 1,1, successive lines are 256 bytes later in memory, rather than at 32-byte intervals as you'd expect from their length. This scrambling enabled the display output circuit to pick up eight bytes of pixel data, and one corresponding attribute byte, in a single very fast 'page mode' access to RAM. Otherwise a 16k Spectrum would run much more slowly, 12K of RAM would be needed for each screen, or precious ULA features would have had to be sacrificed.

```
250 REM Show font from %K on LAYER 0 or 1,1 at %S
260 DEFPROC Show(%k,%s=16384)
270 LOCAL %i,%j
280 FOR %i=@ TO %767 STEP %8
290   FOR %j=%i+k TO %i+k+7
300     POKE %s, % PEEK j
310     %s+=%256
320   NEXT %j
330   %s-=%2047
340 NEXT %i
350 ENDPROC
```

The PIXEL_ADD routine at 8874 in Sinclair's ROM converts vertical and horizontal pixel coordinates in registers B and C into an address in HL and bit number in A. This is one of the routines most-used by budding Spectrum graphics programmers, even in games and applications that avoid most ROM calls for fear of incompatibility, and it's one of the 'entry points' carefully preserved in Next's custom ROMs.

But if you know your program will only run on Next, the entire subroutine call can be replaced by the two-byte Z80n sequence $ED $94 which converts coordinates in DE to an address in HL with a single extended instruction, and $ED $95 to convert the X position into a mask in the accumulator.

These are the PIXELAD and SETAE instructions; you can safely ignore them unless your program uses bit-per-pixel Sinclair or Timex layers, in which case you might also enjoy PIXELDN, $ED $93, which advances HL to the next pixel line of a 6k bitmap, taking account of the interleaving of pixel rows within the three 2k screen sections. LAYER 2 makes this a lot simpler, with one byte per pixel and 256 bytes per line, but requires far more memory.

Since PROC Show() uses a byte for each row of each character, the narrow fonts are spaced out across the eight-pixel wide attribute grid. In between these PEEKed bytes PROC Tell() outputs the narrow fonts as they would normally appear, using PRINT controlled by the CHR$ 30 sequences before the calls on lines 150 and 160:

```
370 DEFPROC TELL()
380 LOCAL %i
390 FOR %i=32 TO 127: PRINT CHR$ (%i);: NEXT %i: PRINT
400 ENDPROC
```

Messing with the ROM

It'd be even more fun to change the system fonts loaded when Next boots, so that they're instantly available. After a few minutes scrolling through the NextBASIC 2.07 **enNextLG.rom** I hit upon the data for both narrow fonts, starting at address offset 9160, but you'll need to do a bit of work to replace either of them as they're tightly packed together.

Only six bytes are reserved for each character – I guess there's an extra step for the few glyphs that need a seventh line, like © – with three-pixel and five-pixel character patterns mashed up into the same byte, squeezing both fonts into 576 bytes of ROM. The first three bits of each byte are for widths 3 and 4, the rest for widths 5 and 6. These are split up and unpacked into BANK 8 later, saving precious ROM space, while keeping the unpacked data in two areas, ready for efficient copying to screen memory, after system initialisation.

There's no reason why Garry should put this data at the same offset in every ROM file, and indeed it starts 42 bytes later, at offset 9202, in the 2.08 RC1 release. It seems that the same offsets apply to both LG and ZX 'ROM' files in a given distro, though that might change in future. A rather more robust approach to finding and patching them is to scan your favourite 64k '.rom' system file for the following sequence of six bytes: $EE, $B1, $F3, $B5, $F3, $B1 which correspond to the packed patterns for the five and (rather cryptic) three-pixel-wide copyright signs. Since this is the last of 96 patterns, each six bytes long, a sensible sanity check is to wind back 570 bytes expecting six zero bytes, the packed pattern for a space character. CHR$ 33 follows, encoding two exclamation marks with $44, $44, $44, $44, $00, $44. The more you check the more sure you can be that you've found the embedded fonts, but the more confused you'll get if Garry changes the packing or moves the data to a different file.

As Chris implies, this is naughty, and fun. I stress that none of us should expect Garry Lancaster to keep any such undocumented secrets consistent between NextZXOS releases. He's still working to extend the system, and we should not do anything to put him off. But Next is a home computer, and digging around the internals can be insightful and entertaining, just as long as we realise the details are likely to change without notice. Even if you carefully scan for the patterns I found by experiment, or any others you discover, they may change if Garry finds a less-illegible way to draw a very small copyright sign. It's his ROM, after all, and his NextZXOS.

Changing the standard font

There's one ROM font which it **is** relatively safe to change by patching the files in machines/next, and that's the standard character set, which appears in the last 768 bytes of original and patched 16k ROMs and right at the end of the 64k Next and +3 files. Always make a backup copy of the original file, just in case. Assuming you have a standard 96-character ¾K file "FONT", this will put it at the end, replacing the system character set. Here's a program to do it:

```
100 REM Patch font in Machines/Next
110 CLEAR 64767
120 R$="EnNextLG.rom":F$="BoldFont"
130 COPY R$ TO R$+".old"
140 CLOSE # 5: OPEN # 5,"U>"+R$
150   L= DIM #5
160   IF (L<16384) OR (L & 16383) THEN STOP
170   GO TO #5,L-768
180   LOAD F$ CODE 64768
190   PRINT #5; PEEK$ (64768,768);
200 CLOSE # 5
```

You'll need to cold-start Next to force it to reload the modified ROM file.

It's possible that some programs will contain hard-coded patterns and go wrong if you do this, but the reverse is equally likely – the screen editor of the original Zeus assembler in the Apps/Dev distro folder won't work if you change the system font by poking CHARS in the documented way, because it uses the ROM data, rather than the system variables, to identify the pixel-patterns of displayed characters. The only way to make Zeus work with a custom font is to patch the ROM, rather than DPOKE CHARS!

Direct Memory Access

The Z80 processor is not the only part of the system that accesses RAM via 8k pages into a 64k address space. Next's FPGA implements a version of a Zilog companion chip, the Z80 DMA controller, which can copy bytes between memory addresses or I/O ports independently of the processor. It's a 1970s design so it is limited to the same 64k address space as the Z80, but since it's implemented inside Next, it can take advantage of the MMU registers to pick and choose 8k pages from the entire Next RAM. A large part of the following discussion deals with programming the DMA controller, since it's barely mentioned in the SpecNext manual but potentially very useful in both BASIC and Z80 programs.

The 8k page scheme is much more flexible and general than the 16k memory bank system born with the Spectrum 128. Although the Spectrum Next hardware still supports 16k banks, for compatibility with old software, we gain nothing by using that approach, so I won't go over it here; it has been exhaustively documented online and in Amstrad and SpecNext manuals.

All we really need to know is that the old scheme still exists and works as a limited and quirky interface on top of the newer MMU page approach. So bank selection via the Spectrum 128 ports also updates the MMU registers, and direct access to the MMU registers takes priority.

Display memory LAYERs

There is another circumstance in which Next works with 16k BANKs rather than 8k pages, and it's associated with LAYER 2 displays. Since LAYER 2 allows each pixel at normal ZX screen resolution to be independently set to one of 256 colours, including transparent, it needs eight times more RAM to keep track of the pixels compared with LAYER 0, where each pixel can take only one of two colours, the INK or PAPER for that attribute cell.

LAYER 0 pixels fit into 6k of the original Spectrum memory map, just after ROM, but LAYER 2 requires 48k to match that resolution while avoiding colour clash and introducing 240 extra colours on a single screen. If we were to map LAYER 2 into the Z80 address space it'd occupy all of the RAM, from 16384 to 65535, leaving no room for anything else!

Next's FPGA allows us to address this 48k pixel-map in three sections, each 16k long, corresponding to the first, second and third slices of the usual 256x192 pixel screen. The system supports two LAYER 2 screen areas, known as the **active layer** (containing pixels being displayed now, often termed the 'front buffer' by computer graphics specialists) and the **shadow layer** or 'back buffer', where you draw things for display when it's complete.

Front and back buffers

This means software can be invisibly drawing to the shadow layer while the active layer is on display, then once all the drawing is complete it can switch them over, usually during the interval between output of one display frame and the following one. This gives smooth animation because the entire scene is complete and static before it is presented to the viewer. It also removes one of the greatest performance bottlenecks of the original Spectrum ULA, caused by the preference to assemble the next full screen image piecemeal in a separate section of memory, to avoid glitches becoming visible as it was drawn and the beam scanned down the display, and then copy everything from that memory to the display once it was ready for viewing.

Classic games like *Manic Miner* and *Atic Atac* typically spent more time copying the finished screen down than they did drawing it. The Spectrum 128 added support for a second hardware screen, selected by setting bit 3 of port 32765, but this was no help for 48k programs, let alone 16k ones which mostly put up with the glitches, as a second screen would have left only 2.5k for everything else.

In the early days of Spectrum emulation this approach was sometimes an advantage, as the LDIR block-move instruction was used to copy down the new image, and that was one of the few that emulators on 16-bit computers had a chance of performing faster than the original machine, with their wider memory and no need to re-interpret the instruction for every byte transferred. This meant that those particular games would run at a playable, if rather stately, pace when emulated on a 16-bit computer clocked at just 7 or 8 MHz.

By the time the Spectrum 128 arrived, Z80 programmers had learned they could marginally out-run LDIR by using a sequence of PUSH and POP instructions to shovel pairs of bytes around, as long as they avoided CALL instructions and disabled interrupts while the hardware stack pointer was being bent to this purpose. We'll soon see that Next can comfortably out-run either approach, but last century this stack-shuffling once more clobbered the instruction-interpreting emulators.

Though the Spectrum 128's second screen removed the need for such bulk copying, the extra overhead of having to translate each Z80 address into a 128k space by looking up bits in the paging registers meant the emulators took another big hit. That meant that – apart from with rare JIT-compiling emulators like Ergon's amazing ZM/HT for the QL – many nostalgic gamers felt the need for a 32-bit computer just to emulate their 8-bit back-catalogue!

Confounding emulators once again, Next has dedicated memory-copying hardware, and supports multiple screens, as well as sprites and layer overlays. That's great for new software, especially games, but needs some explanation so developers can pick the ideal hardware to suit their purpose.

Updating LAYER 2

A couple of registers are provided to tell Next which set of three consecutive BANKs to treat as the active and shadow layers, and these work with 16k BANKs rather than 8k pages, for legacy reasons; there are actually enough bits in the associated registers, REG 18 and 19, for 8k page addressing, but the top bit is reserved, always set to 0, which is slightly limiting but has the pleasant consequence that BASIC BANK numbers 0 to 111 can be directly written to REG 18 (first active layer 2 bank) or REG 19, its shadow.

When NextZXOS starts up both active and shadow screens are mapped to banks 9, 10 and 11, but you can tell the hardware to use any other sets of three consecutive BANKs that suit you. For instance REG 19,12 maps the shadow screen to banks 12, 13 and 14. Draw your next frame by writing pixels to those banks, then use REG 18,12 to make that the front buffer, REG 19,9 to swap the shadow screen to the previous three banks, and so on, swapping bank and forth from frame to frame, avoiding any need to copy memory and giving a perfect glitch-free display, at the cost of 96k RAM.

This is the approach used by Spectrum Next video players, and equally relevant to audio streaming, as we'll soon hear. But it doesn't change the fact that 48k is a lot of memory for an 8-bit processor that can only directly read and write 64k at a time.

Next has another trick up its sleeve, as you may infer from my reference to 'read and write'. Remember that the first 16k of the standard Spectrum memory map is ROM. Read-Only Memory cannot be written; if you try to POKE into it, nothing happens. The bytes in ROM are unchanged. So Next takes another lesson from Bruce Gordon's SAM and allows a different area of memory to be mapped into the first 16k, so that a **read** from that space accesses ROM as usual, but a **write** is diverted to an entirely different *RAM* area. There were a couple of places where the original ZX ROM wrote to ROM, harmlessly and to condense and simplify its code, but these have been patched out long ago.

Next allows either the active or shadow LAYER 2 screen to be mapped underneath the ROM, where it can be written but not read, leaving the upper 48k free for programs and data that may be freely read or written in the usual way. Since you don't have to use LAYER 2, or can put other graphics on top of active parts of it, and you can write invisibly to the shadow screen at any time, this technique can be used to address a total of 80k of memory for any purpose, without any further resort to fiddly MMU or bank-control registers.

Writing through ROM

The following demo procedure writes pixels directly to LAYER 2 with POKEs to low memory addresses. Corresponding output is shown in Figure 69. The missing pixels towards the right of the first examples and on the left of the final one correspond to the transparent palette entry. The difference in the diagonal patterns stems from the STEP values for each POKE loop.

```
2310 DEFPROC ROMLAYER2()
2320 LAYER 2,1
2330 OUT 4667,3:; Enable active layer 2 writes to first 16k
2340 FOR %i=0 TO 4095 STEP 3: POKE %i,%i&255: NEXT %i
2350 PRINT AT 2,1;"ROM POKEs to LAYER 2 top third"
2360 %L= REG 18:;Find layer 2 top front bank
2370 FOR %i=8193 TO 12289 STEP 5:BANK %L POKE %i,%i&255:NEXT %i
2380 PRINT AT 6,5;"LAYER 2 first BANK POKEs"
2390 OUT 4667,67:; Enable active layer 2 writes to second 16k
2400 FOR %i=0 TO 12289 STEP 7: POKE %i,%i&255: NEXT %i
2410 PRINT AT 14,1;"ROM POKEs to LAYER 2 middle 16k"
2420 OUT 4667,131:; Enable active layer 2 writes to third 16k
2430 FOR %i=12289 TO 2 STEP -3: POKE %i,%i&255: NEXT %i
2440 PRINT AT 22,1;"ROM POKEs to LAYER 2 bottom 16k"
2450 PAUSE 0
2670 ENDPROC
```

The first block is written to the top third of the LAYER 2 display, mapped under the ROM by line 2330. The second block is also drawn to the first display BANK but this time using BANK POKE, rather than port 4667 to map that memory under the ROM. It shows that NextBASIC can write to LAYER 2 several different ways. The great advantage of the 'ROM POKE' technique comes when using the Z80n or DMA to copy pixels from main RAM, as there's no need to page any of that out, in order to gain access to the banks assigned to the display.

Line 2390 maps the second, middle 16k section of the active LAYER 2 display under the ROM, with OUT 4667,67. In binary 67 is @01000011; bits 0, 1 and 6 of the port are set. The lower pair of bits enable the LAYER 2 display and mapping for memory writes through ROM, as before when the value 3 was written. Setting bit 6 selects the middle bank of the 48k screen area. Line 2420 sets bit 7 instead, allowing POKEs to the bottom third of the display. If both bits are clear, the first 16k is mapped under ROM.

The fourth option, setting both bits, is incompatible with NextBASIC and usable only with care from machine-code running from the top 16k of Z80 address space, from 49152 to 65535. OUT 4667,195 maps the full LAYER 2 screen to addresses from 0 to 49151. This prevents writes to the NextBASIC system variables and most of the main BASIC program area, which is why it won't work from NextBASIC. It has the great advantage, from a point of view of DMA or Z80 code, that the entire 256x192 pixel layer is all accessible at once. If you try this, make sure system interrupts are disabled, or keyboard input will corrupt the display, and ensure that the Z80 stack is also in the top 16k of RAM. Any graphics data you're copying onto the screen will also need to be in the top 16k, alongside your code.

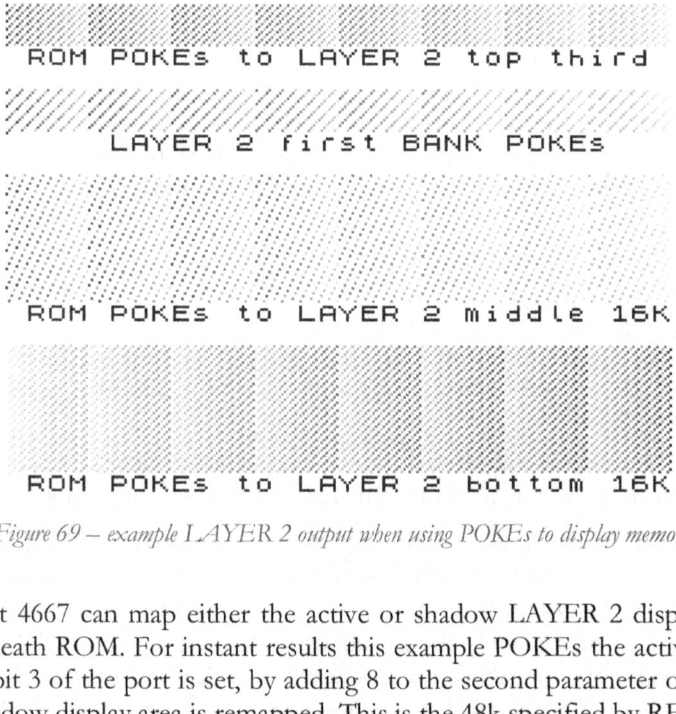

Figure 69 – example LAYER 2 output when using POKEs to display memory

Port 4667 can map either the active or shadow LAYER 2 display area underneath ROM. For instant results this example POKEs the active layer, but if bit 3 of the port is set, by adding 8 to the second parameter of OUT, the shadow display area is remapped. This is the 48k specified by REG 19.

Although the port is intended for display addressing, it can come in handy whenever you need to write to a 16k BANK and don't want to mess with the mapping of the top 48k of Z80 address space, even if LAYER 2 is not on display. The following example uses a combination of POKEs to ROM and specific BANKs, and BANK PEEKs, to show this hack in action:

```
2000 REM 80k config
2010 CLEAR 49151
2020 POKE 49152,17
2030 %v=% REG 19
2040 OUT 4667,9
```

BANK 0 is normally mapped to the top 16k, so the CLEAR protects that area before we POKE 17 into the first byte. Line 2030 finds which bank is mapped to the current shadow RAM page, so we can restore that when we've finished. Then line 2040 maps writes to ROM addresses 0..16363 so that they affect the top part of the invisible shadow LAYER 2 screen.

```
2050 REG 19,0
2060 POKE 0,101
2070 PRINT PEEK 49152;" should be 101"
```

This is a temporary setting; any use of the BASIC editor, or commands like LAYER CLEAR, reset IN 4667 to zero, so you need to repeat the OUT command before ROM POKEs are guaranteed to work. Next we clear REG 19 so BANK 0 is treated as the first shadow display bank. Line 2060 replaces the arbitrary 17 we poked to address 49152 with 101, then displays the new value.

That example works because we know that bank 0 defaults to address 49152. The following version can use whatever memory the system BANK NEW command supplies. This time we poke a magic number into the tenth byte of that bank, and over-write it with a POKE into the ROM area.

```
2080 BANK NEW b
2090 PRINT "Trying bank ";b
2100 REG 19,b
2110 BANK b POKE 9,255
2120 POKE 9,110
2130 PRINT BANK b PEEK 9;" should be 110, from 9 under ROM"
2140 REG 19,%v: REM BANK CLEAR will not free LAYER 2 pages
2150 BANK b CLEAR
```

Line 2130 checks that this has worked as expected. The last two lines tidy up by restoring the previous value of REG 19 and releasing bank **b**.

NextBASIC will ignore you if you pass the number of any bank mapped to LAYER 2 front or back buffers to BANK CLEAR. This reduces the risk of the LAYER 2 display being accidentally corrupted by other BASIC BANK commands. Unfortunately there's no official way in NextBASIC 2.09 or earlier to allocate a group of three consecutive BANKs with BANK NEW, though that'd be useful for applications like multi-frame LAYER 2 animation.

So far, we've been using BASIC POKEs or Z80 LD instructions to write to our memory banks and pages. On a Sinclair Spectrum that's your only option, but Next's FPGA offers a faster alternative, which we'll explore next.

Next's DMA controller

I spent part of my 2021 Xmas holidays exploring the Next's DMA controller. It is a simplified version of Zilog's Z80 DMA chip, the Z8410. DMA stands for 'Direct Memory Access'. Hence the name *DMA Design*, for the company that created the *Lemmings* and *Grand Theft Auto* games. DMACON was the Amiga custom-chip register that controlled its DMA channels. That stuck in the mind of many programmers, including me and former Codemasters CTO Alex MacLean, who geekily used its address ($DFF096) to label his PC on our *Incredibuild* network. For once, we had a CTO who still liked to program!

The following sections show how to access Next's DMA controller from BASIC. They're built upon five demos I posted to Spectrum Next Facebook groups, with improvements and additional explanations. Our controller has only one channel, versus the Amiga's 25, but after the Z80n it's the most convoluted chunk of programmable logic in our Nexts.

The demos show how DMA can copy memory around five times faster than the processor, after a sequence of OUT instructions is used to set up the transfer. This doesn't help if you only want to move a few bytes, but zooms ahead of Z80 code for larger blocks, or repeated transfers that are similar but not identical, when only part of the set-up needs to be redone before dealing with the next block.

The speed is limited by the time it takes RAM to accept an address and store or retrieve a data byte. With nothing else in the way, each byte of our 2MB can potentially be accessed every two ticks of the system clock, whereas the Z80 needs four ticks just to read and decode the simplest single-byte instruction, and 20 or more for some of the more complicated ones. SET 0,(IY) needs three code bytes and 23 ticks just to set a single memory bit, but the DMA controller lacks the finesse for such fiddling – it works strictly with whole bytes, and while the Zilog chip can stop or generate an interrupt when a particular pattern appears, the Next version lacks that capability.

Next's DMA has an added feature called the 'pre-scaler' which lets the processor continue to run while a DMA transfer is underway. At pre-defined intervals the DMA logic grabs the address and data bus from the CPU and performs the next pre-programmed transfer. In between, the Z80 runs as normal. This is great for data streaming, logging and animation because it allows one hard real-time process to be serviced reliably independently of the main program. It can play sampled sound in the background, for example.

You might wonder how DMA can out-run the CPU, since it's using the same memory, peripheral ports, data and address busses. The answer is that a single-minded special-purpose device can be more efficient than a general-purpose processor, which also needs time to decode instructions and make decisions while it's rummaging through RAM.

We've seen that the Z80 has instructions like LDIR to transfer blocks of data between memory addresses, or OTIR and INDR to access hardware ports in a similar way. These are faster than the multi-instruction counting and copying loops used by 8080 programmers, but still hamstrung by depending on the CPU. For every data byte moved those instructions have to re-read both bytes of the corresponding machine-code instruction; along with the extra overhead of counting and addressing subsequent bytes, the processor spends more time housekeeping than it does actually doing what you asked, copying bytes from one place to another.

Some programmers criticise Faggin and Shima for not adding extra silicon to store and re-use the opcodes of looping instructions. This might shave each LDIR repeat cycle-count from 21 to 13, versus DMA at six Ts byte per transfer, or four with fast RAM like Next's. Indeed Motorola did something similar, later. They boosted the C string handling of their 68000 processor range, and similar tiny dual-conditional loops, by adding a six-byte cache to the 68010 remix. But Zilog engineers knew what they were doing – greater complications come when an interrupt occurs during a looping instruction.

LDIR can potentially churn away for more than a million cycles before the count in BC reaches zero and tells it to stop, so just waiting could be disastrous for interrupt latency. Saving and restoring the processor state mid-way through a looping instruction is a lot more complicated than resetting the logic in the usual way before each transfer, and restarting each instruction.

Earlier display and disc controllers had their own simple memory-access logic, working either in conjunction with the main processor, or independently when speed and data volume demanded. Hard disc drives delivered bytes more quickly than Zilog could read, check and store them, so they knew from the start that their Z80 range would need to include a DMA chip, as well as hardware timers and serial ports.

Since all these things can be done, less efficiently, using the CPU, earlier Sinclair machines were cost-reduced to the point that they even used the CPU for video output and cassette filing. More expensive micros from Acorn and Commodore dedicated specialist chips for such tasks. So there was little prospect of finding a Z80 DMA in a Spectrum system, apart from one obscure *Datagear* add-on, and devices like DivMMC and earlier floppy disc controller add-ons rely on the CPU to read and write data. This limits the speed of access to SD cards, but kept pace with data from a double-density disc or Microdrive. That was good enough in the 1980s when customers were skint and hardware was expensive.

Now we Nexters all have a DMA 'chip' of our own, albeit only a single-channel one, it's time to find out what difference that makes. NextBASIC deliberately does not use the DMA hardware, even though it could speed up LOAD, SAVE and the BASIC editor and variable-area manipulations, because Garry decided to leave it available to user programs rather than tie it into the system. From the point of view of NextBASIC programmers, or Z80 fans who still prefer to let the OS take care of boring stuff, this is a good choice; it means we can be sure the DMA is available when we want it, and nobody will have reconfigured it in-between user-accesses, so we can take short cuts when using it over and over again.

Figure 70 – A Zilog DMA chip manufactured in November (week 47) of 1983

DMA registers

Rather like the AY-3-8912 soundchip or Next's dedicated FPGA hardware, the DMA controller contains a bank of registers – byte stores for control information, accessed via a couple of Z80 ports and BASIC or machine-code IN and OUT instructions. There are potentially more registers than free Z80 ports, especially given Sinclair's habit of reserving thousands for each device just to keep the wiring simpler and faster. The Spectrum cassette interface uses a single ULA pin redundantly mapped to 32768 Z80 port addresses! This meant a single input line, A0, could be monitored most economically without including logic to decode a full set of 8 or 16 lines. Peripheral manufacturers like Kempston followed suit, using A5 alone to decode IN 31 – among many others – in fact claiming *half the remaining ports* as collateral.

So, rather as we need to tell the soundchip or FPGA which register we want with one OUT and the data to put there with another, or write repeatedly to the same port to update palette or copper registers, Z80 DMA packs dozens of registers together on a single port, relying on context to determine what ends up where.

SpecNext reserves two ports: OUT 11 for backwards compatibility with a subset of Zilog's Z80 DMA, and OUT 107 for zxnDMA which is simpler. Since life is short and Z8410 manuals are freely available for those intrigued by the differences, I'm going to concentrate on port 107 in this chapter. Being based on the Zilog design, it's quite quirky enough, even without the complications of pattern-matching and the Zilog pipeline which almost guaranteed off-by-one results without careful manipulation of the controls.

As we wade through all these layers of complexity, you might curse Datapoint, Intel, Zilog, Sinclair or Kempston, or maybe Don Lancaster who came up with the CPU-video technique Jim Westwood adapted for the ZX80. But if you are tempted to do so, bear in mind that a more elegant scheme would have cost more, and taken longer to design and bring to market. Haste and penny-pinching is what brought cheap, fairly reliable and somewhat expandable home computers to millions of us. Without that there'd be no Next to enjoy, or curse when it overflows our understanding. Hang in there. It will make sense eventually, and may even seem cool, in an eccentric way.

The zxnDMA logic is described here: www.specnext.com/the-zxndma. Even if you're using the compatibility port, programmers familiar with the Zilog chip should study the zxnDMA documentation to make sure they understand the gaps and differences.

That said, the SpecNext description was written in 2019 and things have improved in the meantime; a 28 MHz clock is now supported and the LAYER 2 slowdown has been eliminated. Newer options allow serial ports, timers, NMI, frame and line interrupts to pre-empt DMA when in Hardware Interrupt mode – see NextRegs 192 to 207 in the updated Spectrum Next manual.

Rather than restate this combined documentary effort by five of the Next team, I'm going to focus on specific examples. This means that when reading the DMA status, for example, my code sometimes collects more information than is strictly needed. That way I know it works, it's simpler to explain, and there's more room for other stuff in this book. It's easier to start from a working example and cut it down, than to write optimised code from scratch.

The following description, like the SpecNext page, skips aspects of Zilog's chip which are not implemented on Next. Even so, it's quite a lot to get your head around.

When particularly puzzled, I've referred to the FPGA source at https://gitlab.com/SpectrumNext/ZX_Spectrum_Next_FPGA/-/blob/master/cores/zxnext/src/device/dma.vhd. The VHDL language used in that file is introduced in Chapter 17, Hardware Programming.

There are seven 'register groups' mapped to the Z80 port that controls DMA. Depending upon the first byte you write to any of those 'registers', up to eight more bytes may be implicated. While you've got the attention of a particular 'register group' that's the only set of values that can be read and written. You need to read or write all the bytes selected in the group before you're allowed to access a different group.

For instance your first output to the WR0 'write register' group may be followed by up to four more bytes, depending on the bit pattern of the first OUT command. Similarly, the WR6 'command register' group implements eleven functions; ten of those are complete in a single byte, but the eleventh is followed by a 'read mask' byte which selects a set of up to seven more bytes which must be read with individual IN commands, depending on the bits set in the mask, before you can get at any other group of registers.

Write Register Group	Group Size	State, functions and controls
WR0 Transfer control	1 to 5 bytes	Transfer from A to B or B to A? 16-bit port A start address 16-bit block length, in bytes
WR1 Port A controls	1 or 2 bytes	Set port A for RAM or I/O access Set transfer cycle count: 2, 3 or 4 Ts Step forward, back or same address
WR2 Port B control and Next prescale feature	1, 2 or 3 bytes	Set port B for RAM or I/O access Set transfer cycle count: 2, 3 or 4 Ts Step forward, back or same address Set Z80n prescalar (fixed timeslots)
WR3 Zilog Z8410-only	1 byte	We can ignore this group on Next
WR4 Port B address & rate	1, 2 or 3 bytes	Port B 16-bit start address Burst or Continuous accessing
WR5 Auto-restart	1 byte	One-shot or loop repeating transfer
WR6 Command issue Read register status	1 to 9 bytes	Enable or Disable DMA transfers Reset, Initialise, Load or Continue Read Internal registers – see below

Table 5 – A summary of zxnDMA register groups and their functions

The above table is a quick summary of the scope of each group. For really deep details refer either to the SpecNext reference page or the VHDL source.

In general I'll explain the complications of register groups in context as we come to use them. WR6 is exceptionally fiddly, so that will get its own discussion, right away.

DMA Commands and Status

Write Register Group six is misnamed since it can *read* seven registers within the DMA hardware. It's also used to issue commands, most importantly the ones to Enable or Disable DMA transfers. Apart from the register read functions, you only need to write one byte to WR6 to issue a command. All the valid commands – and 20 invalid ones – have the two least significant bits and most significant bit set. This being Zilog design at its crankiest, if you enter an invalid command, all bets are off. Anything, but usually nothing, may happen.

In the program snippets later I'll use the @ binary prefix to show each bit written, but in this summary of available commands I'll translate the command codes to decimal as it's a bit harder to get those wrong once you know what you're doing. Either way works, as long as you double-check.

Command	Code
Pause DMA	131
Start DMA	135
Reset Status	139
Set Sequence	167
Read Latches	187
Read Status	191
Reset Rate A	199
Reset Rate B	203
Latch address	207
Resume DMA	211

Table 6 – Key DMA commands

SpecNext documentation uses a mixture of hexadecimal, with either BASIC-friendly dollar or C-style 0x prefixes at the whim of the collator, or unprefixed binary. That soon gets messy since the same page also uses X to represent an unknown or irrelevant bit position, which may hold 0 or 1, so 0x means hexadecimal except in the three places where it refers to a byte with top bit zero and second undefined, and once where 0x11 cites REG 17 rather than either of the 4-bit values 3 or 7!

The SpecNext Wiki sometimes uses % to prefix a binary number, where NextBASIC favours @. Other pages assume that no prefix is necessary as a mixture of 0s and 1s, and occasional Xs, speaks for itself. Perhaps we're lucky they didn't write everything in CAPITALS. Having set myself up for accusations of similar inconsistency, I'll stoop from the general to the specific – what follows, typos and proof-readers permitting, is what works for me.

DMA command summary

The most-used command is 135, which enables DMA with whatever settings have previously been confirmed. The counterpart of this is command 131, which disables any DMA that's currently running. Later you can use command 211 to resume the transfer.

Before starting DMA from scratch, you need to issue command 207 which loads the start addresses for Port A and Port B, from WR0 and WR4 respectively, into the internal hardware counters that will be updated at each subsequent transfer.

The controller has a single-byte 'status' register. Just two of the eight bits are implemented on Next. Bit 5 is set when a transfer has finished, and is labelled **status_endofblock_n** in the VHDL. Bit 0 is labelled **status_at_leastone** there and less cryptically named **DMA transfer has occurred** in Zilog's datasheet. The other status bits don't change; Next hard-wires three bits undocumented in the datasheet to 0 and sets the other three, bits 1, 3 and 4. The Z8410 only clears them if it detects conditions zxnDMA doesn't support.

The logic doesn't rely on these status bits – they're just information for client programmers. But knowing about them helps us understand the four reset commands. Simplest is command 139, named **reinitialise status byte** – this just sets **status_endofblock_n** and clears **status_at_leastone** on Next. Commands 199 and 203 reset the access timing factors, set in WR1 and WR2 for Port A and B respectively, to 1, denoting a midrange cycle transfer count of one access every three cycles. Two is best for current Nexts; the default dates back to when even 14 MHz operation entailed hardware bodges for LAYER 2.

The most general reset command is 195, which combines the functions of the other three while also disabling the prescalar in WR2 and clearing the auto-restart bit in WR5. This combination defines the initial controller state.

Command 179 is dubbed **Force Ready** by Zilog and ignored by Next, which is presumably always ready. Four other commands noted in Zilog's databook, 163, 171, 175 and 177, deal specifically with interrupts, making them irrelevant to Next's subset implementation. Completists should refer to Figure 8.b in Zilog's *Z8410 Z80 DMA Direct Memory Access Controller Product Specification* datasheet for reassurance of their irrelevance. I've read it, so you don't have to.

This leaves two commands for reading, one of which is a subset of the other more complicated one. Command 191, **Read status byte**, checks if DMA is underway. It is simply implemented – after OUT 107,191 an IN 107 reads the status register.

To find out what point the transfer has reached use command 187. This must be followed by writing a 'read mask' containing up to seven set bits. The data returned depends upon which of those bits are set, but requested data bytes always come back in the same order. The least significant bit requests the status byte. The next two ask for the remaining byte count, least-significant byte first, so you can skip that – by clearing bit 1 – if you're only working in 256-blocks. Set bits 3 or 4 to read back the Port A address, and bits 5 and 6 to find out where Port B is pointing. Bit 7 is ignored and should be zero. There seems no way to read the previously set prescalar factor or transfer cycle counts.

This leaves only command 167, 'Initiate Read Sequence', which makes the hardware scan through the previously-delivered 'read mask' and set things up so that subsequent reads start with the data associated with the first set bit in that mask; otherwise it's ignored and you get all seven bytes, in order from status to the high byte of Port B, cyclically from each IN instruction.

Zilog's datasheet is – to be generous – almost impenetrably concise, but that's clearer than the SpecNext wiki page, which assigns two different names to the command, and otherwise doesn't refer to it at all. As I was still a VHDL virgin back then, the NextBASIC DMA5 demo I posted to Facebook in

January 2022 used a mixture of inference and dead reckoning, as explained later, to find and maintain its place in the rota of status bytes. The 2024 Z80n slot-driver version, at the end of this chapter, is based on later analysis of the VHDL and does it properly, I think.

This brings new nuances to the catch-phrases 'if all else fails, read the documentation', and the corollary 'use the source, Luke', beloved of Star Wars fans who enjoy coding but consider documentation beneath them. The latest slogan is 'read the VHDL', or 'read the Verilog'. Should that fail, I dare say we're expected to dig out epoxy-melting acid baths and electron microscopes. I've not needed to go that far. If you're tempted that way, Ken Shirriff's scary but brilliant blog at righto.com may enlighten you, but please finish reading this chapter first!

DMA block-copying

Overview over – this NextBASIC program shows how to use the Direct Memory Access controller to copy or clear memory. It's limited by the RAM bandwidth but whatever the CPU clock and VGA modifier it's at least twice as fast as doing it in Z80 machine-code, because after the DMA is set up there's no need to read instructions as well as data.

```
500 REM ZX NEXT DMA demo 1 – Simon N Goodwin December 2021
510 LAYER 0:dma=107: REM DMA uses port %$6b for everything
520 %s=0:%c=2048:%d=16384
```

This little demo uses DMA to copy the first 2K of ROM to LAYER 0. Line 510 selects the original ZX display format and assigns a symbolic name for the zxnDMA port. The byte-count, source and destination addresses are preset in integer variables %C, %S and %D, with a flurry of fourteen OUT commands before the DMA is initialised, then one more to start the transfer.

Comments from the original posting help you work out the purpose of each line and which register-numbers are encoded in the binary constants, which I derived from tables in the Zilog and SpecNext documentation. Notice how **& 255** and **>> 8** split the 16-bit values into low and high bytes.

```
530 OUT dma,%@01111101:REM WR0 Transfer A -> B, 4 bytes follow
540 OUT dma,%s & 255: OUT dma,%s>>8: REM Source address A
550 OUT dma,%c & 255: OUT dma,%c>>8: REM byte count
560 OUT dma,%@01010100: REM WR1 Port A increments through RAM
570 OUT dma,2: REM Cycle length 2 for 2, 1 for 3, 0 for 4
580 OUT dma,%@01010000: REM WR2 Port B increments through RAM
590 OUT dma,2: REM No prescalar
600 OUT dma,%@10101101: REM WR4, Continuous, 2 bytes follow
610 OUT dma,%d & 255: OUT dma,%d>>8: REM Destination address B
620 OUT dma,%@10000010: REM Set WR5, no loop
630 REM Load hardware, enable DMA after a keypress
640 OUT dma,%@11001111: PAUSE 0: OUT dma,%@10000111
```

As 15 OUT instructions are needed to launch DMA, a POKE loop would be quicker for copying one small block. But after the first block you only need to use OUT to change parameters which are different, so you probably won't need to touch WR2 or WR4 again. Always ignore the Zilog-only WR3. For copying and block-moves, you can treat this example as a black box, as long as you set **dma** first, or use %107 for speed. The Z8410 data sheet is still a useful overview, in conjunction with the terse summary on the SpecNext website.

Remove the PAUSE and append ENDPROC to line 640 to call this code as a procedure. %C bytes (1..65535) are copied from source address %S to destination %D. Addresses are in the 64k Z80 address space so you'll need to CLEAR and set MMU registers to 'directly' access BANK memory.

Like LDIR, DMA can fill or copy memory. This fills a block of %N bytes of memory at %D with the byte value in %B, for any %N between 2 and 65535 inclusive:

```
PROC DMA(%S, %S+1, %N-1)
```

Later examples play sampled audio while allowing the CPU to run between transfers, using Next's custom prescalar. This demo runs flat out, due to the WR2 and WR4 settings, so it blocks the Z80 till it finishes. Even interrupts are blocked, so if you're also relying on those it's wise to break large transfers into sections, setting a lower count and using command 211, Resume DMA, to continue from subsequent addresses once interrupts are serviced. The old count gets re-used till we update the Transfer Control WR0. Avoid counts of zero, which attract 'TO DO' warnings in the VHDL source.

DMA and RAM paging

The next example, DMA3.BAS, is system-friendly for all RAM addresses; it reserved space above 49151 to dodge some NextBASIC 2.06 paging bugs. It shows and copes with the difference between NextBASIC's 16k BANKs and 8k MMU pages, potentially copying up to 2 MB. The principle is to extend the addressing from 0..64k-1 to 0..2048k-1. All ROM and system pages are accessible this way, not just the 16k RAM BANKs usually exposed to BASIC. It uses lines from PROC DMA64k() in my original demo.

The improved PROC DMA() takes the same three parameters but accepts addresses and a count from one to 2 MB-1. It uses the top 16k addressable from BASIC to map in a source page at 48k and destination 8k at 56k, copying up to 8k at a time with PROC DMA64k(). Careful readers could map the output side under the ROM, using the write-only to RAM feature, to free up another 8k for BASIC variables and unbanked program lines, but chances are that a 16k workspace above RAMTOP will be generally useful for Z80 helpers, graphics and audio data. We need at least 8k above CLEAR, to remap any page, to use DMA to read arbitrary addresses from NextBASIC.

```
100 REM ZX NEXT DMA demo 3 - Simon N Goodwin December 2021
110 CLEAR 49151: REM Reserve top 16k for switching 2*8k pages
120 RUN AT 3: LAYER CLEAR : PAPER 0: LAYER 2,1
130 FOR i=0 TO 255: INK i: PLOT i,0: DRAW 255-i,191: NEXT i
140 r=% REG 18:layA2= FN B(r,0): REM Active base, shadow at 19
```

```
150 REM "Layer 2 active screen starts at flat address ";layA2
160 half=256*192/2: REM Half of layer 2 size in bytes & pixels
```

Layer 2 front and back buffers

The first lines set RAMTOP and draw a 256 colour pattern in LAYER 2. Line 140 finds the start of the 48k active LAYER 2 screen, often termed the *front buffer* as it's the immediately visible part of the display. Use REG 19 for the shadow screen (*back buffer*) or both REGs to copy between them. Notice that LAYER 2 screens comprise three contiguous 16k BANKs (not just any six 8k MMU pages) so FN B() converts the REG value into a flat address. The ugly variable names like **layA2** are used because LAYER is a keyword.

```
180 PAUSE 0: PROC DMA(layA2,layA2+half,half): PAUSE 0: STOP
```

After a key-press line 180 copies 24k from the start of LAYER 2 to the second half, in three 8k chunks, as shown in Figure 71:

Figure 71 – The LAYER 2 display after running DMA DEMO 3.BAS

Two little DEF FNs in lines 250 and 260 convert a BANK number 0 to 255, and an offset in the range 0 to 16383, into a flat address anywhere in two megabytes. That's the approach SAM BASIC takes to mapping all its RAM, paging automatically as it it was running on a 24-bit computer. Prioritising backward compatibility, NextBASIC expects us to do all the paging ourselves, with the BANK keyword or MMU registers. The following functions and procedures wrap that up:

```
240 REM Convert Page or Bank & Offset to flat address 0..2MB
250 DEF FN P(b,o)=b*8192+o: REM Page 0..223, offset 0..8191
260 DEF FN B(p,o)=p*16384+o: REM Bank 0..111, offset 0..16383
```

PROC DMA() splits such flat addresses and byte counts into a page number and offset up to 8k so both source and destination can be mapped into the Z80's top 16k. To keep the example simple there are no checks for C, S or D extending beyond physical memory, or C being zero, so SAVE before trying anything you've not checked by hand.

```
290 REM Copy c bytes by DMA from s to d, all values 0..2048k
300 DEFPROC DMA(s,d,c)
310 LOCAL dma,base,sp,dp,cp,K8:K8=8192:base=49152:dma=107
320 sp= INT (s/K8):%s=s-sp*K8: REM split bank and offset
330 dp= INT (d/K8):%d=d-dp*K8 :cp= INT (c/K8):%c=c-cp*K8
350 REM "Source ";s," = offset ";%s;" in 8k page ";sp
360 REM "Destination ";d," = offset ";%d;" in 8k page ";dp
370 REM "Byte count ";c," = ";cp;" 8k banks +";%c;" bytes"
```

Those REMs were originally PRINT statements, written while I was developing the procedure. The following loop breaks the DMA operations into 8k chunks, plus one final call to DMA64k() for any bytes left over.

```
380 FOR %p=1 TO cp: REM Copy complete 8k pages first
390   REG 86,sp: REG 87,dp:sp=sp+1:dp=dp+1
410   PROC DMA64k(base,base+K8,K8)
420 NEXT %p: IF %c=0 THEN ENDPROC
440 REG 86,sp: REG 87,dp: REM Copy last fraction of a page
470 PROC DMA64k(base,base+K8,%c): ENDPROC
```

Because of the way this code is written, shuffling whole pages, the start and destination addresses (but not the count) must be a multiple of 8k, in the range 0 to 2,080,768. 8k page boundaries align nicely with the start of memory allocated to screen layers. Otherwise, copy smaller chunks either side of the page boundaries in the source and destination ranges, or move your data. Finally, here's the wrapper for the previously-listed demo code:

```
510 REM Copy %c bytes from %s to %d, presumes dma=107
520 DEFPROC DMA64k(%s,%d,%c)
…
650 ENDPROC
```

DMA for audio sample replay

If you wondered what happened to DMA2.BAS, here it is. Rather than copy data at top speed from memory to memory, this plays 8-bit sampled audio at a configurable rate to the *SpecDrum* port, using a pair of Next's four analogue to digital converters to send identical mono waveforms to left and right stereo channels, before those are mixed with BEEP, AY and external audio.

The setup sequence is almost identical to that for the ROM-to-RAM and RAM-to-RAM cases. The key difference is that output is to port 223. Alter %D in line 530 to the value 15, 31, 79 etc (listed in hexadecimal on page 264 or 273 of the manuals) you can divert output to just the left or right channel, or a different DAC pair. DAC stands for Digital to Analogue Converter, give or take a few vowels depending on your preferred flavo(u)r of English.

Hz is an abbreviation for Hertz, the SI standard unit formerly known as 'cycles per second'. It indicates the rate at which samples will be presented to the DAC. Low values give a dull sound but reduce the amount of memory needed to store audio of a given duration. In the ZX eras, telephone circuits were sampled at 8 kHz, 8000 seven-bit samples per second. This set the 57,600 bit-per-second limit of analogue modems, and the practical unlikeliness that this full rate would be achieved, as that'd require a perfect match between the two pairs of converters either end of the long copper wire between the modem and the telephone exchange.

The lower the rate, the longer the sample data will play for and the less the CPU's instruction throughput will be affected, but the more muffled it will sound. The higher this value the crisper the audio, but the faster we must feed the DAC with fresh sample bytes from memory.

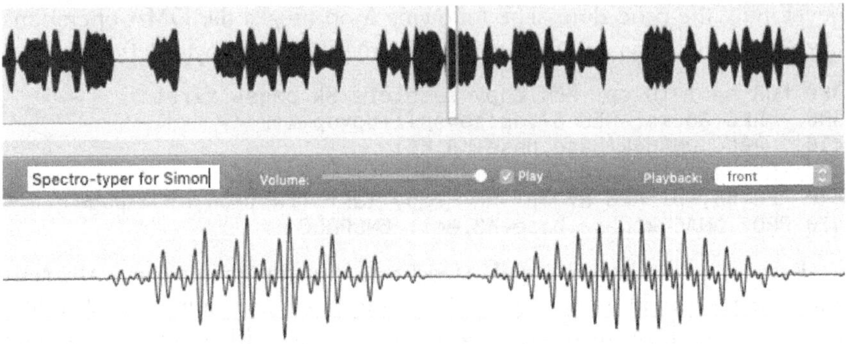

Figure 72 – Zooming in (below) on the section of a sample waveform highlit in the overview (above) – the middle line corresponds to a sample value of 128 in unsigned byte format

For simplicity, the introductory sound sample is a 64-value sine wave POKEd then read from the start of LAYER 0 display memory. Once again %S sets the start address, anywhere in the CPU's 64k, and %C counts the bytes. We've already seen how MMU REGs 80 to 87 can be used to read any part of Next's 2 MB RAM. Later examples use memory paging to 'stream' much longer samples from SD files or RAM BANKs to the DAC.

```
500 REM ZX NEXT DMA demo 2 - Simon N Goodwin December 2021
505 REM replays arbitrary sample data from LAYER 0 VRAM
510 hz=28000:dma=107:REM Hz is sample rate. DMA uses port %$6b
515 LAYER 0: IF hz<3500 OR hz>48000 THEN PRINT "Hertz?": STOP
530 %s=16384:%c=64:%d=223: REM Source, Count, DAC Port
```

Line 535 POKEs in the waveform – try a sawtooth or square wave for different harmonic timbres. The wider the range of values, the louder the sound. For a smooth sound the waveform should return to its start position and gradient at the end, as in the waveforms above, to avoid an audible click – unless that's the sound you want!

```
535 FOR i=0 TO 63: POKE 16384+i,128+ SIN (i/32* PI)*99: NEXT i
540 OUT dma,%@01111101:REM WR0 Transfer A -> B, 4 bytes follow
550 OUT dma,%s & 255: OUT dma,%s >> 8
570 OUT dma,%c & 255: OUT dma,%c >> 8
590 OUT dma,%@01010100: REM WR1, Port A increments through RAM
600 OUT dma,2: REM Cycle length 2 for 2, 1 for 3, 0 for 4
620 OUT dma,%@01101000: REM WR2, Port B doesn't change
```

Lines 540 to 600 match those in the memory-to-memory routines, but the WR2 setting is different because for audio output – and a few other things, like sprite and copper updates – we don't want the Port B address to change even as the Port A index advances through memory. That's ensured by writing @01**101**000 rather than @01**010**000 to WR2. The change also lets us pass an extra parameter byte, specifically designed for Next audio replay.

Sample rate control

Another innovation in this routine is the use of Next's prescalar, a feature tailor-made to allow concurrent audio while your program – in any language – continues to run. This did not feature in Zilog's original Z8410 chip, as that was designed around floppy discs rather than audio transfers.

Bit 5 (weight 32) is set in line 630, indicating that a prescalar (slow-down) value follows in the next write to the DMA port. Only 256 rates are allowed and the exact speed varies (like almost everything else in Next) if video output other than PAL or 50 Hertz VGA is selected – so you may need to retune your guitar (or piano?!) before playing along while viewing an inauthentic PC or HDMI screen.

Tweaks to the 'magic number' 875000 can reduce but not eliminate this discrepancy by factoring in the video timing factors on page 267 for KS1 and page 235 in KS2 manuals, under NextREG 17 – multiply by 28000000 (the correct 50 Hertz value) and divide by the corresponding number documented for alien displays, e.g. 27000000 for HDMI on KS1-vintage cores) to close the gap.

If you are determined to get AY and sampled music in time and in tune, and to support all displays, expect some fiddling. Alternatively, use one device for music and the other for sound effects; few people will notice, unless they have 'golden ears', a sound tech background, carefully read this, or study my game audio book, summarised at http://simon.mooli.org.uk/b2b.

Next's prescalar only has single-byte resolution, so don't expect exactly the rate you ask for, even after adjusting for VGA adaptations. The lowest rate Next supports is a smidge below 4,000 Hertz. Old telephones run at twice that rate, so don't expect HiFi if you decide you need to play 10 seconds of audio without paging or reloading main RAM. The formula on line 640 converts the value in **hz** to the closest rate Next hardware provides, and Table 7 summarises how close that gets it to eight common sample rates.

```
630 OUT dma,34: REM Prescalar byte follows
640 OUT dma,875000/hz: REM Determine sample rate
650 REM Configure WR4 (we ignore WR3 on Next)
660 OUT dma,%@11001101: REM WR4; Burst, 2 bytes follow
670 OUT dma,%d & 255: OUT dma,%d >> 8
700 OUT dma,%@10100010: REM Set WR5 to loop sample
720 REM Load and Enable DMA
730 OUT dma,%@11001111: PAUSE 0: OUT dma,%@10000111
740 PAUSE 100: OUT dma,%@10000011: STOP : REM disable DMA
```

The trick for longer samples, higher fidelity and less reserved RAM is to reload the half of the sample buffer that's not currently being played and let replay wrap round from end to start, so that the new data is picked up next time around. This is 'streaming' and will follow in a fourth example once we've got our heads round this simpler one.

Hertz Requested	Actual frequency	Prescalar	Error
8000	8028	109	+0.34%
12000	11986	73	–0.11%
16000	15909	55	–0.57%
20000	19886	44	–0.57%
22050	21875	40	–0.80%
32000	32407	27	+1.26%
44100	43750	20	–0.79%
48000	48611	18	+1.26%

Table 7 – Prescalar values for common sample rates and error at a 50 Hertz frame rate

Table 7 shows common audio sample rates in the first column, then the actual frequency Next will play them at, assuming a 50 Hertz VGA0 display. The closest-matching prescalar value appears in the third column, with the percentage error at the end. When using VGA1 and above, the pitch is shifted up with the frame rate and system clock frequency, just like AY tones and BEEPs. PROC GETCLOCKRATIO( ), in the next chapter, can help you trim those systems as close as possible to perfect pitch, within the 8-bit limits of the prescalar byte, but be wary of that correction affecting relative timings.

Unlike the memory-copying examples, this routine uses burst rather than continuous access to the processor bus, freeing up the CPU between samples. This aspect is brittle – if you get it wrong you'll hang your Next, so it would be safer if the new hardware had an interlock to prevent bus-hogging if a prescalar is used to limit the DMA rate, otherwise those cycles are wasted, strangling the CPU. Anyhow, you (and I) know, now…

Since we set WR5 to repeat replay from the end back to the start (looping the sample) we need one extra DMA instruction OUT dma,%@10000011 to stop replay or it'll continue endlessly. Lines 730 and 740 load the addresses into the DMA chip then enable it after a key is pressed. The second PAUSE waits a couple of seconds before turning off the loop.

Choosing the sample rate

Even 48 kHz audio DMA leaves more than 99% of memory cycles free at 28 MHz, so the CPU is running at almost full speed in the meantime – and there's nothing to stop you running arbitrary code or animation as the sample plays. RAM is a more significant limitation.

The CD rate of 44100 Hertz is close to the upper practical limit, allowing for less than a second of sample data in DMA-accessible RAM at any time.

48000 is the standard rate for consumer audio this century, but games old and new often use lower rates, 24000 and below, to fit more audio into RAM. The brighter the sound, the higher the rate required. Cheetah's SpecDrum used very carefully recorded 2k and 3k samples, replayed at 20,000 Hz.

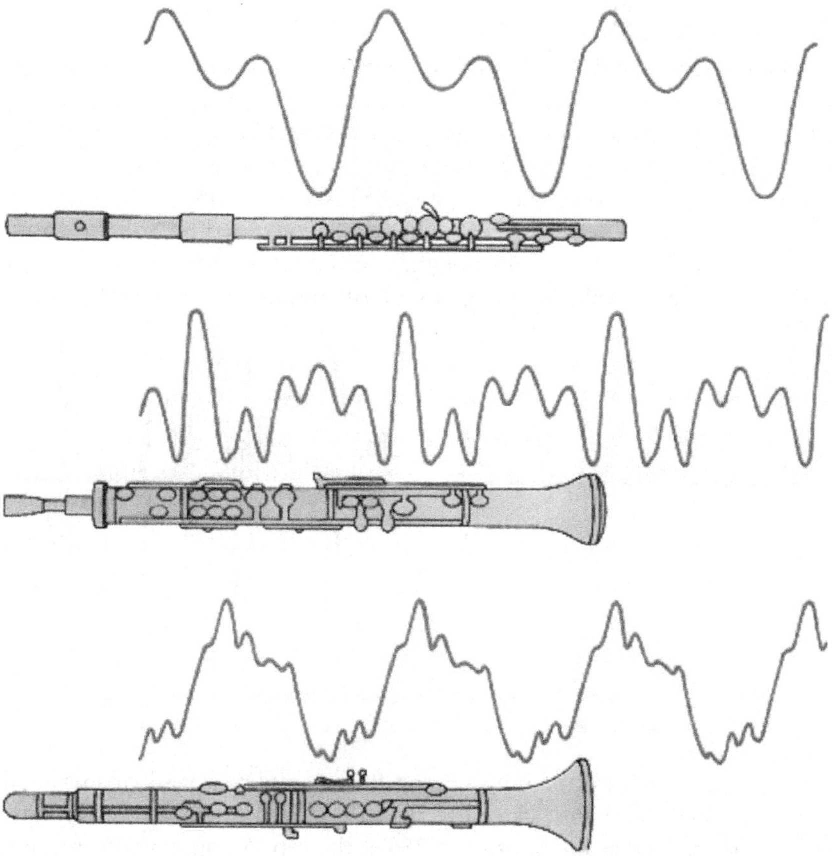

Figure 73 – the sample waveforms created by recording musical instruments (flute, oboe and clarinet shown, from top to bottom) depend on the pitch and the shape of the instrument, especially the mouthpiece. Notice how each of the waveform patterns repeats regularly – this repetition rate determines the pitch, while the wave shape sets the timbre.

NiCam stereo TV was sampled at 32 kHz, and generally considered 'HiFi'.

Amiga games were practically limited to a maximum of just over 28 kHz because of the way audio samples were picked up between TV output lines, but could play at much higher rates if you owned and used a multisync monitor – shades of our VGA6 timing boost! It was normal for much lower rates to be used to save memory, especially on bass-heavy samples.

Since Sony's PS2 arrived at the turn of the century, 48 kHz has been the standard rate for modern 64-bit games, typically using recordings sampled at 96 kHz in 24-bit resolution, to reduce conversion artefacts. But in a 3D game with a moving listener Doppler-shift effects mean that samples rarely play at their original rate, and it remains normal practice to carefully down-sample audio that doesn't need to sparkle, or which will be masked by other sounds playing alongside, to reduce package sizes and loading times. Follow your ears, bearing in mind that as we age our sensitivity to high notes wanes.

The free command SoX (available for most computers from Sinclair QL onwards, but alas not ZX) can adjust sample rates and bit depths to suit Next. Select 8-bit unsigned output and use a decimating filter (sync is slowest but sounds best) so that the sound is not distorted by aliasing of frequencies too high for the reduced sample rate. Amiga 8SVX-format samples are closer to the spec needed by Next and can be losslessly converted by SoX or similar software. Beware: some so-called digital audio workstations, and codecs like WMA, do an acoustically incompetent job of limiting sample-rate distortion.

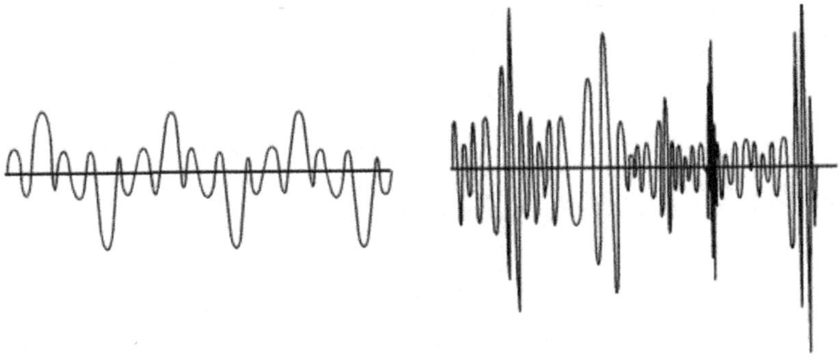

Figure 74 – the waveform of a plucked nylon string, shown on the left, can be convincingly captured at a lower sample rate than the cymbal crash wave on the right

There are two ways of representing 8-bit samples, signed or unsigned. Next uses unsigned bytes, like early IBM PC sound cards, where the wave value varies from 0 at the bottom to 255 at the top. Amiga opted for signed bytes, ranging from -128 to +127. Since the signed approach represents silence as zero, in the middle, it's easier to mix samples together in that format. SoX can convert either way, and it's easy, if slower, to do this with BASIC: add 128 and ignore any byte overflow. A=(B+128)&255 converts unsigned sample A to signed sample B, *or vice versa*, from signed to unsigned!

Don't get hung up on exact rates. Early 44.1 kHz CDs were routinely mastered at 44,096 Hertz to suit the adapted video recorders used to capture them. This was done to fit an exact number of 16-bit samples on each 'video' line. US cinema soundtracks, designed for 24 frame per second replay, were routinely broadcast four per cent fast in Europe – two thirds of a semitone sharp – making playing along with musicals on domestic pianos problematic, but avoiding the 12 Hertz judder when they were chunked up for broadcast on Japanese and North American analog TV.

Streams and banks

I've made a collection of sample files suitable for Next DMA. It was originally compiled for the QL Sampled Sound System which uses the same 8-bit unsigned format. The files are in the QL Sampled Sound section at https://dilwyn.qlforum.co.uk/sound and all have names starting with **qlsss** and ending with **zip**. Compatible audio files often have the **ub** (unsigned byte) extension. Most expect a 20 kHz sample rate.

I have also been given permission to share the 30 second loop I used in the front-end menu system of the mobile versions of Codemasters' *Colin McRae Rally*. This was originally composed for Rally 2 by Jonathan Colling of Octagon Music, and has been auditioned more than a million times on his page at open.spotify.com/artist/7zfvtnlTYE5mLJuF3f12Ql

Here's a player for whatever length of sample, in 8-bit unsigned PCM format, you can fit into main memory – the space potentially used for used for BASIC variables or protected by CLEAR, directly accessible to the Z80. Adjust the CLEAR statement to set the limit (up to about 40k) and the samples will be automatically loaded just above RAMTOP. You can set any reasonable sample rate, and make them loop, while BASIC continues to run, as the decorative line-drawing loop on line 200 shows.

```
100 REM ZX NEXT DMA demo 4 - Simon N Goodwin January 2022
110 REM replays arbitrary 8-bit sample data from above RAMTOP
120 CLEAR 40000
130 Hz=12200:dma=107: REM Hz is sample rate. DMA uses port %$6b
140 RAMTOP=%1+ DPEEK 23730:MAX=65536-RAMTOP: REM Find free RAM
150 f$="Samples/Marvelous.ub"
```

This sample is a low-rate noisy grab from a VHS video tape, but the sneer of Red Dwarf's Rimmer (Chris Barry) is unmistakable. Before we load it we check it'll fit above RAMTOP, then LOAD CODE puts it up there, and the PlayDMA64k() procedure sets the DMA hardware running:

```
170 OPEN # 3,f$: DIM #3 TO length : CLOSE # 3: REM Check size
180 IF length>MAX THEN PRINT f$;" LEN! ";length;">";MAX: STOP
190 LOAD f$ CODE RAMTOP: PROC PlayDMA64k(RAMTOP,length,Hz)
200 FOR i=0 TO 155: PLOT i,0: DRAW 100,i: NEXT i
210 PAUSE 200: PROC StopDMA(): STOP
```

PROC PlayDMA64k() requires two, three or four parameters – at least the start address of the sample and its length in bytes, both integers, then two optional parameters: the sample rate in Hertz, defaulting to the SpecDrum's 20 kHz, and a 'loop flag' which should be set to zero, or omitted, to play the sample only once. Any other value, e.g. 1, makes the sample repeat continuously till DMA is disabled or redirected to some other data.

```
510 REM Play %c sample bytes from %s at Hz Hertz, loop 0/1
520 DEFPROC PlayDMA64k(%s,%c,Hz=20000,loop=0)
```

```
530 IF Hz<3500 OR Hz>48000 THEN PRINT Hz;" Hertz?": STOP
540 OUT dma,%@01111101: REM WR0
550 OUT dma,%s & 255: OUT dma,%s >> 8
570 OUT dma,%c & 255: OUT dma,%c >> 8
590 OUT dma,%@01010100: OUT dma,2: REM WR1
620 OUT dma,%@01101000: REM WR2
630 OUT dma,34: OUT dma,875000/Hz: REM Set sample rate
660 OUT dma,%@11001101: REM WR4
670 OUT dma,223: OUT dma,0: REM Burst to mono SpecDrum port
700 OUT dma,130+(32 AND loop): REM WR5 controls looping
730 OUT dma,%@11001111: OUT dma,%@10000111
740 ENDPROC
```

The only new part of that slightly-condensed re-tread is line 700, which uses the expression 130+(32 AND loop) to set WR5 to 130 or 162 depending on whether or not the **loop** flag is set. DMA would be easier if OUT supported multiple parameters, sent in sequence, as NextBASIC's POKE now does.

OUT 107,131

The counterpart StopDMA() procedure just writes the Disable DMA command to WR6. Like PlayDMA64k() and earlier examples, it expects the DMA port address to be in the variable **dma**, but you can boil the whole thing down to OUT %107,%131 – and remove the need for a DEFPROC – if you prize speed and economy over readability.

```
760 DEFPROC StopDMA()
770 OUT dma,%@10000011
780 ENDPROC
```

Streaming tunes

PlayDMA64k() is great for adding realistic sounds to your software, especially transition jingles and terminal explosions that can be loaded and played by chaining a small program from SD in place of the main game or application.

But the DMA hardware knows nothing about Next's BANKs; it can only read the 64k directly accessible by the Z80. This limits the length of sample that can be played, and the quality – the longer the sample, the lower the sample-rate, and even at half-telephone rate of 4 kHz there's barely room for ten seconds of very rough audio, alongside a little BASIC to play it.

Cheetah squeezed eight percussion samples into one second of 20 kHz samples, leaving the rest of the 48k RAM for the *SpecDrum* rhythm editor and player, stored drum patterns and the display. But this left no room for cymbal crashes, any one recording of which could easily have eaten up all the drum memory, We ended up dubbing them in live from a Korg synth in my 8-bit demo recordings like Norman Hall's Ska anthem *Got to Get Out*, which featured at ZX-92, the Spectrum's 10th birthday party in Cambridge, and is downloadable from http://simon.mooli.org.uk/music/GotToGetOut.mp3

The way to free up most of the memory for other things is to 'stream' longer samples piecemeal from banks or SD, so that only the part about to play – and that which has just played – is in Z80 RAM at any time. Your main program takes a performance hit when the 'buffer' in main memory is being reloaded, but the more often you check if that needs updating the smaller the buffer needs to be, and the less time is spent loading the next morsel.

Ideally the main loop of your game will sustain a 50 Hertz update, like the most responsive classic Spectrum titles. That's quite a challenge in NextBASIC, even at 28 MHz, but possible, especially if you rely on sprites for animation.

Strictly speaking, to stream audio with a guaranteed 50 Hertz (or faster) update, you only need room for 40 milliseconds (ms) of sample data. That's just 800 bytes in two 400-byte buffers, for decent-quality 20 kHz samples. In practice 1k in two 512-byte chunks is more efficient in terms of addressing and SD sector allocation units, and adds 5.6 ms of slack to account for delayed interrupts, such as those caused by BEEP, SD reading, or certain system accesses to banked memory.

While one buffer is playing via DMA you can reload the other from SD, swapping back and forth in a ping-pong fashion, always staying just ahead of the DMA source pointer. But even professional programmers struggle to make games run at a rock-steady 50 or 60 Hertz; unless your game logic is very simple indeed you'll probably want to allocate a larger buffer so you can get more done between reads from the sample file.

By allocating a full 8k page, half of a 16k BANK, you have to check for buffer updates no more than five times per second, which is relatively practical. If your main loop doesn't repeat at least that often, your action game's likely to be unplayably choppy in any case. If all else fails, reduce the sample rate so that you can check less often, or get away with smaller buffers, or a bit of both.

The next example was written as a proof-of-concept for continuous streaming, and posted to the *BASIC on the ZX Spectrum Next* Facebook group on January 3rd 2022. You can still watch the video there, if you're a member of the group.

It's a bit of a hack, so I'll present a more elegant Z80-based solution later, but great for experimentation as it's just a short NextBASIC loop with configurable sample-rate and buffer sizes, and it updates the DMA source address and count in BASIC variables each time round.

DEMO5 starts like the other demos, then sets **f$** to the path of the sample to be streamed and plonks the file length, in bytes, in the variable **total**.

```
100 REM ZX NEXT DMA demo 5 - Simon N Goodwin January 2022
110 REM streams arbitrary 8-bit sample data from SD card
120 CLEAR 32767
```

```
130 Hz=20000:dma=107:REM Hz is sample rate. DMA uses port %$6b
140 RAMTOP=%1+ DPEEK 23730:MAX=65536-RAMTOP
145 REM Bebop.ub,Folk.ub,Funky.ub,Classic.ub,Country.ub etc.
150 f$="Chamber.ub"
155 OPEN #3,f$: DIM #3 TO total:CLOSE #3:PRINT total;" in ";f$
```

The following lines set **buff** to the capacity of each buffer, in bytes, check there's room for two of them – one for playing, one for loading – above RAMTOP and preload both buffers with the first **length** bytes of the file. The audio file ought to be at least that long. Otherwise you could play it all with the previous routine and there'd be no need for streaming.

```
160 buff=10000:length = buff*2 : REM Preload two buffers
170 IF length>MAX THEN PRINT f$;" LEN! ";length;">";MAX: STOP
175 a$=f$+" +0 "+ STR$ length+" -m "+ STR$ RAMTOP
180  .$ extract a$
190 PROC PlayDMA64k(RAMTOP,length,Hz,1)
```

I'm using large buffers in this example because of the **.extract** dot command overhead. That command reads bytes from part of any file. It re-opens the file every time, and also needs to reload the **extract** routine from the dot directory, so it does a lot more work than is really necessary.

Line 175 builds the parameters of the dot command in a string, **a$**, starting with the file name, then the offset within the file, **+0**, the byte count **20000**, and finally the load address, prefixed by **-m** and converted into a string with STR$. For example, it might generate:

```
.extract Funky.ub +0 20000 -m 32768
```

Figure 75 reveals the steps involved in streaming a file through two buffers. Test file sections are A, B, C, D, E and F; F is too short to fill the last buffer.

Line 190 calls PlayDMA64k() with the loop flag set, passing not the **total** file size but just the size of both buffers, in **length**. PROC PlayDMA64k() is just as in the previous demo, DMA4. This is enough to get the stream started, but if we stopped there only the first **length** bytes from the start of the file would play, over and over. These are sections A and B in Figure 75.

The trick to streaming is to monitor the position of the DMA pointer in the buffers, and shovel in a load more samples as soon as we detect that one buffer has fully played, so the next lot are ready in that buffer before the DMA pointer passes over all the bytes in the other buffer and wraps back round to the first. See how sections C, D, E and the final section F are loaded into alternate buffers, shown in grey in Figure 75.

If we get this right, replay is seamless. If not, it stutters. That usually means either the buffers are too small, the sample rate is too high (an equivalent issue) or the update checks are not sufficiently regular or frequent. The fun comes in working out when to update the buffer, where to get the data, and where to put it.

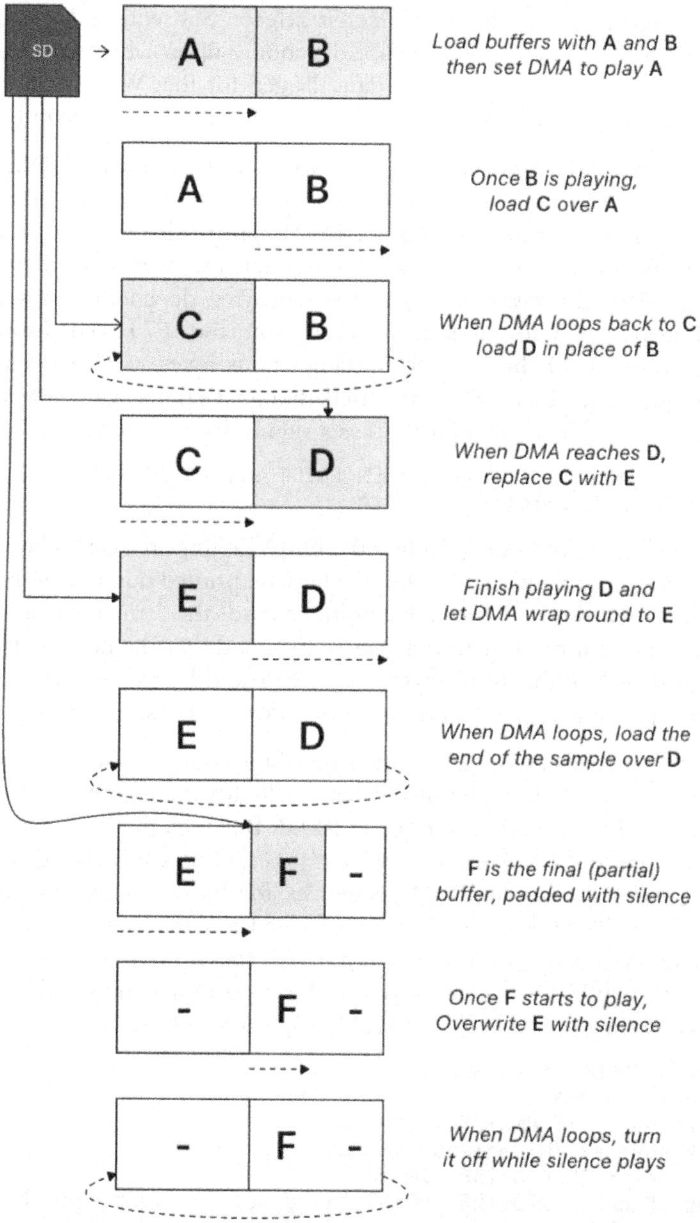

Figure 75 – Continuous streaming of a file larger than the available buffers

Pragmatic guesswork

The next loop is an ugly hack, but one I found necessary when first I wrote this routine, before studying the hardware design to work out the logic underlying the mysterious command 167, **Initiate Read Sequence**. When you send a DMA command with OUT 107, the pattern of bits in the first byte determines which register set it affects. Subsequent OUTs may get stored in the same register group, depending upon which bits were set in previous bytes, but after all the data flagged for that Write Register Group has been output the hardware will be ready for another command.

This stateful behaviour, combined with a lack of any indication of which group is selected and what's still expected, is one of the hazards of Z80 DMA programming. But the handling of IN 107, to read status and some of the other values embedded in the DMA state-machine, is trickier still. We've seen that IN 107 can return any one of seven bytes, depending on what's been read previously. Without understanding command 167 I needed some way to be sure which of those seven possible status bytes would be returned by subsequent INs. Line 197 did the trick, though it's not suitable for production code and even includes a GO TO as a sign of its hackiness!

```
197 s= IN dma: IF s<>59 THEN PRINT s,: GO TO 197
198 GO SUB 820:offset=length
```

The line simply loops, reading the DMA input port over and over, until it sees the 'magic number' 59. Other values are printed out, in columns, till the required byte pops up. From that point onwards the demo code optimistically assumes that it has just read a 'status' byte and that the next six bytes from the port will be the 16-bit byte count, followed by the 'source' address for the next sample transfer, and the 'destination' address, *SpecDrum* port 223.

Of course it's possible that any byte of the count or source address might happen to be 59, though unlikely, especially for the high byte of the source address, which would have to be in ROM. But even that's possible, if you're channelling the 48k game *Way of the Exploding Fist*, which saved bytes by re-using carefully-chosen ROM sequences for its one-bit sound effects. As further evidence that this code was hacked together in desperation, notice how the following line 198 uses a retro GO SUB rather than a new-fangled user-friendly PROC call to work out the latest DMA source address. Here's the code the other side of that GO SUB, warts and all:

```
800 DEFPROC StatusDMA()
810 s= IN dma
820 count= IN dma+256* IN dma
830 source= IN dma+256* IN dma
835 dest= IN dma+256* IN dma
840 IF dest<>223 THEN PRINT "Wild destination: ";dest: STOP
845 RETURN
850 ENDPROC
```

Apart from the patched-in lines 840 and 845, this is a tidily written PROC to read all seven status bytes into variables: the 8-bit status in **s**, remaining buffer contents in **count**, next **source** and **dest**ination addresses. The patches make it work as a subroutine with two entry points – look away, structured programmers! GO SUB 820 is used just after the loop found a plausible status byte, then GO SUB 810 to read subsequent seven-byte status packets once sync is established.

Why am I airing this dirty underware? Because when I was testing this stuff, learning as I went along, I could not be sure where in the status sequence the hardware had reached, as I broke into the demo code, revised and restarted it. So I used line 197, the GO SUBs, plus the sanity check at line 840, to work around the opaque internal state of the DMA controller and crank it round to a point where I could reliably interpret IN 107 values.

Line 840 catches the unlikely possibility of the magic number 59 being part of a count or address, rather than a status byte. Since we're writing to the same destination port every time, the last two bytes of the status seven had better be the *SpecDrum* port number, or something must have gone wrong.

Even that is an imperfect check, but it enabled me to complete and post a working demo before my winter holidays ran out and I was dragged back into the 64-bit world of modern game development. While the original code is prettier, it didn't work, and there's a useful lesson there.

My final DMA example – for this volume, at least – reveals a more robust approach. I'm 'showing my working' because I didn't understand any of this till I worked my way through increasingly sophisticated routines, DMA1 to DMA5, and reckon you've got a better chance of understanding the finished Z80-assisted driver-driven version if you've seen the steps leading up to it. As the saying goes, *great oaks from little acorns grow*.

Keeping streaming going

Once the first samples are playing we're in a race to keep the half-buffers full with subsequent parts of the file as the DMA source pointer trundles on between the two halves of the buffer. Lines 200 and 230 are almost identical, both using GO SUB 810 to read the latest value of the hardware **source** address and looping till it crosses the boundary between one half of the buffer and the other.

The difference is that line 200 loops until **source** points into the second half of the buffer. At that point we must have finished playing the first half, and need to reload that with fresh data from further down the sample file. Line 210 builds the corresponding parameter string for **.extract**, like the one that preloaded the buffer but now trimmed to **buff** bytes starting from **offset** within the file. DMA continues to play from the second half of the buffer, while the dot command does its laborious stuff.

Rows 2, 5 and 9 of Figure 75 are caught by line 200, as sections B, D and F play. The PRINT on line 215 reassures the user that BASIC is still running. You could put more code there – potentially the main update loop of a game – as long as it and the file-reading finishes before DMA reaches the end of the second half of the buffer.

```
200 REPEAT : GO SUB 810: REPEAT UNTIL source>=RAMTOP+buff
210 a$=f$+" +"+ STR$ offset+" "+ STR$ buff+" -m "+ STR$ RAMTOP
215 offset+=buff: PRINT AT 5,0;"LOAD A ";a$
220 .$ extract a$
```

We then enter another holding loop at line 230, waiting till source is pointing back to the *first* half of the buffer. The initial load of samples has now all been played and while DMA is working through the second load, now playing from the first half of the buffer, we can safely extract section C of the file into the second half, and later do the same for section E:

```
230 REPEAT : GO SUB 810: REPEAT UNTIL source<RAMTOP+buff
240 REM Update second half-buffer
250 a$=f$+" +"+ STR$ offset+" "+ STR$ buff+" -m "+
    STR$ (RAMTOP+buff)
260 offset=offset+buff: PRINT AT 5,0;"LOAD B ";a$
270 .$ extract a$
280 IF offset+buff<total THEN GO TO 200
410 PAUSE 50*buff/hz: PROC StopDMA(): STOP
```

Line 280 detects the end of the file, looping until the **total** number of bytes is less than we'd need to fill the last buffer. As previously noted, this relies on the long sample file ending with a fade-out to silence, otherwise we'll hear a click when the partial buffer-load at the end of the sample get chopped off.

The PAUSE at the end waits for the last full buffer to finish playing before StopDMA() cuts it off. Another way to ensure we hear the whole stream is to pad the sample with **length** bytes of silence – the mid-point value 128 in 8-bit unsigned format – though not all of those bytes will be heard. A third more economical way to avoid ending too soon or – even worse – replaying stale data from the penultimate block is to apply padding programmatically when the end of file is reached, so the correct amount is created on the fly to match the exact sample-count to the buffer size and associated worst-case update time.

The resultant video is included in the NextBASIC Facebook report. I was using a twin-SD interface from Richard Spencer's Active Consult service, with the sample on drive D: and the dot command loading from C:, so as well as the buffer-swap messages you can see the drive select lights flashing alternately as the long sample plays.

After I uploaded that video I realised my Next had only been running at 14 MHz, so there's plenty of scope to do more in-between loads, or use smaller buffers, with RUN AT 3. DMA5 was just a proof of concept but it showed that arbitrarily-large files could be streamed smoothly on Next with a handful of periodic IN and OUT commands, while BASIC continues to RUN. Of course it's arguably madness to load from SD at the same time, but it works, even without using banked RAM.

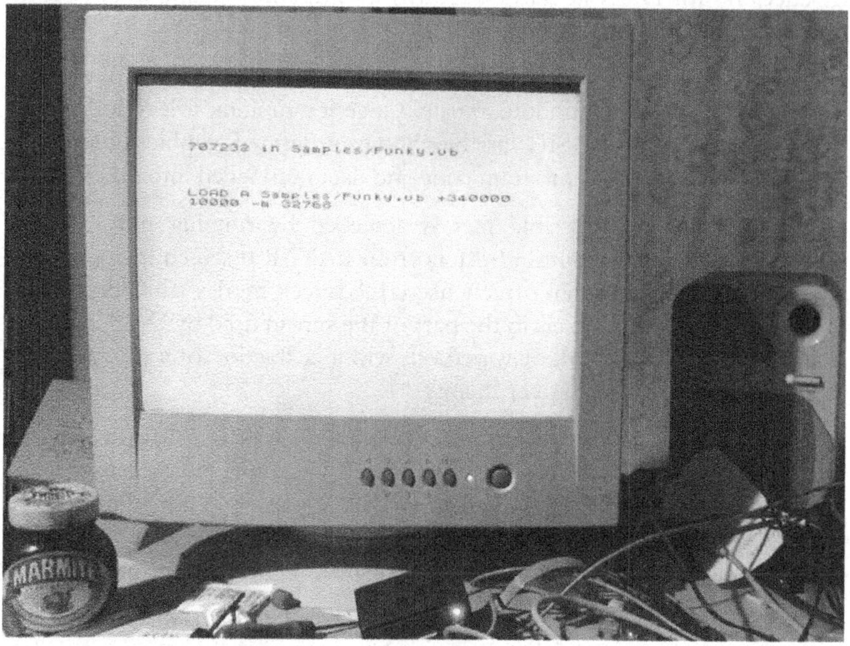

Figure 76 – The prototype Next streaming from SD

Streamlined streaming

The final audio-streaming example draws on research and routines created for this book to fix the dead-reckoning hack, tidy up handling of the end of the stream, and reduce the overhead of buffer-servicing. The checking is moved from BASIC into a DRIVER slot, the end of the file is padded properly, and the data is streamed from pre-loaded BANKs, which limits the total duration but eliminates the SD overhead for every single block update.

If you've got better uses for your RAM banks, consider replacing the bank-swapping and copying in the slot routine with the multi-byte INPUT$ code on page 86. This still requires access to SD, but eliminates the dot command and other file-juggling overhead. The following 140-byte slot routine incorporates the seven-byte INPUT$ code, for convenience in copying chunks of the audio file to the output buffers or memory banks outside the Z80 address space.

The prime purpose of the DMA audio slot method is to monitor the DMA hardware every frame to see if it's finished playing one of the buffers. If so, it pages in the current bank of pre-loaded data and quickly copies the next chunk of that into the buffer that's just finished playing, so it's ready by the time the other buffer is exhausted – and then we can load that, and so on. When the end of the banked sample data is reached, DMA is automatically turned off. The slot routine still runs till either it's disconnected with another DRIVER command, or the driver is unloaded. But since it starts by checking for DMA activity, it returns in little more than a microsecond unless the DMA pointer is changing.

This routine is more than a demo – it's designed to be easy to add into programs that need continuous music. Once it's running it leaves ALL the memory available for BASIC variables and user-defined graphics untouched, and allows free access to program code and data pre-loaded into other banks.

This seemingly-impossible feat is achieved by running not only the method code but both output buffers from LAYER 0 screen memory! The snag of that is that you can't freely use ULA screen modes while the stream is running. If you plot pixels in the part of the screen used by DMA they will either be output as sound, or wiped out within a fraction of a second when fresh audio data is copied over them.

This is not a problem for programs that use a LAYER 2 main screen and sprites, neither of which make any use of ULA memory. In fact there's still about 8.5k available for hardware tiles and TileMaps, if you need a third layer, and the lower part of the standard ZX screen, or the same area of a Timex or LoRes display, can still be used as a layer showing beneath the main screen.

Indeed, the NextBASIC setup routine makes a feature of this, opening up a transparent column of its display where you can see the audio data streaming through the layer below, as a colour vector animation runs alongside. The streaming bank and address offset are continuously updated by a couple of PEEKs that reveal what the DMA is up to by polling the internal state of the slot method that's keeping the hardware busy.

I shall explain this in two sections, starting with a machine-code version of the buffer updating code previously presented in NextBASIC. This is a self-contained slot method, run every frame by the slot driver, capable of swiftly switching in any bank of main memory, copying data from it to the DMA output buffer in a millisecond or so, depending upon the buffer size which determines the maximum sample rate, and returning control to NextBASIC as if main memory had never been touched.

The second section is NextBASIC. It shows how long samples are pre-loaded into banks, so there's no need for slow SD access while the audio plays, and how the slot method is configured to play up to 100 banks, in any order, once the BASIC has gone away. There's also a place-holding GAME() procedure which shows LAYER 2 animation running smoothly at the same time as the sample plays.

Sound Streaming Slot method

The streaming slot code is a concise translation of the NextBASIC we've seen earlier. All the setup work is done in BASIC, because there's no point optimising code that will only run once. The Z80 code deals only with updating output buffers at the right time, like the loop between lines 200 and 280 in the previous example. Since it's machine-code, there's some bit-twiddling to keep it efficient, and as we're streaming from banks rather than SD there's memory paging involved. Details aside, it's familiar stuff, so you can concentrate on how it fits together rather than having to guess what each part is doing.

The source is written as part of the same BASIC program that does the pre-loading and animation. The first lines make sure we're using LAYER 2 rather than ULA graphics. The code is assembled directly to attribute memory at 22K, immediately after the 16k ROM and 6k bitmap areas.

```
2000 REM Stream update method for 2*2K buffers at 16k
2020 REM RUN from here to find interface addresses
2040 LAYER CLEAR : LAYER 2,1
2060 .asm
2080 ; org 22528          ; Assemble to attribute RAM
```

Lines 2120 to 2220 give human-friendly names to magic numbers which appear later in the code. SIZE and BASE are the number of bytes in each buffer, and the address where the first buffer starts. We need two buffers of equal size, used alternately, one to load while the other plays, so the total buffer size is 4k bytes. The term buffer is ambiguous – it could refer to the entire 4k area, or either 2K half, so the term 'half-buffer' refers to whichever section loads next as the stream progresses.

```
2120 ;SIZE   equ 2048    ; Buffer multiple of 256
2140 ;BASE   equ 16384   ; Top 2/3 of LAYER 0 pixels
```

Notice that all these numbers are 'round' from the computer's point of view. If written in binary, each value would have only one bit set; 16k is @0100 0000 0000 0000 and 2K is @0000 **1**000 0000 0000. This property matches the simple way the program determines which half-buffer is being used, and means that – unless the code is rewritten – buffer sizes must be a power of 2: 256, 512, 1024, or 2048 in this case. Since we need two buffers and there's only 6¾K of LAYER 0 memory, 2048 is the upper limit for this approach, but if we moved the buffers to the end of memory, above RAMTOP, we could use two lots of 4k, or more.

Going up to 8k would completely eliminate the need to copy memory around, as we could simply map 8k pages from the start or end of each bank into the area addressed by the DMA, but this would tie down a third of the RAM visible to the Z80 and DMA. If you've got a spare 16k, go for it. That's the most efficient way to stream memory banks on Next, but a high price to pay when that 16k is 40% of all the memory available for BASIC variables.

The top 16k is used by BANK so if you split a large NextBASIC program that way, that leaves only the middle 16k for streaming, and you end up with a 16k Spectrum for your main loop and variables. Hit games have been written for just that space, and they didn't have streaming audio, or access to banks of additional BASIC and data!

Extract overheads

As we've seen when streaming from SD, there's a trade-off between small and large buffers. The smaller the buffer, the sooner you can get started but the more likely it becomes that replay will glitch if you fail to catch the DMA transition from one buffer to the other with enough time to reload the one that's just finished.

When streaming from an already open file, with the INPUT$ call, that involves esxDOS reading each byte from SD, using the CPU, and storing it in RAM. If we use **.extract** it's a lot more work, because the 8k dot command must be reloaded, every time, and before we can even do that we must select the drive containing the dot folder, scan the subdirectory to find one command's name among the 80-plus within it, then use the directory information to find which 16 sectors on the card hold the command code.

Once the command is loaded into paged memory, the first thing it does is re-open the input file, with more directory-scanning, potentially on another drive with even more files to wade through. Rather than pick up from the byte after the last one loaded, as the INPUT$ hook would, **.extract** then has to seek within the file to find the requested chunk. After loading just that, the file is closed and the entire farrago is repeated for every chunk.

All this overhead means each buffer needs to last an appreciable fraction of a second, so there's time to find both files. The actual transfer of the chunk takes a relatively small proportion of the total time, but it still imposes a substantial delay on the entire system, because the Z80 can do nothing else while bytes are being read from the SD card by NextZXOS. We need to read a hefty chunk so we've got enough samples to play to cover all the other overheads of loading.

Finally, remember that we can't even start to reload a buffer till we know it's finished playing. This involved a call to PROC StatusDMA(), which only happens when we've finished anything else we might have been calculating or animating in the meantime, and after that we still need to interpret the results and work out what to do about them, before we go back to the SD. And that applies even if the next chunk is already waiting in RAM. It's nothing to do with the SD, but a factor of the latency, the total time needed to stop one thing and start another.

The slot streamer doesn't just reduce the loading time, it also reduces the latency in two ways. Most significantly it runs on an interrupt, so it runs 50 times every second, whatever else the computer may be in the middle of doing, unless that's one of those time-critical interrupt-blocking operations like cassette loading or saving, SD access, or a traditional BEEP.

If your main program does all its loading up-front, and uses the AY chips rather than software BEEPs, it can get by with much smaller buffers. But we still can't be sure of updating the buffer 50 times a second, because sometimes interrupts are delayed when the system enters a 'critical region', such as moving the area of memory used for the stack, and interrupts have to be disabled then because they rely on the stack for their temporary data and return address.

NextZXOS sometimes uses self-modifying code, in DivMMC RAM, to read a pair of bytes without the risk that an interrupt might put them out of sync. Otherwise even a simple DPEEK of the first bytes of FRAMES might give inconsistent results, requiring multiple attempts, as the clock demo in the manual explains, or momentarily disabling interrupts. There are times when the interrupt just has to wait, and we need to leave some slack to cover for such cases. The maskable Z80 interrupt is level-triggered, not edge-triggered and latched the way the NMI (yellow button) interrupt is, so it may be missed entirely unless the pulse lasts until after the next EI instruction.

The other issue is the amount of time spent finding out what to do, and doing it. With luck and a following wind, at 28 MHz NextBASIC can execute a few thousand statements every second. The Z80n generally manages several million instructions per second, so even if it takes ten times more machine code instructions your program can still end up 100 times faster, if you pick the right instructions and arrange things to suit the simple-minded 8-bit CPU.

The next two equates in the program also appear in the slot driver source:

```
2160 ;SELECT equ 9275     ; NextReg select port
2180 ;MMU6   equ 86       ; 48..56k mapping REG
```

SELECT is the Z80 port address used to select input from a particular NextReg; MMU6 keeps track of the 8k of memory from 48k to 56k in the Z80 address space. That's where we'll momentarily map part of the bank we're streaming from, in order to copy data from there to the stream output buffer. MMU0 and MMU1 are out of bounds because the system uses those, and I've avoided using MMU7, which maps the top 8k, because the way CLEAR reserves memory from the top down means that's the most obvious place for streaming buffers when ULA screens are being used for their intended purpose.

We could just as well use MMU3, MMU4 or MMU5 here, as whatever's originally mapped there will be replaced as soon as the copying is done, while the interrupt routine still runs. MMU2 would be a bad choice for this BASE address since it maps the LAYER 0 screen RAM. It would be a serious mistake to swap out the destination buffer address as the same time as mapping in the source!

```
2200 ;DMA    equ 107      ; Next DMA control port
2220 ;STOP   equ 131      ; DMA STOP command code
```

The last two magic numbers are associated with zxnDMA. 107 is the DMA hardware port number, and 131 is the STOP DMA command byte.

Most times that the slot routine is invoked, it only runs the first nine bytes, five instructions, listed next. Slot execution starts at the label **handler** and usually returns four lines later because there's nothing to be done. The DMA is still stepping through the same half-buffer that it was in when the last check occurred.

```
2260 ;handler in a,(DMA) ; Find current buffer
2300 ; and %01001000     ; Ignore fractions of 2K
2320 ; ld hl,CURRENT
2340 ; cp (hl)           ; Has buffer changed?
2360 ; ret z             ; No need to swap yet
```

The address CURRENT points to a byte which only changes when there's been a buffer-swap. We've set things up so that IN A,(DMA) reads only the high byte of the address from which DMA is loading. The following AND instruction strips out the three least significant bits of that address, which count units of 256, 512 and 1024 bytes, while the next bit, in the middle, is set only when the address is a multiple of 2k but not a multiple of 4k.

To understand this, consider how the least significant bit determines if a single byte value is odd or even. Now imagine the 64k of Z80 address space as 32 areas of 2k each. The middle bit we're isolating indicates whether the full address is in an odd or even-numbered one of those 2k areas.

The other set bit in the binary value corresponds to 16k. Remember that we're reading DMA data from the LAYER 0 screen area, and we have two buffers next to one another there, at 16k and 18k. Since both buffers add up to 4k, valid addresses in either buffer must fall in the range 16k to 20k-1, and we've seen how the middle bit is set only when the second 2k buffer is being addressed.

The 16k arena never changes, for the chosen buffer addresses, so after the AND instruction the value in the accumulator must be either 64 (only the 16k bit set; remember this is the high byte of a 16-bit address, and 64 * 256 =16k) or 72, when both the 16k and 2k-weighted bits are set. If it's 64, DMA must be reading the first 2k buffer. When it changes to 72, DMA has swapped to the second buffer.

This approach can be used for any pair of adjacent buffers which are a power-of-two bytes in length and both start at an exact multiple of their size. The least significant set bit is chosen to match the buffer size, so if we were using two 1k buffers at the start of LAYER 0 the 'mask' would be @0100 0100, and if those were at the top of memory, starting at 62k and 63k, the corresponding mask would be @11111100. The two zeroes exclude offsets of 512 or 256 bytes, as we only care when a 1k boundary is crossed.

The next two lines compare the value in the accumulator with the byte at CURRENT, which records which buffer the DMA handler was playing at the last interrupt-driven check. If they match, the zero flag is set, and the RET Z instruction returns control to the interrupt driver, because there's nothing more to be done. The check has taken one millionth of a second, not counting the return. Compare that with the NextBASIC version and you can see that even 2k buffers are generous.

This is how LAYER 0 looks while the stream is playing:

Figure 77 – music streaming through LAYER 0 display RAM

Swapping buffers

Let's see what happens when the DMA has moved between half-buffers. The first thing we do is store the new value at CURRENT. Handily saving a byte, we already have the address in HL. Register A tells us which buffer is playing now, but what we really want is the start address of the other buffer, the one that's just been consumed and which we now need to update. The XOR instruction flips bits in the accumulator if they're set in the operand, from 0 to 1 or vice versa.

```
2400 ; ld (hl),a            ; Update CURRENT
2420 ; xor %1000            ; Swap to alternate 2K
2440 ; ld d,a               ; Set MSB of destination
```

It's called 'eXclusive OR' because when a bit ends up set when it's set in the input *or* the mask, but *not both*. It has the useful property that exclusive-ORing the same mask twice gets you back to the number you started with. For our double-buffered ping-pong DMA scheme, that's ideal. The exclusive-or operation is written ^| in NextBASIC, flipping up to 16 bits of integers and 32 within floating-point values. It's also used in ZX BASIC when plotting pixels with OVER 1; set pixels are cleared, clear ones are set. Things get more complicated in LoRes or LAYER 2; we'll come to that later.

Now we have the most significant byte of the address of the buffer we'll need to reload. We stash that in register D, for later use as the DEstination in a LDIR block-copy instruction. We already know that the E register will hold zero since buffers always start at exact multiples of 256 bytes – otherwise we'd need to consider more than just the high byte of the DMA source address – but there's no need to set that, yet.

Before we can update the buffer at DE we need to find the data to copy in there. That's the role of the next four instructions. The pre-loader stored the NextBASIC BANK numbers for the entire sample in a 100-byte table at the address labelled BANKS. The total number of entries used in that table is stored at Count, and the value at INDEX tells us which entry in the table holds the number of the 16k BANK we've reached. These lines read that entry from the table.

```
2520 ; ld a,(INDEX)        ; Bank index 0..Count-1
2540 ; ld hl,BANKS         ; Base for offset
2560 ; add hl,a
2580 ; ld a,(hl)           ; Get source bank number
```

The **add hl,a** instruction is a Z80n addition which adds an 8-bit value to a 16-bit address. On a stock Z80 this would need to be done in three or four steps, first adding L to A, then checking for an overflow and incrementing H only if the first total was more than 255, and finally copying A back to L.

It's a similarly fiddly task on earlier and many later Intel processors, but at least Next programmers can now mimic the ABX instruction, first in the dictionary of Motorola 6809 enthusiasts. Our Nextras can equally well add A to DE or BC. Unlike older ADD instructions, the Z80n additions don't update the processor flags, which would be useful for arithmetic but pointless or counterproductive for address manipulations, like this.

Each NextBASIC BANK holds 16384 samples, but we only need a fraction of that for our buffer update, and Next's MMU works in 8k pages rather than 16k banks. The word labelled OFFSET indicates where in the bank we'll read from next, starting at zero and increasing by SIZE as each output buffer is loaded.

```
2600 ; ld hl,(OFFSET)
2620 ; add a,a             ; First page of bank
2640 ; bit 5,h             ; Past 8k boundary?
2660 ; jr z,even
2680 ;
2700 ; res 5,h             ; Take offset modulo 8k
2720 ; inc a               ; Second page of bank
2740 ;
2760 ;even add hl,49152    ; HL points to source
```

When offset reaches 8k, bit 5 of the high byte becomes set. To get from a bank number and offset between 0 and 16k, to a page number and offset less than 8k, we double the bank number by adding A to itself on line 2620, then check if the offset is 8k or more, in which case we must add one to get to the second 8k page within the 16k bank.

Zilog added eighty BIT instructions to the Intel 8080 repertoire to make this a bit easier, and then made it harder again by insisting that if the tested bit is 1, the Z80 Z flag gets set, but if the bit is 0 the flag is cleared, which indicates 'not zero' in other circumstances. You eventually get used to it, or stick with the 8080 subset, which is often faster – but problematic here, because the Intel approach involves clobbering the accumulator and we've already got a useful value in there.

If bit 5 of H is clear we skip to the label EVEN, and if it's set we increment the accumulator, adding one to the page number, and clear that bit so HL remains an offset in the 0 to 7¾K range. Since MMU6 controls the page starting at address 49152 in the memory map, we add that value to HL on line 2760, using another handy Z80n instruction, to turn the offset into an absolute address. If you prefer to use another MMU register, be sure to alter the base address correspondingly, e.g. adding 40960 for MMU5, and so on.

Now HL points to the address want to load fresh samples from. It's time to temporarily page the source data in at 48k, so we can copy from it. Just as with the slot driver support for code at high addresses, regularly swapped around by NextBASIC, before we alter MMU6 we need to read the current value so we can put it back when we're done, before the rest of the system finds unexpected bytes in the paging area.

The only register that can be used to update NextRegs is the accumulator, and we need two such values, for the original and temporary values of MMU6. Faggin and Shima saw this coming and gave the Z80 an extra accumulator and set of processor flags, using one of those precious single-byte opcodes not needed by the 8080 to swap between them. So we temporarily hide the value we really want to put in MMU6 by exchanging the AF register pair with the alternate AF' set (the apostrophe makes all the difference), replacing it first with the MMU6 register number which we write to the NextReg SELECT port, then stepping on economically to the DATA port with INC B, and loading the current MMU6 setting from there into A.

```
2840 ; ex af,af'
2860 ; ld bc,SELECT
2880 ; ld a,MMU6
2900 ; out (c),a          ; Select MMU6 register
2920 ; inc b
2940 ; in a,(c)           ; Current page in MMU6
2960 ; ex af,af'          ; Save current page in A'
2980 ; out (c),a          ; Page-in load buffer
3000 ; ld bc,SIZE         ; Size is a multiple of 256
3020 ; ld e,c             ; Clear destination low byte
3040 ; ldir               ; Transfer load buffer for DMA
3060 ; ex af,af'
3080 ; nextreg MMU6,a     ; Restore previous page
```

The dance continues by swapping AF back again, then stuffing the new MMU6 page number into the DATA port, handily still pointed at by BC. This puts the memory we want to copy from at the source address in HL, and frees up BC for the Byte Count required by the block-copying instruction LDIR. Before we can copy SIZE bytes from (HL) to (DE) we need to clear E, which is easy because we're working in multiples of 256 bytes, to avoid fussing over the low byte of the DMA pointer, so L must be zero.

The LDIR (Load, Increment and Repeat) takes less than a microsecond to copy each byte and step onward, so a 2K buffer can be transferred in less than one tenth of a 20 ms PAL display frame. Even at the DVD sampling rate that's enough data to tide the DMA through for a couple of frames, which is why I chose it as the default for this routine.

If your samples were captured or downsampled to a lower rate, and you're not loading or BEEPing much at the same time, you'll probably get away with 1k buffers, and if telephone-quality 8 kHz samples are good enough for your tin ears, even a pair of 512-byte buffers might just about be enough. Suck it and see. If you squeeze the buffers too far Next won't crash, but the sound will hiccup as stale data gets re-played before the next chunk replaces it. This program won't need any new symbols, but as well as reducing SIZE you'll need to alter which bit gets tested and toggled between the first and second buffer addresses.

At this point both buffers have valid data and DMA can safely wrap from the one it was playing when the slot handler polled it into the fresh chunk. To reduce total latency, before the slot routine returns it updates OFFSET and INDEX to point at the next chunk, if any. Doing this now, while both buffers are full, is better than puzzling it out while the stream was already approaching the point of starvation.

We can also check if we've reached the end of the stream, and make appropriate preparation for it to stop without a disconcerting click at the end. That would usually be followed by an equally irksome counter-click when the next sample starts. That's the purpose of the last few lines of the interrupt handler, and two lines of data-massaging in the pre-loader.

```
3160 ; ld hl,(OFFSET)     ; Increase OFFSET by SIZE
3180 ; add hl,SIZE
3200 ; ld (OFFSET),hl
3220 ; ld a,(COUNT)       ; Is this the last bank?
3240 ; ld b,a
3260 ; dec b              ; Index counts from zero
3280 ; ld a,(INDEX)
3300 ; cp b
3320 ; jr nz,notLast
```

Lines 3160 to 3200 add SIZE to OFFSET, using HL as a 16-bit accumulator. We do this before considering whether or not we've reached the end of the current bank; if so OFFSET will be cleared back to zero when we start the next bank. The check for the last bank is simple in principle – just compare INDEX with COUNT, the total number of banks. But INDEX starts at zero while COUNT starts at 1, for a single bank. I considered making COUNT one less than the number of banks, but that seems error-prone as well as user-hostile, so I prefer to take the hit of a four-cycle DEC B instruction to align the two numbers, even though it makes the 2K chunk update nearly 0.1% slower. It seems a price worth paying.

After checking INDEX we skip ahead to **notLast** unless this is indeed the final bank of the sample. But we can't turn the DMA off till we know that the final buffer from the last bank is playing; for a one-shot sample, the pre-loader will put silence there to avoid a click, and if the sample is looping we need to play all the valid data in the final buffer and wrap immediately back to the start of the sample. The byte flag LAST is set when we're really playing that silence, and can be monitored with PEEK(offset+2) so NextBASIC can find out when the stream has run its course. If the flag is not yet set, we continue at CHECK. Otherwise we write the STOP command to the DMA port and our work is done.

```
3360 ; ld a,(LAST)       ; Are we finished?
3380 ; or a
3400 ; jr z,check
3420 ;
3440 ; ld a,STOP
3460 ; out (DMA),a       ; Issue DMA STOP command
3480 ; ret
```

The CHECK routine below only runs while the final bank of the stream is selected but the last buffer hasn't yet been reached. Since the sample is unlikely to be an exact multiple of 16k long, the final bank is probably not full. The word at TAIL holds the exact number of valid samples in the final bank, and we already have the next offset within that bank in HL, so a 16-bit subtraction is enough to establish whether or not the end is nigh, or there are buffers still to be queued.

```
3520 ;check ld de,(TAIL) ; DE = bytes in last bank
3540 ; sbc hl,de          ; Carry clear, at the end?
3560 ; ret c              ; C set, ready to play more
3580 ;
3600 ; ld a,(ONCE)        ; One-shot or looping?
3620 ; or a
3640 ; jr z,loop          ; Not just once, restart
3660 ;
3680 ; ld (LAST),a        ; Flag final transfer
3700 ; ret
```

There's no simple 16-bit SUB instruction on the Z80, only SBC which also subtracts 1 if the carry flag is set. This is useful for multi-word arithmetic, but often means that a SBC instruction must be preceded by OR A or a similar instruction guaranteed to clear carry, otherwise the result is liable to be off by one. In this specific case we know from the previous code block that we can only reach the label CHECK when LAST is zero. The OR A above to check that is sure to have cleared the carry flag. Register LoaD instructions never affect the Z80 flags, which is why we needed OR A after loading A from LAST, and the interim loading of DE makes no difference. The comment 'carry clear' on line 3540 is a reminder of this assumption. If other code that jumped to CHECK was added, it'd need re-checking. If the carry flag is set after the SBC, we know there's more to play and can return.

The final end-of-sample check copes with the possibility that we might want the entire sample to play again from the start. As far as DMA is concerned a streamed sample is always looping, because the hardware wraps back and forth between the two half-buffers, playing whatever it finds in them till it's deliberately stopped. So we can't use the 'loop' flag of PROC PlayDMA64k() to repeat any sample larger than the output buffer. Instead, the streaming slot method uses another byte flag, ONCE, which is set if the long sample is only meant to play once, and clear otherwise, so the sample automatically plays again from the start every time it reaches TAIL. The LAST flag never gets set unless ONCE is also set.

We're not quite done yet. Remember the conditional jump to **notLast**, when we've yet to reach the last bank? Here's the code to handle that. It checks bit 6 of H, which is set once the offset in HL reaches 16k. If that's clear, we carry on. But if the offset has reached 16k, we need to advance INDEX to the next bank, which we know must exist because COUNT didn't match INDEX.

Back at line 3220 I deliberately put INDEX rather than COUNT in the accumulator when making the comparison. This pays off now because there's no need to re-load it; we just INC A to advance to the next entry in the BANKS table, update INDEX, and clear the high byte of OFFSET ready to load the following buffer from the start of the next bank. Remember that the low byte is always zero because SIZE must be a multiple of 256.

```
3740 ;notLast bit 6,h     ; Reached 16k bank limit?
3760 ; ret z
3780 ;
3800 ; inc a               ; Proceed to next bank
3820 ;
3840 ;loop ld (INDEX),a
3860 ; xor a
3880 ; ld (OFFSET+1),a     ; Back to base of bank
3900 ;
3920 ;done ret
```

That's it, an exercise in Z80 quirk management, real-time programming and Z80n optimisation. The techniques might seem eccentric, especially the assumptions about bits and bytes, but they crop up regularly in most 8-bit micro programs, and become second-nature eventually. I've taken pains to explain them, because while a great deal can be done with NextBASIC, the Spectrum was always designed to support machine-code experimentation, with features like CLEAR and USR building on the ZX80 and ZX81 experience. The trick, especially on a faster machine like Next, is to only use Z80 code for things that absolutely require it, when you've proven that BASIC is just too slow, and

> *We should forget about small efficiencies, say about 97% of the time: premature optimization is the root of all evil*
>
> Donald Knuth

isolate the simple parts that must run many times per second. It's pointless to optimise the rest, and not much fun either.

Native Z80 debugging

Before moving on to the BASIC that sets this magic up, which I deliberately have NOT optimised, here is my advice on testing machine code programs on Next. We're still waiting for a full-featured Next-specific Z80 debugger, which is aware of banks and pages; the NMI debug menu is meant to provide that eventually, unless *Odin* gets there first. It's a topic I plan to revisit in the next volume of this series.

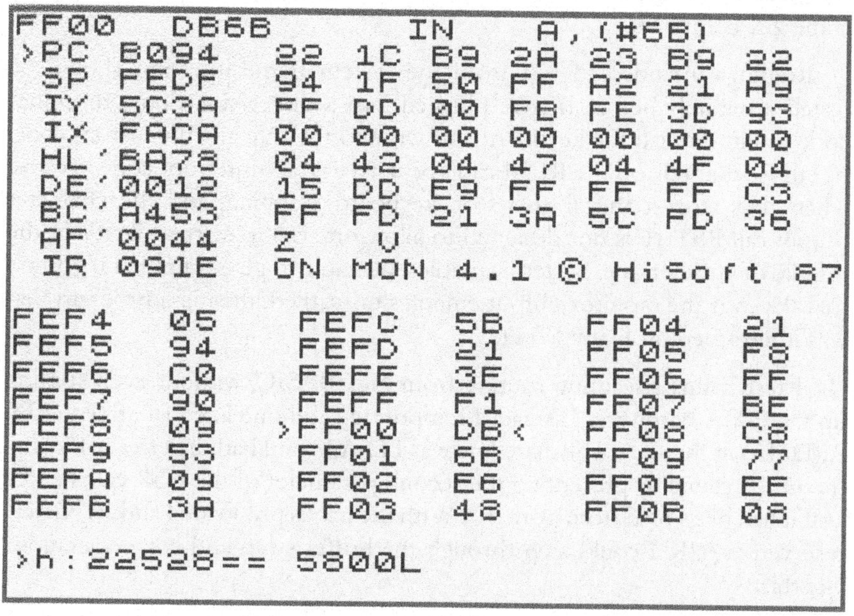

Figure 78 – HiSoft's venerable MONS4, poised to step through the start of SlotStreamer2 code

But in the meantime we have to use the original Spectrum debuggers, which are fine as long as your code fits alongside them in main memory. I used HiSoft's *MONS4* for the few times I needed to step through code in this book to fix bugs. It's a bit fiddly but can run from any address, letting us set breakpoints, where the program will temporarily stop and return to the monitor, or step through code instruction by instruction, watching values change in the registers and memory.

The main thing that lets down *MONS4*, and other familiar tools from the 48k era, is that it doesn't know about Z80n instructions. If you try to step over those, the two-byte ones will be properly handled, apart from the missing mnemonic, but stepping goes wrong for instructions that have embedded operands, like **nextreg**, **push nn** and the 16-bit constant **adds**. The workaround is simple – if you run up to one of those instructions, don't try to step over it.

Press W to set a breakpoint on the next standard Z80 instruction, and use **Symbol Shift K** rather than **Symbol Shift Z** to run past the new and complicated opcode. The register display and flags will be correctly updated, so otherwise you can use whatever machine-code monitor you are used to. Built in disassemblers will also be puzzled by Nextras, which is why my Z80n disassembler has been part of the Next distro since the first update. Look for *Nextramon* in the apps/dev subdirectory – it has a detailed NextGuide accessible by browsing to docs/guides. As well as all the Z80n instructions Nextramon can automatically identify references to system variables, Sinclair error codes and the floating-point calculator language used by the ROM and some ZX compilers.

Routines intended to run from the system frame interrupt should be tested separately before they're plugged into a driver slot. Some machine-code monitors read the keyboard and write to the screen with custom code, but those that rely on the ROM can't be used to trace interrupt code because when they stop it they'll also stop keyboard scanning, and the character output call RST 16 is not designed to allow one call to start while it's in the middle of another one. System variables are liable to get scrambled if you try that. Even if the monitor output emerges unscathed, the main program that was interrupted probably won't.

I tested this streaming routine from NextBASIC, without even starting up the DMA hardware. Instead, I temporarily add one line just after the IN A,(DMA) at the start. The extra line was LD A,E, and had the effect of faking the DMA status by presenting the second parameter of the USR call, 0..255, as if it had been read from port 107. With the banks pre-loaded and 1k buffers reserved at 62K I could step through the buffer swap and copy operations like this:

```
3000 DEFPROC HARNESS()
3030 t= USR (method,248): PROC STATUS()
3040 t= USR (method,252): PROC STATUS()
3300 ENDPROC
```

The first USR call pretends that DMA is consuming the first buffer (at 248*256 = 62K, bBase = 63488) then calls PROC STATUS() to show what's changed. Since DMA was not playing audio I could use test data optimised for eyes rather than ears. A little BASIC loop created a 20k test file containing 20 fake buffers, each 1k long, starting with 1024 copies of the letter A, then 1024 Bs, ending with a kilobyte of Ts. Pre-loading that instead of a sample file meant I could instantly see which part of the file was in each buffer by PEEKing and PRINTing the first 32 characters from both.

```
4000 DEFPROC STATUS()
4010 PRINT DPEEK offset;" in bank "; PEEK (setup+2);" buff ";
4020 PRINT PEEK(offset+3);" not" AND NOT PEEK(offset+2);" last"
4060 PRINT PEEK$ (bbase,32); PEEK$ (bbase+bsize,32);
4080 ENDPROC
```

PROC STATUS() PEEKs the initialisation data at **setup** (pointing at the ONCE flag) adds 2 to find INDEX, the current entry in the BANKS table, then checks the runtime private state at **offset** (the word offset within the bank, followed by the LAST flag and updated CURRENT buffer number) and the start of both buffers at **bBase** and **bBase+bSize**. Skip line 4060 unless you're streaming test text.

Little NextBASIC routines like HARNESS() and STATUS() can be cobbled together in a few minutes and will save hours during testing, even if they're not needed when the program is *perfect*, *finished*, *working* – and, as Marshall McLuhan would add, therefore *obsolete!* Every time you create a data-structure in a block of memory, consider writing a test routine to PEEK and PRINT the contents. You'll almost always save time by doing so.

Divide and USR

The other technique I've used time and again while writing this book, and in 45 years writing machine-code for fun, is to isolate bits of the code by inserting a RET instruction mid-way, copying any result I'm not sure about into BC, which is the 16-bit value returned by USR, and jumping in to the problematic code by making a USR call to its start.

Additional LD instructions can be temporarily inserted to preset register values, and the second parameter of USR can be set up to pass specific 16-bit test data in DE, shuffling it to the most sensitive registers with LD, EX or a PUSH/POP pair. Nine times out of ten this eliminates any need to step through the code.

If we were using a file-based assembler or compiler, designed before interactive micros, the temporary program editing and reassembly might become so tedious we'd prefer to manually set the program counter and other registers in the monitor before stepping through. But with a built-in assembler like **.asm** and the flexibility of NextBASIC at our fingertips, USR calls from a test harness are just as easy.

Test PROCs allow us to flip banks and pages around with REG instructions before and after, following a protective CLEAR, of course. They can format and print crucial values on the way in and out. Best of all, they leave us with useful re-usable test routines as a side-effect: a permanent record of the test conditions rather than evanescent numbers typed in to the monitor, often in an inconvenient number base.

Interfacing the streaming method from NextBASIC

The routines that preload audio samples into NextBASIC BANKs are at the start of the file SlotStreamer.bas, before the assembly-language source. But right after the assembler lines there's data used to link these parts together. The seven-byte esxDOS routine to read a bunch of file bytes into a string is labelled **fread**, and the address of that code is returned to BASIC via the %F variable, using Chris Taylor's elegant LET syntax to copy values created within his assembler into NextBASIC integer variables.

The setup routine also needs to know the start address of the slot handler, returned in %C. It's also useful to know the address of the first free byte after the machine-code and before the interface variables, so that is returned in %L, with the address of the first of those variables in %V, like this:

```
3960 ;fread db 213,221,225,26,207,157,201
3980 ; LET %L=$          ; First free byte after code
3990 ;
4000 ;; NextBASIC interface Variables, POKE to start
4020 ; org 22528+140
4030 ;
4040 ; LET %C=handler
4060 ; LET %V=ONCE
4100 ; LET %F=fread
```

Line 4020 uses ORG to reset the code origin to 140 bytes after the start of the handler. If 140 bytes was not enough, we'd know because %L would be greater than %V after assembly, and it'd be necessary to increase the value 140 to leave more room for code.

I could have omitted the second ORG and just let the variables float around wherever they ended up after the FREAD bytes, but that means the **setup** and **offset** addresses change whenever the code grows and shrinks. It's easier, though a little less efficient, to leave a few bytes 'for future expansion' between the code and data ORG addresses, so I added the second ORG during testing. When every byte counts, and the code is working/obsolete, you can eliminate the wastage by ensuring %L exactly matches %V.

For similar reasons I tuned both ORGs to leave a few bytes of slack after the variables, setting %E to point where that slack starts. By comparing %E with the start address of the system variables, immediately after the LAYER 0 attribute space I've borrowed for streaming code and data, or alternate buffers following code relocated to the end of Z80 RAM, we can tell how much space is left for extra variables, or anything else.

Hence the program ends with these diagnostic lines:

```
4380 PRINT "Method @ ";%C;" Interface @ ";%V
4400 PRINT "Code expansion margin ";%V-L;" bytes"
4410 PRINT "Data expansion margin ";23296-(%E);" bytes"
4420 PRINT "FREAD patch at ";%F;" to ";%L
4440 SAVE "StreamModule3" CODE %C,%L-C
9999 SAVE "SlotStreamer.bas"
```

Check the values printed to make sure the margins are safe. Manually copy the start address of the code and setup data into the NextBASIC loader on the rare occasions when they've changed. There are two automatic steps – line 4440 saves out the assembled code, using %C and %L to isolate the required bytes. The data area is not saved as it'll be set up by the loader to suit the chosen sample and buffer addresses. As is traditional, the last valid line number 9999 is used for a SAVE command. These SAVEs only occur after the assembly succeeds – otherwise it'd stop sooner with an error. Programmers soon learn the wisdom of saving work in progress before attempting to test it, especially if there's machine language or POKEs that could clobber the source involved. The rest become managers.

Before we wind back to the streaming setup in BASIC, here's a summary of all the memory address labels that link the machine-code and BASIC together. There are five data bytes (DB), two 16-bit words (DW), and space for 100 bytes of the sample bank numbers (DS). We'll POKE those so the machine code knows what to play, and PEEK them later to check progress.

```
4140 ;ONCE    db 1       ; Clear to repeat everything
4160 ;COUNT   db 0       ; Number of banks at BANKS
4180 ;INDEX   db 0       ; Entry in BANKS to load next
4200 ;TAIL    dw 0       ; Byte count of last bank
4220 ;BANKS   ds 100     ; Up to 1638400 samples
4240 ;
4260 ;; Runtime private state, read-only
4280 ;
4300 ;OFFSET  dw 0       ; Next chunk in bank, 0..15k
4320 ;LAST    db 0       ; Set if playing final buffer
4340 ;CURRENT db 0       ; High 6 bits of buffer in use
```

Sound Streaming Slot setup

The following lines of BASIC select the audio file and get it playing. The variables **method** and **setup** come from the assembler, pointing at the replay code and data respectively. By tweaking the ORG addresses and reassembling the code, these can be placed anywhere convenient in the 48k Z80 RAM area, other than the 8k from 40960 to 49151, where samples are briefly remapped from BANKs for copying into output buffers, and the locations reserved by NextBASIC, starting with the system variables at 23296 (where the ZX printer buffer lived until 128 BASIC claimed it for paging routines) and extending to the end of your BASIC program and variables.

Use CLEAR to limit that arena and protect higher memory. The Z80 stack used by BASIC must fit into the gap between the last variable value and the CLEAR parameter – e.g. CLEAR 32767 to mimic a 16k Spectrum, with nearly 9k for un-banked BASIC.

The variables **bBase** and **bSize** set the start address of the output buffers and the length in bytes of each of those two buffers. All these values must be exact multiples of 256. If you change **bSize** don't forget to make sure the masks used in the machine-code suit the new buffer size, and both variables meet the alignment requirements set out earlier.

I've assigned variable names to all the interface data addresses, for ease of updating and checking their contents. They are relative to **setUp** so if the second ORG changes you only need to adjust **setUp** and the rest will automatically shift to suit. Here's how the Streamer starts:

```
100 REM Next DMA Audio Streamer, April 2024
120 REM v3.4, uses LAYER 0, copyright 2024 Simon N Goodwin
140 RUN AT 3: SPECTRUM CHR$ 64
160 LAYER CLEAR : OVER 0: INK 1: PAPER 2: LAYER 1,2: CLS
180 dma=107
200 bSize=2048          :; Transfer block size in bytes
220 bBase=16384         :; Double-buffer in LAYER 0
240 method=22528        :; Slot handler in attribute RAM
260 LOAD "StreamModule3" CODE method
280 setUp=22668         :; Embed state later in attributes
300 index=setUp+2       :; INDEX of bank to copy from
320 tail=setup+3        :; TAIL word: bytes in last bank
340 banks=setUp+5       :; Store bank numbers here
360 offset=banks+100    :; Word offset in playing bank
380 last=offset+2:current=last+1:count=setUp+1
390 aBank=16384:%F=22652:; Even FREAD is in attribute RAM
400 rate=20000
410 loop=1
420 .install slot.drv
```

The first lines set Next to 28 MHz speed and the BASIC editor to Timex HiRes 64-column mode. This makes sure error messages or program tweaks don't over-write the StreamModule code tucked away in the LAYER 0 attribute memory area. You could use SPECTRUM CHR$ 85, though most of the lines have been formatted to fit nicely in a clearer 64-column listing. But SPECTRUM CHR$ 32 would be a disaster as the scrolling and syntax-colouring would overwrite the code almost immediately, causing Next to crash when it was called.

Unfortunately the NextZXOS NMI (yellow button) menu *always* uses LAYER 0, at the time of writing, so don't press that button while you have code running in the attribute area, or you'll need to resort to the red reset button soon after! It's absolutely fine to use the NMI menu *before* starting the slot routine, or *after you've turned it off* with a DRIVER command, so long as you return to some other display layer and reload the StreamModule before starting the stream again.

You could still edit in colour if you reassemble the code to run at the top of memory and CLEAR 63199 to protect it and its buffers. But that would lead to nasty noises when NextZXOS puts its own banks in the top 16k, for screen manipulation or BANK commands. If you are using extra BANKs you can probably afford to sacrifice some of the main program and variables memory and move your buffers below the 48k watermark where BASIC swaps stuff around.

There's no ideal memory map – it depends upon your program design and which features of BASIC you value most. For 40k of variables, sacrifice LAYER 0 and stream from display memory. For LAYER 0, put the buffers and code higher up. For extra BANKs *and* LAYER 0, it'll have to go somewhere in the middle, in the 24..48k area.

Beware of LAYER 1,1

Since LAYER 1,1 also uses 8x8 attributes, it's as hostile as LAYER 0 to code at 22K. But Timex HiColor mode uses 8x1 attributes, held in an extra 6k of RAM, hidden from BASIC. If sprites, hardware tiles and LAYER 2 aren't enough you can still tuck code down there and use attribute colour in LAYER 1,3, similar to the CPU-gobbling Radastan hack some demos use to increase vertical colour resolution. But in that case you'll need to move the stream buffers out of ULA memory, or limit the part of the screen where attributes show through to pixels that don't coincide with the screen buffer.

If you don't mind weird stuff flowing by at the top of the screen, and brief graunchy noises if you print over it, you can still use the other ULA layers: LoRes 1,0, Timex HiRes 1,2 or HiColor 1,3 while the music, or any other sampled audio, plays, with both code and buffers in ULA display memory.

If all this bank-management upsets you, you might be happier with SuperBASIC and the brand-new QL core! One of the main reasons Sinclair abandoned the Z80 for the 68008 was because the QL chip can directly address up to a megabyte of RAM – or 4096 MB for later 32-bit processors in the 680xx series.

Apple felt the same way when they ditched the 8-bit 6502 for the 68000-based Lisa and Mac systems. But this is a Sinclair Spectrum Next, an 8-bit processor with a 16-bit address bus and similarly constrained Z80-style DMA. Its quirky addressing is part of its charm, and without it this book would have been a great deal lighter.

Synaesthesia, sort-of

If you leave a stream playing by DMA from LAYER 0 memory, while editing 64 or 85-column BASIC, you'll see the audio data streaming through the top part of the screen as you try to work out where the cursor's hiding. The demo makes a feature of this.

In fact you can tell by eye when a track is fading down, or the run-out samples at the end of a long one-shot sample are reached, because of the characteristic appearance of quiet samples in display memory. File this with niche superpowers like knowing when a ZX tape is about to end by the high tone of trailing zeros, the regular pulse of cassette-borne arrays, or an even rarer and more retro ability to decipher punched cards or paper tape by glancing over the pattern of holes.

It's still possible to edit the program, using the unaffected lower lines of the screen, but when the listing scrolls or the top lines get redrawn you'll hear the graphics data rather than the expected samples, until the interrupt comes in and puts audio back into the corrupted buffers.

As long as the static machine code – as opposed to the streaming sample data – is intact, Next will still work fine despite this memory-sharing. But graphics data is rarely tuneful, and might be interpreted by the DACs as very loud high-frequency noise, so it's sensible to turn your amplifier down to protect your ears and speakers while attempting to edit and stream at the same time.

The drastic command OUT 107,131 will instantly stop the DMA and pause the screeching. The code in the driver slot will still be running, though only for a microsecond each frame as it won't detect any DMA activity signalling the need for buffer updates. So **.uninstall** or turn off the slot with a DRIVER command before you clobber the method code.

It's a pity that the system menus only work in ULA modes, but amusing that the DMA hammers on regardless. If you're willing to give up a couple of K of main memory by using StreamModule2, all the ULA layers are up for grabs again and you can whistle along as you're editing your program, though even a 1.5 MB looping choon may wear thin after much repetition. Version 2 shifts **method** to 65280, **fread** to 65404 and has **setUp** at 65420.

Sample Bank loading

After the sample rate and looping flag are assigned to variables, we load the slot driver and select the sample we want to play. We need at least two buffers-worth of data and no more than 1600k as we only have 100 banks to play with.

```
420 .install slot.drv
440 f$="Folk20k0.ub"
460 CLOSE # 4: OPEN # 4,f$: DIM #4 TO length
480 IF length>100*aBank THEN PRINT "Too long": CLOSE # 4: STOP
500 IF length<bSize*2 THEN PRINT "Too short": CLOSE # 4: STOP
520 %c= INT ((length-1)/aBank)+1:; Bank count
540 DIM b$(bSize): PROC S2H(4) TO h:h$= CHR$ h
550 PRINT ; : PRINT AT 17,1;"Loading ";f$
```

We could load the banks 16k at a time with **.extract**, but we've seen that approach, and its snags, before, so this demo uses the esxDOS FREAD hook to emulate multi-byte INPUT$ to a string. PROC S2H(), listed on page 85, gets the PLUS3DOS handle of an open file which esxDOS needs.

To avoid temporarily gobbling up lots of variable-space, the sample file is transferred to the bank via a string variable B$ dimensioned to the size of one DMA buffer. Bigger transfers use more RAM and may be slightly faster, but the greater benefit comes from using FREAD for multiple bytes, rather than thousands of INKEY$ #4 statements. The main loop, from line 590 to 740, allocates banks and loads samples into them:

```
580 left=length:store=banks
590 FOR %b=1 TO %c
600   PRINT AT 18,1;"Banking ";%b;" of ";%c
620   BANK NEW %t: POKE store,%t: store+=1: %o=0
```

```
640   REPEAT
660     WHILE left>=bSize
680     b$(1)=h$: left-= USR (%f,b$)
700     BANK %t POKE %o,b$: %o+=bSize
720   REPEAT UNTIL (%o)=aBank
740 NEXT %b
```

Unless the sample has been stretched or padded to a block boundary, we'll need to treat the last few bytes specially. The assumption here is that an aligned file, an exact multiple of **bSize** bytes in length, will have been tweaked to loop or tail off nicely. But if there are bytes left over we need to make sure that the final data buffer is full, by padding the end with silence. This is sample value 128, for wave amplitudes that vary up and down between 0 and 255.

```
760 IF left
780   DIM b$(left): b$(1)=h$: h= USR (%f,b$)
800   BANK %t POKE %o,b$+ CHR$ (128)*(bSize-left)
820    IF (%o)=aBank-bSize
840      %o=0: BANK NEW %t: POKE store,%t: %c+=1
860    ELSE %o+=bSize:; Runout continues in the last bank
880    ENDIF : BANK %t POKE %o, CHR$ (128)*bSize: %o+=bSize
900 ENDIF : DIM b$(1): CLOSE # 4
```

To avoid the clicks mentioned earlier, line 880 appends one half-buffer of silence, and line 840 allocates one extra bank for this if the padding filled the last bank already allocated for samples from the file. There is a subtle bug lurking here. Can you spot it, and how would you fix it? Does it really matter?

You might wonder why the array B$ is redimensioned twice in this little sequence. Line 780 trims it so FREAD doesn't read past the end of the sample file. Line 900 reduces it to the minimum size – since NextBASIC does not offer any command to entirely delete an array from memory – so it's not sitting around wasting space once loading is complete, while the main part of the program runs afterwards.

The whole file has now been loaded. Before triggering DMA, it only remains to prepare the **setUp** area. The sample rate and whether or not to loop it continuously is controlled by the **rate** and **loop** variables assigned just after loading the driver.

Setting up for streaming

```
 920 REM Initialise state
 940 POKE setUp, NOT loop,%c,0,%o~
 950 POKE offset,bSize*2~,0,bBase>>8
 960 REM Preload buffers
 980 POKE bBase, BANK PEEK banks PEEK$ (0,bSize)
1000 POKE bBase+bsize, BANK PEEK banks PEEK$ (bsize,bSize)
1020 PROC playDMA64k(bBase,bSize*2,rate,1)
1030 DRIVER 8,1,method
```

Line 940 initialises ONCE and COUNT, clears INDEX and sets TAIL. The tilde ~ at the end of the line ensures the last value is stored as a word, in two bytes, so we don't need a separate DPOKE. Line 950 works similarly for the data after the table of bank numbers, setting the offset word to account for the two preloaded buffers, clearing LAST, and setting CURRENT so the driver waits for the first buffer to pass before paging more in from the preallocated banks. Lines 980 and 1000 prime both output buffers.

PlayDMA64k() is the same PROC we've seen before this chapter, plus one extra line using command 187 to set the Read Mask so the high byte of the source address is returned via IN DMA:

```
1400 OUT dma,%187: OUT dma,%16: REM Report only Source high
```

Line 1030 sets the driver slot running. The method code refers directly to the setup and state bytes alongside, so there's no need for a data address in the driver call. That's hardly a limitation as we've only got one DMA channel. To switch to playing a different sample, pre-load it and POKE the bytes from ONCE to CURRENT for the fresh audio data. There's no need to reload the banks holding these samples to play them again, unless you've handed them back to NextZXOS with BANK CLEAR, **.clear** or NEW. But you must repeat the setup POKEs, to ensure the entire sample plays.

Something to look at

While that's running – and before I explain how to make it stop! – let's set up a display for NextBASIC to animate while the tune plays in the background. Ideally this would be a complete game, but we'll make do with a real-time view of the samples flowing through video memory, and a colourful pattern in LAYER 2.

At first we just loop, continuously updating a HiRes display of which part of the sample is playing. The Timex mode protects code in the LAYER 0 attribute area. Samples stream by in alternate bytes; the blank columns come from a separate 6k hidden in BANK 7, only paged in when NextZXOS explicitly writes to this 'Timex second screen' area.

When the last sample bank is reached, or a key is pressed, the demo falls into a grandly-named PROC GAME() which overlays a cone of radial lines, randomly updated, till you've had enough and press a key:

```
1040 REPEAT : PROC STATUS()
1050 REPEAT UNTIL CODE INKEY$ OR PEEK count-1= PEEK index
1060 PROC GAME()
```

These are the procedures called by the main loop:

```
1720 DEFPROC STATUS()
1740 PRINT AT 20,1; DPEEK offset; TAB 6;" in bank ";
1760 PRINT PEEK (setup+2); TAB 18;" buffer "; PEEK (offset+3)
1780 ENDPROC

1810 DEFPROC GAME()
1820 BORDER 0: LAYER 2,1: PAPER 33: CLS
1830 FOR x=229 TO 255: INK 227: PLOT x,0: DRAW 0,127: NEXT x
```

```
1840    REPEAT : INK RND (128)
1850    x= RND (227):y= RND (192)-96
1860    OVER 1: PLOT 113,96: DRAW 113-x,y: OVER 0
1870    PRINT AT 18,27; INK 255; DPEEK offset,
1880    PRINT AT 20,29; INK 212; PEEK (setup+2);" ";
1890 REPEAT UNTIL CODE INKEY$ : INK 255: PAPER 0
1900 ENDPROC
```

The TAB statements line up the display and insert spaces so that odd digits aren't left lying around when the length of INDEX (PEEK setup+2) decreases as each loop repeats. PROC GAME() put similar information in the right-hand margin, under a 'window' into the stream buffers, with an animated pattern occupying the remainder of the screen.

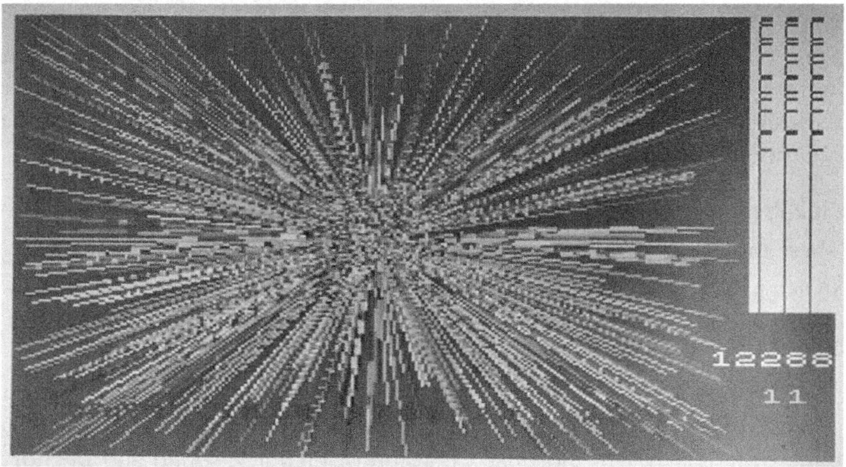

Figure 79 – Layer 2 animation with fading samples in LAYER 0 buffers exposed, top right

Line 1820 wipes LAYER 2, then line 1830 floods the top right corner in transparent 'ink', colour 227. This allows part of the hi-res LAYER 1,2 screen to show through, revealing continuous DMA activity.

Colour combinations

You might wonder why line 1840 only uses half of the potential INK colours. This masks a subtlety of OVER 1, random INKs and transparency. We know that in a default configuration INK 227 is transparent. My first version of this loop used INK RND(256) but I soon noticed that some pixels were flickering even when the random lines didn't touch them. Aha, I thought, I should exclude INK 227 from the random set. But that didn't fix the flicker.

In byte-per pixel modes, OVER 1 works by combining the current pixel colour with the random INK. Since OVER 1 uses exclusive OR, defying patent trolls and allowing two lines of the same INK to cancel out, there's a possibility that two successive PLOT or DRAW statements might leave 227 in the pixel, even though INK 227 wasn't used either time.

Consider the bit-patterns; in binary, 227 is @1110 0011. There are 512 pairs of INK values that will leave a pixel with that pattern. The obvious one is to use INK 0 then INK 227, or vice versa. My dodgy fix precluded that. But what of the other 510 possibilities, like overlaying INK 3 (@0000 0011) with INK 224 (@1110 0000). OVER 1 mashes the bits together and leaves INK 227. Two cheeky Timex HiRes pixels show through the LAYER 2 overlay, fizzing excitedly as streamed samples change their value.

To prevent such artefacts, which might be distracting, we must avoid using any pair of INKs that combine into the transparent index 227. There are many ways to ensure that – we might only pick even INKs, so bit **0** never gets set. I tackled the glitch from the opposite end, using random INK numbers from 0 to 127, so that bit **7** is always zero. Six similar fixes all yield a different subset of colours, all excluding half the palette. Try them all – hint, in three cases you'll need to force bits to be set rather than clear. Many other fixes are available if you can live with fewer than 128 colours. Transparency is a tricky business!

Cleaning up

These three lines turn off the driver and DMA, and release allocated banks:

```
1070 DRIVER 8,1,0: OUT dma,131
1080 FOR %b=banks TO banks+(%c-1): BANK % PEEK b CLEAR: NEXT %b
1090 %c=0:.uninstall slot.drv
```

We have explored the topics of transparency, slot methods and drivers in other chapters. We've seen (and heard) that the best way to enjoy Next is to think of it as a system, not just a mashup of graphics, sound and memory components.

I find the most thrilling experience of hobby programming comes when parts interact, leading to 'emergent behaviour'. If this happens on a modern computer, you may never get to the bottom of what's going on.

After 40-odd years we've just about worked out all the quirks of the 16k Spectrum, though it took most of that time, and the genius of Chris Smith, author of '*The Spectrum ULA, How to Design a Microcomputer*' to fully unravel mysteries like the 'snow effect', or the slight shadow sometimes visible beside flashing characters, which Chris rode down to a single transistor. Grokking Next will take longer, and it's a moving target. Fun, though!

Chapter 14, Better BEEPs

The original ZX Spectrum audio system used a single digital output wire to deliver rudimentary sound via a small speaker – loudspeaker would be a misnomer. In this it was an advance on earlier micros like the ZX80, ZX81, TRS-80 and Pet, closer to the capability of the Apple][, and similarly dependent upon monopolising the processor to generate a sequence of regularly-spaced clicks. A low buzz was the highest 'note' attainable via a loop toggling the corresponding hardware bit, like this:

```
1 OUT 254,16: OUT 254,0: GO TO 1
```

The corresponding Z80 OUT and JP instructions are hundreds of times faster, capable of clicking fast enough to cover the entire audible range of pitches, and upwards into the ultrasonic realm of bats. Programmed delays between the OUT instructions allow arbitrary pitches to sound. For instance a 2 ms delay between OUTs gives a regular pulse that repeats 250 times per second corresponding to a musical note near the middle of a piano keyboard.

Such a pulse sequence should theoretically generate a square wave, like the castellations atop a mediaeval tower, but in practice the measured waveform is not so symmetrical. That's understandable as infinite power would be instantaneously needed to generate a perfectly vertical spike. Real-world components cause the wave to overshoot vertically, in amplitude, and slew horizontally, in time, in a pitch-dependent way, as shown in Figure 80 below for BEEP 8,48 output by a 48k Spectrum.

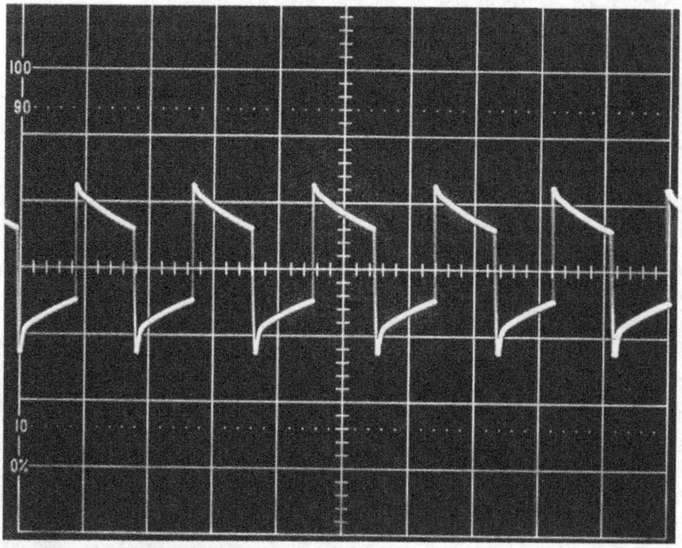

Figure 80 – A BEEP 8,48 waveform, oscillographed by Matthew Logue for Beep to Boom

As Steve Jobs perceptively observed, the natural world is full of curves and (roughly) straight lines are almost always artefacts of human activity.

Speech and music waveforms follow curves, which is why humans struggle to sing like a computer cassette output and BEEP falls some way short of music, to the unpractised ear. Next is not limited to regular rectangular audio pulses, but in this chapter we'll give those a comprehensive work-out, from the earpoints of both sound designers and programmers.

How BEEP works

In principle the equivalent Z80 BEEP code corresponds line-for line with the BASIC, except that the output values and port number must be set in separate lines of machine code:

```
LOOP:  LD A,16
       OUT (254),A
       LD A,0
       OUT (254),A
       JR LOOP
```

An experienced Z80 programmer would save a byte and three cycles by clearing the accumulator with XOR A instead of LD A,0, then potentially use the byte saved to replace the relative jump JR with a JP, which is longer but faster as it doesn't require the CPU to add the loop offset onto the address where the instruction is loaded. Still, the correspondence with BASIC is clear.

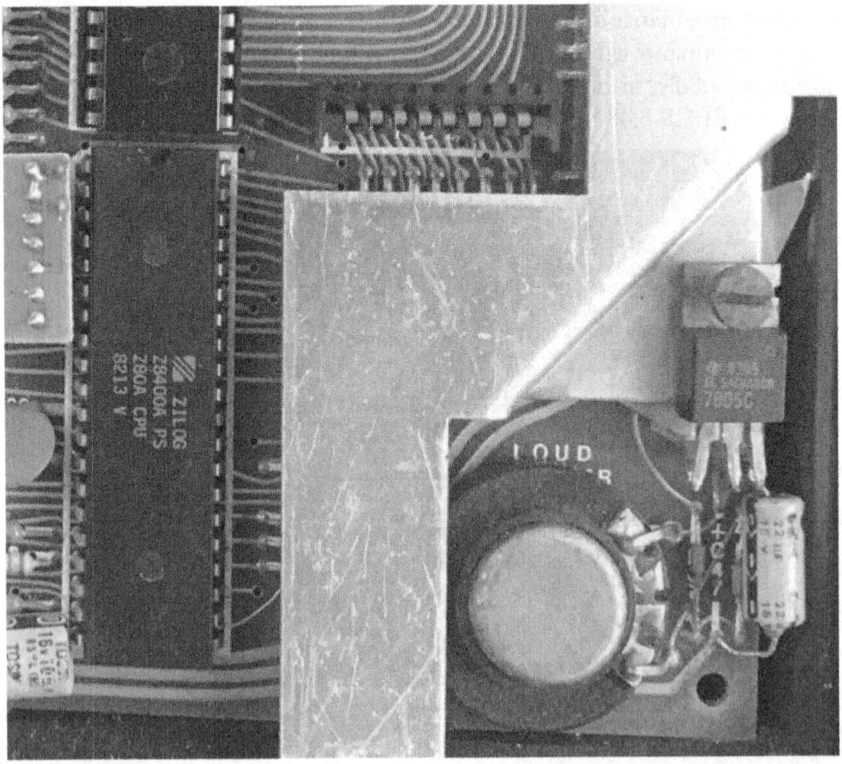

Figure 81 – The speaker squeezed into the corner of the issue 1 Spectrum circuit-board

The word 'LOUD' printed alongside the tiny speaker in the lower right corner of the issue 1 Spectrum circuit board was wisely deleted from later revisions. It never was LOUD by any stretch, though later revisions boosted it somewhat by driving it from a higher supply voltage. KS1 Next boards were designed to drive a similar high-impedance speaker, perhaps via a booster transistor, but KS2 ones expect a small audio amplifier.

Complicated timing

In practice such a simple loop would not be used, for three reasons. Firstly, it offers no way out other than reset. A check for a key-press would be included so the loop can be interrupted. If system interrupts are enabled, we could check the value at address 23560, LASTK, and break the loop if that changes to hold any non-zero value, corresponding to some key other than a shift being pressed, or for a specific value like 32, the ASCII code for a space.

In principle that would work, but the note would sound ragged because 50 or 60 times per second (depending on the display configuration) the system interrupt would momentarily pause the loop as it does its business. We could wrap the loop in DI and EI instructions to disable interrupts before and re-renable them afterwards, but then LASTK won't change however hard you hammer at the keyboard, and reset is still the only way out.

To work around ***that*** we must directly read the keyboard matrix from within the loop. For instance, `XOR A; IN A,(254); AND 31` leaves 31 in A if no key is pressed, otherwise some other value. Different IN instructions are needed if you're fussed about which key is pressed, as noted at the end of Chapter 23 of Spectrum manuals, but this means going beyond the scope of a chapter about sounds, and that's only snag number one.

The second snag of our tiny loop is that it's so short that it will only generate ultrasonic sounds. An additional delay between each OUT instruction is needed to bring the sequence of pulses down to a speed a speaker can move at and mammalian ears can detect.

Snag number three is more subtle, and affects the timbre of the note, most of all in the slower BASIC version but to some extent in machine-code too. The jump or GO TO from the end of the loop back to the start makes the tone asymmetrical, as more time is spent outputting 0 than 16. It sounds buzzy and flat unless the loop is padded so that both paths take exactly the same number of CPU cycles.

Expert Z80 programmers make balanced loops in order to write cassette or MIDI data, or mix and play back samples SpecDrum-style, but to do this you need to carefully look up every line in a table of instruction timings, accounting for the different time spent depending on whether a conditional jump is taken or ignored, and the delay associated with access to these ports, which the ULA gets priority access to.

After all that, there's still no volume control, and the processor remains tied up for the duration of the sound. The tone is harsh, an approximation to the physically-unattainable square waveform, with discordant harmonics at odd intervals across the spectrum and no filters other than the limited range of the toy speaker to smooth the sound.

Nonetheless it was used to add vital audio cues to almost all early Spectrum games, bursts of music and even barely-intelligible speech synthesis, by nothing more than ingenious fine variation of the interval between clicks.

Australian programmer Steve Taylor took this approach to extremes when creating the effects for the Spectrum version of the Melbourne House karate hit *Way of the Exploding Fist.* All of the sound effects in that game were generated by feeding raw data from the original 16k Spectrum ROM directly to the one-bit beeper, experimenting with different start addresses till a suitable sound was discovered.

The history of digital audio synthesis

Books have been written about such experiments. For a detailed analysis of early beep routines, consult Abertay lecturer Ken McAlpine's book '*Bits and Pieces*', or his freely-available 2015 Computer Games Journal paper '*All aboard the Impulse Train*' which deconstructs the two-channel Manic Miner music.

For broader but no less technical insights, the Audio Engineering Society commissioned me to write a book, *Beep to Boom*, published by Routledge in 2019. That book includes a chapter about early audio hardware including three-note home-computer chips like the AY-3-8912 used in Spectrum 128s, the similar SN76489 used in Acorn, Coleco, Memotech, Tatung and some Tandy and IBM micros, and Commodore's unique SID. The entire volume (sic) covers the development of 'advanced interactive runtime sound systems' from Alan Turing's insistence that early British computers should all have speakers, long before they had displays, up to Ambisonic 3D, *Grand Theft Auto* and beyond.

ZX bit-wranglers were rescued in 1985 when Investronica and later Timex and Sinclair soldered up an AY-3-8912 to take these chores away from the CPU. The Spectrum 128's sound chip does all the counting and timing for us, without tying up the processor. It gets the Tech Tips treatment here because it is reimplemented three times over in Next's FPGA core, and both its rivals SN76489 and SID feature in the Acorn BBC Micro cores for Next hardware.

An early proposal to include a SID in Next's core was ruled out for licensing reasons, but 'unofficial' cores need have no such scruples. The Acorn cores and their audio extras are explored later in final last chapter of this volume; this chapter concentrates on taming the AY-3-8912s.

The NextBASIC procedures presented here marshal the chip sub-systems in a programmer-friendly way. Next can also play pre-recorded samples, as we've seen in the previous chapter about DAC and DMA hardware, but that is substantially more expensive in terms of RAM and other scarce hardware resources than setting one of the sound chips warbling away. So it makes sense to use both, favouring the AY-3-8912s for interactive sound effects.

Before delving into the silicon we should pause audio for a moment and consider how Next keeps track of time. This is vital information for anyone programming Next who wants their efforts to work well on computers other than their own. The timings of sound effects and graphical output alike vary depending on the machine's configuration.

The original Spectrums all ran at a clock-speed of around 3.5 MHz (3,500,000 pulses per second) and output a complete screen of 256x192 pixels 50 times per second. Next supports higher clock speeds and – as a practical concession to the global display market – other rates of display output.

Cranking up the CPU speed affects both the pitch and duration of BEEP commands, and display tweaks mean that PAUSE 50 cannot be relied upon to wait exactly a second unless the screen in use happens to work at just the speed which was standard in the UK in 1982. So the next section of this chapter is relevant to anyone planning real-time programming on Next, with sound or without, building on insights from Chapter 3, Screen Selections.

Real-time redefined

Four procedures are provided to keep track of the difference between time as measured by the hardware clocks inside the Spectrum Next and Newtonian time in the world outside. These are irrelevant on a Spectrum 128 as those machines always use the same CPU clock and display rate. Next varies the former to speed up the system, in binary steps nominally from 3.5 to 28 MHz, controlled by RUN AT, REG commands or NextZXOS menus.

Next also combinatorially speeds up or retards the whole system to suit displays made for non-Spectrum locales or applications, which might otherwise reject video frames output 50 times per second, matching the European PAL TV standard targeted by Sinclair and Amstrad. TVs made only for use in Japan or North America expect 60 frames per second, and computer monitors often require other rates. We've seen that the closer the rate is to 50 Hertz (cycles per second) the better the compatibility of Next with games for the original hardware, but the more difficult it may be to find an otherwise-suitable screen, especially outside Europe.

All this matters in the context of sound, as well as the 'twitch game' genre, because changes to the display timing also affect the CPU clock, and that of the soundchip which is synchronised with it in hardware. Without compensation, tunes played on a Spectrum with a PC-spec VGA6 screen (refreshed at 59 Hertz) will play noticeably sharp and too fast compared with an original Spectrum 128 or the same Next with a SCART or VGA0 (50 Hertz monitor) set-up. In fact a 48k Spectrum BEEPs a fifth of a semitone flat compared with a 128, due to a subtle difference in processor clock-speed.

The procedures which enable us to make animations, pitches and durations consistent regardless of display settings are called GETCLOCKFACTOR(), GETCLOCKRATIO(), GETMHz() and GETmsPERFRAME(). They all return a number. None of them take any parameters.

PROC GETCLOCKFACTOR( ) returns the factor by which the CPU and soundchip clocks are adjusted to suit a display not tolerant of authentic 50 frame per second display updates. The factor is 1 for a fully-compatible screen and greater if the frame rate exceeds 50 Hertz. These figures are derived from the table of tiny numbers alongside the documentation for REG 17 in the original Next manual. The correct HDMI (VGA7) value for later cores in the v3.x.x series may be 50.0 rather than 48.2, especially on KS2 shipments, but that depends on the outcome of experiments still underway.

```
4040 DEFPROC GETCLOCKFACTOR()
4080 LOCAL %v,fps:%v=% REG 17 & 7
4090 REM PRINT "VGA ";%v
4100 IF %v<2 THEN fps=%50+v: ENDPROC =fps
4110 IF %v=7 THEN fps=48.2: ENDPROC =fps
4120 IF %v<4 THEN fps=%v:fps=fps+50.6: ENDPROC =fps
4130 IF %v=4 THEN fps=55.4
4140 IF %v=5 THEN fps=57.1
4150 IF %v=6 THEN fps=59
4160 ENDPROC =fps
```

I plan to update this to use REG 1 and REG 14 to check the core version and tweak accordingly, when the dust settles and I'm sure of the implications of each release. In the meantime if your Next has a hardware clock fitted you can find out the actual frame rate for any setting of your own computer with PROC REALTIME() from http://simon.mooli.org.uk/nextech/#Timers though some of the functions earlier in that 2020 demo are redundant since NextBASIC 2.08 gained the TIME keyword.

PROC GETCLOCKRATIO( ) returns the factor by which the clock speed of the Next's CPU and sound chip is accelerated by RUN AT, not including any further change caused by display adaptation. For RUN AT 0, 1, 2 or 3 it returns 1, 2, 4 or 8 respectively.

```
4310 DEFPROC GETCLOCKRATIO()
4320 LOCAL t:t=% REG 7 & 3
4330 IF t<2 THEN ENDPROC =t+1
4340 ENDPROC =4*(t-1)
```

PROC GETMHz( ) returns the effective clock speed of the Next's CPU after allowing for RUN AT and the display output setting, as a decimal number of Megahertz e.g. 3.5 or 33.04.

```
4200 DEFPROC GETMHz()
4210 LOCAL f,r
4220 PROC GETCLOCKFACTOR() TO f
4225 PROC GETCLOCKRATIO() TO r
4230 ENDPROC =f/50*r*3500000
```

The **GETmsPERFRAME()** procedure returns the actual number of milliseconds between display frame updates, taking account of the 50/60 Hertz setting, VGA or HDMI mode, and any acceleration contributed by RUN AT. It can be used to derive consistent delays, within the limited precision of counting complete frames.

```
4250 DEFPROC GETmsPERFRAME()
4260 LOCAL f
4270 PROC GETCLOCKFACTOR() TO f
4280 IF % REG 5&4 THEN f=f*1.2: REM 60 Hz
4290 ENDPROC =1000/f
```

GETmsPERFRAME() will be used later in the helper procedures AYPLAYDATA() and TRUEPAUSE()... With that timely advice we can wave goodbye to BEEP, and any deaf readers who couldn't care less about interactive audio, and spend the rest of this chapter delving into the inner workings of chips that can play tones and noises while leaving the Z80 free for other purposes.

The AY sound chips

Old or new, ZX BASIC lacks interactive support for sound. Whether you use the original BEEP, or the Spectrum 128's three-channel General Instrument soundchip via PLAY, your BASIC program stops and waits for the sound to finish before continuing.

This need not be so. The AY-3-8912 is capable of generating three tones plus pseudo-random digital noise, without any need for intervention from the Z80 processor which runs BASIC. It can also make the combined volume fluctuate, in simple ways, automatically.

The challenge Sinclair left unaddressed was how to control this from BASIC, but the original ROM maestros Nine Tiles left enough capability even in the original ZX BASIC for that to be possible. The trick is to hammer away on two of the Z80 input/output ports which provide byte-wide communication with peripherals.

Each of Next's built-in 'AY chips' has 14 internal audio-control registers (and a pair of redundant ones). These hold numbers that determine channel volume levels, time delays and routing of pulses. They control what's known as a state-machine – selecting and cycling endlessly through a pre-ordained sequence at a preset fraction of Next's system clock rate.

Hundreds of thousands of times a second the AY-3-8912 hardware 'ticks' and cycles through its registers, checking and adjusting them; every 16 ticks it considers whether or not to toggle each of the three tone channel outputs between high and low logic levels, and applies a 16-level ear-compensated volume control to the result; every 256 ticks it considers adjusting any of those volume controls up or down, if the envelope controller is also active.

The next section goes into more detail about the hardware, before we wrap it up in a comprehensive set of BASIC procedures that make all the features relatively easy to control from your own programs.

AY-3-8912 architecture

The following photograph shows the internal structure of the chip; while Next's FPGA is logically and sonically equivalent, the layout differs. Most of the following analysis is equally applicable to Next, the Spectrum 128 or other micros such as Oric, Amstrad CPC, Intellivision, Vectrex, MSX and Atari STs, all built around the same chip with minor wiring variations.

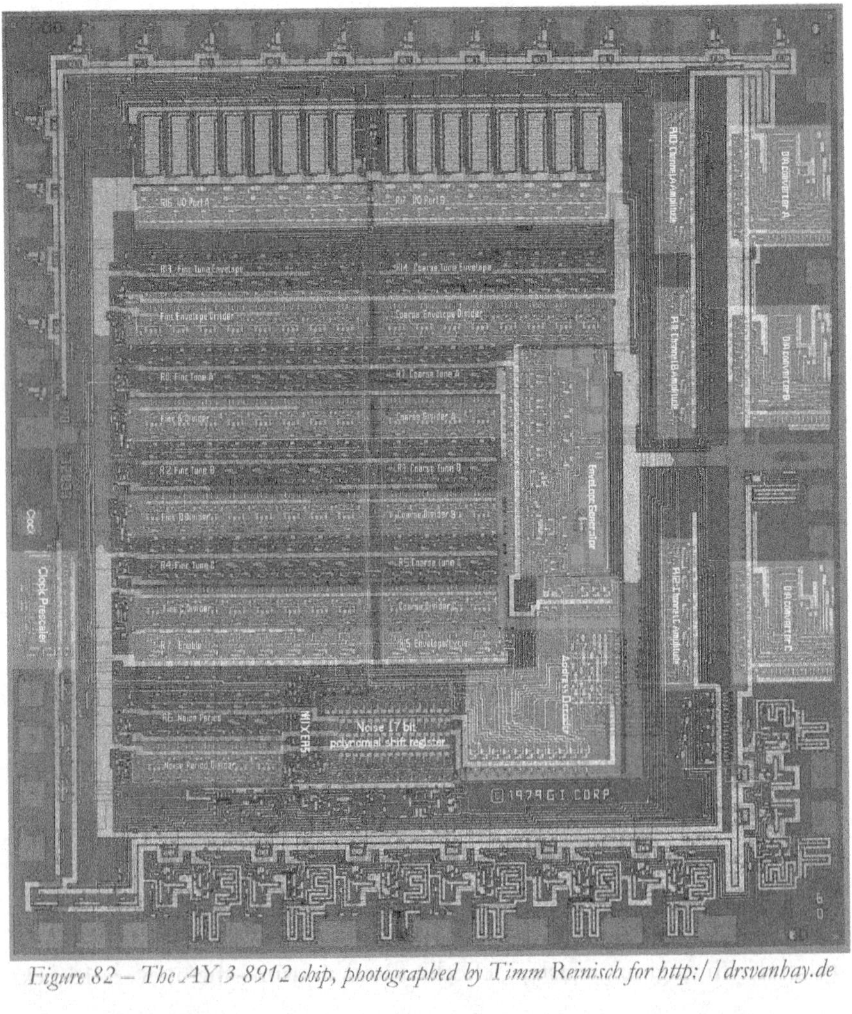

Figure 82 – The AY 3 8912 chip, photographed by Timm Reinisch for http://drsvanhay.de

The photograph of the chip die in Figure 82 makes the Programmable Sound Generator look rather complicated, and the official documentation hardly helps, starting off with wiring details for the peculiar CP1610 processor that first used this chip in Mattel's 1979 Intellivision console. The documentation goes on to number the chip registers in Octal, base 8, so R10 comes right after R7 and R11 is what most humans would call R9. With that in mind, Figure 83 lists the registers and shows how the eight bits within each register are assigned.

The hatched areas are undefined – values written to those bits are ignored – so you can see that although two bytes, 16 bits, are reserved for the 'tone period' control on each of the three channels, A, B and C, only 12 bits are significant and you have to split those with bitwise operations – much easier in Next than ZX BASIC – and write the most significant four bits of the value to the following register, much as addresses in Z80 code and ZX system variables are spread over two bytes, though 16-bit addressing means all the bits are significant to a Z80.

REGISTER		B7	B6	B5	B4	B3	B2	B1	B0
R0	Channel A Tone Period	8-BIT Fine Tune A							
R1						4-BIT Coarse Tune A			
R2	Channel B Tone Period	8-BIT Fine Tune B							
R3						4-BIT Coarse Tune B			
R4	Channel C Tone Period	8-BIT Fine Tune C							
R5						4-BIT Coarse Tune C			
R6	Noise Period				5-BIT Period Control				
R7	Enable	IN/OUT		Noise			Tone		
		IOB	IOA	C	B	A	C	B	A
R10	Channel A Amplitude				M	L3	L2	L1	L0
R11	Channel B Amplitude				M	L3	L2	L1	L0
R12	Channel C Amplitude				M	L3	L2	L1	L0
R13	Envelope Period	8-BIT Fine Tune E							
R14		8-BIT Coarse Tune E							
R15	Envelope Shape/Cycle					CONT.	ATT.	ALT.	HOLD

Figure 83 – The official AY-3-8912 PSG register map (General Instrument)

The separation of controls into byte-sized registers, with between four and eight significant bits in each, is logical enough, but the way they're mapped to Z80 ports is indirect, another consequence of the CP1610 design. Rather than allocate one port address to each register, in the style of Next's own REG array, all of the AY internal registers are selected for reading and writing from the same port number 65533, given the name **ayR** (for AY chip Register number) in the following program snippets.

To determine which register that port accesses you must first write the register number (in octal if you insist, though we'll use decimal here) to another port, with OUT 49149. So the simplest interaction, to set the 'noise period', takes two steps: OUT 49149,6 to pick the register and then OUT 65533,N where N is a value between 1 and 31, to set the pitch of the sound, lower values being higher pitches and 0 being treated the same way as 1. Values above 31 are taken modulo 32, as if the hardware was applying the bitwise mask &31, so 33 is treated as 1 and 255 is interpreted as if 31 had been written, each time considering the top three bits of the byte to be zero.

Stereophonic options

Spectrum 128 output was mixed-down from three channels to one to suit mono TVs, but Next also supports two stereo set-ups. The order in which channels are arranged in stereo from left to right is configurable. Some add-on boards array them left to right from A to C, with B in the middle, and others differently but equally logically still put A on the left but then pan B right and C in the middle. Those follow the traditional mapping of initial channels to Left and Right respectively, and the mnemonic C for Centre.

Toggling between these two conventions may make music authored that way sound more authentic, especially if sounds are deliberately panned across the stereo field. Bit 5 of REG 8 is termed the *PSG Stereo Mode Control*, where "PSG" stands for Programmable Sound Generator. 0 gives ABC order and setting the bit yields ACB.

To avoid changing the other bits in that register – which could turn PSGs 2 and 3 off, or affect other parts of the system including keyboard, Timex video or memory performance – it's necessary to read all the bits first and change only bit 5. NextBASIC's bitwise and operator, **&**, makes this far easier than it would be in ZX BASIC. To force ABC order, clear bit 5 like this:

```
REG 8,%@11011111 & REG 8
```

All three chips are also available in older Spectrum Next personalities, as long as TurboSound is enabled, but the following incantation is required to achieve the same effect in ZX BASIC. For clarity three temporary variables are used: **t8** holds all eight bits from the port; the lower five of those are isolated in **t5**, then the top two bits in **t2**. After finding those we can write back the original value, but with bit 5 excluded, by adding them together:

```
OUT 9275,8
LET t8= IN 9531
LET t5= t8- INT (t8/32)*32
LET t2= INT (t8/64)*64
OUT 9531,t2+t5
```

The NextBASIC pattern %@11011111 in the REG version is equivalent to ZX BASIC's BIN 11011111, but stored in five fewer bytes. The decimal value 223 is identical, as it is 255-32 where 255 represents all bits of a byte set and 32 corresponds to bit 5, as bits on a microprocessor are conventionally numbered from right to left, starting at 0.

Some non-PC IBMs count upwards in the opposite direction – and the committee-created Algol 68 programming language does that starting from 1, so bit one is its most significant – but they're exceptions. When micro enthusiasts refer to bit zero they almost always mean the least-significant bit of a byte or word: the one that makes it either odd or even. Here's how we put Next channels into ACB order:

```
REG 8,%@11011111 & REG 8 | @100000
```

In ZX BASIC you'd need to repeat the five-line spell above and add 32 to the final OUT expression, to set bit 5, making it OUT 9531,t2+t5**+32**.

In NextBASIC, in this case, we can use either **|**, the bitwise OR operator, or **+** (simple addition) to combine the old and new values. If one of the bits may already be set, it's safer to pick **|** as we'll see later. It's normal to call the pattern used to select or exclude bits the 'mask' because of the way it hides some bits and reveals others.

Before returning to music, I should note (sic) that there are three bits which over-ride the stereo setting, mixing the output of the corresponding sound chip equally into both output channels.

Bit 5 of NextReg 9 makes the first AY mono, while bits 6 and 7 do the same for the second and third sound chip. So this NextZXOS instruction puts all three into mono, which may sound better if you have an old single-speaker television or minimal SCART cable:

```
REG 9,%@00011111 & REG 9+@11100000
```

PSG block diagram

Figure 84 shows a block diagram of an AY chip from an audio programmer's point of view. The labels R0 to R13 (in decimal, this time!) appear alongside each register. Timing signals arrive at the top left corner. Identical copies are distributed to the channel and noise counters after scaling down by a factor of 16; this flow is shown by the vertical arrows on the left.

Register numbers 0 to 6 set up the counts for each channel, and the noise option. Only one register, R6, is needed for the noise counter as it has only five bits, versus 12 for the more finely-controlled tones. R6 decides how often bits from the pseudo-random number generator hardware get passed on to the three channels.

Six bits in R7 enable output of either tone or noise, or both, from each channel. Three mixes of tone and noise are fed into three volume controls, shown as Volume A, B and C blocks, before digital to analogue conversion.

Volume control can be manual, by setting registers 8, 9, and 10 (decimal!) to a value from 0 to 15, or automated by setting any of those to 16, which puts the Envelope Shaper, configured by R13, in control. The envelope shapes are explained and diagrammatically represented in Figure 90 alongside the description of PROC AYENVELOPE() later.

Signal flow

The timing clock for the slower-stepping envelope counter is divided again and fed into the Envelope Counter, controlled by R11 and R12, which sends regular pulses at the interval they prescribe to the Shaper. The vertical lines down from that block feed identically into each channel volume control, and are ignored unless those controls are set to 16, to give the envelope priority.

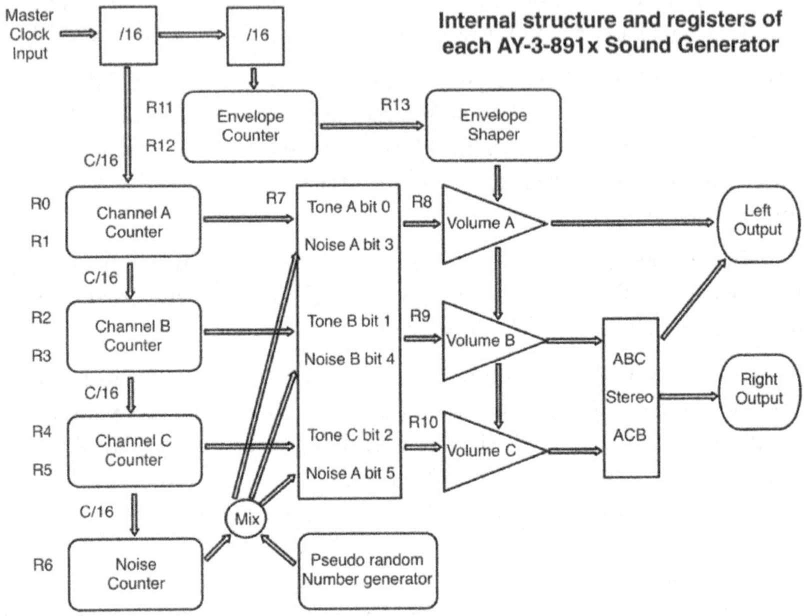

Figure 84 – Blocks and paths in each of Next's three Programmable Sound Generators

Much of the chip logic consists of hardware counters, which are set to a target value by register writes and then trigger an output pulse whenever the count is reached, before resetting the counter so a regular train of pulses is output. The higher the count, the longer the interval between pulses.

The 3.5 MHz master timing clock signal is divided by 16 (accounting for the unused bits in registers 1, 3 and 5) then applied to the tone or noise channel counters. The noise control differs in that it allows pseudo-random bits from a shift register into the mix. There's only one random noise generator but it can be mixed in with any or all of the tone channels, or disabled.

Apart from their stereo endpoint each tone channel is equivalent and they each have an independent volume control, mapped to registers 8, 9 and 10 for channels A, B and C. These affects the volume of the corresponding tone, and any noise mixed in with it. Register 7 contains six single-bit controls – the top two are unimplemented by Next, though one is associated with the keypad and printer ports on a Spectrum 128. The other three pairs of bits select noise or tone output for each channel. They're arranged in two clumps, for tone and noise respectively, rather than adjacent pairs for each channel.

To make this more confusing for programmers, the bits must be set to 0 to turn the output ON, and 1 to turn it OFF. Hardware designers bury this information in their diagrams by drawing a horizontal line above the name of the bit, or the function of several, as they see fit.

One of the key purposes of the NextBASIC routines presented here is to hide such eccentricities and register-slicings from the programmer. The examples can be directly converted to machine code by doing the arithmetic in Z80 registers with instructions like AND, OR and RLCA to sift and align the bits, then putting the port address in BC and using OUT (C) instructions to select and set each register.

The last three registers, numbered 11 to 13 by humans or 13 to 15 by octal enthusiasts, provide automatic volume changes, using a similar counting scheme but with a full 16-bit period, allowing subsonic modulation akin to a tremolo effect. In this case the master clock is divided by 256 rather than 16, which in conjunction with the 16-bit counter gives a maximum interval between automatic volume changes of 4.8 seconds, with an envelope period of 65535, and a minimum interval of just 73 us, fast enough for the envelope to layer an additional tone over a channel – perhaps a bassier triangle or sawtooth waveform, rather than a square beep. There's only one envelope generator per chip. It can be applied to any, all or none of the three channels, using a dummy value of 16 in the channel volume (amplitude) register.

There are three ways of silencing a channel; you can turn it off via control bits in register 7, by setting a volume of zero, or by setting the tone period count so small that the clicks are inaudibly high in pitch. Rather as in Z80 programming, the most efficient choice depends on what you're planning to do next. The NextBASIC procedures AYBEEP and AYNOISE do the bit-fiddling for you, but you can also mute one channel quickly by just clearing its volume. The counters never stop, and the channel will be heard again as soon as you give it a non-zero volume.

Any wave you like, as long as it's square

Figure 85 shows the sorts of waveforms the AY tone channel hardware is designed to generate. The numbers on the left correspond directly to the counter values and inversely to the perceived pitch of the sound. Bigger numbers imply longer delays and hence lower notes. The height of the wave varies with the volume setting.

We've seen that the actual waves that reach our ears are not so square, and should bear in mind that the AY's volume steps are sensibly chosen to match the nonlinearity of human hearing; in practice volume 2 will be more than twice the amplitude of volume 1, and the intervals progressively widen so the step from 12 to 15, say, sounds equivalent to that from three to six or seven to ten.

Such 'psychoacoustic normalisation' occurs in the DAC (Digital to Analogue converter) parts on the right-hand side of the chip; programmers can generally rely on the step between each volume setting sounding smooth even though it doesn't look that way to a linear meter. Bear it in mind if you try to play samples through AY channels, rather than Next's linear DACs.

The Noise outputs are just as square-cornered but introduce variations in pulse-width, randomised within the range set by the noise counter register 6. This roughens up the sound distinctively, if no more naturally. Numerical analysis of the 31 'noise tones' won't get you far – the first part of our demo program lets us audition them, far more productively.

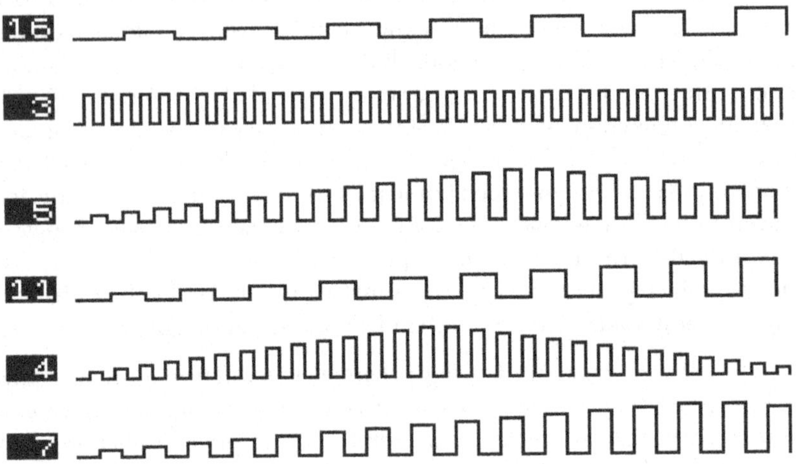

Figure 85 – Idealised PSG channel output waveforms at various fixed frequencies

Making Tones

This remainder of this chapter describes an audio-visual demo program and NextBASIC utility library, VBEEP.BAS, which I created back in 2020 in response to questions from Next pioneers calling for better ways to generate interactive sounds. Unlike PLAY in 128 BASIC, or add-on drivers written to replay custom-baked tunes, the focus here is providing audible feedback to game players and hobbyists, responding smoothly and immediately to their actions. Along the way the strengths and limitations of NextBASIC and the AY-3-8912 hardware are laid bare.

The name VBEEP stands for 'virtual BEEP'. This started out as a way to use the AY chip to mimic the classic Spectrum BASIC BEEP command without monopolising the processor. It has grown to support nine-channel output, manual and automatic volume controls, and other sounds beyond the limited gamut of BEEP.

The first part of VBEEP.BAS sets up a HiRes screen, resets the chips and reports their configuration, then falls into an interactive audio-visual demonstration. The middle of the file comprises NextBASIC procedures to control the sound chips. These can be MERGEd into your own programs or run from a bank. Matt Langley's Next Horizon suite includes these in its Sound module of handy ready-packaged routines.

Main procedures
AYBEEP,
AYBEEPW,
AYENVELOPE,
AYMUTE,
AYNOISE,
AYSELECT,
AYSELECTED,
AYREG,
AYSTATUS,
AYVOLUME,
AYVOLUMES,
GETENV,
GETPERIOD,
GETRATE,
GETVOL

The adjoining tables list the names of 14 procedures used to control and monitor AY sound. Another dozen 'support procedures' in the same file help with testing and configuration. If an invalid parameter is passed to any of these procedures they STOP, showing the number of the checking line and listing the procedure concerned.

To show how these fit together, there are five demo procedures; These are FSCALE, KINETIC, MAHLER, MAHLER2, and TSCALE. KINETIC is the most complicated of those and also includes synchronised graphics.

Support procedures
AYCHORD,
AYEXTRAS,
AYPLAYDATA,
AYSTATUS,
GETCLOCKFACTOR,
GETCLOCKRATIO,
GETMHz,
GETmsPERFRAME,
SH, SH3,
TRUEBEEP,
TRUEPAUSE

Parameter checks soak up processor time and are not always vital, so some of the main procedures are reworked as faster versions, using multi-statement lines and skipping sanity-checks to save time. They'd be even faster without the LOCAL statements, but those make them easier to embed in programs already using integer variables without unwanted side-effects. These 'optimised procedures' have F (for fast) rather than AY at the start of their names.

Beware: FBEEP, FBEEPW, FENV, FINIT, FMUTE and FVOL fail arbitrarily, but without doing any damage, if passed invalid parameters. Test first with the AY equivalents and only replace those with F-versions once you are confident the right values will always be passed to them.

Audio initialisation

VBEEP.BAS starts by assigning symbolic names for key parts of the AY hardware. An OUT instruction to **ayR** selects one of the 14 control registers within the chip. After that, a new value for that register can then be set with another OUT to port address **ayD**, or an IN from **ayD** to check the current value – a feature absent from the first Sinclair implementation.

The names **ayA**, **ayB** and **ayC** correspond to bit-patterns used to select one or several of the sound channels. These run from 1 to 4, rather than 0 to

2, with a deliberate gap at 3, so combinations can be selected with simple addition, e.g. **ayA+ayC** excludes channel **ayB**. These variables make the rest of the program easier to understand than would be the case if the corresponding 'magic numbers' were used, though at some cost in speed.

PROCs are then called to select AY device 0 – the hardware numbers the PSGs from 0 to 2 – and to make sure it's in ready for use, by setting the components to well-defined states. This is important discipline because other programs may have left parts of the chip running but not necessarily audible. State-machine programming can be very frustrating unless the machine starts off in a known state! Here's the complete initialisation routine:

```
1000 REM VBEEP 1.7 by Simon N Goodwin, June 2020..January 2024
1010 REM For all NextBASIC versions 2.0+
1020 LAYER 1,2: REM HiRes gives clearer reports
1030 LET ayD=49149
1040 LET ayR=65533
1050 LET ayA=1: REM Channel masks
1060 LET ayB=2
1070 LET ayC=4
1080 PROC AYSELECT(0): PROC SH(): REM Chip select, 0..2
1090 PROC AYNOISE(0,0): PROC FINIT()
```

These routines have been written for the first release of NextBASIC 2 so they could be optimised for the latest distro, by removing LET statements for example, or making more use of integers. That said, they work fine as they are, on systems old and new. The PROCs are listed and explained later.

To review the current setup at this point, call PROC AYSTATUS() for a report on the currently-selected chip, or PROC AYEXTRAS() to read about the Next-specific aspects of the configuration.

```
AY Unit 6 selected
Last register set 65535
8 bit 8912 port A set for OUTPUT
8 bit 8910 port B set for OUTPUT
Channel A Tone ON  Volume 16
 Period 527 Noise off
Channel B Tone ON  Volume 16
 Period 1406 Noise off
Channel C Tone ON  Volume 16
 Period 703 Noise off
Envelope shape 8 Period 1000
 Noise generator Period 0
```

Figure 86 - AY Status while playing a three-tone chord under envelope control

Data port trickery

PSG Port A is implemented on a Spectrum 128, for serial and keypad connections, but absent from Next. Neither flavour of Spectrum implements Port B, which is only wired up inside AY-3-8910 chips used in Oric, Colour Genie and MSX computers. But that doesn't mean the PSG port hardware cannot be useful.

Some 128k programs use the registers for those ports, which are present on all chip versions regardless of the external connections, as a form of copy-protection. The initial loader for *Match Day 2* stores 94 in the register for Port B, **ayR 15**, and then checks if it's still set to that value while the game runs. If not, it decides that it's running an illegal copy, and wipes memory.

This protection racket worked because standard snapshot files didn't store the sound-chip register settings, so the PSG set-up step is bypassed when running a copy of game RAM, rather than after loading the original tape. *Taipan* for the Spectrum 128 pulls a similar trick, but 229 is its magic number. If you want to transfer these games to SD you'll need to set AY register 15 to the expected value, with a couple of OUT commands, after loading and before running the code, or they'll reset.

Similar tricks can be performed on Next, using any of the six dummy port registers on its three PSGs. You also can use them to persist other more user-friendly information between programs, such as the numbers of pre-allocated memory banks.

Next reserves one of its own registers as a sort of punch-bag for temporary data bytes. REG 127 has been set aside for programmers to use however they wish. It doesn't control anything specific, but gives a safe place to plonk eight arbitrary bits of data, even while system memory is being flushed by NEW or CLEAR.

Configuration probe

PROC AYEXTRAS( ) can tell you if Next is emulating AY or YM chips and whether each works in mono or stereo, showing the channel mapping from left to right. The chips sound very similar but the later YM (Yamaha) version plays envelopes more smoothly, so it's the default. It's rare to find a tune that sounds much different in either setting, but all Spectrum 128s were fitted with the original AY-3-8912 version.

At this point VBEEP is ready to run the KINETIC audio-visual demo, listed at the end of this chapter; otherwise the demonstration continues with simple examples of single-channel tone and filtered random-noise output.

```
1110 PROC AYVOLUMES(7,ayA): PROC AYBEEP(1,ayA): PAUSE 50
1120 PROC AYMUTE(ayA): PROC AYSTATUS(): PROC AYVOLUMES(0,7)
1130 REPEAT
1140   INPUT '"Noise pitch (1..31, 0 to quit) ";p
1150   WHILE p
1160   PROC AYNOISE(p,ayA): PROC AYVOLUME(15,ayA)
1170 REPEAT UNTIL 0
1180 PROC AYNOISE(0,0): PRINT : PROC AYSTATUS()
```

Line 1110 plays a C# note at intermediate volume, via soundchip channel A. The loop after that allows you to audition the 31 noise patterns by typing their number. Type 0 to stop this. If you break into the program the previous noise will keep playing till you mute it with PROC AYNOISE(0,0) or PROC AYVOLUME(0,ayA), or turn off all voices with either PROC AYVOLUMES(0,7), PROC SH() – which also resets the active channels and envelope – or the last resort for a quiet life, PROC SH3( ) which makes all three chips pipe down at once.

AY control PROCedures

This section explains each of the procedures in turn, exposing the inner working of the sound chip along the way.

AYBEEP is very like BEEP in terms of its **p** pitch parameter. First you specify the note as a decimal value around middle C; but rather than give a duration, during which BEEP would stall the Z80 processor, the second parameter **%c** is a channel mask: a value 1, 2 or 4, chosen that way to allow combinations, or the total 7 to pick all three channels. The channel numbers were given names, like the register addresses, in lines 1030 to 1070, so **ayC** refers to channel C, the third, **ayA** is the first channel and **ayB** is the second.

AYBEEP is flexible but slow because it converts **p** arithmetically from the logarithmic musical scale to the reciprocal scale of the hardware. This means it is not limited to an exact pitch in semitones, and can also generate fractional notes 'in the cracks' between piano keys, like the similarly slow (but monophonic and CPU-hogging) BEEP command.

AYBEEP does not set the volume of each note – that would be unnecessary when it's usually the same as the note before it, and classic BEEP has no volume control – so separate procedures like FVOL let you adjust the volume of each channel or several together.

PROC AYBEEPW(p, d, %v, %c) is a combined command which plays a note at pitch **p** for a duration **d**. In principle this is like BEEP, tying up the processor, though the duration **d** consistently expressed in seconds is rounded to a whole number of display frames, then corrected for VGA display compensations by PROC TRUEPAUSE(), as explained later. Again **%c** is a channel mask, while **%v** sets the loudness, from 1 (barely audible) to 15 (the loudest). Values 0 and 16 have special meanings, also detailed below.

```
1210 DEFPROC AYBEEPW(p,t,%v,%c)
1220 IF %v>16 THEN LIST 1210: STOP
1230 PROC AYBEEP(p,%c): PROC FVOL(%v,%c)
1240 PROC TRUEPAUSE(t*50): PROC FVOL(0,%c)
1250 ENDPROC
```

Invalid parameters cause the program to STOP showing the number of the checking line and listing the procedure concerned. Like BEEP, AYBEEPW stops the program for the indicated duration. To avoid this holdup, use a combination of AYBEEP and AYVOLUME calls to set the pitch and start and end volumes separately, from appropriate places and times in your program.

Simple tunes

Demo procedures let us compare AYBEEP with the original BEEP, and sequence simple tunes from DATA lines for either output.

PROC MAHLER( ) plays the snippet of Mahler from the Spectrum manual. It's the same as the original BEEP example except that it reads note durations and pitches from DATA at line 3500 in a NextBASIC REPEAT loop, to gain more control and avoid typing more than one BEEP command. Press any key to prematurely terminate the tune at the end of the current note. The demo sets RUN AT 0 so the pitch and duration of ROM BEEP commands expecting a 3.5 MHz clock is not upset by CPU speed boosts, though non-standard displays requiring VGA1 to VGA6 settings will still bend it, upwards, though to a far lesser extent than RUN AT.

```
3410 REM Mahler BEEPs from the Sinclair manual
3420 DEFPROC MAHLER()
3430 RUN AT 0: RESTORE 3500
3440 REPEAT
3450   READ d,t: WHILE d
3460   BEEP d*.25,t
3470 REPEAT UNTIL CODE INKEY$
3475 IF d=0 AND t<>0 THEN RESTORE t: GO TO 3440
3480 ENDPROC
3490
3500 DATA 4,0,4,2,2,3,2,2,4,0,4,0,4,2,2,3,2,2,4,0,
3505 DATA 4,3,4,5,8,7,4,3,4,5,8,7,3,7,1,8,2,7,2,5,
3510 DATA 2,3,2,2,4,0, 3,7,1,8,2,7,2,5,2,3,2,2
3515 DATA 4,0,4,0,4,-5,8,0,4,0,4,-5,8,0,0,3500
```

The last pair of the DATA items is 0, to mark the end, and an optional line number. If that is non-zero the music continues to play from DATA at the line specified. If it is zero, replay stops at the end of the tune.

The duration values in the DATA are specified in quarter-second units. This whole-number approach is more convenient for integer arithmetic or conversion into a frame count. For a faster tune, shorter units might be appropriate, but after all this is meant to be a Funeral March!

Playing chords

For more impressive results we can trigger several notes at once, to form musical chords. AYCHORD takes the same parameters as AYBEEP and plays the main note on channel A accompanied by deeper tones on the other two channels. The values -5 and -17 shift the pitch downwards by five and seventeen semitones (musical intervals of a perfect fourth, and an octave and a fourth) on channels C and B respectively, making the sound less harsh by augmenting the odd harmonics of the original square wave. Adjusting these factors and the channel volumes alters the timbre of the combined sound. There's nothing special about those particular numbers, so do experiment!

```
3570 REM BEEP a triad chord up to note n for d seconds
3575 DEFPROC AYCHORD(d,n)
3580 IF n<=99 THEN PROC fBEEP(n,ayA): PROC fBEEP(n-5,ayC): PROC
 fBEEP(n-17,ayB): ELSE PROC AYMUTE(7): REM sustained bass voice
3585 PROC TRUEPAUSE(d*50-1): PROC AYMUTE(5): ENDPROC
```

The magic numbers 7 and 5 in the calls to PROC AYMUTE mean that all notes stop at once when a dummy duration greater than 99 is supplied, but only channels A and C get muted at the end of the procedure. This gives an effect similar to that of a piano with a 'loud' pedal bound only to the deepest note. The timbre may be less pleasant, but software synthesisers are not bound by the mechanical constraints of piano manufacture.

```
2430 DEFPROC TSCALE()
2440 PROC AYVOLUMES(16,ayA+ayB+ayC): PROC AYENVELOPE(8,1000)
2450 REM BEEP semitones -60 to +69, AY -39.507..+105ish
2460 FOR i=-22 TO 69: PROC AYCHORD(.2,i): NEXT i
2470 PROC AYVOLUMES(0,7)
2480 ENDPROC
```

Procedure TSCALE uses AYCHORD to bleep a chromatic scale of three-note chords, applying a tremolo effect via the AYENVELOPE procedure. The REM notes that while the semitone units correspond, the pitch range of BEEP extends to deeper notes, up to 60 semitones below middle C, well off the bottom of the piano keyboard or the range of human hearing.

Middle C, most often known as C4 or MIDI note 60, is named because it appears near the middle of a grand piano keyboard. BEEP 69 is termed A9, just beyond the reach of MIDI, the Musical Instrument Digital Interface standard. Our AYBEEP's upper pitch limit is A12, semitone 105. At around 7,000 Hertz, this is far above the piano range which runs out at C8.

The lowest note BEEP can manage is subsonic, matching MIDI note 0 which would be known as C-1 if anyone could hear it. The range of AYBEEP is not quite as generous but it still extends down to semitone –39, corresponding to the leftmost piano key, also known as A0 or MIDI note 21.

Figure 87 – Classic notes

You need to take account of the full range of notes in each chord, not just the top one specified as a parameter, to make sure every note played by AYCHORD falls in the allowed range. AYCHORD(.2, –24) fails because although semitone –24, two octaves below middle C, is within the range for AY channel A, channel B tracks it 17 semitones lower and –41 is too deep for the chip.

Going up, BEEP stops 69 semitones above middle C, due to auditory and software-timing limitations, whereas the 12-bit counter registers in the AY chip can barely reach 39 semitones below middle C, but whistle away about 105 semitones up in the other direction, inaudible even to bats.

The very highest pitches end up widely and rather unmusically spread in frequency. They only exist so that finer control becomes available within the range of human hearing. This was a lesson learned from the earlier Atari sound chips TIA and POKEY which had relatively coarse control; that didn't map accurately to higher notes in the logarithmic musical scale.

Mixing the trick, **PROC MAHLER2( )** replays the BEEP tune from the Spectrum manual at the same tempo, but in three-part harmony using the soundchip. It just passes the line number of the music DATA to **PROC AYPLAYDATA( )**, which can play any tune or sequence of phrases.

```
3540 DEFPROC MAHLER2()
3541 PROC AYPLAYDATA(3500)
3542 ENDPROC

3544 DEFPROC AYPLAYDATA(L)
3545 LOCAL d,t: RESTORE L
3550 PROC AYNOISE(0,0): PROC AYVOLUMES(15,ayA+ayB+ayC)
3551 REPEAT
3552   READ d,t: WHILE d
3553   PROC AYCHORD(d*.25,t)
3554 REPEAT UNTIL CODE INKEY$
3555 IF d=0 AND t<>0 THEN RESTORE t: GO TO 3551
3556 PROC SH(): ENDPROC
```

The Next Horizon Sound bank includes more elaborate versions of AYCHORD and AYBEEP, which work similarly but more robustly, adapting for non-standard display timing and avoiding the potential for keyboard interference associated with using PAUSE to generate delays.

PROC AYPLAYDATA(%L) takes one parameter, the first line number of a sequence of note-duration and pitch DATA pairs. It uses **PROC AYCHORD( )** to play a three-note chord up to the chosen pitch. A pitch value over 100 is interpreted as a rest (silence). At the end of a block of data, the values 0, 0 stop the tune, while 0, **num** continues playing from data at line **num** – which may be a constant, variable or expression – to chain dynamically to the corresponding line. If that line does not exist, the next higher line number that does will be substituted.

Pause rethought

The delay could be implemented with PAUSE, but then pressing a key will hurry it along, and the duration will vary with the screen setup: VGA0 to 6 or HDMI, and 50/60 Hertz setting; all those affect the timing of display updates which drive PAUSE. In a game the PAUSE could be replaced by counting update frames, so useful work can be done in the meantime regardless of key-presses. At the time of writing Next's HDMI framerate was being adjusted in the hardware core; Kickstarter 2 and updated earlier machines can output HDMI at 50 Hertz to compatible screens, while earlier cores slowed down to about 48.2 Hertz in HDMI mode.

If you need consistent timing and can afford to wait, **PROC TRUEPAUSE( )** works like PAUSE but always counts 20 ms (1/50 second) intervals, regardless of any keypresses, and does not allow any count less than 1. It clears the low word of FRAMES when it starts, which may be helpful or annoying if your program uses FRAMES for any other purpose. This limits the time it will wait reliably to around 20 minutes (65535 frames) but avoids the risk of ending prematurely if FRAMES had already reached a point close to that threshold when TRUEPAUSE was called. Since this procedure was written NextBASIC has gained a BBC BASIC-style TIME command and function which pokes FRAMES similarly, but not as obviously.

```
4460 DEFPROC TRUEPAUSE(f)
4465 IF f<1 THEN LIST 4460: STOP
4470 LOCAL %f,m,%n
4480 DPOKE 23672,0:f=f*20: REM ms required
4490 PROC GETmsPERFRAME() TO m:%f=f/m
4495 REM PRINT %f;" actual frames"
4500 REPEAT :%n=% DPEEK 23672: REPEAT UNTIL %n>=f
4510 ENDPROC
```

The DPOKE and DPEEK of 23672, the low-order word of the FRAMES system variable, can be replaced by the equivalent 2.08 keyword TIME once you're sure everyone you share with is using that version or later.

The associated **PROC TRUEBEEP( )** uses helper functions to correct the parameters of a traditional BEEP for consistency in pitch and time, regardless of RUN AT or screen modes. The underlying BEEP has a maximum length of 10 seconds and this further limits the duration of a TRUEBEEP when the Next CPU is running faster than Sinclair intended.

```
3240 DEFPROC TRUEBEEP(d,p)
3250 LOCAL m: PROC GETMHz() TO m:m=m/3.5
3260 BEEP d*m,p-17.31* LN (m): ENDPROC
```

For instance in VGA0 with RUN AT 2 – four times faster than original Spectrum's Z80 – TRUEBEEP is limited to a maximum duration of 2.5s. The pitch is scaled-down correspondingly. The factor 17.31 is 12 divided by the natural logarithm of 2. This logarithmic manipulation extends the gap between notes, though that is reduced pro rata when the CPU is sped up.

Since TRUEBEEP uses the original hardware rather than the AY add-on, it disables interrupts and monopolises the processor while it is running. Unless hardware authenticity is required, perhaps because AY chips are disabled for compatibility, AYBEEPW is generally a better choice, and adds volume control or an optional envelope to the capability.

Mind the gaps

ZX BASIC BEEP always left a short gap between notes, as it cranked the floating-point calculator to convert decimal musical pitches and durations into integer pulse delays. Now we can play sounds continuously, pauses between notes make a big difference, and vary between instruments and musical styles.

For the Mahler the deepest note on **ayB** is deliberately not muted between beeps, to sustain the drone. Change the parameter of AYMUTE after the

TRUEPAUSE from 5 (**ayA**|**ayC**) to 7 (**ayA**|**ayB**|**ayC**) to mute all three, and listen to the difference. The ELSE part on line 3580 is only needed to ensure a rest is entirely silent even if some voices are otherwise deliberately left to drone.

To see how tunes can chain together, changing key and pace between sections, type PROC AYPLAYDATA(%3600). The contrived DATA there hops around five times through a four-note loop (not up Mahler standards) then chains on into the funeral march. If a variable value is substituted for the line-number, such tunes can switch automatically at the end of a phrase to another, neatly enabling context-sensitive in-game tunes.

```
3600 DATA 5,4,5,5,5,6,5,5,0,3620
3610 DATA 4,12,4,13,4,14,4,13,0,3640
3620 DATA 4,4,4,5,4,6,4,5,0,3610
3630 DATA 3,4,3,5,3,6,3,5,3,4,6,-8,3,999,0,3500
3640 DATA 3,12,3,13,3,14,3,13,0,3630
```

Optimisations

The procedure calls make it easy to see how the code fits together, but they slow it down substantially, especially on NextBASIC 2.06 or 2.07. A fast-paced program is better off extracting the called lines, or cut-down versions that do just what you need, to avoid the PROC overhead. Future NextBASIC speed-ups should make such fiddling less important, but the key to fast performance in any interpreted program is to do only the necessary work.

To see the difference, here is the fully-commented source for AYBEEP followed by the condensed skin-of-the-pants FBEEP version. The REM PRINT lines in AYBEEP reveal the steps needed to convert musical note values into AY counter register intervals, and the associated approximations.

```
1730 REM Set one channel's pitch, converting p to AY period
1740 REM p may be a decimal and is rounded to the closest pitch
1750 DEFPROC AYBEEP(p,%c)
1760 IF p<-39 THEN PRINT "AY bass limit=-39, 27.5 Hz": STOP
1770 IF p>105 THEN PRINT "AY top note=105, 110 kHz!": STOP
1780 LOCAL %d,%p,tick,Hz
1790 IF %c=0 | (c>4) | (c=3) THEN LIST 1750: STOP
1800 REM A above middle C is 440 Hz, semitone 9
1810 LET Hz=2^((p-9)/12)*440
1820 REM PRINT "Semitone ";p;" is ";Hz;" Hertz ";
1830 tick=32/3500000
1850 REM PRINT "Maximum frequency ";1/tick;" Hertz"
1860 REM PRINT "Period step is ";tick*1e6;" us"
1870 REM PRINT "Note period is ";1e6/Hz;" us"
1880 LET %p=1/Hz/tick
1890 REM PRINT "Ideal period ";1/Hz/tick;", nearest ";%p
1900 OUT ayR,7:%d= IN ayD
1920 IF %d & c THEN OUT ayD,%d-c
1930 %c=%c-(c=4)
1940 OUT ayR,%c-1<<1: OUT ayD,%p&255
1960 OUT ayR,%c<<1-1: OUT ayD,%p>>8
1980 ENDPROC
```

Temporary variables like **tick** and **clock** could be omitted, replaced by constants or combined into one expression, but they're deliberately used here to show how the magic numbers fit together. 3500000 is the Spectrum clock speed in Hertz, give or take a few kilohertz. 32 is the first factor in the AY chip timing chain.

-9 is the semitone interval from middle C to the 'concert pitch' reference note A, now set at 440 Hertz. This is a 20th century convention – Mozart took 422 Hertz as his reference, about a semitone lower. In 1859 the French government legislated in favour of 435 Hertz. The computer doesn't care but accompanying musicians prefer us to pick one value and stick with it.

Here's the fast version, which uses a pre-computed table in a pair of integer arrays to avoid needlessly repeating the pitch corrections. Insert LOCAL %q if you use that variable elsewhere, though it'll slow things down:

```
2890 REM Fast BEEP on channel (1,2,4) pitch -39..88, no checks
2900 REM Reads N%(),O%(), BEWARE! clobbers %q
2910 DEFPROC FBEEP(p,%c)
2920 OUT %65533,7: %q=% IN 49149: IF %q&c THEN OUT %49149,%q-c
2930 %c=%c-(c>>2):%q=p+39: OUT %65533,%c-1<<1:%q=%n[q]: OUT
  %49149,%q&255: OUT %65533,%c<<1-1: OUT %49149,%q>>8: ENDPROC
```

For this to work you must previously have called PROC FINIT() below, to fill the arrays. Only exact semitones are computed, so we lose the ability to play notes 'in the cracks' where trombones can stretch but pianos cannot. Variables for AY register access are also set here, for convenience in calling programs, but FBEEP uses the corresponding integer constants like %49149 rather than **ayD** to wring a little more speed from the BASIC interpreter:

```
2760 REM Initialise pitch table in arrays N% & O%
2770 DEFPROC FINIT()
2780 LOCAL tick,Hz,%p,p,h
2790 LET tick=3500000/(32*440)
2800 FOR p=-39 TO 127-39
2810   LET h=2^((p-9)/12)
2820   LET %p=p+39
2830   LET %n[p]=tick/h
2840 NEXT p
2850 ayD=49149:ayR=65533:ayA=1:ayb=2:ayc=4
2870 ENDPROC
```

The comparison between AYBEEP and FBEEP reveals tests that can potentially be skipped. But while getting started, AYBEEP will check you're making reasonable requests, and explain otherwise.

Making Noise

As well as regular, reedy square-waves, the sound chips can generate randomly-timed pulses known as 'noise', on each or all of the output channels. The loop at the end of the introductory program, between lines 1130 and 1170, lets us audition such sounds.

PROC AYNOISE(%p, %c) sets the frequency of the random noise generated by the chip to one of 31 pitches and determines which, if any, of the three channels the noise is mixed into. Two parameters are passed to this PROC. The first **%p** is the pitch of the noise, where 1 is highest, like a hiss, and 31 is the deepest, more of a crackle. Intermediate values 2 to 30 descend in-between, changing the tone progressively less. The ordering makes sense when you realise that this register, like the tone counter parameters, represents a delay rather than a frequency.

The second parameter **%c** determines which channel or channels the noise is routed to. It can turn each channel on or off with a single value between 0 and 7. Using 0 turns them all off – so no noise is heard at the output, though the process continues regardless, at the rate set by the first parameter – and 7 turns them all on.

To route noise to any single channel, pass one of the values **ayA**, **ayB** or **ayC** to PROC AYNOISE, thus choosing channel A, B or C. To control two at once, simply add up the values, or mask them together with **|**, the bitwise OR operator. So each controls two channels, one in common. There are 3 combinations, 3, 5, 6, corresponding to channel pairs A and B, A and C and B and C respectively. The English words 'and' in that sentence mean the same thing as the Boolean term 'or'! Ain't maths wonderful.

It makes no difference whether you use **+** or **|** when all the bits are different, as in this case, but if the same bit might already be set in more than one value you need to use| to avoid accidentally setting other bits. For example, 5+6 is 11 (BIN 1011) but 5|6 is 7 (BIN 0111). You can see why if you write 5 and 6 in binary, as BIN 101 and BIN 110.

Now it's clear why **ayC** needs to take the value 4 not 3 – otherwise it would use the same value as **ayA+ayB**. This 1, 2, 4 binary step means that each channel can be controlled independently by a single binary digit (bit) of register 7. It enabled General Instrument to pack six audio routing switches – for tones and noise on each channel – into a single byte. The other two bits of eight in that register are unimplemented by Next and reserved for controls unrelated to sound.

This logic saves hardware and is convenient when setting (or clearing) every route at once, but makes the general case of turning just one signal on or off much fiddlier than it would be if each had its own register. It becomes necessary to read the current byte, save seven of the eight bits, and alter just one before writing back the whole combination.

NextBASIC has special bit operations in its integer expression evaluator which streamline this sort of bit-twiddling. The same effect can still be achieved in ZX BASIC but it's much slower and more complicated as it has to be done with a sequence of 40-bit floating-point division, multiplication, addition and INT operations, as illustrated earlier in the REG 8 stereo setup.

```
1270 REM Toggle channel(s) to produce noise at period 1..31
1280 REM Uses global variables ayR and ayD to address soundchip
1290 DEFPROC AYNOISE(%p,%c)
1310 IF %(p>31) OR (c>7) THEN LIST 1290: STOP
1330 LOCAL %s: OUT ayR,6: OUT ayD,%p: OUT ayR,7
1360 %s= IN ayD:%s=%s & @11000111: OUT ayD,%s|((7-c)<<3)
1390 ENDPROC
```

The brackets in line 1310 would not be needed if it was a conventional expression, but the % prefix makes them essential because the integer expression evaluator works strictly from left to right.

Without them it would OR the result of the first comparison with **%c** and then compare that combination with the value 7, whereas we need results from both comparisons before the OR can combine them. The first pair around (p>31) are not strictly needed as NextBASIC would evaluate the test immediately regardless, but they make it a clearer example.

Notice that once register 7 is selected in line 1330 it is not necessary to update **ayR** again to rewrite the same register. At the end of the PROC, register 7 is read and then written back with one bit reset, to enable output of that channel – or more than one, if parameter **%c** has more than one set bit. This gives a way to get louder noises by mixing them into more channels.

Before finishing with PROC FNOISE, notice that the frequency control **%p** affects all channels. You can't set a different pitch for each, neat though that'd be. Here's the slimline no-checks version, PROC FNOISE, which packs all the work on a single (rather long) line:

```
3230 DEFPROC FNOISE(%p,%c)
3240 LOCAL %s: OUT %65533,6: OUT %49149,%p: OUT %65533,7: %s=
     % IN 49149: %s&=%@11000111: OUT %49149,%s | ((7-c)<<3)
3310 ENDPROC
```

There's only one noise generator per chip, though the choice of channel does allow you to place it simply in stereo: hard left, centre or right, or in two intermediate positions either side, by routing noise to both the centre and one side.

The balance is better if you route the central position to all three channels rather than just the centre one. Otherwise the intermediate positions are noticeably louder, whereas a symmetrical and progressive fall-off in volume to either side is more realistic.

Authentic stereo panning is more complicated and involves constant-power curves and psychoacoustic adjustments, but this five-directional noise comes almost for free thanks to the separate outputs of the AY chip channels.

Games sound more responsive and varied if effects are positioned in this way. It's unfortunate that Spectrum 128 sound was wired in mono.

Amstrad CPC, Spectrum Next, and add-on cards split out the channels to left, right and centre (left **and** right) positions in stereo, but there are two incompatible orders in which channels can be placed. Alphabetically from left to right gives us A = LEFT, B = CENTRE, C = RIGHT but some people argue it's more logical for C to be the Centre and A and B left and right respectively, so stereo backing uses A and B, leaving C for the 'lead' in the middle.

Figure 88 - This mono earpiece from a broken Sony headphone tacked onto Simon's issue 2A Next made sounds audible, but authentically very quiet!

We've seen how Next treats this as an exercise in hardware reprogramming and gives ABC and ACB stereo options, so tunes authored for either standard have the expected stereo channel placement if you first set this to match the composer's set-up. Alternatively everything can be placed incorrectly (in stereo, alone) if you prefer, or forget, or guess wrongly. Beware of options! Every one you add makes full testing that much harder.

Pump up the volumes

Whatever their order, remember that you won't hear any of the three channels unless you turn up its volume control. Which brings us at last to **PROC AYVOLUMES(%v, %c)**:

```
1500 REM Set multiple channels to the same volume
1510 REM mute=0, loudest=15; 16 follows the envelope
1520 REM Add channel numbers ayA, ayB, ayC for combinations
1530 DEFPROC AYVOLUMES(%v,%c)
1540 IF %c>7  THEN LIST 1530: STOP
1550 IF %v>16 THEN LIST 1530: STOP
1560 IF %c & 1 THEN OUT ayR,8: OUT ayD,%v
1570 IF %c & 2 THEN OUT ayR,9: OUT ayD,%v
1580 IF %c & 4 THEN OUT ayR,10: OUT ayD,%v
1590 ENDPROC
```

This sets the output volume of any or all of the three channels. It fades the mixture of noise and tone routed to that channel up or down in 15 acoustically-smooth steps of around 2 dB. A single dB or decibel, almost named after telephone pioneer Alexander Graham Bell, corresponds to the smallest step up or down where humans can generally agree the direction of the change, louder or softer. On a Spectrum, 1 is the softest audible volume, 15 the loudest. 0 means silence – an infinite step down! – while 16 is a special value that puts that channel's volume under automatic control from another part of the chip – the envelope generator – which we'll soon explore.

The second parameter determines which channels have their volume changed. If it is 0, nothing changes. If it is 7, the total of **ayA**, **ayB**, and **ayC**, all three channels are affected. Like PROC AYNOISE(), you can also change one or two channel volumes at once with a single call to PROC AYVOLUMES(). Also similarly, the same value is set to all the selected channels. Others are unaffected.

Whereas there's only one noise source optionally routable to any channels, with a pitch but no volume control, there are three separate channel volume controls, each of which independently fades the *mixture* of noise and tone routed to that channel. There are no separate volume controls for the noise and tone components.

The similarly-named **PROC AYVOLUME()** takes the same pair of parameters – a volume 0 to 16 and a channel mask – but it is slightly faster as it can only set the volume of a single channel. Hence the name is singular, PROC AYVOLUME() rather than PROC AYVOLUMES(). If you only want to alter the volume of one channel, either will do the job but PROC AYVOLUME() will be quicker:

```
1610 REM Single channel (0 or 1=A) fade 0..15
1620 DEFPROC AYVOLUME(%v,%c)
1630 IF %(c=3) | (c>4) | (v>16) THEN LIST 1620: STOP
1640 OUT ayR,%c>>1+8: OUT ayD,%v: ENDPROC
```

PROC FVOL() is faster but fussier, using just the two OUT statements with no sanity checks. To set two or three channels to the same volume with a single procedure call, PROC AYVOLUMES() is required. The typical use for this is to silence all the channels, by setting their volumes to 0.

Making it shut up

When experimenting with the AY chip from BASIC it's easy to end up with a channel or two droning away indefinitely. This is where **PROC SH()** comes in handy. It silences all channels with PROC AYVOLUMES(0,7), turns off the envelope generator, and for good measure also switches off all the noise and tone outputs by setting all bits in register 7, the routing control. On a Spectrum 128 you'd be wise to preserve the top two bits, unused by Next.

```
1660 REM Mute all channels, turn off envelope, noise and tones
1670 REM Addresses chip via globals ayA, ayB, ayC, ayD and ayR
1680 DEFPROC SH()
1690 PROC AYVOLUMES(0,ayA+ayB+ayC)
1700 OUT ayR,7: OUT ayD,255
1705 PROC AYENVELOPE(0,0)
1710 ENDPROC
```

Bits have to be cleared to zero to let corresponding signals through. The encapsulation offered by procedures mean NextZXOS programmers don't have to worry about such hardware details. Similar procedures, perhaps with extra channels or more levels, could be used to control the tone-generators of a Philips six-channel stereo SAA-1099 chip, used in SAM and some Unix workstations, or 8-bit Atari and Acorn home micro four-voice chips. If we reuse the same PROC names, and scale the parameter values, we can use this interface to control other chips, without modifying the calling program, though some of the extra capabilities, like SAA-1099 stereo, may be hidden.

Sound status reports

The helper PROC AYSTATUS( ) is useful while experimenting with the AY chip. It shows the current channel, noise and envelope settings using the corresponding GET procedures, and the configuration of the data ports in real AY-3-8912 and AY-3-8910 chips, which are not implemented on Next but currently allow hackers to stash a few values outside RAM, beyond the reach of CLEAR or NEW.

```
2000 DEFPROC AYSTATUS()
2010 LOCAL %s,%c,%v,%p
2012 PROC AYREG() TO %p
2014 PROC AYSELECTED() TO %s
2016 PRINT "AY Unit ";%p;" selected","Last register set ";%s
2020 OUT ayR,7: LET %s= IN ayD
2040 PRINT "8 bit 8912 port A set for ";
2050 IF %s & 64  THEN PRINT "OUTPUT": ELSE PRINT "INPUT"
2060 PRINT "8 bit 8910 port B set for ";
2070 IF %s & 128 THEN PRINT "OUTPUT": ELSE PRINT "INPUT"
2080 FOR %c=0 TO 2
2090   LET c=%c: PRINT "Channel "; CHR$ (c+65);" Tone ";
2100   IF %1<<c & s THEN PRINT "off";: ELSE PRINT "ON ";
2110   PROC GETVOL( FN M(c)) TO %v: PRINT " Volume ";%v;
2120   PROC GETPERIOD( FN M(c)) TO %v: PRINT " Period ";%v;
2130   PRINT " Noise ";
2140   IF %8<<c & s THEN PRINT "off": ELSE PRINT "ON"
2150 NEXT %c
2160 OUT ayR,12:%c= IN ayD
2170 OUT ayR,11:%s= IN ayD
2180 OUT ayR,13: PRINT "Envelope shape "; IN ayD;
2190 PRINT " Period ";%c<<8+s;
2200 OUT ayR,6
2210 PRINT "  Noise generator Period "; IN ayD
2220 ENDPROC
```

Figure 86 illustrated the output from AYSTATUS(). The tiny PROC AYREG() uses a post-Sinclair hardware improvement to simply retrieve the most recently-selected AY register via `ENDPROC =% IN 49141 & 31.`

Another helper procedure, AYEXTRAS(), discloses the state of the TurboSound implementation on a Spectrum Next. It reports the chip model, channel order and mono/stereo status, and which chip and data register is currently selected.

```
2230 DEFPROC AYEXTRAS()
2235 LOCAL %b,%c,%i
2240 %b=% REG 6 & 3
2245 PRINT "Next ";
2250 IF %b=0 THEN PRINT "YM";: ELSE IF %b=1 THEN PRINT "AY";
2255 PRINT " soundchip configuration"
```

```
2260 %b=% REG 8
2265 %c=% REG 8&2+1
2270 PRINT "Number of chips synthesised ";%c
2275 FOR %i=0 TO %c-1
2280   PRINT "Sound chip ";%i;" outputs in ";
2285   IF %REG 9&(1<<(5+i)) THEN PRINT"mono":ELSE PRINT"stereo"
2290 NEXT %i
2295 PRINT "Channels left to right are ";
2300 IF %b & 32 THEN PRINT "A-B-C": ELSE PRINT "A-C-B"
2305 ENDPROC
```

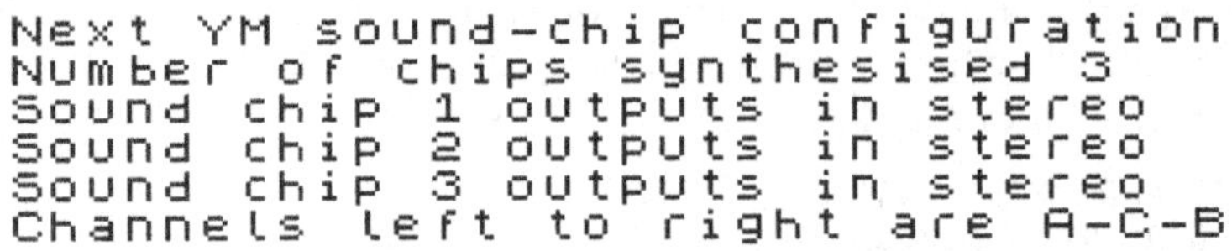

Figure 89 – Default output from PROC AYEXTRAS()

PROC AYSELECT(%a) directs subsequent commands to any one of the three chips, numbered 0, 1 and 2 depending on the value passed to **%a.**

```
2320 REM Select one of the three AY chips, 0, 1 or 2
2330 DEFPROC AYSELECT(%a)
2340 IF %a>2 THEN PRINT "AY chips are numbered 0..2": STOP
2350 OUT ayR,%255-a
2355 ENDPROC
```

This is obviously vital to playing six or nine-channel audio, and also used in **PROC SH3()** which silences all the chips, not just the current one, clobbering **%i** and leaving the third chip selected:

```
2385 REM Silence all three AY sound generators
2390 DEFPROC SH3()
2400 FOR %i=0 TO 2: PROC AYSELECT(%i): PROC SH(): NEXT %i
2410 ENDPROC
```

PROC AYSELECTED( ) works only on Core 3.01.10 and later, and indicates which chip is currently selected, returning 0, 1 or 2 as appropriate.

```
2360 DEFPROC AYSELECTED()
2365 ENDPROC =%3-( IN 49141>>6)
```

The port to query this state was kindly added by Next hardware programmer Allen Albright after Simon N Goodwin pointed out that Next drivers were liable to switch chips and register values while a BASIC program ran, making it impractical to share chips or dedicate some to background music sequences and still use the rest safely from BASIC. If you find this a problem, you have an obsolete DRIVER; contact the author for an update.

Opening up the Envelope

The soundchip can alter its channel output volumes automatically, fading up or down in predefined ways, if the dummy value 16 is set with PROC

AYVOLUME() or PROC AYVOLUMES(). The pattern of fading is set by the first parameter passed to AYENVELOPE(), while the rate is determined by the second parameter, a value between 0 and 65535 (about ten seconds).

The patterns are rudimentary; half of the possible selections are duplicates because of the simple way control bits are interpreted. The bits are labelled Hold, Alternate, Attack and Continue in the datasheet, but when bit 3 (Continue) is zero the two low-order bits are irrelevant, as there's nothing to Hold or Alternate, and when it's set both the one-shot envelopes associated with the redundant settings 0 to 7 can be obtained with settings 9 and 15.

For instance, first parameter settings 0, 1, 2, 3 and 9 all start loud and fade down to silence. Envelopes 4, 5, 6, 7 and 15 each fade up over 16 logarithmic steps, then suddenly mute the channel. You can get all the options just using values 8 to 15, as shown in Figure 90. The first eight are just redundant swaps.

Envelope 13, perhaps the most musically useful, fades up to maximum volume at the chosen rate then stays there till the sound is muted. With a bit of imagination, this resembles the 'soft attack' characteristic of stringed instruments played with a bow. Envelope 11 is the weirdest, starting loud, fading down to silence momentarily then jumping back to full volume and sticking there once the rate runs out. Good luck finding a use for that one.

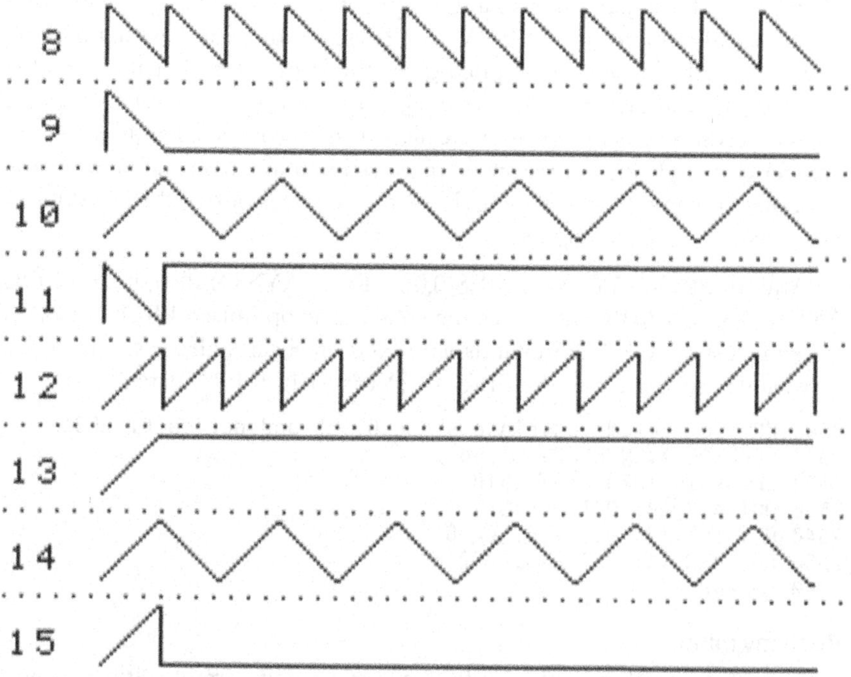

Figure 90, The eight volume envelope shapes supported by AY sound chips

For longer repeating variations, envelope 8 starts loud, fades down then jumps back to loud, over and over. 12 is the same but in the opposite direction, fading up then jumping back to silence before repeating the cycle. Envelope 10 fades down then up over and over, while 14 follows the same pattern but starts by fading upwards.

There is only one envelope generator per chip so if more than one channel volume is set to 16 they all rise and fall at the same rate. The rate is a delay count between changes. Very low values change the volume so fast that they can effectively create new sounds as the pitch and envelope durations, in units 16 times longer, interact.

The envelope counter on the AY-3-8912 has 16 steps per section, whereas the YM2149 has 32, stepping twice as fast. Apart from this subtle difference, the sound is identical. The envelope feature is half-baked but like many hardware lash-ups it can sometimes yield interesting interactions, after patient experimentation.

This example sounds rather like a fast-moving steam train, especially with some railway graphics to guide the ear:

```
PROC AYENVELOPE(8,900)
PROC AYVOLUMES(16,7)
PROC AYNOISE(20,7)
```

For something akin to the sound of a piston-engined aeroplane, substitute the values 14, 50 into the AYENVELOPE() line. In a game with a moving viewpoint, reducing the noise pitch gives the impression that the sound is approaching, and increasing it above 20, in proportion to the relative speed, suits a receding vehicle. For most realistic results you may like to store the transfer curve relating source speed to noise pitch in a table, tailored for the scale of your game-world. Tuning this sort of curve is one of the key skills of a professional sound designer.

Any of PROC AYVOLUMES(0,0), PROC AYNOISE(0,0) or PROC AYENVELOPE(0,0) will silence the sound. The optimised PROC FENV() contains just six OUT commands with literal register addresses. Here's the very similar implementation of PROC AYENVELOPE(%shape,%rate):

```
2500 REM Set volume envelope shape 0..15 and period 0..65355
2510 DEFPROC AYENVELOPE(%s,%p)
2520 IF %s>15 THEN LIST 2510
2530 OUT ayR,13: OUT ayD,%s
2540 OUT ayR,12: OUT ayD,%p>>8
2550 OUT ayR,11: OUT ayD,%p&255
2560 ENDPROC
```

Read my mind

Any interface worth its salt includes facilities to read current settings as well as to change them. Accordingly, two procedures let you read the current pitch and volume for any specified channel of the currently-selected AY chip.

This was not possible on the original Spectrum 128, but Next fixes this in Core 3.1.10, which will also let us find out which of the three chips is selected – that makes it possible for drivers to share the hardware nicely with BASIC programs by detecting the unit in use and switching temporarily to another and back, so foreground programs don't find their OUTs have been diverted to different registers by interrupting code. Drivers are fine for background tunes but much less versatile than direct access to any bit of the hardware, if it's a truly interactive response you're after.

PROC GETVOL(%c) is trivial – after checking for a valid channel bit it converts that to a register number and returns the corresponding data:

```
2580 REM return volume 0..16 of channel ayA, ayB, ayC (1,2,4)
2590 DEFPROC GETVOL(%c)
2600 IF %c<1 OR c=3 OR c>4 THEN LIST 2590: STOP
2610 OUT ayR,%c+7-(c=4)
2620 ENDPROC = IN ayD
```

PROC GETPERIOD(%c) is a little more complicated, as the 16-bit channel pitch period is held in two adjacent registers, so it reads first the high then the low byte and combines them with a fast bit-shift in line 2730:

```
2640 REM return period 0..4095 for channel mask 1, 2 or 4
2650 DEFPROC GETPERIOD(%c)
2660 IF %c<1 OR c=3 OR c>4 THEN LIST 2650: STOP
2670 LOCAL %h:%c=%c-1-(c=4)<<1
2690 OUT ayR,%c+1:%h= IN ayD
2710 OUT ayR,%c:%c= IN ayD
2730 ENDPROC =%h<<8+c
```

Notice how the parameter **%c** is re-used in the last two lines, to save slowing the procedure down by avoidably introducing another local variable. In a compiled language this might be considered poor style but in interpreted BASIC it is a useful economy.

The current envelope repeat rate and shape can be read similarly, with **PROC GETRATE**() and **PROC GENENV**() respectively. These need no parameter as each soundchip only contains a single envelope generator.

```
2740 DEFPROC GETRATE()
2742 LOCAL %h,%l: OUT ayR,12:%h= IN ayD
2744 OUT ayR,11:%l= IN ayD: ENDPROC =%h<<8+l

2734 DEFPROC GETENV()
2736 OUT ayR,13: ENDPROC = IN ayD
```

The fast stuff

Since parameter-checking is expensive in an interpreted language, seven of the most useful VBEEP procedures come in alternative faster versions, with names prefixed by the letter F for Fast rather than AY, whatever that stands for; please let me know if you find out. These are FBEEP, FBEEPW, FENV, FINIT, FMUTE, FNOISE and FVOL, and we've seen the implementation of some of those alongside their more pedestrian counterparts.

These procedures gain speed in three ways – they're earlier in the program, or Horizon bank, so they can be found more quickly by the interpreter, especially before NextBASIC 2.08. Also they skip all the error-checking, intermediate calculations and comments in the normal procedures. If they do not work as expected, replace the F prefix and compare the slower AY versions, stepping through with STOP and CONTINUE if necessary.

Thirdly, FBEEP avoids the overhead of about fifty 40-bit floating-point mathematical operations used to map a musical scale in place of the reciprocal delays used in the soundchip. The 2^ operation grids away internally using logarithms and exponentials computed stepwise to nine decimal places.

Since this is an 8-bit system and none of the soundchip values exceed the 16-bit capacity of NextBASIC's built-in integer evaluator, we can work out in advance the closest channel pitch values for exact notes of the musical scale – including semitones in each key, but ignoring quarter-tones and other fractions inaccessible to pianists – and store those in an integer array. In fact for the full range of semitones the AY can play, from -39 below middle C to +88 above (inaudible to human ears) we need two Next integer arrays as NextZXOS preallocates space for just 64 16-bit values in each.

However an early extension to NextBASIC allows code to use the space allocated for two or more arrays as if it were a single larger one. PROC FBEEP(%p, %c) uses %N[D] to access 128 consecutive elements in arrays %N and the subsequent %O (never a good choice of variable name, because the vowel risks confusion with 0 zero).

PROC FINIT() sets up the required values in that array just once, taking a second or two up front but saving milliseconds on each FBEEP after that, when it matters as the CPU has animation and interaction to consider simultaneously. It follows that you must not use those integer arrays for any other purpose, or NEW or CLEAR without first calling PROC FINIT() to put back the values PROC FBEEP() expects.

You can avoid this setup by using PROC AYBEEP(), but it'll be slower, making it hard to trigger chords without noticeable stepping of the note arrivals, even when running NextBASIC at 28 MHz with RUN AT 3.

PROC FBEEP(%p, %c) is also faster because it requires its first parameter %c to be a signed whole number, ignoring the fractional part which AYBEEP interprets microtonally. The second parameter is a channel number, e.g. **ayA**, **ayB** or **ayC**, though things will go faster if the literal value %1, %2 or %4 is supplied, removing the need for BASIC to search for the named variable.

Matt Langley's Next Horizon framework allows developers free use of those integer arrays by providing an alternative way to store the required values in a dedicated DATA BANK. Rather than using arrays, the 16-bit pitch values are stored in order at the start of that bank, and retrieved from there by FBEEP. The bank number is stored by Horizon in **%x[sound].**

PROC FMUTE(%c) behaves like AYMUTE as long as the channel-number parameter **%c** falls into the expected range 1 to 7. It can mute one, two or three channels at once. A parameter of 0 has no effect. Values greater than 7 affect other parts of the soundchip mixer, for instance 8, 16 and 32 disconnect noise output on channels A, B and C respectively.

```
440 DEFPROC FMUTE(%c)
450 OUT %65533,%7: OUT %49149,%IN 49149|c
460 ENDPROC
```

PROC FBEEPW(%p, d, %c) works like a hybrid of BEEP and FBEEP for the specified duration, twiddling its thumbs while the note plays for approximately **d** seconds. It uses TRUEPAUSE rather than PAUSE, otherwise the interval would be measured in steps of between 1/48 to 1/70 seconds depending on the display configuration. For efficiency, it leaves the volume of the chosen channel **%c** unaltered and rounds the pitch parameter **%p** to the nearest whole-semitone step.

```
300 DEFPROC FBEEPW(%p,t,%c)
310 PROC FBEEP(%p,%c)
320 PROC TRUEPAUSE(t*50)
325 PROC FMUTE(%c)
330 ENDPROC
```

PROC FNOISE(%p, %c) is equivalent to PROC AYNOISE() as long as its parameters **%p** and **%c** do not exceed the expected range, up to 31 or 7 respectively. It is faster because it does not check the first parameter and simply ignores all but the lowest 3 bits of **%c**. It also addresses the soundchip directly by constant port numbers rather than **ayA**, **ayB** and **ayC** mnemonics.

PROC FVOL(%v,%c) quickly sets the volume of a single channel **%c** (1, 2 or 4, unchecked) to 0, muted, 1 to 15 for increasing loudness, or 16 to derive the volume from the envelope set with AYENVELOPE() or FENV().

FENV(%s, %p) works like AYENVELOPE(), but faster as it does not check that **%s**, the envelope shape, is less than 32. The second 'period' value determines the rate at which the loudness of channels set to volume 16 varies. Low values give such fast variation so that new notes may be heard. Larger values add a rhythmic modulation, especially in conjunction with the repeating envelopes 8, 10, 12 and 14. These can be useful to generate continuous pulses of sound

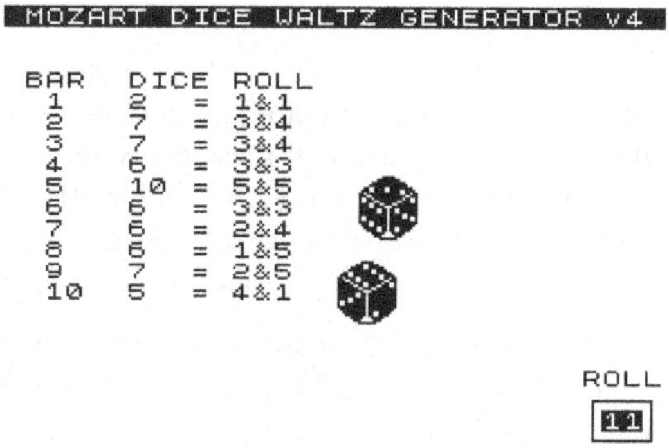

Figure 91 - Musical dice from Minuetz

during an animation, such as the rattling of dice. That's how my remix of the Mozart Dice Waltz generator written by Rod Hopkins and H Laverty, first featured in *Your Computer* magazine and later updated by Ian Collier, generates suitably rattly sound effects while the dice animation runs:

```
PROC AYNOISE(%5+RND 5,ayA|ayB|ayC)
PROC AYVOLUMES(16,ayA|ayB|ayC)
PROC AYENVELOPE(8,%1024+ RND 255)
```

The sound effect continues to play till the animation finishes; then it can be muted with PROC SH(). The calls to RND make the speed and pitch of the effect vary subtly each time it plays, while synaesthesia ensures it always seems to run in time with the animation. The Minuetz4 program can be freely downloaded to your Next over WiFi, via GetIt; its ID is 1e599f.

Sound examples

Small procedures in the main program VBEEP.BAS show how to start and stop runs of notes or sound effects.

The example **PROC FSCALE()** plays notes in ascending from deepest to near-audible, via PROC FBEEP(). The duration is determined by PAUSE 10 in the loop, so you will hear around five notes per second unless you hold down a key, e.g. the spacebar, to speed things up. Notice how it sets the volume for each note at the start. FBEEP does not do this for us – it uses whatever volume was previously set.

FVOL(0,ayA) silences the last note. FMUTE is a quicker way to do this if more than one channel needs to be muted simultaneously. The note continues to play, silently, so the quickest way to hear it again is to call FVOL for the channel concerned, with no need to send the multi-byte pitch value again via FBEEP or AYBEEP.

PROC TSCALE() is similar but sounds more interesting as it plays chords with PROC AYCHORD(), and uses an envelope to make them pulse rhythmically. Notice how this time holding a key speeds up the pitch progression but does not affect the rhythm. That's because the pulse duration is determined by the second parameter of AYENVELOPE, which sets a countdown inside the sound chip independent of BASIC.

The KINETIC demo starting at line 5000 of VBEEP.BAS illustrates NextBASIC sound and animation working simultaneously and interacting – this is the main reason all these procedures exist, and shows the advantages of VBEEPs over the old game-halting BEEP command. The program was written in 2020 for testing rather than as a code demo so it's not been updated for the latest NextBASIC goodies, and uses pidgin ZX BASIC in places.

The program shows an animated pattern, like the central character in the Taito arcade game QIX, bouncing round the screen. The algorithm was devised by Louis Cesa and published a year before in the November 1980 issue of *BYTE* magazine, under the name 'Kinetic String'.

The sounds accompanying the graphics vary with the number of patterns being drawn. Enter a number from 1 to 3 at the start. When only one QIX is shown, simple music data is read and played as the animation is updated. Next Registers 50 and 51 are directly tweaked to scroll a simple low resolution background independently of the animation.

Since NextBASIC is not quick about drawing long lines, you will notice the speed varying as the pattern grows and shrinks. This limits the amount that can be updated while playing music this way, but is not necessarily a bad thing – consider the way the tempo of the four-note bass riff in Space Invaders accelerates towards the end of each wave, a side-effect of the diminishing amount of graphics to be drawn but also a psychoacoustic factor in regulating waves of tension as the game progresses.

While Western games often use pre-recorded filmic music, only vaguely related to the on-screen action, companies built on interaction like Nintendo traditionally use simpler sequenced music to good effect as a gameplay element rather than background.

If background muzak is what you're after, consider dedicating an AY chip to a driver which will play this automatically. These procedures are more suitable to provide live feedback to the player, especially if pitch and volume as well as timings are modulated to provide extra information in context.

If 2 or 3 is entered the demo sounds track the position of the ends of each new QIX line, while bouncing two or three patterns at once.

```
5000 REM NextBASIC QIX animation demo
5001 RUN AT 3:SPRITE CLEAR:SPRITE PRINT 0:LAYER CLEAR:LAYER 0
5002 INPUT "Number of QIX Patterns (1 to 3)?";n: IF n<1 OR
     n<> INT n OR n>3 THEN GO TO 5002
5004 REM Each QIX requires 2 of N position and delta pairs
5005 n=n*2: DIM x(n): DIM y(n): DIM h(n): DIM v(n)
5006 PROC FMUTE(7): PROC FINIT(): PROC AYENVELOPE(10,400):
     PROC AYVOLUMES(12,0): PROC FVOL(15,2): PROC FNOISE(0,4):
     PROC fBEEP(0,1): PROC fBEEP(0,4): PROC fBEEP(0,2)
5008 FOR i=1 TO n
5010   x(i)=% RND 256
5020   y(i)=% RND 183
5030   REPEAT: h(i)=2- INT ( RND *5): REPEAT UNTIL h(i)
5040   v(i)=1+ 2* INT (3* RND )
5042 NEXT i
5044 LAYER 1,0: CLS : FOR %i=0 TO 31:c= INT ( RND *256):
     x= INT ( RND *128) : PLOT INK c,x,%i:
     PLOT INK c,x,%i+32 : PLOT INK c,x,%i+64: NEXT %i
5052 LAYER 2,1: LAYER OVER 0
5055 LAYER PALETTE 0: LAYER PALETTE 0,0,0
5056 LAYER PALETTE 0,1,511-7: REM Yellow
5057 LAYER PALETTE 0,3,56: REM Green
5058 LAYER PALETTE 0,5,384: REM Red
5059 LAYER PALETTE 0,0,0: REM Black
5080 BORDER 0: PAPER 0: INK 7: OVER 1
5086 PRINT AT 23,0; INK 7; PAPER 1;
```

```
     " NextBASIC QIX audiovisual demo ";
5087 PRINT AT 0,0;:%h=0
5090 %v=64:%u=%64-v:%w=%u: REM v is Qix length, 1 to 64
5092 RESTORE 3500: READ %r,t: PROC AYBEEP(t,2)
5095 IF n=2 THEN GO TO 6000: REM 1-Qix version includes vbeeps
```

The following loop is used when two or three animations are running. Apart from one call to FNOISE it relies on direct OUT commands to update just the fine-tune registers with unmusical tones that tracks the horizontal position where the QIX pattern was most recently erased with OVER 1. The DRAW time predominates, showing how long lines affect the frame rate.

```
5100 REPEAT
5102 FOR i=1 TO n
5110   x=x(i):x=x+h(i): IF x<0 OR x>255 THEN h(i)=( SGN x)*
         (- INT (1+ RND *6)): x=x(i)
5116   y=y(i):y=y+v(i): IF y<0 OR y>182 THEN y=y(i): v(i)=-v(i)
5117   y(i)=y:x(i)=x
5118 NEXT i:%w=%u: PROC FNOISE(%w & 15<<1,4)
5119 REG 51,%h:%h=%h+3&63: REG 50,%h<<2
5120 FOR %i=1 TO n STEP 2
5130   %u=%u+2 & 63
5135   INK 0: OVER 0
5140   PLOT %u(u),%v(u):%v=%u+1:x=%256+u(v)-u(u):
         y=%256+v(v)-v(u): DRAW x-256,y-256
5150 NEXT %i
5155 %u=%w
5160 FOR i=1 TO n STEP 2
5170   %u(u)=x(i):%v(u)=y(i): INK i: OVER 1:
         PLOT %u(u),%v(u):%v=%u+1
5175   OUT %65533,i-1: OUT %49149,%u(u)
5180   t=i+1:%u(v)=x(t):%v(v)=y(t): DRAW x(t)-x(i),y(t)-y(i)
5185   %u=%u+2 & 63
5190 NEXT i
5210 REPEAT UNTIL LEN INKEY$
5220 OVER 0: PROC SH(): PROC AYENVELOPE(0,0)
5230 STOP
```

The code for a single animation is a more ambitious variant, though still prone to DRAW-related slow-downs. The drones on channels **ayA** and **ayB** are now associated with both coordinates of the pattern, leaving **ayC** free for background music, somewhat erratically rendered via FVOL and FBEEP calls in the style of AYPLAYDATA. A couple of REMs conceal optional statements that use border stripes and PRINT to track progress, at the expense of additional delay.

This sort of synchronous 'music' works well for player feedback in Space Invaders. If you're trying to get players to dance along, a looped sample or pre-authored tune rendered in the background via a suitable DRIVER will be quicker and more regular.

```
5990 REM QIX loop for 1 pattern, 2 tones and a backing choon
6000 FOR %i=0 TO 63:%u(i)=0:%v(i)=0: NEXT %i: REM clear history
6100 INK 5: OVER 1: REPEAT : REM BORDER 0: PAUSE 1: BORDER 2
6102 FOR i=1 TO n
```

```
6110   x=x(i):x=x+h(i): IF x<0 OR x>255 THEN h(i)=( SGN x)*
         (- INT (1+ RND *6)):x=x(i)
6116   y=y(i):y=y+v(i): IF y<0 OR y>182 THEN y=y(i):v(i)=-v(i)
6117   y(i)=y:x(i)=x
6118 NEXT i:%w=%u
6119 REG 51,%h:%h=%h+3&63: REG 50,%h<<2
6130 %u=%u+2 & 63
6140 PLOT %u(u),%v(u):%v=%u+1:x=%256+u(v)-u(u):
       y=%256+v(v)-v(u): DRAW x-256,y-256
6155 %u=%w
6170 %u(u)=x(1):%v(u)=y(1): PLOT x(1),%v(u):%v=%u+1
6175 OUT %65533,0: OUT %49149,%u(u)
6177 OUT %65533,4: OUT %49149,%v(u)
6180 %u(v)=x(2):%v(v)=y(2): DRAW x(2)-x(1),y(2)-y(1)
6185 %u=%u+2 & 63
6195 IF %r THEN %r=%r-1: GO TO 6210
6199   PROC FVOL(0,2)
6200   READ %r,t:%r=%r<<2
6202   IF %r>0 THEN PROC FBEEP(t,2):PROC FVOL (15,2):GO TO 6210
6205   IF t=0 THEN %r=65535: ELSE RESTORE t: GO TO 6200
6210 REPEAT UNTIL LEN INKEY$
6220 OVER 0: PROC SH(): PROC AYENVELOPE(0,0)
6230 STOP
```

Notice how a mixture of procedures and direct OUT statements are used to control the sounds. The OUTs in lines 6175 and 6177 adjust the pitch of playing sounds directly and quickly, from the coordinate data. There is no need to remap these sound effects to a chromatic scale – indeed to do so sounds odd because since the 1970s effects, as opposed to music, have generally used the reciprocal scale of the hardware.

Our ears have been retuned by experience to the way higher pitches (lower register counts) are perceptually more widely-spaced than deep sounds. Unlike a musical glissando, pitch-sliding sound effects typically change more slowly as they ascend in frequency.

There are no rules for interactive audio, least of all those forced upon classical musicians when the mechanical limitations of keyboards took hold. Use whatever values you have generated already and the changing sound will literally guide the player to understand what's going on.

The ear never blinks
Marty O'Donnell

Chapter 15, Tiles and Layers

T
I
LAYERS
E
S

Extra Layers

One big difference between the Spectrum Next and earlier ZX computers is that Next's display can be composed from several superimposed layers. Besides LAYER 0, the original Spectrum screen, there's a new LAYER 2 with 256 colours and no attribute limitations.

As an alternative to LAYER 0 there are four LAYER 1 variants. Two of these are derived from the Timex 2068 version of the Spectrum, offering additional pixel or colour resolution by using 12K of video RAM rather than just 6¾K. The others provide a LAYER 0 variant with simpler pixel addressing but the same attribute colour limits, and a quarter-resolution version of LAYER 2, with 256 colours in chunky 128x96 pixel resolution.

Layers 0, 1 and 2 are documented in the Spectrum Next manual; this chapter focusses on things that splendid book does not explore, providing access to a powerful third layer which is not officially available to NextBASIC but which I've found ways to use alongside Sprites and Layers 0, 1 and 2.

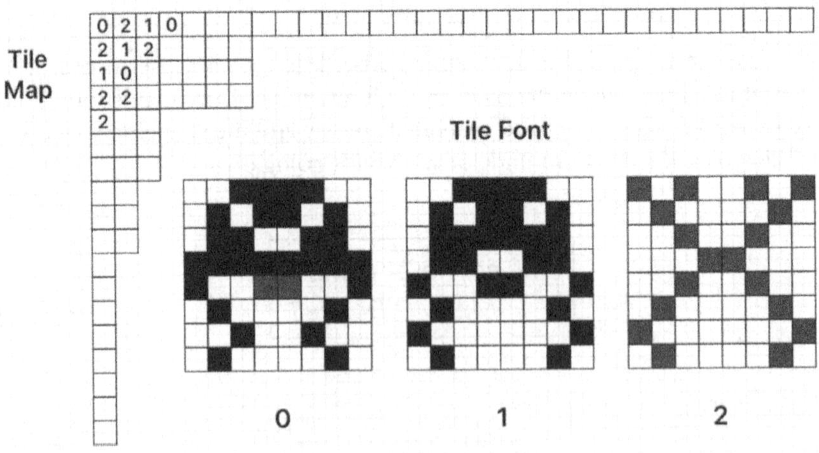

Figure 92 – The start of a Tile Font, and a Map with tile codes in the top left corner

The manual says, correctly, that Layer 3 is *'not currently available to PRINT'* but my custom driver fixes that. It allows many more pixels than the documented 'Timex HiRes' and the display of 8x8 pixel symbols in an array of 80x30 coloured cells, with two additional dedicated palettes.

Layer 3 is an especially efficient way of displaying 8x8 pixel blocks, known as 'tiles'. It supports two resolutions: 40x32 or 80x32 tiles. These extend into the Layer 0 border by 32 pixels all round. They cover the same area as the 320x256 and 640x256 pixel overscan modes of Layer 2, which are likewise not currently supported by NextBASIC but accessible via REG commands.

This chapter introduces a NextZXOS driver which lets us PRINT to Layer 3 just as we would to Layers 0, 1, or 2, so each character code printed displays a complete tile at the cursor position. Just like the default display device "s", output can be confined to a scrolling window, the cursor can be moved around, and characters – or rather, tile patterns and colours – can be redefined. All this is done using standard BASIC statements.

Figure 93 – Layer 3 display of tiles corresponding to the top left of the previous figure

Figure 92 shows the first three tiles in a Tile Font overlaid on part of a TileMap using them. The first tile (0) is used in the top left corner of the Layer 3 display, with instances of the third tile (2) alongside and below. Between those the second tile (1) appears. Like rows, columns, sprites and layers, tiles are numbered from zero. The following Figure 93 reveals how the tile numbers in the top corner of the map create a pattern on the screen, which can be placed above or below sprites and other layers. Typical tiles will be more varied and colourful – the example is deliberately simple.

ZX BASIC fonts and user-defined graphics are converted into pixel and attribute data by PRINT, but tile data is instantly expanded by the hardware, from the current font or 'tile definitions' according to the corresponding bytes in the 'TileMap', into a distinct screen layer. So if you change just the *definition* of one tile, all the positions on the screen that cite that tile will instantly change to match. This is a powerful animation technique, potentially using very little memory or processor effort to alter large areas of the screen. Imagine trees rustling in the breeze, waves processing over water or radar scanners twirling round, achieving each effect with just one or two POKEs.

Tile patterns can also be reflected and rotated *in hardware*, with no change to the tile definitions, just by twiddling one or two bits for that position on the TileMap, or for the whole screen if you set up Layer 3 to share those bits. There are lots of setup options besides the pixel resolution, allowing two, 16 or 256 colours per tile, partial transparency, mirroring and 90 degree rotation. Many of these optional combinations get demonstrated in the following text, but there are other cases to be explored, as concisely documented in the SpecNext manual, Wiki pages and reference books like Tomaz Kragelj's fine *ZX Spectrum Next Assembly Developer Guide.* These will be mentioned along the way and in exercises suggested on page 428.

Types of Tiles

Early home computers like Sinclair's ZX80 and ZX81, Commodore's Pet and the original Tandy TRS-80 could not spare enough RAM for even one bit per displayed pixel. Rather than the bit-mapped graphics of a Spectrum or Apple 2, they used a system where a single byte (or just seven bits, in the chip-trimmed TRS-80) controlled the display of each character on the screen.

The bit patterns for each character were fixed in ROM and unpacked for display by custom hardware. This saved RAM at the price of hard-wiring the character set. There could be no equivalent of the Spectrum's User Defined Graphics, let alone the vector graphics possible by toggling lines of bits associated with specific screen pixels. Scrolling was relatively fast because only the character codes, not the individual pixel data, needed to be copied around to shift the display contents up or down, in character-sized steps.

Those early machines worked only in black and white, or smeary green if you had one of the old monitors derived from radar screens. But chips like Commodore's 6560, used in the VIC 20, also allowed the colour of each character to be controlled by a scheme similar to Spectrum attributes, and with the same limitation of only two colours per character-cell.

When this approach was generalised for colour displays and games like *Centipede* and *Pacman*, the pixel patterns for each cell could be arbitrary graphics, rather than just US standard 'ASCII' characters, and the 'character cells' became known as 'tiles'. Next's Layer 3 is a tile-mapped display. It can work in mono or hybrid colour schemes, at standard or doubled resolution, up to 640x256 pixels using up to 256 colours from a palette of 512.

Only two or 16 colours may appear *within* each 8x8 pixel tile, depending on the RAM space allocated to tile numbers and corresponding colour attributes. To leave room for LAYER 2 and the traditional LAYER 0 to be displayed at the same time as tiles, the NextZXOS driver presented here delivers a 640 by 240-pixel tile layer, composed of 2400 sixteen-colour tiles.

Next hardware allows each tile to pick from sixteen groups of sixteen colours within the 256-entry palette. Thus 256 colours can appear on any single display line or column, but not all in a single tile. It's rather like the LAYER 0 attribute system, but with more choices at each level. This is just one possible Layer 3 configuration. As Figure 94 implies, there are lots more depending on how you apportion ULA memory between tile patterns, visible or hidden tile-maps, NextZXOS and perhaps a LAYER 0 or LAYER 1 display as well.

Layer 3 configurations	*Width in pixels*	*Width in tiles*	*Bytes per map entry*	*Font bytes per tile*	*Bytes in full map*	*Bytes in tile font*
2 colour LoRes	*320*	*40*	*1*	*8*	*1280*	*2048*
16 colour LoRes	*320*	*40*	*1*	*32*	*1280*	*8192*
256 colour LoRes	*320*	*40*	*2*	*64*	*2560*	*16384*
2 colour HiRes	*640*	*80*	*1*	*8*	*2560*	*2048*
16 colour HiRes	*640*	*80*	*1*	*32*	*2560*	*8192*
256 col HiRes	*640*	*80*	*2*	*64*	*5120*	*16384*

Figure 94 – Some of the Layer 3 memory and display options

Muddying the waters, NextBASIC supports another sort of 'tile', implemented entirely in software, as an option for LAYER 2 or LAYER 1,0 (loRes) displays. These tiles are very different from the hardware sort. They may be 8 by 8 pixels in size, like user-defined graphics, or 16 by 16 like sprites, but either way one byte is allocated per pattern pixel.

Those tiles are documented in the Next Manual, at the end of the Graphics chapter, so they're not discussed further here. I only mention them to draw a distinction between those 'tiles' – effectively, square blocks of pixels copied around by the CPU – and Layer 3 hardware tiles which support higher resolutions and are much more economical in memory and bandwidth. It's unfortunate that the same word has been used to describe these two very different approaches to building up graphics. Each has unique strengths and limitations. At long last, I've worked out how we can use hardware tiles in NextBASIC, as well as the software sort. The information is equally relevant to machine-code programmers - they just have more memory for Layer 3 data, as long as they can live without access to NextBASIC system variables.

Three-layer text demo

Before writing a complete Layer 3 driver, with support for dynamic redefinition of characters, custom-sized scrolling windows, cursor control and colours, I cobbled together a ten-line demo for the 2023 Crash Show which put three layers of text on-screen at once, with horizontal and vertical scrolling for different layers, and optional sprites bouncing around over the top, using little more than POKEs and a few REG commands.

Figure 95 – This demo comes alive once all three layers and sprites start moving

Unlike LAYER 2 there are strict rules about which RAM pages can be used for hardware tile and font data. This demo had to be short because it squeezes the program, 8k tile font and a normal LAYER 0 display all into the first 16k of RAM. Of all the RAM BANKs in Next, only BANK 5, usually mapped to addresses 16384 to 32767 (the RAM on a 16k Spectrum) and half of the system BANK 7 support hardware tile data. BANK 7 is protected from BASIC POKEs, though the machine-code driver presented later can work around that, so my little demo packs everything except the tile index and LAYER 2 overlay – including the system variables, 8k of colour font, BASIC program, variables and LAYER 0 display – into that 16k.

This memory map is a contingent hack, and at some point – perhaps as soon as NextBASIC 2.10 – Garry Lancaster may make some of it obsolete by implementing Layer 3 support within NextZXOS. But the examples will remain valid, showing how the third layer uses Next's FPGA-internal and external RAM, and can be directly accessed with BASIC POKEs, Z80 machine code or DMA. They also shows how memory is reserved, allocated and used by the existing system, and how all or part of that can be bypassed – with care – to make NextBASIC and other languages like Forth and Pascal do things that were previously only supported by raw Z80n machine code.

The entire demo program, apart from the tile data, is listed below. It can also be seen scrolling around within the three layers of the demo display, as the program text is LISTed to LAYER 0 to give that some interesting content. Alternatively you could LOAD a SCREEN$, but keep the filename short as there are very few bytes free – this is a rare case where the per cent suffixes are vital to ensure that the program fits into the required RAM area.

```
100 CLEAR %32767: DIM o$($20FF):%v=% DPEEK 23627
110 %o=%v+260 & $ff00: LAYER %0: PAPER %6: CLS : LIST %100
120 LAYER %2,%1: PAPER %0: LAYER OVER %0: LAYER PALETTE %0:
    REG %20,%0: CLS : INK %200
130 PRINT CHR$ (%29); CHR$ (%1); CHR$ (%28); CHR$ (%1)''''
    "   NEXT BASIC      3 LAYER TEXT"
140 LOAD "l3b" CODE %o,%8192: REG %87,%14
150 FOR %f=$e000 TO $e9ff: POKE %f,%f&255: NEXT %f
```

```
160 REG %110,%192: REG %111,%o>>8
170 REG %108,%0: REG %107,%225
180 REPEAT :%f=%f-1&255: SPRITE MOVE INT : REG %49,%f:
    REG %38,%f: REPEAT UNTIL CODE INKEY$
190 LAYER %2,%1: LAYER CLEAR
```

Tile RAM allocation

The hacks start on the first line, after we CLEAR 32767 to stop BASIC using the top 32k of Z80 address space. The string array **o$** is dimensioned to reserve half of the first 16k of RAM, immediately after the BASIC program, plus an extra 255 bytes to make sure that there will always be 8k available within the array after starting from an address which is a multiple of 256. We must do this because the tile data is required to start at such a 'round' address; the hardware presumes that the least significant eight bits of the start address are zero.

0k	SYSTEM ROM
16k	BANK 5 – LAYER 0 pixels and attributes
22¾k	System Variables
24k	BASIC program (starting at PROG)
	BASIC Variables – tile font in o$ (starting at %O)
32k	Unused space, around 24k, all above RAMTOP
56k	Start of BANK 7 – remapped to top of Z80 RAM
	2560 bytes of tile data (32 rows of 80 columns)
59½k	Unused space, around 3.5k (reserved for Timex screen data)
62k	2k of NextZXOS private data (up to the middle of BANK 7)

Figure 96 – Memory Map of how the Z80 sees the Tile demo

Figure 96 shows how the 64k of memory accessible to standard PEEK and POKE commands and the Z80 is arranged while the three-layer demo runs. The first 24k is a normal BASIC configuration, with ROM followed by the LAYER 0 display area – 6k of pixels and 768 bytes of attributes – and the System Variables. Then comes the program and variables, dominated by the big array **o$** dimensioned at the start of **3LayerText.bas.**

All this has to be squished into the first 16k of RAM, because that's most of the 24k the FPGA mirrors for LAYER 0, 1 and 3 graphics. That's why we used CLEAR to keep all of BASIC – including the Z80 stack – under the 32k mid-point. Sprites are held in a separate 16k block inside the FPGA, alongside 2K for the Copper co-processor. The biggest display area, for LAYER 2, is held elsewhere in main memory, in consecutive blocks of banks numbered from 9 upwards, after the banks reserved for system use.

The second half of the 64k memory map is mostly unused by this demonstration, apart from the first half of BANK 7 which we slot into the top 8k of Z80 space with the MMU7 register. Most of BANK 7 is dedicated to undocumented system tables, but we know – from the hardware design, and the way Timex modes are implemented – that about 6k in there is potentially available for LAYER 1.

This demo stomps on 2½K of that to store the TileMap data grid. A similar amount immediately after could be claimed for per-tile attributes, but this little demo uses the same attribute for each tile, to reduce the pressure in the BASIC program area lower down.

The DPEEK at the end of line 100 reads the system variable VARS from address 23627 into %V. Line 110 steps past the variable's name and dimensions, which we know will be first in the VARS space as we used CLEAR immediately before the DIM, to an address beyond allocated for at least 8k of the array. The hardware requires that the least-significant eight bits of the tile font and map addresses must be zero; the &$FF00 term, in conjunction with the extra 255 bytes in **o$**, ensures that **%o** holds just such an address.

Tile font setup

This 8k is where we're going to POKE our custom Layer 3 font. That needs 32 bytes for each 256 characters, with four bits per pixel for 16 colours in the 8x8 tile pattern. If we'd have selected 256-colour tiles, there would only have been room for 128 patterns. Remember that we're aiming to get three layers up at once, plus sprites, without upsetting BASIC.

If we didn't need LAYER 0, or were allowed to overwrite the system variables, we'd gain flexibility but incur a lot more trouble testing. If you wonder why it took me five years to get this demo together, and NextBASIC 2.09 still doesn't support hardware tiles, that's partly why. In some ways Z80 programmers who clobber the system have it easy. But this book is about exploring and extending the entire Next system, firmware as well as hardware, not doing away with NextZXOS as games ports are wont to do.

The rest of line 110 lists the program to LAYER 0, in standard-palette black ink on yellow paper. Lines 120 and 130 switch to LAYER 2 and plonk an orange banner in the middle of it. The CHR$ sequences select double-width and double-height characters, while the REG 20 command sets the global transparency colour so all the layers are visible.

Line 140 loads the 256-entry colour font data from an 8k file. Then REG 87 puts page 14 – the start of BASIC BANK 7 – in the top 8k of address space, where the loop on line 150 stores 2560 character codes. It uses **& 255** to convert each byte address into consecutive values from 0 to 255 so the entire font appears ten times over 32 lines each of 80 columns. That's just test data – you could use anything else, for a more interesting display, by the same technique used to load and copy the pre-baked font.

REG commands from the Next manual follow thick and fast. I shall explain each one briefly now, and go into detail later when fully documenting the driver. Line 160 tells the FPGA where we've put the tile font and index. Line 170 selects the Layer 3 variant we want: one using the first 16 palette 0 colours, without rotation or mirroring, shown on top of LAYER 0, at 80x32 resolution – matching the fifth variant in Figure 94.

Four bits per pixel allow only 15 colours, rather than 16, because REG 76 reserves one of the four-bit patterns for transparent pixels. ULA memory sets a practical limit on the total size of the TileMap and 256-colour Tile Font, even with NextZXOS disabled, especially if you want to use LAYER 0 or 1 at the same time. While NextZXOS running we could put tile data in three places: the first 6¾K of BANK 5, around 8k at the end of that area, BASIC permitting, plus almost 6k in BANK 7, as long as we don't try to use Timex HiColor or HiRes at the same time. This frees up around 20 of the possible 24k, but the system variables split that into three parts, rather than the two we'd prefer.

All three layers are now visible at once; line 180 gets them moving! Variable %F cycles round and round from 255 to 0, scrolling Layer 3 vertically via REG 49 and LAYER 0 horizontally with REG 38, directly without needing LAYER AT. The SPRITE MOVE INT command synchronises these movements with display frame output and updates any previously-configured sprite animations. The loop repeats till a key is pressed, then line 190 does the minimum needed to restore a default display.

I set up a load of moving sprites with a separate program for the Crash Show, then merged this demo over the top of that, so that a fourth layer of sprites bounced around, without having to squeeze any SPRITE statements into the demo program itself. The simple program that creates the Tile Font shown is included in the **TileDriver** download, but not listed here as it's not essential to understanding either the driver or the demo. **MakeL3Bold.bas** reads a standard 96-character 768-byte two-colour Spectrum font – in this case my brother's "BoldFont" from the Crash Tech Tape – and expands each bit into four; that's why we need 8k to define 256 tiles.

Figure 97 - The 80 by 32 character Layer 3 bold text font

Tiles 0 to 31, corresponding to invisible ZX control characters, are left blank, followed by the font patterns for ASCII characters 32 to 127. As each set bit in the standard font is expanded to four set bits in the tile, BIN 1111, our tile INK uses palette entry 15. Changing the bits make the pixels of that character use different colours.

Tile numbers 128 to 143 correspond to Sinclair block-graphics, normally generated on the fly by ROM logic. Some NextBASIC bit-twiddling creates the same patterns, by analysis of the four least significant bits of the index number. The rest of the font is padded out with sixteen solid-colour tiles using codes 144 to 159, and INVERSE 1 versions of the ASCII set from 160 to 255. These correspond to ASCII codes, except with each top bit set.

This is just test data. Artistically-minded readers could put any set of 256 8x8 pixel 15-colour tiles in that 8k. Layer 3 doesn't care what the data is, it just uses the first 32 bytes for index 0, working from left to right and top to bottom, all the way up to index or CHR$ 255 at offset 8160. If you don't need 256 tiles you can stop sooner and save RAM, but then you should avoid using high index numbers, or you'll see random graphics in those positions.

Enter the TileDriver

That little demo is a neat example for people looking for a minimal way to add a fast high-resolution overscan display layer, but it's just a demo. There's no cursor, no scrolling, and integrating the layer with BASIC programs is fiddly. Writing to the layer still requires POKEs, though string parameters often remove the need for a loop to update a line or even the whole screen.

My next project refined this prototype into a NextZXOS system driver that directly supports PRINT, scrolling windows within the screen area, and control codes like those for the standard LAYERs. These place and move the cursor, so that PRINT AT and comma-separated columns work consistently. This is a complementary example to the *NextBASIC Profiler* I wrote using *Zeus* for the 2.08 Next system update, and the *Interrupt Slot handler* written for this book with *Odin*. Those examples do use DRIVER commands and interrupts but they don't support the character-output aspect which is designed for printer, network and similar drivers, as the TileDriver must. In combination the three drivers demonstrate interrupts, transparent paging, driver-local storage, Get and Set commands – and now, faster, device-independent, high-resolution windowed display output too.

Dot ASM

By the time I started this work, Chris Taylor's inline assembler dot command was available, allowing assembly language to be edited and assembled from comments within a BASIC program. This reminded me of ACS *Ultraviolet* which I used in 1982, and the Currah *microSource* ROM released later, but it has full NextBASIC and Z80n support. So **.asm** was the obvious choice for my third Next driver project, with bonus features like interfacing with

NextBASIC integer variables and conditional assembly. The following example has been written and tested entirely from the NextBASIC editor.

In a year **.asm** has leapfrogged *Zeus, Odin, Z80 BBC BASIC* and earlier ZX and CP/M assemblers to become the best-integrated Z80n assembler for Next, as we shall soon see. It does stop assembling at the first error it finds, giving a concise reason. That's no handicap, as it's so fast and well-integrated.

One of Chris's demos, **.bfind**, seemed so useful to NextBASIC devotees that I bundled it into the NextBASIC 2.09 release. That scans the program in memory for a specified string (such as a label, variable name, text or comment, including Z80n source – but not binary tokens like NEXT or RETURN) reporting the next matching line number. The bigger your program, the more useful you'll find it.

TileDriver features

When the American Standard Code for Information Interchange (ASCII) character set was invented in 1973, display screens were rare and printing teletypes were the most common output device. Earlier teletypes used a five-bit character code, first devised for telegraphy by Emile Baudot in 1870, later revised by Donald Murray to minimise wear on the machinery. Five bits were enough for the Latin alphabet but required 'shift' characters reminiscent of Sinclair keyboards to switch to digits and limited punctuation.

Murray also introduced codes for 'Line Feed' to roll the paper to the next line, and 'Carriage Return' to move the print-head back to the left margin. These 'new line' operations were separated to give the option of overprinting and underlining. Another non-printing code was reserved for switching between upper and lower-case, though most teleprinters, like early micros, PRINTED ONLY IN CAPITALS.

Five-bit codes are still used by radio amateurs and communication equipment made for deaf people. ASCII uses seven bits to encode upper and lower-case letters, numerals and a rag-bag of punctuation characters, some of them freshly-invented, as noted in Chapter 6, The NextBASIC Text Editor.

Sinclair's ZX80 and ZX81 micros used a custom 6-bit code, in part to save 256 bytes of precious ROM. A ragged group of lower-case characters was added when Sinclair embraced 7-bit ASCII for the ZX Spectrum. Seven bits permit 128 possible codes, but ASCII only defines 94 symbols, plus the blank space code 32, and one known as DEL which has all bits set, corresponding to punched-paper tape with holes in all seven positions. Rather than delete the previous character, as a key labelled DEL might, this pattern was deliberately ignored, giving an easy way to skip a character previously wrongly punched without having to start a new roll of paper tape.

Never being slaves to standardisation, Sinclair reused that code 127 for the copyright symbol, which does not appear in ASCII. Paper tape was still in use, if not exactly popular, in the 1970s when CP/M was devised, but

Sinclair sensibly decided that fully supporting 7-bit teletypes on the TV-oriented ZX Spectrum was not going to do anything for sales, unlike having a way to display and print a copyright sign.

This accounted for codes from 32 to 127, but left codes below 32 up for grabs. ASCII reserved those for invisible 'control characters' as a handy way to control the behaviour, as opposed to the printed characters, of teletypes and other serial peripherals, marking sections within the data or controlling its flow. Home micros ignored or repurposed most of these esoteric codes, apart from 10 and 13, Line Feed and Carriage Return, which came in handy to separate lines of text.

While sort-of adopting ASCII for the Spectrum, Sinclair ignored about half the control codes and used most of the rest to encode display output modifier keywords like INK, OVER, AT and TAB. Appendix A of the original Spectrum manual summarises these non-character codes in Sinclair's set. A group of four, from 8 to 11, was dedicated to cursor movements in the directions, if not intervals, corresponding to most of those ASCII codes. While developing the +3e ROM and then NextZXOS, Garry Lancaster used up all the 'spare' codes Sinclair left fallow. His additions are in the expanded Appendices of Spectrum Next manuals and the new chapter about *Channels, Streams, Devices and Windows.*

CHR$	TileDriver ID	NextZXOS role	ASCII definition
0..3	N/A	Window and font setup	Null, text start/end
4	HOME	Move cursor to top left	End of transmission
5	LASTL	Cursor to start of last line	Enquire if listening
6	COMMA	Tab in half-window steps	Acknowledge receipt
7	SCROLL	Move text up by one line	Ring bell or beeper
8	LEFTA	Move cursor backward	Backspace cursor left
9	RIGHTA	Move cursor forward	Tabulate cursor right
10	DOWN	Move cursor downward	Feed next paper line
11	UP	Move cursor upward	Tabulate vertically
12	DEL	Erase previous character	Feed new form/page
13	ENTER	Cursor to start of next line	Print Carriage Return
14	CLS	Clear screen (or window)	Switch character set
15..21	N/A	Set PRINT style or wash	Device control, etc.
22	AT	Position cursor Y then X	Synchronous idle
23	TAB	Blank to chosen column	End of transmission

Figure 98 – PRINT control codes implemented by the TileDriver, and ASCII equivalents

Figure 98 shows the dozen control codes which the TileDriver supports on a white background. The first four codes, ignored by Sinclair and re-defined by Garry to set up display windows and fonts, are not implemented in the TileDriver but that does come with NextBASIC procedures to customise the font and window size and position.

Sinclair's print-style codes from 15 to 21 are skipped, as colours are baked into the Tile Font, but the driver understands that those are followed by colour-number bytes when PRINTed from ZX BASIC so it skips those too. This means that the cursor position is not screwed up by orphaned codes meant to select ULA colours like GREEN or CYAN, which would otherwise send the cursor to the start of the first or last line of the window, following Next's extensions.

I wrote code to implement DEL, which moves the cursor back to the left or up to the end of the previous line, blanking the current character, but ran out of space to implement it in a 512-byte driver, mainly because of the complications of moving between lines and checking for window edges. But I did squeeze in the four cursor-control codes 8 to 11, the four PRINT modifiers AT, TAB, comma and apostrophe, and Next-specific codes to scroll and clear the current window or jump to the first or last line.

Full Z80n source to implement these control codes, and trap the others, is presented later. If you've got different priorities, or don't mind extending the driver to use additional memory beyond one of the pre-allocated DRIVER slots, you may drop in additional code. You might prefer to keep only the vital time-critical parts in assembly-language and use NextBASIC PROCs to add optional features. That's the approach I've used to implement user-defined windows, character redefinition and screen lookup without bloating the already-complicated example driver.

Garry uses numeric parameters in the string passed to OPEN to set the bounds of user-defined windows. My approach stores these within the driver, defaulting to full-screen dimensions – unless you patch the code, as explained later – but then provides a set of DRIVER commands to adjust the default window size and position. There are pros and cons to either approach – my way, there's no need to re-open the stream just to adjust the window, but a risk that you might use a sequence of commands that confuses the driver, by setting the top below the bottom line, or leaving the cursor outside the window.

The code to check this would be long and fiddly, so I've wimped out and provided BASIC procedures that collate several DRIVER commands and do the necessary checking. If you bypass those checks, expect trouble. The driver assumes windows have at least one line, two columns, and a cursor within that space. You have the freedom to add cool things like smooth hardware scrolling, or TileMaps taller than the visible display, but it's up to you to make sure each DRIVER command you send makes sense in context.

The driver has ten 'system variables' of its own, which you can tweak to adjust the behaviour of Layer 3 windows. Commands let you read and write any of these bytes, even though they're secreted away in protected system memory. Another three variables are used inside the driver when processing multi-byte sequences like PRINT AT. You can read those just like the first ten, but changing them may either have no effect or gobble up characters.

Those are handy if you add support for other multi-byte sequences. Those date back to dumb dialup computer terminals, so naturally CP/M uses them on Next, as do terminal emulators, Epson parallel printers and similar still useful accessories. These 'escape sequences' are manufacturer-specific, like Sinclair codes but usually prefixed with CHR$ 27, ASCII's ESC code, which the standard says 'alters the meaning of a limited number of following bytes'.

PRINT AT sends three control characters, not just one. CHR$ 22, the Sinclair AT control code, is followed by two code bytes indicating the row then column where the next output (known as the cursor position) should appear. The TileDriver checks AT parameters against the window bounds, providing examples of how to do this in Z80 code if you'd rather adjust the window with a PRINT sequence rather than DRIVER commands or OPEN parameters. Alternatively, you can save bytes by omitting these checks and offsets if you only expect to use full-width 40 or 80-column TileMaps.

For instance, PRINT CHR$ 22; CHR$ 0; CHR$ 0; is functionally identical to PRINT AT 0,0; in BASIC. Either moves the character output position to the top left corner, ready to overwrite the top line. In NextBASIC, or with this TileDriver, PRINT CHR$ 4; is enough, using the new Spectrum's HOME code.

In CP/M and the wider world, that's equivalent to the escape sequence CHR$ 27;"H"… strictly speaking, that is the only 'graphics' command' you need to write a *very* jerky version of *Space Invaders*! My introduction to the ESC-code CHR$ 27;"H" spell came at Racal in 1980, while exploring just such a game running in DEC BASIC+ on a PDP-11 driving a DEC VT-52B terminal at 9600 baud. That was the sort with a CRT screen and an electrolytic wet-wick printer, into which we poured salty water to get soggy thermal screen-prints. Those were the days of truly eccentric hardware; it wasn't just a Sinclair thing!

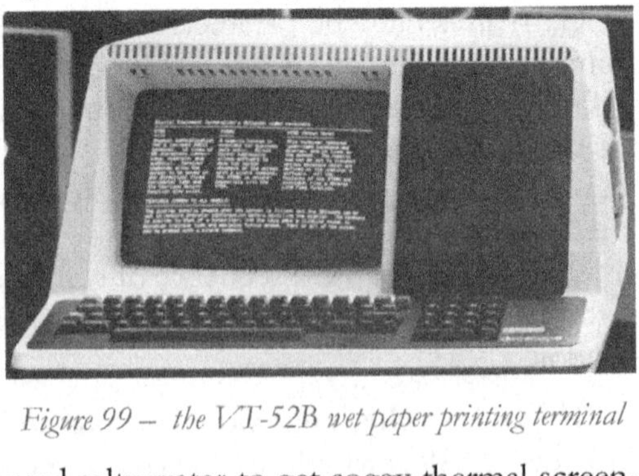

Figure 99 – the VT-52B wet paper printing terminal

Width and Height in Figure 100 give the maximum size of the TileMap, starting from the offset in the first word. The command DRIVER CODE

"T", 2, 64 sets Width to 64 tiles or characters. Output can be limited to a rectangular area within that space by setting Left, Right, Top and Bottom. Top Left is 0,0, as for PRINT AT. The final read-only variable, OldPage, temporary preserves the previous value of MMU7.

Offset	Name	Purpose	Default
0	StartL	Start address of TileMap, low byte	0 (always)
1	StartH	Start address of TileMap, high byte	224
2	Width	Maximum tiles per line e.g. 40, 64, 80	80
3	Height	Maximum lines per screen e.g. 24, 32	30
4	Left	Window left margin in tiles	0
5	Right	Window right margin + 1, in tiles	80 (Width)
6	Top	Window top margin in skipped lines	0
7	Bottom	Window lower margin, line below last	30 (Height)
8	CursorX	Print position on line, Left .. Right	0
9	CursorY	Current print row, Top .. Bottom-1	0
10	Count	Bytes pending in a control sequence	0
11	Seq1	First control byte of this sequence	1
12	Seq2	Second control byte of this sequence	2
13	OldPage	MMU7 register value to be restored	3

Figure 100 – TileDriver internal variables: white lines read/write, grey typically read-only

It's good practice to write helper procedures to display the state of each data-structure in your programs. PROC TILEVARS() outputs a tabulated list of the TileDriver system variable names and values. If you're only interested in the first of these, add a parameter to tell it the offset to stop at, e.g. PROC TILEVARS(7) will skip the cursor and control sequence information.

```
400 REM Tabulate driver state
410 DEFPROC TILEVARS(m=13)
420 LOCAL s,s$,v: RESTORE 470
430 FOR s=0 TO m: READ s$
440   DRIVER 84,s,%-1 TO v
450   PRINT s$;" ";s,v
460 NEXT s
470 DATA "Start L","Start H","Width","Height","Left","Right"
480 DATA "Top","Bottom","Cursor X","Cursor Y","Count"
490 DATA "Seq1","Seq2","Top Page"
500 ENDPROC
```

Unlike some terminal displays there is no visible cursor, but the place where PRINT would output the next character is stored in CursorY for the row and CursorX for the column. CursorX is allowed to point *just past* the last character position on a line, in which case subsequent output will be to the start of the *next* line, scrolling if necessary. This provision for what Sinclair QLs calls a 'pending newline' allows us to print all the way to the bottom corner of a window without immediately forcing the display to scroll up, blanking the last line and losing the first.

Sadly NextBASIC only supports visible INPUT on the built-in channel "S". INPUT from any other channel is neither echoed on screen nor available for editing before entry. Thankfully, streams to other layers can still read the keyboard with INPUT or INKEY$, or the NextBASIC screen editor PEEK LASTK approach may be used.

I asked Garry in March, May and July 2024 about allowing other drivers to call the system line-input routine but got no reply before I had to finish this chapter. I infer that it's hard-coded for the layers he implemented in 2018 and it'd be a lot of work to make that more general. The same lock-in applies to the current CLS command, which does yet not permit a stream parameter like CLS #6, as it would in Sinclair SuperBASIC. However, PRINT CHR$ 6; to a stream works equally well for clearing NextZXOS system screens and TileDriver windows.

The TileSetter utility

TileSetter.bas is a utility program to set up the DRIVER's display format, font and windows. It also shows how to redefine characters on the fly and scan for character codes, like Spectrum BASIC's SCREEN$ function. I've implemented those features in BASIC procedures as they're useful examples but inessential and relatively niche.

Even after that, it was a tight squeeze to pack all the key PRINT features into one 512-byte driver, along with data bytes to keep track of the window and cursor position; but that gives me an opportunity to demonstrate new Z80n features, and traditional Zilog space-saving hacks!

Some of the standard control codes are implemented very concisely: cursor HOME and SCROLL (CHR$ 4 and CHR$ 7 respectively) need just five bytes of code. CHR$ 5, to put the cursor at the start of the last line of the window, takes between six and eight bytes, depending on which others you drop.

The following **TileSetter.bas** program loads the driver, copies the font it needs into BANK 7, then prepares an 80x30 character Layer 3 display centred on the screen. Once everything is set up it places test output on the top and bottom lines, lists itself to the layer ten times, then tidies up.

RAM above address 49151 is reserved for font loading and copying, but once that's done the top 16k can be reclaimed for BASIC, unless you're using PROC TSCREEN() in which case you'll need to leave the top 8k protected so the TileMap can be paged in up there as character-codes are read from the layer.

It's a fiddle to work around the way BANK 7 is hidden from NextBASIC programs. We're not trusted even to PEEK BANK 7, but if you are not also using LAYER 0 or 1 you may shunt the TileMap into the original Spectrum screen RAM area between 16k and 22¾K with PROC TILEBASE(16384), after removing the RAMTOP-checking line 3005 from PROC TSCREEN(). recovering the top 8k and PEEKing just as Sinclair intended. Storing the TileMap there makes a mess of your ULA display but, if you're writing a new program for Next using the TileDriver, you probably won't mind as you've still got LAYER 2 and Sprites to play with.

```
 900 REM TileSetter 20240307
1000 RUN AT 3: CLEAR %48*1024-1
1020 LAYER %0: PAPER %7: BRIGHT %1: INK %1: BORDER %0: CLS
1040 LAYER PALETTE 0,31,511: REM bright layer 0 & overscan
1060 %r=% REG 87: REG %87,%14: REM Map Bank 7 at 56k
1080 PRINT "Populating tiles"
1100 FOR %f=$ec00 TO %80*30+$ebff STEP %2
1120   POKE %f,%f&63+32,%f+1&63+64: NEXT %f
1130 PROC PAL SET()
1140 %c=%48*1024:%f=$e000: PRINT "Uploading font"
1150 LOAD "ASCII.bin" CODE %c
1160 %m=$cccc: REM font colour mask
1170 FOR %f=%f TO %96*32+f-1 STEP $8: DPOKE %f,% DPEEK c&m,%
DPEEK (c+2)&m,% DPEEK (c+4)&m,% DPEEK (c+6)&m
1180   %c=%c+8: NEXT %f
```

The loop at line 1100 puts dummy tile numbers from 32 (space) to 127 (the copyright sign) in the TileMap from address $EC00 (60416), POKEing adjacent codes two at a time to speed up the loop. I've used base 16 here to save space and highlight the need for TileMaps to start at an address which is a multiple of 256, hence the hexadecimal value must end with 00.

The next part of the set-up routine works around system restrictions to prepare memory areas that NextBASIC does not expose. PROC PAL SET() uploads our own TileMap palette 0. This must use direct REG commands since LAYER PALETTE only uploads to the current layer and NextBASIC doesn't yet support Layer 3.

Then the second loop copies the tile font from address 49152, where we initially loaded it above RAMTOP, to address $E000 (56k, start of the top MMU page) which has been temporarily remapped to contain the first half of system BANK 7, not otherwise POKEable. You might expect that LOAD CODE $E000 would do the trick, since we've set RAMTOP below that address and used MMU7 to put the memory we want to load at that address, but no such luck. LOAD CODE resets REG 87 to its default value 1 so the data ends up in BANK 0 rather than BANK 7. A Z80 LDIR routine would fix this, but for demonstration purposes I've used BASIC, speeding it up by copying eight bytes at a time with DPOKE after four consecutive DPEEKs.

The font file has four set bits for each pixel, corresponding to bright white, palette INK 15, but each pixel value is combined with the 'font colour mask' in %M as it is loaded, so that other colours – strictly speaking, other palette entries – can be selected by clearing bits in %M. The value $CCCC excludes red and blue, giving green characters. $DDDD yields cyan, $7777 or $8888 are shades of grey, $1111 and $9999 are dark and bright blue, and so on. You can even have striped characters by using different values for each four-bit nybble, so $3A3A gives red and magenta stripes.

In a graphics application like a game you'd probably use more colours in most of the tiles, and your own palette. This demo uses the 16-colour HiRes configuration from Figure 94, but could be extended to 256 colours or limited to 2 with other settings of the Layer 3 control registers we're about to configure. But first, here's the PAL SET() procedure called from line 1130:

```
4650 DEFPROC PAL SET(%n=@0)
4660 IF %n>1 THEN PRINT "Palettes 0 and 1 available": STOP
4670 LOCAL %t= REG 67 & 15:; Preserve other enabling bits
4680 REG %67,%n<<6+t+48:; Tile palette with auto-increment
4700 LOCAL %c: RESTORE 4780: FOR %t=0 TO 15
4710   READ %c: REG 65,%c: NEXT %t
4780 DATA @0,@10,@10100000,@10100010,@10100,@10110,@10110100
4790 DATA @10110110,@01101101,@11,@11100000,@11100011,@11100
4800 DATA @11111,@11111100,@11111111:;Bits R2R1R0G2G1G0B2B1
```

Memory mapping magic

Line 1200 deals with memory mapping. It restores the old value of MMU7, REG 87, then points registers 110 and 111 to the TileMap and Tile Font respectively. The interpretation of bits in these registers is bizarre; the most significant bit is set to use BANK 7 and clear for BANK 5. Bit 6 is always ignored, and bits 0 to 5 give the offset, in steps of 256 bytes, where the Tile data will start within the selected bank!

```
1200 REG %87,%r: REG %110,@10001100: REG %111,@10011100
```

The TileMap winds up at offset @001100*256 = 3072 in BANK 7, half way through the second screen area. Register 111 tells the hardware that these Tile Definitions start at offset @011100*256. That's 7168 bytes – 7k – into BANK 7. Hang on, you may think: here be dragons! That's past the HiRes pixels in Timex LAYER 1,2, and well into the secret parts of BANK 7. Only Garry knows what's going on there and he is entitled to change it at any time.

In practice, this is how I've mapped the visible ASCII codes 32 to 127 to use the 3k four-bit font I just DPOKEd into the *start* of BANK 7, mapped via MMU7 to address $E000, 56k as the Z80 sees it. Two tricks combine here to put the 3k tile font and the 2400 byte (80x30 character) TileMap back-to-back in the (relatively) safe area at the start of BANK 7.

Firstly, remember that the first 32 ASCII values are reserved for invisible 'control codes'. The 96 visible characters use codes from 32 up to 127, and those are the ones we need to define graphically with tiles so that an ASCII listing is readable. Each character definition uses 64 pixels of four bits (for 15 colours plus transparent) so 32 bytes apiece. Memory usable for Layer 3, yet not already claimed by the system, is scarce. We certainly don't want to waste 1k of it – 32 bytes each for 32 characters – defining tile patterns for invisible control codes!

The penny drops when you realise that the FPGA can only access the first 8k of BANK 7 for ULA and Tile displays. As Phoebus's manual says of these Layer 3 (TileMap) address registers, *'Bank 7 addresses wrap around its 8k boundary'.* We've set REG 111, the Tile Definitions Base Address, to start 7k into BANK 7. Tile codes 0 to 31 will read patterns from the last (24 places) of that 8k space. We don't mind what's there as ASCII doesn't use those codes for character patterns, and simply *reading* there is safe, anyway.

But the 96 *visible* ASCII codes, 32 to 127, can't be rendered from immediately after that because they'd be the other side of that '8k boundary'. The 'wrap around' effect means that the pattern for tile 32, an ASCII space, gets read from the start of BANK 7, our REG 111 setting.

The pattern for tile 127, the copyright sign, comes from the last 32 bytes before the 3k offset where our TileMap starts. Everything fits together nicely and we've squeezed all we need into the first part of BANK 7 which we're able – if not strictly 'allowed' – to reuse for our Layer 3 data.

BANK 5 has not been touched, so standard ZX attribute screens, in LAYER 0 or LAYER 1,1 work normally, the system variables are intact and we've got the full 40k for BASIC variables. From this point onward we could CLEAR 65535 and put anything we like in main Z80 memory. The driver will automatically stuff character codes in BANK 7 and Layer 3 hardware will read the corresponding tile patterns just before that.

In practice you may prefer to CLEAR 56*1024-1 so that MMU7 can still be used to PEEK around in secret banks. The optional TSCREEN procedure puts BANK 7 up there temporarily when its reading codes from chosen positions in the TileMap; that's how I've implemented the Layer 3 equivalent of SCREEN$ in BASIC.

The PROC fails safe, checking that RAMTOP is below the MMU7 space and otherwise returning 0 without attempting paging. If you need SCREEN$ capability but begrudge locking down the top 8k, and don't have other hacks in mind for that area, you could rewrite PROC TSCREEN as a short Z80 routine, temporarily mapping the tile data anywhere your code can access. If you do that, make sure you disable interrupts before paging and restore them immediately afterwards, in case the Z80 stack or some other area used by interrupt code gets momentarily mapped out by your tile-reading routine.

Configuring Layer 3 registers and driver variables

That's a lot of discussion for three little REG commands, but we'll need seven more, and ten DRIVER commands, before we can open a stream and start printing to Layer 3. These six lines complete the job, starting by loading the tile driver itself:

```
1210 .install TILE.DRV
1220 REG %107,@11100001: REG %108,%0
1230 PROC TILEBASE($e000): PROC TILEWIN(%0,%0,%80,%30)
1240 REM Clip outer 8 pixels above and below and centre screen
1250 REG %27,%0: REG %27,%159: REG %27,%8: REG %27,%247
1260 REG %49,%248
```

REG 107, TileMap control, picks the hi-res 15 colour variant from the options in Figure 94 using Layer 3 palette 0. Set bit 4 to use palette 1. Clear bit 5, and allocate two bytes per tile in the TileMap, to enable 256 colours and per-tile reflection and rotation effects. Clear bit 6 for 40 rather than 80 columns; this frees up spare bytes for per-tile attributes.

In this case we're saving memory for a high-resolution 80-column display. Rather than have one attribute byte per tile, interleaved with the TileMap index, all tiles share the same attribute, read from REG 108. Apart from the least significant bit, this control byte works like REG 55, Sprite Attribute 2, which flips, rotates and re-colours four-bit per-pixel hardware sprites.

Tile and sprite attributes

Attributes are additional properties; Spectrum attributes affect rectangular areas of the screen. In Richard Altwasser's LAYER 0 each 8x8 pixel area gets its ink and paper colour, and bright or flash options, from a separately-stored 'colour attribute byte'. Layer 3 attributes determine the orientation, colour-set and composition of tiles into Next's multi-layer display.

Clearing the bottom four bits of REG 108 means that all our tiles are shown the normal way round (neither reflected nor mirrored) and on top of LAYER 0, as bit 0 is clear. If we had set bit 3 with REG 108,16 the tiles would all have been mirrored to face left rather than right. Back in the 80s I made a Spectrum-based TV autocue system, using a standard ZX font flipped so it became readable through a mirror reflecting the script to the TV presenter. Next can do this without changing the font data!

Bit 2 flips tiles vertically, and bit 1 rotates them clockwise a quarter turn. Rotation is done first, so setting all three bits gives an anti-clockwise twist. The rotation options could be handy in authentic versions of games like *Pacman* and *Space Invaders*, which expect a 'portrait' screen aspect, taller than it is wide. If you try this, make sure the rotation doesn't upset the balance or convection cooling of your telly. Dennis Briggs was once called out to fix a monitor that had mysteriously started displaying Sinclair screens upside down. This 'fault' was traced back to the office cleaner not noticing which way up the square steel-cased screen had originally been placed!

Half of the palette entry for each tile pixel comes from the top half of the attribute byte or register, and the lower four bits from the tile (or sprite) itself. Our demo clears those bits so each tile uses colours 0 to 15 from the start of the palette. If we'd set all four of those bits the other end of the palette, from 240 to 255, would be used. The top four-bit nybble of the palette index for each tile pixel is the same throughout the tile, coming from the attribute byte or register, while the lower four bits come from the four-bit tile font. Thus you can use at most sixteen different colours in each tile, but 256-colour tiles can choose from sixteen different palette subsets on a per-tile basis.

There are more combinations than I can comprehensively demonstrate here. The exercises later suggest variations worth trying, and corresponding tweaks to the example driver. For the time being we'll stick with 16-colour high-resolution tiles, but they're just a starting point; compared with LAYER 2, or even Sinclair's LAYER 0, tile displays are very powerful, and relatively complicated. Fun times for hackers!

Layer 3 display dimensions

Back at the set-up code, line 1230 calls two NextBASIC procedures that wrap up DRIVER command sequences. PROC TILEBASE() just copies the supplied address into the first two driver variables, so it knows the start address of the tile-map. The driver uses MMU7 to temporarily put an 8k page of ULA-friendly RAM at the top of the Z80 memory map, between addresses 56k and 64k, so the parameter of TILEBASE should always be at least 57344. Tweak only bits 8 to 12. Our TileMap is at the start of BANK 7, so the offset within the 8k is zero, hence we pass $e000 to the procedure.

PROC TILEWIN() sets the rest of the driver variables for the desired screen and window position. To avoid clobbering an undocumented byte near the middle of BANK 7, the driver is set up for a maximum of 30 lines. If you are willing to sacrifice LAYER 0 you could tweak REG 110 and 111 settings to use the first 6912 bytes of BANK 5, with room for the full 80x32 tile display and 40 extra tile definitions in the remaining space, but be careful not to stray beyond 23295 or you'll clobber the system variables and crash NextZXOS.

256 pixel lines is pushing the limit for a PAL-standard TV display – hence the term 'overscan' to describe graphics drawn into the original Spectrum border area. Some may be lost in the screen border if you're using a CRT or monitor made to non-European standards. The BBC BASIC *TV command was added to fix this. So in our last two set-up lines, 1250 and 1260, REG 49 centres the 80x30 screen by scrolling it backwards eight pixels (the parameter 248 being 256-8) and REG 27 commands limit the visible display to 640 by 240 pixels. The only bizarre thing here is that the X limit counts four pixels at a time, starting from 0, so that it will fit in a byte and still allow counts up to 640; the first two values define a screen width of 160*4 pixels, which is room for 80 columns of 8-pixel-wide tiles.

PRINTing to Layer 3

It's taken quite some explanation, but at last, the set-up is complete. The following five lines prove it all works! Line 1270 opens a channel to the previously-installed TileDriver. The next two lines use PRINT and LIST commands to move the cursor around and display the entire TileSetter program, ten times over, on the Layer 3 display. Press space a couple of times to step through the demo. Notice how much faster it is than other LAYERs, despite the six extra rows.

```
1270 OPEN # 4,"D>T"
1272 PRINT #4; CHR$ 4;"TOP","TAB"; CHR$ 5;"Bottom";: PAUSE 0
1280 FOR %i=0 TO 9: LIST #4: NEXT %i
1285 PRINT #4;"©";: PAUSE 0 :PROC TSCREEN(0,29) TO %c
1290 CLOSE # 4
```

Even though it shows 2400 characters, far more than even Timex HiRes, which requires a narrowed font for more than 64 columns, tile output and scrolling are speedy because only a single byte, rather than between nine and 64, needs to be stored to update each 8x8 pixel cell. Line 1285 prints a copyright sign at the start of the bottom line, after the listing, then uses another helper PROC TSCREEN() to read its character code from that column and row of the display.

Cleaning up

System-friendly programs, even little demos like this, should return NextZXOS and the FPGA hardware to a known state when they're finished, or subsequent experiments might prove hard to replicate! Line 1300 does the necessary minimum, restoring registers we've tweaked to their default values.

```
1300 REG %107,%0: REG %49,%0: REG %111,%12: REG %110,%44
1310 .uninstall TILE.DRV: STOP
```

You don't absolutely need to uninstall the driver after using it. It will wait dormant in system memory till another "D>T" stream is opened. But as there's only room for four custom drivers to be installed at any time, line 1310 represents good practice.

TileSetter Procedures

The following procedures are not essential to use the TileDriver. They just package up DRIVER commands under meaningful names to make programs easier to write and test. If you find yourself regularly calling any of these, especially if the display layout is not liable to change, it's more efficient to copy just the DRIVER commands you need directly into your main program.

```
2000 DEFPROC TILEBASE(%b)
2005 IF %b & @11111111 THEN STOP
2010 DRIVER 84,%0,%b&255: DRIVER 84,%1,%b>>8
2030 ENDPROC
2040
2050 DEFPROC TILEWIN(%x,%y,%w,%h)
2060 IF %x>77 OR (y>28) THEN STOP
2070 IF %w<2 OR (h<2) THEN STOP
2080 IF %x+w>80 OR (y+h>30) THEN STOP
2090 REM This hardware configuration is 80x30
2100 DRIVER 84,%2,%80: DRIVER 84,%3,%30
2150 DRIVER 84,%4,%x: DRIVER 84,%6,%y
2170 DRIVER 84,%5,%x+w: DRIVER 84,%7,%y+h
```

```
2190 REM ENSURE cursor starts in window!
2200 DRIVER 84,%8,%x: DRIVER 84,%9,%y
2300 ENDPROC
```

PROCs TILEBASE() and TILEWIN() set the base address and window position respectively. 84 is CODE "T", identifying the TileDriver. Adjust lines 2080 to 2110 if you've rearranged the memory for something other than the 80x30 character layer presumed by the driver. The next two procedures just return the cursor position within the current window, allowing for any margin. A single in-line DRIVER command will do the job if you are using the full display area, skipping the need for %M and probably the need for a procedure at all:

```
2410 DEFPROC CURSOR X()
2420 LOCAL %x,%m
2430 DRIVER 84,%8,%-1 TO %x: DRIVER 84,%4,%-1 TO %m
2460 ENDPROC =%x-m
2490
2510 DEFPROC CURSOR Y()
2520 LOCAL %y,%m
2530 DRIVER 84,%9,%-1 TO %y: DRIVER 84,%6,%-1 TO %m
2560 ENDPROC =%y-m
```

The next four helpers are very similar, returning the width and height of the current window or the top left origin coordinate, which would be 0,0 to use the whole screen. A structured programming zealot would call the ORIGIN routines from within the WIN size ones, but as NextBASIC is an interpreted language that'd be needlessly slow.

```
2600 DEFPROC WIN WIDTH()
2610 LOCAL %l,%r
2620 DRIVER 84,%5,%-1 TO %r: DRIVER 84,%4,%-1 TO %l
2640 ENDPROC =%r-l
2690
2700 DEFPROC WIN HEIGHT()
2710 LOCAL %t,%b
2720 DRIVER 84,%7,%-1 TO %b: DRIVER 84,%6,%-1 TO %t
2740 ENDPROC =%b-t
2790
2810 DEFPROC ORIGIN X()
2820 LOCAL %m
2830 DRIVER 84,%4,%-1 TO %m
2840 ENDPROC =%m
2900
2910 DEFPROC ORIGIN Y()
2920 LOCAL %m
2930 DRIVER 84,%6,%-1 TO %m
2940 ENDPROC =%m
```

The last and most complicated utility is TSCREEN, a version of SCREEN$ for Layer 3. It returns the tile number 0 to 255 associated with X and Y character coordinates by PEEKing it directly from the TileMap, but this involves seven preparatory DRIVER commands to allow for the window position and screen base address. These make the procedure generic but in combination take much longer than the required paging and ultimate PEEK.

The upside of this, from a demonstration point of view, is that you get to see example DRIVER commands that check the window geometry, and conditional checks that X and Y coordinates make sense, in context. If anything goes wrong an out-of-range code, from 256 to 258, is returned. 256 signifies that the X parameter is outside the window, or 257 if the Y check fails. In either case, the maximum valid coordinate is printed alongside the rejected one. All these checks, and the associated arithmetic, can be simplified or eliminated if you know the base address and bounds of the window won't change. If so, ditch lines 3020 to 3130, presetting %B to the address of the top left corner tile data byte and %T to the number of bytes per line.

The other complication is that the TileMap may be outside the set of pages directly accessible to PEEK – in BANK 7, by default – so 258 is returned if RAMTOP is too low for that page to be temporarily remapped to the top of Z80 memory. The original page is remapped before PROC TSCREEN() returns, but if the Z80 stack could already be up there the procedure fails with code 258 rather than risk crashing the machine. You can remove that check if your TileMap is in BANK 5, competing with LAYER 0 or LAYER 1 displays that try to use the same memory.

```
3000 DEFPROC TSCREEN(%x,%y)
3005 IF DPEEK 23730>=56*1024 THEN ENDPROC =%258
3010 LOCAL %t,%b,%r
3020 DRIVER 84,%0,%-1 TO %t: DRIVER 84,%1,%-1 TO %b
3040 %b=%b<<8+t:; Base address of TileMap
3050 DRIVER 84,%4,%-1 TO %t
3060 %x+=%t: DRIVER 84,%6,%-1 TO %t
3080 %y+=%t: DRIVER 84,%5,%-1 TO %t
3100 IF %x>=t THEN PRINT "Bad X ";%x;">=";%t: ENDPROC =%256
3110 DRIVER 84,%7,%-1 TO %t
3120 IF %y>=t THEN PRINT "Bad Y ";%y;">=";%t: ENDPROC =%257
3130 DRIVER 84,%2,%-1 TO %t
3140 %r=% REG 87: REG %87,%14: REM Map Bank 7 at 56k
3150 %t=% PEEK (y*t+x+b): REG %87,%r
3170 ENDPROC =%t
```

Notice that the variable %T is used as a general-purpose temporary store through the procedure. This is not great programming style – ideally a named variable specific to each role would be created – but declaring five extra variables, each only be needed and used once, is wasteful. NextBASIC has to copy the old value, and any FOR loop properties, for each LOCAL variable to and from the Z80 stack when entering and ending a procedure, so the interpreter runs faster and in less RAM if local variables are re-used this way.

Redefining tiles

Just like ZX BASIC User Defined Graphics, you can redefine individual tile patterns with POKEs to the relevant memory. Unlike UDGs, you don't need to re-print anything to see the new pattern. The hardware picks up each change as soon as it's made and all tiles using that code change to match. The following lines use PROC TILEDEF() to redefine the first three characters of our tile font to a fine checkboard, in place of space, and puts eight-pixel diagonal lines for character 33 and 34, in place of the usual exclamation and quotation marks.

```
3420 %c(0)= BIN 10101010:%c(1)= BIN 01010101
3430 %c(2)= BIN 10101010:%c(3)= BIN 01010101
3440 %c(4)= BIN 10101010:%c(5)= BIN 01010101
3450 %c(6)= BIN 10101010:%c(7)= BIN 01010101
3460 FOR %i=0 TO 7: %c(i+8)=%1<<i: NEXT %i
3470 FOR %i=0 TO 7: %c(i+16)=%128>>i: NEXT %i
3480 PROC TILEDEF(%c(),32,3,14)
```

The data is identical to that for UDGs – eight bytes per character, with one bit per pixel, customarily entered in binary so the pattern is obvious. Since these will need to be unpacked to four or eight bits per pixel for 16 or 256 colour tiles, PROC TILEDEF() reads them from an integer array named by its first parameter. It has room for eight definitions in its elements 0 to 63.

The parameters are the number of the first affected font entry, the number of entries to change, and an optional colour mask akin to %M in the font-copying set up loop. The default is 15 and means that set pixels use that palette entry, usually bright white.

Line 3480 uses 14, for bright yellow or whatever new colour you've programmed into the 15th entry in the active Layer 3 palette. Four unset bits select palette entry 0, unless you modify the following TILEDEF procedure:

```
3190 REM Upload %n UDG patterns to code %c from %c[]
3200 DEFPROC TILEDEF(%a(),%c,%n,%p=%15)
3210 IF %c<32 OR (c>127) THEN PRINT %c;" not ASCII": STOP
3220 IF %c+n>128 THEN PRINT %n;" is too many": STOP
3225 IF DPEEK 23730>=56*1024 THEN PRINT "Set RAMTOP!": STOP
3230 LOCAL %t,%l,%v,%b=%(c-32)*32+$e000,%r=% REG 87
3240 REG %87,%14: REM Map Bank 7 at 56k
3250 FOR %l=%0 TO %n<<3-1
3260   %t=%a[l]
3270   FOR %v=%0 TO %3
3280     POKE %b,%(p<<4 AND (t&128))+(p AND (t&64))
3290     %t<<=%2: %b+=$1
3300   NEXT %v
3310 NEXT %l
3390 REG %87,%r
3400 ENDPROC
```

I deliberately use square rather than round brackets to extract values from the integer array, so more than eight characters can be redefined in one go, if extra ones are specified in integer arrays %D, %E etc. Square brackets are not allowed in the PROC lines, which specify the name of the *first* array to be passed by reference. Once again, the top 8k of memory is paged to access BANK 7.

This is a demo, not a general purpose tile-creation procedure. It assumes that the tile font entry for character 32 is at the start of the ULA memory page, unless you alter the first two references to 32 and the base address $e000. Among other things, you need to change the third 32 to 64 for a 256-colour font. %B holds the base address of the first character to be redefined. The outer loop %L processes each pixel line in turn. The inner loop %V unpacks four pairs of pixels from one to four-bit format.

The mapping of bits to two colours is convenient for reusing standard UDGs but limited to two colours per tile. Much more colourful displays are possible if you modify the procedure to accept and store four or eight bits per tile pixel. In that case it's probably easier to pass in a block of memory from a sprite-creation program, but if your tile font is going into BANK 7 make sure the source block is not paged in before you POKE it.

MemBrowse

I've written another short example for the TileDriver download, adapting Mark Gallop's GetIt project **membrowse.bas** to use an 80x31 tile display, so that it can show 384 bytes from any PEEKable bank in a single screen, in a configurable number base. Press D for decimal and H for Hex, or set %R to 8 for octal or whatever other base, up to 36, you prefer.

This example has PROCs at the end which implement the TileMap and are designed to be adaptable to retarget other NextBASIC programs. It uses only 'legal' LAYER 0 memory and features a custom PROC for numeric input, to work around the current NextZXOS limitation which prevents the echo of INPUTs on channels other than 's'.

Negative and non-numeric entries are ignored, but a $ prefix allows hexadecimal values to be entered. Select bank 5 and offset $E80 to see the TileMap data in the memory browser that's using it – look for the ASCII codes of Z and X in the top left corner.

The yellow button NMI browser clobbers LAYER 0, corrupting both the tile font and the TileMap, and if you find a way to cause a BASIC error that's liable to leave a garbled screen because standard layers are obscured. Fear not, GO TO 400 will restore normal working, though you'll have to type that in 'blind'. This can happen if you use FLASH or similar keywords in PRINT or INPUT to streams not routed to channel 's'. NextBASIC 2.09 passes them through correctly, then fails with a spurious 'nonsense in BASIC' error. PRINT CHR$ of appropriate control codes works fine, rather as with CLS.

Customisation

There are several suggestions for customisation and extension of this driver at the end of the following chapter, which explains precisely how it works and the trade-offs needed to pack all its functions into a single 512-byte driver slot. Don't stop now! But you may want to get a cup of tea, first.

Chapter 16, TileDriver source

It's been a long time coming, but at last we're ready to show how the TileDriver works. Compared with the bit-twiddling needed to get a Layer 3 display up, the code is quite straight-forward, but it is Z80n assembly language, shoehorned into 512 bytes of code and data, so subtle techniques are required. It supports low-resolution 40x32 TileMaps as well as up to 80x32 HiRes, but assumes that all tiles share the same attribute byte from REG 108. Tweaks are needed for per-tile attributes and extra colours, as noted along the way.

The driver code is logically divided into three main sections. The first and shortest handles the 28 DRIVER commands. Another larger block of code interprets invisible control codes by adjusting the 14 variables at the end. In the middle is the routine which puts characters in the TileMap. That needs to access memory outside the driver, so it includes code to page the TileMap into the MMU7 area and restore the original paging when it's done. Driver output is synchronous with BASIC, so other programs never notice this temporary remapping. Sinclair QL drivers are asynchronous, but they don't need to do paging and have a multi-tasking operating system to help out!

Except when scrolling, when up to 2400 bytes may need to be rewritten, TileMap output only takes a few microseconds; the character output speed limit is mostly determined by the system overhead for each byte passed through the stream interface. Whole lines of tiles can be updated faster by paging in the TileMap and poking them all at once, but then we lose the benefit of device-independence, and the code becomes layer-specific.

Test version, conditional assembly

Since this is also our showcase for the inline assembler dot command, we demonstrate some of its neat features. The program uses 'conditional assembly' so the same source can generate two versions, one ready-to-run as a driver and the other designed for interactive testing in main memory.

That variation doesn't need to honour the 512-byte driver slot limit, so it can be used to test alternative or extra routines before deciding which are most important to include in the driver. It can run from anywhere in Z80 memory, as long as you edit the required start address into the source, so it can be positioned safely above RAMTOP and out of the way of MONS or other machine-code utilities you might want to use to test it.

The **.asm** command can read and set NextBASIC integer variables as it does its work. We use this capability to control which source lines get assembled, and find the exact locations of the code and data in each version. The variable %D controls the conditional assembly. If this is set to 1 before assembling, the DRIVER version is generated. If it's zero, we get the test version instead.

```
 990 %d=0:;0 for testing in RAM, 1 for DRIVER version
1000 .asm
1010 ;
1020 ;; ZX PRINT control codes TileDriver implements:
1030 ;
1040 ;SPACE  equ 32    ; First ASCII non-control code
1050 ;TAB    equ 23    ; Not ASCII, 3-byte tab in line
1060 ;AT     equ 22    ; Not ASCII, 3-byte PRINT AT y,x;
1070 ;CLS    equ 14    ; Clear ZX screen
1080 ;ENTER  equ 13    ; CR in ASCII, ZX line separator
1090 ;DEL    equ 12    ; Not in driver; ASCII form feed
1100 ;UP     equ 11    ; ASCII vertical tab   (move up)
1110 ;DOWN   equ 10    ; LF in ASCII        (move down)
1120 ;RIGHTA equ 9     ; TAB in ASCII      (move right)
1130 ;LEFTA  equ 8     ; BACKSPACE          (move left)
1140 ;SCROLL equ 7     ; N.B. Does not alter print position
1150 ;COMMA  equ 6     ; Tab in half-window width steps
1160 ;LASTL  equ 5     ; Move cursor to start of last line
1170 ;HOME   equ 4     ; Move cursor to window top left
1180 ;
1190 ;MMU    equ 87    ; Top 8k paging register number
```

I start by equating symbolic names to the control-code magic numbers from Figure 98. I could just put 11 in the source when I wanted to refer to the code to move the cursor UP, and 22 in place of AT, but the names are easier to read and harder to mistype. EQU is short for equate and one of the 'assembler directives' that don't directly generate machine code but configure the assembly process.

The following directives cater for differences between the test version and the installable driver. Either we assemble directly to our debug address 56000 above RAMTOP, writing code that loads each character we want to test from register E to a file called 'TileDriver', or we tell **.asm** to save us a loadable driver, TILE.DRV, with the required eight-byte header at the start.

```
1210 ; if %d=0
1220 ; org 56000
1230 ; output "TileDriver"
1240 ; ld e,ENTER       ; Testbed setup, POKE ASCII here
1250 ; else
1260 ; output "TILE.DRV"
1270 ; db "NDRVQ",RELOC_COUNT,0,0
1280 ; org 0
1290 ; RELOC_START
```

ORG 0 means the base address before relocation is zero, but this time – unlike in the Profile and Slot drivers – there's no need to label lines that will need relocation after loading and compile a table of words citing those labels, because **.asm** can do that for us. Chris Taylor adapted the *Zeus* source for my NextBASIC profiler while testing, and decided to automate Garry's driver relocation scheme with special directives, derived from an Amstrad CPC emulator, *WinAPE*, via Peter 'Ped' Helcmanovsky's cross-assembler *sjasmplus*. It's great to find such conveniences natively on Next, now.

Address labels created and referenced between RELOC_START and RELOC_END directives are noted as relocation targets. RELOC_TABLE emits a table of RELOC_COUNT offsets at the end of the driver, so Next can customise it to run from the next available driver slot. The system is smart enough to track relocations for labels used in arithmetic, and avoids creating any for labels just used for relative offsets, as they're implicitly self-relocating.

Driver command handling

The following block of code appears in the driver but is not needed in the test version, because it implements the DRIVER commands to read and write internal variables. Those can be readily accessed with PEEK or POKE if they're in main memory. Otherwise, NextZXOS puts the command-code in register B. We use that to sift out our commands, with parameters 0 to 13 corresponding to variable offsets, from 'Standard API function codes' in the NextZXOS_API document, which claim parameters over 127.

In this case it's code 251, requesting character output, that needs sifting. Anything under 128 is potentially a variable byte number, but we only want commands to touch the data bytes between Start and OldPage so the next check ignores values beyond OldPage which might otherwise corrupt bytes outside our driver. Just 21 bytes implement all 28 commands to read or alter internal variables!

```
1320 ; ld a,b
1330 ; cp 251          ; Character Output $fb
1340 ; jr z,output
1345 ;
1350 ; ld a,OldPage-Start ; Variable byte offsets: 0 to 13
1360 ; sub b
1370 ; jp c,ignore1     ; Values 14+ are quietly ignored
```

As you scan this source you'll notice blank lines after changes in the flow of control, such as jumps, calls and returns. These separate logical blocks of code, which typically take several instructions to perform even a simple task. I often put breakpoints before these when stepping through, to help trace key decisions while checking that changes work as planned.

Once we know B has a safe value we add it to the address of the first variable at Start. Next has special instructions to add the accumulator, register A, to 16-bit pairs, but this Z80n special only works with some registers, so we copy B to A first. Now we know which variable is involved we need to check if it is to be read or written. The code to find it comes first, so it can be shared between both cases.

```
1390 ; ld a,b
1400 ; ld hl,Start     ; Point HL at the first variable
1410 ; add hl,a
1420 ; inc d            ; DE = -1 to read a driver variable
1430 ; jr nz,setVar
1440 ;
1450 ; ld c,(hl)        ; Return variable byte in BC
```

```
1460 ; ld b,d           ; Clear high byte of result
1470 ; ret
1480 ;
1490 ;setVar
1500 ; ld (hl),e        ; Update variable
1510 ; ret              ; Carry is clear, signal success
1520 ;
1530 ; endif
```

NextZXOS puts the third parameter of any driver command in the DE register pair. To save bytes I decided that this should be -1, rather than some byte to be stored, when just reading a setting. I can check for this with just three bytes of code, as -1 is internally represented as the value $FFFF, two bytes with the maximum value 255.

The valid range for setting a byte is 0 to 255, which fits entirely in register E, leaving zero in D. In that case INC D is sure to produce one, a non-zero result, so we can safely jump on to **setVar**, store E in the place we just worked out, and return. But if DE is -1, the INC adds one and the byte value wraps round from 255 to zero (with an overflow, which we ignore) setting the Z flag. That's how we know a read is required.

Other small negative numbers would have the same effect, so **DRIVER CODE "T", 4, -99, TO M** would load the X origin offset into M just as well as **DRIVER 84, 4, -1 TO M** would. In either case the command returns with the carry flag clear; if it is set, commands return the generic error 19, *Invalid I/O Device.*

Notice the ENDIF which closes the ELSE block from line 1250. After that, till the next IF, the code is shared by both the driver and test versions. It's time to interpret the character passed from the NextZXOS stream.

Tile and character output

```
1570 ;output            ; character output entry point
1580 ; ld hl,Count
1590 ; ld a,(hl)
1600 ; or a             ; In a multibyte sequence?
1610 ; ld a,e
1620 ; jp nz,multi
1630 ;
1640 ; cp SPACE
1650 ; jr c,control     ; E is not a visible character
```

We need to sift out three possible situations. If the character code in E is less than SPACE we've received an invisible control code and must jump forward to the label **control** to work out what to do with it. But there's another invisible possibility – we might have already received part of a multi-byte control sequence, as explained in Chapter 15 of the first Next manual, Chapter 14 for KS2. If so, the driver variable Count will be non-zero, and we jump forward to **multi** to complete it, leaving HL pointing at the current Count so we can count-down in due course.

Otherwise the code in register E is potentially visible so let's work out where to store it in the TileMap. The next block of code checks the CursorX and CursorY variables against the window bounds, calling subroutines to handle any edge-cases. At the edge of the screen, we might need to wrap to the next line, or scroll the window up if it's full.

You might wonder why the code keeps loading driver variables into the accumulator then immediately copying them to another register before a comparison. The Z80 has no LD D,(RIGHT) or similar instruction. Byte loads from a 16-bit immediate address always end up in A, so we need to copy the byte elsewhere before comparing it with another similar variable.

CALL **Ydown** moves the cursor to the next line, setting the carry flag if successful; otherwise **scrolln** shunts the window contents up, leaving the cursor at the start of a new blank line at the bottom. CALL **left2X** copies the Left margin variable to CursorX, saving three bytes, while calling **lineA** converts a row number in the accumulator into a TileMap address in HL.

```
1670 ; ld c,e
1680 ;; Will the character in C fit on the current line?
1690 ; ld a,(Right)
1700 ; ld d,a
1710 ; ld a,(CursorX)
1720 ; cp d
1730 ; jr c,roomX
1740 ;
1750 ;; Wrap to left margin of next line
1760 ; call Ydown
1770 ;
1780 ; call nc,scrolln
1790 ;
1800 ; jr nc,onLine
1810 ;
1820 ; ld (CursorY),a
1830 ;
1840 ;onLine
1850 ; call left2X
1860 ;
1870 ;roomX ; point HL at the tile at the cursor position
1880 ; ld a,(CursorY)
1890 ; call lineA
1900 ;
1910 ; ld a,(CursorX)
1920 ; add hl,a
```

Now HL points to the place in the TileMap where the tile number in C needs to be stored. Unless we're in the non-paging test version of the driver, it's time to page the TileMap into the MMU7 slot. We call the subroutine **topIn** to do that, sharing instructions also needed for scrolling. Now we can copy the tile index character code from C to HL; we're almost done but before we can return the cursor column, still in A, needs to move right and the driver must restore MMU7 by jumping to **topOut**. The test version skips that, but to make debugging easier it stores the TileMap update address in a test-only word labelled **here**, after the last of the driver variables.

```
1940 ; if %d
1950 ; call topIn        ; Put TileMap in top page
1960 ; endif
1970 ;
1980 ; ld (hl),c         ; Output the character
1990 ; inc a             ; Move cursor right
2000 ; ld (CursorX),a
2020 ; if %d=0
2030 ; ld (here),hl      ; Save tile pointer (testbed only)
2040 ; ret
2050 ; else
2060 ; jp topOut         ; Restore MMU
2070 ; endif
```

Eight short subroutines follow. If speed was more important than size we'd insert the relevant instructions in-line, rather than use CALL and RET sequences, which require four extra bytes of machine code and four data byte transfers, to save and restore the return address. But with only 512 bytes for the whole driver I'm reluctant to duplicate existing code; the subroutine overhead is justified by the space we can claw back.

All but one of these subroutines follows the code we've just seen. The exception is **topIn**, the memory pager, which I shall present out of order. As it's always accessed with CALL, and that instruction requires a full 16-bit address, I've put it right at the end of the assembly code. This lets me use relative jumps more often earlier, where their one-byte range would otherwise be a limitation. But it'd be a poor book that arranged its explanations strictly to suit signed byte offsets in the code it describes, so this is one of the places I've ignored line-number sequence to make the logic easier to follow.

TileMap memory paging

The **topIn** subroutine uses registers A, B and C. It starts by saving those so it can safely be called even when those registers contain values needed later. Before it can change the existing MMU setup it needs to read the current state, so that can be restored later.

While the Z80n adds two instructions to *write* to NextRegs, *reading* those is not so simple. The five lines from 6210 to 6250 use the Z80 port interface to the FPGA to select the MMU register and then update it. The same ten bytes are needed to read any Next register, tweaking only the values in A for the register concerned.

```
6170 ; if %d
6180 ;topIn              ; Driver paging code
6190 ; push af
6200 ; push bc
6210 ; ld a,MMU
6220 ; ld bc,9275        ; Next register Select port
6230 ; out (c),a
```

```
6240 ; inc b           ; Next register data port
6250 ; in a,(c)        ; Read current MMU page
6260 ; ld (OldPage),a
6270 ; ld a,14         ; TileMap page (2 * bank 7)
6290 ; pop bc
6310 ; jp a2mmu
6330 ; endif
```

The BASIC keyword REG can be used to read or write any Next register, but the function still uses the same sequence of Z80 instructions internally. Before REG was added to NextBASIC, this would have to be written:

```
OUT 9275,MMU :LET A=IN 9531
```

That still works, but REG is quicker as it only needs to evaluate one parameter rather than three.

Another Z80 trick saves bytes when reading the FPGA Data register immediately after writing to the Select port. The seemingly-unrelated port numbers 9275 and 9531 differ by 256 so we can quickly switch between the two by incrementing or decrementing just the high byte of the BC register pair used for 16-bit port addressing. This is no accident. In context, the INC B at line 6240 is equivalent to LD BC,9531 but two bytes shorter.

Even though this is a subroutine, and should logically finish with a RET instruction to return from the most recent CALL, in fact it ends by jumping to the label **a2mmu**. That's actually the end of the corresponding **topOut** routine. **TopIn** shares its RET instruction because – whichever way we're switching the pages – before returning we update the MMU with a new page number, passed via the accumulator. This re-uses a NextReg MMU instruction, as well as the POP AF needed so either subroutine can be called without losing important data in register A, saving two precious bytes!

Cursor subroutines

The cursor placement subroutines are fairly simple, but sometimes need extra register-copying or flag-setting to make them useful wherever they are called from. Notice how tightly interwoven these routines are. **findTop** puts the cursor at the top left corner of the currently-defined window, reusing **lineA**, then falls into **Cwidth** which puts the width of the line into C. The second reading of the Left margin variable at line 2330 is sometimes redundant, but a relative jump over it would be two bytes longer and only one cycle quicker.

```
2090 ;Ydown
2100 ; ld a,(Bottom)
2110 ; ld e,a
2120 ; ld a,(CursorY)
2130 ; inc a
2140 ; cp e
2150 ; ret
2160 ;
2230 ;findTop          ; Point HL at top line of window
2250 ; ld a,(Top)      ; Number of first line
```

```
2260 ; Call lineA
2270 ;
2280 ; ld a,(Left)
2290 ; add hl,a           ; Offset HL into window
2300 ; ld b,0             ; Count bytes per line in BC
2310 ;
2320 ;Cwidth
2330 ; ld a,(Left)        ; Reload left for callers
2340 ; ld c,a
2350 ; ld a,(Right)       ; Assume left+1 < right
2360 ; sub c
2370 ; ld c,a             ; A and BC = right-left
2380 ; ret
```

The **lineA** subroutine uses the Z80n MUL instruction to multiply the line width by the chosen line number, then adds the TileMap base address. Two more single-byte opcodes are needed to get values from the accumulator, which can be loaded from any explicit address, to the DE register pair MUL insists upon using.

```
2400 ;lineA
2410 ; ld e,a             ; Copy target line number to E
2420 ; ld a,(Width)
2430 ; ld d,a
2440 ; mul d,e            ; DE is offset to target line
2450 ; ld hl,(Start)
2460 ; add hl,de          ; HL is base of line A
2470 ; ret
```

The following five lines implement three cursor-wangling subroutines, though they all end up in a fourth similarly-simple one, **SetX**, used in three places to update the CursorX data byte. **GoHome** implements the HOME control CHR$ 4, placing the cursor in the top left corner of the window, sharing code with CLS, and **setYX** that selects the bottom line after CHR$ 5. In turn, this falls into **left2X**, which selects the leftmost column.

```
2490 ;goHome
2500 ; ld a,(Top)
2510 ;
2520 ;setYX
2530 ; ld (CursorY),a
2540 ;
2550 ;left2X
2560 ; ld a,(Left)
2570 ; jp setX
```

Now we're ready to interpret the invisible character codes, which involves checking for the ones we implement and carefully ignoring the others as well as whatever data trails after them, such as FLASH or INK parameters. I tried using a look-up table to convert the codes 0 to 31 into routine addresses, or place-holders, but although that would have been quicker in many cases the combination of code and data offsets was more verbose, so I've taken a tip from the example driver source and done most of the sifting with DJNZ instructions, which Zilog introduced as a concise way to write short loops.

DJNZ stands for Decrement and Jump relative if Not Zero. It subtracts one from the value in the B register then branches back or forth up to a hundred or so bytes unless the result is zero, in which case it carries on to the next line. Traditionally this would come at the end of a loop, branching back to the point just after the number of loops was loaded into B, but drivers use it to sift consecutive byte values in ascending order for custom processing.

The more obvious alternative code would use pairs of **CP n** and **JR Z,case_n** instructions, comparing the value in the accumulator with various values of **n** and branching onward to **case_n** if it matches. DJNZ uses half as many bytes per case, but requires you to process them in ascending order and decrements the value every time. This is potentially quite confusing, and problematic when skipping gaps. Ideally we'd pick off the most likely cases first, for speed. But DJNZ saves precious bytes, so we use that.

Sifting control codes

Before we copy the code into B we use a three-way test to handle codes 0 to 4. CHR$ 4 is the only one of those implemented, to home the cursor. After comparing the accumulator with that code, and branching to **goHome** if it matches, codes in the range 0 to 3 leave the carry flag set. They're all dealt with by jumping to **ignore1**, which also ignores DRIVER parameters that refer to non-existent variables.

```
2610 ;control
2620 ; sub HOME          ; First supported control code
2630 ;
2640 ; jr z,goHome       ; 4
2650 ;
2660 ; jr c,ignore1      ; Codes <4 are ignored
2670 ;
2680 ; ld b,a            ; Prepare for DJNZ tests
2690 ;
2700 ;notHome            ; LASTL, CHR$ 5
2730 ; djnz notEnd
2740 ;
2750 ; ld a,(Bottom)
2760 ; dec a
2770 ; jr setYX
```

CHR$ 5, LASTL, is implemented with eight bytes of code, labelled notHome. It works like CHR$ 5 but instead of clearing CursorY it sets it to Bottom-1, placing the cursor on the window's last line, rather than the first.

So far we've ignored four of six control codes, but the next few, from 6 to 11, are all implemented to match their behaviour in NextBASIC layers. The DJNZ trick wraps each case with a conditional branch over the routine to handle the next control code. So the label **notEnd** marks the end of the code for CHR$ 5, **notCom** comes after the CHR$ 6 routine invoked by a comma in a PRINT statement, then **notScrl** after the code for CHR$ 7, which scrolls the window under the cursor, and so on. As long as each block of code is within the 127-byte forward range of DJNZ, everything fits.

CHR$ 6, commas and columns in PRINT

CHR$ 6 implements the PRINT comma separator, advancing the cursor to the next line if it's in the second half of the current row, or to the middle if it's nearer the start. This splits output across two columns, whatever the window width.

```
2820 ;notEnd                ; COMMA, CHR$ 6
2840 ;  djnz notCom
2850 ;
2860 ;; If cursor is before half-way move there, else next line
2870 ; call Cwidth          ; Set C and A to line width, right-left
2880 ;
2890 ; srl a                ; Column width is line width >> 1
2900 ; ld b,a               ; Save column width
2910 ; ld a,(Left)
2920 ; ld c,a
2930 ; ld a,(CursorX)
2940 ; sub c
2950 ; ret z                ; Already at start of first column
2960 ;
2970 ; cp b                 ; Compare with middle of line
2980 ; ret z                ; Already at start of second column
2990 ; jr nc,tabA
3000 ;
3010 ; neg                  ; A = -offset in line
3020 ; add b                ; A = column width-offset
3030 ; jr spacer            ; A = space count to middle column
```

My first implementation of this just moved the cursor without spitting out spaces, but that was inconsistent with ZX BASIC so I added a loop to print spaces until the required position was reached. The logic so far just returns if the cursor is already in the right place; otherwise it has left the number of spaces needed to reach the start of next column in register A. The label **padLine** is also used to implement PRINT TAB statements.

```
3050 ;tabA                  ; Advance cursor by printing spaces
3060 ; add c                ; Add margin to find absolute X
3070 ; ld c,a
3080 ;
3090 ;padline
3100 ; ld a,(Right)         ; A = offset past right margin
3110 ; sub c                ; A = space count to fill line
3120 ;
3130 ;spacer
3140 ; ld c,SPACE
3150 ; push af              ; Preserve space count
3160 ; call roomX           ; Re-entrant call emits one space
3170 ;
3180 ; pop af
3190 ; dec a                ; Space countdown ;-)
3200 ; jr nz,spacer
3203 ;
3206 ;ignore1
3210 ; or a                 ; Carry clear denotes success
3220 ; ret
```

The **spacer** loop calls back into the driver output code to output spaces, counting down in register A. There's no risk of infinite recursion, because the count is temporarily preserved on the stack between calls and that's the only register the loop uses other than C, the space character code reloaded each time round. We already know our position on the current line, and its length, so we can be sure we won't put spaces beyond the end.

The OR A clears the carry flag, preventing any error report on return to NextZXOS. Zilog provide SCF and CCF instructions to set and complement (flip) the carry flag, but no specific instruction to clear it. This doesn't matter since neither OR A nor AND A can cause an overflow; thus they always clear the carry flag, without changing the value in A.

TileMap scrolling

Scrolling occurs when the window is too full for the next character, or when CHR$ 7 is printed, forcing a scroll regardless of the cursor position. It clears the bottom line after moving other lines upwards one row. The contents of the top line are lost. Since this involves reading and writing the TileMap, the driver version must call **topIn** to put that in the MMU7 area, and exit via **topOut** which restores the previous paging.

```
3240 ;notCom              ; SCROLL, CHR$ 7
3260 ; djnz notScrl
3270 ;
3280 ;scrolln
3290 ; push bc            ; Save character code in C
3300 ; if %d
3310 ; call topIn         ; Driver version must set page
3320 ; endif
3330 ;
3340 ; call findTop
3350 ;
3360 ; ld d,h
3370 ; ld e,l             ; Save HL in DE for destination
3380 ; ld a,(Width)
3390 ; add hl,a           ; Point HL to source line below
3400 ; ld a,(Top)
3410 ; ld (CursorY),a     ; CursorY counts rows from the top
```

Now BC is the width of the window, HL points to the first line to be moved up and DE to the line above. We use the LDIR instruction to copy lines, one by one, from bottom to top. We have to work line-by-line because the window being scrolled may not be the full width of the screen, and scrolling applies to the window contents, not tiles that may be outside that on either side.

```
3430 ;scroll1
3440 ; push bc            ; Reuse count for each row
3450 ; ldir                ; Copy one line upwards
3460 ; push de            ; Save destination address
3470 ; call Ydown         ; The MUL in this clobbers DE
3480 ; pop de             ; Restore DEstination
```

```
3500 ; jr nc,rolled     ; Carry clear for exit
3510 ;
3520 ; ld (CursorY),a   ; Consider the next row
3530 ; call Cwidth
3540 ;
3550 ; ld a,(Width)     ; N.B. 3 loop invariants
3560 ; sub c
3570 ; add hl,a         ; Advance over margins
3580 ; add de,a
3590 ; pop bc           ; Recover LDIR count
3600 ; jr scroll1
```

After moving each line we must find the next and repeat the process until **CALL Ydown** clears the carry flag, indicating that we've reached the top, and have to stop – aping Disney swinger King Louie! The comment about 'loop invariants' notes that some of this recalculation could be simplified by working out the margin interval outside the loop and re-using that value, which won't have changed, rather than recalculating it. But the wastage is slight compared with the LDIR overhead, and the code was longer when I tried it, so this is another subtle case where economy trumps efficiency. Scrolling Layer 3 in software is still simpler than for other layers; even LAYER 0 needs nine LDIR instructions to move each line of characters.

Clearing one line

With the window contents shifted up one line, it only remains to clear the bottom one. The following subroutine **clear1** does the trick, but we can't just fall into it as it uses the register-hungry LDIR block-copy instruction and we must hang onto the tile number in register C so we can output that pending character once we've made room for it. This caters for the more common case when scrolling is triggered because the window is full, rather than when CHR$ 7 is printed. Notice that we have to push B at the same time as C, since Z80 PUSH and POP instructions always transfer two bytes even if we only need to preserve one of them.

```
3620 ;rolled
3630 ; pop bc           ; Discard count of row width
3640 ; ex de,hl
3650 ; sbc hl,bc        ; Should not set carry
3660 ; call clear1      ; Wipe bottom line of window
3670 ;
3680 ; pop bc           ; Retrieve character code in C
3690 ; ret              ; Carry clear from jr nc,rolled
3700 ;
3710 ;clear1
3720 ; ld (hl),SPACE
3730 ; dec c            ; B should be 0, LDIR clears 2+
3740 ; jr z,topOut      ; That one was enough
3750 ;
3760 ; ld d,h
3770 ; ld e,l
3780 ; inc de           ; Point DE at the next space
3790 ; ldir             ; Clear the full width required
```

This time, LDIR is used to copy within a line rather than between rows. It shows how LDIR can clear, rather than copy, a block of memory.

First the byte we want to replicate is stored at the start of the row by LD (HL),SPACE. Then line 3780 points DE at the following byte, and LDIR counts down in BC as spaces are copied till the whole row has been blanked.

Note the check at 3740 for a column width of one. We may presume that B is zero, because a visible row of tiles cannot be anywhere near 256 bytes (2048 pixels) long, but must still check for the possibility of a single-byte window-width because LDIR counts first and checks afterwards... if BC starts at zero it copies not 0 bytes but 65536, potentially wiping the entire Z80 address space, probably only stopping when it overwrites its own code!

This approach saves code bytes but wastes some time as the blank tile value is re-read from the previous location as we advance from column to column. It'd be faster to clear a large area by putting two blank codes into a register pair and repeatedly PUSHing that into the target space after temporarily diverting SP to point there, but that would make the driver longer, especially for odd-length rows.

The **topOut** subroutine is empty, leaving only a RET instruction, in the test build, but the driver version adds four vital lines to reset MMU7. The key lines are 3840 and 3870, which retrieve the saved OldPage value and restore it to MMU7. But this value must be transferred via the accumulator, which might still have some value important to the caller in it, so we push and pop AF to preserve A. We don't really need to save F, but Z80 stack operations transfer two 8-bit registers, not just one.

```
3810 ;topOut              ; Restore OldPage
3820 ; if %d
3830 ; push af
3840 ; ld a,(OldPage)
3850 ;
3860 ;a2mmu
3870 ; nextreg MMU,a     ; Restore OldPage
3880 ; pop af
3890 ; endif
3900 ;
3910 ; ret
```

> *Get it to work,*
> *Get it to fit,*
> *Make it fast*
> *Adam Sawkins*

We've now seen everything needed to access more than 64k from a running Z80n program. Call something like **topIn** to access any other page from Next's megabytes, then **topOut** when you're done. Just make sure that code you're running, and the Z80 stack, are not in the area you're swapping out, or your code will never return!

Drivers are benign as far as MMU2 to MMU7 are concerned, because their main code, and their stack, runs from the area Sinclair reserved for ROM, using MMU0 and MMU1.

Cursor movement

Four consecutive control codes move the cursor left and right within the line or up and down between lines. The lines labelled **setX** are used at the end of both routines, also when homing the cursor and if DEL is implemented. Horizontal motion stops at the window edge, so you can't cursor left or right to another line. Attempts to do so are ignored, which is consistent with NextBASIC, thereby fixing four related bugs in the original Spectrum ROM, described in Ian Logan's 1982 book *Understanding Your Spectrum*.

```
3930 ;notScrl              ; LEFT, CHR%$ 8
3950 ; djnz notLeft
3955 ;
3960 ; ld a,(CursorX)
3965 ; ld c,a
3970 ; ld a,(Left)
3980 ; cp c
3990 ; ret nc               ; Already at left margin
4000 ;
4010 ; dec c                ; Move left
4020 ; ld a,c
4030 ; jr setX
4040 ;
4050 ;notLeft              ; RIGHT, CHR$ 9
4070 ; djnz notRite
4080 ;
4090 ; ld a,(Right)
4100 ; ld c,a
4110 ; ld a,(CursorX)
4120 ; inc a                ; Consider right move
4130 ;
4140 ;checkXc
4150 ; cp c
4160 ; ret nc               ; Already at right margin
4170 ;
4180 ;setX
4190 ; ld (CursorX),a
4200 ; or a                 ; Carry clear denotes success
4210 ; ret
```

The logic for vertical movement is simplified by the **Ydown** subroutine:

```
4240 ;notRite              ; DOWN, CHR$ 10
4250 ; djnz notDown
4260 ;
4270 ; call Ydown
4280 ;
4290 ; ret nc               ; Already at bottom
4300 ;
4310 ;setY
4320 ; ld (CursorY),a
4330 ;
4340 ;ignore
4350 ; or a                 ; Clear carry, it worked
4360 ; ret
```

The code labelled **ignore** is identical to that at **ignore1** but those two bytes are used often enough that it's more concise to duplicate them here than to replace several two-byte relative jump instructions with three-byte absolute jumps, given how tight we are for space.

That said, Intel's original JP transfers control two cycles faster than Zilog's JR, which has to add an 8-bit offset to the program counter rather than just replace that value with the 16-bit operand. A JR to a JR would be similarly brief, doubling the allowable offset, but slower than either. It would still be the best choice for simple code intended to run from any address, since JP and CALL instructions use absolute addressing rather than relative offsets.

The driver RELOC_TABLE addresses that during loading to the system managed slot, but LOAD CODE does no such relocation so if you can write your code without any calls, entirely using relative jumps, you'll find it easier to use. My *MultiSearch* (first published in issue 12 of *Your Spectrum* magazine, still handy on Next for renaming variables and removing ugly per cent signs) works that way, so it can be loaded and called via USR from any address.

```
4380 ;notDown              ; UP, CHR$ 11
4400 ; djnz notUp
4410 ;
4420 ; ld a,(CursorY)
4430 ; ld c,a
4440 ; ld a,(Top)
4450 ; cp c
4460 ; ret nc              ; Already at top
4470 ;
4480 ; dec c               ; Move up a line
4490 ; ld a,c
4500 ; jr setY
```

CHR$ 12, DELETE

CHR$ 12, the delete code, is an oddity. It moves the cursor left, or up to the end of the previous line if already at the start, then emits a blank space, overwriting the character before the cursor but leaving its position unchanged.

PRINT CHR$ 12 is ignored when the cursor is at the top left, as there's nowhere for it to go. It's ideal for scrubbing out the just-typed symbol while editing a line. Unfortunately Next drivers don't yet support interactive input, where it would be most handy. CHR$ 12 works fine in LAYER 1 and LAYER 2 but ZX ROMs just print a question mark! The *Delete Editing* routine, at 4117 in Sinclair's ROM, deals directly with LAYER 0 input.

The eccentric motion and implicit output mean DEL takes 35 bytes to implement, which was more than I had spare in the DRIVER slot after implementing more often-used codes, so DEL is only implemented in the test version. This tested routine could be squeezed back in if DEL is more important for your terminal emulator than, say, windowing or the output of spaces by PRINT TAB or comma.

```
4520 ;notUp            ; DEL, CHR$ 12
4540 ; if %d
4550 ; dec b           ; Ignore DELETE to make driver fit
4560 ; else
4570 ; djnz notDel
4580 ;
4590 ;DELETE
4600 ; ld hl,CursorX
4610 ; ld a,(Left)
4620 ; cp (hl)         ; Set Z only at left margin
4630 ; jr nz,inLine
4640 ;
4650 ; ld a,(Top)      ; Try to move to the previous line
4660 ; ld c,a
4670 ; ld a,(CursorY)
4680 ; cp c
4690 ; ret z           ; Out Of Screen: already at top left
4700 ;
4710 ; dec a           ; Move up one line
4720 ; ld (CursorY),a
4730 ; ld a,(Right)
4740 ; ld (hl),a       ; Go to end of previous line
4750 ;
4760 ;inLine           ; Move left on this line
4770 ; dec (hl)
4780 ; ld c,SPACE      ; Emit a space, CHR$ 32
4790 ; call roomX      ; Returns with CursorX updated in A
4800 ;
4810 ; dec a           ; Move back over the space
4820 ; jr setX
4830 ;
4840 ; endif
```

New Line, ENTER, CHR$ 13

ASCII calls CHR$ 13 'Carriage Return'. It encodes the Enter key and the apostrophe separator in PRINT statements, which is why PRINT ' ' (two apostrophes, not one speech-mark) moves the cursor down two lines. PRINT alone moves to the following line, so adding a single apostrophe after it makes no difference, rather unexpectedly.

CHR$ 13 is often called 'New Line', and marks the end of BASIC lines in both .BAS and .TXT program files. The driver implementation uses four subroutines we've seen before. **Left2X** moves the cursor to the left window margin, then **Ydown** attempts to move it down a row. If that succeeds it sets the carry flag and we return via **setY**; otherwise the **scroll** subroutine shunts the window contents up, leaving the cursor at the start of a new blank line at the bottom.

```
4860 ;notDel           ; ENTER, CHR$ 13
4880 ; djnz notENT
4890 ;
4900 ;newline
4910 ; call left2X
4920 ;
```

```
4930 ; call Ydown
4940 ;
4950 ; jp nc,scrolln
4960 ;
4970 ;setY2
4980 ; jr setY
```

Clear Screen, CLS, CHR$ 14

The code CHR$ 14 generally clears the entire NextBASIC screen, or the current window if you've set one up. The CLS command does the same thing for officially-supported layers, including LAYER 0 where PRINT CHR$ 14; just spits out a question mark, consistent with ZX BASIC.

Unfortunately CLS cannot be directed to any other stream in the way PRINT can, so the Layer 3 driver expects PRINT CHR$ 14 in place of CLS. LAYER 1 and LAYER 2 variants work either way, so it's easy enough to write programs that can consistently output to LAYERs 1, 2 or 3, by using the control code rather than CLS which NextBASIC versions up to 2.09 always apply to channel "s".

As with SCROLL, windows smaller than the full screen complicate things. CHR$ 14 must wipe the entire window, but leave any border around it intact. The implementation is not optimal because it saves bytes by reusing the **clear1** subroutine to wipe every line of the window, and that pages the TileMap out each time, so we must precede each wipe with a call to **topIn**.

To save bytes, control code 14 is implemented later in the listing but I've hoisted that routine back into a more logical order for this chapter, so that the four-part logic for the multibyte control codes PRINT AT and PRINT TAB can be discussed in a single section after this:

```
5240 ;notENT             ; CLS, CHR$ 14 (Next lacks CLS #)
5260 ; djnz notCLS
5270 ;
5280 ; call findTop      ; HL->window start, BC=window width
5290 ;
5300 ; ld a,(Width)
5310 ; sub c
5320 ; inc a
5330 ; ld e,a            ; E=unused bytes in row
5340 ; ld a,(Top)        ; Find window height
5350 ; ld d,a
5360 ; ld a,(Bottom)
5370 ; sub d             ; A=line count
5380 ; ld d,b            ; DE=gap to next window line
5390 ;
5400 ;doLine
5410 ; push bc           ; Save row width
5420 ;
5430 ; if %d
5440 ; call topIn        ; Page in TileMap
5450 ; endif
5460 ;
```

```
5470 ; push de
5480 ; call clear1      ; N.B. exits via topOut
5490 ;
5500 ; pop de           ; Restore gap count
5510 ; add hl,de        ; Advance over gap
5520 ; pop bc           ; Restore row width
5530 ; dec a
5540 ; jr nz,doLine
5550 ;
5560 ; jp goHome        ; Too far for jr
```

The final step is to reposition the cursor at the top left corner of the window, and a three-byte JP instruction is used here because the **goHome** subroutine is more than 128 bytes away from the end of the line-clearing loop so a shorter JR would not reach it. But it works, and it fits. Even with this palaver the simplicity of the TileMap means it's acceptably quick, though a non-windowing version could be faster *and* shorter.

Three-byte control sequences

The PRINT AT and PRINT TAB control codes are followed by two data characters, all interpreted together. We can't act immediately when either of those codes reaches the driver. Subsequent character-codes are needed to work out which column or row the cursor is being sent to. That data is not interpreted as an ASCII character or tile index, even if it happens to have a corresponding code. So when CHR$ 64 appears after the AT or TAB control it refers to column 64 of the display, not the ASCII character "@".

This context-dependency requires us to trap instances of control codes 22 and 23, representing AT and TAB, buffering them and the subsequent data byte until the third byte completes the set. Three read-only driver variables Count, Seq1 and Seq2 implement this buffer. Count holds the number of data bytes required to complete the current sequence. Normally it's zero, so tile numbers pass straight through to the TileMap. Sometimes it's set to one, so the data byte after irrelevant control codes like BRIGHT and INK is skipped without messing up the text.

When either an AT or TAB control code is encountered, that code is stashed in Seq1 and Count gets set to 2. For the time being, this is all we can do. The complete sequence is needed before we can act on the control code. Here's how CHR$ 22, PRINT AT, is initially handled:

```
5000 ;notCLS
5010 ; ld a,e           ; Restore input control code
5020 ; cp AT            ; AT takes Y and X parameters
5030 ; jr nz,notAT
5040 ;
5050 ;await2
5060 ; ld (Seq1),a
5070 ; ld a,2           ; Two data bytes needed
5080 ;
5090 ;await
5100 ; ld (count),a
```

```
5110 ; ret
5120 ;
5130 ;notAT
5140 ; cp TAB
5150 ; jr z,await2      ; TAB also needs 2 bytes
```

CHR$ 23, PRINT TAB, is so similar that only two lines are needed to catch it. More will be needed later, to wind on to the chosen column. But there are other control codes which BASIC might pass to a driver, and since 23 is the highest our TileDriver implements we must suppress remaining codes in the range 24 to 31. Lines 5170 to 5220 do the trick, setting Count to one along the way, so the following character is ignored.

All of these unsupported codes are followed by a data byte, which is neither a tile number, control or ASCII character code. For instance BASIC emits CHR$ 18 followed by either CHR$ 0 or CHR$ 1 to control whether or not subsequent characters have their FLASH attribute set. This LAYER 0 legacy does not apply to TileMaps, or LAYER 2, or HiRes and LoRes layers for that matter, so we skip both bytes to keep the display clear.

This works nicely for eight of the nine codes, but the new pixel-positioning CHR$ 25 requires a *four* byte sequence. The pixel line number 0 to 255 will fit a single byte, immediately after the 25 code, but the potential for HiRes and Overscan screens to have more than 256 pixels on each line mean that the horizontal offset needs two more bytes, as it could range up to 509 when placing 3-dot-wide text on LAYER 1,2.

The logic to catch this exception is simple enough – set Count to 3 after detecting a CHR$ 25 – but it would require eight more bytes of code we can ill-afford, so if you attempt to send that sequence to a TileMap stream the X coordinate bytes will not be filtered. Pixel addressing makes no sense in the context of 8x8 tiles, in any case.

I'm happy enough to have caught the similarly irrelevant INK, PAPER, BRIGHT, INVERSE and OVER cases, which may well appear in partly-converted ZX BASIC programs. Higher codes to adjust character sizes are inapplicable to Layer 3 and we're out of bytes to implement justification or automatic pausing, neither of which are much help when using hardware tiles for their intended purpose.

The logic to skip the remaining control codes uses another simple trick. After sifting out AT and TAB, line 5170 adds 240 to the accumulator. If this does not overflow the code must be less than 16, and we can ignore it with RET NC. This catches CHR$ 15 (wash window with current attributes) and any other parameterless codes we've skipped to save bytes. But if the code is 16 or more, adding 240 to it causes the accumulator to overflow, setting the carry flag, as the largest number an 8-bit register can hold is 255:

```
5170 ; add 240          ; Exploit byte overflow
5180 ; ret nc           ; Code <16, discard it
5190 ;
```

```
5200 ; xor a              ; Clear A and carry
5210 ; inc a              ; Ignore 1 parameter byte
5220 ; jr await
```

We want to set Count to 1 to ignore the parameter byte and return, but if we used the obvious LD A,1 before exiting via **await** that would leave the carry flag set, implying that an error was detected. The sequence XOR A: INC A also sets A to 1 in two bytes, and guarantees that the carry flag will be clear. It takes one clock tick longer than the LD but we're optimising for space, not time.

CPUs like the 6502 update their flags when they load a value, but Zilog and Intel chips only set them after arithmetic operations. There are pros and cons to both conventions, which is why PowerPC and ARM chips give programmers the choice. If you need to test the Zilog Z and N flags after loading the accumulator, to identify zero or negative values, interpose an AND A or OR A instruction.

Multibyte sequences

Way back at line 1620, the first test in the character output routine jumps forward to the label **multi** if Count is non-zero. Here it is at last. We continue with HL pointing to Count and the latest code in register E.

```
5580 ;; Count is non-zero, store rest of sequence
5590 ;multi
5600 ; dec (hl)
5610 ; jr nz,stash2      ; Save second byte
5620 ;
5630 ;; Interpret the sequence in Seq1, Seq2 and register E
5640 ; inc hl            ; Point HL at Seq1
5650 ; ld a,AT
5660 ; cp (hl)
5670 ; inc hl            ; Point HL at Seq2
5680 ; jr z,doAt
```

To work out where we are in the sequence we decrement Count. If this leaves zero we're ready to process the whole thing. Immediately after Count there is space for two bytes, the first parts of the sequence. When the third one turns up we'll combine it with the second and do whatever the first byte implies.

Otherwise we jump forward to **stash2** which saves this parameter byte in Seq2. The first was already stashed in Seq1 by the **await2** routine. But if Count was 1 and is now clear, we have a sequence ready for interpretation.

The Seq bytes are deliberately stored immediately after Count so we can find them with a single-byte INC HL, rather than use a three-byte absolute or indexed LD instruction, which would be slower as well as more verbose.

It's poor programming style to make code dependent upon the implicit order of variables in memory, but this is Z80 and bytes are precious. Style is not our priority. It's no good if it won't fit.

> *Optimum things are fragile. We don't build optimum bridges, cars or planes. We overbuild them. So, in programming, there is a point of diminishing returns where you start paying with flexibility. And that makes the program fragile!*
>
> *Richard Wesley Hamming*

Before we can interpret the sequence we need to know if it start with AT or TAB. After tweaking Count we check Seq1 by advancing HL there and comparing the code for AT at line 5660. Either way, we're soon going to need Seq2 so we step HL forward again, ready to read that. Another Zilog quirk helps us. The 16-bit INC and DEC instructions, intended for addressing, do not alter any flags, unlike their eight-bit counterparts.

If this is a PRINT AT sequence the Z flag will still be set from the comparison, and we can press on to **doAt**. Otherwise we consider a TAB sequence. Sinclair provided for up to 65536 columns – I'd like to see that ZX Printer! 255 seems plenty, so we ignore the high byte of the column number in E, as it's always going to be zero for any plausible window width, whether tiled or pixelated. There's not enough room for 257 columns, even in the unsupported combination of HiRes overscan with three-pixel wide characters. It would require a lot of system updates just to reach column 212!

```
5780 ;doTab
5790 ; ld a,(Left)      ; Check window bounds
5800 ; ld b,a
5805 ; ld a,(CursorX)
5810 ; ld c,a
5820 ; sub b            ; A = relative X
5830 ; ld b,a
5840 ; ld a,(hl)        ; Get X from seq2, ignore nHigh
5850 ; sub b
5860 ; ret z            ; We are already there
5870 ;
5875 ; push af
5880 ; jp c,padline     ; Fill to end of line with spaces
5885 ; pop af
5890 ;
5900 ; jp spacer        ; Emit A spaces
```

As the manual explains, TAB outputs spaces to advance the cursor to the specified column, moving to the next line if there's not room. Line 5860 handles the possibility that it's already there, and we've nothing left to do.

Otherwise there are two possibilities. If the cursor is before the requested column, we exit via **spacer**, the loop we also use for a comma separator that advances to the next PRINT column. But if it's already too far over, the carry flag will be set, and we need to blank the remainder of the current line with a call to **padLine**; this explains why line 5810 saves CursorX in register C.

The only remaining TileDriver routine is **doAT**. That uses SEQ2 to set the cursor row and the last parameter, from register E, for the column. If the row is below the Bottom line, after adjusting for the window start at TOP, we simply ignore the sequence. NextBASIC would stop with an *Integer Out of Range* or *Out of Screen* error, depending on the layer.

If the row number passes muster we check the column similarly, and only set CursorX and CursorY if *both* checks pass. The long-awaited **stash2** subroutine brings up the rear.

```
5970 ;doAT
5980 ; ld a,(Bottom)      ; Check Y first
5990 ; ld b,a
6000 ; ld a,(Top)
6010 ; add (hl)          ; Offset line from top by seq2
6020 ; cp b
6030 ; ret nc            ; Too far down, ignore
6040 ;
6050 ; ld d,a            ; Save Y to set later
6060 ; call Cwidth       ; Get width in c and a
6070 ;
6080 ; sub e             ; A = width - X
6090 ; jp c,ignore       ; Too far over, ignore
6100 ;
6110 ; ld a,(Left)
6120 ; add e             ; Make X absolute
6130 ; ld (CursorX),a
6140 ; ld a,d
6145 ; jr setY2
6150 ;
6152 ;stash2            ; Store second parameter byte
6154 ; ld a,e
6156 ; ld (seq2),a
6158 ; ret
```

The END is nigh

Fingers crossed, we're still within the 512-byte driver slot limit. A little **.asm** magic enables us to check that automatically, rather than trust to luck. The inline assembler can associate integer variables with its own symbols.

We've seen how we control conditional assembly from BASIC by reading the variable %D at key points in this listing. It's also possible to set variables from within the assembler, using LET.

```
6350 ;end
6360 ; LET %e=end
6370 ; if %d
6380 ; LET %v=14           ;Cannot yet be computed by .asm
6390 ; assert 512+1-%v>end
6400 ; ds 512-end-14       ;Pad variable bytes to end of driver
6410 ; else
```

```
6420 ; assert 56512-14>end
6430 ; ds 56512-end-15      ; Testbed uses 1 more variable byte
6440 ;varPad equ last-Start   ; Not yet usable with ORG 0
6450 ; LET %v=varPad
6460 ; endif
```

Line 6360 passes the address of the label **end** back to BASIC variable %E. Since we know the start address, from the ORG directive, we can use this to make sure there's still room for the variables.

Ideally we'd be able to work this out with some more arithmetic within the **.asm** source, but this gets complicated because of differences between the way **.asm** handles relocatable code, for the driver, compared with absolute code, like the test version. Chris has since added a VAR directive to make this sort of thing easier.

The driver always puts its 14 variables right at the end of the 512-byte slot, padding out the code if necessary, for ease of reconfiguration by a separate BASIC program. The test version uses three more bytes and its origin is 56000 bytes later in memory. Either way, the conditional code passes the number of bytes of driver data to BASIC in %V. The assembly code checks, at build-time, that there's at least enough room for both code and data, while it is trying to apply the padding.

The ASSERT directive takes a numeric expression, which may include assembler symbols or integer variable names, and stops the build unless the expression is logically true. ASSERT 0 always fails. The two ASSERT lines check this for either version. Only if they succeed do we reach the DS (define space) directive that ensures the driver variables are in their expected space, regardless of the value of %E. This finagling allows the BASIC to print the length of the code and data from %E and %V, assuming it fits.

Driver internal variables

The table of driver variables comes last. Feel free to change the default values. The demos use BASIC procedures to adjust them after loading the driver, but you can avoid that overhead by patching or reassembling in whatever your application needs.

```
9000 ;; variables
9020 ;Start   dw 57344      ; 56k + TileMap start offset in page
9040 ;Width   db 40 ;80     ; Characters per line e.g. 40,64,80
9060 ;Height  db 20 ;30     ; Lines per screen (spare) 24,30,32
9080 ;Left    db 10 ;0      ; Window left margin, default 0
9100 ;Right   db 40 ;80     ; Window right margin+1,default maxX
9120 ;Top     db 10 ;0      ; Window top margin, default 0
9140 ;Bottom  db 20 ;30     ; Window bottom margin, default maxY
9160 ;CursorX db 10         ; Cursor column, leftX..rightX
9180 ;CursorY db 10         ; Cursor row, topY..bottomY-1
9200 ;Count   db 0          ; Bytes awaited in CTRL sequence
9220 ;Seq1    db 1          ; First control byte of sequence
9240 ;Seq2    db 2          ; Second byte of sequence
```

Wrapping up

A final conditional test appends either the diagnostic's **Here** pointer or the **OldPage** variable, followed by the driver's relocation data:

```
9250 ; if %d
9253 ;OldPage db 3          ; MMU register value to be restored
9255 ; RELOC_END
9256 ; RELOC_TABLE
9257 ;
9258 ; else
9260 ;Here     dw 9999       ; Only used for testbed
9280 ;          dw end        ; Appears at offset 512
9290 ; endif
9295 ;last equ $
9300 ;
9310 PRINT "Code end ";%E;" ";%V;" variables"
```

The PRINT is only reached if neither of the earlier Asserts has prevented the assembly of an outsize driver. The closer their total gets to 512, the less slack you have to play with when adding features.

TileDriver testbeds

There are two testbeds for the TileDriver. One calls the code directly, making it easy to debug as it's in main memory alongside the TileMap it manipulates. Thus there's no need for a font or NextReg setup, but no display either, at least not in Layer 3. Instead a couple of simple procedures are used to extract the character codes from the TileMap and PRINT them to a Timex HiRes display. If you're only interested in using the existing driver there's not much to see here – but if you are tempted to adapt the code for your own purposes, adding per-tile attributes, or switching to a 40 line display to allow more ULA RAM for colours and tile data, this gives you the same framework for your tweaks that I used to develop this complicated driver:

```
10 CLEAR 49151:; Thursday 20240729 ©SNG
13 LOAD "TileDriver" CODE 56000:REM 1344 before base of tiles
16 t$= CHR$ 5+"12345678901234567890123456 78"+ CHR$ 6
   +"0123456789012345"+ CHR$ 13+"test unphased by the length"
19 base=57344:width=40:lines=20
20 PROC WIPE(127)
25 LAYER 1,2
30 PROC REDRAW()
34 REM Code variable addresses
35 start=56497:wide=56499:height=56500:left=56501:right=56502
37 top=56503:bottom=56504:cursor X=56505:cursor Y=56506
39 count=56507:seq1=56508:seq2=56509:here=56510:end=56512
41 PRINT(DPEEK end)-56000;" ";PEEK cursor X;" ";PEEK cursor Y
42 PAUSE 0: REPEAT : POKE 56001, CODE t$:t$=t$(2 TO )
45 %r= REG 87: REG 87,14:t= USR 56000: REG 87,%r
50 PROC REDRAW()
55 PRINT PEEK cursor X;",";  PEEK cursor Y;": "; PEEK count;
   " "; STR$ PEEK seq1+" " AND count; STR$ PEEK seq2 AND
   count;" @ "; DPEEK here;" with "; LEN t$
60 PAUSE 0: REPEAT UNTIL NOT LEN t$: STOP
```

Here are PROC WIPE() and PROC REDRAW(), the test routines that echo the contents of the TileMap onto the LAYER 1,2 screen. These use the variables **base**, **lines** and **width** to find the start address of the TileMap and the part of it that's being tested. Since Timex HiRes mode does not support printing into the border area, as the overscan Layer 3 can, **lines** and **width** should not exceed 22 and 64 when the standard character-set is used, as that's the character-capacity limit of the upper screen.

```
9420 DEFPROC REDRAW()
9430 LOCAL %r,y,t=base
9440 %r= REG 87: REG 87,14
9450 PRINT AT 0,0;
9460 FOR y=1 TO lines
9480   PRINT PEEK$ (t,width)
9500   t+=width
9520 NEXT y
9530 REG 87,%r
9540 ENDPROC
9560
9580 DEFPROC WIPE(c=32)
9600 LOCAL %r,y,t=base
9610 %r= REG 87: REG 87,14
9620 FOR y=1 TO lines
9640   POKE t, CHR$ (c-y)*width
9660   t+=width
9680 NEXT y
9710 REG 87,%r
9720 ENDPROC
```

The second testbed starts at line 100 in TileDriver.bas It updates the TileMap directly, with DRIVER commands rather than PEEKs and POKEs to set and query the variables inside it. The same routines are used to echo the contents of a trimmed-down window to a Timex HiRes display. Once again the purpose of these is to show how a driver can be tested from BASIC, but this time it's not practical to step through the code because it runs from system memory paged under the ROM.

```
100 REM NextBASIC Testbed for driver control codes
102 REM This renders from and draws to the top 8k
105 LAYER 1,2:.install TILE.DRV
107 CLEAR 56*1024-1:base=56*1024
108 DRIVER 84,3,%-1 TO lines: DRIVER 84,2,%-1 TO width
109 PRINT "Map is ";width;" * ";lines;" characters"
110 DRIVER 84,8,%-1 TO x: DRIVER 84,9,%-1 TO y
120 PRINT "Original Cursor X,Y = ";x;",";y
124 DRIVER 84,13,%-1 TO q
126 PRINT "Default top page was ";q
130 CLOSE # 4: OPEN # 4,"D>T"
132 DRIVER 84,11,%-1 TO x: DRIVER 84,12,%-1 TO y
136 PRINT "Open; Seq1, Seq2 = ";x;",";y
138 PRINT "Testing LASTL, TAB, RIGHT"
140 PRINT #4; CHR$ 5, CHR$ 9;
150 DRIVER 84,8,%-1 TO x: DRIVER 84,9,%-1 TO y
160 PRINT "Revised Cursor X,Y = ";x;",";y
```

```
170 PRINT "Press a key when bored...": PAUSE 0
200 PROC WIPE(91): PROC REDRAW()
210 PRINT #4; CHR$ 4;"New text on top line"; CHR$ 8;"!";
212 DRIVER 84,13,%-1 TO q
214 PRINT #4'';"Saved top page now ";q
220 PROC REDRAW(): PAUSE 1: PAUSE 0
230 PRINT #4; CHR$ 14;"©";
240 PROC REDRAW(): PAUSE 1: PAUSE 0: CLS : PROC TILEVARS()
250 FOR i=0 TO 3: PRINT #4;"Ping Pong";: NEXT i
260 PROC REDRAW(): PAUSE 1: PAUSE 0
270 DRIVER 84,13,%-1 TO q
280 PRINT "Saved top page now ";q
360 CLOSE # 4
370 .uninstall TILE.DRV
380 STOP
```

These lines are examples from my own testing. Feel free to add more. They call PROC WIPE() to fill the screen and PROC REDRAW() to echo the changes from the TileMap to the Timex HiRes screen. These rely on the **base**, **lines** and **width** variables set by line 108. Make sure the settings of driver variables 2 and 3 fit within the smaller space available in LAYER 1,2.

TileDriving the NextBASIC Text Editor

We've seen that there are important differences between Next's built-in screen drivers and the capabilities available to a custom Layer 3 driver. Font handling is different, INVERSE and OVER can't work as the tiles are rendered directly from the Tile Font without the opportunity to toggle pixel values en route to a bitmap, and INPUT is not echoed the screen.

That said, tiles are drawn and scrolled faster and can use the screen border for increased resolution and clearer 80-column text. How much work would it be to make a complicated utility like the NextBASIC Text Editor use Layer 3 rather than Timex HiRes Layer 1,2? Once we know that, we'll have a good guide to converting other text-heavy programs to use the TileDriver.

Cosmetics like the double-width heading and block graphic separators in the menu are no great loss. Sinclair-standard fonts must be stored in main memory, competing with BASIC variables. Tile fonts are larger but can be tucked away in BANK 7, as long as we're careful not to clobber them.

Let's see what we need to change, assuming we are running NextBASIC 2.08 or 2.09 and TILE.DRV. The main principle is to use an 80x24 TileMap instead of Timex HiRes for the text being edited. This leaves us some additional screen lines, originally part of the Sinclair and Timex screen border, which we can use for INPUT in one of the standard layers.

For a good chance of making everything fit, let's start the TileMap one row down from the top of the sprite overscan area, on pixel lines eight to 199 (-24 to 167 in ZX PLOT coordinates). This uncovers three lines of the Sinclair screen lower down, pixel lines 168 to 191, where we can INPUT file names and patterns for Find and Replace. The menu stays at the bottom of the TileMap, remaining visible during INPUT. The NextZXOS file browser always uses a 256x192 pixel attribute layer, but with some REG magic we can make sure that whatever layers need to be seen are not obscured.

The font and pointer files need to be changed, as we'll use a 16-colour font and a colour sprite, rather than OVER 1, for the text input cursor. And we'll compromise the all-BASIC implementation by adding a little code file, **AnyPage**, from page 272, to streamline our access to BANK 7 memory. This can quickly copy up to 8k from any RAM page to any other, regardless of NextZXOS restrictions, at a price of just 55 bytes at the top of main memory, so it's not just useful for tiling and text editing.

In turns out that PROC Init Display() is the only one needs to be completely re-written. A few other lines need tweaks to remove unsupported attributes and divert INPUT to a suitable layer. The following sections list and explain all the tweaks needed in Editor.bas and the banked EditorProcs.

Tile-friendly changes to Editor.bas

Twenty lines of Editor.bas have been updated, though not all of the changes are essential. The other 200-odd are unchanged. At the start I revise a couple of comments, then shift RAMTOP down so we can use BASIC to load our tiles. Once they are tucked away in BANK 7, before we set up the big text arrays, RAMTOP can move back up – in fact, it can go 713 bytes higher than it would be if we were using a bitmapped character set:

```
  3 ; 20240806 TileDriver Version 2.1 for NextBASIC 2.08+
 90 CLEAR $d3ff
140 ; "L3bold.bin" and "Cursors.spr". Edit if needed.
```

This sequence loads the USR code and tile data, then calls the code to move the tiles to BANK 7. I've used hexadecimal for the load address just below RAMTOP, and saved a few bytes by writing the constant 0 as a degenerate binary value: NextBASIC interprets a lone @ just like %0, but even more concisely.

```
151 LOAD F$+"AnyPage" CODE %65480
153 %c=$d400: LOAD F$+"Bold96x16" CODE %c
155 POKE %65520,@: DPOKE %65515,%c: POKE %65510,%14:
  IF % USR 65480 THEN
157 DPOKE %65515,@: REG %110,@10001100: REG %111,@10011100:
  CLEAR %65479
160 %w=%80: F$=""
```

The line width is fixed at 80 columns to make full use of a high-resolution TileMap. The path prefix F$ must be re-stated after the additional CLEAR, though we could just edit the path on line 250, which loads the banked BASIC, if it's not in the same directory as the main program. Those EditorProcs also assume the drivers are in the current directory. Unlike dot commands there's no dedicated system directory for drivers, so the **.install** and **.uninstall** lines will need tweaking if you have your own preferred place for shared NextZXOS DRIVER files.

> *IF USR THEN...*
> *Carol Brooksbank*

I learned the eccentric idiom IF USR THEN from prolific *ZX Computing* and MGT *FORMAT* magazine columnist Carol Brooksbank, who realised it was the most concise way to call 48k USR code when you don't care about the result but don't want to mess up random number generation, as the keyword classic RANDOMIZE USR would. NextBASIC makes this a little easier to type by accepting abbreviated commands RAND and CONT.

Assigning the function with something like LET t=USR needs more bytes and involves a slow search through VARS for the place to store the value we don't care about. The IF evaluates the expression without needing to store the result, and the empty THEN clause completes the statement. Only use this at the end of a line, unless you're sure the USR call will never return zero! NextBASIC doesn't need the syntactic sugar of standard BASIC's LET keyword either, and has pre-placed integer variables that can be found and updated faster, but even %T=USR takes more space than IF USR THEN. I've used it here in memory of Carol, a rare female journalist and developer on the '80s ZX scene, who used Spectrum and SAM computers to administer her church as well as to develop and explain clever BASIC and Z80 projects.

The speed-up hacks for fast horizontal cursor movement are no longer needed, or possible in the absence of OVER 1, simplifying three of the cursor-movement lines. BANK ProcArea PROC Display Cursor() now uses a sprite, so there's no need to clear and re-draw characters.

```
610 IF Last Key Pressed=9 THEN IF Cursor Col<(%w-1) THEN
  IF PosIn Current Paragraph<>L(Current Paragraph)+1 THEN
  cursor col+=%1: BANK ProcArea PROC DisplayCursor():
  PosIn Current Paragraph+=%1: REPEAT UNTIL %0
620 IF Last Key Pressed=8 THEN IF Cursor Col>0 THEN Cursor
  Col-=%1: BANK ProcArea PROC Display Cursor():PosIn Current
  Paragraph-=%1: REPEAT UNTIL %0
640 IF Last Key Pressed>=8 AND Last Key Pressed<=11 THEN
  BANK ProcArea PROC MoveCursor()
```

Lines 860 and 870 used to unload the bitmapped character set, and should be removed. This means the old RAMTOP is not restored; 56 bytes remain allocated at the top of RAM, and could be clawed back with CLEAR 65535.

The only other changes in the main program make file operations tile-friendly. It turns out that **.browse** stashes temporary data in the second screen – which helps explain why it uses condensed characters rather than a HiRes display, but also clashes with our wish to put tiles there, in one of the few pages accessible to the TileMap hardware. And that's the main reason I resorted to machine code to upload the tile font. The AnyPage routine that copied the tiles up there is equally adept at copying them out again, to the WorkArea bank which we won't need till we've finished browsing and start to load the chosen text, and then puts it back. These three lines momentarily hide Layer 3, stashing and restoring the tile data either side of the **.browse** call, during PROC Open File().

```
4128 REG %107,@: POKE %65510,WorkArea*2
4129 POKE 65506,%14: POKE %65520,@: IF % USR 65480 THEN

4140 @Bad Browse: ON ERROR : PRINT #%4; CHR$(%14); :
    REG %107,@11100001: POKE %65520,%235: IF % USR 65480 THEN
```

The REG 107 commands turn Layer 3 off and on. The POKEs configure AnyPage to copy from the work area to BANK 7 (doubling the bank numbers to address 8k pages) or back again. The instruction at 65520 simplifies this by swapping source and target addresses when it's 235 (the EX DE,HL opcode) and leaving them alone when it's 0 (NOP). The PRINT clears the ULA screen so it doesn't interact with the tiles when they're back.

PROC Save File() uses stream #4 again, this time for INPUT, and a helper procedure CL4() to clear the ULA screen and put the cursor at the bottom, underneath the TileMap. Line 5175 can be deleted as we're no longer using the menu line for text entry:

```
5130 IF saveAs OR F$="Untitled.txt" THEN BANK ProcArea PROC
  CL4(): INPUT #%4;"Save as: "; LINE X$: BANK ProcArea PROC
  CL4(): IF X$="" THEN ENDPROC
5630 BANK ProcArea PROC CL4(): PRINT #%4;" Save changes (y/n)?",
5650 IF k= CODE "y" THEN PRINT #%4; "y";: PROC SaveFile(%0): EXIT
5685 BANK ProcArea PROC CL4()
```

Those 18 lines are all that need tweaking in the main program, but I found two others useful just while I was testing, because without them if an error occurs the report appears underneath the tiles, making it rather hard to see:

```
522 ON ERROR GO TO %950
950 FOR %i=0 TO 3:%e(i)= ERROR (%i): NEXT %i: ON ERROR :
  PROC Quit(): PRINT "Error ";: FOR %i=0 TO 3: PRINT %e(i);
  " ";: NEXT %i: STOP
```

Values from the ERROR function that identify what went wrong are copied into the array %E before calling Quit(), in case that clobbers them, then reported in order: reason, statement, line and bank number. Those lines can be removed, and the standard break and error-trap at line 525 reinstated, once you're sure your changes haven't broken anything. They're equally useful when testing other Layer 3 conversions.

Making EditorProcs.bas use Layer 3

The Init Display() procedure at the start of EditorProcs.bas must be entirely replaced now we're using Layer 3 and LAYER 1,1 (for INPUT) rather than LAYER 1,2 for everything:

```
1600 ;------------------------------------------------------------
1610 ;-             Load and Initialise tile driver              -
1620 ;------------------------------------------------------------
```

```
1630 DEFPROC Init Display()
1640 SPECTRUM CHR$ %32: LAYER CLEAR : LAYER %1,%1: PAPER %7:
  BRIGHT %1: PALETTE CLEAR
1645 LAYER PALETTE %0,%31,%511: LAYER PALETTE %0,%23,%511:
  CLS : CLOSE # %4: OPEN # %4,"k"
1650 LOCAL %i,%d
1660 .install TILE.DRV: OPEN # %2,"D>T"
1670 RESTORE:FOR %i=%0 TO %9: READ %d:DRIVER %84,%i,%d: NEXT %i
1680 DATA @,%236,%80,%24,@,%80,@,%24,@,@
1690 REG %49,%248: REG %107,@11100001: REG %108,%0
1700 REG %27,%0: REG %27,%159: REG %27,%8: REG %27,%199
1710 REG %67,% REG 67 & 15+48:;Tile palette with auto-increment
1720 FOR %i=%0 TO %15: READ %d: REG %65,%d: NEXT %i
1730 DATA @,@10,@10100000,@10100010,@10100,@10110,@10110100
1740 DATA @10110110,@01101101,@11,@11100000,@11100011,@11100
1750 DATA @11111,@11111100,@11111111:;Bits R2R1R0G2G1G0B2B1
1760 ENDPROC
```

This is a useful template for other Layer 3 conversions. It stops the NextBASIC editor using Timex HiRes, as that would mess up tiles in BANK 7 during testing, then selects a LAYER 1,1 attribute display with bright white paper, preventing the print-through blending featured in the 3-layer text demo. Stream #4 is OPEN for input via the "k" channel. The CLOSE is just in case some other program might have left it open, and ignored otherwise.

Once the Tile Driver is loaded line 1660 directs the default PRINT stream #2 to use it and 1670 sets the driver variables for an 80x24 screen. The DATA values could be assembled directly into the driver code, saving a couple of lines, but this way we don't need a special version of the TileDriver. Lines 1690 to 1700 are copied from TileSetter.bas lines 1220 to 1260, but this time they move Layer 3 output to allow INPUT from LAYER 1,1 below it.

The lines 1710 to 1750 make up for an understandable gap in current NextBASICs – the LAYER PALETTE command can't set the Layer 3 colours because it only groks LAYERs 0, 1 and 2. So these lines set up custom colours, using REG 67 to select the Layer 3 palette 0 hardware then REG 65 to plonk 8-bit colour values into the first 16 slots.

The DATA is written in binary so the correspondence between bits and levels of red, green and blue intensity is easier to see. Leading zeros are omitted to save space, leaving only an @ sign for the first, black, value. Alter entries 1 and 15 to recolour the tile ink and paper respectively, but check you can still see the mouse pointer and text cursor, which use the sprite palette.

Here are the lines that load and place the sprites. Sprite 0 is the mouse pointer, which uses its own driver, and the added Sprite 1 is the text cursor. The old lines 1860 and 1870 should be deleted; they've been moved up so that we still get a text cursor, even if the mouse driver fails to load:

```
1822 LOAD "Cursors.spr" BANK SpriteArea
1824 SPRITE CLEAR : SPRITE %1,@,$F,%1,%1
1826 SPRITE BANK SpriteArea: SPRITE PRINT %1: SPRITE BORDER %1
```

The Refresh Display procedure needs to use CHR$ 14 rather than CLS to wipe the screen, and eschews the widener heading as tiles are fixed-width:

```
2040 PRINT CHR$ 14;
2050 PRINT AT %0,%0;F$;" ";
```

Display Cursor now positions sprite 1 over the active character, rather than incompatibly flipping its ink and paper with OVER 1. The SPRITE X coordinate is in low-res pixels (four rather than eight per character) so we convert that tile coordinate by shifting two places to the left, rather than three for Cursor Row where the full range 0..255 still fits into one byte. The extra 8 pixels accounts for the TileMap starting one row below the upper border limit, to reduce the chance of the title line getting lost on an old telly.

```
2475 SPRITE %1,Cursor Col<<2,Cursor Row<<3+8
```

PROC FIND() contains a couple of INPUT statements which need to be redirected to the bottom lines of LAYER 1 via stream #4. The new one-line helper function PROC CL4() is called before and after showing each prompt.

```
3737 PROC CL4()
3740 INPUT #%4;"Find: "; LINE X$
3750 IF NOT LEN X$ THEN PROC CL4(): ENDPROC

3780 First Visible Paragraph=i: PROC Refresh Display(): Cursor
  Row= %t/w+1: Cursor Col=%t MOD w-1: PROC Display Cursor():
  PROC CL4():PRINT #%4;"Next [";X$;"] Replace or Quit (n/r/q)";

3796 IF R$="" THEN PROC CL4():INPUT #4;"Replacement? "; LINE R$

3840 PROC ClearMessage(): PROC CL4()

3870 DEFPROC CL4()
3880 PRINT #%4; CHR$ (%14); AT %22,@;: ENDPROC
```

These additional lines in PROC QUIT() turn off Layer 3 and restore the standard display. The **uninstall** statement will fail if TILE.DRV is not in the current directory, so if you've set up a dedicated place for drivers it makes sense to put that path before the driver name on line 5495:

```
5485 REG %107,@: REG %49,@: REG %111,%12: REG %110,%44
5490 CLOSE # %4: CLOSE # %2: OPEN # %2,"s"
5495 .uninstall TILE.DRV
```

The Timex-layer mouse menu used INVERSE and block graphics to divide HiRes menu elements. The tiled version just puts a + sign before letters associated with Symbol-shifted commands. The prompt for the **Delete** command has been shortened to fit 80 rather than 85 columns, and line 5750 can be deleted as there's no room for the optional **Find** menu item:

```
5720 LOCAL T$="+"
5730 PRINT AT %23,%0;"Sym Shift Commands ";T$;"Erase all ";
 T$;"Get file  ";T$;"Save   Save";T$;"As   ";T$;"Quit";
5740 PRINT AT %23,%66;T$;"Insert  ";T$;"Del";
5750
```

The last two lines we need to alter strip the INVERSE attributes from messages displayed at the bottom of the TileMap, and take advantage of the fixed 8x8 tile size when converting mouse coordinates in PROC Handle Mouse Click(). The IF test ignores the empty top line of the border, without any risk of puzzling the integer expression evaluator with a negative number.

```
6020 PRINT AT %22,%0;" ";T$;" ";

8030 LOCAL %k,%c=%x/8,%r=%y/8:IF %r<2 THEN ENDPROC: ELSE %r-=%1
```

The TileDriver integration was one of the last experiments I carried out before the deadline for this book, so it's not had as much testing as I would have liked. Please check on GetIt or at http://simon.mooli.org.uk/nextbook for updates, and let me know if you find reproducible problems, or (even better) improvements for this experimental code.

Now it's your turn

This demo only uses the two-colour HiRes version of a TileMap. By tweaking REG settings and the driver code, or the supporting BASIC, it can do lots more. Here are a few suggestions, in order of increasing difficulty. Implementing these will show that you've understood the driver and the Layer 3 hardware, and open up even more potential for exciting and original displays.

a) Experiment with modifying the font to colour characters differently depending on their position in the ASCII set. Play with the palette.

b) Move the TileMap to use 2.5k at address 16384. Alter TSCREEN and TileSetter to suit. Set up a full-sized 80x32 tile overscan screen.

c) Move the tile font to follow that, at 18944. There's 4¼K left in the LAYER 0 memory area: room for 136 characters, enough for the full ASCII set and 40 custom tiles, but you'll have to reload the font after using the NextBASIC editor or browser, which clobbers it.

d) Convert the display to use 40x32 resolution. How many more tile definitions can you fit into memory? Design new and colourful ones.

e) Use the extra memory freed up to support one attribute per tile. Tweak the character output code to skip the attribute bytes. Test the changes by writing PROCs to set the attributes for given positions.

f) Add INK and PAPER control codes 0..255, to PRINT attributes. You'll need to trim something else to make room for extra code in 512 bytes; maybe simplify this version to use a fixed-sized window?

g) Extend the driver to load and use extra code in an additional page, allocated when it is installed. Reinstate support for DELETE and configurable windows. Try to make sure the variables stay at the same offsets, for patching.

Chapter 17, Hardware Programming

One of the most exciting things about Next is that the hardware, as well as the software, is programmable. Better still, and unlike the system software NextZXOS, the exact hardware specification is open-source, downloadable from GitLab, in the form of VHSIC Hardware Design Language (VHDL) files which can be *synthesised* with freely-available software into a *bitstream* that can be loaded into Next, changing the behaviour of the FPGA once the corresponding core is selected. FPGA stands for Field Programmable Gate Array.

In turn, the embedded acronym VHSIC stands for Very High Speed Integrated Circuit. The nesting of technology is very much what it's all about, and acronyms, always popular with the Military-Industrial Complex (MIC – *I made that one up*) are commonplace. Don't let them put you off. VHDL is as old as the Spectrum, though it was originally intended for circuit simulators; the hardware synthesis part came along later.

This chapter is a taster of the potential of VHDL, comparing analogue and digital electronics, then software and hardware programming. My aim is to learn and encourage other enthusiasts to understand and eventually be able to make their own VHDL patches or even complete cores, but that's way beyond the scope of this article. This time, I'm going to explore one small part of the Next hardware design, showing how 8-bit samples are converted into analogue sounds. But first, a bit of history.

Back in the 1980s, computers were designed using a mixture of LSI and TTL chips. LSI stands for Large Scale Integration and refers to RAM, ROM and CPU chips, each containing thousands of components wired together in a fixed pattern to meet a specification. TTL chips are smaller, logically and often physically, and provide the 'glue' that links up LSI components into a complete and unique computer. The term stands for 'Transistor Transistor Logic', a step up from RTL and DTL which mixed Resistors and Diodes onto early chips to reduce the need for initially-expensive transistors.

Sinclair's ZX80 was designed by Jim Westwood using four LSI chips, for CPU, ROM and RAM, and seventeen simpler TTL logic chips to complete the design. TTL took up most of the board, even though each of those chips was much simpler, internally, than the LSI parts. Implementing a complete computer with keyboard, tape and TV display in 21 chips was an impressive feat – most single-board computers used at least twice as many, and the simplest 4k RAM Apple used more than sixty, with sockets for another 20, despite Steve Wozniak's well-deserved reputation for using fewer chips to do more than most rival circuit designers.

Since all the ZX80 parts were available on the open market, apart from the 4k ROM, programmed to a specification created by John Grant of Sinclair contract mathematicians Nine Tiles, it was easy for rivals to copy it.

Chris Cary, Irish pirate radio pioneer and co-owner of the UK computer dealer Comp Shop, copied the ROM (swapping over a couple of data lines, to scramble the data without affecting the Z80 code) and started selling clones under the Micro Ace brand. When Sinclair took Comp Shop to court the judge refused to rule that the ROM breached Sinclair's copyright, saying "I cannot see it" and leading to hasty changes in UK copyright law so that software, visible or not, was also covered.

But the judge *could* see the unusual ZX80 keyboard layout, with BASIC keywords associated with each key, and ruled that, at least, was an unlicensed copy. So the case was settled, Comp Shop got a brief licence to sell Micro Ace kits in the USA in return for royalty payments to Sinclair, as Clive Sinclair had already described the ZX80 as a 'nine day wonder' and was on the point of releasing the much-improved yet even more minimal ZX81, cut down to four or five chips by eliminating the fiddly TTL.

This is the point at which 'custom chips' enter the Sinclair scene. With a lot of help from one of the few UK chip-makers, Ferranti in Manchester, Jim Westwood replaced the TTL with a semi-custom chip, the Ferranti Uncommitted Logic Array (ULA) and still had room for improvements. Ferranti's ULA was a grid of simple logic gates, repeated across the chip, but in this 'uncommitted' form they were left unconnected from one another and the IC pins round the outside. Jim Westwood worked out a 'final metal mask' to hook these gates up into the required circuit, giving Sinclair a product that was more capable, cheaper to manufacture, and much harder for opportunist rogues to copy.

Modern FPGA design, used in our Next, is based on the same principle of standard components 'wired up' after manufacture, except that components on a chip are now so plentiful and cheap that it's practical to include all the possible wiring, with extra transistors controlled by a pattern in embedded memory that determine which of those wires is active in a given design. Small memories, known as 'registers', hold temporary values inside the chip till the next stage is ready for them.

This is wasteful compared with a full-custom design, like the Z80 CPU or 4116 RAM chips, but saves months of effort working out and checking all the connections, which used to be done literally by hand, cutting traces in rubylith photographic masking material, on a zoomed-up floorplan of the chip, before piling up all the layers for lithographic projection onto silicon, and doing it over and over till (with luck) the LSI chip came near enough to the required specification to be saleable.

The culture of logic design has also changed since the 1980s, when circuits were often 'asynchronous', each part working at just the speed needed to service the next in the chain. This made the whole system brittle, as a slight change in the timing anywhere, caused by heat, power or production variations, could stop the whole thing working. Trading additional components for predictability and scalability, modern designs are 'synchronous' which means that 'clock' timing signals regulate each step of the logic. Next FPGA maestro Allen Albright explains that, this way, the design becomes independent of the implementation.

"At a little higher view, all synchronous logic (i.e. almost everything) is just logic between registers triggered by a common clock. The design happens at this level and then you target a specific technology. If it's TTL parts you want to use to build the circuit, you map the logic to as few available TTL parts as possible."

The process of converting the design into a core is known as synthesis. It's analogous to compiling a program, but more subtle, as we shall soon see. Rather than the logic gates of TTL, which combine signals with Boolean operations like AND, OR and NOT, or the few transistors in each Ferranti logic block or 'cell', our Xilinx chip is a mass of Configurable Logic Blocks known, to acronym fans, as CLBs. An intermediate technology, called ASIC (Application Specific Integrated Circuit) uses ULA-style metal layers to connect larger pre-designed logic blocks, some of which may be complete processors.

Each Xilinx CLB has six inputs and two outputs, with an optional register to hold the value of each output bit. The formula that converts inputs to outputs is held in a tiny static RAM, the LUT (Look Up Table), making it 'field programmable'. Allen explains:

"If it's an FPGA you want to use to build the circuit, you map the logic to CLBs... If you know the target technology ahead of time, that can affect the design process too, and the FPGA "parts" (the CLB, in the main) are much more amenable than TTL.

"The other thing is the FPGA synthesis step will optimise your circuit, slide registers around, possibly duplicate logic to make things smaller and faster. That's fairly important because there are other details to worry about when circuits are implemented on such a small scale like clock skew, temperature variation, routing delay, etc, that aren't an issue on larger scale devices like TTL.

FPGA manufacturers work out standard ways to arrange CLBs to make complex components like adders and comparators, and allow those rather than simple logic expressions to be included as part of the VHDL for synthesis. In a simpler way, Ferranti did the same, so a simple TTL buffer or three-input NOR gate could be made with a single cell, whereas a binary divider might need three, or six for a differential amplifier. Allen added:

"So it's normal to estimate CLB/LUT usage when considering alternate implementations of something and there is less concern about using higher level blocks like adders since adders just become some number of LUTs on an FPGA but with TTL an adder could be something expensive in terms of number of parts."

As the design is elaborated, the VHDL synthesiser finds ways to combine existing parts more economically, aided by hints from the designer. The more we try to squeeze in, the longer this takes and the greater the risk that the design will need to be manually simplified to fit. As the KS1 FPGA filled up with great ideas from the team this has required hours and sometimes days of semi-automatic tweaking, just to keep up.

The GA suffix in FPGA corresponds to Ferranti's earlier LA (Logic Array), and the Field Programmable bit to the 'Uncommitted' aspect of Sinclair's chips. By the time they were built into a ZX81, ZX Spectrum, Sinclair QL (twice), Interface 1, ZX microdrives, C5 trikes or for that matter Acorn's BBC and Electron micros, they were fully committed and not re-programmable.

This is unlike Next's FPGA which can be – and indeed must be – recommitted to a particular circuit or 'core', every single time it's powered up. We get a choice of 'core' configurations for our Nexts, because the Flash memory chip that initialises our FPGA has room for dozens of different cores, selected from a menu once the first one, known as the 'anti-brick system', has set the ball rolling.

In practice there are still some fixed elements of the Next system, because of the way on-board peripherals are wired up to specific pins of the FPGA. There's only one analogue video mixer circuit, for example, so we only get one VGA port, and the final audio output uses a dedicated connection to the stereo jack socket. We could only extend those, or the keyboard, tape, joystick, HDMI, WiFi, Pi or expansion edge connections, by changing the circuit board as well as the FPGA core.

To explain in detail how a representative part of this works, I'm going to concentrate on the stereo audio output in this chapter. There are several DAC (Digital to Audio Converter) designs in the Next FPGA source and I've chosen one of the simpler ones. Current Nexts use a different implementation from the same GitLab source folder, based on the Xilinx application note XAPP154. This sigma-delta scheme works progressively, which takes more FPGA space but improves the 12-bit audio quality. Part of the beauty of FPGA is that by the time you read this it might have changed again, but the principles remain the same.

Analogue to digital – the traditional way

We want to convert numbers between 0 and 255 into a voltage that varies smoothly between those values. To start with, let's consider how this would be done with multiple digital outputs to analogue electronics. The 8-bit sample corresponds to a varying voltage, lowest for the value 0 and highest for 255. Each of the eight bits of the byte contributes twice as much to the output as the lower-numbered bit, so bit 0 – the difference between values 0 and 1 – makes 1/128th the difference contributed when bit 7 is set, thereby adding 128 to the total.

Imagine that all eight bits are set or cleared at once, their combined value 0 to 255 corresponding to a required output level. The same voltage is delivered from each set bit, whether it's the least or most significant.

We want to make the higher bits contribute proportionately more. For 256 equal steps, we need a way to pass through the entire output of bit 7, the most significant; half that for bit 6; half again for bit 5, and so on down to bit 0, the least significant, which makes 1/128th the contribution of bit 7.

Figure 101 shows a suitable circuit to divide all eight bits by binary factors and add up the result.

The aim is to get the maximum output (actually 255/256th of the unresisted output level) given a sample value of 255, progressively decreasing to 0/256, usually known as 0, for lower sample values.

When a voltage is applied to two otherwise-isolated resistors connected end to end, it is distributed between them in proportion to their resistances.

If we connect a 9v battery to two 1k resistors wired end-to-end in series, the voltage measured across each resistor will be 4.5v, as the resistors match so the voltage is evenly distributed.

If one resistor was 8k and the other was 1k, we'd see eight volts across the higher resistance and only one volt on the 1k side.

For bit 0 of our converter we need 1/128th of the full voltage. We could get that with a 255k resistor from the bit 0 output, mixing it to a 1k resistor across which our output will appear.

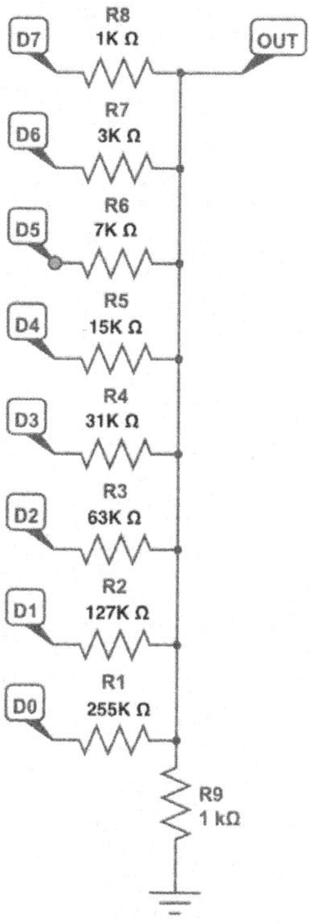

Figure 101 – The circuit diagram for a summing digital to analogue converter

Now consider bit 1. This needs to have twice the weight of bit 0, so we use a 127k resistor. If only output bit 1 is set, the level is 1/128, or 2/256. If both bits 0 and 1 are set at the same time, the mix rises to 3/256.

Bit 2 is needs to be twice as potent again, so we feed it via a 63k resistor to the output mix.

That resistor soaks up 63/64 of the bit 2 output level, leaving 1/64 which corresponds to 4/256. Now we have a three-bit Digital to Analogue converter (DAC), and can get output levels from 0/256 to 7/256 by setting combinations of bits 0, 1 and 2.

The rest follows logically. Bit 3 takes a 31k resistor for a weight of 1/32. Bit 5 uses 7k, Bit 6 drives 3k, and the most significant bit 7 contributes half the maximum output on its own, so it is connected to the mixer via a 1k resistor, matching the one between the output and earth, and thereby splitting the voltage into matching halves, a weight of 1 / 2 or 128/256.

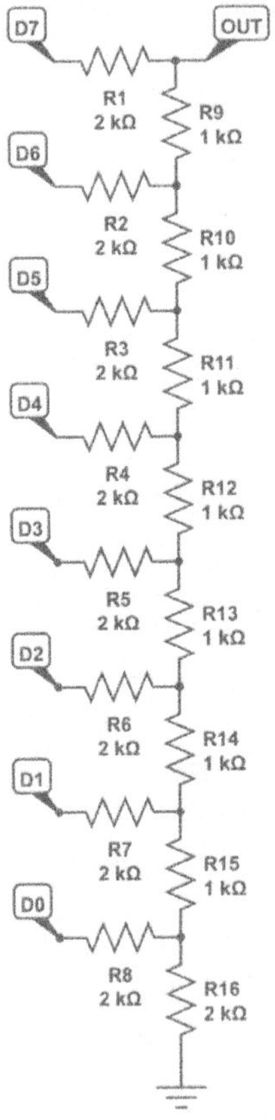

Figure 102, The circuit digram of an R2R summing Digital to Analogue converter

The principle is sound, but in practice, it's very difficult to get a set of resistors with exactly the right values. The lower the resistance, the more accurate the value must be.

If the 1k resistor connected to output bit 7 was just half of one per cent less than it should be, 995 ohms, it'd make more difference to the output than the state of bit 0 (1/200 versus 1/256) and the ladder performs worse than a 7-bit DAC. The circuit needs nine matched resistors in eight very specific values, accurate overall to a fraction of one per cent.

A more practical discrete DAC

In practice this sort of 'analogue summing DAC' is built another way, known as R2R since it uses a ladder of matched resistors, some exactly twice the resistance of the others, but no tricky ratios like 1/127 or 1/255. This arrangement gives equivalent results but only requires two values of resistor. Since the output is analogue, we're not much fussed about the exact value of R, but care passionately about the ratios being spot on, because if they're not then the accuracy suffers.

It's much easier to manufacture lots of identical components, to a close tolerance, than a wide range of them with precise differences. The cost of making extra identical ones is relatively low. So it's straightforward to make a precise 2R resistor by connecting two 1Rs in series. This leads to the design in Figure 102, where R1 to R8 and R16 will typically be implemented with two identical resistors equal in value to R9 to R15.

The maths of proving that network equivalent to the binary-weighted one is explained in many places online, such as http://www.electronics-tutorials.ws/combination/r-2r-dac.html. But the purpose of this chapter is not to teach electronics – indeed, I have run rather roughshod over distinctions between voltage and current, in a bid to keep the principles clear. It's the underlying principle that matters, and especially how it relates to the Spectrum Next we know and love.

In fact, as we'll soon see, the stereo DAC in the Next audio output works an entirely different way, which is easier to implement with digital components – but if you look at the SpecNext Wiki you'll see three analogue circuits very similar to the first one presented here, in the schematic diagram for the analogue VGA output, Figure 103. Nine digital outputs from the FPGA are mixed into three analogue pins at the VGA socket, using sets of binary-weighted resistors. The values chosen are approximate – 510 ohm resistors are cheaper than 500 ohm ones, and the eye can't tell the difference. They also assume that the monitor internally presents a low resistance to ground (typically just 75 ohms), so the ratios can ignore that. Precision is not vital because the difference between the darkest and brightest shades of each component is only a factor of 1 in 7, about 14.3%. This approach works fine for a 3-bit linear video DAC but it's not even close to audio quality.

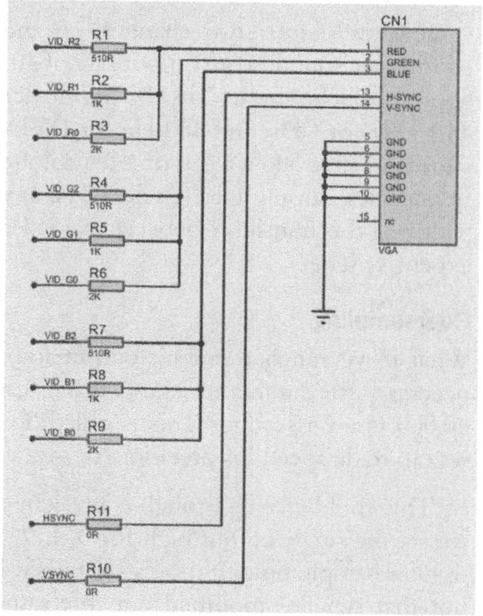

Figure 103 - the Spectrum Next VGA analogue video mixer – image used with permission, from https://wiki.specnext.dev/Circuit_Diagrams

Analogue to digital – the VHDL way

Next manages to eliminate the need for precision-matched components by converting from digital to analogue in a completely different way, that makes more sense for the FPGA hardware. Hardware is good at doing the same thing over and over again very fast indeed, and this is the key to the difference between Next's video and audio outputs.

Imagine that you've got only one hardware output signal, and can only switch it on and off. On is logic 1, off is logic 0, and the difference between the two may be a couple of volts. So what if you want to send the world a voltage half way between 0 and 1? There's no 'maybe' (logic level ½) in Boolean algebra, let alone ¼ or ¾, but for two-bit resolution we'd need to be able to output those levels, not just 0s and 1s.

However, remember the computer is potentially much faster than our ears, which ignore changes happening faster than 20,000 times a second. This is the upper limit of human hearing, which declines with age – so if you had an original 48k Spectrum you're doing well still to be able to hear the 15.6

kHz whistle on an old analogue TV, generated when the CRT flips the beam across the tube every 64 microseconds.

It takes at least two changes, up and down or vice versa, to make a continuous sound, so an output rate of 40,000 samples per second should be good for pitches up to 20 kHz. In practice slightly higher rates are used, like 44.1 kHz for CDs, and 48 kHz for DVD, Minidisc, DAT and many online streams. These allow a gap of a few kilohertz for a filter that stops inaudible frequencies causing interference. The steeper that filter is, in terms of the width of the transition between passed and suppressed pitches, the more expensive it gets.

Oversampling

What if we run our one-bit output four times as fast as the highest rate necessary for audible tones, so that it can be wiggled 160,000 rather than 40,000 times a second? This is called 'four-times oversampling' and a neat way to trade speed for precision, or vice versa.

This could give us a rough equivalent of five different levels at 40 kHz, if we set the single output high for 0, 1, 2, 3, or 4 of the four quarters of the original sample time. It'd be a bit buzzy, because of the sudden transitions, but that can be smoothed out, the same way the CD people do it – or probably in a simpler but still acceptable way.

So if one of the four intervals is at level 1, and the other three at logic 0, the *average* will be ¼. If we wiggle the output so it's on half the time and off the other half, the average is ½; three out of four averages to ¾; and 1 and 0 work as before.

The faster the hardware, compared with our old analogue ears, and the more carefully designed the smoothing filter, the more finely this scheme works. Next implements its 8-bit digital to analogue conversion by running the hardware 256 times faster than it reckons our ears can keep up. Each doubling of rate is equivalent – on average – to an extra bit of output resolution.

From theory to VHDL

The following walk-through is adapted from an early version of the PWM.VHD file, written by Allen Albright in 2019. It is just an example, with no warranty, and I'm grateful to him for permission to Bowdlerise it here, and for checking over a draft of this chapter and sending me clarifications and additional explanations.

The latest version of the file, and the associated licences, can be downloaded from the **cores/zxnext/src/audio** folder of the official repository, here:

https://gitlab.com/SpectrumNext/ZX_Spectrum_Next_FPGA/

The file can be considered in three parts. The first part states the library functions it may depend upon. Then comes the 'entity' which defines the interface between the logic block and other parts of the design, in other VHDL files. Finally comes the 'architecture' part, which implements the required behaviour. Entity is just a posh word for a 'thing', or lump of logic.

VHDL looks rather like a program in C or some similar procedural language, but appearances are deceptive. Whereas a C, or BASIC, program is processed sequentially, line by line, the architecture section contains a mixture of logic equations, which are evaluated continuously, and 'processes' which contain sequential statements that are performed in the order written, though several processes are typically active at once. Processes are typically triggered into action when a condition, such as a control signal, changes state.

Library tickets

Our VHDL conforms to a standard agreed in 1987 by the US Institute of Electrical and Electronic Engineers, IEEE. The first line of the example file declares that it depends upon the **ieee library** and says we're going to use three parts of it, known to their friends as **std_logic_1164**, for logic values, and **numeric_std**, a job-lot of ready-made vector arithmetic functions; **std_logic_unsigned** contains a commonly-used set of extensions to handle unsigned vectors, originally crafted by Synopsys and intended to limit the sort of ambiguity between positive and negative values which NextBASIC's implicitly-unsigned **%** prefix can cause.

```
library ieee;
use ieee.std_logic_1164.all;
use ieee.numeric_std.all;
use ieee.std_logic_unsigned.all;
```

These files of helper functions are referenced by most of the Next hardware sources. We don't need to know all the details to use them. Vectors are just collections of bits. They're handy when you want to treat several signals together, as a set, without duplicating logic equations for each bit.

Now let's look at the PWM 'entity'. This defines what the inputs and outputs signals are and how they should be interpreted. It has two parts. The 'generic' section contains configuration values to make the rest easier to re-use. In this case the values are all derived from the first, **Bits_per_sample**, which should be clear enough. Since bits are numbered from 0, the top bit of an 8-bit sample is bit 7, which I've called **Top_bit** to avoid surprises later.

We're also going to need to know the maximum sample value, **Max**, which is one less than two to the power of the number of bits. The ****** operator, borrowed from Fortran, is the equivalent of ^ in ZX BASIC. 2^8 is 256 so **Max** is 255. We write it this way so that if **Bits_per_sample** gets changed one day, **Top_bit** and **Max** will automagically change to suit.

```
entity pwm is
  generic
  (
    Bits_per_sample : integer := 8;
    Top_bit         : integer := Bits_per_sample-1;
    Max             : integer := 2**Bits_per_sample-1;
  );
```

The inner interface

The second part of the entity is the 'port' block. This lists all the external signals that the entity will read or write. The **i_** and **o_** suffixes stand for input and output. See that the PWM entity takes two digital inputs, a signal called **i_clock** which ticks regularly (28 million times per second, varying slightly with display options) and one called **i_reset** which is true, logic level 1, while the system starts up. Most of Next's VHDL entities use both of these.

```
  port
  (
    i_clock     : in std_logic;
    i_reset     : in std_logic;

    i_pcm       : in std_logic_vector(Top_bit downto 0);
    o_pwm       : out std_logic
  );
end entity;
```

The specific purpose of this entity is to convert 8-bit sample values, arriving in the vector **i_pcm**, into a single digital logic signal, **i_pwm**. PCM stands for Pulse Code Modulation, another term for sampling, and PWM for Pulse Width Modulation which is a way of conveying arbitrary values on a single wire by varying the timing of on/off transitions. At this point you may be able to guess how this DAC works – but if not, we'll find out by analysing the subsequent *architecture* part.

The 'signal' lines might be thought of as the VHDL equivalent of local variables. Unlike the ports, these bits or vectors are only visible to logic expressions inside the architecture block. Signals **sample** and **period** are 8-bit level and time values, while **tally** and **delta** have an ninth bit (remember that off-by-one sometimes starting-at-zero hassle with arrays and addresses?) so they have room – literally, a bit extra – for values that might crop up after adding or subtracting a pair of 8-bit numbers.

If hardware values overflow you don't normally get an error message, just an incorrect answer (again, much like NextBASIC's %land). But since VHDL works bit-by-bit, we're not limited to 1, 8, 16 or 40 bit values, as we generally are in BASIC. Signals **tally** and **delta** are nine-bit words. There's also a one-bit internal signal, **pwm_one**. Unlike those in the port block, these are implicitly bi-directional, and can be freely read or written.

```
architecture rtl of pwm is

  signal sample  : std_logic_vector(Top_bit downto 0);
```

```
signal period  : std_logic_vector(Top_bit downto 0);

signal tally  : std_logic_vector(Bits_per_sample downto 0);
signal delta  : std_logic_vector(Bits_per_sample downto 0);

signal pwm_one  : std_logic;
```

The reason the bits are numbered **downto 0** stems from another holy war. Bit 0 could be considered the most or least significant bit of a byte or word. For reasons which date back to the first electronic programmable computers, such as EDSAC at Cambridge and the Ferranti Mark One in Manchester, bit zero is generally considered the least significant. This makes working out arithmetic carries between columns during addition much easier on a bit-serial computer, like those.

Zilog and hence Next work that way, even though they're not bit-serial. But it's just a convention. IBM prefer to count bits the opposite way, even now, and in the processors they made for Wii, Xbox 360 and PS3 consoles, so VHDL gives us the choice.

The hardware architecture

At last we've reached the active logic, defined in a block between the first **begin** and the **end architecture** keywords. VHDL comments are preceded by two dashes. Allen has divided the logic into three sections, labelled **period counter**, **pwm output** and simply **output** at the end. The first listed, and most program-like, is the **period** counter.

```
begin

  -- period counter

  process(i_clock)
  begin
    if rising_edge(i_clock) then
      if i_reset = '1' then
        period <= (others => '0');
      elsif period = Max then
        period <= (others => '0');
      else
        period <= period + 1;
      end if;
    end if;
  end process;
```

The lines between process and end process are evaluated in order. The parameters in brackets after the process keyword are called the *sensitivity list* and tell the logic synthesis tool which symbols could activate the process when they change state. The **i_clock** ticks between Boolean true, written 1, and false, written 0. The period counter process needs to wake up as soon as **i_clock** goes from false to true, which is known as the *rising edge* of the clock pulse. All the signals being combined must settle before the clock next ticks, when the register takes the current state of the logic.

The rest of the process proceeds line by line, much like a procedure in a BASIC program. The second **if** test checks whether the reset line is set true. If so, it clears the period vector. The symbol **<=** denotes assignment, like the = following LET in ZX BASIC, or **:=** in Algol or Pascal.

The expression **(others => '0')** is shorthand for 'as many zero bits as needed to fill the vector'. If we wanted to set bit two and clear all the others we could write **(2 => '1', others => '0')** instead. Since **period** is more than one bit, **period <= '0'** would be ambiguous, and might only set one bit of the vector, or fail to synthesise.

The **elsif** keyword marks the start of an alternative case only active if previous **if** or **elseif** tests were not true. This condition also clears all the bits in **period**, but only when it matches the constant **Max**, the highest sample value. The final possibility, after **else**, runs if neither of the previous two conditions are true. Using the grammar of an imperative programming-language, it adds one to the vector **period**.

NextBASIC 2.08 fans must resist the temptation to re-write this with +=, and realise that this doesn't just copy the value in the vector and the value 1 to some shared arithmetic unit, crank the handle and copy the result back to period. It tells the VHDL synthesiser to create a dedicated adding circuit, in place, which will add 1 to **period** when conditions dictate. There are hundreds of circuits like this in the Next core, and they are all capable of working simultaneously.

This is just a simple example of a process; it could also have an optional symbolic name before the process keyword, or declare additional signals for internal use between the **process** and **begin** lines. Unlike a sequential program, it's very important to keep track of which signals are changed by a process. Unpredictable things happen if two or more processes try to change a signal at once. Mostly, the VHDL synthesiser will notice and warn you.

Allen Albright adds that the acronym RTL has changed meaning since it was the parent of TTL: "This is RTL (register transfer logic) where everything is a wire, register or logic and a design is just specifying logic between registers. It was the first synthesizable subset of HDLs and it's how designers thought about digital circuits. The VHDL process() block with sensitivity list is really an artefact of the simulation aspect of HDLs. They are supposed to inform the simulator when it has to change the output of the process block.

"But when you are using HDL for synthesizing real hardware, the sensitivity list has specific meaning. There is a style for a synchronous register (sensitivity = clock only), a style for a synchronous register with asynchronous reset (sensitivity = clock and a signal), a style for a latch and so on. If the process block is for combinatorial logic only then you need to list every single input signal in the list. It's very common to miss something when the list becomes long but the synthesizer can normally figure out there are no registers intended there so it will do the combinatorial logic with a warning.

"Synthesizers became more powerful and the so-called behavioural description of circuits has started to take hold. Previously behavioural descriptions were used for simulation only and sometimes verification where you matched the outputs of an RTL design with a higher level behavioural description which was more likely to be correct. And now larger subsets of the HDLs can be synthesized by the tools and as a result you see more and more behavioural descriptions being used as the final design.

" The good thing is it's easier to make something with a behavioural description. The bad thing is you don't know exactly what the final circuit will be so you lose track of resource control and speed, instead relying on the tool to do a good job of it. When I was working in ASIC design, I never saw behavioural design anywhere but in FPGAs, where it seems common for semi-complex circuits. The Next project contains source code from a variety of sources and that includes some behaviourally defined circuits and you run into nuances of syntax, for example using = or <= has different meaning in behavioural circuits."

The next section contains one process and two 'concurrent statements'. The lines starting with **pwm_one <=** and **delta <=** synthesise logic which is continuously active. Unlike the previous and following processes, they don't wait for the clock to tick. The outputs change as soon as the signals which they test, **tally** and **pwm_one**, do.

```
-- pwm output

pwm_one <= '1' when tally >= ('0' & std_logic_vector(
  to_unsigned(Max, Bits_per_sample))) else '0';
```

What this line does is set the **pwm_one** bit to '1' when **tally** is greater or equal to **Max**, and '0' otherwise. The instructions look more complicated than they really are, because VHDL is a strongly-typed language. In BASIC you can use a Boolean value, from AND or NOT, as if it was an arbitrary number. Multiplying by true, or (2=2) makes sense, preserving the first value. Multiplying by false logically yields zero. You can assign %0 to a variable even if it's not an integer.

Sinclair's later SuperBASIC went even further, automatically converting numbers into strings without need of STR$ if you write something like A$=PI/2. This means that strings must be joined with a different symbol, **&**, because A$="1" + "3" would yield "4", whereas A$="1" & "3" gives "13". There's no VAL() function, let alone VAL$(). Such 'coercion' is anathema to VHDL, which expects every vector to exactly fit the one you're stashing it into. It also uses **&** to tack values together, but in a different way.

Remember that some of our vectors are nine bits wide, and some only eight? And numbers like **Max** are not the same thing as VHDL vectors which might hold that number. The long-winded incantation **('0' & std_logic_vector (to_unsigned(Max, Bits_per_sample)))** converts the number **Max** into an unsigned logic vector **Bits_per_sample** bits wide, then prefixes it with an extra '0' bit so it matches the 9-bit vector **tally**.

The following line runs concurrently, checking if pwm_one is '0'. If so, it extends the value in **sample** vector to 9 bits and copies it to **delta**. Otherwise, it sets **delta** to the difference between **sample** and **Max**. This difference may need nine bits, hence the extra width of the **delta** vector and the three **'0' &** expressions. The when-else structure is called a 'priority conditional assignment'.

```
delta <= ('0' & sample) when pwm_one = '0' else (('0' &
  sample) - ('0' & std_logic_vector(to_unsigned(Max,
  Bits_per_sample))));
```

The final process is also synchronised with **i_clock**. It does three different things every time the clock ticks, depending on the state of **i_reset** and the **period** counter. If **i_reset** is true it simply clears the values of **tally** and **samples**. Otherwise it compares **period** with **Max** and does different things depending upon whether or not they match.

We saw earlier, in the period counter process, that **period** counts round and round from 0 to **Max**. When **period** reaches **Max**, once every 256 clock pulses, **sample** and **value** both get set to the input sample level, from **i_pcm**. As **tally** can hold nine bits, it's padded with a leading zero. On the other 255 out of 256 steps, the value of **delta** is added to **tally**.

```
process(i_clock)
begin
  if rising_edge(i_clock) then
    if i_reset = '1' then
      tally <= (others => '0');
      sample <= (others => '0');
    elsif period = Max then
      tally <= '0' & i_pcm;
      sample <= i_pcm;
    else
      tally <= tally + delta;
    end if;
  end if;
end process;
```

The changing value of **tally** is detected by the pwm_output logic, which sets **pwm_one** when **tally** reaches the **Max**. The subsequent line of pwm_output adjusts delta, and the cycle continues.

The final line of the VHDL logic, as the comment suggests, delivers the output. It copies the internal **pwm_one** signal to the one-bit output port, **o_pwm**:

```
-- output

o_pwm <= pwm_one;

end architecture;
```

It's vital to realise that the interactions between **pwm_one**, **tally** and **delta** happen in parallel, but if you're used to sequential programming the necessary intermediate steps make the logic hard to follow, at first. Translating from BASIC to VHDL is tempting but bad practice because it fails to exploit the hardware parallelism. This means more logic has to be synthesised than is really needed – perhaps more than will fit the FPGA – and can fail entirely if it contains circular dependencies or fails to synchronise itself to **i_clock**. But a comparison in the other direction helps to illustrate – and graph – what's going on.

Show me a picture, or some BASIC!

Here's a BASIC program that generates the 256 possible patterns of changes in **pwm_one** which correspond to each sample value, 0 to 255. I've used variable names that match the signal names, though **delta**, **o_pcm** and **i_pcm** have been lost in the rough translation. They're needed, in practice, so that the hardware can work in parallel rather than sequentially like BASIC.

```
110 tally=0,Max=255
120 FOR sample=0 TO Max
130   FOR period=0 TO Max
140     tally=tally+sample
150     pwm1=tally>Max
160     IF pwm1 THEN tally-=256
180   NEXT period
200 NEXT sample
```

Figure 104 was generated with a version of that BASIC program.

To graph what it's doing, add the following lines and alter line 120 to start from 4 and use a STEP of 7 or 8. Without the larger step, there are more lines than we can fit on the screen. It's not necessary to see the output for every sample value to recognize the pattern.

```
100 LAYER 1,2
170 IF pwm1 PLOT p*2,s/1.5: DRAW 0,3
```

The missing and messy line 190 added the captions down the left side of the screen, which correspond to values of **sample** for the pattern of lines alongside. These captions use the standard font so there wasn't room for all the numbers, but you can easily work out the intermediate ones.

Looking at the first row, captioned 4, the output is mostly zero (blank) with four evenly-spaced pulses in the 256 columns. When these are smoothed out by the averaging filter they'll settle out to a level of 4 on a scale from 0 to 255. We didn't start at zero, because that'd give a blank line, with no pulses at all.

Figure 104 shows 0 and 1 levels as pulses with a one-pixel gap between each of them, in a 512-pixel wide HiRes image, to make counting easier, but in reality there should be no gap between successive logic 1 (high) outputs in pwm1, but only when pwm1 gets set to 0, which happens less and less as the required average output level increases.

The next row, captioned 12, shows a dozen pulses. Count them. They're not quite evenly spaced because 256 doesn't divide exactly into 12; ideally the pulses would be at intervals of 21.33 samples, but in practice they're spaced by 21 or 22 to give the same average, but with some irregularity. The higher the oversampling factor (the number of internal steps for each single sample output) the smaller this 'jitter' becomes. In practice we rely on the filter to average it out.

Successive lines show **pwm1** set more and more of the time, corresponding to increasing output levels after smoothing. The final line in the figure, captioned with the level 252, is the counterpart to the first. For an output value of 252, **pwm1** is high (marked) in all but four of the 256 slots.

The filter is required for all sample values other than 0, silence, because of the way the **pwm1** output toggles on and off. Even if the maximum byte value, 255, is presented to the DAC, **pwm1** still spends one pulse low rather than high out of each 256, because there's no provision for a sample value of 256, which would leave **pwm1** on all the time, in an 8-bit port.

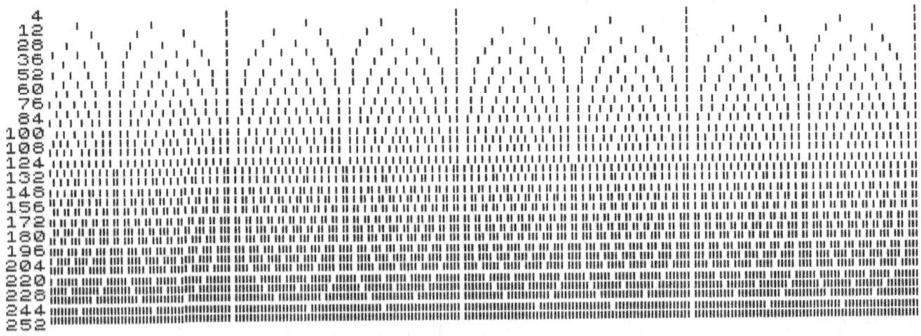

Figure 104 – Patterns of output pulses corresponding to output levels between 4 and 252

You might argue that this could be done more simply by only turning the output on then off once for each value from 1 to 255. An output of 8 would then correspond to eight consecutive intervals at a high level, followed by a run of 248 at low level, or 128 high and 128 low for a mid-range output of 128.

This would indeed work, but for all but extreme values (1 and 255 already do exactly that) it would sound harsh, requiring more corrective hardware to hide the relatively few transitions. For intermediate values, with a simple filter, spreading out the changes as evenly as possible makes averaging easier and more effective, as the distortion associated with lots of brief transitions is at a much higher frequency than the two transitions per sample output if long blocks at the same level were generated.

The recommended filter for this sort of low-cost DAC is a simple resistor and capacitor combination which works rather like a mechanical shock absorber, storing the energy from pulses, releasing it in the gaps. The bigger the capacitor, the smoother the output. However a smooth filter also slows and delays fast output level transitions which are intentional, so that high notes are dulled and cymbal sounds get lost, along with the distortion, if the capacitor is larger. It's a compromise, just what's necessary to smooth out typical values that change many times within each sample interval, generating distortion that's relatively easy to filter away.

Improving the hardware

There are three ways to reduce the distortion, none of them used by Next. One would be to clock the entire system faster, for a given output frequency. But we have to double the speed of the hardware for each six decibel (dB) improvement in quality. And 1 dB is a step so small that listeners can only just tell there's been any change at all. A crying baby can be 100 dB louder than a whisper.

Another refinement would to be to use several stages of filter, with analogue amplifiers between them. Each active stage can shave 12 dB of noise away, as well as a proportion of the high frequencies in the expected output.

That would be a good external add-on project for those discomfited by the harshness of Next's audio output, but Spectrum users brought up on the 1-bit beeper are probably used to it. The crackling in Tim Follin's multichannel beeper tunes is an inevitable consequence of hammering a one-bit output with a 3.5 MHz Z80, capable of toggling the beeper at best a few hundreds of thousands of times per second, rather than tens of millions the SpecNext FPGA way.

The third approach would be to use multiple digital outputs and a resistor array, like Next's digital output, probably in a hybrid arrangement combining oversampling with analogue mixing and filtering. But we're not making a HiFi here – the pragmatic approach taken by Allen and Victor uses very little hardware, almost all of it 'free' inside the FPGA, and still sounds pretty good, by either AY or Beeper standards.

How Amiga did it

Jay Miner and Sam Dicker, respectively chief hardware designer and audio guru at Amiga, thought just that way. Amiga's Paula chip uses both PCM for 8-bit sample output, and PWM for volume control. The giveaway is that sample values range from -128 to +127 – the signed representation makes mixing easier – but the corresponding sample volume controls go from 0 to 64 – not 0 to 63 as they would to fit a six-bit register.

The 0 setting gives silence, but the others allow from 1 to 64 copies of the sample to be output, using a clock at least 64 times faster than the required sample rate. I've yet to see schematics of the analogue part of Next, but if VHDL data-sheets cited in the source are any guide I expect that Next's filter is probably the minimalist passive arrangement of one capacitor and one resistor per output, giving a 'roll off' slope of just 6 dB per octave.

By contrast, the upmarket Amiga (unlike many pale emulations) uses steeper, more effective 24 or 12 dB per octave active analogue filters on each channel. A 'spare bit' in the digital hardware, also connected to the A500 power light, switches between those settings, trading smooth sound for brightness, which is why you see it pulsing in time with the music as some modules play on the original hardware.

Time marches on; by the miracle of lithographical scaling, digital gear get cheaper while analogue parts don't. Next's hardware clock is faster so the noise typically added to its output is higher-pitched, making it easier to filter. But if you want to listen to 8-bit modules as intended, a real Amiga is the way to do it.

More about VHDL

This Chapter is a first step in explaining the principles and one aspect of Next's VHDL design. By the time you read it, the machine may have changed, to save gates, add features, or improve quality. Perhaps one of the early readers of this chapter will be responsible for the update!

I shall focus my Tech Tips for Next itself, rather than other computers used or needed to update it, but I'm keen to return to the subject of VHDL in future books for Next enthusiasts, and hope this exploration has whetted your appetite.

The Next source on GitLab, the following Chapter about BBC Micros on Next and Hoglet's repurposing of our FPGA and Pi0, provide plenty of food for thought and further reading:

https://github.com/hoglet67/BeebFpga

> *People who are really serious about software should make their own hardware*
>
> *Alan Kay*

Chapter 18, Alternative Cores

The FPGA hardware-programable design means that Next can be literally rewired to work like other computers. There's provision to store details of up to 30 cores and select any one of them when Next starts up. Two slots are reserved for NextZXOS and the 'anti-brick' core which only runs if the system has been misconfigured, allowing normal operation to be restored.

Originally we needed to put a **.bit** file on to the SD card in the root of the card (the same location as TBBLUE.FW and TBBLUE.TBU) and name it core0001.bit. Then we had to start the flashing process; reboot the computer, hold down the C key and press F1 so it goes into the core flashing utility. From here it would ask you if you want to flash the core. Press Y, and wait a few seconds while the core flashes. When it was done, we'd either unplug the power or hold the reset button for a couple of seconds.

Then, once Next had started back into the main NextZXOS menu, we had to open the command line option, type REG 16, 255 and press Enter. That rebooted Next into the old-style flashed core. When you turned the power off and on it returned to the default Next core, though you didn't have to reflash the alternate core again unless wanting to use a different one.

The current flashing process is much the same, but easier. Now cores go in a platform-specific folder in the MACHINES subdirectory. These work on KS1 Nexts and their clones, but as I write we're still awaiting cores for KS2, complicated by the fact that the FPGA is structurally different so there ought to be a new file-format that supports both releases, and future ones.

Up to half of Next's memory can be pre-loaded with data that the incoming core will need. Some Arcade cores have the game ROMs built in, others allow you to select a ROM image from the SD card (for example the NES and Atari 2600 cores) and others like the Amstrad CPC core requires ROM files and DSK images on the SD card in the root of the card with the core file.

Acorn Cores for Next

It might seem strange to find a section of a book about the new Sinclair Spectrum going into detail about another venerable home computer designed in Cambridge, but there's method in my madness. Back in 1982 the choice between following Acorn and Sinclair was a subtle one, with profound consequences in terms of costs, capabilities and software support. But nowadays we can have the best of both worlds, and a lot more, because all versions of Next can run the much-lauded BBC BASIC, in versions customised for the capabilities of Spectrums old and new, including support for Z80 assembly language programming. But that's just the start.

If ever you want a real 6502 (or two) in place of your Z80, give thanks for the reprogrammability of Next's FPGA hardware, and many years of hobbyist effort retargeting the BBC Micro system to new hardware. In a few seconds we can swap out the Next's Z80n and replace it with a pair of closely-coupled 6502s, running at Acorn's original speed and double that, reading and writing files from Next's SD drive, with stereo audio output, plus VGA and HDMI displays at standard Beeb resolutions.

Thus we can run the original Acorn *Elite* game, or the ultimate 8-bit version *Tube Elite* which uses two processors in parallel, plus mountains of other software, particularly aimed at UK education, including games, programming languages, and serious applications – maybe even the Domesday video history project, or software created to recolour BBC TV broadcasts only archived in black and white.

The 'tube' refers to a co-processor adapter which was part of Acorn's 1981 BBC Micro spec. Originally intended to allow Z80 and 32-bit National Semiconductor processors to be bolted onto the Beeb, it was later adapted for many flavours of 8, 16 and 32-bit CPU, obviously and most conveniently for us including Acorn's own 32-bit RISC (Reduced Instruction Set Computer) chip: the Acorn RISC Machine, doubly-condensed to ARM.

It just so happens that every 'accelerated' Next has one of those chips packed away inside it, running more than a hundred times faster than the ARM2 which wowed CPU watchers in the late 80s. ARM chips went on to become the mainstay of Nokia, Apple and Android phones, and literally billions of other 21st century devices.

Acorn's first co-processor add-ons linked via Ferranti ULA chips, like those used in Sinclair's ZX81, Spectrum, QL and the BBC Model B video circuits. In a bid to relight the fires of 1980s DIY Computing, a six-year effort led by Cambridge University's Eben Upton meant that tiny, cheap but powerful ARM systems became available in 2012 at pocket-money prices – some even cover-mounted as 'free gifts' on news-stand magazines! – thanks to the non-profit Raspberry Pi Foundation.

Eben explained, *"There was a massive decline in the number of people applying to study computer science… There was a feeling that if we could get a program or a piece of hardware into the hands of young people at the right point in their lives, we might be able to do something to reverse that decline."* Sinclair hobbyists surely recognise that feeling. Many of us, starting as Spectrum hackers, acquired the skills that powered the UK entertainment software industry for decades.

These fast, cheap 32-bit Raspberries soon came to the attention of both Acorn and Sinclair enthusiasts. In 2016 Acorn fans worked out how to hook the Pi board's standard parallel interface, known as GPIO (General Purpose Input Output) to their BBC Micro tube ports, giving them a super-fast and cheap alternative to Acorn's ARM2 add-on, with decades of mature support in terms of system and client software. This open-source community project is known as PiTubeDirect, and soon thrived.

Soon after, as the Spectrum Next was planned, there were doubts that the hobbyists involved would be able to afford to licence the HDMI (High Density Multimedia Interface) standard preferred to put retro graphics on modern TVs. As the Pi boards were so cheap, and came with HDMI licensed and built-in, it made good sense to incorporate a slot for one of those, and its HDMI output, into the prototype Nexts.

The success of our Kickstarters meant that production Nexts gained their own HDMI, but the Pi GPIO socket remained. It was re-billed as suitable for an optional 'accelerator' with a digital audio link from the Pi to the Next's FPGA sound mixer. This was programmed by volunteer D. Rimron-Soutter, also known as xalior or simply 'D'.

His approach runs a custom Linux distribution on the ARM to decode TZX files from PC ZX emulators as if they were ZX cassettes, stream various sorts of retro music files, issue Linux commands, and other barely-documented but intriguing things, online at https://zx.xalior.com/NextPi/ – bear in mind that there are other unrelated projects called 'NextPi'.

After a burst of activity around 2018 and 2019 progress slowed. Meanwhile NextPi was leapfrogged in capabilities, documentation and usability when PiTubeDirect was ported from Acorn to Next hardware. Along with the BBC Micro FPGA cores, this turns any accelerated Next into a state-of-the-art expanded BBC Micro.

Already we can all run BBC BASIC natively within NextZXOS, but the Tube interface requires Acorn rather than ZX FPGA cores. Work to bridge this gap hotted up in 2023, boosted by demos to Next maestro Henrique Olifers at the Crash show in Kenilworth. Part of the rationale for this chapter is that bridging NextZXOS and PiTubeDirect is now one of the aims of the SpecNext team. It's high time to spread the word and gather hobbyist support for this exciting convergence.

For context, I should explain that I am no Acorn guru and have sought valuable advice from those who are, in compiling this section. I did buy one of the first 32k BBC Model Bs early in 1982, in a brown box from a shop in Hereford, while I was waiting for the issue 1 Spectrum I'd ordered from Sinclair. I wrote some BBC BASIC programs, including a labelling disassembler published in the UK news-stand magazine *A&B Computing*, but was frustrated by Acorn's buggy 0.1 MOS and BASIC.

When my grey-keyed wonder arrived that summer I soon found the Spectrum was taking up most of my time, more enjoyably than the seemingly over-engineered BBC. I sold my early Model B later that same year, to a student upgrading from a TRS-80, for the £399 I'd paid for it.

I continued to follow and advise about Acorn machines through the mid-80s, as sole compiler of the *Personal Computer World* agony column *Computer Answers*, and later when PCW needed someone to review the streamlined, even more expensive, BBC Master Compact, for a Christmas comparative review against Amstrad's first 128 +2 and Commodore's reboxed C64C. Don't hold your breath for a C64 core review here. Though a SID chip accessible from ZX BASIC would (still) be rather cool…

These days I have a couple of second-hand Acorn Archimedes' propped up in my shed, and until my recent retirement from deadlines I was programming modern 64-bit ARM chips down to the metal as part of the 'day job' as a games system technology programmer, since Codemasters embarked on their belated 'dash for mobile' and later with DTS and Natural Motion. But when it comes to ARM and Acorn arcana, I'm still learning – like most readers of this book.

This chapter explains what can be done on Next at the time of writing, as demonstrated at Crash. Bear in mind three things: so far, you need the free Acorn cores to access PiTubeDirect, and only the co-processors running on the Pi have direct access to its USB and second HDMI ports. Also, only the Next core has been adapted for the new KS2 FPGA. By the time you read this the Artix-7 should be catching up with the earlier Spartan-6 implementations. While different, that was selected for ease of upgrading.

Figure 105 – The original BBC Micro came in 16k Model A and 32k Model B versions

Acorn versus Sinclair

Sinclair's 1982 advertisements mocked Acorn's BBC Micro Model A as less elegant and less powerful than the 16k Spectrum, not even mentioning that the Beeb machine was more than twice the price, with twice the ROM, and a lot more expansion potential.

That extra ROM meant that Acorn's system software is best thought of in three parts – the BASIC interpreter, the Visual Display Unit (VDU) drivers, and the Machine Operating System (MOS), which provided shared facilities including memory and peripheral control for any language, not just BASIC, a full-screen-editor and a command line for system configuration and selecting system language ROMs by bank switching. Sixteen could be plugged in at once, but only one was active at a time.

Acorn produced ROMs for most of the programming languages in vogue, including BCPL (the precursor to C, also invented at Cambridge, later used to write Commodore's AmigaDOS, several Sinclair-endorsed Metacomco QL products, and HeliOS for the Inmos Transputer), teaching languages Logo, Pascal and COMAL (a Scandinavian structured BASIC), traditional Forth and Fortran, Lisp (weapon of choice for old-school hackers at Massachusetts Institute of Technology), and the functional programming AI framework Prolog. Compilers for these languages, other than BCPL, were also published for the Spectrum, though not in ROM form.

You can run all these systems, and many utility ROMs, on Hoglet's cores. They replace the 'language ROM' part of the Acorn system, sharing the MOS part for configuration, filing and peripheral access.

The VDU drivers are crucial. In a simple but elegant way they abstract Acorn's display away from the rest of the system, allowing the base machine to work as a graphics monitor for separate plug-in processors connected via the Tube.

These drivers don't just allow text to be entered and output. They support graphics, including custom fonts, vector outline and solid polygon rendering, in an extensible range of resolutions and colour depths.

Right from the start, coordinates used a virtual space 1280 pixels wide and 1024 high, though the actual resolution of the Model B display was no more than 640 by 256. This soaked up 20k, more than half the available RAM, although limited to just two colours. After allowing for system variables and buffers, this left less memory for the user's program than was available on a 16k Spectrum, albeit with three times more pixels, which analogue TVs struggled to fully display.

This is an unfair comparison, as the Spectrum has just one graphics mode – Next's LAYER 0 – while the BBC Micro supported 4 modes on the 16k Model A and eight on the 32k Model B, both including Teletext in 40x25 characters and eight-colours. using only 1k of RAM, capable of blisteringly fast scrolling but lacking pixel graphics, and with colour limitations even more restrictive than those of Spectrum attributes – like the Oric, another British micro with pretentions to Prestel, Ceefax and Oracle compatibility. Next's TileMap hardware can do similar things, and a lot more besides.

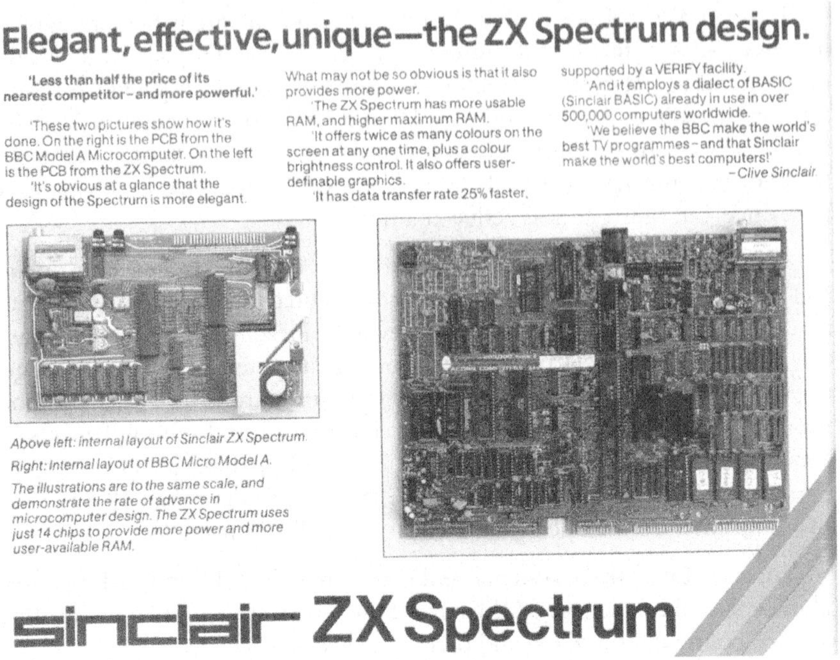

Figure 106 - Sinclair's early advertisements for the ZX Spectrum, in October and November 1982 issues of Practical Computing and Personal Computer World, set the £125 16k Spectrum head to head against Acorn's £299 16k BBC Micro Model A. Guess which one Clive thought was 'more elegant'. Later ads replaced this rhetoric with a page of 'technical data'

Hoglet's BBC Micro cores

David Banks, known online as Hoglet, has done an amazing job of not only bringing the BBC Micro experience to the Next hardware, but going beyond the typical quick-port subset experience, with open-source resources including hardware and software details, user and developer documentation, example files and friendly forum support at **stardot.org.uk**.

His two cores for Next, based on the original BBC Micro Model B and later BBC Master versions, support not only all the graphics, sound and firmware of the Acorn machines but PS/2 and native keyboards, HDMI as well as VGA output and, most impressively of all, a fast inbuilt co-processor.

This runs at twice the speed of the already-quick 6502B, with its own dedicated RAM, BASIC interpreter and Tube interface, building on expansion capabilities baked into the 1981 BBC Micro spec which have extended its life and usefulness since.

Files in Acorn DFS (Disc Filing System) format are accessed from a large file which must be placed early on Next's SD. BEEB.MMB contains hundreds of single-sided disc (.SSD) images, which I've written NextBASIC tools to access.

Hoglet's latest cores can access our optional Pi0 co-processor over the same GPIO interface, with Pi machine-code implementing the Tube expansion protocol. This allows native programming of the 32-bit ARM as if it was an Acorn RISC co-processor or emulation of a dozen other chips, including fast Z80s and souped-up 6502s. Next hardware serves as a linked display and peripheral device host, also running MOS and BBC BASIC, controlling the Pi0 which runs Acorn software hundreds of times faster than the Model B.

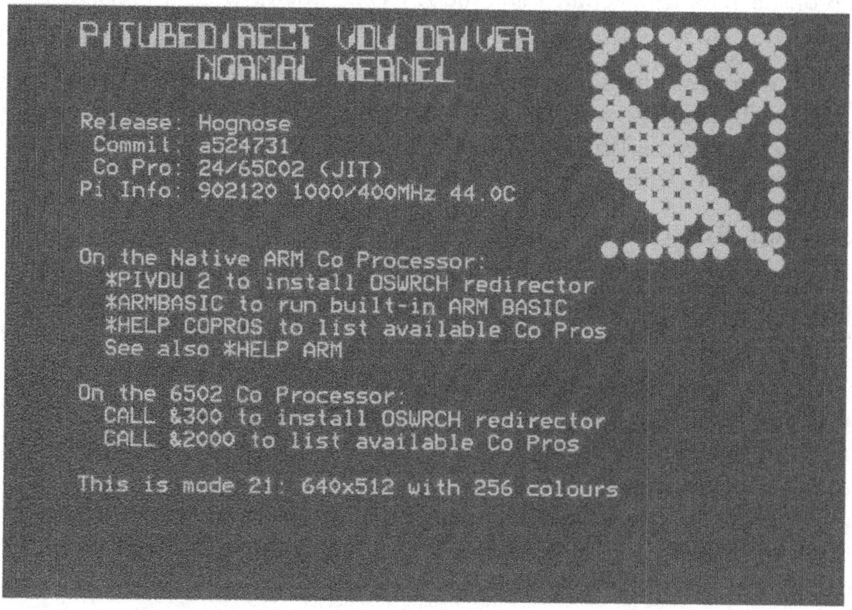

Figure 107 – The moment you power up PiTubeDirect, this screen is output to the Pi's HDMI

And if that's *still* not enough, the Pi0 can run custom firmware which makes the Raspberry widget's HDMI port work as a true-colour high-res second screen, separately and simultaneously with Next's display outputs.

Spectrum BBC BASIC

In fact you can have half the BBC Micro experience, the BBC BASIC part, without leaving NextZXOS. Two implementations of BBC BASIC run natively on our Z80n. Both are comparable in power with the 6502 original though they include a built-in assembler for Z80 rather than 6502 code.

The first of these was adapted long ago from the Sinclair Z88 and Amstrad NC100 versions of BBC BASIC, developed for Z80 computers by former BBC project consultant Richard Russell. It runs on *any* Spectrum with 48k or more RAM, not just Next.

Version 0.4 supports microdrives as well as tape filing, but not OPEN-type files, printers, SOUND or TIME. It lacks support for windows or

Spectrum HiRes graphics, let alone Next LAYERs, having only a simple VDU driver.

Floating point performance runs rings around NextBASIC on the same CPU, yielding identical five-byte precision. Almost 23k is free for BBC BASIC 2.2 programs after loading from a TAP file into RAM, or more if BBC BASIC is loaded into the bottom 16k of Z80 address space, where the ZX ROM normally goes. Not all Spectrums can do that natively, but several add-ons, including Spectranet and the ZX Diag Board, bring that capability to pre-Amstrad systems.

For more information about this 2006 BBC BASIC port, look here: http://mdfs.net/Software/Spectrum/BBCBasic. The author Jonathan 'J.G.' Harston is a revered British micro all-rounder; you'll find lots more Acorn, Spectrum and CP/M tech treats on his pages at http://mdfs.net.

Next BBC BASIC

The other, more recent, Spectrum port of BBC BASIC is the work of Dean Belfield, the guru behind www.breakintoprogram.co.uk, the 'L Break into Program 0:1' retro blog. It runs as a dot command inside NextZXOS.

It builds upon BBC BASIC and adds three Next-specific video modes, in 16 or 256 colours, resolutions from 256x192 to 512x256 pixels, plus REG commands and direct Next-friendly SD file access via esxDOS. A buffered command queue drives the three AY sound chips, and the built-in assembler supports all Next extension instructions. This makes it a very effective platform for Z80n experimentation, even though it doesn't directly support multiple layers, sprites or the Copper.

The following tables contrasts the performance of BBC BASIC Z80 3.0, NextBASIC 2.08 and Microsoft BASIC 5.2 for CP/M, all running at 28 MHz on Next. PCW benchmarks were used, as in earlier NextBASIC comparisons.

Platform	BM1	BM2	BM3	BM4	BM5	BM6	BM7	BM8
BBC float 0	0.14	0.6	1.92	2.12	2.28	3.26	4.72	0.56
BBC Float.5	0.34	0.84	1.84	2.3	2.42	3.42	4.88	0.62
MBASIC	0.22	0.67	1.82	1.78	1.94	3.9	5.71	0.94
NextBASIC	0.55	0.69	1.97	1.91	2.2	5.8	8.02	3.08

Table 8 – Floating-point Z80 BASIC Benchmarks, showing Richard Russell's optimisation

The BBC BASIC Z80 tests were repeated with initial values of K set to the default 0 and also 0.5, as there's a sneaky but very effective optimisation in Richard Russell's code which makes it handle whole numbers as if they were integers, even in floating point expressions. The effect is most apparent for FOR loops, which are particularly unoptimised in Sinclair BASICs. BM8 shows how much the concise ZX ROM code sacrifices mathematical speed.

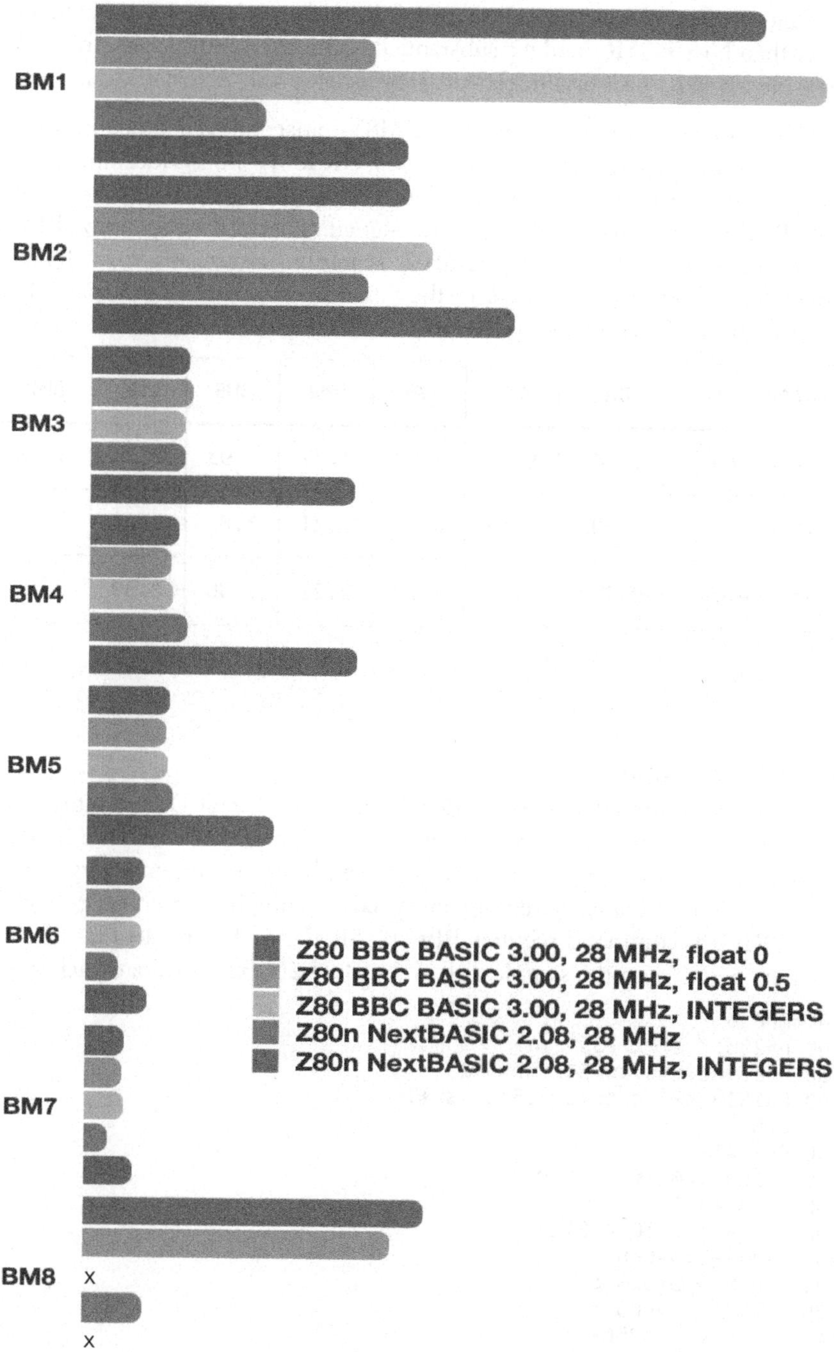

Figure 108 - BASIC interpreter benchmark performance on the Z80n: wider means faster

Figure 108 graphically reveals that BBC BASIC runs BM8 five to six times faster than NextBASIC, and it's substantially-optimised FOR loops. In other tests, NextBASIC's 16-bit integers progressively outrun Acorn's 32-bit ones.

When integers are used, excluding BM8's transcendental function tests, the results are closer. Next lags on BM1 FOR loops but strides ahead on BM3, 4 and 5. Bear in mind that Next integers are unsigned 16-bit values, but BBC BASIC ones are 32-bits wide and signed. The relative speed of BBC BASIC integers, especially on the 6502, is partly because the extra ROM space allows code for each byte in the value to be written out separately, rather than processed in a loop. However, Z80s handle 16 bits in one step.

Interpreter	BM1	BM2	BM3	BM4	BM5	BM6	BM7
Microsoft	0.147	0.54	1.93	1.77	1.93	3.31	5.32
NextBASIC	0.302	0.45	0.72	0.71	1.01	3.00	3.83
BBC BASIC	0.130	0.56	1.98	2.22	2.36	3.30	4.6

Table 9 – Kilobaud integer benchmark timings (higher means slower) for Z80 BBC BASIC 3, Microsoft CP/M MBASIC and NextBASIC, all running on the same 28 MHz Z80n CPU

BBC Micro graphics

Here's a rather attractive graphics demo, courtesy of Paul Dunn, author of SpecBAS, a modern take on Spectrum BASIC. It's a good example of how a complex image can be generated from a simple algorithm, and very CPU intensive so it dramatically reveals the speed of Tube-hosted co-processors. The ORIGIN command requires BBC BASIC V, so I've made a BASIC 2 version, included on the sample disk in the **Beeb2Next** download package.

```
80 MODE 0
100 n=200:r=2*PI/235
120 u=0:v=0:t=0:sw=512:sh=512
160 ORIGIN sw,sh:sw=sw*.5:sh=sh*.5
180 CLG
200 REPEAT
220   FOR i=0 TO n STEP 2
240   k=r*i+t
260   FOR j=0 TO n STEP 2
280   p=i+v:q=k+u
300   u=SIN p+SIN q
320   v=COS p+COS q
340     GCOL i*256+j*.5
360     PLOT 69,u*sw,v*sh
380     NEXT
400   NEXT
420   t=t+.025
440 UNTIL INKEY(0)>0
```

The BBC screen resolution is 1280 horizontal logical pixels by 1024 vertical logical pixels. Each mode maps those coordinates to fill the screen, so in MODE 1 each neighbour of its 320x256 pixels is addressed by adding four to the X or Y coordinate, starting from the origin at 0,0 in the lower left corner. Table 10 shows the resolution in seven of the Model B screen modes. Notice how greedy they are for RAM compared with Spectrums of the time. The top four modes wouldn't fit in the 16k Model A. MODE 7, used at startup, is an exception as it is character-mapped, a bit like a Next's TileMaps but using a fixed and rather different ROM font, with fractions and other niche characters in place of some of the C-programming symbols.

Graphics	Columns	Rows	X pixels	Y pixels	Colours	RAM
MODE 0	80	32	640	256	2	20k
MODE 1	40	32	320	256	4	20k
MODE 2	20	32	160	256	8/16	20k
MODE 3	80	25	-	-	2	16k
MODE 4	40	32	320	256	2	10k
MODE 5	20	32	160	256	4	10k
MODE 6	40	25	-	-	2	8k

Table 10 – Resolution and memory usage for BBC Micro Model B non-Teletext modes

These are all available on Next; accelerated Nexts can render another 64 modes, and shadow variants, via the GPIO interface and Pi0 HDMI output.

Teletext MODE 7 spreads an eight-colour 40-column 25-row display over 480x250 pixels using just one byte per character, at the price of requiring a blank space for each change of ink or paper colour. Optional flashing and double-sized characters match the 1972 Prestel and Teletext specifications.

MODEs 3 and 6 are intended for text, so they use 8x8 character patterns like the others but with two blank pixel lines between character rows. This claws back some memory and improves readability, but makes them unsuitable for hires graphics. ZX BetaBASIC, Sinclair QL SuperBASIC and SAM BASIC do this more flexibly, in software, with commands like CSIZE.

The BBC Master core allows screens to be moved out of main memory into 'shadow RAM' by adding 128 to the mode number. That leaves far more space for BASIC but confuses old programs, especially games, that don't know about the extra memory. So while the BBC Master core is more convenient for developers, only the Model B suits some older games. Bear this in mind when trying out Beeb software.

VideoNULA

Even by Spectrum standards the BBC Micro's colour graphics were limited, because only eight colours, including black and white, could be output, by turning any of the three red, green and blue binary outputs on or off. There's no equivalent of Sinclair's BRIGHT bit, so even in MODE 2, which reserves four bits per pixel on each 160-pixel line, half the combinations were reserved for flashing or palette-hiding effects, with no more than eight colours visible.

Decades later hobbyists boiled up a replacement for yet another Ferranti ULA, the Acorn BBC video output chip, in the form of VideoNULA. This adds four-bit control over each of the red, green and blue outputs, giving 4096 colours like the first Amigas, allowing each of the two, four or sixteen Acorn pixel states (depending on the MODE) to be remapped to a 12-bit colour. The approach resembles the way Next bolts a nine-bit palette onto the original Spectrum scheme, except with more shades but far fewer entries.

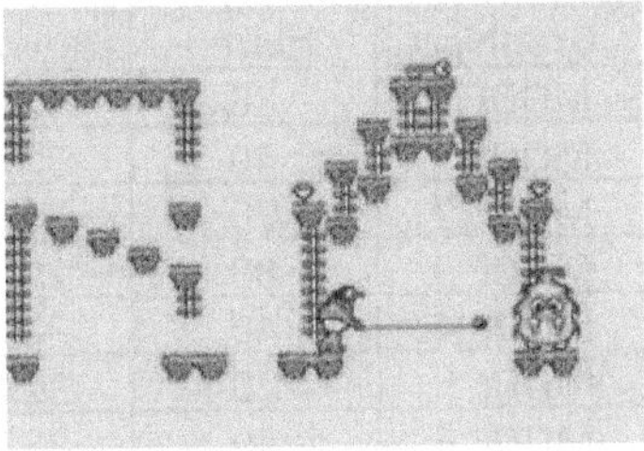

Figure 109 - FRAK as first rendered

VideoNULA is built into the Next Beeb cores, and the disc set includes example screens and palette data to recolour classic Beeb titles. *DBOOT 370 from BEEB.MMB to set the 12-bit HDMI palette for 16 base colours, or chose replacement colour sets for games like *Match Day, Revs, Frak and Snapper.* There's even a 15-colour 'Speccy' set. *FX 151,35 lets you reprogram the palette, from any processor in the BBC Micro system.

The ULA replacement also adds single-pixel scrolling to the Beeb's display capability, and three 'attribute' modes which trade pixel data for finer control over the colour of nearby pixels. Unlike the Spectrum's 8 by 8 pixel attribute grid, these attributes work with rows of six or eight pixels, independently selecting two or four colours from the palette of 16.

One of these attribute modes is similar to our Layer 1,3 HiColor mode, previously available on Timex, Memotech, MSX and Tatung micros. With Next, Timex and original Spectrum attribute layers to call on I doubt many ZX fans will explore VideoNULA attributes, but they have certainly helped original Acorn owners get ZX screens up on their Beebs.

BBC sounds

Just as Next extends the capabilities of the Spectrum by adding interfaces that previously had to be connected externally, such as Multiface, SpecDrum, mouse and joystick adapters, Hoglet's cores build in some of the best-BBC Micro add-ons. Mice and digital joysticks are supported, though not the two-axis analogue sticks ideal for playing *Elite*, as Next lacks analogue inputs.

The SN76489 beeper chip in every Beeb is fully emulated, sounding like an AY with poor pitch control (using only 10 rather than 12 bits for the count-down) and better envelopes, added in software by MOS interrupts that apply pitch or volume variations up to 100 times a second.

Some fans hacked on a Commodore SID imitation, like the one first mooted for Next and dropped in favour of three AYs and four DACs. SID supports even better pitch control, more timbral variety and originally a powerful analogue filter, but most Beeb software ignores this add-on option. That said, there are 15 discs of SID demos in the BEEB.MMB collection.

The peak of Beeb-enhancing audio excellence, closely related to the later Archimedes sound system, was an eight channel synthesiser known as Music 5000. This loops very short samples via a 12-bit DAC driven non-linearly with 8-bit data, similar to the way analogue phone lines are digitised or the muLaw output of **/dev/dsp** in BSD and Linux. The results sound more musical than SN, AY or even SID output, but are still grainy compared with FM or sample-playing keyboards of the era. The Music 5000 system and thirty demo discs are in BEEB.MMB.

There are clear instructions on how to fire up any of these goodies in the Spectrum section of the BeebFPGA wiki. You really do need to type *DBOOT 320 twice to start up the Music 5000.

Remember that some commands only take effect after a soft reset (Ctrl F12 on the PS/2 keyboard, Graph + Break on Next's) and this hides your previous BASIC program, though you can recover it with OLD if you've not entered another in the meantime.

The BBC cores can output stereo analogue audio via the 3.5mm port, or digital audio over HDMI, but the analogue Audio output sounds better because the digital system is generated at 125 kHz and then crudely interpolated by picking 48 of each 125 samples and chucking the other 77 away at irregular intervals. Even if this is fixed, you should not expect quite the fidelity of original hardware from the FPGA – as I explain in the VHDL chapter, the tricks used to mimic analogue components in commodity digital hardware introduce unwanted noise alongside the expected signal.

That said, analogue filters, similar to the Amiga ones, could be added on the Next's outputs, and would smooth the sound of Next, BBC and other cores – though not HDMI. If you're happy with the sound of existing MOD players for Next – and frankly, I'm not, though well aware of the challenges they must address – you're unlikely to complain about Hoglet's, except perhaps when playing high notes over HDMI.

Keyboard woes and workarounds

A ZX Spectrum has 40 keys. A Spectrum Next has 58. The BBC Micro has 74. Something has to give. A PS/2 keyboard has over 100, so mapping those for the BBC Cores is straight-forward except that the keys are assigned to the places they'd appear on a Beeb, so Shift 2 gives quotes, most of the other shifted digit characters are offset one place, F12 is Break, End is the Copy key, vital when editing, and backspace works like Acorn's Delete. It's a bit confusing when moving back and forth, unless your other micro is a BBC, in which case it's splendid.

PS/2 suits most keyboard-controlled games, which is less often the case when using Next's own keyboard. Symbol Shift brings up the fifteen ASCII punctuation characters that lack unique keys; the yellow button is used as a shift so that the Next digits mimic Acorn's ten programmable function keys, TRUE VIDEO and INV VIDEO stand in for TAB and COPY, GRAPH for CTRL. This works fine for BASIC but can lead to contortions when playing games expecting the Acorn layout.

The green button is ignored. A tap on the red button reboots the current BBC core, while a longer press brings back NextZXOS, or the core selection menu if you hold down C in the usual way.

There are four display output settings, set with CTRL-ALT and a function key on PS/2, Yellow button and a digit on Next. CTRL-ALT-F10 stands in for the Beeb's F10, adding a border to check for cropping of the screen edges. As on any Beeb, the *TV command shifts the picture up or down a line at a time, since 256 rows is a lot to expect of most analogue tellies. *TV 2 moves it down two lines, while *TV 255 and *TV 254 etc progressively shunt it up.

Config-2 is the default and works best for most people, using the same 27 MHz Pixel clock as Next's original HDMI output. Config-1 is for a SCART TV and turns off the HDMI output and scan-doubler on the analogue video port. Configs 3 and 4 adjust the scan-doubler and pixel clock to 24 or 32 MHz, to suit some VGA displays, but give a shaky picture on my HDMI TV.

All of these work only at 50 Hertz. If you need to use VGA 1 or above to get a picture, Acorn cores won't work for you; there's no attempt to speed them up to suit PC-style monitors or Japanese TVs. Config-5 turns off audio to suit some DVI monitors connected via HDMI, and Configs 6 to 8 drop HDMI hints to the screen about the required aspect ratio. When using the Model B core, Config-9 toggles the internal 4 MHz co-processor on and off.

BBC BASIC versus NextBASIC

Back in the 1980s versions of BASIC competed on unique features and approaches, which was exciting but made program translation tricky unless you knew both platforms and were willing to experiment. For a few years I revelled in this, compiling the 'Computer Answers' column for *Personal Computer World* magazine. Table 11 – NextBASIC and BBC BASIC equivalent statements – lists NextBASIC keywords alongside their BBC equivalents.

There's no ideal order for such a table so the keywords have been indexed to make them easier to find without laborious searching. Later versions of BBC BASIC (for the Archimedes, or PiTubeDirect) also include Nextras such as bitwise shifts, accumulation assignments, CIRCLE, ENDIF and WHILE, plus matrix operations not yet seen on Next.

Over time the BASIC dialects have grown and borrowed features from one another. It's notable that many of the latest features of NextBASIC were first seen on Acorn micros, and that's one of the reasons it's illuminating to compare them. This summary, and especially the table, provides a quick way of determining how easily (or not) a given program line can be translated. The section after that goes into detail about differences and equivalents.

NextBASIC	BBC BASIC
PAUSE 1	*FX 19
PAUSE N	t$=INKEY$(N*2)
PAUSE 0: %T=CODE INKEY$	T%=GET
INKEY$	INKEY$(0)
LAYER	MODE
LLIST	^B LIST ^C
LPRINT T$	PRINT CHR$(2);T$: VDU 3
PRINT CHR$ 1;CHR$(%T);	VDU 1,T%
INK %T (text or pixels)	COLOUR %T (GCOL for pixels)
PAPER %T (text or pixels)	GCOL or COLOUR %T+128
PROC T()	PROC T
ERASE 1,9	DELETE 1,9
T*180/PI	DEG(T)
T*PI/180	RAD(T)
GOTO 1E4	END
ERROR TO %R	R%=ERR
ERROR TO %R,%L	R%=ERR: L%=ERL
ON ERROR	ON ERROR OFF
T=VAL T$	T=EVAL(T$)
R$=VAL$ T$	R$=EVAL(T$)
DIM #	EXT #
0	FALSE
LOAD “program”	CHAIN “program”
|	OR
&	AND
CODE T$	ASC(T$)
CODE INKEY$ #4	BGET #4
INKEY$ #4	CHR$(BGET #4)
PRINT #4;CHR$ 33;	BPUT# 4,33
IF USR %T THEN	CALL T%
BEEP 0.3,11.75	VDU 7
BEEP D,P	SOUND 0,-15,53+P/4,D/20
PEEK 23688 (S_POSN)	POS
POKE 23561,%T (REPDEL)	*FX 11,T%*2
POKE 23562,%T (REPPER)	*FX 12,T%2
(POINT #4)=DIM #4	EOF #4
%R ^| %T	R% EOR T%
%R | %T	R% OR T%
%R & %T	R% AND T%
%R/%T	R% DIV T%
DIM #4	EXT #4
%T=%DPEEK 23730 (RAMTOP)	T%=HIMEM
%T=IN(A$,B$)	T%=INSTR(A$,B$)
R=LN(T)*0.434294482	R=LOG(T)
R$=T$(TO 3)	R$=LEFT$(T$,3)
R$=T$(3 TO)	R$=MID$(T$,3)

R$=T$(LEN T$-2 TO)	R$=RIGHT$(T$,3)
OPEN #%S,T$	S%=OPENIN(T$)
OPEN #%S,"O>"+T$	S%=OPENOUT(T$)
PLOT OVER 1;INVERSE 1;X,Y	MOVE X,Y
PLOT X,Y	PLOT 68,X,Y
POKE USR "A",1,2,3,4,5,6,7,8	VDU23,144,1,2,3,4,5,6,7,8
DRAW X,Y	PLOT 1,X,Y
POINT #4	PTR#4
LINE start,step	RENUMBER start,step
LINE NEW start,step	AUTO start,step
ERROR	REPORT
RANDOMIZE T	T=RND(-T)
RND	RND(1)
RND(%T)	RND(T%-1)
PRINT CHR$(32)*T	PRINT SPC(T)
T$*T	STRING$(T,T$)
PRINT AT X,Y;T	PRINT TAB(X,Y);T
PRINT TAB X;T	PRINT TAB(X);T
TIME	TIME*2
-1	TRUE
REPEAT UNTIL T	UNTIL T
PEEK 23689 (S_POSN)	VPOS
CAT	*CAT
PRINT POINT X,Y	MOVE X,Y:VDU 5
%T=PEEK B	T%=?B
POKE B,A	?B=A
POKE B+10,A	B?10=A
POKE B,T$+CHR$ 13	$A=T$
%CODE=%CODE|2	*FX 229,1
SAVE "T:"	*TAPE
PRINT 65536-USR 7962	DIM A%-1:PRINT HIMEM-A%-
PRINT STR$(T,16)	PRINT ~T

Table 11 – NextBASIC and BBC BASIC equivalent statements

These 13 keywords are only available in BBC BASIC: ADVAL, CLG, COUNT, ENVELOPE, GCOL, LISTO, LOMEM, OPT, PAGE, SOUND, TOP, TRACE, WIDTH.

ZX and Next only: ATTR, BORDER, BRIGHT, CONTINUE, COPY, FLASH, IN, MERGE, OUT, OVER, PEEK, POKE, VAL$, VERIFY.

These, with variants and combinations, only in NextBASIC: BANK, LAYER, PALETTE, PEEK$, PWD, REG, RUN AT, SPRITE, TILE.

Equivalents and translations

As the table shows, a question mark in BBC BASIC can stand in for either PEEK or POKE. This is one of the eccentricities of Acorn's earlier Atom

BASIC which the BBC let pass, probably because they dismissed the educational value of PEEKing and POKEing. We know better!

The Beeb were not so permissive about the Atom's single-letter variable names (doubled-up for a further 26 arrays), let alone the different sorts of IF, PRINT and INPUT statements it required for integer and optional floating-point expressions, and strings that could only be sliced or compared one character at a time! But the Atom was fast.

All arrays are indexed from 0, whereas Next's array base is 0 for integer arrays and 1 for others. Strings are counted from character 1 in both cases.

There's no BBC BASIC equivalent of Next's two-byte DPEEK and DPOKE but, as on the Atom, an exclamation mark can be used to read or write a 32-bit value in ascending order of byte weights, so !T%=#7890ABCD works like DPOKE %T,#ABCD,#7890

Figure 110 - the best edition of the BBC Micro manual

I've not exhaustively listed the file-system commands for Acorn's MOS and DFS. These start with an asterisk *, so all languages can share them. Some of these 'star commands' have dot and default equivalents on Next, such as CD, MKDIR and CAT, but many dot and * commands are system-specific. Consult Acorn manuals for details.

*COPY and *RENAME work like Sinclair's MOVE, while *LOAD and *SAVE are Acorn syntax for Sinclair LOAD CODE and SAVE CODE. The set of four *REMOVE, *DELETE, *DESTROY and *WIPE are all variants of ERASE. *COMPACT works like .DEFRAG but is used more often because Acorn file systems can't split files across parts of a disc, as *FREE reveals, whereas the FAT (File Allocation Table) filesystem used on Next SD cards is able to distribute the contents of the file across the card to soak up gaps left by deleted files, so that .DEFRAG is only needed when a data file has to be streamed at top speed from a card.

By default both BASICs save programs in tokenised binary form. Use .bas2txt and .txt2bas to convert Next tokenised files to and from text, and *SPOOL and *EXEC to divert Acorn LIST output and keyboard input to and from a text file, for equivalent results, easier bulk editing, and transferring program source between the systems. BBC BASIC does not check syntax on entry, unlike ZX BASIC, so append the **-a** switch to .txt2bas if your program hasn't yet been fully converted for NextBASIC, so dodgy lines are converted into REMs rather than rejected.

Some BBC BASIC equivalents of Sinclair's OVER and INVERSE graphics modifiers use special values of the first parameter of the PLOT command. Acorn's PLOT can also draw and fill-in triangles.

Multi-line IF/THEN/ELSE structures require Acorn BASIC V or NextBASIC 2.08+ and the ENDIF keyword to explain when to stop. This also enables proper nesting, so each ELSE matches the corresponding THEN rather than the most recent IF to fail. ELSE within a line requires a colon before it, on Next. UNTIL conditionally terminates a repeat loop, without the redundant REPEAT keyword prefix that Next requires.

BBC BASIC AND, OR and NOT work bitwise e.g. 5 AND 3 = 2 whereas ZX BASIC treats them as Boolean (true or false, so 5 AND 3 = 1, TRUE) and allows the first operand of AND to be a string, e.g. PRINT c;“item”;”s” AND c<>1. Hence TRUE in BBC BASIC is -1, not 1, as -1 is represented with all bits set in two's complement arithmetic.

ZX BASIC skips code within a FOR if **start** exceeds **end**, but BBC BASIC follows Microsoft and always executes the loop body at least once! Like Microsoft, Acorn allow the variable names after NEXT to be omitted.

GOTO and GOSUB allow the line number to be calculated, not just a label or number, in ZX BASIC but not BBC BASIC. GOSUB is limited to 26 nested calls in BBC BASIC, versus free memory/3 in ZX BASIC, or free memory/12 in NextBASIC. Where PRINT 65536-USR 7962 shows the amount of free memory in ZX and NextBASIC, BBC BASIC requires DIM A%-1:PRINT HIMEM-A%-256 or similar; the 256 is a guess at the extent of system stack usage.

LOCAL arrays are not allowed by Acorn. There are no resident arrays akin to our 64-element %A() to %Z() but integer arrays can be DIMensioned.

Apart from ON ERROR, ON can only be followed by an expression then GOTO or GOSUB in BBC BASIC, where the value of the expression determines which of the subsequent line numbers is targeted. In NextBASIC ON can be followed by any number of single statements, not just GOs. The closest equivalent in ZX BASIC is **GO TO/SUB expression** where **expression** evaluates to the desired line number.

Acorn's INKEY can be used to test for a specific key, by passing a negative parameter. The equivalent for a Spectrum is IN as explained in Chapter 23 of Phoebus's KS1 manual and Chapter 22 of the KS2 remix.

Values separated by commas in PRINT statements appear in two columns in ZX BASIC, or ten character-spaces apart (by default) on a Beeb. Semicolons and apostrophes work identically in both dialects. Prefix a BBC BASIC value with a tilde ~ to print it in hexadecimal.

Neither BASIC has the Fortran-style PRINT USING extension, but BBC BASIC can control the formatting of numbers by assigning a four-byte pattern to @% while NextBASIC 2.08 gives STR$ two additional optional parameters to set the base and number of significant digits.

So Next's **PRINT STR$(PI,10,3)** and Acorn's **%@131850: PRINT PI** both print 3.142, as does **PI=4*ATN(1):PRINT USING "#.###";PI** in Mallard BASIC for +3 CP/M, or extended variants of Microsoft BASIC. Their manuals reveal more of the arcane details.

Acorn LIST can specify a single line or a range separated by commas. ZX LIST only states the first line, implicitly to the end of the program or BANK.

Uncontrolled scrolling is prevented in different ways. On the Acorn, Control N and Control O character codes pause and restart scrolling. After PRINT CHR$ 26;CHR$ N; NextBASIC scrolls N lines till pausing, whereas ZX BASIC (and Next LAYER 0) scrolls (PEEK 23692)-1 lines till pausing.

Next integer variables appear in expressions that start with a % sign, whereas in BBC BASIC integer variables are marked with a per cent suffix.

The BBC NEW command does not alter the 'resident integer variables' A%..Z%; OLD brings back the program after NEW, as long as you've not typed anything to replace it. This enables us to include demo programs in the version of BASIC pre-loaded into Pi0 memory. Set the value of PAGE to the start address of a stored program to make it accessible to LIST and RUN. There's no equivalent of PAGE in Sinclair BASICs.

HIMEM sets or reads the upper bounds of BBC BASIC RAM. That can be set in Spectrum BASIC by appending a parameter to Sinclair's CLEAR and read from DPEEK 23730, the system variable RAMTOP.

DRAW uses relative coordinates in ZX BASIC, but absolute ones on the BBC. Valid coordinate ranges depend on the chosen LAYER in NextBASIC, but the same range encompasses every BBC BASIC MODE.

Trivial differences

The Beeb VAL function only works with numbers, not variables, functions or expressions. Similarly, INPUT only accepts literals, not expressions or variable names. Use EVAL on a string to evaluate an arbitrary expression.

Like VAL and INPUT, DATA only allows constants in BBC BASIC, whereas ZX BASIC allows variable names or expressions in those contexts. String DATA in BBC BASIC doesn't need to be in quotes unless leading spaces are significant, or the string contains a comma.

Random number generation is slightly different but easily convertible, as shown in Table 11. RND(-n) is equivalent to RANDOMIZE n, and by default BBC BASIC's RND returns a signed 32-bit random number, in the range -2147483648 to +2147483647. Add a parameter to limit the range, e.g. RND(2) gives 1 or 2 and RND(1) returns 0..0.999999, like Sinclair's RND.

NextBASIC has separate operators for logical and bitwise operations, such as AND and &, whereas BBC BASICs OR, AND, NOT and EOR operators work on each bit, so NOT -2 is 1 and TRUE has to be -1 rather than +1. FALSE is still 0, thankfully.

> The following 47 keywords are almost-identically handled in both BASICs: ABS, ACS, ASN, ATN, CLOSE #, CLEAR*, CLS, COS, DIM*+, DRAW+, ELSE, ENDPROC*, EXP, FN, FOR, IF, INPUT, INPUT LINE, INT, LEN, LIST+, LN, LOAD*, LOCAL*, MOD, NEW, ON ERROR*, PLOT+, PI, POINT, PRINT, READ, REM, REPEAT, RESTORE, RETURN, RUN, SAVE*, SGN, SIN, SQR, STEP, STOP, STR$*, TAN, THEN and TIME.

** NextBASIC has extra variants* *+ BBC BASIC has extra variants*

BBC graphic codes

BBC Micros support eight colours, using codes from 0 to 7, but not in the same GRB order as on the Spectrum, which gives a smooth greyscale. Acorn prefer BGR bit order and skip the BRIGHT option, as shown in Table 12. In practice this doesn't matter much as ZX and BBC cores support palettes that translate colour codes into 256 * 512 (Next) or 16 * 4096 (VideoNULA) hues, so you can match them by palette shuffling.

ZX	BBC	Colour
0	0	BLACK
1	4	BLUE
2	1	RED
3	5	MAGENTA
4	2	GREEN
5	6	CYAN
6	3	YELLOW
7	7	WHITE

Table 12 – RGB colour codes

Table 12 is useful when translating programs written for the original Beeb.

ZX and BBC BASICs agree on control codes 8 through 11 to move the cursor, but whereas Sinclair assigned codes 16 to 23 for INK, PAPER, FLASH, BRIGHT, INVERSE, OVER, AT and TAB, Acorn – like MGT's SAM – reserved various control codes and subsequent data bytes for PLOT, MOVE and DRAW. Subsequent bytes control many variations, for over-plotting, pen or contrast colours, with relative or absolute coordinates, not just for single dots but also for complete or continuing solid or dotted lines, ellipses and circles (on BASIC V only) and filled triangle meshes where each new point completes a triangle with the pair before. But not texture-mapping!

Acorn's VDU shorthand for PRINT CHR$ saves bytes and allows easy re-targeting of screen, output between co-processors but the many parameters for graphics commands take a while to learn. The 1982 BBC Micro manual is the best source of such detail – the later BBC Master ones skimp on BASIC details in favour of documenting built-in ROM-based applications, and the first 'provisional' manual is fit only for swatting wasps.

VDU commands can be up to 12 bytes long, so the Tube interface includes a buffer so they can be batched together, rather than slowly passed byte-by-byte between processors. Use VDU 24 or 28 to set graphics or text window bounds, a bit like OPEN "W>" in NextBASIC. VDU 135 provides an equivalent of SCREEN$, but you have to call it via the corresponding OSBYTE function to read back the result in a processor register.

This is the basis of the BBC BASIC program editor, which displays a second 'copy cursor' if the arrow keys are used to move off the current line. In an approach pioneered by Commodore's PET, you can then copy any characters visible elsewhere into the current line by moving the cursor over them and pressing the COPY key (INV VIDEO on Next's keyboard, or END on PS/2). Next cannot match this efficient screen-scraping access to previous commands; QL SuperBASIC needs the free add-on *SuperToolkit 2* ROM, or a disk expansion card, to recall past entries.

The copy cursor provides a handy way to repeat previous commands without retyping them. Neither Acorn nor Next systems support command-line history or tab completion, except in a NextPi shell, but a full stop can be used when entering commands to save typing, once enough characters have been entered to make the selection unambiguous to BBC BASIC or MOS.

An extreme example of this is *. which completes the default MOS command, which happens to be *CAT. Hence the name of the StarDot website! *CO. completes as *CONFIGURE, showing a list of setup options, whereas *C. yields *CAT again.

AUTO provides line numbers in sequence without requiring them to be typed by hand, like LINE NEW in NextBASIC 2.09, and the Microsoft-style TRACE spews newly-encountered line numbers to the screen as a program runs. I know of no Acorn equivalent of Next's .RET, or QL Turbo Toolkit's HOW_COME demo procedure, to show the sequence of calls and parameter changes from when a program starts until it's interrupted.

MODE works like LAYER but without the potential for transparent overlays, and COLOUR can set either ink or paper depending on the value of bit 7, or adjust the palette with extra MODE-specific parameters. COLOUR sets only the text colour, combining INK, PAPER, OVER in one statement. GCOL controls graphics colours, OVER and various types of logical blending.

The BBC machines support 16 colour codes including 8 flashing pairs, half of which are swaps, but GCOL lets us map logical colours 0..1, 0..3 or 0..15 to any of the 8 possible, depending on the mode. This also allows basic palette animation, when we have more logical than physical colours, by shuffling physical colour numbers or VideoNULA palette indices.

Star commands

If a command might be useful to other languages besides BASIC, or does operating-system setup tasks, it's handled by MOS, the Machine Operating System, which picks up and processes any input which starts with an asterisk.

Many file-system operations use * commands such as *CAT, and *LOAD for LOAD CODE. *-prefixed commands to MOS are conceptually similar to our **.dot** commands but directed to ROMs not SD, and available in all Acorn programming languages. Many *SPOOL diverts screen output to a file, *EXEC reads keyboard input from a file. These use text rather than tokens, like Nexts .bas2txt and .txt2bas dot commands. Combining those gives a limited MERGE capability, for program lines only. Variable values cannot be saved with programs, nor can arrays be saved as on a Spectrum, but line numbers can exceed the 9999 limit of ZX BASIC.

*KEY allows keys to be redefined to produce other codes or short strings of characters when they're pressed. It'd be nice to have something like this on Next, but we've got relatively few keys to play with.

Like the VDU command, *FX can be followed by magic numbers, such as *FX 19 which waits for the screen refresh, like PAUSE 1 but without being disturbed by keyboard input. These are passed through the OSBYTE system vector so they can be redirected or called from assembly language, if you want to get a value back. Other OSBYTE calls are like Sinclair's SVAR POKES to adjust RAMTOP, key repeat and serial baud rates, PAUSE, SCREEN$, screen output copying or diversion to serial and parallel ports, Spectrum-compatible UDG definition and buffered input and output.

Machine code from BASIC

It has always been easy to write a mixture of BASIC and machine code on BBC systems, regardless of host processor, because they include a built-in assembler! Machine code mnemonics and labels are embedded into the BASIC listing within square brackets, and assembled to memory by 'running' the lines. This must be done twice, under control of the OPT keyword, if the code includes forward references to labels not yet encountered the first time.

Key routines in BASIC and MOS are accessible via fixed addresses at the end of ROM, each of which jumps to the corresponding code via a 'vector' in RAM, which can be patched to change or extend the system. SAM BASIC includes a similar scheme, but in Sinclair BASICs the only equivalents are the input and output code addresses associated with each open stream, which can direct characters to and from RAM, screen output or input areas, files other devices. A similar set of vectors for NextZXOS might make it a little slower, but much more readily extensible. In fact Sinclair made a start on this when the ROM was expanded for the Spectrum 128, adding a table of editor ROM routines at a fixed offset, but Amstrad soon scrapped that. I suspect it's not something they wanted to have to support.

In some respects Acorn's system is old-fashioned; it's not truly device independent – the display, printers, networks and disc files all have their own dedicated system hooks – so it can't redirect input and output with a tweak to OPEN command parameters as Next can, except for INPUT and CLS.

Machine code is invoked with CALL or the Next-like USR function, but the integer variables are neatly mapped to CPU registers so that variables %a, %x and %y pass 24 bits of data in as parameters into 6502 code , and 32 bits of result come back from USR, combining registers P, Y, X, A where P in the top byte is the 6502 processor status register. In assembly language P% sets and reads the program counter, like ORG and * in Zeus.

The Z80 CPU has a lot more registers, so in BBC BASIC Z80 variables A%, B%, C%, D%, E%, F%, H%, L%, X% and Y% pass values to CPU registers in CALL and USR routines, with further command parameters at IX. USR generally returns a 32-bit integer made up of the contents of the H, L, H' and L' registers, most significant first.

Z80 MOS CALLs and USR routines jump through standard documented addresses in the range &FF00 to &FFFF just as on a BBC micro. In that case IY holds the entry address and the processor's A, H, L and E registers are initialised with the least significant bytes of the integer variables A%, X%, Y% and E% respectively, and the returned 32-bit integer is copied from the F,H,L,A registers. System-calls at &FFCE to &FFF7 include OSFIND, OSGBPB, OSBPUT, OSBGET, OSARGS, OSFILE, OSRDCH, OSASCI, OSNEWL, and the powerful OSWORD, OSBYTE and OSCLI.

There's not room here for all the details which are documented in Acorn manuals, but most VDU commands use OSBYTE, system calls requiring more parameters tend to use OSWORD. OSFIND works like OPEN, with various other hooks to read and write bytes or blocks, while OSFILE can load and invoke files up to 4 GB long within the address space of any co-processor. 32-bit forward planning has turned out well for Acorn aficionados.

Mind the Gaps

There are profound but hidden differences between the BASIC dialects. Whereas you can edit your program and CONTINUE testing in ZX BASICs, or on Next since corrections for the new structure keywords in NextBASIC 2.08, BBC BASIC discards variable values and the context of the program, such as active loops, locals and returns, as soon as you make any change. This helps make Sinclair BASIC programmers more productive when debugging.

There is no Acorn equivalent of Sinclair BASIC's hidden floating-point values within a program, which saves some memory but slows down the BBC BASIC interpreter when dealing with decimal constants. BBC BASIC strings waste RAM when they're edited, as I'll graphically demonstrate below, and are limited to a maximum length of 255 characters. But unlike Sinclair BASIC, Acorn string array elements are of variable-length.

Like Microsoft dialects, but unlike Atari and Sinclair BASICs, BBC BASIC uses string-slicing functions copied from DEC minicomputers, rather than follow the original Dartmouth BASIC or the later ANSI standard. LEFT$(A$,n) works like A$(TO n), MID$(A$,n,n+m-1) apes A$(n TO m) and RIGHT$(A$,n) for A$(LEN A$-N TO). But beware, as some other BASICs, including Zilog's own, RIGHT$(A$,n) gives A$(N TO)! There's no direct way to insert characters into a string without copying it.

BASIC incompatibility

For reasons best known to Richard Russell, his Z80 versions of BBC BASIC use the same keyword tokens and three-byte encoding for line numbers as Acorn, but mark the start and end of each program line differently. There are many more programs for the Acorn BASICs, though they often make assumptions about display layout, but Next uses a Z80 by default so we can't even try the Acorn programs under NextZXOS unless we can fix this incompatibility. So I've written two little NextBASIC PROCs to do the job.

PROC Acorn 2 BBCz80() takes one or two parameters – the name of a file containing Acorn-encoded BASIC, and optionally a new name for a corresponding file in Z80 format. Otherwise the new file has the same name as the Acorn one but with the extension, typically .BBC, replaced with .BAC.

If the file exists, but is not valid, three error messages can still halt the procedure. Acorn files start with a CR, CHR$ 13, and repeat this at the start of each line, while ZX BASIC has a CR at the *end* of each line. If those are not found, at the start or later, **Not Acorn BBC BASIC** is printed. **End junk** appears if there's unexpected data at the end of the input file – in which case the output might still work – and **Bad sync** denotes a logic error indicated by the output file not being one byte longer than the input, as it should be.

```
1450 REM Convert Acorn BASIC token file to Z80 BBC BASIC
1460 DEFPROC Acorn 2 BBCz80(in$,out$="")
1470 IF out$="" THEN out$=in$(1 TO LEN in$-3)+"BAC"
1480 PRINT in$;" to ";out$
1490 LOCAL t$,%i,%n,%c
1500 CLOSE # 4: OPEN # 4,in$
1510 CLOSE # 5: OPEN # 5,"o>"+out$
1520 REPEAT
1525   IF 13<> NEXT #4 THEN PRINT "Not Acorn BBC BASIC": GO TO 1680
1530    %n= NEXT #4
1540    WHILE %n<>255
1550    %n= NEXT #4+(%n<<8)
1555    %c= NEXT #4
1560    t$=""
1570    FOR %i=1 TO %c-4
1580      t$+= INKEY$ #4
1590    NEXT %i
1610    ;PRINT "Scanned line ";%n
1620    PRINT #5; CHR$ (%c); CHR$ (%n&255); CHR$ (%n>>8);t$
1630 REPEAT UNTIL 0
1640 PRINT #5; CHR$ 0; CHR$ 255*2;
```

```
1660 IF POINT #4<> DIM #4 THEN PRINT "End junk"
1670 IF POINT #5<>1+ POINT #4 THEN PRINT "Bad sync"
1680 CLOSE # 5: CLOSE # 4
1690 ENDPROC
```

Given all the goodies available in Hoglet's cores and PiTube, it's also useful to be able to move programs from our own CPU flavour to suit the alternatives. Hence this PROC BBCz80 2 Acorn() which works similarly but outputs a filename ending with .BBC and catches one more error, **Bad End**, if the Z80-style input file doesn't end with two CHR$ 255s.

```
1170 REM Convert Z80 BBC BASIC token file to Acorn BBC BASIC
1180 DEFPROC BBCz80 2 Acorn(in$,out$="")
1190 IF out$="" THEN out$=in$(1 TO LEN in$-3)+"BBC"
1200 PRINT in$;" to ";out$
1210 LOCAL t$,%i,%n,%c
1220 CLOSE # 4: OPEN # 4,in$
1230 CLOSE # 5: OPEN # 5,"o>"+out$
1240 REPEAT
1250   %c= NEXT #4
1260   WHILE %c
1270   %n= NEXT #4+256* NEXT #4
1280   t$=""
1290   FOR %i=1 TO %c-4
1300     t$+= INKEY$ #4
1310   NEXT %i
1320   IF 13<> NEXT #4 THEN PRINT "Not BBC BASIC Z80": GO TO 1400
1340   PRINT #5;CHR$ 13; CHR$ (%n>>8); CHR$ (%n&255); CHR$ (%c);t$;
1350 REPEAT UNTIL 0
1360 PRINT #5; CHR$ 13; CHR$ 255;
1370 IF INKEY$ #4+ INKEY$ #4<> CHR$ 255*2 THEN PRINT "Bad End"
1380 IF POINT #4<> DIM #4 THEN PRINT "End junk"
1390 IF POINT #4<>1+ POINT #5 THEN PRINT "Bad sync"
1400 CLOSE # 5: CLOSE # 4
1410 ENDPROC
```

These file manipulation examples use NextBASIC 2.08 features like optional parameters, random-access functions, and integers in a string context. The following PROC determines the flavour (if any) of a file. Refer to http://beebwiki.mdfs.net/ Program_format for more details of BBC BASIC encodings.

```
1000 REM Test Acorn or Z80 BBC BASIC token file, SNG after JGH
1010 DEFPROC BBClines(f$)
1020 LOCAL t$,z80,acorn
1030 CLOSE # 4: OPEN # 4,f$
1040 GO TO #4, DIM #4-2
1050 t$= INKEY$ #4+ INKEY$ #4
1060 z80=t$= CHR$ 255*2
1070 acorn=t$= CHR$ 13+ CHR$ 255
1080 IF z80
1090   PRINT "Z80/x86 BASIC"
1100 ELSE IF acorn
1110   PRINT "Acorn BASIC"
1120 ELSE
1130   PRINT "Unknown"
```

```
1140 ENDIF
1150 CLOSE # 4
1160 ENDPROC
```

BBC BASIC and MOS demonstration

There are thousands of BBC BASIC programs available for download, for many purposes, especially education. The following small example (which is in BBC BASIC, not NextBASIC) gives an insight into the inner workings of the BBC Micro, and works best in the Model B configuration, not on a co-processor, because it directly accesses Acorn hardware.

```
100 ENVELOPE 1,4,8,-1,-3,8,24,13,1,-1,0,0,99,45
110 SOUND 1,1,99,-1
120 SOUND 0,-5,7,90
130 CLEAR:MODE 4
140 VDU 19,0,1,0,0,0
150 VDU 23;12;0;0;0
160 MODE 4:HIMEM=10240:A$=""
170 DIM S-1
180 REPEAT
190   A$=A$+CHR$(RND(256)-1)
200   IF LEN(A$)>220 A$=""
210   B$=A$
220   A=INKEY(1)
230 UNTIL A=32
240 DIME-1
250 MODE 4
260 PRINT E-S;" Bytes used"
270 SOUND 16+1,0,0,0
```

The program uses HiRes graphics and multi-channel sound, continuously updated as it runs. The first three lines set up the audio, declaring an 'envelope' which rises quickly in pitch then falls, slowly then faster, initially rising and falling in volume. On Next this would call for a DRIVER slot.

Sound channel 1 is then set playing continuously (duration -1) by line 110, using envelope 1 to vary the pitch which starts at 99, 2.5 semitones above note A4 (440 Hertz). It is updated 25 times a second (determined by the factor 4 in the envelope line, counting 10 ms ticks) first in eight steps of a full tone (the two 8s) then downwards in 24 steps of a quarter semitone (24 and -1) and back to the start near enough, over 13 steps of -3 pitch units. The whole pitch wobble repeats after 1.8 seconds and the last six parameters vary the volume up and down.

Meanwhile the 'noise' channel 0, playing more quietly (volume -5, where -15 is loudest, 0 is silent, in steps of around 2 dB) tracks the pitch of channel 1 (the 7 parameter) for a few seconds then stops; the parameter 90 counts 50 ms intervals. You hear a continuous irregular siren, with accompanying noise that stops 4.5 seconds later. It's a powerful but number-heavy approach – see the Acorn manuals for details. It makes the 128 BASIC PLAY command, which can't even work alongside a running program, seem feeble.

Custom memory display

Line 130 clears all variables (except the 'resident integers' A% to Z%) and puts the display into the 10k two-colour 320x256 MODE 4. Line 140 sets one of those colours to red, by sending CHR$ 19, CHR$ 0, CHR$ 1 and three padding null bytes (set aside 'for future expansion' in 1981) to the display (VDU, Visual Display Unit) driver.

The next line goes directly to the FPGA's 6845 display controller, telling it to get pixel data from memory range 0 to 10239 as this is a 10k mode. When semicolons are used instead of commas in a VDU line, the previous 16-bit value is sent as two bytes, low then high, so VDU 23;12;0;0;0 outputs nine bytes, clearing CRTC register 12. You get used to the extra zeros eventually.

The aim of this is to display every bit of the first 10k of memory. You can see values changing constantly in the first 256 bytes, the 'zero page' which holds system variables that won't fit in the three 8-bit CPU registers, then the processor stack, operating system workspace (including the varying sound state, near the top in the middle), the BASIC program (by default at address PAGE, 3.5k in) and the variables. HIMEM is the equivalent of RAMTOP, set by the CLEAR address in ZX BASIC, and we set it to 10k so all the variable values are visible, too.

The main loop of the program fiddles with a couple of strings, showing how BBC BASIC struggles to find space for them. Even though neither can exceed a length of 220 characters, more than 5.5k is allocated for their values, a dozen times more than strictly necessary. ZX BASIC wouldn't waste a byte in this case – and allows much longer strings – but 8-bit BBC BASIC works this way for speed, perhaps over-reacting to the faults in Microsoft's 6502 BASIC. That was prone to halt for a minute or more in 'garbage collection' while tidying up its similarly-short strings, or hang altogether in some buggy releases!

Line 160 re-asserts the screen mode after our rude prodding of the CRTC, creates an empty string variable A$, then line 170 puts the upper limit of RAM being used by BASIC in variable S, for comparison later. When applied to a scalar variable, DIM reserves one more byte than is specified after the variable name and a space, and puts the address in the variable. This is a handy if arcane way to reserve memory – much easier than poking a REM, ZX81 style, and more capacious than stashing code in memory reserved for Spectrum user-defined graphics. We'll use DIM again after the main loop to see how much memory the strings have grabbed.

Tied up with strings

Lines 180 to 230 mimic a typical string-building function by adding random characters one by one to A$ and copying the result so far to B$. In this mean but unexceptional way BASIC is forced to keep allocating fresh memory for

A$, since design rules don't allow it to be extended. Our window on RAM shows the string being copied back and forth between the fixed-sized string buffer early in memory and the variables area. I had to limit the length of both strings to 220 characters as otherwise, between the two of them, they'd out-run the 10k display window!

Notice that THEN is not needed after IF in line 200. The loop continues (using UNTIL, without NextBASIC's redundant REPEAT), furiously churning RAM as the sounds play under interrupt control, till the space key (ASCII code 32) is pressed.

The cryptic DIME-1 shows how BBC BASIC does not require spaces after keywords. It sets E to the new limit of BASIC memory, for comparison with S gathered before the loop. After restoring the usual MODE it shows that those two 220-byte strings have gobbled up 5716 bytes – on a computer shipped with 16k or 32k RAM, requiring 10 or 20k for high-resolution graphics, and several kilobytes for its elaborate and powerful operating system. The final line mutes sound channel 1 (phew!)

Whereas ZX BASIC always inserts spaces around keywords, these are stored in the BBC BASIC program as typed, so even a space between each line number and the following keyword eats up precious RAM. BBC programmers got used to missing out spaces wherever possible, and then using the 'pretty printing' option LISTO 7 to make the listing more readable, indenting lines and loops by adding spaces only on output.

The ZX BASIC superset SAM BASIC has a more powerful capability, controlled by LIST FORMAT, which copes with a dozen structured keywords and can optionally put each statement on a separate display line. It'd be great to have something like that for Next, perhaps exploiting .BAS2TXT and a NextBASIC program to reformat the output for readability.

NextBASIC's REG 18,0 command can put the first 48k of Next RAM into LAYER 2. It won't look as exciting, though, because NextBASIC doesn't use interrupts and main memory in the same way.

Unravelling the MMB file

Packing files into 'images' of original discs is handy for backward-compatibility, but limits their size, as do Plus3DOS floppy .DSK containers, making individual files harder to access. This is not a problem when using Dean's Next-optimised BBC BASIC Z80, as that saves and loads individual files in Next subdirectories, but it does complicate importing files to Next from Acorn-style .SSD and .MMB containers.

The following NextBASIC scans through all the disc images in an MMB file and displays the directory of each in turn. It's a preparatory step to being able to extract and insert 200k disc images, letting us update the contents of the MMB file, to suit other versions of BBC BASIC or convert and use specific programs.

```
100 REM MMB2NEXT November 2023
110 CLEAR %$DFFF
120 %b=$E000
130 LAYER 1,2: PRINT CHR$ 26; CHR$ 0;
140 mmb$="BEEB.MMB"
150 PROC GetMMB(mmb$,1)
155 DIM d$(31,9)
160 FOR %i=0 TO 510
170   IF %a[i]<16 THEN CLS : PROC BBCAT(%i): PAUSE 0
180 NEXT %i: STOP
190
200 DEFPROC GetMMB(f$,noisy=0)
210 LOCAL e$,%s,%d,invalid,blank
220 IF %b<>$E000 THEN PRINT "CLEAR %B-1 first": STOP
230 e$=f$+" +0 8192 -m "+ STR$ (%b)
240 .$ extract e$
250 e$= CHR$ 0+ CHR$ 1+ CHR$ 2+ CHR$ 3+( CHR$ 0)*12
260 IF PEEK$ (%b,16)<>e$ THEN PRINT "Not MMB": STOP
290 IF noisy THEN PRINT f$
300 FOR %d=%b+16 TO %510*16+b STEP 16
310   %s=% PEEK (d+15)
320   %a[d-b>>4-1]=%s
330   IF %(s=0) OR (s=15)
340     e$= PEEK$ (%d,12)[>]
350     IF noisy
360       PRINT %d-b>>4-1; TAB 5;e$; TAB 20;"  READ";
370       IF %s THEN PRINT "/WRITE": ELSE PRINT "-ONLY"
380     ENDIF
390   ELSE
400     blank+=%s=240
410     invalid+=%s=255
420   ENDIF
430 NEXT %d
440 IF noisy
450   PRINT blank;" blank disc";"s" AND blank<>1
460   IF invalid THEN PRINT "and ";invalid;" invalid."
470 ENDIF
480 ENDPROC
490
500 DEFPROC BBCAT(%c)
510 IF %b<>$E000 THEN PRINT "GetMMB first": STOP
515 %d=%c: REM Global copy for later
520 IF %d>510 THEN PRINT "0..510": STOP
525 LOCAL e$
530 IF %(a[d]=0) OR (a[d]=15)
540   e$=mmb$+" +"+ STR$ ((%d)*1024*200+8192,10)
550   e$+=" 512 -m "+ STR$ (%b)
560   .$ extract e$
570   PROC ShowCAT()
580 ELSE IF %a[d]=240
590   PRINT "Unformatted disc ";%d: STOP
600 ELSE
610   PRINT "Invalid disc ";%d: STOP
620 ENDIF
630 ENDPROC
640
650 REM Show SSD catalogue of disc %d from %b, leaving
```

```
655 REM the file count in %f and names in d$(1 to %f)
660 DEFPROC ShowCAT()
670 IF %b<>$E000 THEN PRINT "CLEAR %b-1 first": STOP
680 LOCAL %s,%r,%n,n$:n$= PEEK$ (%b,8)+ PEEK$ (%b+256,4)
690 INVERSE 1: PRINT n$[>];"  Disc ";%d;"  ";
700 %f=% PEEK (b+261)>>3: PRINT %f;" file";
710 IF %f<>1 THEN PRINT "s";
720 PRINT ,: INVERSE 0: PRINT ''
730 FOR %n=%f TO 1 STEP %-1
740   %r=%n<<3+b
750   %s=% PEEK (r+7) & 127
760   IF (%s)<> CODE ("$") THEN PRINT CHR$ (%s);".";
770   PRINT PEEK$ (%r,7);
775    d$(%n)= CHR$ (%s)+"."+ PEEK$ (%r,7)
780   PRINT " "; DPEEK (%r+260)+ ( PEEK (%r+262)&48<<12),
790 NEXT %n
800 PRINT
810 ENDPROC
```

PROC GetMMB() sets up half a dozen global variables with information needed to access individual files and disc images. The path to the MMB file should be in MMB$. %B points to an 8k buffer in high memory, to hold both the MMB and SSD directories, and %D is the current disc number, 0 to 510. %F is the number of files in its directory and the file names are in the array F$, from F$(1) to F$(%F). Integer arrays %A to %H contain the type of each disc image, typically 240 if it's unformatted, 15 if write-protected and 0 for a disc that may be written as well as read.

Now we're ready to pass PROC MB 2 ZX() the name of the file we want – remember, Acorn DFS file names, like BBC BASIC keywords and variable names, are case-sensitive, so Ok, ok and OK are three different variables and files! The same name suffixed with the .BBC extension is used for the output NextBASIC file, unless a preferred name is specified in a second parameter.

```
2020 DEFPROC MMB 2 ZX(in$,out$="")
2025 IF %b<>$E000 THEN PRINT "CLEAR %b-1 first": STOP
2030 IF out$="" THEN out$=in$+".BBC"
2040 LOCAL %i,%r,bytes,offset,e$,t$
2050 DIM t$(9): t$=in$
2070 IF t$(2)<>"." THEN t$="$."+in$
2080 FOR %i=%f TO 1 STEP -1
2090   IF t$=d$(%i)
2110     %r=%i<<3+b
2120     bytes= DPEEK (%r+260)+ (( PEEK (%r+262)&48)<<12)
2130     offset=(%d)*204800+8192:; Disc start in MMB
2140     offset+= ( PEEK (%r+263)+ (( PEEK (%r+262))&3)<<8)<<8
2150     e$=mmb$+" +"+ STR$ (offset,10)+" "
2160     e$+= STR$ (bytes)+" -f -o "+out$
2170     .$ extract e$
2180     EXIT
2290   ENDIF
2300 NEXT %i
2310 IF % NOT i THEN PRINT in$;" not found"
2360 ENDPROC
```

Once the SSD directory is scanned to find the name, first sector and its length, the entire file can be extracted in one step because Acorn's disc filing systems – even the later 'Advanced' version – require that the entire file is in a single contiguous group of sectors, and that all files are placed in the directory in the order in which they occur on the disc surface.

The MOS command *COMPACT recovers space when files are deleted or replaced with longer versions. It resembles the NextZXOS **.defrag** command except that *COMPACT is often necessary when editing disc contents, whereas **.defrag** is only needed to simplify direct access to the media when playing music or streaming video from large files with quick, simple code.

Text files can be read and written more simply using *SPOOL file to copy all display output e.g. PRINT or LIST to the specified file till an empty *SPOOL command is entered (and ends up in the output!) and the companion *EXEC file reads input from the file rather than the keyboard. Darren hadn't implemented those when I tested his Next port of BBC BASIC, but by the time you read this we expect they'll have been added, reducing the need for a relatively complicated PROC ZX 2 MMB().

In the meantime I have written three little procedures to allow downloaded SSD images to be catalogued, inserted into slots in an MMB container, or individual SSDs to be extracted. PROC MMB 2 SSD() again uses the global mmb$ to find the container, and requires the number of the disc therein and an output filename as parameters:

```
840 DEFPROC MMB 2 SSD(%d,f$)
850 IF %d>510 THEN PRINT "0..510": STOP
860 LOCAL e$
870 e$=mmb$+" +"+ STR$ ((%d)*204800+8192,10)
880 e$+=" 204800 -o "+f$
890 .$ extract e$
900 ENDPROC
```

PROC SSDCAT loads the directory of the specified SSD file into the buffer at %B then calls ShowCAT to display the directory. This explains why ShowCAT and BBCAT are separate procedures.

```
930 DEFPROC SSDCAT(f$,%c=0)
940 IF %b<>$E000 THEN PRINT "CLEAR %b-1 first": STOP
950 LOCAL e$
960 e$=f$+" +0 512 -m "+ STR$ (%b)
970 .$ extract e$
975 %d=%c
980 PROC ShowCAT()
990 ENDPROC
```

A slightly trickier procedure inserts an SSD file into the current MMB. The first parameter is the name of the SSD file, the second is the slot number to update in the MMB. Some SSD files online have empty sectors trimmed off the end to reduce download time. These should be extended to the full 200k length before inserting them, e.g. by with a NextBASIC PRINT loop to add arbitrary padding characters.

```
2840 DEFPROC SSD 2 MMB(f$,%d)
2850 IF %d>510 THEN PRINT "0..510": STOP
2860 LOCAL %i,%k,bytes,k200=1024*200,n$,k2$
2865 DIM n$(12): DIM k2$(2048)
2870 CLOSE # 4: OPEN # 4,f$
2880 bytes= DIM #4
2890 IF bytes<>k200 THEN PRINT f$;" not SSD": STOP
2900 FOR %i=1 TO 8:n$(%i)= INKEY$ #4
2903   IF n$(%i)<" " OR n$(%i)>"©" THEN n$(%i)=" "
2906 NEXT %i
2910 GO TO #4,256
2920 FOR %i=9 TO 12:n$(%i)= INKEY$ #4
2923   IF n$(%i)<" " OR n$(%i)>"©" THEN n$(%i)=" "
2926 NEXT %i
2930 CLS : PRINT "SSD ";n$;" 0  % copied"
2940 GO TO #4,0
2950 CLOSE # 5: OPEN # 5,"u>"+mmb$
2960 GO TO #5,8192+(%d)*k200
2970 FOR %k=1 TO 100
2980   FOR %i=1 TO 2048:k2$(%i)= INKEY$ #4: NEXT %i
2990   PRINT AT 0,17;%k;
3000   PRINT #5;k2$;
3010 NEXT %k
3020 REM Set name and mark disc as read/write
3030 GO TO #5,%d+1<<4
3040 PRINT #5;n$+ CHR$ 0*3+ CHR$ 15;
3050 CLOSE # 5: CLOSE # 4
3070 PRINT AT 1,0;
3080 ENDPROC
```

I've not found much use for this PROC so it's quite slow, taking more than five minutes even at 28 MHz. The byte reading loop, in line 2980, is the bottleneck, and could be replaced by calls to **.extract** chunks to memory and print them via PEEK$. If you have plenty of spare Z80 RAM, allocate chunks of more than 2K to reduce the overhead of repeatedly reloading the dot command, or use the esxDOS F_READ hook from page 86.

I could carry on, but space is limited; the Beeb wiki and StarDot forums are the places to look and ask, if you want to build on these examples. The SpecNext Beeb FPGA thread alone has already had more then 290,000 views!

PiTubeDirect

The Hoglet cores are extraordinary in the way they make use of the Next's Pi0 co-processor. In the hands of David Banks, building on decades of efforts to expand the BBC Micro via it's 'tube' co-processor interface, the Pi0 becomes not just an accelerator of prodigious capability (running some unmodified BBC Micro programs more than four thousand times faster than the originals) but also a very capable graphics interface, allowing BBC BASIC, 6502 and ARM programs access to a 24-bit colour HDMI screen at resolutions up to 1280 by 1024 pixels.

And all this works on any stock Next with a Pi fitted, requiring no extra hardware and just a few megabytes of software in the Pi's SD card. Compare that with NextPi2's 16 Gigabyte minimum installation, usable just for audio decoding as I write, and it's clear we've collectively got some catching up to do – and great opportunities still to improve the Next, whatever the cores you're running.

Even if you side with Sinclair against Acorn in the BBC's made-up conflict of Micro Men, thinking 256x192 pixels should be enough for anyone, and a 28 MHz Z80n makes programming too easy, PiTubeDirect is an exciting development and an example of how future-proof the Spectrum Next's design is.

It's unfair to compare the current and growing capability of NextPi with PiTubeDirect, even though the hardware is identical, because Hoglet's efforts build on more than 40 years of accelerator development designed in by Acorn before the ZX Spectrum even existed, let alone the Next. One of the criticisms of the Acorn BBC Micro was its dependence on the 6502 processor. Clive Sinclair pointedly told the BBC that any CPU choice other than the Z80 would be a mistake. Besides the nascent Spectrum, the Z80A was used in his ZX80 and ZX81, and crucially the Newbrain computer, developed at an earlier Sinclair company which had been the BBC's first choice till the schedule slipped unacceptably.

Acorn countered this stinging charge of built-in obsolescence by promising a Z80 co-processor addon for the BBC micro, designing their machine operating system around 32 rather than 16-bit addresses (to suit the National Semiconductor 16032 CPU, which never works properly and was eventually ditched for the home-grown ARM 32 architecture). One of the BBC technical staff charged with making sure the BBC Micro was up to snuff went on to write a Z80-based version of BBC BASIC, used on that co-processor, Sinclair's Z88 and Amstrad's NC notebook computers.

In conjunction with Sinclair's ULA-making suppliers at Ferranti, Acorn devised a simple 8-bit buffering interface they called 'the tube' to allow data to be passed quickly – by 1980s standards – between the 6502 host and all sorts of 'parasite' co-processor. A Ferranti tube ULA in each Acorn add-on, along with the logical separation of BASIC, MOS and the peripheral interfaces, provided a 'fire and forget' interface between collaborating CPUs, and an expansion plan for the BBC Micro which is still effective – and expanding – decades later.

There's no Tube ULA in a Next, but before Next was thought of metal-bashing ARM programmers, fresh from Acorn's Archimedes, had come up with a scheme exploiting the exceptionally fast interrupt handling capability of Raspberry Pis to do the whole job with interrupt-driven software on a bare metal system, with no operating system to get in the way. They were able to get the Pi0 to reliably respond to activity on the GPIO bus which links the

Next FPGA to the Pi0, in less than a third of a millionth of a second, implementing an equivalent of the Ferranti buffers with no extra hardware.

At first this invention was used on BBC Micros and later systems to turn various versions of the Pi into a 32-bit ARM co-processor. BBC BASIC was used to develop the ARM and had been promptly ported onto it, so there was a ready-to-run compatible high-level programming language, updated to include an ARM assembler in place of the Model B's 6502 one, or the Z80 equivalent in the Zilog ports of BBC BASIC. This runs on Next's Pi0, just as it does on any ARM connected to Acorn 8-bit micros.

If you wonder where many of the new features in NextBASIC 2.08 hail from, or indeed several extensions to ZX BASIC in previous releases, look no further than Archimedes BBC BASIC V. Shift operators, multi-line IF statements, array parameters and local arrays, increment assignments, long-named strings and arrays, the TIME function, the general DEFPROC scheme (plus those annoying extra brackets) all came before in extensions to BBC BASIC. They're not unique of course – some are in Python, C and other contemporary programming languages. Versions of many of them also appeared in Sinclair's own SuperBASIC, which built almost the entire language, and it's unique extensibility, on a generalisation of the Acorn CALL statement. But that's another core entirely…

Acorn's first Tube co-processors included updates of the 6502, running faster since there was no need to share RAM with the display system as that was running on the 'host' leaving the 'parasite' coprocessor uncontended. A Souped-up version of Elite, the BBC Micro's killer app, was adapted to run on 3 MHz and 4 MHz 6502s, using the original 2 MHz chip just for input, audio and display output. BBC BASIC was ported to these co-processors, where it was still limited to 64k RAM but no longer fighting for space with the 16k MOS, 20k MODE 0 screen, disc and other system buffers which stayed on the 'host' side.

The ARM can't run 6502 code directly, but it's fast enough to emulate it very quickly, so Beeb fans for whom 4 MHz was small beer soon ported emulators for the 6502 and later supersets like the 65C02 and 65816 (a 16/24 bit chip used in the Apple GS and Super Nintendo). These run original or enhanced versions of BBC BASIC, as well as 6502 code, with faster clocks, extra instructions and more RAM. The ReCo 65816 models a 14.7 MHz system but is substantially faster at transcendental arithmetic. The Turbo 65C02 emulating interpreter averages 30 times the speed of a 6502A in tests on my Pi0. All these and a dozen more are built in to PiTubeDirect.

But the default is an on-the-fly compiler which uses JIT (Just in Time) techniques and abundant extra memory to translate rather than interpret 8 bit code into 32-bit instructions for the 1 GHz Pi, necessarily supporting self-modifying code as well as static routines. This runs standard BBC BASIC

ClockSp tests 400 times faster than a BBC Micro, and manages a factor of 809 times on common mathematics functions.

Remember, this CPU suits virtually all the code written for the 6502 in forty years. If that's not enough, and you're using BASIC, BBC BASIC V for the ARM benchmarks as if it was a 6502 running at between 4.3 and 8.5 ***GigaHertz*** – thousands of times faster, which is probably a bit much for games but great for fractals and graphics manipulation.

Figure 111 shows how much faster custom BBC BASIC benchmarks run on PiTubeDirect. I've not tried to print a bar-chart here, because if the 'fast' BBC Model B bar was 5mm wide I'd need a page more than two metres across to fit in the ARM Native results. Notice that in BBC BASIC, unlike NextBASIC, PROC calls perform marginally *faster* than simple GO SUBs.

BBC ClockSp	REP	REP%	FOR	FOR%	Maths	Strings	PROC	GOSUB
BBC Model B	2.0	2.0	2.0	2.0	2.0	2.0	2.0	2.0
ARM Native	4260	7100	5120	7286	5910	7275	8030	8500
JIT 6502	394	435	474	424	809	505	438	441
Turbo 6502	61.3	65.1	68.1	62.7	132.6	82.8	56.6	58.8
Dossytronics	21.9	71.4	27.7	53.6	CRASH	85.7	52.2	50.1
ReCo 65816	13.7	16.0	15.6	14.6	50.1	18.5	13.4	13.0

Figure 111 – The BBC BASIC ClockSp test works out the effective speed of BBC BASIC in MHz compared with a 2 MHz Model B running BASIC 1.2. Others used BBC BASIC IV or BASIC V on the 1 GHz ARM32 Pi0.The Maths test crashes the Dossytronics 65816!

Of course, PiTubeDirect doesn't speed up access to the SD card – though the file format is identical – and the tube interface is still slower than writing directly to BBC Micro video memory, but the Acorn aficionados have a ready answer to that, too…

Pi VDU Driver

When the Next was first mooted, one of the obstacles to small-scale production was the high cost of an HDMI licence. Eventually the Kickstarter raised enough money for the Next FPGA to afford its own dedicated digital video output, but while that was in doubt the GPIO/Pi0 solution was hatched as a way to allow HDMI output through the already-licenced Pi in parallel with VGA directly from the FPGA. This means most of us have two HDMI ports on the back of our Next's – one directly connected to the Spectrum, and another indirectly available on the Pi0 board. The 'bump' to accommodate this on the Spectrum Next's case was one of the aspects of the design most regretted by Rick Dickinson, but it is here now and it works – though apart from a brief demo using Linux, it's not seen much limelight.

The Pi VDU driver changes all that. This is an extra capability of the 'Hognose' development branch of PiTubeDirect, and I tested the June 2023 release for this chapter. It still has a few gaps, especially in terms of graphics features added later by Acorn, such as video block and arc manipulation, scroll suppression or printer redirection, and attempts to read the remote screen from the 6502 sometimes read the host instead, but even at this early stage it's very capable and quite stable.

Even in 1981 BBC Micro graphs were plotted in 1280 x 1024 pixel coordinate system, which was scaled appropriately by the MOS for the actual capability of the BBC Micro, ranging from 160 pixel lines in MODEs 2 and 5 to 640x256 pixels in MODE 0. Later Acorn RISCOS systems added 46 more modes, some only suitable for specialist displays, but never reached the design limit of 1,310,720 pixels – till now, on our Spectrum Nexts and other Hognose clients, which offer the full resolution in 24 bit and 16-bit direct colour, or 8 bits via a palette. The extra screen modes 8 to 53 are listed at http://www.riscosopen.org/wiki/documentation/show/Screen Modes

If that's not enough, the Pi VDU driver adds eight more! Modes 64, 66 and 68 offer 640x512 resolution with 8, 16 or 24 colour bits per pixel. Add one to quadruple those resolutions, so MODE 69 gives 1280x1024 pixels in 24 bit colour. The 8-bit modes are palette-mapped so each byte value selects a chosen 24-bit colours, and the 16bit modes allocate 6 bits to green and 5 each to red and blue. There are no Next-style sprites or overlapping layers.

The last two modes 70 and 71 give Teletext-style displays with 60 or 80 columns and a choice from dozens of custom fonts. The highest resolution modes are much the fastest, capable of updating 8000 characters without scrolling in about 60 ms, whereas scrolling makes the teletext modes about ten times slower. That's where I really want to put my debugger panes!

It's important to note that the Pi's video output is only directly available to 'external co-processors' also running on the Pi. Hoglet's core on the Next is still handling keyboard input, SD card access and sound, but BASIC or machine code is running on the Pi. This removes the video performance bottleneck of the PI, but makes it trickier for us to do the same thing when running NextBASIC, as we need to funnel messages and display output via the Acorn MOS VDU interface, over GPIO.

It will take software and maybe FPGA tweaks to make full use of the potential, and at the moment you can only easily access the Pi0 VDU driver from an ARM or 6502 emulation, not your Z80n. It's possible that NextPi2 will catch up in the meantime, though unlikely that it'll be as snappy, given that it's running Linux rather than the bare-metal PiTubeDirect driver.

When the Pi0 runs ARM code it can access the frame buffer directly, or use the VDU and MOS system protocols. The documentation includes a few lines of ARM BBC BASIC that can query the dimensions, bit depth and base address of the frame buffer, allowing 8 or 32-bit PEEKs and POKEs, via the Acorn-standard ? and ! operators, or arbitrary screen manipulation via the built-in assembler. Writing OpenGL in BBC BASIC will still be rather a big job.

When emulating a 6502 there's nowhere near enough address space for 4 megabytes of pixels, so the VDU interface is retargeted to the Pi's display by a 256-byte 'driver' that transparently implements text, pixel and graphics redirection, including support for the screen editor, to read the edit cursor position and character there. You need to type CALL &300 to start this up (on 6502 only).

The Pi VDU driver documentation shows how this can be called from the host, with a couple of writes to memory-mapped 'tube registers'. This is a hint of how we could do the same from NextZXOS! My dream is to be able to run the existing NextPi audio players and TZX decoder, and future abilities, alongside PiTubeDirect, on their efficient Linux-free platform. But that would make it harder to unleash the Pi's USB port.

As with all Next developments, the key will be co-operation, and in the short term it's necessary to swap firmware depending on what you most want to do. A big step for Next users, unwilling to open their cases, would be for PiTubeDirect to allow firmware updates via GPIO. At that point it's just software – time and enthusiasm – holding us back. At the moment you need to pick the one you want most, or two micro-SD cards and a willingness to swap them.

Turning on the Driver

Even if you have the latest Hognose release you need to make a one-character change to one of the text files on the Pi's micro-SD card to unleash the PI VDU driver. This is a simple matter of changing a 0 to a 1 after **vdu=** in the cmdline.txt file on the PiTubeDirect card. As soon as you power up Next after doing this you'll get a friendly colour screen on the second HDMI output, with clear instructions on how to link up your chosen co-processor with a command or two from either BBC core.

On the native ARM, copro 15, you need to type *PIVDU 2 to divert output from Next's FPGA to the PI's HDMI, and load BASIC with *ARMBASIC. There are a few other embedded MOS commands, including a blisteringly fast Conway's game of Life (effortlessly updating millions of pixels a second in any screen mode) and an ARM disassembler.

To show off the power of the display and ARM combination, select mode 21 or 64 and type *PILIFE 640 640 512, or full-screen MODE 71 with *PILIFE 100 960 500. These commands implement John Conway's cellular-automaton-based Game of Life very fast. MODE 70 is just MODE 71 with a blank area on the right, there are substantial borders on a widescreen display in most of the other modes, as they're designed for a 4x3 TV aspect ratio.

The 6502s (copro 0, 1, 2, 3, 16, 17, or 25 the fast JIT one) start up in BASIC IV but continue to use the Next's 50 Hertz display until you re-direct them to the PI VDU with CALL &300. Unlike Hoglet's support for Next's own outputs, which work only with 50 Hertz PAL-like displays compatible with the original BBC Micro, output from the Pi seems stable on HDMI monitors as well as TVs. I've tested a few which struggled with the original KS1 Next HDMI output – out of thousands of display models, with varying HDMI specs – and found the Pi0 HDMI more rather than less-compatible.

If the BBC, Archimedes and custom HDMI modes are not enough, you can roll your own by specifying the pixel, character and colour resolutions with a VDU 23,22 command sequence, but not beyond 1280 pixel width and with a risk of having to power down and start again if you are unlucky or overambitious. The same applies, of course, to experiments with VDU 23 aimed at reprogramming the standard 6845 video CRTC (CRT display controller). You already have 60-odd modes to play with.

Many of these leave wide borders on a modern 16:9 aspect LCD display, but the Teletext modes soak those up, apart from the 720x500 pixel MODE 70 which looks like the full-screen 960x500 MODE 71 with an offset and narrower work area (for 60x25 rather than 80x25 Teletext characters).

The larger fonts in Teletext modes are a pleasure to read, but not redefinable like the Spectrum-style 8x8 fonts Acorn used in other MODEs. The original Teletext display is 40x25 and uses a dedicated ROM chip; the Pi driver lets you shuffle between dozens of preset fonts optimised for various languages and resolutions, ranging from 6x8 to 8x14 pixels with options for rounding, integer scaling and custom spacing. All very BBC.

Apart from screwing things up with VDU 23, the only bug I found was that while the *SPOOL command, to redirect output to a file, works in *PIVDU 1 and 3 configurations, which respectively use the Next screen output or both Next and PI simultaneously (with formatting to suit the PI, lines wrapping on the smaller screen) but nothing is output to the file when *PIVDU 2 is used to direct output only to the second screen.

I should stress that the entire Hoglet system, including PiTubeDirect, is exceptionally stable and well-documented compared with every other extension, software, emulator or core, which I've tested on Next, other than the official SpecNext cores, of course!

When it came to deciding which optional core to document in this book, there was really no contest. I only hope that planned MGT and ZX8x cores will come close to this quality. The Sinclair QL core is tantalising close, as this book goes to press. Time will tell; so far the team focus has rightly been on KS2 and NextZXOS. Watch SpecNext.com, and Facebook Next groups, for news of new cores and multicore support for Kickstarter 2 systems. I've seen some encouraging but unfinished prototypes.

Exotic processors

PiTube doesn't stop just at Acorn-favoured chips like ARM and 6502. Since it's generally running software emulators, albeit on bare metal, and the Tube interface is CPU-agnostic, you can also configure the tube for a Motorola 6809, the finest 8-bit microprocessor, though it seems only Microsoft's BASIC (used in Dragon and Tandy Color computers) has been ported to it.

There are ARM emulators for various flavours of Z80 CP/M (requiring additional disc images), an 896k Intel x86 core (which strangely ignored input till I pressed ESC), the rudimentary 'Pandora' OS for the 1MB National Semiconductor 16032, which rebranding as a 32016 could not save, a slick DEC PDP-11 minicomputer, three DIY processors in the OPC line, a Ferranti F100-L with 32k words of memory ready for all your old UK military software, and this decade's CPU darling, a RISC-V implementation, including a built-in RISC assembler, of course.

I haven't spent much time on these, but noticed that the Dossy 65C816 core fails some maths tests, unlike the slower ReCo implementation of the same chip. I wasn't able to get Z80 or PDP-11 BBC BASIC to run in these emulations, though I gather some people have managed it. I fired up Microsoft 6809 BASIC with *RUN BASIC09 and Archimedes BASIC V on the ARM2 with *RUN ABASIC. Jonathan Harston's **mdfs.net** web site is a good place to look for files and applications for such spin-off systems.

The main BBC Micro games archive, established by actively seeking permission from authors and publishers, was once a website called *Stairway to Hell*, and now occupies discs 200 to 252 of BEEB.MMFS, with an index on disc 0 which can be launched with *DBOOT 0. Bear in mind that some software only works on the Model B, rather than the Master, or vice versa. That's why we have both Acorn cores, and numerous Next personalities. For educational software – and there's a lot of it, as the Beeb was a standard fixture in UK schools for more than a decade – visit **flaxcottage.com**

That's a wrap for Next Tech Volume 1, after around 500 pages, over 210,000 words and arguably half as much again in diagrams. If you want more, for instance on CP/M, compilers, CTCs, Forth, graphics, networking, SuperBASIC, Z80n programming and other cores and languages, please send your suggestions to me at spectrumnextbook@gmail.com, and **encourage your friends to buy this book!**

> *We shall not cease from exploration*
> *And the end of all our exploring*
> *Will be to arrive where we started*
> *And know the place for the first time*
>
> *T.S. Eliot*

Symbols

Digits

A

D

N

O

P

Q

R

Made in United States
Orlando, FL
04 November 2026

90219745R00272